EPICTETUS

EPICTETUS

THE DISCOURSES AS REPORTED BY ARRIAN, THE MANUAL, AND FRAGMENTS

WITH AN ENGLISH TRANSLATION BY

W. A. OLDFATHER

UNIVERSITY OF ILLINOIS

IN TWO VOLUMES
VOL. I

DISCOURSES, BOOKS I AND II

CAMBRIDGE, MASSACHUSETTS
HARVARD UNIVERSITY PRESS
LONDON
WILLIAM HEINEMANN LTD
MCMLXI

First printed 1925
Reprinted 1946, 1956, 1961

Printed in Great Britain

CONTENTS

INTRODUCTION

Slave, poor as Irus, halting as I trod,
I, Epictetus, was the friend of God.[1]

EPICTETUS was a slave woman's son, and for many
years a slave himself.[2]   The tone and temper of
his whole life were determined thereby.   An all-
engulfing passion for independence and freedom so

---

[1] Δοῦλος Ἐπίκτητος γενόμην καὶ σῶμ' ἀνάπηρος καὶ πενίην
Ἶρος καὶ φίλος ἀθανάτοις.   An anonymous epigram (John
Chrys., *Patrol. Gr.* LX. 111; Macrob. *Sat.* I. 11, 45; *Anth.
Pal.* VII. 676), as translated by H. Macnaghten. The ascrip-
tion to Leonidas is merely a palaeographical blunder in part
of the MS. tradition, that to Epictetus himself (by Macrobius)
a patent absurdity.

[2] This is the explicit testimony of an undated but fairly
early inscription from Pisidia (J. R. S. Sterrett: *Papers
of the Amer. School of Class. Stud. at Athens*, 1884–5, 3, 315 f. ;
G. Kaibel : *Hermes*, 1888, 23, 542 ff.), and of Palladius
(Ps.–Callisthenes, III. 10, ed. C. Müller), and is distinctly
implied by a phrase in a letter professedly addressed to him
by one of the Philostrati (Ep. 69: ἐκλανθάνεσθαι τίς εἶ καὶ
τίνων γέγονας).   I see, therefore, no reason to doubt the
statement, as does Schenkl (2nd ed., p. xvi).   The phrase
δοῦλος...γενόμην in the epigram cited above cannot be used
as certain evidence, because γίγνεσθαι, as Schenkl observes,
too frequently equals εἶναι in the poets, but, in view of the
other testimony, it is probable that servile origin was what
the author of it had in mind.—There is little reason to
think, with Martha (*Les Moralistes*, etc., 159), that Epictetus
was not his real name, and that the employment of it is
indicative of a modesty so real that it sought even a kind of
anonymity, since the designation is by no means restricted
to slaves, while his modesty, because coupled with Stoic
straightforwardness, is far removed from the shrinking
humility that seeks self-effacement.

preoccupied him in his youth, that throughout his life he was obsessed with the fear of restraint, and tended to regard mere liberty, even in its negative aspect alone, as almost the highest conceivable good. It is perhaps no less noteworthy that he came from Hierapolis in Phrygia. From of old the Phrygians had conceived of their deities with a singular intensity and entered into their worship with a passion that was often fanaticism, and sometimes downright frenzy. It is, therefore, not unnatural that the one Greek philosopher who, despite the monistic and necessitarian postulates of his philosophy, conceived of his God in as vivid a fashion as the writers of the New Testament, and almost as intimately as the founder of Christianity himself, should have inherited the passion for a personal god from the folk and land of his nativity.[1]

Beside these two illuminating facts, the other details of his life history are of relatively little importance. He was owned for a time by Epaphroditus, the freedman and administrative secretary of Nero, and it was while yet in his service that he began to take lessons from Musonius Rufus, the greatest Stoic teacher of the age, whose influence was the dominant one in his career.[2] He was of

---

[1] It is noteworthy, as Lagrange, p. 201, observes, that Montanus, who soon after the time of Epictetus "threatened Christianity with the invasion of undisciplined spiritual graces," was also a Phrygian.

[2] So many passages in Epictetus can be paralleled closely from the remaining fragments of Rufus (as Epictetus always calls him) that there can be no doubt but the system of thought in the pupil is little more than an echo, with changes of emphasis due to the personal equation, of that of the master.

feeble health, and lame, the latter probably because
of the brutality of a master in his early years ; [1]

[1] This is generally doubted nowadays, especially since
Bentley's emphatic pronouncement (cf. *Trans. Am. Philol.
Assoc.*, 1921, 53, 42) in favour of the account in Suidas,
to the effect that his lameness was the result of rheumatism.
Ceteris paribus one would, of course, accept as probable the
less sensational story. But it requires unusual powers of
credulity to believe Suidas *against* any authority whomso-
ever, and in this case the other authorities are several,
early, and excellent. In the first place Celsus (in Origen,
contra Celsum, VII, 53), who was probably a younger
contemporary of Epictetus and had every occasion to be
well informed ; further, Origen (*l.c.*), who clearly accepted
and believed the story, since his very answer to the
argument admits the authenticity of the account, while
the easiest or most convincing retort would have been to
deny it ; then Gregory of Nazianzus and his brother
Caesarius (in a number of places, see the *testimonia* in
Schenkl², pp. viii–ix ; of course the absurdities in Pseudo-
Nonnus, Cosmas of Jerusalem, Elias of Crete, *et id genus
omne*, have no bearing either way). Now the fact that such
men as Origen and Gregory accepted and propagated the
account (even though Epictetus, and in this particular
instance especially, had been exploited as a pagan saint, the
equal or the superior of even Jesus himself) is sufficient to
show that the best-informed Christians of the third and
fourth centuries knew of no other record. To my feeling
it is distinctly probable that the denial of the incident
may have emanated from some over-zealous Christian, in
a period of less scrupulous apologetics, who thought to take
down the Pagans a notch or two. The very brief statement
in Simplicius, "that he was lame from an early period of
his life" (*Comm. on the Encheiridion*, 102b Heins.), establishes
nothing and would agree perfectly with either story. The
connection in which the words occur would make any
explanatory digression unnatural, and, whereas similar
conciseness in Plutarch might perhaps argue ignorance of
further details, such an inference would be false for
Simplicius, the dullness of whose commentary is so por-
tentous that it cannot be explained as merely the unavoidable

long unmarried, until in his old age he took a wife to help him bring up a little child whose parents, friends of his, were about to expose it ;[1] so simple in his style of living, that in Rome he never locked the doors of a habitation, whose only furniture was said to be a pallet and a rush mat, and in Nicopolis (in Epirus, opposite Actium) contented himself with an earthenware lamp after the theft of his iron one.

Of the external aspects of his career it should be noted that he had a recognized position as a philosopher when Domitian banished all such persons from Rome (presumably in A.D. 89 or 92); that he settled in Nicopolis, where he conducted what seems to have been a fairly large and well-regarded school ; that he travelled a little, probably to Olympia, and certainly once to Athens.[2]   In

[1] He had been stung, no doubt, by the bitter and in his case unfair gibe of Demonax, who, on hearing Epictetus' exhortation to marry, had sarcastically asked the hand of one of his daughters (Lucian, *Demon.* 55).

[2] Philostratus, *Epist.* 69 ; Lucian, *Demon.* 55 would not be inconsistent with the idea of such a visit, but does not necessarily presuppose it.

---

concomitant of vast scholarship and erudition, but must have required a deliberate effort directed to the suppression of the elements of human interest.   Epictetus' own allusions to his lameness are non-committal, but of course he would have been the last person to boast about such things.   And yet, even then, the references to the power of one's master, or tyrant, to do injury by means of chains, sword, rack, scourging, prison, exile, crucifixion, and the like (although the general theme is a kind of Stoic commonplace), are so very numerous as compared with the physical afflictions which come in the course of nature, that it is altogether reasonable to think of his imagination having been profoundly affected during his impressionable years by a personal experience of this very sort.

this connection it should also be observed that his general literary education was not extensive— Homer, of course, a little Plato and Xenophon, principally for their testimony about Socrates, a few stock references to tragedy, and the professional's acquaintance with the philosophy of the later schools, and this is practically all. It can scarcely be doubted, as Schenkl observes (p. xci), that this literary apparatus comes almost entirely from the extensive collections of Chrysippus. And the same may be said of his aesthetic culture. He seems to have seen and been impressed by the gold-and-ivory statues of Zeus and Athena, at Olympia and Athens respectively, but he set no very high value upon the work of artists, for he allowed himself once the almost blasphemous characterization of the Acropolis and its incomparable marbles as "pretty bits of stone and a pretty rock." Epictetus was merely moralist and teacher, but yet of such transcendent attainments as such that it seems almost impertinent to expect anything more of him.

The dates of his birth and of his death cannot be determined with any accuracy. The burning of the Capitol in A.D. 69 was yet a vivid memory while he was still a pupil of Musonius;[1] he enjoyed the personal acquaintance of Hadrian, but not of Marcus Aurelius, for all the latter's admiration of him; and he speaks freely of himself as an old man, and is characterized as such by Lucian (*Adv.*

---

[1] The Capitol was burned in 69 and again in A.D. 80, but the reference to the event (I. 7, 32) as a crime suggests that the earlier date should be understood, since the burning then was due to revolution, while that in A.D. 80 was accidental.

Indoctum, 13); accordingly his life must have covered roughly the period *ca.* A.D. 50–120, with which limits the rare and rather vague references to contemporary events agree. He was, accordingly, an almost exact contemporary of Plutarch and Tacitus.

Like Socrates and others whom he admired, he wrote nothing for publication,[1] and but little memory would have survived of him had not a faithful pupil, successful as historian and administrator, Flavius Arrian, recorded many a discourse and informal conversation. These are saved to us in four books of Διατριβαί, or *Discourses,*[2] out of the original eight, and in a very brief compendium, the Ἐγχειρίδιον,[3] a *Manual* or *Handbook,* in which,

[1] Although he must have written much for his own purposes in elaborating his argumentation by dialectic, since he lauds Socrates for such a practice and speaks of it as usual for a "philosopher." Besides, in his own discourses he is always looking for an interlocutor, whom he often finds in the person of pupil or visitor, but, failing these, he carries on both sides of the debate himself. Cf. Colardeau, p. 294 f.

[2] Some, especially Schenkl, have believed in the existence of other collections, and it was long thought that Arrian had composed a special biography. But the evidence for the other works seems to be based entirely upon those variations in title and form of reference which ancient methods of citation freely allowed, and it is improbable that there ever existed any but the works just mentioned. See the special study by R. Asmus, whose conclusions have been accepted by Zeller, 767, n., and many others.

[3] This has occasionally been translated by *Pugio,* or Dagger, in early modern editions, possibly with a half-conscious memory of Hebrews iv. 12 : *For the word of God is quick and powerful, and sharper than any two-edged sword, piercing even to the dividing asunder of soul and spirit, and of the joints and marrow, and is a discerner of the thoughts*

for the sake of a general public which could not take time to read the larger ones, the elements of his doctrine were somewhat mechanically put together out of verbatim, or practically verbatim, extracts from the *Discourses*. That Arrian's report is a stenographic [1] record of the *ipsissima verba* of the master there can be no doubt. His own compositions are in Attic, while these works are in the *Koine*, and there are such marked differences in style, especially in the use of several of the prepositions, as Mücke has pointed out, that one is clearly dealing with another personality. Add to that the utter difference in spirit and tempo, and Arrian's inability when writing *propria persona* to characterize sharply a personality, while the conversations of Epictetus are nothing if not vivid.

We have, accordingly, in Arrian's *Discourses* a work which, if my knowledge does not fail me, is really unique in literature, the actual words of an extraordinarily gifted teacher upon scores, not to say hundreds, of occasions in his own class-room, conversing with visitors, reproving, exhorting, encouraging his pupils, enlivening the dullness of the formal instruction, and, in his own parable, shooting it through with the red stripe of a conscious moral purpose in preparation for the

---

[1] Hartmann, p. 252 ff., has settled this point.

---

and intents of the heart. But despite the not inappropriate character of such a designation, and the fact that Simplicius himself (preface to his commentary) misunderstood the application, there can be no doubt but the word βιβλίον is to be supplied and that the correct meaning is *Handbook* or *Compendium*; cf. Colardeau's discussion, p. 25.

xiii

problem of right living.[1] The regular class exercises were clearly reading and interpretation of characteristic portions of Stoic philosophical works, somewhat as in an oral examination; problems in formal logic, these apparently conducted by assistants, or advanced pupils; and the preparation of themes or essays on a large scale which required much writing and allowed an ambitious pupil to imitate the style of celebrated authors. The Master supervised the formal instruction in logic, even though it might be conducted by others, but there is no indication that he delivered systematic lectures, although he clearly made special preparation to criticize the interpretations of his pupils (I. 10, 8). From the nature of the comments, which presuppose a fair elementary training in literature, we can feel sure that only young men and not boys were admitted to the school, and there are some remarks which sound very much like introductions to the general subject of study, while others are pretty clearly addressed to those who were about to leave —constituting, in fact, an early and somewhat rudimentary variety of *Commencement Address*.[2] Some of the pupils were preparing to teach, but the majority, no doubt, like Arrian, were of high social position and contemplated entering the public service.

For a proper understanding of the *Discourses* it is important to bear in mind their true character,

[1] Colardeau, pp. 71–113, has an admirable discussion of the method and technique of instruction employed. In view of the singularly valuable nature of the material it seems strange that more attention has not been paid to Epictetus in the history of ancient education.

[2] See Halbauer, p. 45 ff., for a good discussion of these points and a critique of the views of Bruns, Colardeau, and Hartmann.

which Halbauer in a valuable study has most clearly stated thus (p. 56): "The *Diatribae* are not the curriculum proper, nor even a part of that curriculum. On the contrary, this consisted of readings from the Stoic writings, while the *Diatribae* accompany the formal instruction, dwell on this point or on that, which Epictetus regarded as of special importance, above all give him an opportunity for familiar discourse with his pupils, and for discussing with them in a friendly spirit their personal affairs." They are not, therefore, a formal presentation of Stoic philosophy, so that it is unfair to criticize their lack of system and their relative neglect of logic and physics, upon which the other Stoics laid such stress, for they were not designed as formal lectures, and the class exercises had dwelt *satis superque*, as Epictetus must have felt, upon the physics and logic, which were after all only the foundation of conduct, the subject in which he was primarily interested. They are class-room comment, in the frank and open spirit which was characteristic of the man, containing not a little of what we should now be inclined to restrict to a private conference, often closely connected, no doubt, with the readings and themes, but quite as often, apparently, little more than *obiter dicta*.[1]

---

[1] *Cf.* Bonhöffer, 1890, 22. The arrangement of topics by Arrian is a point which seems not to have been discussed as fully as it deserves. Hartmann's view, that the order is that of exact chronological sequence, seems to be an exaggeration of what may be in the main correct, but I think I can trace evidences of a somewhat formal nature in some of the groupings, and it seems not unlikely that a few of the chapters contain remarks delivered on several occasions. However, this is a point which requires an elaborate investigation and cannot be discussed here.

They constitute a remarkable self-revelation of a character of extraordinary strength, elevation, and sweetness, and despite their frequent repetitions and occasional obscurity must ever rank high in the literature of personal portrayal, even were one inclined to disregard their moral elevation. For Epictetus was without doubt, as the great wit and cynic Lucian calls him, "a marvellous old man."

It may not be amiss to dwell a few moments upon the outstanding features of his personality, before saying a few words upon his doctrines, for his doctrines, or at all events the varying emphasis laid on his doctrines, were to a marked degree influenced by the kind of man that he was.

And first of all I should observe that he had the point of view of a man who had suffered from slavery and abhorred it, but had not been altogether able to escape its influence. He was predisposed to suffer, to renounce, to yield, and to accept whatever burden might be laid upon him.[1] He was not a revolutionist, or a cultured gentleman, or a statesman, as were other Stoics before and after. Many of the good things of life which others enjoyed as a matter of course he had grown accustomed never to demand for himself ; and the social obligations for the maintenance and advancement of order and civilization, towards which men of higher station were sensitive, clearly did not weigh heavily upon his conscience. His whole teaching was to make men free and happy by a severe restriction of effort to the realm of the moral

---

[1] Compare the excellent remarks of E. V. Arnold upon this point, *Encyclop.*, *etc.*, 324.

nature.[1] The celebrated life-formula, ἀνέχου καὶ ἀπέχου, which one feels inclined to retranslate as "Endure and Renounce," in order to give it once more the definite meaning of which the *cliché*, "Bear and Forbear," has almost robbed it, is, to speak frankly, with all its wisdom, and humility, and purificatory power, not a sufficient programme for a highly organized society making towards an envisaged goal of general improvement.

And again, in youth he must have been almost consumed by a passion for freedom. I know no man upon whose lips the idea more frequently occurs. The words "free" (adjective and verb) and "freedom" appear some 130 times in Epictetus, that is, with a relative frequency about six times that of their occurrence in the New Testament and twice that of their occurrence in Marcus Aurelius, to take contemporary works of somewhat the same general content. And with the attainment of his personal freedom there must have come such an upwelling of gratitude to God as that which finds expression in the beautiful hymn of praise concluding the sixteenth chapter of the first book, so that, while most Stoics assumed or at least recognized the possibility of a kind of immortality, he could wholly dispense with that desire for the survival of personality after death which even Marcus Aurelius felt to be almost necessary for his own austere ideal of happiness.[2]

[1] See Zeller's admirable discussion of this topic, p. 776.

[2] "Sich aber als Menschheit (und nicht nur als Individuum) ebenso vergeudet zu fühlen, wie wir die einzelne Blüthe von der Natur vergeudet sehen, ist ein Gefühl über alle Gefühle.—Wer ist aber desselben fähig?" F. Nietzsche: *Menschliches, Allzumenschliches*, I. 51.

INTRODUCTION

Almost as characteristic was his intensity. He speaks much of tranquillity, as might be expected of a Stoic, but he was not one of those for whom that virtue is to be achieved only by Henry James's formula of successive accumulations of "endless" amounts of history, and tradition, and taste. His was a tranquillity, if there really be such a thing, of moral fervour, and of religious devotion. His vehemence gave him an extraordinarily firm and clean-cut character, and made him a singularly impressive teacher, as Arrian in the introductory epistle attests. For he was enormously interested in his teaching, knowing well that in this gift lay his single talent; made great efforts to present his material in the simplest terms and in well-arranged sequence; and sharply reproved those who blamed the stupidity of their pupils for what was due to their own incompetence in instruction. It also gave a notable vigour to his vocabulary and utterance, his παρρησία, or freedom of speech, *suo quamque rem nomine appellare*, as Cicero (*Ad. Fam.* IX. 22, 1) characterizes that Stoic virtue, which few exemplified more effectively than Epictetus; but it also, it must be confessed, made him somewhat intolerant of the opinions of others, were they philosophic or religious, in a fashion which for better or for worse was rapidly gaining ground in his day.[1]

But he was at the same time extremely modest. He never calls himself a "philosopher," he speaks frankly of his own failings, blames himself quite as much as his pupils for the failure of his instruction ofttimes to produce its perfect work, and quotes

[1] See Bonhöffer's remarks upon this point (1911, 346).

freely the disrespectful remarks of others about him.
He is severe in the condemnation of the unrepentant
sinner, but charitable towards the naïve wrong-
doer, going so far, in fact, in this direction as to
advocate principles which would lead to the abolition
of all capital punishment.[1] He is much more an
angel of mercy than a messenger of vengeance.[2]
And this aspect of his character comes out most
clearly perhaps in his attitude towards children, for
with them a man can be more nearly himself than
with his sophisticated associates. No ancient author
speaks as frequently of them, or as sympathetically.
They are one of his favourite parables,[3] and though
he is well aware that a child is only an incomplete
man, he likes their straightforwardness in play,
he claps his hands to them and returns their
"Merry Saturnalia!" greeting, yearns to get down
on hands and knees and talk baby talk with them.
There is, of course, a sense in which Pascal's
stricture of Stoic pride applies to Epictetus, for
the Stoic virtues were somewhat self-consciously
erected upon the basis of self-respect and self-
reliance; but a more humble and charitable Stoic
it would have been impossible to find, and what
pride there is belongs to the system and not to
the man.[4] Towards God he is always devout,

---

[1] I. 18, especially sections 5 ff.
[2] See Colardeau, p. 209 ff., and Zeller, p. 780 f.
[3] *Cf.* Renner's interesting study.
[4] Pascal's judgment (to say nothing of the grotesque
misconceptions of J. B. Rousseau) was undoubtedly influenced by his preoccupation with the *Encheiridion*, which,
as necessarily in such a compendium of doctrine, is more
Stoic than Epictetean, and suppresses many of the more
amiable traits of personality. The actual man of the

grateful, humble, and there is a little trace in him
of that exaltation of self which in some of the
Stoics tended to accord to the ideal man a moral
elevation that made him sometimes the equal if not
in certain aspects almost the superior of God.[1]

His doctrines were the conventional ones of
Stoicism, representing rather the teaching of the
early Stoics than that of the middle and later
schools, as Bonhöffer has elaborately proven. There
is, accordingly, no occasion to dwell at length upon
them, but for the sake of those who may wish
to fit a particular teaching into his general scheme,
a very brief outline may here be attempted.[2]

Every man bears the exclusive responsibility
himself for his own good or evil, since it is impossible to imagine a moral order in which one
person does the wrong and another, the innocent,
suffers. Therefore, good and evil can be only those
things which depend entirely upon our moral
purpose, what we generally call, but from the
Stoic's point of view a little inaccurately, our free

[1] As expressed, *e.g.*, in Seneca, *De Prov.* VI. 6: *Hoc est
quo deum antecedatis: ille extra patientiam malorum est, vos
supra patientiam.* *Cf.* also Zeller, 257.
[2] I am following here in the main, but not uniformly,
Von Arnim's admirable summary.

Discourses is a very much more attractive figure than the
imaginary reconstruction of the man from the abstracted
principles of the *Manual*; there he is a man, here a statue
(Martha, 162 f.). It would go hard with many to have
their personal traits deduced from the evidence supplied by
the grammars, indices, or even confessions of faith that
they have written; especially hard if the compendium
were drawn up somewhat mechanically by another's hand.

will; they cannot consist in any of those things which others can do either to us or for us. Man's highest good lies in the reason, which distinguishes him from other animals. This reason shows itself in assent or dissent, in desire or aversion, and in choice or refusal,[1] which in turn are based upon an external impression, φαντασία, that is, a prime *datum*, a "constant," beyond our power to alter. But we remain free in regard to our attitude towards them. The use which we make of the external impressions is our one chief concern, and upon the right kind of use depends exclusively our happiness. In the realm of judgement the truth or falsity of the external impression is to be decided. Here our concern is to assent to the true impression, reject the false, and suspend judgement regarding the uncertain. This is an act of the moral purpose, or free will. We should never forget this responsibility, and never assent to an external impression without this preliminary testing. In order to escape from being misled by fallacious reasoning in the formation of these judgements we need instruction in logic, although Epictetus warns against undue devotion to the subtleties of the subject.

Corresponding to assent or dissent in the realm of the intellectual are desire or aversion in the realm of good and evil, which is the most important

[1] This triple division of philosophy, with especial but not exclusive application to ethics, is the only notably original element which the minute studies of many investigators have found in Epictetus, and it is rather a pedagogical device for lucid presentation than an innovation in thought. See Bonhöffer, 1890, 22 ff.; Zeller, p. 769; especially More, p. 107 f.

thing for man, since from failing to attain one's desire, and from encountering what one would avoid, come all the passions and sorrows of mankind. In every desire or aversion there is implicit a value-judgement concerning the good or evil of the particular thing involved, and these in turn rest upon general judgements (δόγματα) regarding things of value. If we are to make the proper use of our freedom in the field of desire or aversion we must have the correct judgements concerning good and evil. Now the correct judgement is, that nothing outside the realm of our moral purpose is either good or evil. Nothing, therefore, of that kind can rightly be the object of desire or aversion, hence we should restrict the will to the field in which alone it is free, and cannot, therefore, come to grief. But herein we need not merely the correct theoretical conviction, but also continual practice in application (ἄσκησις), and it is this which Epictetus attempts to impart to his pupils, for it is the foundation of his whole system of education.

Finally, in the field of choice or refusal belongs the duty[1] (τὸ καθῆκον) of man, his intelligent action in human and social relations. Externals, which are neither good nor evil, and so indifferent (ἀδιά-φορα), because not subject to our control, play a certain rôle, none the less, as matters with which we have to deal, indeed, but should regard no more seriously than players treat the actual ball with which they play, in comparison with the game itself. It is characteristic of Epictetus that, although he recognizes this part of Stoic doctrine in which the theoretical indifference of externals is in practice

[1] On the use of this term, cf. More, p. 116, 12.

largely abandoned, he manifests but slight interest in it.

Among duties he is concerned principally with those of a social character. Nature places us in certain relations to other persons, and these determine our obligations to parents, brothers, children, kinsmen, friends, fellow-citizens, and mankind in general. We ought to have the sense of fellowship and partnership (κοινωνικοί), that is, in thought and in action we ought to remember the social organization in which we have been placed by the divine order. The shortcomings of our fellow-men are to be met with patience and charity, and we should not allow ourselves to grow indignant over them, for they too are a necessary element in the universal plan.

The religious possibilities of Stoicism are developed further by Epictetus than by any other representative of the school. The conviction that the universe is wholly governed by an all-wise, divine Providence is for him one of the principal supports of the doctrine of values. All things, even apparent evils, are the will of God, comprehended in his universal plan, and therefore good from the point of view of the whole. It is our moral duty to elevate ourselves to this conception, to see things as God sees them. The man who reconciles his will to the will of God, and so recognizes that every event is necessary and reasonable for the best interest of the whole, feels no discontent with anything outside the control of his free will. His happiness he finds in filling the rôle which God has assigned him, becoming thereby a voluntary co-worker with God, and in filling this rôle no man can hinder him.

INTRODUCTION

Religion as reconciliation to the inevitable—ἑκόντα δέχεσθαι τὰ ἀναγκαῖα (frg. 8), *in gratiam cum fato revertere* [1]—is almost perfectly exemplified in Epictetus, for with him philosophy has definitely turned religion, and his instruction has become less secular than clerical.[2]   But it is astonishing to what heights of sincere devotion, of intimate communion, he attained, though starting with the monistic preconceptions of his school, for the very God who took, as he felt, such personal interest in him, was after all but "a subtle form of matter pervading the grosser physical elements . . . this Providence only another name for a mechanical law of expansion and contraction, absolutely predetermined in its everlasting recurrences."[3]   Of his theology one can scarcely speak.   His personal needs and his acquiescence with tradition led him to make of his God more than the materials of his philosophical tenets could allow.   The result is for our modern thinking an almost incredible mixture of Theism, Pantheism, and Polytheism, and it is impossible, out of detached expressions, to construct a consistent system.   As a matter of fact, with a naïve faith in God as a kind of personification of the soul's desire, he seems to have cherished simultaneously all of these mutually exclusive views of his nature.   His moral end was eudaemonism,

---

[1] Seneca, *Ep.* 91, 15.   "Dass der Mensch ins Unvermeidliche sich füge, darauf dringen alle Religionen; jede sucht auf ihre Weise mit dieser Aufgabe fertig zu werden."—Goethe.

[2] Cf. Lagrange, p. 211.—"The school of the philosophers is a hospital" (*cf.* Epict. III. 23, 30).

[3] More, p. 167, and *cf.* the whole brilliant passage, p. 162 ff.

to which, in a singularly frank expression (I. 4, 27),
he was ready to sacrifice even truth itself. No
wonder, then, he cared little for logic as such and
not at all for science.[1] " The moralist assumes
that what lies upon his heart as an essential need,
must also be the essence and heart of reality. . . .
In looking at everything from the point of view
of happiness men bound the arteries of scientific
research." Though spoken of the Socratic schools
in general, this word of Nietzsche's [2] seems especially apt of Epictetus. He was of an age when
the search for happiness by the process of consulting
merely the instincts of the heart was leading
rapidly to an alienation from scientific truth and
a prodigious decline in richness of cultural experience.

Yet even in his happiness, which we cannot dismiss
as a mere pose, there was something wanting. The
existence of evil was in one breath denied, and in
another presumed by the elaborate preparations that
one must make to withstand it. " And having done
all, to stand ? " No, even after having done all, " the
house might get too full of smoke," the hardships of
life too great any longer to endure ; the ominous
phrase, " the door is open," or its equivalent, the final
recourse of suicide, recurs at intervals through his
pages like a tolling bell. And beyond ? Nothing.
Nothing to *fear* indeed ; " the dewdrop sinks into the
shining sea." " When He provides the necessities
no longer, He sounds the recall ; He opens the door
and says, ' Go.' Where ? To nothing you need
fear, but back to that from which you came, to what

[1] *Cf.* Zeller, p. 770.
[2] *Menschliches, Allzumenschliches*, I. 21 ; 23.

is friendly and akin to you, to the physical elements"
(III. 13, 14). But at the same time there is nothing
to hope for.[1]

That Epictetus was influenced by the writings of
the New Testament has often been suggested.
There were those in late antiquity who asserted
it,[2] and it was natural enough in an age when
Tertullian and Jerome believed that Seneca had
conversed with Paul, and in Musonius Rufus, the
teacher of Epictetus, Justin (II. 8) recognizes a
kindred spirit. But despite the recrudescence of
the idea from time to time, and the existence of a
few scholars in our own generation who seem yet
to believe it, this question can be regarded as
definitely settled by the elaborate researches of
Bonhöffer (1911). Of course Epictetus knew about
the existence of Christians, to whom he twice refers,
calling them once Jews (II. 9, 19 ff.), and a second
time Galilaeans (IV. 7, 6), for there was an early
community at Nicopolis (Paul's Epistle to Titus, iii.
12), but he shared clearly in the vulgar prejudices
against them, and his general intolerance of variant
opinion, even when for conscience' sake, makes it
certain that he would never have bothered to read
their literature. The linguistic resemblances, which
are occasionally striking, like " Lord, have mercy ! "
κύριε, ἐλέησον, are only accidental, because Epictetus
was speaking the common language of ethical
exhortation in which the evangelists and apostles
wrote ; while the few specious similarities are
counterbalanced by as many striking differences
In the field of doctrine, the one notable point of

[1] See More, p. 168 ff.
[2] A Byzantine scholiast in Schenkl[2] xv.

disregard for the things of this world[1] is offset by
so many fundamental differences in presupposition,
if not in common ethical practice, that any kind
of a sympathetic understanding of the new religion
on the part of Epictetus is inconceivable.   A certain
ground-tone of religious capability, a fading of
interest in the conventional fields of human achievement, a personal kindliness and " harmlessness " of
character, a truly pathetic longing as of tired men
for a passive kind of happiness, an ill-defined
yearning to be " saved " by some spectacular and
divine intervention, these things are all to be found
in the *Discourses,* yet they are not there as an
effect of Christian teaching, but as a true reflection
of the tone and temper of those social circles to
which the Gospel made its powerful appeal.[2]

His influence has been extensive and has not
yet waned.   Hadrian was his friend, and, in the
next generation, Marcus Aurelius was his ardent
disciple.   Celsus, Gellius, and Lucian lauded him,
and Galen wrote a special treatise in his defence.
His merits were recognized by Christians like
Chrysostom, Gregory of Nazianzus, and Augustine,
while Origen rated him in some respects even

---

[1] " I find in Epictetus," says Pascal, " an incomparable
art to disturb the repose of those who seek it in things
external, and to force them to recognize that it is impossible
for them to find anything but the error and the suffering
which they are seeking to escape, if they do not give
themselves without reserve to God alone."

[2] " For it is doubtful if there was ever a Christian of
the early Church," remarks von Wilamowitz (*Kultur der
Gegenwart*[3], I. 8, 244), " who came as close to the real teaching
of Jesus as it stands in the synoptic gospels as did this
Phrygian."

above Plato. His *Manual,* with a few simple changes, principally in the proper names, was adapted by two different Christian ascetics as a rule and guide of monastic life.[1]

In modern times his vogue started rather slowly with translations by Perotti and Politian, but vernacular versions began to appear in the sixteenth century, and at the end of that century and the first part of the subsequent one, Epictetus was one of the most powerful forces in the movement of Neo-Stoicism, especially under the protagonists Justus Lipsius and Bishop Guillaume Du Vair.[2] His work and the essays of Montaigne were the principal secular readings of Pascal, and it was with Epictetus and his disciple Marcus Aurelius that the Earl of Shaftesbury "was most thoroughly conversant." [3] Men as different as Touissant L'Ouverture and Landor, Frederick the Great and Leopardi, have been among his admirers. The number of editions and new printings of his works, or of portions or translations of the same, averages considerably more than one for each year since the invention of printing. In the twentieth century, through the inclusion of Crossley's *Golden Sayings of Epictetus* in Charles William Eliot's *Harvard Series of Classics,* and of the *Manual* in Carl Hilty's *Glück,* of which two works upwards of three hundred and

[1] The same was done again in the seventeenth century for the Carthusians by Matthias Mittner (1632), who took the first 35 of his 50 precepts *Ad conservandam animi pacem* from the *Encheiridion.* See *Acta Erudit.* 1726, 264.

[2] See Zanta's elaborate work upon the share taken by these men in the movement.

[3] B. Rand: *The Life, etc., of Anthony, Earl of Shaftesbury* (author of the *Characteristics*), (1900), p. **xi.**

fifty thousand copies had, at a recent date, been sold, it may safely be asserted that more copies of portions of his work have been printed in the last two decades than ever existed all told from his own day down to that time.

In concluding one can hardly refrain from translating a portion of the sincere and stirring passage in which Justus Lipsius, a great man and a distinguished scholar, paid Epictetus the tribute of his homage:

"So much for Seneca; another brilliant star arises, Epictetus, his second in time, but not in merit; comparable with him in the weight, if not in the bulk, of his writings; superior in his life. He was a man who relied wholly upon himself and God, but not on Fortune. In origin low and servile, in body lame and feeble, in mind most exalted, and brilliant among the lights of every age. . . .

"But few of his works remain: the *Encheiridion*, assuredly a noble piece, and as it were the soul of Stoic moral philosophy; besides that, the *Discourses*, which he delivered on the streets, in his house, and in the school, collected and arranged by Arrian. Nor are these all extant. . . . But, so help me God, what a keen and lofty spirit in them! a soul aflame, and burning with love of the honourable! There is nothing in Greek their like, unless I am mistaken; I mean with such notable vigour and fire. A novice or one unacquainted with true philosophy he will hardly stir or affect, but when a man has made some progress or is already far advanced, it is amazing how Epictetus stirs him up, and though he is always touching some tender

spot, yet he gives delight also. . . . There is no one who better influences and shapes a good mind. I never read that old man without a stirring of my soul within me, and, as with Homer, I think the more of him each time I re-read him, for he seems always new; and even after I *have* returned to him I feel that I ought to return to him yet once more."

BIBLIOGRAPHY [1]

THE *editio princeps* of Epictetus was prepared by Victor Trincavelli at Venice, in 1535, from a singularly faulty MS., so that it is valueless for the purposes of textual criticism. The first substantial work of a critical character was done by Jacob Schegk, a distinguished professor of medicine at Tübingen, in the edition of Basel, 1554. Although few changes were made in the Greek text, Schegk employed his admirable Latin version as a medium for the correction of hundreds of passages. Even greater were the services of Hieronymus Wolf, whose edition, with translation and commentary, Basel, 1560, is perhaps the most important landmark in Epictetean studies, but for some reason failed to influence markedly the common tradition, which long thereafter continued to reproduce the inferior Greek text of Schegk (Trincavelli).

The next advance is connected with the name of John Upton, whose work appeared in parts, London, 1739–41. Upton had some knowledge of a number of MSS., and in particular a " codex," which was a copy of the Trincavelli edition that contained in the margins numerous readings of a MS. now in Mutina, and possibly other MSS., together with notes and emendations from Wolf, Salmasius, and others, so that one cannot be certain always just what "authority" is behind any particular reading whose

[1] For details see my forthcoming *Contributions toward a Bibliography of Epictetus.*

source is otherwise not accounted for. He had, moreover, the annotations of Anthony, Earl of Shaftesbury, and the assistance of the learned James Harris, and his contributions to the interpretation of Epictetus in the elaborate commentary are numerous. Richard Bentley's sagacious and often brilliant emendations entered in the margins of his copy of the Trincavelli edition remained unfortunately unknown until quite recently, as also the ingenious and stimulating, but on the whole less carefully considered, annotations of J. J. Reiske (in H. Schenkl's edition).

Appropriately designated *Monumenta* (*Epicteteae Philosophiae Monumenta*) is the great work in five large volumes by Johannes Schweighäuser, Leipzig, 1799–1800, immediately following a notable edition, in fact the only really critical edition, of the *Encheiridion* (1798), which, despite its imperfections, subsequent editors have been content merely to reprint. Schweighäuser's work is characterized by acumen, industry, and lucidity, and it will be long before it is entirely superseded. The edition by A. Koraes, Paris, 1826, although its author was a learned and ingenious scholar, is marred by a number of unnecessary rewritings.

A substantial critical edition we owe to the painstaking labours of Heinrich Schenkl (Leipzig, 1894; *editio minor*, 1898; second edition, 1916). This is based upon the Bodleian MS. Misc. Graec. 251, s. xi/xii, which Schenkl and, it would appear, J. L. G. Mowat before him (*Journ. of. Philol.* 1877, 60 ff. ; *cf.* J. B. Mayor, *Cl. Rev.* 1895, 31 f., and Schenkl, *ed. minor*, 1898, p. iv; *ed.* 1916, p. iv) have shown to be the archetype of all the numerous existing MSS. of

the *Discourses*.[1] For the *editio minor* (1898) a new collation was prepared by the skilled hand of W. M. Lindsay, and for the second edition (1916) Schenkl himself had photographs of the complete MS. to work with, while T. W. Allen furnished an expert's transcription of the Scholia, with the result that, although the first edition by Schenkl left something to be desired in the accuracy and fullness of its MS. readings, one can approach the *apparatus criticus* of the second edition with all reasonable confidence. Schenkl's own contributions to the constitution of the text by way of emendation are considerable, the number of emendations, however, wisely somewhat reduced in the latest printing. A very full *index verborum* greatly facilitates studies of all kinds.

Of the *Encheiridion* scores of editions have appeared, but hardly any that deserve mention either for critical or exegetical value, except those that form parts of the above-mentioned editions by Wolf, Upton, and Schweighäuser (a better text in his separate edition of the *Encheiridion*, Leipzig, 1798). But a few necessary remarks about that work and the *Fragments* will be given in the introduction to the second volume of the present work.

A brief list of some of the most important titles bearing upon the criticism of Epictetus:—

H. von Arnim, article "Epiktetos," in Pauly's *Realencyclopädie, etc., Zweite Bearbeitung,* VI.

---

[1] For some account of a large number of these, see Schenkl[2], LV–LVIII. Their value is very slight indeed, and only for purposes of emendation, since as yet there seem to exist no authentic traces of the existence of a second early MS. of Epictetus, so that the *Discourses* must have survived the Middle Ages in only a single exemplar.

126–31.   Contains an excellent summary of his teaching.

E. V. Arnold, *Roman Stoicism*. Cambridge, 1911. Article "Epictetus," in *Hastings, Enc. of Rel.* VI, 323 f.

R. Asmus, *Quaestiones Epicteteae*. Freiburg i. B. 1888.

R. Bentley's critical notes on Arrian's "Discourses of Epictetus"; *Trans. Amer. Philol. Assoc.* 1921, 53, 40–52 (by W. A. Oldfather).

A. Bonhöffer, *Epiktet und die Stoa*. Stuttgart, 1890. *Die Ethik des Stoikers Epiktet*. Stuttgart, 1894. *Epiktet und das Neue Testament*. Giessen, 1911. "Epiktet und das Neue Testament," *Zeitschr. für die neutest. Wiss.* 1912, 13, 281–92. These are incomparably the most important critical works on the subjects which they cover, and on many points have reached definitive conclusions.

R. Bultmann, *Der Stil der paulinischen Predigt und die kynisch-stoische Diatribe*. Marburg, 1910. "Das religiöse Moment in der ethischen Unterweisung des Epiktets und das Neue Testament," *Zeitschr. für die neutest. Wiss.* 1912, 13, 97 ff., 177 ff.

Th. Colardeau, *Étude sur Épictète*. Paris, 1903.

F. W. Farrar, *Seekers after God*. London, 1863, and often reprinted.

H. Gomperz, *Die Lebensauffassung der griechischen Philosophen und das Ideal der inneren Freiheit*. Jena, 1904. P. 186, and especially 195 ff. 2nd ed. 1915.

O. Halbauer, *De diatribis Epicteti*. Leipzig, 1911.

K. Hartmann, "Arrian und Epiktet," *Neue Jahrb.* 1905, 15, 248–75.

E. Hatch, *The Influence of Greek Ideas and Usages upon the Christian Church*. Sixth ed., London, 1897.

BIBLIOGRAPHY

Fr. M. J. Lagrange, "La philosophie religieuse d'Épictète, etc." *Revue Biblique*, 1912, 91 ff. ; 192 ff.

W. S. Landor, *Imaginary Conversations of Greeks and
   Romans.* London, 1853, and often reprinted.
   " Epictetus and Seneca."

J. Lipsius, *Manuductio ad Stoicam philosophiam.* I. xix,
   pp. 62–64. ed. Antwerp, 1604. Vol. IV, p.
   681 f., ed. Wesel, 1625.

C. Martha, *Les moralistes sous l'empire romain, philo-
   sophes et poètes.* Paris, 1865, and often reprinted.

J. B. Mayor, Rev. of H. Schenkl's " Epictetus," *Class.
   Rev.*, 1895, 9, 31–7.

P. E. H. Melcher, " De sermone Epicteteo quibus
   rebus ab Attica regula discedat," *Diss. philol.
   Hallenses*, 17, 1905.

G. Misch, *Geschichte der Autobiographie.* Leipzig and
   Berlin, 1907. Pp. 257–65.

P. E. More, *Hellenistic Philosophies.* Princeton, 1923.
   Epictetus, pp. 94–171.

R. Mücke, *Zu Arrians und Epiktets Sprachgebrauch.*
   Nordhausen, 1887.

B. Pascal, *Entretien avec de Saci sur Épictète et Montaigne.* First published in authentic form in M.
   Havet : *Pensées de Pascal*, Paris, 1852, and frequently since that time. For discussions of
   Pascal's very interesting views see especially
   M. J. Guyau : *Pascal, etc.*, Paris, 1875. C. A.
   Saint-Beuve : *Port Royal*, fifth edition. Paris,
   1888 ff., Vol. II. pp. 381 ff. F. Strowski : *Histoire
   du sentiment religieux en France au xviii sècle*,
   fourth edition. Paris, 1909.

R. Renner. *Zu Epiktets Diatriben.* Amberg, 1904.
   Das Kind. Ein Gleichnismittel des Epiktets
   München, 1905.

BIBLIOGRAPHY

D. S. Sharp, *Epictetus and the New Testament*. London, 1914.

Rt. Rev. J. L. Spalding, *Glimpses of Truth*, with essays on Epictetus and Marcus Aurelius. Chicago, 1903. Third edition, 1913.

L. Stein, *Die Psychologie der Stoa*. Berlin, 1886, 1888.

J. Stuhrmann, *De vocabulis notionum philosophicarum in Epicteti libris*. Neustadt, 1885.

K. Vorlander, "Christliche Gedanken eines heidnischen Philosophen," *Preuss. Jahrb.*, 1897, pp. 89, 193–222.

Louis Weber, "La morale d'Épictète et les besoins présents de l'enseignement moral," *Rev. de Metaph. et de Moral*, six articles, 1905–1909.

U. von Wilamowitz-Möllendorff, "Die griechische Literatur des Altertums," in *Kultur der Gegenwart*[3], I. 8 (Leipzig and Berlin, 1912), 244. Compare also the admirable statement in his *Griechisches Lesebuch*, I. (Berlin, 1902), pp. 230–1.

Th. Zahn, *Der Stoiker Epiktet und sein Verhältnis zum Christentum*. Erlangen, 1894. Second edition, Leipzig, 1895. The thesis, that Epictetus was acquainted with the New Testament, has been very generally rejected, but the address has value apart from that contention.

L. Zanta, *La renaissance du stoicisme au xvie siècle*. Paris, 1914. *La traduction française du Manuel d'Épictète d'André de Rivaudeau, etc.* Paris, 1914.

E. Zeller, *Die Philosophie der Griechen*[4], III. 1 (Leipzig, 1909), 765–81; III. 2 (1902), 910–14.

There have been three notable translations into

BIBLIOGRAPHY

English of Epictetus; a vigorous and idiomatic repro-
duction by Elizabeth Carter (1758, and often thereafter), a learned and exact rendition by George Long
(1877, and frequently reproduced), and a most fluent
and graceful version by P. E. Matheson (1916). To
all of these, but especially to the last mentioned, I
have been indebted upon occasion.

SYMBOLS

S = Cod. Bodleianus Misc. Graec. 251, s. xi/xii.
Sa, Sb, Sc, Sd = corrections of different periods, as
    discriminated by Schenkl.
s = one or more copies of S.

In general only the important deviations from S
have been recorded in the *apparatus criticus*. All
substantial emendations, when made by modern
scholars, are recorded, but the obvious corrections
made by Greek scholars themselves, either on S
itself or in its numerous copies, have generally been
passed over in silence, since the number of these is
so large (for S is full of errors of all kinds) that they
would seriously clutter up the page without adding
anything important to our knowledge. For details
of the MS. tradition the reader is referred to the
elaborate *apparatus* in Schenkl's second ed. (Leipzig,
1916), upon which the present text is dependent,
although I have not hesitated to depart from his
reading or his punctuation in a number of passages.

W. A. OLDFATHER.

Urbana, Illinois.
   March 6, 1925.

ARRIAN'S DISCOURSES
OF EPICTETUS

ΑΡΡΙΑΝΟΥ
ΤΩΝ ΕΠΙΚΤΗΤΟΥ ΔΙΑΤΡΙΒΩΝ
$\overline{\text{Α}}$ $\overline{\text{Β}}$ $\overline{\text{Γ}}$ $\overline{\text{Δ}}$[1]

$\overline{\text{Α}}$

ΚΕΦΑΛΑΙΑ ΤΟΥ $\overline{\text{Α}}$ ΒΙΒΛΙΟΥ

α'. Περὶ τῶν ἐφ' ἡμῖν καὶ οὐκ ἐφ' ἡμῖν.

β'. Πῶς ἄν τις σῴζοι τὸ κατὰ πρόσωπον ἐν παντί;

γ'. Πῶς ἄν τις ἀπὸ τοῦ τὸν θεὸν πατέρα εἶναι τῶν ἀνθρώπων ἐπὶ τὰ ἑξῆς ἐπέλθοι;

δ'. Περὶ προκοπῆς.

ε'. Πρὸς τοὺς Ἀκαδημαικούς.

ϛ'. Περὶ προνοίας.

ζ'. Περὶ τῆς χρείας τῶν μεταπιπτόντων καὶ ὑποθετικῶν καὶ τῶν ὁμοίων.

η'. Ὅτι αἱ δυνάμεις τοῖς ἀπαιδεύτοις οὐκ ἀσφαλεῖς.

θ'. Πῶς ἀπὸ τοῦ συγγενεῖς ἡμᾶς εἶναι τῷ θεῷ ἐπέλθοι ἄν τις ἐπὶ τὰ ἑξῆς;

ι'. Πρὸς τοὺς περὶ τὰς ἐν Ῥώμῃ προαγωγὰς ἐσπουδακότας.

ια'. Περὶ φιλοστοργίας.

ιβ'. Περὶ εὐαρεστήσεως.

ιγ'. Πῶς ἕκαστα ἔστι ποιεῖν ἀρεστῶς θεοῖς;

ιδ'. Ὅτι πάντας ἐφορᾷ τὸ θεῖον.

[1] The whole title supplied by Schenkl.

ARRIAN'S DISCOURSES OF EPICTETUS

IN FOUR BOOKS

BOOK I

Chapters of the First Book

3

Ἀρριανὸς Λουκίῳ Γελλίῳ χαίρειν

1 Οὔτε συνέγραψα ἐγὼ τοὺς Ἐπικτήτου λόγους
οὕτως ὅπως ἄν τις συγγράψειε τὰ τοιαῦτα οὔτε
ἐξήνεγκα εἰς ἀνθρώπους αὐτός, ὅς γε οὐδὲ συγ-
2 γράψαι φημί. ὅσα δὲ ἤκουον αὐτοῦ λέγοντος,
ταῦτα αὐτὰ ἐπειράθην αὐτοῖς ὀνόμασιν ὡς οἷόν
τε ἦν γραψάμενος ὑπομνήματα εἰς ὕστερον
ἐμαυτῷ διαφυλάξαι τῆς ἐκείνου διανοίας καὶ
3 παρρησίας. ἔστι δὴ τοιαῦτα ὥσπερ εἰκὸς ὁποῖα
ἄν τις αὐτόθεν ὁρμηθεὶς εἴποι πρὸς ἕτερον, οὐχ
ὁποῖα ἂν ἐπὶ τῷ ὕστερον ἐντυγχάνειν τινὰς
4 αὐτοῖς συγγράφοι. τοιαῦτα δ᾽ ὄντα οὐκ οἶδα
ὅπως οὔτε ἑκόντος ἐμοῦ οὔτε εἰδότος ἐξέπεσεν εἰς

---

[1] The contrast intended is between γράφω, "write," § 2,
and συγγράφω, "compose." Arrian had in mind, no doubt,
the works of Plato and Xenophon, which, although they pur-
ported to reproduce the words of Socrates, were in fact
highly finished literary compositions.

BOOK I

ARRIAN TO LUCIUS GELLIUS, greeting:

I HAVE not composed these *Words of Epictetus* as one might be said to "compose" books of this kind, nor have I of my own act published them to the world; indeed, I acknowledge that I have not "composed" them at all.[1] But whatever I heard him say I used to write down, word for word, as best I could, endeavouring to preserve it as a memorial, for my own future use, of his way of thinking and the frankness of his speech. They are, accordingly, as you might expect, such remarks as one man might make off-hand to another, not such as he would compose for men to read in after time. This being their character, they have fallen, I know not how, without my will or knowledge, into the hands

5

5 ἀνθρώπους. ἀλλ' ἐμοί γε οὐ πολὺς λόγος, εἰ οὐχ
ἱκανὸς φανοῦμαι συγγράφειν, Ἐπικτήτῳ τε οὐδ'
ὀλίγος, εἰ καταφρονήσει τις αὐτοῦ τῶν λόγων,
ἐπεὶ καὶ λέγων αὐτοὺς οὐδενὸς ἄλλου δῆλος ἦν
ἐφιέμενος ὅτι μὴ κινῆσαι τὰς γνώμας τῶν ἀκου-
6 όντων πρὸς τὰ βέλτιστα. εἰ μὲν δὴ τοῦτό γε
αὐτὸ διαπράττοιντο οἱ λόγοι οὗτοι, ἔχοιεν ἂν
οἶμαι ὅπερ χρὴ ἔχειν τοὺς τῶν φιλοσόφων λόγους·
7 εἰ δὲ μή, ἀλλ' ἐκεῖνο ἴστωσαν οἱ ἐντυγχάνοντες
ὅτι, αὐτὸς ὁπότε ἔλεγεν αὐτούς, ἀνάγκη ἦν τοῦτο
πάσχειν τὸν ἀκροώμενον αὐτῶν ὅπερ ἐκεῖνος
8 αὐτὸν παθεῖν ἠβούλετο. εἰ δ' οἱ λόγοι αὐτοὶ ἐφ'
αὑτῶν τοῦτο οὐ διαπράττονται, τυχὸν μὲν ἐγὼ
αἴτιος, τυχὸν δὲ καὶ ἀνάγκη οὕτως ἔχειν. ἔρρωσο.

α′. Περὶ τῶν ἐφ' ἡμῖν καὶ οὐκ ἐφ' ἡμῖν

1 Τῶν ἄλλων δυνάμεων οὐδεμίαν εὑρήσετε αὐτὴν
αὑτῆς θεωρητικήν, οὐ τοίνυν οὐδὲ δοκιμαστικὴν
2 ἢ ἀποδοκιμαστικήν. ἡ γραμματικὴ μέχρι τίνος
κέκτηται τὸ θεωρητικόν; μέχρι τοῦ διαγνῶναι
τὰ γράμματα. ἡ μουσική; μέχρι τοῦ διαγνῶναι
3 τὸ μέλος. αὐτὴ οὖν αὑτὴν θεωρεῖ τις αὐτῶν;
οὐδαμῶς. ἀλλ' ὅτε μέν, ἄν τι γράφῃς τῷ ἑταίρῳ,
δεῖ τούτων τῶν γραπτέων, ἡ γραμματικὴ ἐρεῖ·
πότερον δὲ γραπτέον τῷ ἑταίρῳ ἢ οὐ γραπτέον,
ἡ γραμματικὴ οὐκ ἐρεῖ. καὶ περὶ τῶν μελῶν

---

[1] δυνάμεις includes arts as well as faculties, and both are
dealt with in this context.

of men. Yet to me it is a matter of small concern
if I shall be thought incapable of "composing" a
work, and to Epictetus of no concern at all if anyone
shall despise his words, seeing that even when he
uttered them he was clearly aiming at nothing else
but to incite the minds of his hearers to the best
things. If, now, these words of his should produce
that same effect, they would have, I think, just that
success which the words of the philosophers ought
to have; but if not, let those who read them be
assured of this, that when Epictetus himself spoke
them, the hearer could not help but feel exactly
what Epictetus wanted him to feel. If, however,
the words by themselves do not produce this effect,
perhaps I am at fault, or else, perhaps, it cannot
well be otherwise. Farewell.

CHAPTER I

*Of the things which are under our control and not
under our control*

AMONG the arts and faculties [1] in general you will
find none that is self-contemplative, and therefore
none that is either self-approving or self-disapproving.
How far does the art of grammar possess the power
of contemplation? Only so far as to pass judgement
upon what is written. How far the art of music?
Only so far as to pass judgement upon the melody.
Does either of them, then, contemplate itself? Not
at all. But if you are writing to a friend and are at
a loss as to what to write, the art of grammar will
tell you; yet whether or no you are to write to your
friend at all, the art of grammar will not tell. The

7

ὡσαύτως ἡ μουσική· πότερον δ' ᾀστέον νῦν καὶ
κιθαριστέον ἢ οὔτε ᾀστέον οὔτε κιθαριστέον οὐκ
4 ἐρεῖ. τίς οὖν ἐρεῖ; ἡ καὶ αὑτὴν θεωροῦσα καὶ
τἆλλα πάντα. αὕτη δ' ἐστὶ τίς; ἡ δύναμις ἡ
λογική· μόνη γὰρ αὕτη καὶ αὑτὴν κατανοήσουσα
παρείληπται, τίς τέ ἐστι καὶ τί δύναται καὶ
πόσου ἀξία οὖσα ἐλήλυθεν, καὶ τὰς ἄλλας ἀπά-
5 σας. τί γάρ ἐστιν ἄλλο τὸ λέγον ὅτι χρυσίον
καλόν ἐστιν; αὐτὸ γὰρ οὐ λέγει. δῆλον ὅτι ἡ
6 χρηστικὴ δύναμις ταῖς φαντασίαις. τί ἄλλο
τὸ μουσικήν, γραμματικήν, τὰς ἄλλας δυνάμεις
διακρῖνον, δοκιμάζον τὰς χρήσεις αὐτῶν καὶ τοὺς
καιροὺς παραδεικνύον; οὐδὲν ἄλλο.

7 Ὥσπερ οὖν ἦν ἄξιον, τὸ κράτιστον ἁπάντων
καὶ κυριεῦον οἱ θεοὶ μόνον ἐφ' ἡμῖν ἐποίησαν, τὴν
χρῆσιν τὴν ὀρθὴν ταῖς φαντασίαις, τὰ δ' ἄλλα
8 οὐκ ἐφ' ἡμῖν. ἆρά γε ὅτι οὐκ ἤθελον; ἐγὼ μὲν
δοκῶ ὅτι, εἰ ἠδύναντο, κἀκεῖνα ἂν ἡμῖν ἐπέ-
9 τρεψαν· ἀλλὰ πάντως οὐκ ἠδύναντο. ἐπὶ γῆς
γὰρ ὄντας καὶ σώματι συνδεδεμένους τοιούτῳ καὶ
κοινωνοῖς τοιούτοις πῶς οἷόν τ' ἦν εἰς ταῦτα ὑπὸ
τῶν ἐκτὸς μὴ ἐμποδίζεσθαι;

10 Ἀλλὰ τί λέγει ὁ Ζεύς; "'Ἐπίκτητε, εἰ οἷόν
τε ἦν, καὶ τὸ σωμάτιον ἄν σου καὶ τὸ κτησίδιον
11 ἐποίησα ἐλεύθερον καὶ ἀπαραπόδιστον. νῦν δέ,

8

same holds true of the art of music with regard to melodies; but whether you are at this moment to sing and play on the lyre, or neither sing nor play, it will not tell. What art or faculty, then, will tell? That one which contemplates both itself and everything else. And what is this? The reasoning faculty; for this is the only one we have inherited which will take knowledge both of itself—what it is, and of what it is capable, and how valuable a gift it is to us—and likewise of all the other faculties. For what else is it that tells us gold is beautiful? For the gold itself does not tell us. Clearly it is the faculty which makes use of external impressions. What else judges with discernment the art of music, the art of grammar, the other arts and faculties, passing judgement upon their uses and pointing out the seasonable occasions for their use? Nothing else does.

As was fitting, therefore, the gods have put under our control only the most excellent faculty of all and that which dominates the rest, namely, the power to make correct use of external impressions, but all the others they have not put under our control. Was it indeed because they would not? I for one think that had they been able they would have entrusted us with the others also; but they were quite unable to do that. For since we are upon earth and trammelled by an earthy body and by earthy associates, how was it possible that, in respect of them, we should not be hampered by external things?

But what says Zeus? "Epictetus, had it been possible I should have made both this paltry body and this small estate of thine free and unhampered.

9

μή σε λανθανέτω, τοῦτο οὐκ ἔστιν σόν, ἀλλὰ
12 πηλὸς κομψῶς πεφυραμένος. ἐπεὶ δὲ τοῦτο οὐκ
ἠδυνάμην ἐδώκαμέν σοι μέρος τι ἡμέτερον, τὴν
δύναμιν ταύτην τὴν ὁρμητικήν τε καὶ ἀφορ-
μητικὴν καὶ ὀρεκτικήν τε καὶ ἐκκλιτικὴν καὶ
ἁπλῶς τὴν χρηστικὴν ταῖς φαντασίαις, ἧς ἐπι-
μελούμενος καὶ ἐν ᾗ τὰ σαυτοῦ τιθέμενος οὐδέποτε
κωλυθήσῃ, οὐδέποτ' ἐμποδισθήσῃ, οὐ στενάξεις,
13 οὐ μέμψῃ, οὐ κολακεύσεις οὐδένα. τί οὖν; μή
τι μικρά σοι φαίνεται ταῦτα;" "μὴ γένοιτο."
"ἀρκῇ οὖν αὐτοῖς;" "εὔχομαι δὲ τοῖς θεοῖς."

14 Νῦν δ' ἑνὸς δυνάμενοι ἐπιμελεῖσθαι καὶ ἑνὶ
προσηρτηκέναι ἑαυτοὺς μᾶλλον θέλομεν πολλῶν
ἐπιμελεῖσθαι καὶ πολλοῖς προσδεδέσθαι καὶ τῷ
σώματι καὶ τῇ κτήσει καὶ ἀδελφῷ καὶ φίλῳ καὶ
15 τέκνῳ καὶ δούλῳ. ἅτε οὖν πολλοῖς προσδεδε-
μένοι βαρούμεθα ὑπ' αὐτῶν καὶ καθελκόμεθα.
16 διὰ τοῦτο, ἂν ἄπλοια ᾖ, καθήμεθα σπώμενοι καὶ
παρακύπτομεν συνεχῶς· "τίς ἄνεμος πνεῖ;"
βορέας. "τί ἡμῖν καὶ αὐτῷ; πότε ὁ ζέφυρος
πνεύσει;" ὅταν αὐτῷ δόξῃ, ὦ βέλτιστε, ἢ τῷ
Αἰόλῳ. σὲ γὰρ οὐκ ἐποίησεν ὁ θεὸς ταμίαν τῶν
17 ἀνέμων, ἀλλὰ τὸν Αἴολον. "τί οὖν;" δεῖ τὰ
ἐφ' ἡμῖν βέλτιστα κατασκευάζειν, τοῖς δ' ἄλλοις
χρῆσθαι ὡς πέφυκεν. "πῶς οὖν πέφυκεν;" ὡς
ἂν ὁ θεὸς θέλῃ.

18 "Ἐμὲ οὖν νῦν τραχηλοκοπεῖσθαι μόνον;" τί
οὖν; ἤθελες πάντας τραχηλοκοπηθῆναι, ἵνα σὺ
19 παραμυθίαν ἔχῃς; οὐ θέλεις οὕτως ἐκτεῖναι τὸν
τράχηλον, ὡς Λατερανός τις ἐν τῇ Ῥώμῃ κελευ-

---

[1] Compare I. ii. 38.
[2] The exact meaning of σπώμενοι is uncertain.

But as it is—let it not escape thee—this body is not thine own, but only clay cunningly compounded. Yet since I could not give thee this, we have given thee a certain portion of ourself, this faculty of choice and refusal, of desire and aversion, or, in a word, the faculty which makes use of external impressions; if thou care for this and place all that thou hast therein, thou shalt never be thwarted, never hampered, shalt not groan, shalt not blame, shalt not flatter any man. What then? Are these things small in thy sight?" "Far be it from me!" "Art thou, then, content with them?" "I pray the Gods I may be." [1]

But now, although it is in our power to care for one thing only and devote ourselves to but one, we choose rather to care for many things, and to be tied fast to many, even to our body and our estate and brother and friend and child and slave. Wherefore, being tied fast to many things, we are burdened and dragged down by them. That is why, if the weather keeps us from sailing, we sit down and fidget [2] and keep constantly peering about. "What wind is blowing?" we ask. Boreas. "What have we to do with it? When will Zephyrus blow?" When it pleases, good sir, or rather when Aeolus pleases. For God has not made you steward of the winds, but Aeolus. [3] "What then?" We must make the best of what is under our control, and take the rest as its nature is. "How, then, is its nature?" As God wills.

"Must I, then, be the only one to be beheaded now?" Why, did you want everybody to be beheaded for your consolation? Are you not willing to

[3] Alluding to Homer, *Odyssey*, X. 21.

σθεὶς ὑπὸ τοῦ Νέρωνος ἀποκεφαλισθῆναι ; ἐκτείνας
γὰρ τὸν τράχηλον καὶ πληγεὶς καὶ πρὸς αὐτὴν
τὴν πληγὴν ἀσθενῆ γενομένην ἐπ' ὀλίγον συνελ-
20 κυσθεὶς πάλιν ἐξέτεινεν. ἀλλὰ καὶ ἔτι πρότερον
προσελθόντι τις Ἐπαφροδίτῳ τῷ ἀπελευθέρῳ
τοῦ Νέρωνος καὶ ἀνακρίνοντι αὐτὸν ὑπὲρ τοῦ
συγκρουσθῆναι "Ἄν τι θέλω," φησίν, "ἐρῶ σου
τῷ κυρίῳ."

21   "Τί οὖν δεῖ πρόχειρον ἔχειν ἐν τοῖς τοιούτοις ;"
τί γὰρ ἄλλο ἢ τί ἐμὸν καὶ τί οὐκ ἐμὸν καὶ τί μοι
22 ἔξεστιν καὶ τί μοι οὐκ ἔξεστιν ; ἀποθανεῖν με δεῖ·
μή τι οὖν καὶ στένοντα ; δεθῆναι· μή τι καὶ
θρηνοῦντα ; φυγαδευθῆναι· μή τις οὖν κωλύει
γελῶντα καὶ εὐθυμοῦντα καὶ εὐροοῦντα ; "εἰπὲ
23 τὰ ἀπόρρητα." οὐ λέγω· τοῦτο γὰρ ἐπ' ἐμοί
ἐστιν. "ἀλλὰ δήσω σε." ἄνθρωπε, τί λέγεις ;
ἐμέ ; τὸ σκέλος μου δήσεις, τὴν προαίρεσιν δὲ
24 οὐδ' ὁ Ζεὺς νικῆσαι δύναται. "εἰς φυλακήν σε
βαλῶ." τὸ σωμάτιον. "ἀποκεφαλίσω σε." πότε
οὖν σοι εἶπον, ὅτι μόνου ἐμοῦ ὁ τράχηλος ἀναπό-
25 τμητός ἐστιν ; ταῦτα ἔδει μελετᾶν τοὺς φιλο-
σοφοῦντας, ταῦτα καθ' ἡμέραν γράφειν, ἐν τούτοις
γυμνάζεσθαι.

26   Θρασέας εἰώθει λέγειν "Σήμερον ἀναιρεθῆναι
27 θέλω μᾶλλον ἢ αὔριον φυγαδευθῆναι." τί οὖν
αὐτῷ Ῥοῦφος εἶπεν ; "Εἰ μὲν ὡς βαρύτερον
ἐκλέγῃ, τίς ἡ μωρία τῆς ἐκλογῆς ; εἰ δ' ὡς
κουφότερον, τίς σοι δέδωκεν ; οὐ θέλεις μελετᾶν
ἀρκεῖσθαι τῷ δεδομένῳ ;"

---

[1] For all ordinary proper names the reader is referred to
the Index.
[2] The point of the retort lies in the defiance of the officious
but all-powerful freedman.

stretch out your neck as did a certain Lateranus[1] at
Rome, when Nero ordered him to be beheaded?
For he stretched out his neck and received the
blow, but, as it was a feeble one, he shrank back
for an instant, and then stretched out his neck
again. Yes, and before that, when Epaphroditus,
a freedman of Nero, approached a certain man and
asked about the ground of his offence, he answered,
" If I wish anything, I will speak to your master."[2]

" What aid, then, must we have ready at hand in
such circumstances?" Why, what else than the
knowledge of what is mine, and what is not mine,
and what is permitted me, and what is not permitted me? I must die: must I, then, die groaning
too? I must be fettered: and wailing too? I must
go into exile: does anyone, then, keep me from
going with a smile and cheerful and serene? " Tell
your secrets." I say not a word; for this is under
my control. " But I will fetter you." What is that
you say, man? fetter *me*? My leg you will fetter,
but my moral purpose not even Zeus himself has
power to overcome. " I will throw you into prison."
My paltry body, rather! " I will behead you."
Well, when did I ever tell you that mine was the
only neck that could not be severed? These are
the lessons that philosophers ought to rehearse,
these they ought to write down daily, in these they
ought to exercise themselves.

Thrasea used to say: " I would rather be killed
to-day than banished to-morrow." What, then, did
Rufus say to him? " If you choose death as the
heavier of two misfortunes, what folly of choice!
But if as the lighter, who has given you the choice?
Are you not willing to practise contentment with
what has been given you?"

28 Διὰ τοῦτο γὰρ Ἀγριππῖνος τί ἔλεγεν; ὅτι
"Ἐγὼ ἐμαυτῷ ἐμπόδιος οὐ γίνομαι." ἀπηγγέλη
29 αὐτῷ ὅτι "κρίνῃ ἐν συγκλήτῳ."—"Ἀγαθῇ τύχῃ.
ἀλλὰ ἦλθεν ἡ πέμπτη" (ταύτῃ δ' εἰώθει γυμνα-
σάμενος ψυχρολουτρεῖν)· "ἀπέλθωμεν καὶ γυ-
30 μνασθῶμεν." γυμνασαμένῳ λέγει τις αὐτῷ ἐλθὼν
ὅτι "Κατακέκρισαι."—"Φυγῇ," φησίν, "ἢ θανάτῳ;"—"Φυγῇ."—"Τὰ ὑπάρχοντα τί;"—
"Οὐκ ἀφῃρέθη."—"Εἰς Ἀρίκειαν οὖν ἀπελθόντες
31 ἀριστήσωμεν."—Τοῦτ' ἔστι μεμελετηκέναι ἃ δεῖ
μελετᾶν, ὄρεξιν ἔκκλισιν ἀκώλυτα ἀπερίπτωτα
32 παρεσκευακέναι. ἀποθανεῖν με δεῖ. εἰ ἤδη, ἀπο-
θνήσκω· κἂν[1] μετ' ὀλίγον, νῦν ἀριστῶ τῆς ὥρας
ἐλθούσης, εἶτα τότε τεθνήξομαι. πῶς; ὡς προσήκει τὸν τὰ ἀλλότρια ἀποδιδόντα.

β'. Πῶς ἄν τις σῴζοι τὸ κατὰ πρόσωπον ἐν
παντί;

1 Τῷ λογικῷ ζῴῳ μόνον ἀφόρητόν ἐστι τὸ ἄλο-
2 γον, τὸ δ' εὔλογον φορητόν. πληγαὶ οὐκ εἰσὶν
ἀφόρητοι τῇ φύσει.—Τίνα τρόπον;—Ὅρα πῶς·
Λακεδαιμόνιοι μαστιγοῦνται μαθόντες ὅτι εὔλογόν
3 ἐστιν.—Τὸ δ' ἀπάγξασθαι οὐκ ἔστιν ἀφόρητον;—
Ὅταν γοῦν πάθῃ τις ὅτι εὔλογον, ἀπελθὼν

---

[1] C. Schenkl: καί S.

[1] The idea seems to be: By disregarding externals I do
not hinder the natural course of my mind and character,
that is, my true self.

[2] The word πρόσωπον carries something of the figurative
meaning "rôle" from the language of drama.

[3] Referring to the scourging of Spartan youths before the
altar of Artemis.

Wherefore, what was it that Agrippinus used to remark? "I am not standing in my own way."[1] Word was brought him, "Your case is being tried in the Senate."—"Good luck betide! But it is the fifth hour now" (he was in the habit of taking his exercise and then a cold bath at that hour); "let us be off and take our exercise." After he had finished his exercise someone came and told him, "You have been condemned."—"To exile," says he, "or to death?"—"To exile."—"What about my property?"—"It has not been confiscated."—"Well then, let us go to Aricia and take our lunch there." This is what it means to have rehearsed the lessons one ought to rehearse, to have set desire and aversion free from every hindrance and made them proof against chance. I must die. If forthwith, I die; and if a little later, I will take lunch now, since the hour for lunch has come, and afterwards I will die at the appointed time. How? As becomes the man who is giving back that which was another's.

CHAPTER II

How may a man preserve his proper character[2] upon every occasion?

To the rational being only the irrational is unendurable, but the rational is endurable. Blows are not by nature unendurable.—How so?—Observe how: Lacedaemonians take a scourging[3] once they have learned that it is rational.—But is it not unendurable to be hanged?—Hardly; at all events whenever a man feels that it is rational he goes and

15

1 ἀπήγξατο. ἁπλῶς ἐὰν προσέχωμεν, ὑπ' οὐδενὸς
οὕτως εὑρήσομεν τὸ ζῷον θλιβόμενον ὡς ὑπὸ τοῦ
ἀλόγου καὶ πάλιν ἐπ' οὐδὲν οὕτως ἑλκόμενον ὡς
ἐπὶ τὸ εὔλογον.

5 Ἄλλῳ δ' ἄλλο προσπίπτει τὸ εὔλογον καὶ
ἄλογον, καθάπερ καὶ ἀγαθὸν καὶ κακὸν ἄλλο
6 ἄλλῳ καὶ συμφέρον καὶ ἀσύμφορον. διὰ τοῦτο
μάλιστα παιδείας δεόμεθα, ὥστε μαθεῖν τοῦ εὐλόγου καὶ ἀλόγου πρόληψιν ταῖς ἐπὶ μέρους[1]
7 οὐσίαις ἐφαρμόζειν συμφώνως τῇ φύσει. εἰς δὲ
τὴν τοῦ εὐλόγου καὶ ἀλόγου κρίσιν οὐ μόνον ταῖς
τῶν ἐκτὸς ἀξίαις συγχρώμεθα, ἀλλὰ καὶ τῶν
8 κατὰ τὸ πρόσωπον ἑαυτοῦ ἕκαστος. τῷ γάρ τινι
εὔλογον τὸ ἀμίδαν παρακρατεῖν αὐτὸ μόνον βλέ-
ποντι, ὅτι μὴ παρακρατήσας μὲν πληγὰς λήψεται
καὶ τροφὰς οὐ λήψεται, παρακρατήσας δ' οὐ
9 πείσεταί τι τραχὺ ἢ ἀνιαρόν· ἄλλῳ δέ τινι οὐ
μόνον τὸ αὐτὸν παρακρατῆσαι ἀφόρητον δοκεῖ,
ἀλλὰ καὶ τὸ ἄλλου παρακρατοῦντος ἀνασχέσθαι.
10 ἂν οὖν μου πυνθάνῃ "παρακρατήσω τὴν ἀμίδαν
ἢ μή;" ἐρῶ σοι ὅτι μείζονα ἀξίαν ἔχει τὸ λαβεῖν τροφὰς τοῦ μὴ λαβεῖν καὶ μείζονα ἀπαξίαν
τὸ δαρῆναι τοῦ μὴ δαρῆναι· ὥστ' εἰ τούτοις
11 παραμετρεῖς τὰ σαυτοῦ, ἀπελθὼν παρακράτει.
"ἀλλ' οὐκ ἂν κατ' ἐμέ." τοῦτο σὲ δεῖ συνεισφέρειν εἰς τὴν σκέψιν, οὐκ ἐμέ. σὺ γὰρ εἶ
ὁ σαυτὸν εἰδώς, πόσου ἄξιος εἶ σεαυτῷ καὶ
πόσου σεαυτὸν πιπράσκεις· ἄλλοι γὰρ ἄλλων
πιπράσκουσιν.

Wolf: μέρος S.

hangs himself. In short, if we observe, we shall find mankind distressed by nothing so much as by the irrational, and again attracted to nothing so much as to the rational.

Now it so happens that the rational and the irrational are different for different persons, precisely as good and evil, and the profitable and the unprofitable, are different for different persons. It is for this reason especially that we need education, so as to learn how, in conformity with nature, to adapt to specific instances our preconceived idea of what is rational and what is irrational. But for determining the rational and the irrational, we employ not only our estimates of the value of external things, but also the criterion of that which is in keeping with one's own character. For to one man it is reasonable to hold a chamber-pot for another, since he considers only that, if he does not hold it, he will get a beating and will not get food, whereas, if he does hold it, nothing harsh or painful will be done to him; but some other man feels that it is not merely unendurable to hold such a pot himself, but even to tolerate another's doing so. If you ask me, then, "Shall I hold the pot or not?" I will tell you that to get food is of greater value than not to get it, and to be flayed is of greater detriment than not to be; so that if you measure your interests by these standards, go and hold the pot. "Yes, but it would be unworthy of me." That is an additional consideration, which you, and not I, must introduce into the question. For you are the one that knows yourself, how much you are worth in your own eyes and at what price you sell yourself. For different men sell themselves at different prices.

12 Διὰ τοῦτο Ἀγριππῖνος Φλώρῳ σκεπτομένῳ,
εἰ καταβατέον αὐτῷ ἐστιν εἰς Νέρωνος θεωρίας,
ὥστε καὶ αὐτόν τι λειτουργῆσαι, ἔφη "Κατά-
13 βηθι." πυθομένου δ' αὐτοῦ "Διὰ τί σὺ οὐ κατα-
14 βαίνεις ;" ἔφη ὅτι "Ἐγὼ οὐδὲ βουλεύομαι." ὁ
γὰρ ἅπαξ εἰς τὴν περὶ τῶν τοιούτων σκέψιν καὶ
τὰς τῶν ἐκτὸς ἀξίας συγκαθεὶς καὶ ψηφίζων
ἐγγύς ἐστι τῶν ἐπιλελησμένων τοῦ ἰδίου προ-
15 σώπου. τί γάρ μου πυνθάνῃ ; "θάνατος αἱρε-
16 τώτερόν ἐστιν ἢ ζωή ;" λέγω ζωή. "πόνος ἢ
ἡδονή ;" λέγω ἡδονή. "ἀλλά, ἂν μὴ τραγῳδήσω,
τραχηλοκοπηθήσομαι." ἄπελθε τοίνυν καὶ τρα-
17 γῴδει, ἐγὼ δ' οὐ τραγῳδήσω. "διὰ τί ;" ὅτι σὺ
σεαυτὸν ἡγῇ μίαν τινὰ εἶναι κρόκην τῶν ἐκ τοῦ
χιτῶνος. τί οὖν ; σὲ ἔδει φροντίζειν πῶς ἂν
ὅμοιος¹ ᾖς τοῖς ἄλλοις ἀνθρώποις, ὥσπερ οὐδ'
ἡ κρόκη πρὸς τὰς ἄλλας κρόκας θέλει τι ἔχειν
18 ἐξαίρετον. ἐγὼ δὲ πορφύρα εἶναι βούλομαι, τὸ
ὀλίγον ἐκεῖνο καὶ στιλπνὸν καὶ τοῖς ἄλλοις αἴτιον
τοῦ εὐπρεπῆ φαίνεσθαι καὶ καλά. τί οὖν μοι
λέγεις ὅτι "ἐξομοιώθητι τοῖς πολλοῖς" ; καὶ πῶς
ἔτι πορφύρα ἔσομαι ;

19 Ταῦτα εἶδεν καὶ Πρίσκος Ἑλουίδιος καὶ ἰδὼν
ἐποίησε. προσπέμψαντος αὐτῷ Οὐεσπασιανοῦ, ἵνα
μὴ εἰσέλθῃ εἰς τὴν σύγκλητον, ἀπεκρίνατο "Ἐπὶ
σοί ἐστι μὴ ἐᾶσαί με εἶναι συγκλητικόν· μέχρι
20 δὲ ἂν ὦ, δεῖ με εἰσέρχεσθαι." "ἄγε ἀλλ' εἰσ-

¹ ἀνόμοιος Schenkl, after Blass.

---

[1] This was clearly the contribution to Nero's festival
which Florus was expected to make.

Wherefore, when Florus was debating whether he should enter Nero's festival, so as to make some personal contribution to it, Agrippinus said to him, "Enter." And when Florus asked, "Why do you not enter yourself?" he replied, "I? why, I do not even raise the question." For when a man once stoops to the consideration of such questions, I mean to estimating the value of externals, and calculates them one by one, he comes very close to those who have forgotten their own proper character. Come, what is this you ask me? "Is death or life preferable?" I answer, life. "Pain or pleasure?" I answer, pleasure. "But unless I take a part in the tragedy[1] I shall be beheaded." Go, then, and take a part, but I will not take a part. "Why not?" Because you regard yourself as but a single thread of all that go to make up the garment. What follows, then? This, that *you* ought to take thought how you may resemble all other men, precisely as even the single thread wants to have no point of superiority in comparison with the other threads. But *I* want to be the red,[2] that small and brilliant portion which causes the rest to appear comely and beautiful. Why, then, do you say to me, "Be like the majority of people?" And if I do that, how shall I any longer be the red?

This is what Helvidius Priscus also saw, and, having seen, did. When Vespasian sent him word not to attend a meeting of the Senate, he answered, "It is in your power not to allow me to be a member of the Senate, but so long as I am one I must attend its meetings." "Very well then, but

---

[2] The reference is to the band of bright red (commonly called "purple") woven into the hem of the *toga praetexta*.

ελθών," φησίν, " σιώπησον.'' "μή μ' ἐξέταζε καὶ
σιωπήσω.'' "ἀλλὰ δεῖ με ἐξετάσαι.'' "κἀμὲ
21 εἰπεῖν τὸ φαινόμενον δίκαιον.'' " ἀλλ' ἐὰν εἴπῃς,
ἀποκτενῶ σε.'' "πότε οὖν σοι εἶπον, ὅτι ἀθά-
νατός εἰμι ; καὶ σὺ τὸ σὸν ποιήσεις κἀγὼ τὸ
ἐμόν. σόν ἐστιν ἀποκτεῖναι, ἐμὸν ἀποθανεῖν μὴ
τρέμοντα· σὸν φυγαδεῦσαι, ἐμὸν ἐξελθεῖν μὴ
22 λυπούμενον.'' τί οὖν ὠφέλησε Πρῖσκος εἷς ὤν ;
τί δ' ὠφελεῖ ἡ πορφύρα τὸ ἱμάτιον ; τί γὰρ ἄλλο
ἢ διαπρέπει ἐν αὑτῷ ὡς πορφύρα καὶ τοῖς ἄλλοις
23 δὲ καλὸν παράδειγμα ἔκκειται ; ἄλλος δ' ἂν
εἰπόντος αὐτῷ Καίσαρος ἐν τοιαύτῃ περιστάσει
μὴ ἐλθεῖν εἰς σύγκλητον εἶπεν "ἔχω χάριν, ὅτι
24 μου φείδῃ.'' τὸν τοιοῦτον οὐδ' ἂν ἐκώλυεν εἰσελθεῖν, ἀλλ' ᾔδει, ὅτι ἢ καθεδεῖται ὡς κεράμιον ἢ
λέγων ἐρεῖ, ἃ οἶδεν ὅτι ὁ Καῖσαρ θέλει, καὶ
προσεπισωρεύσει ἔτι πλείονα.

25 Τοῦτον τὸν τρόπον καὶ ἀθλητής τις κινδυνεύων
ἀποθανεῖν, εἰ μὴ ἀπεκόπη τὸ αἰδοῖον, ἐπελθόντος
αὐτῷ τοῦ ἀδελφοῦ (ἦν δ' ἐκεῖνος φιλόσοφος) καὶ
εἰπόντος " ἄγε, ἀδελφέ, τί μέλλεις ποιεῖν ; ἀπο-
κόπτομεν τοῦτο τὸ μέρος καὶ ἔτι εἰς γυμνάσιον
προερχόμεθα ;'' οὐχ ὑπέμεινεν, ἀλλ' ἐγκαρτερήσας
26 ἀπέθανεν. πυθομένου δέ τινος· Πῶς τοῦτο ἐποίησεν ; ὡς ἀθλητὴς ἢ ὡς φιλόσοφος ; Ὡς [1] ἀνήρ,
ἔφη, ἀνὴρ δ' Ὀλύμπια κεκηρυγμένος καὶ ἠγωνισ-

---

[1] Added by s.

when you attend, hold your peace." "Do not ask
for my opinion and I will hold my peace." "But I
must ask for your opinion." "And I must answer
what seems to me right." "But if you speak, I
shall put you to death." "Well, when did I ever
tell you that I was immortal? You will do your
part and I mine. It is yours to put me to death,
mine to die without a tremor; yours to banish, mine
to leave without sorrow." What good, then, did
Priscus do, who was but a single individual? And
what good does the red do the mantle? What
else than that it stands out conspicuous in it as
red, and is displayed as a goodly example to the
rest? But had Caesar told another man in such
circumstances not to attend the meetings of the
Senate, he would have said, "I thank you for
excusing me." A man like that Caesar would not
even have tried to keep from attending, but would
have known that he would either sit like a jug, or,
if he spoke, would say what he knew Caesar wanted
said, and would pile up any amount more on the
top of it.

In like manner also a certain athlete acted, who
was in danger of dying unless his private parts were
amputated. His brother (and he was a philosopher)
came to him and said, "Well, brother, what are
you going to do? Are we going to cut off this
member, and step forth once more into the gymnasium?" He would not submit, but hardened his
heart and died. And as someone asked, "How did
he do this? As an athlete, or as a philosopher?"
As a man, replied Epictetus; and as a man who had
been proclaimed at the Olympic games and had
striven in them, who had been at home in such

μένος, ἐν τοιαύτῃ τινὶ χώρᾳ ἀνεστραμμένος, οὐχὶ
27 παρὰ τῷ Βάτωνι¹ ἀλειφόμενος. ἄλλος δὲ κἂν τὸν
τράχηλον ἀπετμήθη, εἰ ζῆν ἠδύνατο δίχα τοῦ τρα-
28 χήλου. τοιοῦτόν ἐστι τὸ κατὰ πρόσωπον· οὕτως
ἰσχυρὸν παρὰ τοῖς εἰθισμένοις αὐτὸ συνεισφέρειν
29 ἐξ αὐτῶν ἐν ταῖς σκέψεσιν. " ἄγε οὖν, Ἐπίκτητε,
διαξύρησαι." ἂν ὦ φιλόσοφος, λέγω, " οὐ διαξυ-
ρῶμαι." " ἀλλ' ἀφελῶ σου τὸν τράχηλον." εἰ σοὶ
ἄμεινον, ἄφελε.

30 Ἐπύθετό τις· Πόθεν οὖν αἰσθησόμεθα τοῦ κατὰ
πρόσωπον ἕκαστος ;—Πόθεν δ' ὁ ταῦρος, ἔφη,
λέοντος ἐπελθόντος μόνος αἰσθάνεται τῆς αὑτοῦ
παρασκευῆς καὶ προβέβληκεν ἑαυτὸν ὑπὲρ τῆς
ἀγέλης πάσης ; ἢ δῆλον ὅτι εὐθὺς ἅμα τῷ τὴν
παρασκευὴν ἔχειν ἀπαντᾷ καὶ συναίσθησις αὐτῆς ;
31 καὶ ἡμῶν τοίνυν ὅστις ἂν ἔχῃ τοιαύτην παρα-
32 σκευήν, οὐκ ἀγνοήσει αὐτήν. ἄφνω δὲ ταῦρος
οὐ γίνεται οὐδὲ γενναῖος ἄνθρωπος, ἀλλὰ δεῖ
χειμασκῆσαι, παρασκευάσασθαι καὶ μὴ εἰκῆ
προσπηδᾶν ἐπὶ τὰ μηδὲν προσήκοντα.

33 Μόνον σκέψαι, πόσου πωλεῖς τὴν σεαυτοῦ
προαίρεσιν. ἄνθρωπε, εἰ μηδὲν ἄλλο, μὴ ὀλίγου
αὐτὴν πωλήσῃς. τὸ δὲ μέγα καὶ ἐξαίρετον ἄλλοις
τάχα προσήκει, Σωκράτει καὶ τοῖς τοιούτοις.—
34 Διὰ τί οὖν, εἰ πρὸς τοῦτο πεφύκαμεν, οὐ πάντες

¹ Scaliger : βάτωι S.

---

¹ Bato seems to have been a well-known athletic trainer of
the time. At least one, and possibly two gladiators at Rome
bore this name. C.I.L. I. 718, VI. 10188.
² Philosophers, especially Stoics and Cynics, regularly
wore beards in antiquity. See I. 16, 9 ff.

places, and had not merely been rubbed down with oil in Bato's[1] wrestling school. But another would have had even his neck cut off, if he could have lived without his neck. This is what we mean by regard for one's proper character; and such is its strength with those who in their deliberations habitually make it a personal contribution. "Come then, Epictetus, shave off your beard."[2] If I am a philosopher, I answer, "I will not shave it off." "But I will take off your neck." If that will do you any good, take it off.

Someone inquired, "How, then, shall each of us become aware of what is appropriate to his own proper character?" How comes it, replied he, that when the lion charges, the bull alone is aware of his own prowess and rushes forward to defend the whole herd? Or is it clear that with the possession of the prowess comes immediately the consciousness of it also? And so, among us too, whoever has such prowess will not be unaware of it. Yet a bull does not become a bull all at once, any more than a man becomes noble, but a man must undergo a winter training,[3] he must prepare himself and must not plunge recklessly into what is inappropriate for him.

Only consider at what price you sell your freedom of will. If you must sell it, man, at least do not sell it cheap. But the great and pre-eminent deed, perhaps, befits others, Socrates and men of his stamp.—Why then, pray, if we are endowed by nature for such

---

[3] Ancient armies generally disbanded or went into permanent quarters during the winter. To continue military training throughout the winter months was indicative of a sincere and strenuous endeavour.

ἢ πολλοὶ γίνονται τοιοῦτοι ;—Ἵπποι γὰρ ὠκεῖς
ἄπαντες γίνονται, κύνες γὰρ ἰχνευτικοὶ πάντες ;
35 τί οὖν ; ἐπειδὴ ἀφυής εἰμι, ἀποστῶ τῆς ἐπιμελείας
36 τούτου ἕνεκα ; μὴ γένοιτο. Ἐπίκτητος κρείσσων Σωκράτους οὐκ ἔσται· εἰ δὲ μή, οὐ χείρων,
37 τοῦτό μοι ἱκανόν ἐστιν. οὐδὲ γὰρ Μίλων ἔσομαι
καὶ ὅμως οὐκ ἀμελῶ τοῦ σώματος· οὐδὲ Κροῖσος
καὶ ὅμως οὐκ ἀμελῶ τῆς κτήσεως· οὐδ' ἁπλῶς
ἄλλου τινὸς τῆς ἐπιμελείας διὰ τὴν ἀπόγνωσιν
τῶν ἄκρων ἀφιστάμεθα.

γ΄. Πῶς ἄν τις ἀπὸ τοῦ τὸν θεὸν πατέρα εἶναι
τῶν ἀνθρώπων ἐπὶ τὰ ἑξῆς ἐπέλθοι ;

1 Εἴ τις τῷ δόγματι τούτῳ συμπαθῆσαι κατ'
ἀξίαν δύναιτο, ὅτι γεγόναμεν ὑπὸ τοῦ θεοῦ πάντες
προηγουμένως καὶ ὁ θεὸς πατήρ ἐστι τῶν τ'
ἀνθρώπων καὶ τῶν θεῶν, οἶμαι ὅτι οὐδὲν ἀγεννὲς
2 οὐδὲ ταπεινὸν ἐνθυμηθήσεται περὶ ἑαυτοῦ. ἀλλ'
ἂν μὲν Καῖσαρ εἰσποιήσηταί σε, οὐδείς σου τὴν
ὀφρῦν βαστάσει· ἂν δὲ γνῷς, ὅτι τοῦ Διὸς υἱός
3 εἶ, οὐκ ἐπαρθήσῃ ; νῦν δ' οὐ ποιοῦμεν, ἀλλ'
ἐπειδὴ δύο ταῦτα ἐν τῇ γενέσει ἡμῶν ἐγκατα-
μέμικται, τὸ σῶμα μὲν κοινὸν πρὸς τὰ ζῷα, ὁ
λόγος δὲ καὶ ἡ γνώμη κοινὸν πρὸς τοὺς θεούς,
ἄλλοι μὲν ἐπὶ ταύτην ἀποκλίνουσιν τὴν συγγένειαν τὴν ἀτυχῆ καὶ νεκράν, ὀλίγοι δέ τινες
4 ἐπὶ τὴν θείαν καὶ μακαρίαν. ἐπειδὴ τοίνυν

greatness, do not all men, or many, become like him? What, do all horses become swift, all dogs keen to follow the scent? What then? Because I have no natural gifts, shall I on that account give up my discipline? Far be it from me! Epictetus will not be better than Socrates; but if only I am not worse, that suffices me. For I shall not be a Milo, either, and yet I do not neglect my body; nor a Croesus, and yet I do not neglect my property; nor, in a word, is there any other field in which we give up the appropriate discipline merely from despair of attaining the highest.

CHAPTER III

*From the thesis that God is the father of mankind
how may one proceed to the consequences?*

IF a man could only subscribe heart and soul, as he ought, to this doctrine, that we are all primarily begotten of God, and that God is the father of men as well as of gods, I think that he will entertain no ignoble or mean thought about himself. Yet, if Caesar adopts you no one will be able to endure your conceit, but if you know that you are a son of Zeus, will you not be elated? As it is, however, we are not, but inasmuch as these two elements were comingled in our begetting, on the one hand the body, which we have in common with the brutes, and, on the other, reason and intelligence, which we have in common with the gods, some of us incline toward the former relationship, which is unblessed by fortune and is mortal, and only a few toward that which is divine and blessed. Since, then, it is inevit-

ἀνάγκη πάνθ' ὁντινοῦν οὕτως ἑκάστῳ χρῆσθαι
ὡς ἂν περὶ αὐτοῦ ὑπολάβῃ, ἐκεῖνοι μὲν οἱ ὀλίγοι,
ὅσοι πρὸς πίστιν οἴονται γεγονέναι καὶ πρὸς
αἰδῶ καὶ πρὸς ἀσφάλειαν τῆς χρήσεως τῶν φαντασιῶν, οὐδὲν ταπεινὸν οὐδ' ἀγεννὲς ἐνθυμοῦνται
5 περὶ αὑτῶν, οἱ δὲ πολλοὶ τἀναντία. "τί γὰρ
εἰμί; ταλαίπωρον ἀνθρωπάριον" καὶ "τὰ δύστηνά
6 μου σαρκίδια." τῷ μὲν ὄντι δύστηνα, ἀλλὰ ἔχεις
τι καὶ κρεῖσσον τῶν σαρκιδίων. τί οὖν ἀφεὶς
ἐκεῖνο τούτοις προστέτηκας;

7 Διὰ ταύτην τὴν συγγένειαν οἱ μὲν ἀποκλίναντες
λύκοις ὅμοιοι γινόμεθα, ἄπιστοι καὶ ἐπίβουλοι
καὶ βλαβεροί, οἱ δὲ λέουσιν, ἄγριοι καὶ θηριώδεις
καὶ ἀνήμεροι, οἱ πλείους δ' ἡμῶν ἀλώπεκες καὶ
8 ὡς ἐν ζῴοις ἀτυχήματα. τί γάρ ἐστιν ἄλλο λοί-
δορος καὶ κακοήθης ἄνθρωπος ἢ ἀλώπηξ ἤ τι
9 ἄλλο ἀτυχέστερον καὶ ταπεινότερον; ὁρᾶτε οὖν
καὶ προσέχετε, μή τι τούτων ἀποβῆτε τῶν ἀτυ-
χημάτων.

δ. Περὶ προκοπῆς

1 Ὁ προκόπτων μεμαθηκὼς παρὰ τῶν φιλοσόφων
ὅτι ἡ μὲν ὄρεξις ἀγαθῶν ἐστιν, ἡ δ' ἔκκλισις πρὸς
κακά,[1] μεμαθηκὼς δὲ καὶ ὅτι οὐκ ἄλλως τὸ
εὔρουν καὶ ἀπαθὲς περιγίνεται τῷ ἀνθρώπῳ ἢ
ἐν ὀρέξει μὲν μὴ ἀποτυγχάνοντι, ἐν ἐκκλίσει δὲ

---

[1] *Sd: καλὰ S.*

---

[1] The characteristic moral achievement which the Stoics
sought. The metaphor in the first expression, τὸ εὔρουν, is
admirably rendered by Seneca, *Epist.* 120. 11, *beata vita,
secundo defluens cursu.*

able that every man, whoever he be, should deal
with each thing according to the opinion which he
forms about it, these few, who think that by their
birth they are called to fidelity, to self-respect, and to
unerring judgement in the use of external impressions,
cherish no mean or ignoble thoughts about themselves, whereas the multitude do quite the opposite. "For what am I? A miserable, paltry man,"
say they, and, "Lo, my wretched, paltry flesh!"
Wretched indeed, but you have also something
better than your paltry flesh. Why then abandon
that and cleave to this?

It is because of this kinship with the flesh that
those of us who incline toward it become like wolves,
faithless and treacherous and hurtful, and others
like lions, wild and savage and untamed; but most
of us become foxes, that is to say, rascals of the
animal kingdom. For what else is a slanderous
and malicious man but a fox, or something even
more rascally and degraded? Take heed, therefore, and beware that you become not one of these
rascally creatures.

CHAPTER IV

Of progress

HE who is making progress, having learned of the
philosophers that desire is for things good and
aversion is toward things evil, and having also
learned that serenity and calm[1] are not attained by a
man save as he succeeds in securing the objects of
desire and as he avoids encountering the objects of

27

μὴ περιπίπτοντι, τὴν μὲν ὄρεξιν ἦρκεν ἐξ αὑτοῦ
εἰσάπαν ἢ [1] ὑπερτέθειται, τῇ ἐκκλίσει δὲ πρὸς
2 μόνα χρῆται τὰ προαιρετικά. τῶν γὰρ ἀπροαιρέτων ἄν τι ἐκκλίνῃ, οἶδεν ὅτι περιπεσεῖταί ποτέ
τινι παρὰ τὴν ἔκκλισιν τὴν αὑτοῦ καὶ δυστυχήσει.
3 εἰ δ᾽ ἡ ἀρετὴ ταύτην ἔχει τὴν ἐπαγγελίαν εὐδαιμονίαν ποιῆσαι καὶ ἀπάθειαν καὶ εὔροιαν, πάντως
καὶ ἡ προκοπὴ ἡ πρὸς αὐτὴν πρὸς ἕκαστον τού-
4 των ἐστὶ προκοπή. ἀεὶ γὰρ πρὸς ὃ ἂν ἡ τελειότης
τινὸς καθάπαξ ἄγῃ, πρὸς αὐτὸ ἡ προκοπὴ συνεγ-
γισμός ἐστιν.

5   Πῶς οὖν τὴν μὲν ἀρετὴν τοιοῦτόν τι ὁμολογοῦμεν, τὴν προκοπὴν δ᾽ ἐν ἄλλοις ζητοῦμεν καὶ
6 ἐπιδείκνυμεν; τί ἔργον ἀρετῆς; εὔροια. τίς οὖν
προκόπτει; ὁ πολλὰς Χρυσίππου συντάξεις
7 ἀνεγνωκώς; μὴ γὰρ ἡ ἀρετὴ τοῦτ᾽ ἔστι Χρυσίπ-
πον νενοηκέναι; εἰ γὰρ τοῦτ᾽ ἔστιν, ὁμολογου-
μένως ἡ προκοπὴ οὐδὲν ἄλλο ἐστὶν ἢ τὸ πολλὰ
8 τῶν Χρυσίππου νοεῖν. νῦν δ᾽ ἄλλο μέν τι τὴν
ἀρετὴν ἐπιφέρειν ὁμολογοῦμεν, ἄλλο δὲ τὸν συν-
9 εγγισμόν, τὴν προκοπήν, ἀποφαίνομεν. "οὗτος,"
φησίν, "ἤδη καὶ δι᾽ αὑτοῦ δύναται Χρύσιππον
ἀναγιγνώσκειν." εὖ, νὴ τοὺς θεούς, προκόπτεις,
10 ἄνθρωπε· ποίαν προκοπήν. "τί ἐμπαίζεις αὐτῷ;
τί δ᾽ ἀπάγεις αὐτὸν τῆς συναισθήσεως τῶν αὑτοῦ
κακῶν; οὐ θέλεις δεῖξαι αὐτῷ τὸ ἔργον τῆς ἀρε-

---

[1] Koraes: καὶ S.

28

aversion—such a one has utterly excluded desire from himself, or else deferred it to another time,[1] and feels aversion only toward the things which involve freedom of choice. For if he avoids anything that is not a matter of free choice, he knows that some time he will encounter something in spite of his aversion to it, and will come to grief. Now if it is virtue that holds out the promise thus to create happiness and calm and serenity, then assuredly progress toward virtue is progress toward each of these states of mind. For it is always true that whatsoever the goal toward which perfection in anything definitely leads, progress is an approach thereto.

How comes it, then, that we acknowledge virtue to be a thing of this sort, and yet seek progress and make a display of it in other things? What is the work[2] of virtue? Serenity. Who, then, is making progress? The man who has read many treatises of Chrysippus? What, is virtue no more than this—to have gained a knowledge of Chrysippus? For if it is this, progress is confessedly nothing else than a knowledge of many of the works of Chrysippus. But now, while acknowledging that virtue produces one thing, we are declaring that the approach to virtue, which is progress, produces something else. "So-and-so," says someone, "is already able to read Chrysippus all by himself." It is fine headway, by the gods, that you are making, man! Great progress this! "Why do you mock him? And why do you try to divert him from the consciousness of his own shortcomings? Are you not willing to show him the

[1] See the *Encheiridion*, II. 2: "But for the present totally make way with desire."

[2] *i.e.*, the result at which virtue aims.

11 τῆς, ἵνα μάθῃ ποῦ τὴν προκοπὴν ζητῇ ;" ἐκεῖ
ζήτησον αὐτήν, ταλαίπωρε, ὅπου σου τὸ ἔργον.
ποῦ δέ σου τὸ ἔργον ; ἐν ὀρέξει καὶ ἐκκλίσει, ἵν'
ἀναπότευκτος ᾖς καὶ ἀπερίπτωτος, ἐν ὁρμαῖς
καὶ ἀφορμαῖς, ἵν' ἀναμάρτητος, ἐν προσθέσει καὶ
12 ἐποχῇ, ἵν' ἀνεξαπάτητος. πρῶτοι δ' εἰσὶν οἱ
πρῶτοι τόποι καὶ ἀναγκαιότατοι. ἂν δὲ τρέμων
καὶ πενθῶν ζητῇς ἀπερίπτωτος εἶναι, ἆρα πῶς
προκόπτεις ;

13 Σὺ οὖν ἐνταῦθά μοι δεῖξόν σου τὴν προκοπήν.
καθάπερ εἰ ἀθλητῇ διελεγόμην " δεῖξόν μοι τοὺς
ὤμους," εἶτα ἔλεγεν ἐκεῖνος "ἴδε μου τοὺς ἁλ-
τῆρας." ἄπιθι¹ σὺ καὶ οἱ ἁλτῆρες, ἐγὼ τὸ ἀπο-
14 τέλεσμα τῶν ἁλτήρων ἰδεῖν βούλομαι. "λάβε τὴν
περὶ ὁρμῆς σύνταξιν καὶ γνῶθι πῶς αὐτὴν ἀνέγνωκα." ἀνδράποδον, οὐ τοῦτο ζητῶ, ἀλλὰ πῶς ὁρμᾷς
καὶ ἀφορμᾷς, πῶς ὀρέγῃ καὶ ἐκκλίνεις, πῶς ἐπιβάλ-
λῃ² καὶ προτίθεσαι³ καὶ παρασκευάζῃ, πότερα
15 συμφώνως τῇ φύσει ἢ ἀσυμφώνως. εἰ γὰρ συμφώνως, τοῦτό μοι δείκνυε καὶ ἐρῶ σοι ὅτι προκόπτεις. εἰ δ' ἀσυμφώνως, ἄπελθε καὶ μὴ μόνον
ἐξηγοῦ τὰ βιβλία, ἀλλὰ καὶ γράφε αὐτὸς τοι-

---

¹ ἄπιθι (cf. ἄπελθε § 15) Capps: ὄψει S.
² Schweighäuser: ἐπιβάλλεις S.
³ Salmasius and Upton's 'codex': προστίθεσαι S.

---

¹ These are the three spheres or fields (τόποι) of human
activity, inclination, choice, and intellectual assent, upon
which the Stoics laid great stress. For a fuller discussion see
below III. 2, 1 ff.
² Broad-jumpers in antiquity carried weights which on
being thrust backwards while the jumper was in mid-air
seem to have added materially to the distance covered.

work of virtue, that he may learn where to look for his progress?" Look for it there, wretch, where your work lies. And where is your work? In desire and aversion, that you may not miss what you desire and encounter what you would avoid; in choice and in refusal, that you may commit no fault therein; in giving and withholding assent of judgement, that you may not be deceived.[1] But first come the first and most necessary points. Yet if you are in a state of fear and grief when you seek to be proof against encountering what you would avoid, how, pray, are you making progress?

Do you yourself show me, therefore, your own progress in matters like the following. Suppose, for example, that in talking to an athlete I said, "Show me your shoulders," and then he answered, "Look at my jumping-weights."[2] Go to, you and your jumping-weights! What I want to see is the *effect* of the jumping-weights. "Take the treatise *Upon Choice*[3] and see how I have mastered it." It is not *that* I am looking into, you slave, but how you act in your choices and refusals, your desires and aversions, how you go at things, and apply yourself to them, and prepare yourself, whether you are acting in harmony with nature therein, or out of harmony with it. For if you are acting in harmony, show me that, and I will tell you that you are making progress; but if out of harmony, begone, and do not confine yourself to expounding your books, but go and write

These same weights were also used like our dumb-bells for the development of the arm and trunk muscles, as is apparently the case here.

[3] The title, apparently, of a short work by Chrysippus, but known only from this passage. Zeno and Cleanthes wrote also on the subject.

16 αὐτά. καὶ τί σοι ὄφελος; οὐκ οἶδας ὅτι ὅλον
τὸ βιβλίον πέντε δηναρίων ἐστίν; ὁ οὖν ἐξηγού-
μενος αὐτὸ δοκεῖ ὅτι πλείονος ἄξιός ἐστιν ἢ πέντε
17 δηναρίων; μηδέποτε οὖν ἀλλαχοῦ τὸ ἔργον ζητεῖτε, ἀλλαχοῦ τὴν προκοπήν.

18 Ποῦ οὖν προκοπή; εἴ τις ὑμῶν ἀποστὰς τῶν
ἐκτὸς ἐπὶ τὴν προαίρεσιν ἐπέστραπται τὴν αὑτοῦ,
ταύτην ἐξεργάζεσθαι καὶ ἐκπονεῖν, ὥστε σύμφωνον ἀποτελέσαι τῇ φύσει, ὑψηλὴν ἐλευθέραν
19 ἀκώλυτον ἀνεμπόδιστον πιστὴν αἰδήμονα· με-
μάθηκέν τε, ὅτι ὁ τὰ μὴ ἐφ' αὑτῷ ποθῶν ἢ
φεύγων οὔτε πιστὸς εἶναι δύναται οὔτ' ἐλεύθερος,
ἀλλ' ἀνάγκη μεταπίπτειν καὶ μεταρριπίζεσθαι
ἅμα ἐκείνοις καὶ αὐτόν, ἀνάγκη δὲ καὶ ὑποτετα-
χέναι ἄλλοις ἑαυτόν, τοῖς ἐκεῖνα περιποιεῖν ἢ
20 κωλύειν δυναμένοις· καὶ λοιπὸν ἔωθεν ἀνιστάμενος
ταῦτα τηρεῖ καὶ φυλάσσει, λούεται ὡς πιστός, ὡς
αἰδήμων ἐσθίει, ὡσαύτως ἐπὶ τῆς ἀεὶ παραπιπτού-
σης ὕλης τὰ προηγούμενα ἐκπονῶν, ὡς ὁ δρομεὺς
21 δρομικῶς καὶ ὁ φώνασκος φωνασκικῶς· οὗτός
ἐστιν ὁ προκόπτων ταῖς ἀληθείαις καὶ ὁ μὴ εἰκῇ
22 ἀποδεδημηκὼς οὗτός ἐστιν. εἰ δ' ἐπὶ τὴν ἐν τοῖς
βιβλίοις ἕξιν τέταται καὶ ταύτην ἐκπονεῖ καὶ
ἐπὶ τοῦτο ἐκδεδήμηκε, λέγω αὐτῷ αὐτόθεν πο-
23 ρεύεσθαι εἰς οἶκον καὶ μὴ ἀμελεῖν τῶν ἐκεῖ· τοῦτο

some of the same kind yourself. And what will you gain thereby? Do you not know that the whole book costs only five denarii? Is the expounder of it, then, think you, worth *more* than five denarii? And so never look for your work in one place and your progress in another.

Where, then, is progress? If any man among you, withdrawing from external things, has turned his attention to the question of his own moral purpose, cultivating and perfecting it so as to make it finally harmonious with nature, elevated, free, unhindered, untrammelled, faithful, and honourable; and if he has learned that he who craves or shuns the things that are not under his control can be neither faithful nor free, but must himself of necessity be changed and tossed to and fro with them, and must end by subordinating himself to others, those, namely, who are able to procure or prevent these things that he craves or shuns; and if, finally, when he rises in the morning he proceeds to keep and observe all this that he has learned; if he bathes as a faithful man, eats as a self-respecting man,— similarly, whatever the subject matter may be with which he has to deal, putting into practice his guiding principles, as the runner does when he applies the principles of running, and the voice-trainer when he applies the principles of voice-training,—this is the man who in all truth is making progress, and the man who has not travelled at random is this one. But if he has striven merely to attain the state which he finds in his books and works only at that, and has made that the goal of his travels, I bid him go home at once and not neglect his concerns there, since the goal to which

γὰρ ἐφ' ὃ ἀποδεδήμηκεν οὐδέν ἐστιν· ἀλλ' ἐκεῖνο,
μελετᾶν ἐξελεῖν τοῦ αὐτοῦ βίου πένθη καὶ οἰμωγὰς
καὶ τὸ[1] "οἴμοι" καὶ τὸ "τάλας ἐγὼ" καὶ δυστυ-
24 χίαν καὶ ἀτυχίαν καὶ μαθεῖν, τί ἐστι θάνατος,
τί φυγή, τί δεσμωτήριον, τί κώνειον, ἵνα δύνηται
λέγειν ἐν τῇ φυλακῇ "ὦ φίλε Κρίτων, εἰ ταύτῃ
τοῖς θεοῖς φίλον, ταύτῃ γινέσθω," καὶ μὴ ἐκεῖνα
"τάλας ἐγώ, γέρων ἄνθρωπος, ἐπὶ ταῦτά μου τὰς
25 πολιὰς ἐτήρησα." τίς λέγει ταῦτα; δοκεῖτε ὅτι
ὑμῖν ἄδοξόν τινα ἐρῶ καὶ ταπεινόν; Πρίαμος
αὐτὰ οὐ λέγει; Οἰδίπους οὐ λέγει; ἀλλ' ὁπόσοι
26 βασιλεῖς λέγουσιν; τί γάρ εἰσιν ἄλλο τραγῳδίαι
ἢ ἀνθρώπων πάθη τεθαυμακότων τὰ ἐκτὸς διὰ
27 μέτρου τοιοῦδ' ἐπιδεικνύμενα; εἰ γὰρ ἐξαπατη-
θέντα τινὰ ἔδει μαθεῖν, ὅτι τῶν ἐκτὸς καὶ[2] ἀπροαιρέτων οὐδέν ἐστι πρὸς ἡμᾶς, ἐγὼ μὲν ἤθελον
τὴν ἀπάτην ταύτην, ἐξ ἧς ἤμελλον εὐρόως καὶ
ἀταράχως βιώσεσθαι, ὑμεῖς δ' ὄψεσθ' αὐτοὶ τί
θέλετε.

28   Τί οὖν ἡμῖν παρέχει Χρύσιππος; "ἵνα γνῷς,"
φησίν, "ὅτι οὐ ψευδῆ ταῦτά ἐστιν, ἐξ ὧν ἡ
29 εὔροιά ἐστι καὶ ἀπάθεια ἀπαντᾷ, λάβε μου τὰ
βιβλία καὶ γνώσῃ ὡς ἀκόλουθά[3] τε καὶ σύμ-
φωνά ἐστι τῇ φύσει τὰ ἀπαθῆ με ποιοῦντα."
ὦ μεγάλης εὐτυχίας, ὦ μεγάλου εὐεργέτου τοῦ
30 δεικνύοντος τὴν ὁδόν. εἶτα Τριπτολέμῳ μὲν ἱερὰ

---

[1] Added by Schweighäuser.
[2] Supplied by Upton.
[3] Supplied by Schenkl.

he has travelled is nothing; but not so that other goal—to study how a man may rid his life of sorrows and lamentations, and of such cries as "Woe is me!" and "Wretch that I am!" and of misfortune and failure, and to learn the meaning of death, exile, prison, hemlock;[1] that he may be able to say in prison, "Dear Crito, if so it pleases the gods, so be it,"[2] rather than, "Alas, poor me, an old man, it is for this that I have kept my grey hairs!" Who says such things? Do you think that I will name you some man held in small esteem and of low degree? Does not Priam say it? Does not Oedipus? Nay more, all kings say it! For what are tragedies but the portrayal in tragic verse of the sufferings of men who have admired things external? If indeed one had to be deceived[3] into learning that among things external and independent of our free choice none concerns us, I, for my part, should consent to a deception which would result in my living thereafter serenely and without turmoil; but as for you, you will yourselves see to your own preference.

What, then, does Chrysippus furnish us? "That you may know," he says, "that these things are not false from which serenity arises and tranquillity comes to us, take my books and you shall know how conformable and harmonious with nature are the things which render me tranquil." O the great good fortune! O the great benefactor who points the way! To Triptolemus, indeed, all men have

---

[1] The poison with which Socrates was put to death.

[2] Plato, *Crito*, 43 D.

[3] Probably by witnessing tragedies, the plots of which, although fictitious, may teach moral lessons.

35

καὶ βωμοὺς πάντες ἄνθρωποι ἀνεστάκασιν, ὅτι
31 τὰς ἡμέρους τροφὰς ἡμῖν ἔδωκεν, τῷ δὲ τὴν
ἀλήθειαν εὑρόντι καὶ φωτίσαντι καὶ εἰς πάντας
ἀνθρώπους ἐξενεγκόντι, οὐ τὴν περὶ τὸ ζῆν, ἀλλὰ
τὴν πρὸς τὸ εὖ ζῆν, τίς ὑμῶν ἐπὶ τούτῳ βωμὸν
ἱδρύσατο ἢ ναὸν ἢ ἄγαλμα ἀνέθηκεν ἢ τὸν θεὸν
32 ἐπὶ τούτῳ προσκυνεῖ; ἀλλ' ὅτι μὲν ἄμπελον
ἔδωκαν ἢ πυρούς, ἐπιθύομεν τούτου ἕνεκα, ὅτι δὲ
τοιοῦτον ἐξήνεγκαν καρπὸν ἐν ἀνθρωπίνῃ διανοίᾳ,
δι' οὗ τὴν ἀλήθειαν τὴν περὶ εὐδαιμονίας δείξειν
ἡμῖν ἤμελλον, τούτου δ' ἕνεκα οὐκ εὐχαριστή-
σωμεν τῷ θεῷ;

ε΄. Πρὸς τοὺς Ἀκαδημαικούς

1 Ἄν τις, φησίν, ἐνίστηται πρὸς τὰ ἄγαν ἐκ-
φανῆ, πρὸς τοῦτον οὐ ῥᾴδιόν ἐστιν εὑρεῖν λόγον,
2 δι' οὗ μεταπείσει τις αὐτόν. τοῦτο δ' οὔτε παρὰ
τὴν ἐκείνου γίνεται δύναμιν οὔτε παρὰ τὴν τοῦ
διδάσκοντος ἀσθένειαν, ἀλλ' ὅταν ἀπαχθεὶς ἀπο-
λιθωθῇ, πῶς ἔτι χρήσηταί τις αὐτῷ διὰ λόγου;

---

[1] The phrase is from Plato, *Crito*, 48 B.
[2] Referring probably to the mind of Chrysippus.
[3] See also II. 20. 4. Epictetus condemns the exaggerations
of the Academic principle of suspended judgement, which

established shrines and altars, because he gave us as food the fruits of cultivation, but to him who has discovered, and brought to light, and imparted to all men the truth which deals, not with mere life, but with a good life,[1]—who among you has for that set up an altar in his honour, or dedicated a temple or a statue, or bows down to God in gratitude for him? But because the gods have given us the vine or wheat, for that do we make sacrifice, and yet because they have brought forth such a fruit in a human mind,[2] whereby they purposed to show us the truth touching happiness, shall we fail to render thanks unto God for this?

CHAPTER V

Against the Academics [3]

IF a man, says Epictetus, resists truths that are all too evident, in opposing him it is not easy to find an argument by which one may cause him to change his opinion. The reason for this is neither the man's ability nor the teacher's weakness; nay, when a man who has been trapped in an argument hardens to stone, how shall one any longer deal with him by argument?

was based on the doctrine that nothing could be actually known. Cf. Cicero Acad. I. 45: Arcesilas (a prominent Academic) negabat esse quidquam quod sciri posset . . . sic omnia latere in occulto: neque esse quidquam quod cerni aut intellegi posset: quibus de causis nihil oportere neque profiteri neque adfirmare quemquam neque adsensione approbare, etc.

3 Ἀπολιθώσεις δ' εἰσὶ διτταί· ἡ μὲν τοῦ νοη-
τικοῦ ἀπολίθωσις, ἡ δὲ τοῦ ἐντρεπτικοῦ, ὅταν
τις παρατεταγμένος ᾖ μὴ ἐπινεύειν τοῖς ἐναργέσι
4 μηδ' ἀπὸ τῶν μαχομένων ἀφίστασθαι. οἱ δὲ
πολλοὶ τὴν μὲν σωματικὴν ἀπονέκρωσιν φοβούμεθα καὶ πάντ' ἂν μηχανησαίμεθα ὑπὲρ τοῦ μὴ
περιπεσεῖν τοιούτῳ τινί, τῆς ψυχῆς δ' ἀπονεκρου-
5 μένης οὐδὲν ἡμῖν μέλει. καὶ νὴ Δία ἐπὶ αὐτῆς
τῆς ψυχῆς ἂν μὲν ᾖ οὕτως διακείμενος, ὥστε
μηδενὶ[1] παρακολουθεῖν μηδὲ συνιέναι μηδέν, καὶ
τοῦτον κακῶς ἔχειν οἰόμεθα· ἂν δέ τινος τὸ ἐντρεπτικὸν καὶ αἰδῆμον ἀπονεκρωθῇ, τοῦτο ἔτι
καὶ δύναμιν καλοῦμεν.

6 Καταλαμβάνεις ὅτι ἐγρήγορας; "οὔ," φησίν·
"οὐδὲ γάρ, ὅταν ἐν τοῖς ὕπνοις φαντάζωμαι, ὅτι
ἐγρήγορα." οὐδὲν οὖν διαφέρει αὕτη ἡ φαντασία
7 ἐκείνης; "οὐδέν." ἔτι τούτῳ διαλέγομαι; καὶ
ποῖον αὐτῷ πῦρ ἢ ποῖον σίδηρον προσαγάγω,
ἵν' αἴσθηται ὅτι νενέκρωται; αἰσθανόμενος οὐ
8 προσποιεῖται· ἔτι χείρων ἐστὶ τοῦ νεκροῦ. μάχην
οὗτος οὐ συνορᾷ· κακῶς ἔχει. συνορῶν οὗτος οὐ
9 κινεῖται οὐδὲ προκόπτει· ἔτι ἀθλιώτερον ἔχει.
ἐκτέτμηται τὸ αἰδῆμον αὐτοῦ καὶ ἐντρεπτικὸν καὶ
τὸ λογικὸν οὐκ ἀποτέτμηται, ἀλλ' ἀποτεθη-
10 ρίωται. ταύτην ἐγὼ δύναμιν εἴπω; μὴ γένοιτο,
εἰ μὴ καὶ τὴν τῶν κιναίδων, καθ' ἣν πᾶν τὸ
ἐπελθὸν ἐν μέσῳ καὶ ποιοῦσι καὶ λέγουσι.

---

[1] Salmasius : μηδὲν S.

Now there are two kinds of petrifaction: one is the petrifaction of the intellect, the other of the sense of shame, when a man stands in array, prepared neither to assent to manifest truths nor to leave the fighting line. Most of us dread the deadening of the body and would resort to all means so as to avoid falling into such a state, but about the deadening of the soul we care not at all. Indeed, by Zeus, even in the case of the soul itself, if a man be in such a state that he cannot follow an argument step by step, or even understand one, we regard him too as being in a bad way; but if a man's sense of shame and self-respect be deadened, this we go so far as to call strength of character!

Do your senses tell you that you are awake? "No," he answers, "any more than they do when in dreams I have the impression that I am awake." Is there, then, no difference between these two impressions? "None." Can I argue with this man any longer? And what cautery or lancet shall I apply to him, to make him realize that he is deadened? He does realize it, but pretends that he does not; he is even worse than a corpse. One man does not notice the contradiction—he is in a bad way; another man notices it, indeed, but is not moved and does not improve—he is in a still worse state. His self-respect and sense of shame have been lopped off, and his reasoning faculty has been—I will not say cut away, but brutalized. Am I to call this strength of character? Far from it, unless I am so to describe the strength that lewd fellows have, which enables them to say and do in public anything that comes into their heads.

ϛʹ. Περὶ προνοίας

1 Ἀφ' ἑκάστου τῶν ἐν τῷ κόσμῳ γινομένων
ῥᾴδιόν ἐστιν ἐγκωμιάσαι τὴν πρόνοιαν, ἂν δύο
ἔχῃ τις ταῦτα ἐν ἑαυτῷ, δύναμίν τε συνορατικὴν
2 τῶν γεγονότων ἑκάστῳ καὶ τὸ εὐχάριστον. εἰ
δὲ μή, ὁ μὲν οὐκ ὄψεται τὴν εὐχρηστίαν τῶν
γεγονότων, ὁ δ' οὐκ εὐχαριστήσει ἐπ' αὐτοῖς οὐδ'
3 ἂν ἴδῃ.[1] χρώματα ὁ θεὸς εἰ[2] πεποιήκει, δύναμιν δὲ θεατικὴν αὐτῶν μὴ πεποιήκει, τί ἂν ἦν
4 ὄφελος ;—Οὐδ' ὁτιοῦν.—Ἀλλ' ἀνάπαλιν εἰ τὴν
μὲν δύναμιν πεποιήκει, τὰ ὄντα δὲ μὴ τοιαῦτα
οἷα ὑποπίπτειν τῇ δυνάμει τῇ ὁρατικῇ, καὶ οὕτως
5 τί ὄφελος ;—Οὐδ' ὁτιοῦν.[3]—Τί δ', εἰ καὶ ἀμφό-
6 τερα ταῦτα πεποιήκει, φῶς δὲ μὴ πεποιήκει ;—
Οὐδ' οὕτως τι ὄφελος.—Τίς οὖν ὁ ἁρμόσας τοῦτο
πρὸς ἐκεῖνο κἀκεῖνο πρὸς τοῦτο ; τίς δ' ὁ ἁρμόσας
τὴν μάχαιραν πρὸς τὸ κολεὸν καὶ τὸ κολεὸν πρὸς
7 τὴν μάχαιραν ; οὐδείς ; καὶ μὴν ἐξ αὐτῆς τῆς
κατασκευῆς τῶν ἐπιτετελεσμένων ἀποφαίνεσθαι
εἰώθαμεν, ὅτι τεχνίτου τινὸς πάντως τὸ ἔργον,
οὐχὶ δ' εἰκῇ κατεσκευασμένον.

8 Ἆρ' οὖν τούτων μὲν ἕκαστον ἐμφαίνει τὸν
τεχνίτην, τὰ δ' ὁρατὰ καὶ ὅρασις καὶ φῶς οὐκ
ἐμφαίνει ; τὸ δ' ἄρρεν καὶ τὸ θῆλυ καὶ ἡ προ-
θυμία ἡ πρὸς τὴν συνουσίαν ἑκατέρου καὶ δύναμις
ἡ χρηστικὴ τοῖς μορίοις τοῖς κατεσκευασμένοις
οὐδὲ ταῦτα ἐμφαίνει τὸν τεχνίτην ; ἀλλὰ ταῦτα
10 μὲν οὕτω·[4] ἡ δὲ τοιαύτη τῆς διανοίας κατασκευή,

---

[1] Added by Meineke (εἰδῇ Stobaeus).
[2] Stobaeus : an erasure in S.
[3] Here follows in S an erasure of about 110 letters.
[4] Stobaeus : omitted by S.

CHAPTER VI

Of providence

From everything that happens in the universe it is easy for a man to find occasion to praise providence, if he has within himself these two qualities: the faculty of taking a comprehensive view of what has happened in each individual instance, and the sense of gratitude. Otherwise, one man will not see the usefulness of what has happened, and another, even if he does see it, will not be grateful therefor. If God had made colours, but had not made the faculty of seeing them, of what good had it been?—None at all.—But, conversely, if He had made the faculty, but in making objects, had made them incapable of falling under the faculty of vision, in that case also of what good had it been?—None at all.—What then, if He had even made both of these, but had not made light?—Even thus it would have been of no use.—Who is it, then, that has fitted this to that and that to this? And who is it that has fitted the sword to the scabbard, and the scabbard to the sword? No one? Assuredly from the very structure of all made objects we are accustomed to prove that the work is certainly the product of some artificer, and has not been constructed at random.

Does, then, every such work reveal its artificer, but do visible objects and vision and light not reveal him? And the male and the female, and the passion of each for intercourse with the other, and the faculty which makes use of the organs which have been constructed for this purpose, do these things not reveal their artificer either? Well, admit it for these things; but the marvellous constitution of the intellect

καθ᾽ ἣν οὐχ ἁπλῶς ὑποπίπτοντες[1] τοῖς αἰσθη-
τοῖς τυπούμεθα ὑπ᾽ αὐτῶν, ἀλλὰ καὶ ἐκλαμβάνο-
μέν τι καὶ ἀφαιροῦμεν καὶ προστίθεμεν καὶ
συντίθεμεν τάδε τινὰ δι᾽ αὐτῶν καὶ νὴ Δία μετα-
βαίνομεν ἀπ᾽ ἄλλων ἐπ᾽ ἄλλα τινὰ[2] οὕτω πως
παρακείμενα, οὐδὲ ταῦτα ἱκανὰ κινῆσαί τινας καὶ
διατρέψαι πρὸς τὸ μὴ ἀπολιπεῖν τὸν τεχνίτην;
11 ἢ ἐξηγησάσθωσαν ἡμῖν τί τὸ ποιοῦν ἐστιν ἕκαστον τούτων ἢ πῶς οἷόν τε τὰ οὕτω θαυμαστὰ
καὶ τεχνικὰ εἰκῇ καὶ ἀπὸ ταὐτομάτου γίνεσθαι.
12 Τί οὖν; ἐφ᾽ ἡμῶν μόνων γίνεται ταῦτα; πολλὰ
μὲν ἐπὶ μόνων, ὧν ἐξαιρέτως χρείαν εἶχεν τὸ
λογικὸν ζῷον, πολλὰ δὲ κοινὰ εὑρήσεις ἡμῖν καὶ
13 πρὸς τὰ ἄλογα. ἆρ᾽ οὖν καὶ παρακολουθεῖ τοῖς
γινομένοις ἐκεῖνα; οὐδαμῶς. ἄλλο γάρ ἐστι
χρῆσις καὶ ἄλλο παρακολούθησις. ἐκείνων
χρείαν εἶχεν ὁ θεὸς χρωμένων ταῖς φαντασίαις,
14 ἡμῶν δὲ παρακολουθούντων τῇ χρήσει. διὰ
τοῦτο ἐκείνοις μὲν ἀρκεῖ τὸ ἐσθίειν καὶ πίνειν
καὶ τὸ ἀναπαύεσθαι καὶ ὀχεύειν καὶ τἆλλ᾽ ὅσα
ἐπιτελεῖ τῶν αὐτῶν ἕκαστον, ἡμῖν δ᾽, οἷς καὶ
15 τὴν παρακολουθητικὴν δύναμιν ἔδωκεν, οὐκέτι
ταῦτ᾽ ἀπαρκεῖ, ἀλλ᾽ ἂν μὴ κατὰ τρόπον καὶ
τεταγμένως καὶ ἀκολούθως τῇ ἑκάστου φύσει
καὶ κατασκευῇ πράττωμεν, οὐκέτι τοῦ τέλους
16 τευξόμεθα τοῦ ἑαυτῶν. ὧν γὰρ αἱ κατασκευαὶ
17 διάφοροι, τούτων καὶ τὰ ἔργα καὶ τὰ τέλη. οὐ
τοίνυν ἡ κατασκευὴ μόνον χρηστική, τούτῳ χρή-

---

[1] Meineke : ἐπιπίπτοντες S.
[2] Schenkl : τὰ S.

whereby, when we meet with sensible objects, we
do not merely have their forms impressed upon us,
but also make a selection from among them, and
subtract and add, and make these various combinations by using them, yes, and, by Zeus, pass from some
things to certain others which are in a manner
related to them—is not even all this sufficient to
stir our friends and induce them not to leave the
artificer out of account? Else let them explain to
us what it is that produces each of these results, or
how it is possible that objects so wonderful and so
workmanlike should come into being at random and
spontaneously.

What then? Is it in the case of man alone that
these things occur? You will, indeed, find many
things in man only, things of which the rational animal
had a peculiar need, but you will also find many
possessed by us in common with the irrational animals.
Do they also, then, understand what happens? No! for
use is one thing, and understanding another. ⌊God
had need of the animals in that they make use of
external impressions, and of us in that we understand
the use of external impressions. And so for them it
is sufficient to eat and drink and rest and procreate,
and whatever else of the things within their own
province the animals severally do; while for us, to
whom He has made the additional gift of the faculty
of understanding, these things are no longer sufficient,
but unless we act appropriately, and methodically,
and in conformity each with his own nature and
constitution, we shall no longer achieve our own
ends. For of beings whose constitutions are different,
the works and the ends are likewise different. So
for the being whose constitution is adapted to use

43

σθαι ὁπωσοῦν ἀπαρκεῖ· οὐ δὲ καὶ παρακολουθη-
τικὴ τῇ χρήσει, τούτῳ τὸ κατὰ τρόπον ἂν μὴ
18 προσῇ οὐδέποτε τεύξεται τοῦ τέλους. τί οὖν;
ἐκείνων ἕκαστον κατασκευάζει τὸ μὲν ὥστ'
ἐσθίεσθαι, τὸ δ' ὥστε ὑπηρετεῖν εἰς γεωργίαν, τὸ
δ' ὥστε τυρὸν φέρειν, τὸ δ' ἄλλο ἐπ' ἄλλῃ χρείᾳ
παραπλησίῳ, πρὸς ἃ τίς χρεία τοῦ παρακολουθεῖν ταῖς φαντασίαις καὶ ταύτας διακρίνειν δύ-
19 νασθαι; τὸν δ' ἄνθρωπον θεατὴν εἰσήγαγεν
αὐτοῦ τε καὶ τῶν ἔργων τῶν αὐτοῦ, καὶ οὐ μόνον
20 θεατήν, ἀλλὰ καὶ ἐξηγητὴν αὐτῶν. διὰ τοῦτο
αἰσχρόν ἐστι τῷ ἀνθρώπῳ ἄρχεσθαι καὶ καταλήγειν ὅπου καὶ τὰ ἄλογα, ἀλλὰ μᾶλλον ἔνθεν
μὲν ἄρχεσθαι, καταλήγειν δὲ ἐφ' ὃ κατέληξεν ἐφ'
21 ἡμῶν καὶ ἡ φύσις. κατέληξεν δ' ἐπὶ θεωρίαν
καὶ παρακολούθησιν καὶ σύμφωνον διεξαγωγὴν
22 τῇ φύσει. ὁρᾶτε οὖν, μὴ ἀθέατοι τούτων ἀπο-
θάνητε.
23 Ἀλλ' εἰς Ὀλυμπίαν μὲν ἀποδημεῖτε, ἵν' ἴδητε[1]
τὸ ἔργον τοῦ Φειδίου, καὶ ἀτύχημα ἕκαστος ὑμῶν
24 οἴεται τὸ ἀνιστόρητος τούτων ἀποθανεῖν· ὅπου δ'
οὐδ' ἀποδημῆσαι χρεία ἐστίν, ἀλλ' ἔστιν ἤδη καὶ
πάρεστιν τοῖς ἔργοις, ταῦτα δὲ θεάσασθαι καὶ
25 κατανοῆσαι οὐκ ἐπιθυμήσετε; οὐκ αἰσθήσεσθε
τοίνυν, οὔτε τίνες ἐστὲ οὔτ' ἐπὶ τί γεγόνατε οὔτε
τί τοῦτό ἐστιν, ἐφ' οὗ τὴν θέαν παρελήφθε;—
26 Ἀλλὰ γίνεταί τινα ἀηδῆ καὶ χαλεπὰ ἐν τῷ
βίῳ.—Ἐν Ὀλυμπίᾳ δ' οὐ γίνεται; οὐ καυμα-
τίζεσθε; οὐ στενοχωρεῖσθε; οὐ κακῶς λούεσθε;

---

[1] Schweighäuser: εἰδῆτε S.

only, mere use is sufficient, but where a being has also the faculty of understanding the use, unless the principle of propriety be added, he will never attain his end. What then? Each of the animals God constitutes, one to be eaten, another to serve in farming, another to produce cheese, and yet another for some other similar use; to perform these functions what need have they to understand external impressions and to be able to differentiate between them? But God has brought man into the world to be a spectator of Himself and of His works, and not merely a spectator, but also an interpreter. Wherefore, it is shameful for man to begin and end just where the irrational animals do; he should rather begin where they do, but end where nature has ended in dealing with us. Now she did not end until she reached contemplation and understanding and a manner of life harmonious with nature. Take heed, therefore, lest you die without ever having been spectators of these things.

But you travel to Olympia to behold the work[1] of Pheidias, and each of you regards it as a misfortune to die without seeing such sights; yet when there is no need to travel at all, but where Zeus is already, and is present in his works, will you not yearn to behold these works and know them? Will you decline, therefore, to perceive either who you are, or for what you have been born, or what that purpose is for which you have received sight?—But some unpleasant and hard things happen in life.—And do they not happen at Olympia? Do you not swelter? Are you not cramped and crowded? Do you not

---

[1] The famous gold and ivory statue of Zeus.

οὐ καταβρέχεσθε, ὅταν βρέχῃ ; θορύβου δὲ καὶ
βοῆς καὶ τῶν ἄλλων χαλεπῶν οὐκ ἀπολαύετε ;
27 ἀλλ' οἶμαι ὅτι ταῦτα πάντα ἀντιτιθέντες πρὸς
28 τὸ ἀξιόλογον τῆς θέας φέρετε καὶ ἀνέχεσθε. ἄγε
δυνάμεις δ' οὐκ εἰλήφατε, καθ' ἃς οἴσετε πᾶν τὸ
συμβαῖνον ; μεγαλοψυχίαν οὐκ εἰλήφατε ; ἀν-
29 δρείαν οὐκ εἰλήφατε ; καρτερίαν οὐκ εἰλήφατε ;
καὶ τί ἔτι μοι μέλει μεγαλοψύχῳ ὄντι τῶν ἀπο-
βῆναι δυναμένων ; τί μ' ἐκστήσει ἢ ταράξει ἢ τί
ὀδυνηρὸν φανεῖται ; οὐ χρήσομαι τῇ δυνάμει
πρὸς ἃ εἴληφα αὐτήν, ἀλλ' ἐπὶ τοῖς ἀποβαίνουσιν
πενθήσω καὶ στενάξω ;
30 "Ναί· ἀλλ' αἱ μύξαι μου ῥέουσιν." τίνος οὖν
ἕνεκα χεῖρας ἔχεις, ἀνδράποδον ; οὐχ ἵνα καὶ
31 ἀπομύσσῃς σεαυτόν ;—Τοῦτο οὖν εὔλογον μύξας
32 γίνεσθαι ἐν τῷ κόσμῳ ;—Καὶ πόσῳ κρεῖττον
ἀπομύξασθαί σε ἢ ἐγκαλεῖν ; ἢ τί οἴει ὅτι ὁ
Ἡρακλῆς ἂν ἀπέβη, εἰ μὴ λέων τοιοῦτος ἐγένετο
καὶ ὕδρα καὶ ἔλαφος καὶ σῦς καὶ ἄδικοί τινες
ἄνθρωποι καὶ θηριώδεις, οὓς ἐκεῖνος ἐξήλαυνεν
33 καὶ ἐκάθαιρεν ; καὶ τί ἂν ἐποίει μηδενὸς τοιούτου γεγονότος ; ἢ δῆλον ὅτι ἐντετυλιγμένος ἂν
ἐκάθευδεν ; οὐκοῦν πρῶτον μὲν οὐκ ἂν ἐγένετο
Ἡρακλῆς ἐν τρυφῇ τοιαύτῃ καὶ ἡσυχίᾳ νυστάζων
ὅλον τὸν βίον· εἰ δ' ἄρα καὶ ἐγένετο, τί ὄφελος
34 αὐτοῦ ; τίς δὲ χρῆσις τῶν βραχιόνων τῶν ἐκείνου καὶ τῆς ἄλλης ἀλκῆς καὶ καρτερίας καὶ
γενναιότητος, εἰ μὴ τοιαῦταί τινες αὐτὸν περι-
35 στάσεις καὶ ὗλαι διέσεισαν καὶ ἐγύμνασαν ; τί

bathe with discomfort?   Are you not drenched whenever it rains?   Do you not have your fill of tumult
and shouting and other annoyances?   But I fancy
that you hear and endure all this by balancing it off
against the memorable character of the spectacle.
Come, have you not received faculties that enable
you to bear whatever happens?   Have you not
received magnanimity?   Have you not received
courage?   Have you not received endurance?   And
what care I longer for anything that may happen, if
I be magnanimous?   What shall perturb me, or
trouble me, or seem grievous to me?   Shall I fail to
use my faculty to that end for which I have received
it, but grieve and lament over events that occur?

   "Yes, but my nose is running."   What have you
hands for, then, slave?   Is it not that you may wipe
your nose?   "Is it reasonable, then, that there should
be running noses in the world?"—And how much
better it would be for you to wipe your nose than to
find fault!   Or what do you think Heracles would
have amounted to, if there had not been a lion like
the one which he encountered, and a hydra, and a
stag, and a boar, and wicked and brutal men, whom
he made it his business to drive out and clear away?
And what would he have been doing had nothing of
the sort existed?   Is it not clear that he would have
rolled himself up in a blanket and slept?   In the first
place, then, he would never have become Heracles by
slumbering away his whole life in such luxury and
ease; but even if he had, of what good would he
have been?   What would have been the use of those
arms of his and of his prowess in general, and his
steadfastness and nobility, had not such circumstances
and occasions roused and exercised him?   What

οὖν ; αὐτῷ ταύτας ἔδει κατασκευάζειν καὶ ζητεῖν
ποθεν λέοντα εἰσαγαγεῖν εἰς τὴν χώραν τὴν

36 αὐτοῦ καὶ σῦν καὶ ὕδραν ; μωρία τοῦτο καὶ
μανία. γενόμενα δὲ καὶ εὑρεθέντα εὔχρηστα ἦν
πρὸς τὸ δεῖξαι καὶ γυμνάσαι τὸν Ἡρακλέα.

37 Ἄγε οὖν καὶ σὺ τούτων αἰσθόμενος ἀπόβλεψον
εἰς τὰς δυνάμεις ἃς ἔχεις καὶ ἀπιδὼν εἰπὲ " φέρε
νῦν, ὦ Ζεῦ, ἣν θέλεις περίστασιν· ἔχω γὰρ
παρασκευὴν ἐκ σοῦ μοι δεδομένην καὶ ἀφορμὰς
πρὸς τὸ κοσμῆσαι διὰ τῶν ἀποβαινόντων ἐμαυ-

38 τόν." οὔ· ἀλλὰ κάθησθε τὰ μὲν μὴ συμβῇ τρέμοντες, τῶν δὲ συμβαινόντων ὀδυρόμενοι καὶ
πενθοῦντες καὶ στένοντες· εἶτα τοῖς θεοῖς ἐγκα-

39 λεῖτε. τί γάρ ἐστιν ἄλλο ἀκόλουθον τῇ τοιαύτῃ

40 ἀγεννείᾳ ἢ καὶ ἀσέβεια ; καίτοι ὅ γε θεὸς οὐ
μόνον ἔδωκεν ἡμῖν τὰς δυνάμεις ταύτας, καθ' ἃς
οἴσομεν πᾶν τὸ ἀποβαῖνον μὴ ταπεινούμενοι μηδὲ
συγκλώμενοι ὑπ' αὐτοῦ, ἀλλ' ὃ ἦν ἀγαθοῦ βασιλέως καὶ ταῖς ἀληθείαις πατρός, ἀκώλυτον τοῦτο
ἔδωκεν, ἀνανάγκαστον, ἀπαραπόδιστον, ὅλον
αὐτὸ ἐφ' ἡμῖν ἐποίησεν οὐδ' αὐτῷ τινα πρὸς
τοῦτο ἰσχὺν ἀπολιπών, ὥστε κωλῦσαι ἢ ἐμπο-

41 δίσαι. ταῦτα ἔχοντες ἐλεύθερα καὶ ὑμέτερα μὴ
χρῆσθε αὐτοῖς μηδ' αἰσθάνεσθε τίνα εἰλήφατε

42 καὶ παρὰ τίνος, ἀλλὰ κάθησθε πενθοῦντες καὶ
στένοντες οἱ μὲν πρὸς αὐτὸν τὸν δόντα ἀποτε-
τυφλωμένοι μηδ' ἐπιγινώσκοντες τὸν εὐεργέτην,
οἱ δ' ὑπ' ἀγεννείας εἰς μέμψεις καὶ τὰ ἐγκλήματα

43 τῷ θεῷ ἐκτρεπόμενοι. καίτοι πρὸς μεγαλοψυ-

then? Ought he to have prepared these for himself, and sought to bring a lion into his own country from somewhere or other, and a boar, and a hydra? This would have been folly and madness. But since they did exist and were found in the world, they were serviceable as a means of revealing and exercising our Heracles.

Come then, do you also, now that you are aware of these things, contemplate the faculties which you have, and, after contemplating, say: "Bring now, O Zeus, what difficulty Thou wilt; for I have an equipment given to me by Thee, and resources wherewith to distinguish myself by making use of the things that come to pass." But no, you sit trembling for fear something will happen, and lamenting, and grieving, and groaning about other things that are happening. And then you blame the gods! For what else can be the consequence of so ignoble a spirit but sheer impiety? And yet God has not merely given us these faculties, to enable us to bear all that happens without being degraded or crushed thereby, but—as became a good king and in very truth a father—He has given them to us free from all restraint, compulsion, hindrance; He has put the whole matter under our control without reserving even for Himself any power to prevent or hinder. Although you have these faculties free and entirely your own, you do not use them, nor do you realize what gifts you have received, and from whom, but you sit sorrowing and groaning, some of you blinded toward the giver himself and not even acknowledging your benefactor, and others, —such is their ignoble spirit—turning aside to fault-finding and complaints against God. And yet,

χίαν μὲν καὶ ἀνδρείαν ἐγὼ σοὶ δείξω ὅτι ἀφορμὰς
καὶ παρασκευὴν ἔχεις, πρὸς δὲ τὸ μέμφεσθαι καὶ
ἐγκαλεῖν ποίας ἀφορμὰς ἔχεις σὺ δ' ἐμοὶ δείκνυε.

ζ'. Περὶ τῆς χρείας τῶν μεταπιπτόντων καὶ
ὑποθετικῶν καὶ τῶν ὁμοίων

1 Ἡ περὶ τοὺς μεταπίπτοντας καὶ ὑποθετικούς,
ἔτι δὲ τῷ ἠρωτῆσθαι περαίνοντας καὶ πάντας
ἁπλῶς τοὺς τοιούτους λόγους πραγματεία λαν-
θάνει τοὺς πολλοὺς περὶ καθήκοντος οὖσα.
2 ζητοῦμεν γὰρ ἐπὶ πάσης ὕλης πῶς ἂν εὕροι[1]
ὁ καλὸς καὶ ἀγαθὸς τὴν διέξοδον καὶ ἀναστροφὴν
3 τὴν ἐν αὐτῇ καθήκουσαν. οὐκοῦν ἢ τοῦτο λεγέ-
τωσαν, ὅτι οὐ συγκαθήσει εἰς ἐρώτησιν καὶ
ἀπόκρισιν ὁ σπουδαῖος ἢ ὅτι συγκαθεὶς οὐκ
ἐπιμελήσεται τοῦ μὴ εἰκῇ μηδ' ὡς ἔτυχεν ἐν
4 ἐρωτήσει καὶ ἀποκρίσει ἀναστρέφεσθαι, ἢ[2] τούτων μηδέτερον προσδεχομένοις ἀναγκαῖον ὁμολογεῖν, ὅτι ἐπίσκεψίν τινα ποιητέον τῶν τόπων
τούτων, περὶ οὓς μάλιστα στρέφεται ἐρώτησις
καὶ ἀπόκρισις.
5 Τί γὰρ ἐπαγγέλλεται ἐν λόγῳ; τἀληθῆ τι-

---

[1] Meibom : εὑροῖ S.
[2] Schenkl : μὴ S.

---

[1] With the Stoics, whose sole standard of judgement in
problems of conduct was the appeal to reason, the proper
training of the reasoning faculties was an indispensable pre-
requisite to the good life. Three modes of sophistical
reasoning are here differentiated. " Equivocal premisses "

though I can show you that you have resources and endowment for magnanimity and courage, do you, pray, show me what resources you have to justify faultfinding and complaining!

CHAPTER VII

Of the use of equivocal premises, hypothetical arguments and the like

MOST men are unaware that the handling of arguments which involve equivocal and hypothetical premisses, and, further, of those which derive syllogisms by the process of interrogation, and, in general, the handling of all such arguments,[1] has a bearing upon the duties of life. For our aim in every matter of inquiry is to learn how the good and excellent man may find the appropriate course through it and the appropriate way of conducting himself in it. Let them say, then, either that the good man will not enter the contest of question and answer, or that, once he has entered, he will be at no pains to avoid conducting himself carelessly and at haphazard in question and answer; or else, if they accept neither of these alternatives, they must admit that some investigation should be made of those topics with which question and answer are principally concerned.

For what is the professed object of reasoning?

(μεταπίπτοντες λόγοι) are those that contain ambiguities in terms which are intended to mean one thing at one step in the argument, another at another. "Hypothetical premisses" involve assumptions, or conditions. The last class proceeds by drawing unexpected conclusions from the answers to questions.

θέναι, τὰ ψευδῆ αἴρειν, πρὸς¹ τὰ ἄδηλα ἐπέχειν.

6 ἆρ' οὖν ἀρκεῖ τοῦτο μόνον μαθεῖν ;—Ἀρκεῖ, φησίν.—Οὐκοῦν καὶ τῷ βουλομένῳ ἐν χρήσει νομίσματος μὴ διαπίπτειν ἀρκεῖ τοῦτο ἀκοῦσαι, διὰ τί τὰς μὲν δοκίμους δραχμὰς παραδέχῃ, τὰς

7 δ' ἀδοκίμους ἀποδοκιμάζεις ;—Οὐκ ἀρκεῖ.—Τί οὖν δεῖ τούτῳ προσλαβεῖν ; τί γὰρ ἄλλο ἢ δύναμιν δοκιμαστικήν τε καὶ διακριτικὴν τῶν

8 δοκίμων τε καὶ ἀδοκίμων δραχμῶν ; οὐκοῦν καὶ ἐπὶ λόγου οὐκ ἀρκεῖ τὸ λεχθέν, ἀλλ' ἀνάγκη δοκιμαστικὸν γενέσθαι καὶ διακριτικὸν τοῦ ἀλη-

9 θοῦς καὶ τοῦ ψεύδους καὶ τοῦ ἀδήλου ;—Ἀνάγκη. —Ἐπὶ τούτοις τί παραγγέλλεται ἐν λόγῳ ; τὸ ἀκόλουθον τοῖς δοθεῖσιν ὑπὸ σοῦ καλῶς παραδέ-

10 χου. ἄγε ἀρκεῖ οὖν κἀνταῦθα γνῶναι τοῦτο ; οὐκ ἀρκεῖ, δεῖ δὲ μαθεῖν πῶς τί τισιν ἀκόλουθον γίνεται καὶ ποτὲ μὲν ἐν ἑνὶ ἀκολουθεῖ, ποτὲ δὲ

11 πλείοσιν κοινῇ. μή ποτε οὖν καὶ τοῦτο ἀνάγκη προσλαβεῖν τὸν μέλλοντα ἐν λόγῳ συνετῶς ἀναστραφήσεσθαι καὶ αὐτόν τ' ἀποδείξειν ἕκαστα ἀποδόντα καὶ τοῖς ἀποδεικνύουσι παρακολου-θήσειν μηδ' ὑπὸ τῶν σοφιζομένων διαπλανη-

12 θήσεσθαι ὡς ἀποδεικνυόντων ; οὐκοῦν ἐλήλυθεν ἡμῖν περὶ τῶν συναγόντων λόγων καὶ τρόπων πραγματεία καὶ γυμνασία καὶ ἀναγκαία πέφηνεν.

13 Ἀλλὰ δὴ ἔστιν ἐφ' ὧν δεδώκαμεν ὑγιῶς τὰ

¹ Added by Meibom.

To state the true, to eliminate the false, to suspend judgement in doubtful cases. Is it enough, then, to learn this alone?—It is enough, says one.—Is it, then, also enough for the man who wants to make no mistake in the use of money to be told the reason why you accept genuine drachmas and reject the counterfeit?—It is not enough.—What, then, must be added to this? Why, what else but the faculty that tests the genuine drachmas and the counterfeit and distinguishes between them? Wherefore, in reasoning also the spoken word is not enough, is it? On the contrary, is it not necessary to develop the power of testing the true and the false and the uncertain and of distinguishing between them?—It is necessary.—What else besides this is proposed in reasoning? Pray accept the consequence of what you have properly granted. Come, is it enough, then, in this case also merely to know that this particular thing is true? It is not enough, but one must learn in what way a thing follows as a consequence upon certain other things, and how sometimes one thing follows upon one, and at other times upon several conjointly. Is it not, then, necessary that a man should also acquire this power, if he is to acquit himself intelligently in argument, and is himself not only to prove each point when he tries to prove it, but also to follow the argument of those who are conducting a proof, and is not to be misled by men who quibble as though they were proving something? There has consequently arisen among us, and shown itself to be necessary, a science which deals with inferential arguments and with logical figures and trains men therein.

But of course there are times when we have

λήμματα καὶ συμβαίνει τουτὶ ἐξ αὐτῶν· ψεῦδος
14 δὲ ὂν οὐδὲν ἧττον συμβαίνει. τί οὖν μοι κα-
15 θήκει ποιεῖν; προσδέχεσθαι τὸ ψεῦδος; καὶ
πῶς οἷόν τ'; ἀλλὰ λέγειν ὅτι "οὐχ ὑγιῶς
παρεχώρησα τὰ ὡμολογημένα"; καὶ μὴν οὐδὲ
τοῦτο δίδοται. ἀλλ' ὅτι "οὐ συμβαίνει διὰ τῶν
παρακεχωρημένων"; ἀλλ' οὐδὲ τοῦτο δίδοται.
16 τί οὖν ἐπὶ τούτων ποιητέον; ἢ μή ποτε ὡς οὐκ
ἀρκεῖ τὸ δανείσασθαι πρὸς τὸ ἔτι ὀφείλειν, ἀλλὰ
δεῖ προσεῖναι καὶ τὸ ἐπιμένειν ἐπὶ τοῦ δανείου
καὶ μὴ διαλελύσθαι αὐτό, οὕτως οὐκ ἀρκεῖ πρὸς
τὸ δεῖν παραχωρεῖν τὸ ἐπιφερόμενον τὸ δεδωκέναι
τὰ λήμματα, δεῖ δ' ἐπιμένειν ἐπὶ τῆς παρα-
17 χωρήσεως αὐτῶν; καὶ δὴ μενόντων μὲν αὐτῶν
εἰς τέλος ὁποῖα παρεχωρήθη πᾶσα ἀνάγκη ἡμᾶς
ἐπὶ τῆς παραχωρήσεως ἐπιμένειν καὶ τὸ ἀκό-
19 λουθον αὐτοῖς προσδέχεσθαι·[1] . . . οὐδὲ γὰρ ἡμῖν
ἔτι οὐδὲ καθ' ἡμᾶς συμβαίνει τοῦτο τὸ ἐπιφερόμενον, ἐπειδὴ τῆς συγχωρήσεως τῶν λημμάτων
20 ἀπέστημεν. δεῖ οὖν καὶ τὰ τοιαῦτα τῶν λημμάτων ἱστορῆσαι καὶ τὴν τοιαύτην μεταβολήν τε
καὶ μετάπτωσιν αὐτῶν, καθ' ἣν ἐν αὐτῇ τῇ
ἐρωτήσει ἢ τῇ ἀποκρίσει ἢ τῷ συλλελογίσθαι
ἤ τινι ἄλλῳ τοιούτῳ λαμβάνοντα τὰς μετα-

---

[1] At this point Upton introduced from his 'codex' a
sentence intended to express fully the transition in the
argument (§ 18): μὴ μενόντων δὲ αὐτῶν ὁποῖα παρεχωρήθη, καὶ
ἡμᾶς πᾶσα ἀνάγκη τῆς παραχωρήσεως ἀφίστασθαι καὶ ⟨τοῦ Schw.⟩
τὸ ἀνακόλουθον αὐτοῖς λόγοις προσδέχεσθαι. "If, however,
they do not remain as they were granted, we are also bound
to abandon our concession and our acceptance of what is

with sound reasoning granted the premises, and
the inference from them is so-and-so ; and, in spite
of its being false, it is none the less the inference.
What, then, should I do ? Accept the fallacy ?
And how is that possible ? Well, should I say, " It
was not sound reasoning for me to grant the premisses " ? Nay, but this is not permissible either.
Or, " This does not follow from what has been
granted " ? But that is not permissible, either.
What, then, must be done in these circumstances ?
Is it not this, that the fact of having borrowed is
not enough to prove that one is still in debt, but we
must add the circumstance that one abides by the
loan—that is, has not paid it—and just so our having
once granted the premises is not enough to compel
us to accept the inference, but we must abide by our
acceptance of the premises ? And what is more,
if the premises remain until the end what they
were when they were granted, there is every necessity for us to abide by our acceptance of them, and
to allow the conclusion that has been drawn from
them ; . . . for from our point of view and to our way
of thinking this inference does not now result from
the premises, since we have withdrawn from our
previous assent to the premises. It is necessary,
therefore, to enquire into premises of this kind and
into such change and equivocal modification of them,
whereby, at the very moment the question is put,
or the answer made, or the deduction drawn, or at
some other similar stage in the argument, the premisses take on modified meanings and give occasion

---

inconsistent with the premises." Schenkl indicates a
lacuna.

πτώσεις ἀφορμὴν παρέχει τοῖς ἀνοήτοις τοῦ
ταράσσεσθαι μὴ βλέπουσι τὸ ἀκόλουθον. τίνος
21 ἕνεκα; ἵν᾿ ἐν τῷ τόπῳ τούτῳ μὴ παρὰ τὸ
καθῆκον μηδ᾿ εἰκῆ μηδὲ συγκεχυμένως ἀνα-
στρεφώμεθα.

22 Καὶ τὸ αὐτὸ ἐπί τε τῶν ὑποθέσεων καὶ τῶν
ὑποθετικῶν λόγων. ἀναγκαῖον γὰρ ἔστιν ὅτ᾿
αἰτῆσαί τινα ὑπόθεσιν ὥσπερ ἐπιβάθραν τῷ ἑξῆς
23 λόγῳ. πᾶσαν οὖν τὴν δοθεῖσαν παραχωρητέον
24 ἢ οὐ πᾶσαν; καὶ εἰ οὐ πᾶσαν, τίνα;[1] πα-
ραχωρήσαντι δὲ μενετέον εἰς ἅπαν ἐπὶ τῆς
τηρήσεως ἢ ἔστιν ὅτε ἀποστατέον, τὰ δ᾿ ἀκόλουθα
προσδεκτέον καὶ τὰ μαχόμενα οὐ προσδεκτέον;—
25 Ναί.—᾿Αλλὰ λέγει τις ὅτι "ποιήσω σε δυνατοῦ
δεξάμενον ὑπόθεσιν ἐπ᾿ ἀδύνατον ἀπαχθῆναι."
πρὸς τοῦτον οὐ συγκαθήσει ὁ φρόνιμος, ἀλλὰ
26 φεύξεται ἐξέτασιν καὶ κοινολογίαν; καὶ τίς ἔτι
ἄλλος ἐστὶ λόγῳ χρηστικὸς καὶ δεινὸς ἐρωτήσει
καὶ ἀποκρίσει καὶ νὴ Δία ἀνεξαπάτητός τε καὶ
27 ἀσόφιστος; ἀλλὰ συγκαθήσει μέν, οὐκ ἐπι-
στραφήσεται δὲ τοῦ μὴ εἰκῆ καὶ ὡς ἔτυχεν
ἀναστρέφεσθαι ἐν λόγῳ; καὶ πῶς ἔτι ἔσται
28 τοιοῦτος οἷον αὐτὸν ἐπινοοῦμεν; ἀλλ᾿ ἄνευ τινὸς
τοιαύτης γυμνασίας καὶ παρασκευῆς φυλάττειν
29 οἷός τ᾿ ἐστὶ τὸ ἑξῆς; τοῦτο δεικνύτωσαν καὶ
παρέλκει τὰ θεωρήματα ταῦτα πάντα, ἄτοπα
ἦν καὶ ἀνακόλουθα τῇ προλήψει τοῦ σπου-
δαίου.

30 Τί ἔτι ἀργοὶ καὶ ῥάθυμοι καὶ νωθροί ἐσμεν

[1] The words περὶ τίνος ἡ σκέψις; περὶ καθήκοντος at this
point were deleted by Wolf.

to the unthinking to be disconcerted, if they do not see what follows in consequence. Why is it necessary? In order that in this matter we may not behave unsuitably, nor at haphazard, nor confusedly.

And the same holds true of hypotheses and hypothetical arguments. For it is necessary at times to postulate some hypothesis as a sort of stepping-stone for the subsequent argument. Are we, therefore, to grant any and every hypothesis that is proposed, or not every one? And if not every one, what one? And when a man has granted an hypothesis, must he abide for ever by it and maintain it, or are there times when he should abandon it and accept only the consequences which follow from it without accepting those which are opposed to it?—Yes.—But some-one says, "If you once admit an hypothesis that involves a possibility, I will compel you to be drawn on to an impossibility." Shall the prudent man refuse to engage with this person, and avoid enquiry and discussion with him? Yet who but the prudent is capable of using argument and skilful in question and answer, and, by Zeus, proof against deceit and sophistic fallacies? But shall he argue, indeed, and then not take pains to avoid conducting himself recklessly and at haphazard in argument? And if he does not, how will he any longer be the sort of man we think he is? But without some such exercise and preparation in formal reasoning, how will he be able to maintain the continuity of the argument? Let them show that he will be able, and all these speculations become mere superfluity; they were absurd and inconsistent with our preconception of the good man.

Why are we still indolent and easy-going and

καὶ προφάσεις ζητοῦμεν, καθ' ἃς οὐ πονήσομεν
οὐδ' ἀγρυπνήσομεν ἐξεργαζόμενοι τὸν αὑτῶν[1]
31 λόγον ;—Ἂν οὖν ἐν τούτοις πλανηθῶ, μή τι
τὸν πατέρα ἀπέκτεινα ;—'Ανδράποδον, ποῦ γὰρ
ἐνθάδε πατὴρ ἦν, ἵν' αὐτὸν ἀποκτείνῃς ; τί οὖν
ἐποίησας ; ὃ μόνον ἦν κατὰ τὸν τόπον ἁμάρτημα,
32 τοῦτο ἡμάρτηκας. ἐπεί τοι τοῦτ' αὐτὸ καὶ ἐγὼ
Ῥούφῳ εἶπον ἐπιτιμῶντί μοι ὅτι τὸ παραλειπόμενον ἓν ἐν συλλογισμῷ τινι οὐχ εὕρισκον.
"Οὐχ οἷον μέν," φημί, "εἰ[2] τὸ Καπιτώλιον κατέ-
καυσα,"[3] ὁ δ' "'Ανδράποδον," ἔφη, "ἐνθάδε τὸ
33 παραλειπόμενον Καπιτώλιόν ἐστιν." ἢ ταῦτα
μόνα ἁμαρτήματά ἐστι τὸ Καπιτώλιον ἐμπρῆσαι
καὶ τὸν πατέρα ἀποκτεῖναι, τὸ δ' εἰκῇ καὶ μάτην
καὶ ὡς ἔτυχεν χρῆσθαι ταῖς φαντασίαις ταῖς
αὑτοῦ καὶ μὴ παρακολουθεῖν λόγῳ μηδ' ἀποδείξει
μηδὲ σοφίσματι μηδ' ἁπλῶς βλέπειν τὸ καθ'
αὑτὸν καὶ οὐ καθ' αὑτὸν ἐν ἐρωτήσει καὶ ἀποκρίσει, τούτων δ' οὐδέν ἐστιν ἁμάρτημα ;

η'. Ὅτι αἱ δυνάμεις τοῖς ἀπαιδεύτοις οὐκ
ἀσφαλεῖς

1 Καθ' ὅσους τρόπους μεταλαμβάνειν ἔστι τὰ
ἰσοδυναμοῦντα ἀλλήλοις, κατὰ τοσούτους καὶ
τὰ εἴδη τῶν ἐπιχειρημάτων τε καὶ ἐνθυμημάτων
2 ἐν τοῖς λόγοις ἐκποιεῖ μεταλαμβάνειν. οἷον φέρε

---

[1] Salmasius : αὐτὸν S.　　[2] Added by Blass.
[3] Schenkl : κατεσκεύασα S.

sluggish, seeking excuses whereby we may avoid
toiling or even late hours, as we try to perfect our
own reason?—If, then, I err in these matters, I have
not murdered my own father, have I?—Slave, pray
where was there in this case a father for you to
murder? What, then, have you done, you ask?
You have committed what was the only possible
error in the matter. Indeed this is the very remark
I made to Rufus when he censured me for not discovering the one omission in a certain syllogism.
"Well," said I, "it isn't as bad as if I had burned
down the Capitol." But he answered, "Slave, the
omission here *is* the Capitol." Or are there no other
errors than setting fire to the Capitol and murdering
one's father? But to make a reckless and foolish
and haphazard use of the external impressions that
come to one, to fail to follow an argument, or demonstration, or sophism—in a word, to fail to see in
question and answer what is consistent with one's
position or inconsistent—is none of these things an
error?

CHAPTER VIII

That the reasoning faculties, in the case of the
uneducated, are not free from error

IN as many ways as it is possible to vary the meaning of equivalent terms, in so many ways may a man
also vary the forms of his controversial arguments
and of his enthymemes [1] in reasoning. Take this

---

[1] An enthymeme is defined by Aristotle (*Rhet.* I. i. 11) as
"a rhetorical demonstration," that is, an argument expressed
in ordinary literary style, not in the formal fashion of a
syllogism. It is thus called an "incomplete syllogism" (§ 3
below), as falling short of the "definite proof" accorded by
the syllogism.

τὸν τρόπον τοῦτον· εἰ ἐδάνεισω καὶ μὴ ἀπέδωκας,
ὀφείλεις μοι τὸ ἀργύριον· οὐχὶ ἐδάνεισω μὲν καὶ
οὐκ ἀπέδωκας· οὐ μὴν ὀφείλεις μοι τὸ ἀργύριον.
3 καὶ τοῦτο οὐδενὶ μᾶλλον προσήκει ἢ τῷ φιλοσόφῳ
ἐμπείρως ποιεῖν. εἴπερ γὰρ ἀτελὴς συλλογισμός
ἐστι τὸ ἐνθύμημα, δῆλον ὅτι ὁ περὶ τὸν τέλειον
συλλογισμὸν γεγυμνασμένος οὗτος ἂν ἱκανὸς εἴη
καὶ περὶ τὸν ἀτελῆ οὐδὲν ἧττον.

4 Τί ποτ᾽ οὖν οὐ γυμνάζομεν αὐτούς τε καὶ
5 ἀλλήλους τὸν τρόπον τοῦτον ; ὅτι νῦν καίτοι μὴ
γυμναζόμενοι περὶ ταῦτα μηδ᾽ ἀπὸ τῆς ἐπιμελείας
τοῦ ἤθους ὑπό γε ἐμοῦ περισπώμενοι ὅμως
6 οὐδὲν ἐπιδίδομεν εἰς καλοκἀγαθίαν. τί οὖν χρὴ
προσδοκᾶν, εἰ καὶ ταύτην τὴν ἀσχολίαν προσλά-
βοιμεν ; καὶ μάλισθ᾽, ὅτι οὐ μόνον ἀσχολία τις
ἀπὸ τῶν ἀναγκαιοτέρων αὐτὴ προσγένοιτ᾽ ἄν,
ἀλλὰ καὶ οἰήσεως ἀφορμὴ καὶ τύφου οὐχ ἡ
7 τυχοῦσα. μεγάλη γάρ ἐστι δύναμις ἡ ἐπι-
χειρητικὴ καὶ πιθανολογική, καὶ μάλιστ᾽ εἰ τύχοι
γυμνασίας ἐπιπλέον καί τινα καὶ εὐπρέπειαν ἀπὸ
8 τῶν ὀνομάτων προσλάβοι. ὅτι καὶ ἐν τῷ καθόλου
πᾶσα δύναμις ἐπισφαλὴς τοῖς ἀπαιδεύτοις καὶ
ἀσθενέσι προσγενομένη πρὸς τὸ ἐπᾶραι καὶ
9 χαυνῶσαι ἐπ᾽ αὐτῇ. ποίᾳ γὰρ ἄν τις ἔτι μηχανῇ
πείσαι τὸν νέον τὸν ἐν τούτοις διαφέροντα, ὅτι
οὐ δεῖ προσθήκην αὐτὸν ἐκείνων γενέσθαι, ἀλλ᾽
10 ἐκεῖνα αὐτῷ προσθεῖναι ; οὐχὶ δὲ πάντας τοὺς
λόγους τούτους καταπατήσας ἐπηρμένος ἡμῖν καὶ
πεφυσημένος περιπατεῖ μηδ᾽ ἀνεχόμενος, ἄν τις
ἅπτηται[1] αὐτοῦ ὑπομιμνήσκων, τίνος ἀπολελειμ-
μένος ποῦ ἀποκέκλικεν ;

---

[1] τι after ἅπτηται deleted in s.

syllogism, for instance: *If you have borrowed and have not repaid, you owe me the money; now you have not borrowed and have not repaid; therefore you do not owe me the money.* And no man is better fitted to employ such variations skilfully than the philosopher. For if, indeed, the enthymeme is an incomplete syllogism, it is clear that he who has been exercised in the perfect syllogism would be no less competent to deal with the imperfect also.

Why, then, do we neglect to exercise ourselves and one another in this way? Because, even now, without receiving exercise in these matters, or even being, by me at least, diverted from the study of morality, we nevertheless make no progress toward the beautiful and the good. What, therefore, must we expect, if we should take on this occupation also? And especially since it would not merely be an additional occupation to draw us away from those which are more necessary, but would also be an exceptional excuse for conceit and vanity. For great is the power of argumentation and persuasive reasoning, and especially if it should enjoy excessive exercise and receive likewise a certain additional ornament from language. The reason is that, in general, every faculty which is acquired by the uneducated and the weak is dangerous for them, as being apt to make them conceited and puffed up over it. For by what device might one any longer persuade a young man who excels in these faculties to make them an appendage to himself instead of his becoming an appendage to them? Does he not trample all these reasons under foot, and strut about in our presence, all conceited and puffed up, much less submitting if any one by way of reproof reminds him of what he lacks and wherein he has gone astray?

11 Τί οὖν; Πλάτων φιλόσοφος οὐκ ἦν; Ἱπποκράτης γὰρ ἰατρὸς οὐκ ἦν; ἀλλ᾽ ὁρᾷς πῶς
12 φράζει Ἱπποκράτης. μή τι οὖν Ἱπποκράτης οὕτω
φράζει, καθὸ ἰατρός ἐστιν; τί οὖν μιγνύεις πράγματα ἄλλως ἐπὶ τῶν αὐτῶν ἀνθρώπων συνδρα-
13 μόντα; εἰ δὲ καλὸς ἦν Πλάτων καὶ ἰσχυρός, ἔδει
κἀμὲ καθήμενον ἐκπονεῖν, ἵνα καλὸς γένωμαι ἢ
ἵνα ἰσχυρός, ὡς τοῦτο ἀναγκαῖον πρὸς φιλοσοφίαν, ἐπεί τις φιλόσοφος ἅμα καὶ καλὸς ἦν καὶ
14 φιλόσοφος; οὐ θέλεις αἰσθάνεσθαι καὶ διακρῖναι
κατὰ τί οἱ ἄνθρωποι γίνονται φιλόσοφοι καὶ τίνα
ἄλλως αὐτοῖς πάρεστιν; ἄγε εἰ δ᾽ ἐγὼ φιλόσοφος
ἤμην, ἔδει ὑμᾶς καὶ χωλοὺς γενέσθαι; τί οὖν;
15 αἴρω[1] τὰς δυνάμεις ταύτας; μὴ γένοιτο· οὐδὲ
16 γὰρ τὴν ὁρατικήν. ὅμως δ᾽, ἄν μου πυνθάνῃ τί
ἐστιν ἀγαθὸν τοῦ ἀνθρώπου, οὐκ ἔχω σοι ἄλλο
εἰπεῖν ἢ ὅτι ποιὰ προαίρεσις.[2]

θ΄. Πῶς ἀπὸ τοῦ συγγενεῖς ἡμᾶς εἶναι τῷ θεῷ
ἐπέλθοι ἄν τις ἐπὶ τὰ ἑξῆς;

1 Εἰ ταῦτά ἐστιν ἀληθῆ τὰ περὶ τῆς συγγενείας
τοῦ θεοῦ καὶ ἀνθρώπων λεγόμενα ὑπὸ τῶν φιλοσόφων, τί ἄλλο ἀπολείπεται τοῖς ἀνθρώποις ἢ
τὸ τοῦ Σωκράτους, μηδέποτε πρὸς τὸν πυθόμενον
ποδαπός ἐστιν εἰπεῖν ὅτι Ἀθηναῖος ἢ Κορίνθιος,
2 ἀλλ᾽ ὅτι κόσμιος; διὰ τί γὰρ λέγεις Ἀθηναῖον

---

[1] Schenkl: ἐρῶ S.
[2] φαντασιῶν after προαίρεσις deleted by Schenkl.

What then? Was not Plato a philosopher? Yes, and was not Hippocrates a physician? But you see how eloquently Hippocrates expresses himself. Does Hippocrates, then, express himself so eloquently by virtue of his being a physician? Why, then, do you confuse things that for no particular reason have been combined in the same man? Now if Plato was handsome and strong, ought I to sit down and strive to become handsome, or become strong, on the assumption that this is necessary for philosophy, because a certain philosopher was at the same time both handsome and a philosopher? Are you not willing to observe and distinguish just what that is by virtue of which men become philosophers, and what qualities pertain to them for no particular reason? Come now, if I were a philosopher, ought you to become lame like me? What then? Am I depriving you of these faculties? Far be it from me! No more than I am depriving you of the faculty of sight. Yet, if you enquire of me what is man's good, I can give you no other answer than that it is a kind of moral purpose.

CHAPTER IX

How from the thesis that we are akin to God may a man proceed to the consequences?

If what is said by the philosophers regarding the kinship of God and men be true, what other course remains for men but that which Socrates took when asked to what country he belonged, never to say "I am an Athenian," or "I am a Corinthian," but "I am a citizen of the universe"? For why do you

εἶναι σεαυτόν, οὐχὶ δ' ἐξ ἐκείνης μόνον τῆς γωνίας,
3 εἰς ἣν ἐρρίφη γεννηθέν σου τὸ σωμάτιον ; ἢ δῆλον
ὅτι ἀπὸ τοῦ κυριωτέρου καὶ περιέχοντος οὐ μόνον
αὐτὴν ἐκείνην τὴν γωνίαν, ἀλλὰ[1] καὶ ὅλην σου
τὴν οἰκίαν καὶ ἁπλῶς ὅθεν σου τὸ γένος τῶν
προγόνων εἰς σὲ κατελήλυθεν ἐντεῦθέν ποθεν
4 καλεῖς σεαυτὸν Ἀθηναῖον καὶ Κορίνθιον ; ὁ τοίνυν
τῇ διοικήσει τοῦ κόσμου παρηκολουθηκὼς καὶ
μεμαθηκώς, ὅτι "τὸ μέγιστον καὶ κυριώτατον καὶ
περιεκτικώτατον πάντων τοῦτό ἐστι τὸ σύστημα
τὸ ἐξ ἀνθρώπων καὶ θεοῦ, ἀπ' ἐκείνου δὲ τὰ
σπέρματα καταπέπτωκεν οὐκ εἰς τὸν πατέρα τὸν
ἐμὸν μόνον οὐδ' εἰς τὸν πάππον, ἀλλ' εἰς ἅπαντα
μὲν τὰ ἐπὶ γῆς γεννώμενά τε καὶ φυόμενα, προ-
5 ηγουμένως δ' εἰς τὰ λογικά, ὅτι κοινωνεῖν μόνον
ταῦτα πέφυκεν τῷ θεῷ τῆς συναναστροφῆς κατὰ
6 τὸν λόγον ἐπιπεπλεγμένα," διὰ τί μὴ εἴπῃ[2] αὑτὸν
κόσμιον ; διὰ τί μὴ υἱὸν τοῦ θεοῦ ; διὰ τί δὲ
φοβηθήσεταί τι τῶν γιγνομένων ἐν ἀνθρώποις ;
7 ἀλλὰ πρὸς μὲν τὸν Καίσαρα ἢ συγγένεια ἢ ἄλλον
τινὰ τῶν μέγα δυναμένων ἐν Ῥώμῃ ἱκανὴ παρέχειν ἐν ἀσφαλείᾳ διάγοντας καὶ ἀκαταφρονήτους
καὶ δεδοικότας μηδ' ὁτιοῦν, τὸ δὲ τὸν θεὸν ποιητὴν
ἔχειν καὶ πατέρα καὶ κηδεμόνα οὐκέτι ἡμᾶς ἐξαι-
8 ρήσεται λυπῶν καὶ φόβων ;—Καὶ πόθεν φάγω,

---

[1] Added by Schenkl.
[2] τις after εἴπῃ deleted by von Wilamowitz.

---

[1] The terms "Athenian," "Corinthian," etc., characterize
citizens of a country, not merely of a locality, i.e., citizens of
Attica or Corinthia. The "corner" in which one was born

say that you are an Athenian, instead of mentioning
merely that corner into which your paltry body was
cast at birth? Or is it clear you take the place
which has a higher degree of authority and compre-
hends not merely that corner of yours, but also your
family and, in a word, the source from which your
race has come, your ancestors down to yourself, and
from some such entity call yourself " Athenian," or
" Corinthian "?[1] Well, then, anyone who has atten-
tively studied the administration of the universe and
has learned that " the greatest and most authoritative
and most comprehensive of all governments is this
one, which is composed of men and God,[2] and that
from Him have descended the seeds of being, not
merely to my father or to my grandfather, but to
all things that are begotten and that grow upon
earth, and chiefly to rational beings, seeing that by
nature it is theirs alone to have communion in the
society of God, being intertwined with him through
the reason,"—why should not such a man call himself
a citizen of the universe? Why should he not call himself a son of God? And why shall he fear anything
that happens among men? What! Shall kinship
with Caesar or any other of them that have great
power at Rome be sufficient to enable men to live
securely, proof against contempt, and in fear of
nothing whatsoever, but to have God as our maker,
and father, and guardian,—shall this not suffice to
deliver us from griefs and fears?—And wherewithal

[1] might have been Marathon, Rhamnus, Lechaeum, Tenea, or
the like.
[2] This seems to be a quotation from Poseidonius (Diogenes
Laertius, VII. 138), but is also ascribed variously to the Stoics
in general and especially to Chrysippus (see Diels, *Doxographi
Graeci*, 464, 20 and 465, 15, comparing 20 f.).

φησίν, μηδὲν ἔχων ;—Καὶ πῶς οἱ δοῦλοι, πῶς οἱ
δραπέται, τίνι πεποιθότες ἐκεῖνοι ἀπαλλάττονται
τῶν δεσποτῶν ; τοῖς ἀγροῖς ἢ τοῖς οἰκέταις ἢ τοῖς
ἀργυρώμασιν ; οὐδενί, ἀλλ' ἑαυτοῖς· καὶ ὅμως οὐκ

9 ἐπιλείπουσιν αὐτοὺς τροφαί. τὸν δὲ φιλόσοφον
ἡμῖν δεήσει ἄλλοις θαρροῦντα καὶ ἐπαναπαυόμενον
ἀποδημεῖν καὶ μὴ ἐπιμελεῖσθαι αὐτὸν αὑτοῦ καὶ
τῶν θηρίων τῶν ἀλόγων εἶναι χείρονα καὶ δειλό-
τερον, ὧν ἕκαστον αὐτὸ αὑτῷ ἀρκούμενον οὔτε
τροφῆς ἀπορεῖ τῆς οἰκείας οὔτε διεξαγωγῆς τῆς
καταλλήλου καὶ κατὰ φύσιν ;

10 Ἐγὼ μὲν οἶμαι, ὅτι ἔδει καθῆσθαι τὸν πρεσβύτερον ἐνταῦθα οὐ τοῦτο μηχανώμενον, ὅπως
μὴ ταπεινοφρονήσητε μηδὲ ταπεινοὺς μηδ' ἀγεν-
νεῖς τινας διαλογισμοὺς διαλογιεῖσθε αὐτοὶ περὶ

11 ἑαυτῶν, ἀλλὰ μή, ἄν¹ τινες ἐμπίπτωσιν τοιοῦτοι
νέοι, ἐπιγνόντες τὴν πρὸς τοὺς θεοὺς συγγένειαν
καὶ ὅτι δεσμά τινα ταῦτα προσηρτήμεθα τὸ σῶμα
καὶ τὴν κτῆσιν αὐτοῦ καὶ ὅσα τούτων ἕνεκα
ἀναγκαῖα ἡμῖν γίνεται εἰς οἰκονομίαν καὶ ἀναστροφὴν τὴν ἐν τῷ βίῳ, ὡς βάρη τινὰ καὶ ἀνιαρὰ
καὶ ἄχρηστα ἀπορρίψαι θέλωσιν καὶ ἀπελθεῖν

12 πρὸς τοὺς συγγενεῖς· καὶ τοῦτον ἔδει τὸν ἀγῶνα
ἀγωνίζεσθαι τὸν διδάσκαλον ὑμῶν καὶ παιδευτήν,
εἴ τις ἄρα ἦν· ὑμᾶς μὲν ἔρχεσθαι λέγοντας
"'Ἐπίκτητε, οὐκέτι ἀνεχόμεθα μετὰ τοῦ σωματίου

---

¹ Added by Elter.

---

¹ Referring to himself.
² There is less need of his urging them to regard themselves as sons of God than of preventing them, if they are

shall I be fed, asks one, if I have nothing?—And how of slaves, how of runaways, on what do they rely when they leave their masters? On their lands, their slaves, or their vessels of silver? No, on nothing but themselves; and nevertheless food does not fail them. And shall it be necessary for our philosopher, forsooth, when he goes abroad, to depend upon others for his assurance and his refreshment, instead of taking care of himself, and to be more vile and craven than the irrational animals, every one of which is sufficient to himself, and lacks neither its own proper food nor that way of life which is appropriate to it and in harmony with nature?

As for me, I think that the elder man[1] ought not to be sitting here devising how to keep you from thinking too meanly of yourselves or from taking in your debates a mean or ignoble position regarding yourselves;[2] he should rather be striving to prevent there being among you any young men of such a sort that, when once they have realized their kinship to the gods and that we have these fetters as it were fastened upon us,—the body and its possessions, and whatever things on their account are necessary to us for the management of life, and our tarrying therein,—they may desire to throw aside all these things as burdensome and vexatious and unprofitable and depart to their kindred. And this is the struggle in which your teacher and trainer, if he really amounted to anything, ought to be engaged; you, for your part, would come to him saying: "Epictetus, we can no longer endure to be

convinced of this, from acting as if the life of the body were a thing to throw aside, and so committing suicide,—a practice which was defended by many Stoics.

67

τούτου δεδεμένοι καὶ τοῦτο τρέφοντες καὶ ποτί-
ζοντες καὶ ἀναπαύοντες καὶ καθαίροντες, εἶτα δι᾽

13 αὐτὸ συμπεριφερόμενοι τοῖσδε καὶ τοῖσδε. οὐκ
ἀδιάφορα ταῦτα καὶ οὐδὲν πρὸς ἡμᾶς; καὶ ὁ
θάνατος οὐ κακόν¹; καὶ συγγενεῖς τινες τοῦ θεοῦ

14 ἐσμεν κἀκεῖθεν ἐληλύθαμεν; ἄφες ἡμᾶς ἀπελθεῖν
ὅθεν ἐληλύθαμεν, ἄφες λυθῆναί ποτε τῶν δεσμῶν

15 τούτων τῶν ἐξηρτημένων καὶ βαρούντων. ἐνταῦθα
λησταὶ καὶ κλέπται καὶ δικαστήρια καὶ οἱ καλού-
μενοι τύραννοι δοκοῦντες ἔχειν τινὰ ἐφ᾽ ἡμῖν
ἐξουσίαν διὰ τὸ σωμάτιον καὶ τὰ τούτου κτήματα.
ἄφες δείξωμεν αὐτοῖς, ὅτι οὐδενὸς ἔχουσιν ἐξου-

16 σίαν." ἐμὲ δ᾽ ἐνταῦθα² λέγειν ὅτι "ἄνθρωποι,
ἐκδέξασθε τὸν θεόν. ὅταν ἐκεῖνος σημήνῃ καὶ
ἀπολύσῃ ὑμᾶς ταύτης τῆς ὑπηρεσίας, τότ᾽ ἀπο-
λύεσθε πρὸς αὐτόν· ἐπὶ δὲ τοῦ παρόντος ἀνά-
σχεσθε ἐνοικοῦντες ταύτην τὴν χώραν, εἰς ἣν

17 ἐκεῖνος ὑμᾶς ἔταξεν. ὀλίγος ἄρα χρόνος οὗτος
ὁ τῆς οἰκήσεως καὶ ῥᾴδιος τοῖς οὕτω διακειμένοις.
ποῖος γὰρ ἔτι τύραννος ἢ ποῖος κλέπτης ἢ ποῖα
δικαστήρια φοβερὰ τοῖς οὕτως παρ᾽ οὐδὲν πε-
ποιημένοις τὸ σῶμα καὶ τὰ τούτου κτήματα;
μείνατε, μὴ ἀλογίστως ἀπέλθητε."

18   Τοιοῦτόν τι ἔδει γίνεσθαι παρὰ τοῦ παιδευτοῦ

19 πρὸς τοὺς εὐφυεῖς τῶν νέων. νῦν δὲ τί γίνεται;
νεκρὸς μὲν ὁ παιδευτής, νεκροὶ δ᾽ ὑμεῖς. ὅταν
χορτασθῆτε σήμερον, κάθησθε κλαίοντες περὶ τῆς

20 αὔριον, πόθεν φάγητε. ἀνδράποδον, ἂν σχῇς,
ἕξεις· ἂν μὴ σχῇς, ἐξελεύσῃ· ἤνοικται ἡ θύρα.
τί πενθεῖς; ποῦ ἔτι τόπος δακρύοις; τίς ἔτι

---

¹ Reiske: κακὸς S.
² Capps: ἐν τῶι S.

imprisoned with this paltry body, giving it food and drink, and resting and cleansing it, and, to crown all, being on its account brought into contact with these people and those. Are not these things indifferent—indeed, nothing—to us? And is not death no evil? And are we not in a manner akin to God, and have we not come from Him? Suffer us to go back whence we came; suffer us to be freed at last from these fetters that are fastened to us and weigh us down. Here are despoilers and thieves, and courts of law, and those who are called tyrants; they think that they have some power over us because of the paltry body and its possessions. Suffer us to show them that they have power over no one." And thereupon it were my part to say: "Men, wait upon God. When He shall give the signal and set you free from this service, then shall you depart to Him; but for the present endure to abide in this place, where He has stationed you. Short indeed is this time of your abiding here, and easy to bear for men of your convictions. For what tyrant, or what thief, or what courts of law are any longer formidable to those who have thus set at naught the body and its possessions? Stay, nor be so unrational as to depart."

Some such instruction should be given by the teacher to the youth of good natural parts. But what happens now? A corpse is your teacher and corpses are you. As soon as you have fed your fill to-day, you sit lamenting about the morrow, where-withal you shall be fed. Slave, if you get it, you will have it; if you do not get it, you will depart; the door stands open. Why grieve? Where is there yet room for tears? What occasion longer

κολακείας ἀφορμή; διὰ τί ἄλλος ἄλλῳ φθονήσει;
διὰ τί πολλὰ κεκτημένους θαυμάσει ἢ τοὺς ἐν
δυνάμει τεταγμένους, μάλιστ' ἂν καὶ ἰσχυροὶ
21 ὦσιν καὶ ὀργίλοι; τί γὰρ ἡμῖν ποιήσουσιν; ἃ
δύνανται ποιῆσαι, τούτων οὐκ ἐπιστρεψόμεθα·
ὧν ἡμῖν μέλει, ταῦτα οὐ δύνανται. τίς οὖν ἔτι
ἄρξει τοῦ οὕτως διακειμένου;
22 Πῶς Σωκράτης εἶχεν πρὸς ταῦτα; πῶς γὰρ
ἄλλως ἢ ὡς ἔδει τὸν πεπεισμένον ὅτι ἐστὶ τῶν
23 θεῶν συγγενής; "'Άν μοι λέγητε," φησίν, "νῦν
ὅτι 'ἀφίεμέν σε ἐπὶ τούτοις, ὅπως μηκέτι διαλέξῃ
τούτους τοὺς λόγους οὓς μέχρι νῦν διελέγου
μηδὲ παρενοχλήσεις ἡμῶν τοῖς νέοις μηδὲ τοῖς
24 γέρουσιν,' ἀποκρινοῦμαι ὅτι γελοιοί ἐστε, οἵτινες
ἀξιοῦτε, εἰ μέν με ὁ στρατηγὸς ὁ ὑμέτερος ἔταξεν
εἴς τινα τάξιν, ὅτι ἔδει με τηρεῖν αὐτὴν καὶ
φυλάττειν καὶ μυριάκις πρότερον αἱρεῖσθαι
ἀποθνήσκειν ἢ ἐγκαταλιπεῖν αὐτήν, εἰ δ' ὁ θεὸς
ἔν τινι χώρᾳ καὶ ἀναστροφῇ κατατέταχεν, ταύτην
25 δ' ἐγκαταλιπεῖν δεῖ ἡμᾶς." τοῦτ' ἔστιν ἄνθρωπος
26 ταῖς ἀληθείαις συγγενὴς τῶν θεῶν. ἡμεῖς οὖν
ὡς κοιλίαι, ὡς ἔντερα, ὡς αἰδοῖα, οὕτω περὶ
αὐτῶν διανοούμεθα, ὅτι φοβούμεθα, ὅτι ἐπιθυ-
μοῦμεν· τοὺς εἰς ταῦτα συνεργεῖν δυναμένους
κολακεύομεν, τοὺς αὐτοὺς τούτους δεδοίκαμεν.
27 Ἐμέ τις ἠξίωκεν ὑπὲρ αὐτοῦ γράψαι εἰς τὴν
Ῥώμην ὡς ἐδόκει τοῖς πολλοῖς ἠτυχηκὼς καὶ
πρότερον μὲν ἐπιφανὴς ὢν καὶ πλούσιος, ὕστερον
δ' ἐκπεπτωκὼς ἁπάντων καὶ διάγων ἐνταῦθα.

---

[1] A very free paraphrase of Plato, *Apology*, 29 c and 28 E.
[2] At Nicopolis.

for flattery? Why shall one man envy another? Why shall he admire those who have great posses- sions, or those who are stationed in places of power, especially if they be both strong and prone to anger? For what will they do to us? As for what they have power to do, we shall pay no heed thereto; as for the things we care about, over them they have no power. Who, then, will ever again be ruler over the man who is thus disposed?

How did Socrates feel with regard to these matters? Why, how else than as that man ought to feel who has been convinced that he is akin to the gods? "If you tell me now," says he, "'We will acquit you on these conditions, namely, that you will no longer engage in these discussions which you have conducted hitherto, nor trouble either the young or the old among us,' I will answer, 'You make your- selves ridiculous by thinking that, if your general had stationed me at any post, I ought to hold and maintain it and choose rather to die ten thousand times than to desert it, but if God has stationed us in some place and in some manner of life we ought to desert that.'"[1] This is what it means for a man to be in very truth a kinsman of the gods. We, however, think of ourselves as though we were mere bellies, entrails, and genitals, just because we have fear, because we have appetite, and we flatter those who have power to help us in these matters, and these same men we fear.

A certain man asked me to write to Rome in his behalf. Now he had met with what most men account misfortune: though he had formerly been eminent and wealthy, he had afterwards lost every- thing and was living here.[2] And I wrote in humble

28 κἀγὼ ἔγραψα ὑπὲρ αὐτοῦ ταπεινῶς. ὁ δ' ἀνα-
γνοὺς τὴν ἐπιστολὴν ἀπέδωκέν μοι αὐτὴν καὶ ἔφη
ὅτι "'Εγὼ βοηθηθῆναί τι ὑπὸ σοῦ ἤθελον, οὐχὶ
29 ἐλεηθῆναι· κακὸν δέ μοι οὐθέν ἐστιν." οὕτως
καὶ 'Ροῦφος πειράζων μ' εἰώθει λέγειν "Συμβήσε-
ταί σοι τοῦτο καὶ τοῦτο ὑπὸ τοῦ δεσπότου."
30 κἀμοῦ πρὸς αὐτὸν ἀποκριναμένου ὅτι "'Ανθρώ-
πινα," "Τί οὖν; ἔτι ἐκεῖνον παρακαλῶ παρὰ σοῦ
31 ταὐτὰ¹ λαβεῖν δυνάμενος;" τῷ γὰρ ὄντι, ὃ ἐξ
αὐτοῦ τις ἔχει, περισσὸς καὶ μάταιος παρ' ἄλλου
32 λαμβάνων. ἐγὼ οὖν ἔχων ἐξ ἐμαυτοῦ λαβεῖν τὸ
μεγαλόψυχον καὶ γενναῖον, ἀγρὸν παρὰ σοῦ λάβω
καὶ ἀργύριον ἢ ἀρχήν τινα; μὴ γένοιτο. οὐχ
οὕτως ἀναίσθητος ἔσομαι τῶν ἐμῶν κτημάτων.
33 ἀλλ' ὅταν τις ἢ δειλὸς καὶ ταπεινός, ὑπὲρ τούτου
τί ἄλλο ἢ ἀνάγκη γράφειν ἐπιστολὰς ὡς ὑπὲρ
νεκροῦ "τὸ πτῶμα ἡμῖν χάρισαι τοῦ δεῖνος καὶ
34 ξέστην αἱματίου"; τῷ γὰρ ὄντι πτῶμα ὁ τοιοῦτός
ἐστι καὶ ξέστης αἱματίου, πλέον δ' οὐδέν. εἰ δ'
ἦν πλέον τι, ἠσθάνετ' ἄν, ὅτι ἄλλος δι' ἄλλον
οὐ δυστυχεῖ.

ιʹ. Πρὸς τοὺς περὶ τὰς ἐν 'Ρώμῃ προαγωγὰς
ἐσπουδακότας

1 Εἰ οὕτως σφοδρῶς συνετετάμεθα περὶ τὸ ἔργον
τὸ ἑαυτῶν ὡς οἱ ἐν 'Ρώμῃ γέροντες περὶ ἃ

¹ Schweighäuser : αὐτὰ S.

---

[1] In his youth Epictetus had been a slave.
[2] The thought seems to be: If the punishment can be

terms in his behalf. But when he had read the letter he handed it back to me, and said, "I wanted your help, not your pity; my plight is not an evil one." So likewise Rufus was wont to say, to test me, "Your master [1] is going to do such-and-such a thing to you." And when I would say in answer, "'Tis but the lot of man," he would reply. "What then? Am I to go on and petition him, when I can get the same result from you?" [2] For, in fact, it is foolish and superfluous to try to obtain from another that which one can get from oneself. Since, therefore, I am able to get greatness of soul and nobility of character from myself, am I to get a farm, and money, or some office, from you? Far from it! I will not be so unaware of what I myself possess. But when a man is cowardly and abject, what else can one possibly do but write letters in his behalf as we do in behalf of a corpse: "Please to grant us the carcase of so-and-so and a pint of paltry blood?" [3] For really, such a person is but a carcase and a pint of paltry blood, and nothing more. But if he were anything more he would perceive that one man is not unfortunate because of another.

CHAPTER X

To those who have set their hearts on preferment at Rome

If we philosophers had applied ourselves to our own work as zealously as the old men at Rome

humanly borne, I need not petition your master to remit it, for you have within yourself the power to endure it.

[3] As when a friend might ask for the body of an executed criminal.

ἐσπουδάκασιν, τάχα ἄν τι ἠνύομεν καὶ αὐτοί.

2 οἶδα ἐγὼ πρεσβύτερον ἄνθρωπον ἐμοῦ τὸν νῦν
ἐπὶ τοῦ σίτου ὄντα ἐν Ῥώμῃ, ὅτε ταύτῃ παρῆγεν
ἀπὸ τῆς φυγῆς ἀναστρέφων, οἷα εἶπέν μοι,
κατατρέχων τοῦ προτέρου ἑαυτοῦ βίου καὶ
περὶ τῶν ἑξῆς ἐπαγγελλόμενος, ὅτι ἄλλο οὐδὲν
ἀναβὰς σπουδάσει ἢ ἐν ἡσυχίᾳ καὶ ἀταραξίᾳ
διεξαγαγεῖν τὸ λοιπὸν τοῦ βίου· "Πόσον γὰρ
3 ἔτι ἐστὶν ἐμοὶ τὸ λοιπόν;"—Κἀγὼ ἔλεγον αὐτῷ
ὅτι "Οὐ ποιήσεις, ἀλλ' ὀσφρανθεὶς μόνον τῆς
Ῥώμης ἁπάντων τούτων ἐπιλήσῃ." ἂν δὲ καὶ εἰς
αὐλὴν πάροδός τις δίδωται, ὅτι χαίρων καὶ
4 τῷ θεῷ εὐχαριστῶν ὤσεται.—"Ἄν μ' εὕρῃς,"
ἔφη, "Ἐπίκτητε, τὸν ἕτερον πόδα εἰς τὴν αὐλὴν
5 τιθέντα, ὃ βούλει ὑπολάμβανε." νῦν οὖν τί
ἐποίησεν; πρὶν ἐλθεῖν εἰς τὴν Ῥώμην, ἀπήντη-
σαν αὐτῷ παρὰ Καίσαρος πινακίδες· ὁ δὲ λαβὼν
πάντων ἐκείνων ἐξελάθετο καὶ λοιπὸν ἓν ἐξ ἑνὸς
6 ἐπισεσώρευκεν. ἤθελον αὐτὸν νῦν παραστὰς
ὑπομνῆσαι τῶν λόγων, οὓς ἔλεγεν παρερχόμενος,
καὶ εἰπεῖν ὅτι "πόσῳ σου ἐγὼ κομψότερος μάντις
εἰμί."

7 Τί οὖν; ἐγὼ λέγω, ὅτι ἄπρακτόν ἐστι τὸ
ζῷον; μὴ γένοιτο. ἀλλὰ διὰ τί ἡμεῖς οὐκ ἐσμὲν
8 πρακτικοί; εὐθὺς ἐγὼ πρῶτος, ὅταν ἡμέρα
γένηται, μικρὰ ὑπομιμνήσκομαι, τίνα ἐπανα-

have applied themselves to the matters on which they have set their hearts, perhaps we too should be accomplishing something. I know a man older than myself who is now in charge of the grain supply [1] at Rome. When he passed this place on his way back from exile, I recall what a tale he told as he inveighed against his former life and announced for the future that, when he had returned to Rome, he would devote himself solely to spending the remainder of his life in peace and quiet, " For how little is yet left to me ! "—And I told him, " You will not do it, but when once you have caught no more than a whiff of Rome you will forget all this." And if also admission to court should be granted, I added that he would rejoice, thank God and push his way in.—"If you find me, Epictetus," said he, " putting so much as one foot inside the court, think of me what you will." Well, now, what did he do? Before he reached Rome, letters from Caesar met him ; and as soon as he received them, he forgot all those resolutions of his, and ever since he has been piling up one property after another. I wish I could stand by his side now and remind him of the words that he uttered as he passed by here, and remark, " How much more clever a prophet I am than you ! "

What then? Do I say that man is an animal made for inactivity? [2] Far be it from me ! But how can you say that we philosophers are not active in affairs? For example, to take myself first: as soon as day breaks I call to mind briefly what author

[1] *Praefectus annonae*, a very important official during the Empire.
[2] As opposed in the 'active' lives of business or politics.

γνῶναί με δεῖ. εἶτα εὐθὺς ἐμαυτῷ· "τί δέ μοι
καὶ μέλει πῶς ὁ δεῖνα ἀναγνῷ; πρῶτόν ἐστιν,
9 ἵνα ἐγὼ κοιμηθῶ." καίτοι τί ὅμοια τὰ ἐκείνων πράγματα τοῖς ἡμετέροις; ἂν ἐπιστῆτε,
τί ἐκεῖνοι ποιοῦσιν, αἰσθήσεσθε. τί γὰρ ἄλλο
ἢ ὅλην τὴν ἡμέραν ψηφίζουσιν, συζητοῦσι,
συμβουλεύουσι περὶ σιταρίου, περὶ ἀγριδίου,
10 περί τινων προκοπῶν τοιούτων; ὅμοιον οὖν
ἐστιν ἐντευξίδιον παρά τινος λαβόντα ἀναγιγνώσκειν "παρακαλῶ σε ἐπιτρέψαι μοι σιτάριον
ἐξαγαγεῖν" ἢ "παρακαλῶ σε παρὰ Χρυσίππου
ἐπισκέψασθαι τίς ἐστιν ἡ τοῦ κόσμου διοίκησις
καὶ ποίαν τινὰ χώραν ἐν αὐτῷ ἔχει τὸ λογικὸν
ζῷον· ἐπίσκεψαι δὲ καὶ τίς εἶ σὺ καὶ ποῖόν τι
11 σοῦ τὸ ἀγαθὸν καὶ τὸ κακόν"; ταῦτα ἐκείνοις
ὅμοιά ἐστιν; ἀλλ' ὁμοίας σπουδῆς χρείαν ἔχοντα;
12 ἀλλ' ὡσαύτως ἀμελεῖν αἰσχρὸν τούτων κἀκείνων;
τί οὖν; ἡμεῖς μόνοι ῥᾳθυμοῦμεν καὶ νυστάζομεν;
13 οὔ· ἀλλὰ πολὺ πρότερον ὑμεῖς οἱ νέοι. ἐπεί
τοι καὶ ἡμεῖς οἱ γέροντες, ὅταν παίζοντας ὁρῶμεν
νέους, συμπροθυμούμεθα καὶ αὐτοὶ συμπαίζειν.
πολὺ δὲ πλέον, εἰ ἑώρων διεγηγερμένους καὶ
συμπροθυμουμένους, προεθυμούμην ἂν συσπου-
δάζειν καὶ αὐτός.

---

[1] The passage is somewhat obscure, because the precise
expression employed here occurs elsewhere only in *Ench.* 49.
Apparently Epictetus read over, or made special preparation
upon a certain text, before meeting his pupils.   In class then
he would have a pupil read and interpret an assignment, some-

I must read over.[1]   Then forthwith I say to myself:
"And yet what difference does it really make to
me how so-and-so reads?   The first thing is that
I get my sleep."   Even so, in what are the occupa-
tions of those other men comparable to ours?   If
you observe what they do, you will see.   For what
else do they do but all day long cast up accounts,
dispute, consult about a bit of grain, a bit of land,
or similar matters of profit?   Is it, then, much the
same thing to receive a little petition from someone
and read: "I beseech you to allow me to export a
small quantity of grain," and this one: "I beseech
you to learn from Chrysippus what is the administration of the universe, and what place therein the
rational animal has; and consider also who you are,
and what is the nature of your good and evil"?
Is this like that?   And does it demand the like
kind of study?   And is it in the same way shameful to neglect the one and the other?   What
then?   Is it we philosophers alone who take things
easily and drowse?   No, it is you young men far
sooner.   For, look you, we old men, when we see
young men playing, are eager to join in the play ourselves.   And much more, if I saw them wide-awake
and eager to share in our studies, should I be eager
to join, myself, in their serious pursuits.

what as in our "recitation," and follow that by a reading
and exposition of his own (ἐπαναγνῶναι), which was intended
to set everything straight and put on the finishing touches.
See Schweighäuser's note and especially Ivo Bruns, *De Schola
Epicteti* (1897), 8 f.   By changing μέ to μοί, as Capps suggests,
a satisfactory sense is secured, *i.e.*, "what pupil must read
to me," but the ἐπί in the compound verb would thus be
left without any particular meaning, and perhaps it is not
necessary to emend.

ια΄. Περὶ φιλοστοργίας

1 Ἀφικομένου δέ τινος πρὸς αὐτὸν τῶν ἐν τέλει
πυθόμενος παρ᾽ αὐτοῦ τὰ ἐπὶ μέρους ἠρώτησεν,
2 εἰ καὶ τέκνα εἴη αὐτῷ καὶ γυνή. τοῦ δ᾽ ὁμολογήσαντος προσεπύθετο· Πῶς τι οὖν χρῇ τῷ
πράγματι ; — Ἀθλίως, ἔφη.—Καὶ ὅς· Τίνα
3 τρόπον ; οὐ γὰρ δὴ τούτου γ᾽ ἕνεκα γαμοῦσιν
ἄνθρωποι καὶ παιδοποιοῦνται, ὅπως ἄθλιοι ὦσιν,
4 ἀλλὰ μᾶλλον ὅπως εὐδαίμονες.—Ἀλλ᾽ ἐγώ, ἔφη,
οὕτως ἀθλίως ἔχω περὶ τὰ παιδάρια, ὥστε πρῴην
νοσοῦντός μου τοῦ θυγατρίου καὶ δόξαντος
κινδυνεύειν οὐχ ὑπέμεινα οὐδὲ παρεῖναι αὐτῷ
νοσοῦντι, φυγὼν δ᾽ ᾠχόμην, μέχρις οὗ προσήγ-
γειλέ τις μοι ὅτι ἔχει καλῶς.—Τί οὖν ; ὀρθῶς
5 φαίνει σαυτῷ ταῦτα πεποιηκέναι ;—Φυσικῶς,
ἔφη.—Ἀλλὰ μὴν τοῦτό με πεῖσον, ἔφη, σύ, διότι
φυσικῶς, καὶ ἐγώ σε πείσω, ὅτι πᾶν τὸ κατὰ
6 φύσιν γινόμενον ὀρθῶς γίνεται.—Τοῦτο, ἔφη,
πάντες ἢ οἵ γε πλεῖστοι πατέρες πάσχομεν.—
Οὐδ᾽ ἐγώ σοι ἀντιλέγω, ἔφη, ὅτι οὐ γίνεται, τὸ
δ᾽ ἀμφισβητούμενον ἡμῖν ἐκεῖνό ἐστιν, εἰ ὀρθῶς.
7 ἐπεὶ τούτου γ᾽ ἕνεκα καὶ τὰ φύματα δεῖ λέγειν
ἐπ᾽ ἀγαθῷ γίνεσθαι τοῦ σώματος, ὅτι γίνεται,
καὶ ἁπλῶς τὸ ἁμαρτάνειν εἶναι κατὰ φύσιν, ὅτι
πάντες σχεδὸν ἢ οἵ γε πλεῖστοι ἁμαρτάνομεν.

CHAPTER XI

Of family affection

WHEN an official came to see him, Epictetus, after making some special enquiries about other matters, asked him if he had children and a wife, and when the other replied that he had, Epictetus asked the further question, What, then, is your experience with marriage?—Wretched, he said.—To which Epictetus, How so? For men do not marry and beget children just for this surely, to be wretched, but rather to be happy.—And yet, as for me, the other replied, I feel so wretched about the little children, that recently when my little daughter was sick and was thought to be in danger, I could not bear even to stay by her sick bed, but I up and ran away, until someone brought me word that she was well again.—What then, do you feel that you were acting right in doing this?—I was acting naturally, he said.—But really, you must first convince me of this, that you *were* acting naturally, said he, and then I will convince you that whatever is done in accordance with nature is rightly done.—This is the way, said the man, all, or at least most, of us fathers feel.—And I do not contradict you either, answered Epictetus, and say that it is not done, but the point at issue between us is the other, whether it is rightly done. For by your style of reasoning we should have to say of tumours also that they are produced for the good of the body, just because they occur, and in brief, that to err is in accordance with nature, just because practically all of us, or at least most of us, do err. Do you show me, therefore, how your

8 δεῖξον οὖν μοι σύ, πῶς κατὰ φύσιν ἐστίν.—Οὐ
δύναμαι, ἔφη· ἀλλὰ σύ μοι μᾶλλον δεῖξον, πῶς
9 οὐκ ἔστι κατὰ φύσιν οὐδ᾿ ὀρθῶς γίνεται.—Καὶ
ὅς· Ἀλλ᾿ εἰ ἐζητοῦμεν, ἔφη, περὶ λευκῶν καὶ
μελάνων, ποῖον ἂν κριτήριον παρεκαλοῦμεν πρὸς
διάγνωσιν αὐτῶν;—Τὴν ὅρασιν, ἔφη.—Τί δ᾿ εἰ
περὶ θερμῶν καὶ ψυχρῶν καὶ σκληρῶν καὶ μαλα-
10 κῶν, ποῖόν τι ;—Τὴν ἁφήν.—Οὐκοῦν, ἐπειδὴ περὶ
τῶν κατὰ φύσιν καὶ τῶν ὀρθῶς ἢ οὐκ ὀρθῶς γινομένων ἀμφισβητοῦμεν, ποῖον θέλεις κριτήριον
11 παραλάβωμεν ; — Οὐκ οἶδ᾿, ἔφη.—Καὶ μὴν τὸ
μὲν τῶν χρωμάτων καὶ ὀσμῶν, ἔτι δὲ χυλῶν
κριτήριον ἀγνοεῖν τυχὸν οὐ μεγάλη ζημία, τὸ
δὲ τῶν ἀγαθῶν καὶ τῶν κακῶν καὶ τῶν κατὰ
φύσιν καὶ παρὰ φύσιν τῷ ἀνθρώπῳ δοκεῖ σοι
μικρὰ ζημία εἶναι τῷ ἀγνοοῦντι ;—Ἡ μεγίστη
12 μὲν οὖν.—Φέρε εἰπέ μοι, πάντα ἃ δοκεῖ τισιν
εἶναι καλὰ καὶ προσήκοντα, ὀρθῶς δοκεῖ ; καὶ
νῦν Ἰουδαίοις καὶ Σύροις καὶ Αἰγυπτίοις καὶ
Ῥωμαίοις οἷόν τε πάντα τὰ δοκοῦντα περὶ
13 τροφῆς ὀρθῶς δοκεῖν ;—Καὶ πῶς οἷόν τε ;—Ἀλλ᾿
οἶμαι πᾶσα ἀνάγκη, εἰ ὀρθά ἐστι τὰ¹ Αἰγυπτίων,
μὴ ὀρθὰ εἶναι τὰ τῶν ἄλλων, εἰ καλῶς ἔχει τὰ
Ἰουδαίων, μὴ καλῶς ἔχειν τὰ τῶν ἄλλων.—Πῶς
14 γὰρ οὔ ;—Ὅπου δ᾿ ἄγνοια, ἐκεῖ καὶ ἀμαθία καὶ
ἡ περὶ τὰ ἀναγκαῖα ἀπαιδευσία.—Συνεχώρει.
15 Σὺ οὖν, ἔφη, τούτων αἰσθόμενος οὐδὲν ἄλλο τοῦ

¹ Added by Schweighäuser.

conduct is in accordance with nature.—I cannot, said the man; but do you rather show me how it is not in accordance with nature, and not rightly done. And Epictetus said: Well, if we were enquiring about white and black objects, what sort of criterion should we summon in order to distinguish between them?—The sight, said the man.—And if about hot and cold, and hard and soft objects, what criterion?—The touch.—Very well, then, since we are disputing about things which are in accordance with nature and things which are rightly or not rightly done, what criterion would you have us take?—I do not know, he said.—And yet, though it is, perhaps, no great harm for one not to know the criterion of colours and odours, and so, too, of flavours, still do you think that it is a slight harm for a man to be ignorant of the criterion of good and evil things, and of those in accordance with nature and those contrary to nature?—On the contrary, it is the very greatest harm. Come, tell me, are all the things that certain persons regard as good and fitting, rightly so regarded? And is it possible at this present time that all the opinions which Jews, and Syrians, and Egyptians and Romans hold on the subject of food are rightly held?—And how can it be possible?—But, I fancy, it is absolutely necessary, if the views of the Egyptians are right, that those of the others are not right; if those of the Jews are well founded, that those of the others are not.—Yes, certainly.—Now where there is ignorance, there is also lack of knowledge and the lack of instruction in matters which are indispensable.—He agreed.—You, then, said he, now that you perceive this, will henceforth study no other

λοιποῦ σπουδάσεις οὐδὲ πρὸς ἄλλῳ τινὶ τὴν
γνώμην ἕξεις ἢ ὅπως τὸ κριτήριον τῶν κατὰ
φύσιν καταμαθὼν τούτῳ προσχρώμενος διακρινεῖς
τῶν ἐπὶ μέρους ἕκαστον.

16 Ἐπὶ δὲ τοῦ παρόντος τὰ τοσαῦτα ἔχω σοι
17 πρὸς ὃ βούλει βοηθῆσαι. τὸ φιλόστοργον δοκεῖ
σοι κατὰ φύσιν τ' εἶναι καὶ καλόν ;—Πῶς γὰρ
οὔ ;—Τί δέ ; τὸ μὲν φιλόστοργον κατὰ φύσιν τ'
ἐστὶ καὶ καλόν, τὸ δ' εὐλόγιστον οὐ καλόν ;—
18 Οὐδαμῶς.—Μὴ τοίνυν μάχην ἔχει τῷ φιλο-
στόργῳ τὸ εὐλόγιστον ;—Οὐ δοκεῖ μοι.—Εἰ δὲ
μή, τῶν μαχομένων ἀνάγκη θατέρου κατὰ φύσιν
ὄντος θάτερον εἶναι παρὰ φύσιν ; ἢ γὰρ οὔ ;—
19 Οὕτως, ἔφη.—Οὐκοῦν ὅ τι ἂν εὑρίσκωμεν ὁμοῦ
μὲν φιλόστοργον ὁμοῦ δ' εὐλόγιστον, τοῦτο
θαρροῦντες ἀποφαινόμεθα ὀρθόν τε εἶναι καὶ
20 καλόν ;—Ἔστω, ἔφη.—Τί οὖν ; ἀφεῖναι νοσοῦν
τὸ παιδίον καὶ ἀφέντα ἀπελθεῖν ὅτι μὲν οὐκ
εὐλόγιστον οὐκ οἶμαί σ' ἀντερεῖν. ὑπολείπεται δ'
ἡμᾶς σκοπεῖν εἰ φιλόστοργον.—Σκοπῶμεν δή.—
21 Ἆρ' οὖν σὺ μὲν ἐπειδὴ φιλοστόργως διέκεισο πρὸς
τὸ παιδίον, ὀρθῶς ἐποίεις φεύγων καὶ ἀπολείπων
αὐτό ; ἡ μήτηρ δ' οὐ φιλοστοργεῖ τὸ παιδίον ;—
22 Φιλοστοργεῖ μὲν οὖν.—Οὐκοῦν ἔδει καὶ τὴν
μητέρα ἀφεῖναι αὐτὸ ἢ οὐκ ἔδει ;—Οὐκ ἔδει.—Τί
δ' ἡ τιτθή ; στέργει αὐτό ;—Στέργει, ἔφη.—Ἔδει
οὖν κἀκείνην ἀφεῖναι αὐτό ;—Οὐδαμῶς.—Τί δ' ὁ
23 παιδαγωγός ; οὐ στέργει αὐτό ;—Στέργει.—Ἔδει

---

[1] The course of thought is, " You will have to do much
studying before you have mastered this subject ; but for the
present," etc.

subject and will give heed to no other matter than the problem of how, when you have learned the criterion of what is in accordance with nature, you shall apply that criterion and thus determine each special case.

But for the present[1] I can give you the following assistance toward the attainment of what you desire. Does family affection seem to you to be in accordance with nature and good?—Of course.—What then? Is it possible that, while family affection is in accordance with nature and good, that which is reasonable is not good?—By no means.—That which is reasonable is not, therefore, incompatible with family affection?—It is not, I think.—Otherwise, when two things are incompatible and one of them is in accordance with nature, the other must be contrary to nature, must it not?—Even so, said he.— Whatever, therefore, we find to be at the same time both affectionate and reasonable, this we confidently assert to be both right and good?—Granted, said he.—What then? I suppose you will not deny that going away and leaving one's child when it is sick is at least not reasonable. But we have yet to consider whether it is affectionate.—Yes, let us consider that.—Were you, then, since you were affectionately disposed to your child, doing right when you ran away and left her? And has the mother no affection for her child?—On the contrary, she has affection.— Ought then the mother also to have left her child, or ought she not?—She ought not.—What of the nurse? Does she love her child?—She does, he said.—Ought, then, she also to have left her?—By no means.—What about the school attendant? Does not he love the child?—He does.—Ought, then, he

οὖν κἀκεῖνον ἀφέντα ἀπελθεῖν, εἶθ' οὕτως ἔρημον
καὶ ἀβοήθητον ἀπολειφθῆναι τὸ παιδίον διὰ τὴν
πολλὴν φιλοστοργίαν τῶν γονέων ὑμῶν καὶ τῶν
περὶ αὐτὸ ἢ ἐν ταῖς χερσὶν τῶν οὔτε στεργόντων
24 οὔτε κηδομένων ἀποθανεῖν;—Μὴ γένοιτο.—Καὶ
μὴν ἐκεῖνό γε ἄνισον καὶ ἄγνωμον, ὅ τις αὑτῷ[1]
προσῆκον οἴεται διὰ τὸ φιλόστοργος εἶναι, τοῦτο
τοῖς ὁμοίως φιλοστοργοῦσιν μὴ ἐφιέναι;—
25 Ἄτοπον.—Ἄγε, σὺ δ' ἂν νοσῶν ἠβούλου φιλο-
στόργους οὕτως ἔχειν τοὺς προσήκοντας τούς
τ' ἄλλους καὶ αὐτὰ τὰ τέκνα καὶ τὴν γυναῖκα,
ὥστ' ἀφεθῆναι μόνος ὑπ' αὐτῶν καὶ ἔρημος;—
26 Οὐδαμῶς.—Εὔξαιο δ' ἂν οὕτως στερχθῆναι ὑπὸ
τῶν σαυτοῦ, ὥστε διὰ τὴν ἄγαν αὐτῶν φιλοστοργίαν ἀεὶ μόνος ἀπολείπεσθαι ἐν ταῖς νόσοις,
ἢ τούτου γ' ἕνεκα μᾶλλον ἂν ὑπὸ τῶν ἐχθρῶν,
εἰ δυνατὸν ἦν, φιλοστοργεῖσθαι ηὔχου, ὥστ'
ἀπολείπεσθαι ὑπ' αὐτῶν; εἰ δὲ ταῦτα, ὑπολείπεται μηδαμῶς ἔτι φιλόστοργον εἶναι τὸ πραχθέν.
27 Τί οὖν; οὐδὲν ἦν τὸ κινῆσάν σε καὶ ἐξορμῆσαν
πρὸς τὸ ἀφεῖναι τὸ παιδίον; καὶ πῶς οἷόν τε;
ἀλλὰ τοιοῦτόν τι ἦν,[2] οἷον καὶ ἐν Ῥώμῃ τινὰ
ἦν τὸ κινοῦν, ὥστ' ἐγκαλύπτεσθαι τοῦ ἵππου
τρέχοντος ᾧ[3] ἐσπουδάκει, εἶτα νικήσαντός ποτε
παραλόγως σπόγγων δεῆσαι αὐτῷ πρὸς τὸ
28 ἀναληφθῆναι λιποψυχοῦντα. τί οὖν τοῦτό ἐστιν;
τὸ μὲν ἀκριβὲς οὐ τοῦ παρόντος καιροῦ τυχόν·
ἐκεῖνο δ' ἀπαρκεῖ πεισθῆναι, εἴπερ ὑγιές ἐστι τὸ
ὑπὸ τῶν φιλοσόφων λεγόμενον, ὅτι οὐκ ἔξω που

---

[1] ὅ τις Sb : αὑτῶι Sc : ὅτι σαυτῶι S.
[2] Bentley : ἂν S (ἦν or ἂν ἦν J. B. Mayor).
[3] Salmasius and Upton's 'codex' : ὡς S.

as well to have gone away and left her, so that the
child would thus have been left alone and helpless
because of the great affection of you her parents and
of those in charge of her, or, perhaps, have died in
the arms of those who neither loved her nor cared for
her?—Far from it!—And yet is it not unfair and
unfeeling, when a man thinks certain conduct fitting
for himself because of his affection, that he should
not allow the same to others who have as much affection as he has?—That were absurd.—Come, if it had
been you who were sick, would you have wanted all
your relatives, your children and your wife included,
to show their affection in such a way that you would
be left all alone and deserted by them?—By no
means.—And would you pray to be so loved by your
own that, because of their excessive affection, you
would always be left alone in sickness? Or would you,
so far as this is concerned, have prayed to be loved
by your enemies rather, if that were possible, so as to
be left alone by *them?* And if this is what you
would have prayed for, the only conclusion left us is
that your conduct was, in the end, not an act of
affection at all.

What, then; was the motive nothing at all which
actuated you and induced you to leave your child?
And how can that be? But it was a motive like
that which impelled a certain man in Rome to cover
his head when the horse which he backed was
running,—and then, when it won unexpectedly, they
had to apply sponges to him to revive him from his
faint! What motive, then, is this? The scientific
explanation, perhaps, is not in place now ; but it is
enough for us to be convinced that, if what the
philosophers say is sound, we ought not to look

δεῖ ζητεῖν αὐτό, ἀλλ' ἓν καὶ ταὐτόν ἐστιν ἐπὶ
πάντων τὸ αἴτιον τοῦ ποιεῖν τι ἡμᾶς ἢ μὴ ποιεῖν,
τοῦ λέγειν τινὰ ἢ μὴ λέγειν, τοῦ ἐπαίρεσθαι ἢ
29 συστέλλεσθαι ἢ φεύγειν τινὰ ἢ διώκειν, τοῦθ'
ὅπερ καὶ νῦν ἐμοί τε καὶ σοὶ γέγονεν αἴτιον, σοὶ
μὲν τοῦ ἐλθεῖν πρὸς ἐμὲ καὶ καθῆσθαι νῦν
ἀκούοντα, ἐμοὶ δὲ τοῦ λέγειν ταῦτα. τί δ' ἐστὶ
30 τοῦτο ; ἆρά γε ἄλλο ἢ ὅτι ἔδοξεν ἡμῖν ;—
Οὐδέν.—Εἰ δ' ἄλλως ἡμῖν ἐφάνη, τί ἂν ἄλλο ἢ
31 τὸ δόξαν ἐπράττομεν ; οὐκοῦν καὶ τῷ Ἀχιλλεῖ
τοῦτο αἴτιον τοῦ πενθεῖν, οὐχ ὁ τοῦ Πατρόκλου
θάνατος (ἄλλος γάρ τις οὐ πάσχει ταῦτα τοῦ
32 ἑταίρου ἀποθανόντος), ἀλλ' ὅτι ἔδοξεν αὐτῷ. καὶ
σοὶ τότε φεύγειν τοῦτο αὐτὸ ὅτι ἔδοξέν σοι· καὶ
πάλιν, ἐὰν μείνῃς, ὅτι ἔδοξέν σοι. καὶ νῦν ἐν
Ῥώμῃ ἀνέρχῃ, ὅτι δοκεῖ σοι· κἂν μεταδόξῃ, οὐκ
33 ἂν ἀπελεύσῃ. καὶ ἁπλῶς οὔτε θάνατος οὔτε
φυγὴ οὔτε πόνος οὔτε ἄλλο τι τῶν τοιούτων
αἴτιόν ἐστι τοῦ πράττειν τι ἢ μὴ πράττειν ἡμᾶς,
ἀλλ' ὑπολήψεις καὶ δόγματα.

34   Τοῦτό σε πείθω ἢ οὐχί ;—Πείθεις, ἔφη.—Οἶα
δὴ τὰ αἴτια ἐφ' ἑκάστου, τοιαῦτα καὶ τὰ ἀποτε-
35 λούμενα. οὐκοῦν ὅταν μὴ ὀρθῶς τι πράττωμεν,
ἀπὸ ταύτης τῆς ἡμέρας οὐδὲν ἄλλο αἰτιασόμεθα
ἢ τὸ δόγμα, ἀφ' οὗ αὐτὸ ἐπράξαμεν, κἀκεῖνο
86

for the motive anywhere outside of ourselves, but that in all cases it is one and the same thing that is the cause of our doing a thing or of our not doing it, of our saying things, or of our not saying them, of our being elated, or of our being cast down, of our avoiding things, or of our pursuing them—the very thing, indeed, which has even now become a cause of my action and of yours; yours in coming to me and sitting here now listening, mine in saying these things. And what is that? Is it, indeed, anything else than that we wanted to do this?—Nothing.—And supposing that we had wanted to do something else, what else would we be doing than that which we wanted to do? Surely, then, in the case of Achilles also, it was this that was the cause of his grief—not the death of Patroclus (for other men do not act this way when their comrades die), but that he wanted to grieve. And in your case the other day, the cause of your running away was just that you wanted to do so; and another time, if you stay with her, it will be because you wanted to stay. And now you are going back to Rome, because you want to do so, and if you change your mind and want something else, you will not go. And, in brief, it is neither death, nor exile, nor toil, nor any such thing that is the cause of our doing, or of our not doing, anything, but only our opinions and the decisions of our will.

Do I convince you of this, or not?—You convince me, said he.—Of such sort, then, as are the causes in each case, such likewise are the effects. Very well, then, whenever we do anything wrongly, from this day forth we shall ascribe to this action no other cause than the decision of our will which led us to

ἐξαίρειν καὶ ἐκτέμνειν πειρασόμεθα μᾶλλον ἢ τὰ
φύματα καὶ τὰ ἀποστήματα ἐκ τοῦ σώματος.
36 ὡσαύτως δὲ καὶ τῶν ὀρθῶς πραττομένων ταὐτὸν
37 τοῦτο αἴτιον ἀποφανοῦμεν. καὶ οὔτ' οἰκέτην ἔτι
αἰτιασόμεθα οὔτε γείτονα οὔτε γυναῖκα οὔτε τέκνα
ὡς αἴτιά τινων κακῶν ἡμῖν γινόμενα πεπεισμένοι
ὅτι, ἂν μὴ ἡμῖν δόξῃ τοιαῦτά τινα εἶναι, οὐ πράττο-
μεν τὰ ἀκόλουθα· τοῦ δόξαι δὲ ἢ μὴ δόξαι, ἡμεῖς
38 κύριοι καὶ οὐ τὰ ἐκτός.—Οὕτως, ἔφη.—Ἀπὸ τῆς
σήμερον τοίνυν ἡμέρας οὐδὲν ἄλλο ἐπισκοπήσομεν
οὐδ' ἐξετάσομεν, ποῖόν τι ἐστὶν ἢ πῶς ἔχει, οὔτε
τὸν ἀγρὸν οὔτε τὰ ἀνδράποδα οὔτε τοὺς ἵππους
ἢ κύνας, ἀλλὰ τὰ δόγματα.—Εὔχομαι, ἔφη.—
39 Ὁρᾷς οὖν, ὅτι σχολαστικόν σε δεῖ γενέσθαι,
τοῦτο τὸ ζῷον οὗ πάντες καταγελῶσιν, εἴπερ
ἄρα θέλεις ἐπίσκεψιν τῶν σαυτοῦ δογμάτων
40 ποιεῖσθαι. τοῦτο δ' ὅτι μιᾶς ὥρας ἢ ἡμέρας οὐκ
ἔστιν, ἐπινοεῖς καὶ αὐτός.

ιβ'. Περὶ εὐαρεστήσεως

1   Περὶ θεῶν οἱ μέν τινές εἰσιν οἱ λέγοντες μηδ'
εἶναι τὸ θεῖον, οἱ δ' εἶναι μέν, ἀργὸν δὲ καὶ
2 ἀμελὲς καὶ μὴ προνοεῖν μηδενός· τρίτοι δ' οἱ καὶ
εἶναι καὶ προνοεῖν, ἀλλὰ τῶν μεγάλων καὶ
οὐρανίων, τῶν δὲ ἐπὶ γῆς μηδενός· τέταρτοι δ'

---

[1] As, for example, good, or pleasant.
[2] So Epicurus ; see Usener, *Epicurea*, frg. 368.

do it, and we shall endeavour to destroy and excise that cause more earnestly than we try to destroy and excise from the body its tumours and abscesses And in the same way we shall declare the same thing to be the cause of our good actions. And we shall no longer blame either slave, or neighbour, or wife, or children, as being the causes of any evils to us, since we are persuaded that, unless we decide that things are thus-and-so,[1] we do not perform the corresponding actions; and of our decision, for or against something, we ourselves, and not things outside of ourselves, are the masters.—Even so, he said.—From this very day, therefore, the thing whose nature or condition we shall investigate and examine will be neither our farm, nor our slaves, nor our horses, nor our dogs, but only the decisions of our will.—I hope so, he said.—You see, then, that it is necessary for you to become a frequenter of the schools,—that animal at which all men laugh,—if you really desire to make an examination of the decisions of your own will. And that this is not the work of a single hour or day you know as well as I do.

CHAPTER XII

Of contentment

CONCERNING gods there are some who say that the divine does not so much as exist; and others, that it exists, indeed, but is inactive and indifferent, and takes forethought for nothing;[2] and a third set, that it exists and takes forethought, though only for great and heavenly things and in no case for terrestrial things; and a fourth set, that it also takes

οἱ[1] καὶ τῶν ἐπὶ γῆς καὶ τῶν ἀνθρωπίνων, εἰς
κοινὸν δὲ μόνον καὶ οὐχὶ δὲ καὶ κατ' ἰδίαν
3 ἑκάστου· πέμπτοι δ', ὧν ἦν καὶ Ὀδυσσεὺς καὶ
Σωκράτης, οἱ λέγοντες ὅτι

οὐδέ σε λήθω
κινύμενος.

4 Πολὺ πρότερον οὖν ἀναγκαῖόν ἐστι περὶ
ἑκάστου τούτων ἐπεσκέφθαι, πότερα ὑγιῶς ἢ
5 οὐχ ὑγιῶς λεγόμενόν ἐστιν. εἰ γὰρ μὴ εἰσὶν
θεοί, πῶς ἐστι τέλος ἕπεσθαι θεοῖς ; εἰ δ' εἰσὶν
μέν, μηδενὸς δ' ἐπιμελούμενοι, καὶ οὕτως πῶς
6 ὑγιὲς ἔσται ; ἀλλὰ δὴ καὶ ὄντων καὶ ἐπιμελο-
μένων εἰ μηδεμία διάδοσις εἰς ἀνθρώπους ἐστὶν
ἐξ αὐτῶν καὶ νὴ Δία γε καὶ εἰς ἐμέ, πῶς ἔτι
7 καὶ οὕτως ὑγιές ἐστιν ; πάντα οὖν ταῦτα ὁ
καλὸς καὶ ἀγαθὸς ἐπεσκεμμένος τὴν αὑτοῦ
γνώμην ὑποτέταχεν τῷ διοικοῦντι τὰ ὅλα
καθάπερ οἱ ἀγαθοὶ πολῖται τῷ νόμῳ τῆς
8 πόλεως. ὁ δὲ παιδευόμενος ταύτην ὀφείλει τὴν
ἐπιβολὴν ἔχων ἐλθεῖν ἐπὶ τὸ παιδεύεσθαι, "πῶς
ἂν ἑποίμην ἐγὼ ἐν παντὶ τοῖς θεοῖς καὶ πῶς ἂν
εὐαρεστοίην τῇ θείᾳ διοικήσει καὶ πῶς ἂν γε-
9 νοίμην ἐλεύθερος ;" ἐλεύθερος γάρ ἐστιν, ᾧ γίνεται
πάντα κατὰ προαίρεσιν καὶ ὃν οὐδεὶς δύναται
10 κωλῦσαι. τί οὖν ; ἀπόνοιά ἐστιν ἡ ἐλευθερία ;
μὴ γένοιτο. μανία γὰρ καὶ ἐλευθερία εἰς ταὐτὸν
11 οὐκ ἔρχεται. "ἀλλ' ἐγὼ θέλω πᾶν τὸ δοκοῦν μοι
12 ἀποβαίνειν, κἂν ὁπωσοῦν δοκῇ." μαινόμενος εἶ,
παραφρονεῖς. οὐκ οἶδας, ὅτι καλόν τι ἐλευθερία

---

[1] Schenkl : δὲ S, οἱ Stobaeus.

forethought for things terrestrial and the affairs of men, but only in a general way, and not for the individual in particular ; and a fifth set, to which Odysseus and Socrates belonged, who say

Nor when I move am I concealed from thee.[1]

We must, therefore, first of all enquire about each of these statements, to see whether it is sound or not sound. For if gods do not exist, how can it be an end to follow the gods ? And if they exist, indeed, but care for nothing, how even thus will that conclusion be sound ? But if, indeed, they both exist and exercise care, yet there is no communication from them to men,—yes, and, by Zeus, to me personally,—how even in this case can our conclusion still be sound ? The good and excellent man must, therefore, inquire into all these things, before he subordinates his own will to him who administers the universe, precisely as good citizens submit to the law of the state. And he that is being instructed ought to come to his instruction with this aim, " How may I follow the gods in everything, and how may I be acceptable to the divine administration, and how may I become free ? " Since he is free for whom all things happen according to his moral purpose, and whom none can restrain. What then ? Is freedom insanity ? Far from it ; for madness and freedom are not consistent with one another. "But I would have that which seems best to me happen in every case, no matter how it comes to seem so." You are mad ; you are beside yourself. Do you not know that

---

[1] Homer, *Iliad*, X. 279 f. ; compare Xenophon, *Memorabilia*, I. 1, 19.

ἐστὶ καὶ ἀξιόλογον ; τὸ δ' ὡς ἔτυχέν με βούλεσθαι τὰ¹ ὡς ἔτυχεν δόξαντα γίνεσθαι, τοῦτο
κινδυνεύει οὐ μόνον οὐκ εἶναι καλόν, ἀλλὰ καὶ
πάντων αἴσχιστον εἶναι. πῶς γὰρ ἐπὶ γραμμα-
13 τικῶν ποιοῦμεν ; βούλομαι γράφειν ὡς θέλω
τὸ Δίωνος ὄνομα ; οὔ· ἀλλὰ διδάσκομαι θέλειν,
ὡς δεῖ γράφεσθαι. τί ἐπὶ μουσικῶν ; ὡσαύτως.
14 τί ἐν τῷ καθόλου, ὅπου τέχνη τις ἢ ἐπιστήμη
ἐστίν ; εἰ δὲ μή, οὐδενὸς ἦν ἄξιον τὸ ἐπίστασθαί
τι, εἰ ταῖς ἑκάστων βουλήσεσι προσηρμόζετο.
15 ἐνταῦθα οὖν μόνον ἐπὶ τοῦ μεγίστου καὶ
κυριωτάτου, τῆς ἐλευθερίας, ὡς ἔτυχεν ἐφεῖταί
μοι θέλειν ; οὐδαμῶς, ἀλλὰ τὸ παιδεύεσθαι τοῦτ'
ἔστι μανθάνειν ἕκαστα οὕτω θέλειν ὡς γίνεται.
πῶς δὲ γίνεται ; ὡς διέταξεν αὐτὰ ὁ διατάσσων.
16 διέταξε δὲ θέρος εἶναι καὶ χειμῶνα καὶ φορὰν καὶ
ἀφορίαν καὶ ἀρετὴν καὶ κακίαν καὶ πάσας τὰς
τοιαύτας ἐναντιότητας ὑπὲρ συμφωνίας τῶν ὅλων
ἡμῶν θ' ἑκάστῳ σῶμα καὶ μέρη τοῦ σώματος καὶ
κτῆσιν καὶ κοινωνοὺς ἔδωκεν.
17 Ταύτης οὖν τῆς διατάξεως μεμνημένους ἔρχεσθαι δεῖ ἐπὶ τὸ παιδεύεσθαι, οὐχ ἵν' ἀλλά-
ξωμεν τὰς ὑποθέσεις (οὔτε γὰρ δίδοται ἡμῖν οὔτ'
ἄμεινον), ἀλλ' ἵνα οὕτως ἐχόντων τῶν περὶ ἡμᾶς
ὡς ἔχει καὶ πέφυκεν αὐτοὶ τὴν γνώμην τὴν
αὑτῶν συνηρμοσμένην τοῖς γινομένοις ἔχωμεν.
18 τί γάρ ; ἐνδέχεται φυγεῖν ἀνθρώπους ; καὶ πῶς
οἷόν τε ; ἀλλὰ συνόντας αὐτοῖς ἐκείνους ἀλλάξαι ;
19 καὶ τίς ἡμῖν δίδωσιν ; τί οὖν ἀπολείπεται ἢ τίς

----

¹ Schweighäuser : τὰ δ' S.

freedom is a noble and precious thing? But for me to desire at haphazard that those things should happen which have at haphazard seemed best to me, is dangerously near being, not merely not noble, but even in the highest degree shameful. For how do we act in writing? Do I desire to write the name " Dio " as I choose? No, but I am taught to desire to write it as it ought to be written. What do we do in music? The same. And what in general, where there is any art or science? The same; otherwise knowledge of anything would be useless, if it were accommodated to every individual's whims. Is it, then, only in this matter of freedom, the greatest and indeed the highest of all, that I am permitted to desire at haphazard? By no means, but instruction consists precisely in learning to desire each thing exactly as it happens. And how do they happen? As he that ordains them has ordained. And he has ordained that there be summer and winter, and abundance and dearth, and virtue and vice, and all such opposites, for the harmony of the whole, and he has given each of us a body, and members of the body, and property and companions.

Mindful, therefore, of this ordaining we should go to receive instruction, not in order to change the constitution of things,—for this is neither vouchsafed us nor is it better that it should be,—but in order that, things about us being as they are and as their nature is, we may, for our own part, keep our wills in harmony with what happens. For, look you, can we escape from men? And how is it possible? But can we, if they associate with us, change them? And who vouchsafes us that power? What alterna-

εὑρίσκεται μηχανὴ πρὸς τὴν χρῆσιν αὐτῶν;
τοιαύτη, δι' ἧς ἐκεῖνοι μὲν ποιήσουσι τὰ φαινόμενα αὐτοῖς, ἡμεῖς δ' οὐδὲν ἧττον κατὰ φύσιν
20 ἕξομεν. σὺ δ' ἀταλαίπωρος εἶ καὶ δυσάρεστος
κἂν μὲν μόνος ᾖς, ἐρημίαν καλεῖς τοῦτο, ἂν δὲ
μετὰ ἀνθρώπων, ἐπιβούλους λέγεις καὶ λῃστάς,
μέμφῃ δὲ καὶ γονεῖς τοὺς σεαυτοῦ καὶ τέκνα καὶ
21 ἀδελφοὺς καὶ γείτονας. ἔδει δὲ μόνον μένοντα
ἡσυχίαν καλεῖν αὐτὸ καὶ ἐλευθερίαν καὶ ὅμοιον
τοῖς θεοῖς ἡγεῖσθαι αὐτόν, μετὰ πολλῶν δ' ὄντα
μὴ ὄχλον καλεῖν μηδὲ θόρυβον μηδ' ἀηδίαν, ἀλλ'
ἑορτὴν καὶ πανήγυριν καὶ οὕτως πάντα εὐαρέστως
δέχεσθαι.

Τίς οὖν ἡ κόλασις τοῖς οὐ προσδεχομένοις;
22 τὸ οὕτως ἔχειν ὡς ἔχουσιν. δυσαρεστεῖ τις τῷ
μόνος εἶναι; ἔστω ἐν ἐρημίᾳ. δυσαρεστεῖ τις
τοῖς γονεῦσιν; ἔστω κακὸς υἱὸς καὶ πενθείτω.
δυσαρεστεῖ τοῖς τέκνοις; ἔστω κακὸς πατήρ.
23 "βάλε αὐτὸν εἰς φυλακήν." ποίαν φυλακήν;
ὅπου νῦν ἐστιν. ἄκων γάρ ἐστιν· ὅπου δέ τις
ἄκων ἐστίν, ἐκεῖνο φυλακὴ αὐτῷ ἐστιν. καθὸ
καὶ Σωκράτης οὐκ ἦν ἐν φυλακῇ, ἑκὼν γὰρ
24 ἦν. "σκέλος οὖν μοι γενέσθαι πεπηρωμένον."
ἀνδράποδον, εἶτα δι' ἓν σκελύδριον τῷ κόσμῳ
ἐγκαλεῖς; οὐκ ἐπιδώσεις αὐτὸ τοῖς ὅλοις; οὐκ
ἀποστήσῃ; οὐ χαίρων παραχωρήσεις τῷ δε-
25 δωκότι; ἀγανακτήσεις δὲ καὶ δυσαρεστήσεις τοῖς
ὑπὸ τοῦ Διὸς διατεταγμένοις, ἃ ἐκεῖνος μετὰ τῶν
Μοιρῶν παρουσῶν καὶ ἐπικλωθουσῶν σου τὴν
26 γένεσιν ὥρισεν καὶ διέταξεν; οὐκ οἶσθα, ἡλίκον

tive remains, then, or what method can we find for living with them? Some such method as that, while they will act as seems best to them, we shall none the less be in a state comformable to nature. But you are impatient and peevish, and if you are alone, you call it a solitude, but if you are in the company of men, you call them schemers and brigands, and you find fault even with your own parents and children and brothers and neighbours. But you ought, when staying alone, to call that peace and freedom, and to look upon yourself as like the gods; and when you are in the company of many, you ought not call that a mob, nor a tumult, nor a disgusting thing, but a feast and a festival, and so accept all things contentedly.

What, then, is the punishment of those who do not accept? To be just as they are. Is one peevish because he is alone? Let him be in solitude! Is he peevish with his parents? Let him be an evil son and grieve! Is he peevish with his children? Let him be a bad father! "Throw him into prison." What sort of prison? Where he now is. For he is there against his will, and where a man is against his will, that for him is a prison. Just as Socrates was not in prison, for he was there willingly. "Alas, that I should be lame in my leg!" Slave, do you, then, because of one paltry leg blame the universe? Will you not make a free gift of it to the whole? Will you not relinquish it? Will you not gladly yield it to the giver? And will you be angry and peevish at the ordinances of Zeus, which he defined and ordained together with the Fates who spun in his presence the thread of your begetting? Do you not know how small a part you are compared with

μέρος πρὸς τὰ ὅλα; τοῦτο δὲ κατὰ τὸ σῶμα,
ὡς κατά γε τὸν λόγον οὐδὲν χείρων τῶν θεῶν
οὐδὲ μικρότερος· λόγου γὰρ μέγεθος οὐ μήκει
οὐδ' ὕψει κρίνεται, ἀλλὰ δόγμασιν.

27 Οὐ θέλεις οὖν, καθ' ἃ ἴσος εἶ τοῖς θεοῖς, ἐκεῖ
28 που τίθεσθαι τὸ ἀγαθόν; "τάλας ἐγώ, τὸν
πατέρα ἔχω τοιοῦτον καὶ τὴν μητέρα." τί οὖν;
ἐδίδοτό σοι προελθόντι ἐκλέξασθαι καὶ εἰπεῖν
"ὁ δεῖνα τῇ δεῖνι συνελθέτω τῇδε τῇ ὥρᾳ, ἵνα
29 ἐγὼ γένωμαι"; οὐκ ἐδίδοτο. ἀλλ' ἔδει προυπο-
στῆναί σου τοὺς γονεῖς, εἶτα οὕτως γεννηθῆναι.
30 ἐκ ποίων τινῶν; ἐκ τοιούτων, ὁποῖοι ἦσαν. τί
οὖν; τοιούτων αὐτῶν ὄντων οὐδεμία σοι δίδοται
μηχανή; εἶτ' εἰ μὲν τὴν ὁρατικὴν δύναμιν ἠγνόεις
πρὸς τί κέκτησαι, δυστυχὴς ἂν ἦς καὶ ἄθλιος,
εἰ κατέμυες, προσαγόντων σοι τῶν χρωμάτων τι[1]
ὅτι δὲ μεγαλοψυχίαν ἔχων καὶ γενναιότητα πρὸς
ἕκαστα τούτων ἀγνοεῖς, οὐ δυστυχέστερος εἶ καὶ
31 ἀθλιώτερος; προσάγεταί σοι τὰ κατάλληλα τῇ
δυνάμει ἣν ἔχεις· σὺ δ' αὐτὴν τότε μάλιστα
ἀποστρέφεις, ὁπότε ἠνοιγμένην καὶ βλέπουσαν
32 ἔχειν ἔδει. οὐ μᾶλλον εὐχαριστεῖς τοῖς θεοῖς,
ὅτι σε ἐπάνω τούτων ἀφῆκαν ὅσα μηδ' ἐποίησαν
ἐπὶ σοί, μόνον δ' ὑπεύθυνον ἀπέφηναν τῶν ἐπὶ
33 σοί; γονέων ἕνεκα ἀνυπεύθυνον ἀφῆκαν· ἀδελ-

---

[1] Added by Diels.

the whole? That is, as to the body; for as to the reason you are not inferior to the gods, nor less than they; for the greatness of the reason is not determined by length nor by height, but by the decisions of its will.

Will you not, therefore, set what is for you the good in that wherein you are equal to the gods? " Wretched man that I am; such a father and such a mother as I have!" Well, was it permitted you to step forward and make selection, saying, " Let such-and-such man have intercourse with such-and-such woman at this hour, that I may be born "? It was not permitted you; but your parents had to exist first, then you had to be born as you were born. Of what kind of parents? Of such as they were. What then? Since they are such, is no remedy given you? Again, supposing that you were ignorant of the purpose for which you possess the faculty of vision, you would be unfortunate and wretched if you closed your eyes when men brought some colour before them; but in that you have greatness of mind and nobility for use for everyone of the things may happen to you, and know it not, are you not yet more unfortunate and wretched? Things proportionate to the faculty which you possess are brought before you, but you turn that faculty away at the very moment when you ought to keep it wide open and discerning. Do you not rather render thanks to the gods that they have allowed you to be superior to all the things that they did not put under your control, and have rendered you accountable only for what is under your control? As for parents, the gods have released you from accountability; as for brothers, they have released you;

φῶν ἕνεκα ἀφῆκαν, σώματος ἕνεκα ἀφῆκαν,
34 κτήσεως, θανάτου, ζωῆς. τίνος οὖν ὑπεύθυνόν
σε ἐποίησαν; τοῦ μόνου ὄντος ἐπὶ σοί, χρήσεως
35 οἵας δεῖ φαντασιῶν. τί οὖν ἐπισπᾷς σεαυτῷ
ταῦτα ὧν ἀνυπεύθυνος εἶ; τοῦτό ἐστιν ἑαυτῷ
παρέχειν πράγματα.

ιγ΄. Πῶς ἕκαστα ἔστιν ποιεῖν ἀρεστῶς θεοῖς

1 Πυθομένου δέ τινος, πῶς ἔστιν ἐσθίειν ἀρεστῶς
θεοῖς, Εἰ δικαίως ἔστιν, ἔφη, καὶ εὐγνωμόνως καὶ
ἴσως καὶ ἐγκρατῶς καὶ κοσμίως, οὐκ ἔστι καὶ ἀρεσ-
2 τῶς τοῖς θεοῖς; ὅταν δὲ θερμὸν αἰτήσαντός σου
μὴ ὑπακούσῃ ὁ παῖς ἢ ὑπακούσας χλιαρώτερον
ἐνέγκῃ ἢ μηδ᾽ εὑρεθῇ ἐν τῇ οἰκίᾳ, τὸ μὴ χαλεπαίνειν
μηδὲ ῥήγνυσθαι οὐκ ἔστιν ἀρεστὸν τοῖς θεοῖς;—
3 Πῶς οὖν τις ἀνάσχηται τῶν τοιούτων;—'Ανδράποδον, οὐκ ἀνέξῃ τοῦ ἀδελφοῦ τοῦ σαυτοῦ, ὃς
ἔχει τὸν Δία πρόγονον, ὥσπερ υἱὸς ἐκ τῶν αὐτῶν
σπερμάτων γέγονεν καὶ τῆς αὐτῆς ἄνωθεν κατα-
4 βολῆς, ἀλλ᾽ εἰ ἔν τινι τοιαύτῃ χώρᾳ κατετάγης
ὑπερεχούσῃ, εὐθὺς τύραννον καταστήσεις σεαυτόν; οὐ μεμνήσῃ τί εἶ καὶ τίνων ἄρχεις; ὅτι
συγγενῶν, ὅτι ἀδελφῶν φύσει, ὅτι τοῦ Διὸς
5 ἀπογόνων;—'Αλλ᾽ ὠνὴν αὐτῶν ἔχω, ἐκεῖνοι δ᾽
ἐμοῦ οὐκ ἔχουσιν.—῾Ορᾷς ποῦ βλέπεις; ὅτι εἰς τὴν

as for body, they have released you; and for property, death, life. Well, for what have they made you accountable? For the only thing that is under your control—the proper use of impressions. Why, then, do you draw upon yourself that for which you are not responsible? This is to make trouble for yourself.

CHAPTER XIII

How may each several thing be done acceptably to the gods?

Now when someone asked him how it is possible to eat acceptably to the gods, he said, If it is done justly and graciously and fairly and restrainedly and decently, is it not also done acceptably to the gods? And when you have asked for warm water and the slave does not heed you; or if he does heed you but brings in tepid water; or if he is not even to be found in the house, then to refrain from anger and not to explode, is not this acceptable to the gods?— How, then, can a man bear with such persons?— Slave, will you not bear with your own brother, who has Zeus as his progenitor and is, as it were, a son born of the same seed as yourself and of the same sowing from above; but if you have been stationed in a like position above others, will you forthwith set yourself up as a tyrant? Do you not remember what you are, and over whom you rule—that they are kinsmen, that they are brothers by nature, that they are the offspring of Zeus?—But I have a deed of sale for them, and they have none for me.—Do you see whither you bend your gaze, that it is to

99

γῆν, ὅτι εἰς τὸ βάραθρον, ὅτι εἰς τοὺς ταλαιπώρους τούτους νόμους τοὺς τῶν νεκρῶν, εἰς δὲ τοὺς τῶν θεῶν οὐ βλέπεις;

ιδ. Ὅτι πάντας ἐφορᾷ τὸ θεῖον

1 Πυθομένου δέ τινος, πῶς ἄν τις πεισθείη, ὅτι ἕκαστον τῶν ὑπ᾽ αὐτοῦ πραττομένων ἐφορᾶται ὑπὸ τοῦ θεοῦ, Οὐ δοκεῖ σοι, ἔφη, ἡνῶσθαι τὰ 2 πάντα;—Δοκεῖ, ἔφη.—Τί δέ; συμπαθεῖν τὰ ἐπίγεια τοῖς οὐρανίοις οὐ δοκεῖ σοι;—Δοκεῖ, 3 ἔφη.—Πόθεν γὰρ οὕτω τεταγμένως καθάπερ ἐκ προστάγματος τοῦ θεοῦ, ὅταν ἐκεῖνος εἴπῃ τοῖς φυτοῖς ἀνθεῖν, ἀνθεῖ, ὅταν εἴπῃ βλαστάνειν, βλαστάνει, ὅταν ἐκφέρειν τὸν καρπόν, ἐκφέρει, ὅταν πεπαίνειν, πεπαίνει, ὅταν πάλιν ἀποβάλλειν καὶ φυλλορροεῖν καὶ αὐτὰ εἰς αὑτὰ συνειλούμενα ἐφ᾽ ἡσυχίας μένειν καὶ ἀναπαύεσθαι, μένει 4 καὶ ἀναπαύεται; πόθεν δὲ πρὸς τὴν αὔξησιν καὶ μείωσιν τῆς σελήνης καὶ τὴν τοῦ ἡλίου πρόσοδον καὶ ἄφοδον τοσαύτη παραλλαγὴ καὶ ἐπὶ τὰ ἐναντία μεταβολὴ τῶν ἐπιγείων θεωρεῖται; 5 ἀλλὰ τὰ φυτὰ[1] μὲν καὶ τὰ ἡμέτερα σώματα οὕτως ἐνδέδεται τοῖς ὅλοις καὶ συμπέπονθεν, αἱ

---

[1] Stobaeus: φύλλα S.

---

[1] This is the famous principle of συμπάθεια (συμπαθεῖν and συμπέπονθεν in the text here), *i.e.*, the physical unity of the cosmos in such a form that the experience of one part necessarily affects every other. This doctrine, especially popular with the Stoics, is essentially but a philosophic formulation of the vague ideas that underlie the practices of

the earth, that it is to the pit, that it is to these wretched laws of ours, the laws of the dead, and that it is not to the laws of the gods that you look?

CHAPTER XIV

That the Deity oversees all men

Now when someone asked him how a man could be convinced that each thing which he does is under the eye of God, Do you not think, he answered, that all things are united in one?—I do, said the other.—Very well, do you not think that what is on earth feels the influence [1] of that which is in heaven?—I do, he replied.—For how else comes it that so regularly, as if from God's command, when He bids the plants flower, they flower, when He bids them put forth shoots, they put them forth, when He bids them bear their fruit, they bear it, when to ripen, they ripen; when again He bids them drop their fruit and let fall their leaves and gather themselves together and remain quiet and take their rest, they remain quiet and take their rest? And how else comes it that at the waxing and waning of the moon and at the approach and recession of the sun we see among the things that are on earth so great an alteration and change to the opposite? But are the plants and our own bodies so closely bound up with the universe, and do they so intimately share its affections,[1] and is not the

sympathetic magic. For the literature on this topic see Pease on Cicero's *De Divinatione*, ii. 34, where συμπάθεια is defined by Cicero as a *coniunctio naturae et quasi concentus et consensus.*

6 ψυχαὶ δ' αἱ ἡμέτεραι οὐ πολὺ πλέον ; ἀλλ' αἱ
ψυχαὶ μὲν οὕτως εἰσὶν ἐνδεδεμέναι καὶ συναφεῖς
τῷ θεῷ ἅτε αὐτοῦ μόρια οὖσαι καὶ ἀποσπάσματα,
οὐ παντὸς δ' αὐτῶν κινήματος ἅτε οἰκείου καὶ
7 συμφυοῦς ὁ θεὸς αἰσθάνεται ; ἀλλὰ σὺ μὲν
περὶ τῆς θείας διοικήσεως καὶ περὶ ἑκάστου
τῶν θείων, ὁμοῦ δὲ καὶ περὶ τῶν ἀνθρωπίνων πραγμάτων ἐνθυμεῖσθαι δύνασαι καὶ ἅμα μὲν αἰσθη-
τικῶς ἀπὸ μυρίων πραγμάτων κινεῖσθαι, ἅμα δὲ
διανοητικῶς, ἅμα δὲ συγκαταθετικῶς, τοῖς δ' ἀνα-
8 νευστικῶς ἢ ἐφεκτικῶς, τύπους δὲ τοσούτους ἀφ'
οὕτω πολλῶν καὶ ποικίλων πραγμάτων ἐν τῇ σαυτοῦ ψυχῇ φυλάττεις καὶ ἀπ' αὐτῶν κινούμενος εἰς
ἐπινοίας ὁμοειδεῖς ἐμπίπτεις τοῖς πρώτως τετυπω-
κόσι τέχνας τ' ἄλλην ἐπ' ἄλλη [1] καὶ μνήμας ἀπὸ
9 μυρίων πραγμάτων διασῴζεις· ὁ δὲ θεὸς οὐχ οἷός
τ' ἐστὶ πάντα ἐφορᾶν καὶ πᾶσιν συμπαρεῖναι
10 καὶ ἀπὸ πάντων τινὰ ἴσχειν διάδοσιν ; ἀλλὰ
φωτίζειν οἷός τ' ἐστὶν ὁ ἥλιος τηλικοῦτον μέρος
τοῦ παντός, ὀλίγον δὲ τὸ ἀφώτιστον ἀπολιπεῖν
ὅσον οἷόν τ' ἐπέχεσθαι ὑπὸ σκιᾶς, ἣν ἡ γῆ ποιεῖ·
ὁ δὲ καὶ τὸν ἥλιον αὐτὸν πεποιηκὼς καὶ περιάγων
μέρος ὄντ' αὐτοῦ μικρὸν ὡς πρὸς τὸ ὅλον, οὗτος δ'
οὐ δύναται πάντων αἰσθάνεσθαι ;

[1] Schenkl : ἄλλην ἐπ' ἄλλας S.

same much more true of our own souls? But if our
souls are so bound up with God and joined together
with Him, as being parts and portions of His being,
does not God perceive their every motion as being
a motion of that which is His own and of one
body with Himself? And yet you have power to
think about the divine dispensation and about each
several item among things divine, and at the same
time also about human affairs, and you have the
faculty of being moved by myriads of matters at the
same time both in your senses and in your intelligence, and at the same time you assent to some,
while you dissent from others, or suspend judgement
about them; and you guard in your own soul so
many impressions derived from so many and various
matters, and, on being moved by these impressions,
your mind falls upon notions corresponding to the
impressions first made, and so from myriads of matters
you derive and retain arts, one after the other, and
memories. All this you do, and is God not able
to oversee all things and to be present with all
and to have a certain communication from them all?
Yet the sun is capable of illuminating so large a
portion of the universe, and of leaving unilluminated
only the small space which is no larger than can
be covered by the shadow that the earth casts; and
is He who has created the sun, which is but a small
portion of Himself[1] in comparison with the whole,
and causes it to revolve, is *He* not able to perceive
all things?

---

[1] Chrysippus identified the Universe, of which the sun
is but a part, with God. See Cicero, *De Natura Deorum*,
ii. 38 f.

11 Ἀλλ' ἐγώ, φησίν, οὐ δύναμαι πᾶσιν ἅμα τούτοις παρακολουθεῖν.—Τοῦτο δέ σοι καὶ λέγει τις,

12 ὅτι ἴσην ἔχεις δύναμιν τῷ Διί ; ἀλλ' οὖν οὐδὲν
ἧττον καὶ ἐπίτροπον ἑκάστῳ παρέστησεν τὸν
ἑκάστου δαίμονα καὶ παρέδωκεν φυλάσσειν αὐτὸν
αὐτῷ καὶ τοῦτον ἀκοίμητον καὶ ἀπαραλόγιστον.

13 τίνι γὰρ ἄλλῳ κρείττονι καὶ ἐπιμελεστέρῳ φύ-
λακι παρέδωκεν ἂν [1] ἡμῶν ἕκαστον ; ὥσθ', ὅταν
κλείσητε τὰς θύρας καὶ σκότος ἔνδον ποιήσητε,

14 μέμνησθε μηδέποτε λέγειν ὅτι μόνοι ἐστέ· οὐ γὰρ
ἐστέ, ἀλλ' ὁ θεὸς ἔνδον ἐστὶ καὶ ὁ ὑμέτερος δαί-
μων ἐστίν. καὶ τίς τούτοις χρεία φωτὸς εἰς τὸ

15 βλέπειν τί ποιεῖτε ; τούτῳ τῷ θεῷ ἔδει καὶ ὑμᾶς
ὀμνύειν ὅρκον, οἷον οἱ στρατιῶται τῷ Καίσαρι.
ἀλλ' ἐκεῖνοι μὲν τὴν μισθοφορίαν λαμβάνοντες
ὀμνύουσιν πάντων προτιμήσειν τὴν τοῦ Καίσαρος
σωτηρίαν, ὑμεῖς δὲ δὴ [2] τοσούτων καὶ τηλικούτων
ἠξιωμένοι οὐκ ὀμόσετε ἢ ὀμόσαντες οὐκ ἐμμενεῖτε ;

16 καὶ τί ὀμόσετε ; μὴ ἀπειθήσειν μηδέποτε μηδ'
ἐγκαλέσειν μηδὲ μέμψεσθαί τινι τῶν ὑπ' ἐκείνου
δεδομένων μηδ' ἄκοντες ποιήσειν τι ἢ πείσεσθαι

17 τῶν ἀναγκαίων. ὅμοιός γ' ὁ [3] ὅρκος οὗτος ἐκείνῳ ;
ἐκεῖ μὲν ὀμνύουσιν αὐτοῦ μὴ προτιμήσειν ἕτερον,
ἐνταῦθα δ' αὐτοὺς ἁπάντων.

---

[1] Suggested by Upton (after γὰρ Schweighäuser).
[2] Schenkl (δὲ δὴ οἱ von Wilamowitz): δὲ δέ S.
[3] von Wilamowitz (γε ὁ Diels): γε ὅρκος S.

---

[1] Compare Seneca, *Epist.* 41, 2 : *sacer intra nos spiritus sedet,
malorum bonorumque nostrorum observator et custos,* and

And yet, says one, I cannot follow all these things at one and the same time.—But does anyone go so far as to tell you *this*, namely, that you possess a faculty which is *equal* to that of Zeus? Yet none the less He has stationed by each man's side as guardian his particular genius,[1]—and has committed the man to his care,—and that too a guardian who never sleeps and is not to be beguiled. For to what other guardian, better and more careful, could He have committed each one of us? Wherefore, when you close your doors and make darkness within, remember never to say that you are alone, for you are not alone; nay, God is within, and your own genius is within. And what need have they of light in order to see what you are doing? Yes, and to this God you also ought to swear allegiance, as the soldiers do to Caesar. They are but hirelings, yet they swear that they will put the safety of Caesar above everything; and shall you, indeed, who have been counted worthy of blessings so numerous and so great be unwilling to swear, or, when you have sworn, to abide by your oath? And what shall you swear? Never to disobey under any circumstances, never to prefer charges, never to find fault with anything that God has given, never to let your will rebel when you have either to do or to suffer something that is inevitable. Can the oath of the soldiers in any way be compared with this of ours? Out there men swear never to prefer another in honour above Caesar; but here we swear to prefer ourselves in honour above everything else.

especially Menander, *Epitr.* 881 ff., with Capps's note. Almost exactly the same idea appears also in Marcus Aurelius, V. 27.

ιε΄. Τί ἐπαγγέλλεται φιλοσοφία ;

1 Συμβουλευομένου τινός, πῶς τὸν ἀδελφὸν πείσῃ
2 μηκέτι χαλεπῶς αὐτῷ ἔχειν, Οὐκ ἐπαγγέλλεται,
ἔφη, φιλοσοφία τῶν ἐκτός τι περιποιήσειν τῷ
ἀνθρώπῳ· εἰ δὲ μή, ἔξω τι τῆς ἰδίας ὕλης
ἀναδέξεται.¹ ὡς γὰρ τέκτονος ὕλη τὰ ξύλα,
ἀνδριαντοποιοῦ ὁ χαλκός, οὕτως τῆς περὶ βίον
3 τέχνης ὕλη ὁ βίος αὐτοῦ ἑκάστου.—Τί οὖν ὁ τοῦ
ἀδελφοῦ ;—Πάλιν τῆς αὐτοῦ ἐκείνου τέχνης ἐστίν,
πρὸς δὲ τὴν σὴν τῶν ἐκτός ἐστιν, ὅμοιον ἀγρῷ,
ὅμοιον ὑγείᾳ, ὅμοιον εὐδοξίᾳ. τούτων δ᾽ οὐδὲν
4 ἐπαγγέλλεται φιλοσοφία. " ἐν πάσῃ περιστάσει
τηρήσω τὸ ἡγεμονικὸν¹ κατὰ φύσιν ἔχον."—Τὸ
5 τίνος ;—"Τὸ ἐκείνου, ἐν ᾧ εἰμί."—Πῶς οὖν
ἐκεῖνός μοι μὴ ὀργίζηται ;—"Φέρε μοι ἐκεῖνον
κἀκείνῳ ἐρῶ, σοὶ δὲ περὶ τῆς ἐκείνου ὀργῆς
οὐδὲν ἔχω λέγειν."

6 Εἰπόντος δὲ τοῦ συμβουλευομένου ὅτι Τοῦτο
ζητῶ, πῶς ἂν ἐκείνου καὶ μὴ διαλλασσομένου
7 κατὰ φύσιν ἔχοιμι, Οὐδέν, ἔφη, τῶν μεγάλων
ἄφνω γίνεται, ὅπου γε οὐδ᾽ ὁ βότρυς οὐδὲ σῦκον.
ἄν μοι νῦν λέγῃς ὅτι "θέλω σῦκον," ἀποκρινοῦμαί
σοι ὅτι "χρόνου δεῖ." ἄφες ἀνθήσῃ πρῶτον, εἶτα
8 προβάλῃ τὸν καρπόν, εἶτα πεπανθῇ. εἶτα συκῆς

---

¹ Reiske : ἀνέξεται S.

¹ The soul of man, as feeling and thinking, often equivalent
to " reason," but not exclusively intellectual. See Bonhöffer,
Epictet und die Stoa, i. 9 ff.

CHAPTER XV

What does philosophy profess?

WHEN someone consulted Epictetus as to how he could persuade his brother to cease being angry with him, he replied, Philosophy does not profess to secure for man any external possession. Otherwise it would be undertaking something that lies outside its proper subject-matter. For as wood is the material of the carpenter, bronze that of the statuary, just so each man's own life is the subject-matter of the art of living.—Well, what about my brother's life?—That again is the subject-matter of his own art of living, but with respect to *your* art of living it comes under the category of externals, like a farm, like health, like good repute. Philosophy promises none of these things, but rather, "In every circumstance I will keep the governing principle[1] in a state of accord with nature."—Whose governing principle?—"His in whom I am."—How, then, shall I keep my brother from being angry at me?—Bring him to me and I will tell him, but I have nothing to say to *you* on the subject of *his* anger.

And when the man who was consulting him said, What I seek to know is this, how, even if my brother refuses to be reconciled with me, I may yet be in accord with nature, Epictetus replied: Nothing great comes into being all at once; why, not even does the bunch of grapes, or a fig. If you say to me now, "I want a fig," I shall answer, "That requires time." Let the tree blossom first, then put forth its fruit, and finally let the fruit ripen. Now although the

μὲν καρπὸς ἄφνω καὶ μιᾷ ὥρᾳ οὐ τελειοῦται,
γνώμης δ' ἀνθρώπου καρπὸν θέλεις οὕτως δι'
ὀλίγου καὶ εὐκόλως κτήσασθαι; μηδ' ἂν ἐγώ σοι
λέγω προσδόκα.

ιϛ'. Περὶ προνοίας

1 Μὴ θαυμάζετ' εἰ τοῖς μὲν ἄλλοις ζῴοις τὰ πρὸς
τὸ σῶμα ἕτοιμα γέγονεν, οὐ μόνον τροφαὶ καὶ
πόμα, ἀλλὰ καὶ κοίτη καὶ τὸ μὴ δεῖσθαι ὑποδημάτων, μὴ ὑποστρωμάτων, μὴ ἐσθῆτος, ἡμεῖς δὲ
2 πάντων τούτων προσδεόμεθα. τὰ γὰρ οὐκ αὑτῶν
ἕνεκα, ἀλλὰ πρὸς ὑπηρεσίαν γεγονότα οὐκ
ἐλυσιτέλει προσδεόμενα ἄλλων πεποιηκέναι.
3 ἐπεὶ ὅρα οἷον ἂν¹ ἦν ἡμᾶς φροντίζειν μὴ περὶ
αὑτῶν μόνον ἀλλὰ καὶ περὶ τῶν προβάτων καὶ
τῶν ὄνων, πῶς ἐνδύσηται καὶ πῶς ὑποδήσηται,
4 πῶς φάγῃ, πῶς πίῃ. ἀλλ' ὥσπερ οἱ στρατιῶται
ἕτοιμοί εἰσι τῷ στρατηγῷ ὑποδεδεμένοι ἐνδεδυ-
μένοι ὡπλισμένοι, εἰ δ' ἔδει περιερχόμενον τὸν
χιλίαρχον ὑποδεῖν ἢ ἐνδύειν τοὺς χιλίους, δεινὸν
ἂν ἦν, οὕτω καὶ ἡ φύσις πεποίηκε τὰ πρὸς
ὑπηρεσίαν γεγονότα ἕτοιμα παρεσκευασμένα
5 μηδεμιᾶς ἐπιμελείας ἔτι προσδεόμενα. οὕτως ἓν
παιδίον μικρὸν καὶ ῥάβδῳ ἐλαύνει τὰ πρόβατα.
6 Νῦν δ' ἡμεῖς ἀφέντες ἐπὶ τούτοις εὐχαριστεῖν,
ὅτι μὴ καὶ αὑτῶν τὴν ἴσην ἐπιμέλειαν ἐπιμελού-

---

¹ Added by von Wilamowitz.

fruit of even a fig-tree is not brought to perfection all
at once and in a single hour, would you still seek to
secure the fruit of a man's mind in so short a while
and so easily? Do not expect it, not even if I should
tell you so myself.

CHAPTER XVI

Of providence

MARVEL not that the animals other than man have
furnished them, ready prepared by nature, what
pertains to their bodily needs—not merely food and
drink, but also a bed to lie on,—and that they have
no need of shoes, or bedding, or clothing, while we
are in need of all these things. For in the case of
animals, born not for their own sake, but for service,
to have created them in need of other things
was not beneficial. Why, consider what it would
be for us to have to take thought not for merely
ourselves, but also for our sheep and our asses,
how they are to be clothed and shod, how they are
to find food and drink. But just as soldiers appear
before their general, all ready for service, shod,
clothed and armed, and it would be shocking if the
colonel had to go around and equip his regiment
with shoes or uniforms; so also nature has made
animals, which are born for service, ready for use,
equipped, and in need of no further attention.
Consequently one small child with a rod can drive a
flock of sheep.

But as it is, we first forbear to give thanks for
these beasts, because we do not have to bestow upon
them the same care as we require for ourselves, and

7 μεθα, ἐφ' αὑτοῖς ἐγκαλοῦμεν τῷ θεῷ. καίτοι νὴ
τὸν Δία καὶ τοὺς θεοὺς ἓν τῶν γεγονότων ἀπήρκει
πρὸς τὸ αἰσθέσθαι τῆς προνοίας τῷ γε αἰδήμονι
8 καὶ εὐχαρίστῳ. καὶ μή μοι νῦν τὰ μεγάλα· αὐτὸ
τοῦτο τὸ ἐκ πόας γάλα γεννᾶσθαι καὶ ἐκ γάλα-
κτος τυρὸν καὶ ἐκ δέρματος ἔρια τίς ἐστιν ὁ
πεποιηκὼς ταῦτα ἢ ἐπινενοηκώς; "οὐδὲ εἷς" φησίν.
ὦ μεγάλης ἀναισθησίας καὶ ἀναισχυντίας.

9   Ἄγε ἀφῶμεν τὰ ἔργα τῆς φύσεως, τὰ πάρεργα
10 αὐτῆς θεασώμεθα. μή τι ἀχρηστότερον τριχῶν
τῶν ἐπὶ γενείου; τί οὖν; οὐ συνεχρήσατο καὶ
ταύταις ὡς μάλιστα πρεπόντως ἐδύνατο; οὐ
11 διέκρινεν δι' αὐτῶν τὸ ἄρρεν καὶ τὸ θῆλυ; οὐκ
εὐθὺς μακρόθεν κέκραγεν ἡμῶν ἑκάστου ἡ φύσις
"ἀνήρ εἰμι· οὕτω μοι προσέρχου, οὕτω μοι λάλει,
12 ἄλλο μηδὲν ζήτει· ἰδοὺ τὰ σύμβολα"; πάλιν ἐπὶ
τῶν γυναικῶν ὥσπερ ἐν φωνῇ τι ἐγκατέμιξεν
ἀπαλώτερον, οὕτως καὶ τὰς τρίχας ἀφεῖλεν. οὔ·
ἀλλ' ἀδιάκριτον ἔδει τὸ ζῷον ἀπολειφθῆναι καὶ
13 κηρύσσειν ἕκαστον ἡμῶν ὅτι "ἀνήρ εἰμι." πῶς δὲ
καλὸν τὸ σύμβολον καὶ εὐπρεπὲς καὶ σεμνόν,
πόσῳ κάλλιον τοῦ τῶν ἀλεκτρυόνων λόφου, πόσῳ
14 μεγαλοπρεπέστερον τῆς χαίτης τῶν λεόντων. διὰ
τοῦτο ἔδει σῴζειν τὰ σύμβολα τοῦ θεοῦ, ἔδει αὐτὰ
μὴ καταπροίεσθαι, μὴ συγχεῖν ὅσον ἐφ' ἑαυτοῖς
τὰ γένη τὰ διῃρημένα.

then proceed to complain against God on our own account! Yet, by Zeus and the gods, one single gift of nature would suffice to make a man who is reverent and grateful perceive the providence of God. Do not talk to me now of great matters: take the mere fact that milk is produced from grass, and cheese from milk, and that wool grows from skin— who is it that has created or devised these things? "No one," somebody says. Oh, the depth of man's stupidity and shamelessness!

Come, let us leave the chief works of nature, and consider merely what she does in passing. Can anything be more useless than the hairs on a chin? Well, what then? Has not nature used even these in the most suitable way possible? Has she not by these means distinguished between the male and the female? Does not the nature of each one among us cry aloud forthwith from afar, "I am a man; on this understanding approach me, on this understanding talk with me; ask for nothing further; behold the signs"? Again, in the case of women, just as nature has mingled in their voice a certain softer note, so likewise she has taken the hair from their chins. Not so, you say; on the contrary the human animal ought to have been left without distinguishing features, and each of us ought to proclaim by word of mouth, "I am a man." Nay, but how fair and becoming and dignified the sign is! How much more fair than the cock's comb, how much more magnificent than the lion's mane! Wherefore, we ought to preserve the signs which God has given; we ought not to throw them away; we ought not, so far as in us lies, to confuse the sexes which have been distinguished in this fashion.

15 Ταῦτα μόνα ἐστὶν ἔργα ἐφ' ἡμῶν τῆς προνοίας ;
καὶ τίς ἐξαρκεῖ λόγος ὁμοίως αὐτὰ ἐπαινέσαι ἢ
παραστῆσαι ; εἰ γὰρ νοῦν εἴχομεν, ἄλλο τι ἔδει
ἡμᾶς ποιεῖν καὶ κοινῇ καὶ ἰδίᾳ ἢ ὑμνεῖν τὸ θεῖον
16 καὶ εὐφημεῖν καὶ ἐπεξέρχεσθαι τὰς χάριτας ; οὐκ
ἔδει καὶ σκάπτοντας καὶ ἀροῦντας καὶ ἐσθίοντας
ᾄδειν τὸν ὕμνον τὸν εἰς τὸν θεόν ; " μέγας ὁ θεός,
17 ὅτι ἡμῖν παρέσχεν ὄργανα ταῦτα δι' ὧν τὴν γῆν
ἐργασόμεθα· μέγας ὁ θεός, ὅτι χεῖρας δέδωκεν, ὅτι
κατάποσιν, ὅτι κοιλίαν, ὅτι αὔξεσθαι λεληθότως,
18 ὅτι καθεύδοντας ἀναπνεῖν·" ταῦτα ἐφ' ἑκάστου
ἐφυμνεῖν ἔδει καὶ τὸν μέγιστον καὶ θειότατον
ὕμνον ἐφυμνεῖν, ὅτι τὴν δύναμιν ἔδωκεν τὴν παρακολουθητικὴν τούτοις καὶ ὁδῷ χρηστικήν. τί
19 οὖν ; ἐπεὶ οἱ πολλοὶ ἀποτετύφλωσθε, οὐκ ἔδει
τινὰ εἶναι τὸν ταύτην ἐκπληροῦντα τὴν χώραν
καὶ ὑπὲρ πάντων ᾄδοντα [1] τὸν ὕμνον τὸν εἰς τὸν
20 θεόν ; τί γὰρ ἄλλο δύναμαι γέρων χωλὸς εἰ μὴ
ὑμνεῖν τὸν θεόν ; εἰ γοῦν ἀηδὼν ἤμην, ἐποίουν τὰ
τῆς ἀηδόνος, εἰ κύκνος, τὰ τοῦ κύκνου. νῦν δὲ
21 λογικός εἰμι· ὑμνεῖν με δεῖ τὸν θεόν. τοῦτό μου
τὸ ἔργον ἐστίν, ποιῶ αὐτὸ οὐδ' ἐγκαταλείψω τὴν
τάξιν ταύτην, ἐφ' ὅσον ἂν διδῶται, καὶ ὑμᾶς ἐπὶ
τὴν αὐτὴν ταύτην ᾠδὴν παρακαλῶ.

ιζ'. Ὅτι ἀναγκαῖα τὰ λογικά

1 Ἐπειδὴ λόγος ἐστὶν ὁ διαρθρῶν καὶ ἐξεργαζό-
μενος τὰ λοιπά, ἔδει δ' αὐτὸν μὴ ἀδιάρθρωτον

---

[1] Schweighäuser: διαδόντα S.

Are these the only works of Providence in us?
Nay, what language is adequate to praise them all or
bring them home to our minds as they deserve?
Why, if we had sense, ought we to be doing anything
else, publicly and privately, than hymning and
praising the Deity, and rehearsing His benefits?
Ought we not, as we dig and plough and eat, to sing
the hymn of praise to God? " Great is God, that
He hath furnished us these instruments wherewith
we shall till the earth. Great is God, that He hath
given us hands, and power to swallow, and a belly,
and power to grow unconsciously, and to breathe
while asleep." This is what we ought to sing on
every occasion, and above all to sing the greatest and
divinest hymn, that God has given us the faculty to
comprehend these things and to follow the path of
reason. What then? Since most of you have
become blind, ought there not to be someone to
fulfil this office for you, and in behalf of all sing the
hymn of praise to God? Why, what else can I, a
lame old man, do but sing hymns to God? If,
indeed, I were a nightingale, I should be singing as
a nightingale; if a swan, as a swan. But as it is, I
am a rational being, therefore I must be singing
hymns of praise to God. This is my task; I do it,
and will not desert this post, as long as it may be
given me to fill it; and I exhort you to join me in
this same song.

CHAPTER XVII

That the art of reasoning is indispensable

SINCE it is reason that analyzes and perfects all else,
and reason itself ought not to remain unanalyzed,
113

2 εἶναι, ὑπὸ τίνος διαρθρωθῇ; δῆλον γὰρ ὅτι ἢ ὑφ'
αὑτοῦ ἢ ὑπ' ἄλλου. ἤ τοι λόγος ἐστὶν ἐκεῖνος ἢ
ἄλλο τι κρεῖσσον ἔσται τοῦ λόγου, ὅπερ ἀδύνατον.

3 εἰ λόγος, ἐκεῖνον πάλιν τίς διαρθρώσει; εἰ γὰρ
αὐτὸς ἑαυτόν, δύναται καὶ οὗτος. εἰ ἄλλου
δεησόμεθα, ἄπειρον ἔσται τοῦτο καὶ ἀκατάληκτον.

4   "Ναί,¹ ἀλλ' ἐπείγει μᾶλλον θεραπεύειν" καὶ τὰ
ὅμοια. θέλεις οὖν περὶ ἐκείνων ἀκούειν; ἄκουε.

5 ἀλλ' ἄν μοι λέγῃς ὅτι "οὐκ οἶδα πότερον ἀληθῶς
ἢ ψευδῶς διαλέγῃ," κἄν τι κατ' ἀμφίβολον φωνὴν
εἴπω καὶ λέγῃς μοι "διάστιξον," οὐκ ἔτι ἀνέξομαί

6 σου, ἀλλ' ἐρῶ σοι "ἀλλ' ἐπείγει μᾶλλον." διὰ
τοῦτο γὰρ οἶμαι προτάσσουσιν τὰ λογικά,
καθάπερ τῆς μετρήσεως τοῦ σίτου προτάσσομεν

7 τὴν τοῦ μέτρου ἐπίσκεψιν. ἂν δὲ μὴ διαλάβωμεν
πρῶτον τί ἐστι μόδιος μηδὲ διαλάβωμεν πρῶτον
τί ἐστι ζυγός, πῶς ἔτι μετρῆσαί τι ἢ στῆσαι

8 δυνησόμεθα; ἐνταῦθα οὖν τὸ τῶν ἄλλων κριτήριον καὶ δι' οὗ τἄλλα καταμανθάνεται μὴ
καταμεμαθηκότες μηδ' ἠκριβωκότες δυνησόμεθά
τι τῶν ἄλλων ἀκριβῶσαι καὶ καταμαθεῖν; καὶ

9 πῶς οἷόν τε; "ναί· ἀλλ' ὁ μόδιος ξύλον ἐστὶ καὶ

10 ἄκαρπον." ἀλλὰ μετρητικὸν σίτου. "καὶ τὰ

¹ Upton : εἶναι S.

---

¹ Reason, therefore, can be analyzed only by itself.
² The course of the argument is highly condensed here,
but this is the plain sense of the passage.
³ A Roman dry measure, slightly less than half a bushel.

wherewithal shall it be analyzed? Why, clearly,
either by itself, or by something else. This latter is
assuredly either reason, or it will prove to be something else superior to reason, which is impossible. If it
be reason, who again will analyze *that* reason? For
if it analyzes its own self, the reason with which we
started can do as much. If we are going to require
something else at each step, our process will be
endless and unceasing.[1]

"Yes," says someone, "but the cure (of the
decisions of our will) is a much more pressing need
(than the study of logic),"[2] and the like. Do you
then wish to hear about this other matter? Very
well, listen. But if you say to me, "I do not know
whether your argument is true or false," and, if I
use some ambiguous term, and you should then say,
"Distinguish," I shall bear with you no longer, but
shall tell you, "'Nay, but there is a much more
pressing need.'" This is the reason, I suppose, why
the Stoic philosphers put Logic first, just as in the
measuring of grain we put first the examination of
the measure. And if we do not define first what a
modius[3] is, and do not define first what a scale is,
how shall we be able to proceed with measuring
or weighing anything? So, in the field of our present
enquiry, if we have neglected the thorough knowledge and intellectual mastery of our standard of
judgement for all other things, whereby they come
to be known thoroughly, shall we ever be able to
attain intellectual mastery and thorough knowledge
of the rest of the world? And how could we
possibly? "Yes," we are told, "but the *modius* is
made out of wood and bears no fruit." True, but it
is something with which we can measure grain.

λογικὰ ἄκαρπά ἐστι." καὶ περὶ τούτου μὲν
ὀψόμεθα. εἰ δ' οὖν καὶ τοῦτο δοίη τις, ἐκεῖνο
ἀπαρκεῖ ὅτι τῶν ἄλλων ἐστὶ διακριτικὰ καὶ
ἐπισκεπτικὰ καὶ ὡς ἄν τις εἴποι μετρητικὰ καὶ
11 στατικά. τίς λέγει ταῦτα ; μόνος Χρύσιππος καὶ
12 Ζήνων καὶ Κλεάνθης ; Ἀντισθένης δ' οὐ λέγει ;
καὶ τίς ἐστιν ὁ γεγραφὼς ὅτι " ἀρχὴ παιδεύσεως ἡ
τῶν ὀνομάτων ἐπίσκεψις "; Σωκράτης δ' οὐ λέγει ;
καὶ περὶ τίνος γράφει Ξενοφῶν, ὅτι ἤρχετο ἀπὸ
τῆς τῶν ὀνομάτων ἐπισκέψεως, τί σημαίνει
ἕκαστον ;
13   Ἆρ' οὖν τοῦτό ἐστι τὸ μέγα καὶ τὸ θαυμαστόν,
νοῆσαι Χρύσιππον ἢ ἐξηγήσασθαι ; καὶ τίς λέγει
14 τοῦτο ; τί οὖν τὸ θαυμαστόν ἐστιν ; νοῆσαι τὸ
βούλημα τῆς φύσεως. τί οὖν ; αὐτὸς διὰ
σεαυτοῦ παρακολουθεῖς ; καὶ τίνος ἔτι χρείαν
ἔχεις ; εἰ γὰρ ἀληθές ἐστι τὸ πάντας ἄκοντας
ἁμαρτάνειν, σὺ δὲ καταμεμάθηκας τὴν ἀλήθειαν,
15 ἀνάγκη σε ἤδη κατορθοῦν. ἀλλὰ νὴ Δία οὐ
παρακολουθῶ τῷ βουλήματι τῆς φύσεως. τίς
οὖν ἐξηγεῖται αὐτό ; λέγουσιν ὅτι Χρύσιππος.
16 ἔρχομαι καὶ ἐπιζητῶ τί λέγει οὗτος ὁ ἐξηγητὴς
τῆς φύσεως. ἄρχομαι μὴ νοεῖν τί λέγει, ζητῶ
τὸν ἐξηγούμενον. " ἴδε ἐπίσκεψαι, πῶς τοῦτο
17 λέγεται, καθάπερ εἰ Ῥωμαϊστί." ποία οὖν ἐνθάδ'
ὀφρὺς τοῦ ἐξηγουμένου ; οὐδ' αὐτοῦ Χρυσίππου

---

[1] See Xenophon, *Memorabilia*, IV. 6, I.
[2] The famous dictum of Socrates, formulated as, " No man errs voluntarily," in Plato, *Protagoras*, 345 D.

" Logic also bears no fruit." Now as for this statement we shall see later; but if one should grant even this, it is enough to say in defence of Logic that it has the power to discriminate and examine everything else, and, as one might say, to measure and weigh them. Who says this? Only Chrysippus and Zeno and Cleanthes? Well, does not Antisthenes say it? And who is it that wrote, " The beginning of education is the examination of terms "? Does not Socrates,[1] too, say the same thing? And of whom does Xenophon write, that he began with the examination of terms, asking about each, " What does it mean?"

Is this, then, your great and admirable achievement—the ability to understand and to interpret Chrysippus? And who says that? What, then, is your admirable achievement? To understand the will of nature. Very well; do you understand it all by yourself? And if that is the case, what more do you need? For if it is true that "all men err involuntarily,"[2] and you have learned the truth, it must needs be that you are doing right already. But, so help me Zeus, I do not comprehend the will of nature. Who, then, interprets it? Men say, Chrysippus. I go and try to find out what this interpreter of nature says. I begin not to understand what he says, and look for the man who can interpret him. " Look and consider what this passage means," says the interpreter, "just as if it were in Latin!"[3] What place is there here, then, for pride on the part of the interpreter? Why,

[3] Epictetus seems to be placing himself in the position of one of his Roman pupils, who would understand Chrysippus more easily if translated into Latin.

δικαίως, εἰ μόνον ἐξηγεῖται τὸ βούλημα τῆς
φύσεως, αὐτὸς δ' οὐκ ἀκολουθεῖ· πόσῳ πλέον
18 τοῦ ἐκεῖνον ἐξηγουμένου ; οὐδὲ γὰρ Χρυσίππου
χρείαν ἔχομεν δι' αὐτόν, ἀλλ' ἵνα παρακολου-
θήσωμεν τῇ φύσει. οὐδὲ γὰρ τοῦ θύτου δι'
αὐτόν, ἀλλ' ὅτι δι' ἐκείνου κατανοήσειν οἰόμεθα
τὰ μέλλοντα καὶ σημαινόμενα ὑπὸ τῶν θεῶν,
19 οὐδὲ τῶν σπλάγχνων δι' αὐτά, ἀλλ' ὅτι δι'
ἐκείνων σημαίνεται, οὐδὲ τὸν κόρακα θαυμάζομεν
ἢ τὴν κορώνην, ἀλλὰ τὸν θεὸν σημαίνοντα διὰ
τούτων.
20   Ἔρχομαι τοίνυν ἐπὶ τὸν ἐξηγητὴν τοῦτον καὶ
θύτην καὶ λέγω ὅτι "ἐπίσκεψαί μοι τὰ σπλάγχνα,
21 τί μοι σημαίνεται." λαβὼν καὶ ἀναπτύξας ἐκεῖνος
ἐξηγεῖται ὅτι "ἄνθρωπε, προαίρεσιν ἔχεις ἀκώλυτον
φύσει καὶ ἀνανάγκαστον. τοῦτο ἐνταῦθα ἐν τοῖς
22 σπλάγχνοις γέγραπται. δείξω σοι αὐτὸ πρῶτον
ἐπὶ τοῦ συγκαταθετικοῦ τόπου. μή τίς σε κωλῦσαι
δύναται ἐπινεῦσαι ἀληθεῖ ; οὐδὲ εἷς. μή τίς σε
ἀναγκάσαι δύναται παραδέξασθαι τὸ ψεῦδος ; οὐδὲ
23 εἷς. ὁρᾷς ὅτι ἐν τούτῳ τῷ τόπῳ τὸ προαιρετικὸν
ἔχεις ἀκώλυτον ἀνανάγκαστον ἀπαραπόδιστον ;
24 ἄγε ἐπὶ δὲ τοῦ ὀρεκτικοῦ καὶ ὁρμητικοῦ ἄλλως
ἔχει ; καὶ τίς ὁρμὴν νικῆσαι δύναται ἢ ἄλλη ὁρμή ;
τίς δ' ὄρεξιν καὶ ἔκκλισιν ἢ ἄλλη ὄρεξις καὶ ἔκκλι-
25 σις ;" "ἄν μοι," φησί, "προσάγῃ θανάτου φόβον,
ἀναγκάζει με." "οὐ τὸ προσαγόμενον, ἀλλ' ὅτι
δοκεῖ σοι κρεῖττον εἶναι ποιῆσαί τι τούτων ἢ

there is no just place for pride even on the part
of Chrysippus, if he merely interprets the will of
nature, but himself does not follow it; how much
less place for pride, then, in the case of his interpreter! For we have no need of Chrysippus on his
own account, but only to enable us to follow nature.
No more have we need of him who divines through
sacrifice, considered on his own account, but simply
because we think that through his instrumentality
we shall understand the future and the signs given
by the gods; nor do we need the entrails on their
own account, but only because through them the
signs are given; nor do we admire the crow or the
raven, but God, who gives His signs through them.

Wherefore, I go to this interpreter and diviner
and say, "Examine for me the entrails, and tell me
what signs they give." The fellow takes and spreads
them out and then interprets: "Man, you have a
moral purpose free by nature from hindrances and
constraint. This stands written here in these entrails. I will prove you that first in the sphere of
assent. Can anyone prevent you from assenting to
truth? No one at all. Can anyone force you to
accept the false? No one at all. Do you see that
in this sphere you have a moral purpose free from
hindrance, constraint, obstruction? Come, in the
sphere of desire and choice is it otherwise? And
what can overcome one impulse but another impulse?
And what can overcome one desire or aversion but
another desire or aversion?" "But," says someone,
"if a person subjects me to the fear of death, he compels me." "No, it is not what you are subjected to that
impels you, but the fact that you decide it is better
for you to do something of the sort than to die.

26 ἀποθανεῖν. πάλιν οὖν τὸ σὸν δόγμα σε ἠνάγκα-
27 σεν, τοῦτ᾽ ἔστι προαίρεσιν προαίρεσις. εἰ γὰρ
τὸ ἴδιον μέρος, ὃ ἡμῖν ἔδωκεν ἀποσπάσας ὁ θεός,
ὑπ᾽ αὐτοῦ ἢ ὑπ᾽ ἄλλου τινὸς κωλυτὸν ἢ ἀναγ-
καστὸν κατεσκευάκει, οὐκέτι ἂν ἦν θεὸς οὐδ᾽
28 ἐπεμελεῖτο ἡμῶν ὃν δεῖ τρόπον. ταῦτα εὑρίσκω,"
φησίν, " ἐν τοῖς ἱεροῖς. ταῦτά σοι σημαίνεται.
ἐὰν θέλῃς, ἐλεύθερος εἶ· ἐὰν θέλῃς, μέμψῃ
οὐδένα, ἐγκαλέσεις οὐδενί, πάντα κατὰ γνώμην
29 ἔσται ἅμα τὴν σὴν καὶ τὴν τοῦ θεοῦ." διὰ
ταύτην τὴν μαντείαν ἔρχομαι ἐπὶ τὸν θύτην
τοῦτον καὶ τὸν φιλόσοφον, οὐκ αὐτὸν θαυμάσας
ἕνεκά γε τῆς ἐξηγήσεως, ἀλλὰ ἐκεῖνα ἃ ἐξηγεῖται.

ιη΄. Ὅτι οὐ δεῖ χαλεπαίνειν τοῖς ἁμαρτανομένοις

1 Εἰ ἀληθές ἐστι τὸ ὑπὸ τῶν φιλοσόφων λεγόμενον ὅτι πᾶσιν ἀνθρώποις μία ἀρχή, καθάπερ τοῦ
συγκαταθέσθαι· τὸ παθεῖν ὅτι ὑπάρχει καὶ τοῦ
ἀνανεῦσαι τὸ παθεῖν ὅτι οὐχ ὑπάρχει καὶ νὴ
Δία τοῦ ἐπισχεῖν τὸ παθεῖν ὅτι ἄδηλόν ἐστιν,
2 οὕτως καὶ τοῦ ὁρμῆσαι ἐπί τι τὸ παθεῖν ὅτι ἐμοὶ
συμφέρει, ἀμήχανον δ᾽ ἄλλο μὲν κρίνειν τὸ
συμφέρον, ἄλλου δ᾽ ὀρέγεσθαι καὶ ἄλλο μὲν
κρίνειν καθῆκον, ἐπ᾽ ἄλλο δὲ ὁρμᾶν, τί ἔτι τοῖς

---

[1] It is not known just what persons are here referred to, but the doctrine that feeling (πάθος) is a kind of judge-ment (κρίσις) or opinion (δόξα) is common among the Stoics. See Bonhöffer, *Epiktet und die Stoa*, I. 265 ff., and on the general argument in this chapter, p. 276 f.

Once more, then, it is the decision of your own will which compelled you, that is, moral purpose compelled moral purpose. For if God had so constructed that part of His own being which He has taken from Himself and bestowed upon us, that it could be subjected to hindrance or constraint either from Himself or from some other, He were no longer God, nor would He be caring for us as He ought. This is what I find," says the diviner, "in the sacrifice. These are the signs vouchsafed you. If you will, you are free; if you will, you will not have to blame anyone, or complain against anyone; everything will be in accordance with what is not merely your own will, but at the same time the will of God." This is the prophecy for the sake of which I go to this diviner—in other words, the philosopher,—not admiring *him* because of his interpretation, but rather the interpretation which he gives.

CHAPTER XVIII

That we ought not to be angry with the erring

IF what the philosophers [1] say is true, that in all men thought and action start from a single source, namely feeling—as in the case of assent the feeling that a thing is so, and in the case of dissent the feeling that it is not so, yes, and, by Zeus, in the case of suspended judgement the feeling that it is uncertain, so also in the case of impulse towards a thing, the feeling that it is expedient for me and that it is impossible to judge one thing expedient and yet desire another, and again, to judge one thing fitting, and yet be impelled to another—if all this be true, why

3 πολλοῖς χαλεπαίνομεν ;—Κλέπται, φησίν, εἰσὶ
καὶ λωποδύται.—Τί ἐστι τὸ κλέπται καὶ λωποδύται ; πεπλάνηνται περὶ ἀγαθῶν καὶ κακῶν.

4 χαλεπαίνειν οὖν δεῖ αὐτοῖς ἢ ἐλεεῖν αὐτούς; ἀλλὰ
δεῖξον τὴν πλάνην καὶ ὄψει πῶς ἀφίστανται τῶν
ἁμαρτημάτων. ἂν δὲ μὴ βλέπωσιν, οὐδὲν ἔχουσιν ἀνώτερον τοῦ δοκοῦντος αὐτοῖς.

5 Τοῦτον οὖν τὸν λῃστὴν καὶ τοῦτον τὸν μοιχὸν

6 οὐκ ἔδει ἀπολωλέναι ;—Μηδαμῶς, ἀλλ' ἐκεῖνο
μᾶλλον " τοῦτον τὸν πεπλανημένον καὶ ἐξηπατη-
μένον περὶ τῶν μεγίστων καὶ ἀποτετυφλωμένον
οὐ τὴν ὄψιν τὴν διακριτικὴν τῶν λευκῶν καὶ
μελάνων, ἀλλὰ τὴν γνώμην τὴν διακριτικὴν τῶν
ἀγαθῶν καὶ τῶν κακῶν μὴ ἀπολλύναι ; " κἂν οὕτως

7 λέγῃς, γνώσῃ πῶς ἀπάνθρωπόν ἐστιν ὃ λέγεις καὶ
ὅτι ἐκείνῳ ὅμοιον " τοῦτον οὖν τὸν τυφλὸν μὴ

8 ἀπολλύναι καὶ τὸν κωφόν ; " εἰ γὰρ μεγίστη βλάβη
ἡ τῶν μεγίστων ἀπώλειά ἐστιν, μέγιστον[1] δ' ἐν
ἑκάστῳ προαίρεσις οἵα δεῖ καὶ τούτου στέρεταί

9 τις, τί ἔτι χαλεπαίνεις αὐτῷ ; ἄνθρωπε, εἰ σὲ δεῖ
παρὰ φύσιν ἐπὶ τοῖς ἀλλοτρίοις κακοῖς διατί-
θεσθαι, ἐλέει αὐτὸν μᾶλλον ἢ μίσει· ἄφες τοῦτο τὸ

10 προσκοπτικὸν καὶ μισητικόν· μὴ εἰσενέγκῃς[2] τὰς
φωνὰς ταύτας ἃς οἱ πολλοὶ τῶν φιλοψογούντων[3]
" τούτους οὖν τοὺς καταράτους καὶ μιαροὺς

11 μωρούς.[4] " ἔστω· σὺ πῶς ποτ' ἀπεσοφώθης ἄφνω

---

[1] ἀπώλειά ἐστιν, μέγιστον, supplied by Schenkl.
[2] Mowat: ἐ . . . . . . πης S.
[3] Schenkl: φ . . . . των S.
[4] Supplied by Capps for a lacuna of about five letters in S.

are we any longer angry with the multitude?—"They are thieves," says someone, "and robbers."—What do you mean by "thieves and robbers?" They have simply gone astray in questions of good and evil. Ought we, therefore, to be angry with them, or rather pity them? Only show them their error and you will see how quickly they will desist from their mistakes. But if their eyes are not opened, they have nothing superior to their mere opinion.

Ought not this brigand, then, and this adulterer to be put to death? you ask. Not at all, but you should ask rather, "Ought not this man to be put to death who is in a state of error and delusion about the greatest matters, and is in a state of blindness, not, indeed, in the vision which distinguishes between white and black, but in the judgement which distinguishes between the good and the evil?" And if you put it this way, you will realize how inhuman a sentiment it is that you are uttering, and that it is just as if you should say, "Ought not this blind man, then, or this deaf man to be put to death?" For if the loss of the greatest things is the greatest harm that can befall a man, while the greatest thing in each man is a right moral purpose, and if a man is deprived of this very thing, what ground is left for you to be angry at him? Why, man, if you must needs be affected in a way that is contrary to nature at the misfortunes of another, pity him rather, but do not hate him; drop this readiness to take offence and this spirit of hatred; do not introduce those words which the multitude of the censorious use: "Well, then, these accursed and abominable fools!" Very well; but how is it that you have so suddenly been converted to wisdom that you are

ὥστε ἄλλοις μωροῖς [1] χαλεπὸς εἶ ; διὰ τί οὖν χαλεπαίνομεν ; ὅτι τὰς ὕλας θαυμάζομεν, ὧν ἡμᾶς
ἀφαιροῦνται. ἐπεί τοι μὴ θαύμαζέ σου τὰ ἱμάτια
καὶ τῷ κλέπτῃ οὐ χαλεπαίνεις· μὴ θαύμαζε τὸ
κάλλος τῆς γυναικὸς καὶ τῷ μοιχῷ οὐ χαλεπαίνεις.

12 γνῶθι ὅτι κλέπτης καὶ μοιχὸς ἐν τοῖς σοῖς τόπον
οὐκ ἔχει, ἐν δὲ τοῖς ἀλλοτρίοις καὶ τοῖς οὐκ ἐπὶ σοί.
ταῦτα ἂν ἀφῇς καὶ παρὰ μηδὲν ἡγήσῃ, τίνι ἔτι
χαλεπαίνεις ; μέχρι δ' ἂν ταῦτα θαυμάζῃς, σεαυτῷ

13 χαλέπαινε μᾶλλον ἢ ἐκείνοις. σκόπει γάρ· ἔχεις
καλὰ ἱμάτια, ὁ γείτων σου οὐκ ἔχει· θυρίδα ἔχεις,
θέλεις αὐτὰ ψῦξαι. οὐκ οἶδεν ἐκεῖνος τί τὸ
ἀγαθόν ἐστι τοῦ ἀνθρώπου, ἀλλὰ φαντάζεται ὅτι

14 τὸ ἔχειν καλὰ ἱμάτια, τοῦτο ὃ καὶ σὺ φαντάζῃ.
εἶτα μὴ ἔλθῃ καὶ ἄρῃ αὐτά ; ἀλλὰ σὺ πλακοῦντα
δεικνύων ἀνθρώποις λίχνοις καὶ μόνος αὐτὸν
καταπίνων οὐ θέλεις ἵνα αὐτὸν ἁρπάσωσι ; μὴ
ἐρέθιζε αὐτούς, θυρίδα μὴ ἔχε, μὴ ψῦχέ σου τὰ
ἱμάτια.

15 Κἀγὼ πρῴην σιδηροῦν λύχνον ἔχων παρὰ τοῖς
θεοῖς ἀκούσας ψόφον τῆς θυρίδος κατέδραμον.
εὗρον ἡρπασμένον τὸν λύχνον. ἐπελογισάμην
ὅτι ἔπαθέν τι ὁ ἄρας οὐκ ἀπίθανον. τί οὖν ;

16 αὔριον, φημί, ὀστράκινον εὑρήσεις. ἐκεῖνα γὰρ
ἀπολλύει, ἃ ἔχει. " ἀπώλεσά μου τὸ ἱμάτιον."
εἶχες γὰρ ἱμάτιον. " ἀλγῶ τὴν κεφαλήν." μὴ
τι κέρατα ἀλγεῖς ; τί οὖν ἀγανακτεῖς ; τούτων

---

[1] ὥστε (Mowat) μωροῖς supplied by Capps for a lacuna of
about eleven letters in *S*.

[1] An illustration of the famous principle, *nil admirari*
(Horace, *Epist.* I. 6, 1).

angry at fools? Why, then, are we angry? Because
we admire the goods of which these men rob us
For, mark you, stop admiring¹ your clothes, and you
are not angry at the man who steals them; stop admiring your wife's beauty, and you are not angry at
her adulterer. Know that a thief or an adulterer
has no place among the things that are your own,
but only among the things that are another's and
that are not under your control. If you give these
things up and count them as nothing, at whom have
you still ground to feel angry? But so long as you
admire these things, be angry at yourself and not at
the men that I have just mentioned. For consider;
you have fine clothes and your neighbour does not;
you have a window and wish to air them. *He* does not
know wherein the true good of man consists, but
fancies that it consists in having fine clothes, the very
same fancy that you also entertain. Shall he not
come, then, and carry them off? Why, when you
show a cake to gluttonous men and then gulp it
down all to yourself, are you not wanting them to
snatch it? Stop provoking them, stop having a
window, stop airing your clothes.

Something similar happened to me also the other
day. I keep an iron lamp by the side of my household gods, and, on hearing a noise at the window, I
ran down. I found that the lamp had been stolen.
I reflected that the man who stole it was moved by
no unreasonable motive. What then? To-morrow,
I say, you will find one of earthenware. Indeed, a man
loses only that which he already has. "I have lost
my cloak." Yes, for you had a cloak. "I have a
pain in my head." You don't have a pain in your
horns, do you? Why, then, are you indignant? For

γὰρ αἱ ἀπώλειαι, τούτων οἱ πόνοι, ὧν καὶ αἱ κτήσεις.

17 "'Αλλ' ὁ τύραννος δήσει"—τί; τὸ σκέλος· "ἀλλ' ἀφελεῖ"—τί; τὸν τράχηλον. τί οὖν οὐ δήσει οὐδ' ἀφελεῖ; τὴν προαίρεσιν. διὰ τοῦτο παρ-

18 ήγγελλον οἱ παλαιοὶ τὸ Γνῶθι σαυτόν. τί οὖν; ἔδει νὴ τοὺς θεοὺς μελετᾶν ἐπὶ τῶν μικρῶν καὶ ἀπ' ἐκείνων ἀρχομένους διαβαίνειν ἐπὶ τὰ μείζω.

19 "κεφαλὴν ἀλγῶ." "οἴμοι" μὴ λέγε. "ὠτίον ἀλγῶ." "οἴμοι" μὴ λέγε. καὶ οὐ λέγω ὅτι οὐ δέδοται στε-νάξαι, ἀλλὰ ἔσωθεν μὴ στενάξῃς. μηδ' ἂν βραδέως τὸν ἐπίδεσμον ὁ παῖς φέρῃ, κραύγαζε καὶ σπῶ καὶ λέγε "πάντες με μισοῦσιν." τίς γὰρ μὴ μισήσῃ

20 τὸν τοιοῦτον; τούτοις τὸ λοιπὸν πεποιθὼς τοῖς δόγμασιν ὀρθὸς περιπάτει, ἐλεύθερος, οὐχὶ τῷ μεγέθει πεποιθὼς τοῦ σώματος ὥσπερ ἀθλητής· οὐ γὰρ ὡς ὄνον ἀήττητον εἶναι δεῖ.

21 Τίς οὖν ὁ ἀήττητος; ὃν οὐκ ἐξίστησιν οὐδὲν τῶν ἀπροαιρέτων. εἶτα λοιπὸν ἑκάστην τῶν περιστάσεων ἐπερχόμενος καταμανθάνω ὡς ἐπὶ τοῦ ἀθλητοῦ. "οὗτος ἐξεβίασε τὸν πρῶτον κλῆρον.

22 τί οὖν τὸν δεύτερον; τί δ' ἂν καῦμα ᾖ; τί δ' ἐν Ὀλυμπίᾳ; " καὶ ἐνταῦθα ὡσαύτως. ἂν ἀργυρί-διον προβάλῃς, καταφρονήσει. τί οὖν ἂν κορασί-διον; τί οὖν ἂν ἐν σκότῳ; τί οὖν ἂν δοξάριον;

---

[1] That is, a man should prove himself invincible by reason and reflection, not by brute strength, or the sheer obstinacy of passive resistance.

our losses and our pains have to do only with the things which we possess.

"But the tyrant will chain——" What? Your leg. "But he will cut off——" What? Your neck. What, then, will he neither chain nor cut off? Your moral purpose. This is why the ancients gave us the injunction, "Know thyself." What follows, then? Why, by the Gods, that one ought to practise in small things, and beginning with them pass on to the greater. "I have a head-ache." Well, do not say "Alas!" "I have an ear-ache." Do not say "Alas!" And I am not saying that it is not permissible to groan, only do not groan in the centre of your being. And if your slave is slow in bringing your bandage, do not cry out and make a wry face and say, "Everybody hates me." Why, who would not hate such a person? For the future put your confidence in these doctrines and walk about erect, free, not putting your confidence in the size of your body, like an athlete; for you ought not to be invincible in the way an ass is invincible.[1]

Who, then, is the invincible man? He whom nothing that is outside the sphere of his moral purpose can dismay. I then proceed to consider the circumstances one by one, as I would do in the case of the athlete. "This fellow has won the first round. What, then, will he do in the second? What if it be scorching hot? And what will he do at Olympia?" It is the same way with the case under consideration. If you put a bit of silver coin in a man's way, he will despise it. Yes, but if you put a bit of a wench in his way, what then? Or if it be in the dark, what then? Or if you throw a bit of reputation in his way, what then? Or abuse, what

τί οὖν ἂν λοιδορίαν; τί οὖν ἂν ἔπαινον; τί δ' ἂν
23 θάνατον; δύναται ταῦτα πάντα νικῆσαι. τί οὖν
ἂν καῦμα ᾖ, τοῦτό ἐστι· τί, ἂν οἰνωμένος[1] ᾖ; τί ἂν
μελαγχολῶν; τί ἐν ὕπνοις; οὗτός μοί ἐστιν ὁ
ἀνίκητος ἀθλητής.

ιθ΄. Πῶς ἔχειν δεῖ πρὸς τοὺς τυράννους;

1   Ὅτι ἄν τινι προσῇ τι πλεονέκτημα ἢ δοκῇ γε
προσεῖναι μὴ προσόν, τοῦτον πᾶσα ἀνάγκη, ἐὰν
2 ἀπαίδευτος ᾖ, πεφυσῆσθαι δι' αὐτό. εὐθὺς ὁ
τύραννος λέγει "ἐγώ εἰμι ὁ πάντων κράτιστος."
καὶ τί μοι δύνασαι παρασχεῖν; ὄρεξίν μοι
δύνασαι περιποιῆσαι ἀκώλυτον; πόθεν σοί; σὺ
γὰρ ἔχεις; ἔκκλισιν ἀπερίπτωτον; σὺ γὰρ
3 ἔχεις; ὁρμὴν ἀναμάρτητον; καὶ ποῦ σοι
μέτεστιν; ἄγε, ἐν νηὶ δὲ σαυτῷ θαρρεῖς ἢ τῷ
4 εἰδότι; ἐπὶ δ' ἅρματος τίνι ἢ τῷ εἰδότι; τί δ'
ἐν ταῖς ἄλλαις τέχναις; ὡσαύτως. τί οὖν
δύνασαι; "πάντες με θεραπεύουσιν." καὶ γὰρ
ἐγὼ τὸ πινάκιον θεραπεύω καὶ πλύνω αὐτὸ καὶ
ἐκμάσσω καὶ τῆς ληκύθου ἔνεκα πάσσαλον

---

[1] Upton: οἰώμενος S.

---

[1] Under all ordinary circumstances the man who is being
tested will resist the temptations of money, a maid, secrecy,
reputation, and the like. But if, like the athlete, he be
tested under abnormal conditions, as when drunk, or mad, or
asleep, will he hold out against these temptations even then?
If he can, he is indeed invincible.

then? Or praise, what then? Or death, what
then? All these things he can overcome. What,
then, if it be scorching hot—that is, what if he be
drunk? What if he be melancholy-mad?[1] What
if asleep? The man who passes all these tests is
what I mean by the invincible athlete.

CHAPTER XIX

How ought we to bear ourselves toward tyrants?

IF a man possesses some superiority, or thinks at
least that he does, even though he does not, it is
quite unavoidable that this man, if he is uneducated,
becomes puffed up on account of it. For example,
the tyrant exclaims, "I am the mightiest in the
world." Very well, what can you do for me? Can
you secure for me desire that is free from any
hindrance? How can you? Do you have it yourself? Can you secure for me aversion proof against
encountering what it would avoid? Do you have it
yourself? Or infallible choice? And where can
you claim a share in that? Come, when you are on
board ship, do you feel confidence in yourself, or in
the skilled navigator? And when you are in a chariot,
in whom do you feel confidence other than the skilled
driver. And how is it in the other arts? The same
way. What does your power amount to, then? "All
men pay attention[2] to me." Yes, and I pay attention
to my little plate and wash it and wipe it out, and
for the sake of my oil-flask I drive a peg in the wall.

---

[2] The whole passage turns on the various meanings of
θεραπεύω, which include *serve, attend to, give medical care to,
pay attention to, pay court to, flatter, etc.*

πήσσω. τί οὖν ; ταῦτά μου κρείττονά ἐστιν ;
οὔ· ἀλλὰ χρείαν μοι παρέχει τινά. ταύτης οὖν
ἕνεκα θεραπεύω αὐτά. τί δέ ; τὸν ὄνον οὐ θερα-
5 πεύω ; οὐ νίπτω αὐτοῦ τοὺς πόδας ; οὐ περικα-
θαίρω ; οὐκ οἶδας ὅτι πᾶς ἄνθρωπος ἑαυτὸν
θεραπεύει, σὲ δ' οὕτως ὡς τὸν ὄνον ; ἐπεὶ τίς σε
6 θεραπεύει ὡς ἄνθρωπον ; δείκνυε. τίς σοι θέλει
ὅμοιος γενέσθαι, τίς σου ζηλωτὴς γίνεται ὡς
Σωκράτους ; "ἀλλὰ δύναμαί σε τραχηλοκοπῆ-
σαι." καλῶς λέγεις. ἐξελαθόμην ὅτι σε δεῖ θεραπεύειν καὶ ὡς πυρετὸν καὶ ὡς χολέραν καὶ βωμὸν
στῆσαι, ὡς ἐν Ῥώμῃ Πυρετοῦ βωμός ἐστιν.
7 Τί οὖν ἐστι τὸ ταράσσον καὶ καταπλῆττον
τοὺς πολλούς ; ὁ τύραννος καὶ οἱ δορυφόροι ;
πόθεν ; μὴ γένοιτο· οὐκ ἐνδέχεται τὸ φύσει
ἐλεύθερον ὑπ' ἄλλου τινὸς ταραχθῆναι ἢ κωλυ-
8 θῆναι πλὴν ὑφ' ἑαυτοῦ. ἀλλὰ τὰ δόγματα
αὐτὸν ταράσσει. ὅταν γὰρ ὁ τύραννος εἴπῃ τινὶ
"δήσω σου τὸ σκέλος," ὁ μὲν τὸ σκέλος τετιμη-
κὼς λέγει "μή· ἐλέησον," ὁ δὲ τὴν προαίρεσιν
τὴν ἑαυτοῦ λέγει "εἴ σοι λυσιτελέστερον φαίνεται,
δῆσον." "οὐκ ἐπιστρέφῃ ;" "οὐκ ἐπιστρέφομαι."
9 "ἐγώ σοι δείξω ὅτι κύριός εἰμι." "πόθεν σύ ; ἐμὲ
ὁ Ζεὺς ἐλεύθερον ἀφῆκεν. ἢ δοκεῖς ὅτι ἔμελλεν
τὸν ἴδιον υἱὸν ἐᾶν καταδουλοῦσθαι ; τοῦ νεκροῦ
10 δέ μου κύριος εἶ, λάβε αὐτόν." "ὥσθ' ὅταν μοι
προσίῃς, ἐμὲ οὐ θεραπεύεις ;" "οὔ· ἀλλ' ἐμαυ-

What follows, then? Are these things superior to
me? No, but they render me some service, and
therefore I pay attention to them. Again, do I not
pay attention to my donkey? Do I not wash his
feet? Do I not curry him? Do you not know that
every man pays attention to himself, and to you just
as he does to his donkey? For who pays attention
to you as to a *man*? Point him out to me. Who
wishes to become like you? Who becomes a zealous
follower of yours as men did of Socrates? "But I
can cut off your head." Well said! I had forgotten
that I ought to pay attention to you, as to fever or
cholera, and set up an altar to you, just as in Rome
there is an altar to the God Fever.

What is it, then, that disturbs and bewilders the
multitude? Is it the tyrant and his bodyguards?
How is that possible? Nay, far from it! It is not
possible that that which is by nature free should be
disturbed or thwarted by anything but itself. But
it is a man's own judgements that disturb him. For
when the tyrant says to a man, "I will chain your
leg," the man who has set a high value on his leg
replies, "Nay, have mercy upon me," while the man
who has set a high value on his moral purpose replies,
"If it seems more profitable to you to do so, chain
it." "Do you not care?" "No, I do not care."
"I will show you that I am master." "How can
you be my master? Zeus has set me free. Or do
you really think that he was likely to let his own
son be made a slave? You are, however, master of
my dead body, take it." "You mean, then, that
when you approach me you will not pay attention
to me?" "No, I pay attention only to myself.
But if you wish me to say that I pay attention to

τόν. εἰ δὲ θέλεις με λέγειν ὅτι καὶ σέ, λέγω σοι
οὕτως ὡς τὴν χύτραν."

11 Τοῦτο οὐκ ἔστιν φίλαυτον· γέγονε γὰρ οὕτως
τὸ ζῷον· αὑτοῦ ἕνεκα πάντα ποιεῖ. καὶ γὰρ ὁ
ἥλιος αὑτοῦ ἕνεκα πάντα ποιεῖ καὶ τὸ λοιπὸν

12 αὐτὸς ὁ Ζεύς. ἀλλ' ὅταν θέλῃ εἶναι Ὑέτιος καὶ
Ἐπικάρπιος καὶ πατὴρ ἀνδρῶν τε θεῶν τε, ὁρᾷς
ὅτι τούτων τῶν ἔργων καὶ τῶν προσηγοριῶν οὐ
δύναται τυχεῖν, ἂν μὴ εἰς τὸ κοινὸν ὠφέλιμος ᾖ.

13 καθόλου τε τοιαύτην τὴν¹ φύσιν τοῦ λογικοῦ
ζῴου κατεσκεύασεν, ἵνα μηδενὸς τῶν ἰδίων ἀγαθῶν δύνηται τυγχάνειν, ἂν² μή τι εἰς τὸ κοινὸν

14 ὠφέλιμον προσφέρηται. οὕτως οὐκέτι ἀκοινώνη-

15 τον γίνεται τὸ πάντα αὑτοῦ ἕνεκα ποιεῖν. ἐπεὶ
τί ἐκδέχῃ ; ἵνα τις ἀποστῇ αὑτοῦ καὶ τοῦ ἰδίου
συμφέροντος ; καὶ πῶς ἔτι μία καὶ ἡ αὐτὴ ἀρχὴ
πᾶσιν ἔσται ἡ πρὸς αὐτὰ οἰκείωσις ;

16 Τί οὖν ; ὅταν ὑπῇ δόγματα ἀλλόκοτα περὶ
τῶν ἀπροαιρέτων ὡς³ ὄντων ἀγαθῶν καὶ κακῶν,

17 πᾶσα ἀνάγκη θεραπεύειν τοὺς τυράννους. ὤφελον γὰρ τοὺς τυράννους μόνον, τοὺς κοιτωνίτας
δ' οὔ. πῶς δὲ καὶ φρόνιμος γίνεται ἐξαίφνης ὁ
ἄνθρωπος, ὅταν Καῖσαρ αὐτὸν ἐπὶ τοῦ λασάνου
ποιήσῃ. πῶς εὐθὺς λέγομεν "φρονίμως μοι λελά-

18 ληκεν Φηλικίων." ἤθελον αὐτὸν ἀποβληθῆναι

19 τοῦ κοπρῶνος, ἵνα πάλιν ἄφρων σοι δοκῇ. εἶχέν
τινα Ἐπαφρόδιτος σκυτέα, ὃν διὰ τὸ ἄχρηστον
εἶναι ἐπώλησεν. εἶτα ἐκεῖνος κατά τινα δαίμονα

---

¹ Added by Koraes.   ² Added by Trincavelli.
³ Wolf : πῶς S.

---

¹ That is, the whole order of nature requires every living
thing to appropriate, or make its own, whatever it needs in
order to maintain life.

you too, I tell you that I do so, but only as I pay attention to my pot."

This is not mere self-love; such is the nature of the animal man; everything that he does is for himself. Why, even the sun does everything for its own sake, and, for that matter, so does Zeus himself. But when Zeus wishes to be " Rain-bringer," and " Fruit-giver," and "Father of men and of gods," you can see for yourself that he cannot achieve these works, or win these appellations, unless he proves himself useful to the common interest; and in general he has so constituted the nature of the rational animal man, that he can attain nothing of his own proper goods unless he contributes something to the common interest. Hence it follows that it can no longer be regarded as unsocial for a man to do everything for his own sake. For what do you expect? That a man should neglect himself and his own interest? And in that case how can there be room for one and the same principle of action for all, namely, that of appropriation [1] to their own needs?

What then? When men entertain absurd opinions about what lies outside the province of the moral purpose, counting it good or bad, it is altogether unavoidable for them to pay attention to the tyrant. Aye, would that it were merely the tyrants and not their chamberlains too! And yet how can the man suddenly become wise when Caesar puts him in charge of his chamberpot? How can we forthwith say " Felicio has spoken wisely to me"? I would that he were deposed from the superintendency of the dunghill, that you may think him a fool again! Epaphroditus owned a certain cobbler whom he sold because he was useless; then by some chance the

ἀγορασθεὶς ὑπό τινος τῶν Καισαριανῶν τοῦ
Καίσαρος σκυτεὺς ἐγένετο. εἶδες ἂν πῶς αὐτὸν
20 ἐτίμα ὁ Ἐπαφρόδιτος· "τί πράσσει Φηλικίων ὁ
21 ἀγαθός, φιλῶ σε ;" εἶτα εἴ τις ἡμῶν ἐπύθετο "τί
ποιεῖ αὐτός ;" ἐλέγετο ὅτι "μετὰ Φηλικίωνος
22 βουλεύεται περί τινος." οὐχὶ γὰρ πεπράκει
23 αὐτὸν ὡς ἄχρηστον ; τίς οὖν αὐτὸν ἄφνω φρό-
νιμον ἐποίησεν ; τοῦτ' ἔστι τὸ τιμᾶν ἄλλο τι
ἢ τὰ προαιρετικά.

24 "Ἠξίωται δημαρχίας." πάντες οἱ ἀπαντῶντες
συνήδονται· ἄλλος τοὺς ὀφθαλμοὺς καταφιλεῖ,
ἄλλος τὸν τράχηλον, οἱ δοῦλοι τὰς χεῖρας.
ἔρχεται εἰς οἶκον, εὑρίσκει λύχνους ἁπτομένους.
25 ἀναβαίνει εἰς τὸ Καπιτώλιον, ἐπιθύει. τίς οὖν
πώποτε ὑπὲρ τοῦ ὀρεχθῆναι καλῶς ἔθυσεν ;
ὑπὲρ τοῦ ὁρμῆσαι κατὰ φύσιν ; ἐκεῖ γὰρ καὶ
θεοῖς εὐχαριστοῦμεν, ὅπου τὸ [1] ἀγαθὸν τιθέμεθα.

26 Σήμερόν τις ὑπὲρ ἱερωσύνης ἐλάλει μοι τοῦ
Αὐγούστου. λέγω αὐτῷ "ἄνθρωπε, ἄφες τὸ
27 πρᾶγμα· δαπανήσεις πολλὰ εἰς οὐδέν."—"Ἀλλ'
οἱ τὰς ὠνάς," [2] φησί, "γράφοντες γράψουσι τὸ
ἐμὸν ὄνομα."—"Μή τι οὖν σὺ τοῖς ἀναγιγνώ-
28 σκουσι λέγεις παρών· ἐμὲ γεγράφασιν ; εἰ δὲ καὶ
νῦν δύνασαι παρεῖναι πᾶσιν, ἐὰν ἀποθάνῃς, τί
ποιήσεις ;"—"Μενεῖ μου τὸ ὄνομα."—"Γράψον
αὐτὸ εἰς λίθον καὶ μενεῖ. ἄγε ἔξω δὲ Νικο-

---

[1] ὅπου τὸ Shaftesbury : οἱ τοῦτο S.
[2] O. Hirschfeld (γ' ὠνάς Diels) : φωνάς S.

fellow was bought by a member of Caesar's household and became cobbler to Caesar. You should have seen how Epaphroditus honoured him! "How is my good Felicio, I pray you?" he used to say. And then if someone asked us, "What is your master [1] doing?" he was told, "He is consulting Felicio about something or other." Why, had he not sold him as being useless? Who, then, had suddenly made a wise man out of him? This is what it means to honour something else than what lies within the province of the moral purpose.

"He has been honoured with a tribuneship," someone says. All who meet him offer their congratulations; one man kisses him on the eyes, another on the neck, his slaves kiss his hands. He goes home; he finds lamps being lighted. He climbs up the Capitol and offers sacrifice. Now who ever sacrificed as a thank-offering for having had right desire, or for having exercised choice in accordance with nature? For we give thanks to the gods for that wherein we set the good.

To-day a man was talking to me about a priesthood of Augustus. I say to him, "Man, drop the matter; you will be spending a great deal to no purpose." "But," says he, "those who draw up deeds of sale will inscribe my name." "Do you really expect, then, to be present when the deeds are read and say, 'That is my name they have written'? And even supposing you are now able to be present whenever anyone reads them, what will you do if you die?" "My name will remain after me." "Inscribe it on a stone and it will remain after you. Come now, who will remember you outside

---

[1] Epaphroditus once owned Epictetus.

29 πόλεως τίς σου μνεία ; "—"Ἀλλὰ χρυσοῦν στέ-
φανον φορήσω."—"Εἰ ἅπαξ ἐπιθυμεῖς στεφάνου,
ῥόδινον λαβὼν περίθου· ὄψει γὰρ κομψότερον."

κ'. Περὶ τοῦ λόγου πῶς αὑτοῦ θεωρητικός ἐστιν.

1 Πᾶσα τέχνη καὶ δύναμις προηγουμένων τινῶν
2 ἐστι θεωρητική. ὅταν μὲν οὖν ὁμοειδὴς τοῖς
θεωρουμένοις καὶ αὐτή, ἀναγκαίως καὶ αὐτῆς
γίνεται θεωρητική· ὅταν δ᾽ ἀνομογενής,[1] οὐ δύνα-
3 ται θεωρεῖν ἑαυτήν. οἷον σκυτικὴ περὶ δέρματα
ἀναστρέφεται, αὐτὴ δὲ παντελῶς ἀπήλλακται
τῆς ὕλης τῶν δερμάτων· διὰ τοῦτο οὐκ ἔστιν
4 αὑτῆς θεωρητική. γραμματικὴ πάλιν περὶ τὴν
ἐγγράμματον φωνήν. μή τι οὖν ἐστι καὶ αὐτὴ
ἐγγράμματος φωνή ; οὐδαμῶς. διὰ τοῦτο οὐ
5 δύναται θεωρεῖν ἑαυτήν. ὁ οὖν λόγος πρὸς τί
ποτε ὑπὸ τῆς φύσεως παρείληπται ; πρὸς χρῆσιν
φαντασιῶν οἵαν δεῖ. αὐτὸς οὖν τί ἐστιν ;
σύστημα ἐκ ποιῶν φαντασιῶν· οὕτως γίνεται
6 φύσει καὶ αὐτοῦ θεωρητικός. πάλιν ἡ φρόνησις
τίνα θεωρήσουσα παρελήλυθεν ; ἀγαθὰ καὶ κακὰ
καὶ οὐδέτερα. αὐτὴ[2] οὖν τί ἐστιν ; ἀγαθόν.
ἡ δ᾽ ἀφροσύνη τί ἐστιν ; κακόν. ὁρᾷς οὖν ὅτι

---

[1] Meibom : ἀι ὁμογενῆς S.
[2] Schegk : αὗτη S.

---

[1] The city in which Epictetus taught during the latter
part of his life, and where the present conversation is clearly
thought of as taking place. Greek and Roman documents,
instead of being attested, as most commonly among us, by a

of Nicopolis?"[1] "But I shall wear a crown of gold."
"If you desire a crown at all, take a crown of roses
and put it on; you will look much more elegant in
that."

CHAPTER XX

How the reasoning faculty contemplates itself

EVERY art and faculty makes certain things the
special object of its contemplation. Now when the
art or faculty itself is of like kind with what it
contemplates, it becomes inevitably self-contemplative; but when it is of unlike kind, it cannot
contemplate itself. For example, the art of leather-
working has to do with hides, but the art itself is
altogether different from the material of hides, wherefore it is not self-contemplative. Again, the art of
grammar has to do with written speech; it is not,
therefore, also itself written speech, is it? Not at
all. For this reason it cannot contemplate itself.
Well then, for what purpose have we received reason
from nature? For the proper use of external impressions. What, then, is reason itself? Something
composed out of a certain kind of external impressions. Thus it comes naturally to be also self-
contemplative. Once more, what are the things that
wisdom has been given us to contemplate? Things
good, bad, and neither good nor bad. What, then,
is wisdom itself? A good. And what is folly? An
evil. Do you see, then, that wisdom inevitably comes

single notary, contained many names of witnesses, eponymous
magistrates, supervising officials, and the like. A priest of
Augustus would naturally be called in often to sign formal
documents in one capacity or another.

ἀναγκαίως καὶ αὐτῆς γίνεται καὶ τῆς ἐναντίας
7 θεωρητική; διὰ τοῦτο ἔργον τοῦ φιλοσόφου τὸ
μέγιστον καὶ πρῶτον δοκιμάζειν τὰς φαντασίας
καὶ διακρίνειν καὶ μηδεμίαν ἀδοκίμαστον προσφέ-
8 ρεσθαι. ὁρᾶτε ἐπὶ τοῦ νομίσματος, ὅπου δοκεῖ
τι εἶναι πρὸς ἡμᾶς, πῶς καὶ τέχνην ἐξευρήκαμεν
καὶ ὅσοις ὁ ἀργυρογνώμων προσχρῆται πρὸς
δοκιμασίαν τοῦ νομίσματος, τῇ ὄψει, τῇ ἀφῇ,
9 τῇ ὀσφρασίᾳ, τὰ τελευταῖα τῇ ἀκοῇ· ῥίψας¹ τὸ
δηνάριον τῷ ψόφῳ προσέχει καὶ οὐχ ἅπαξ ἀρκεῖται ψοφήσαντος, ἀλλ᾽ ὑπὸ τῆς πολλῆς προσοχῆς
10 μουσικὸς γίνεται. οὕτως ὅπου διαφέρειν οἰόμεθα
τὸ πλανᾶσθαι τοῦ μὴ πλανᾶσθαι, ἐνταῦθα πολλὴν προσοχὴν εἰσφέρομεν εἰς διάκρισιν τῶν δια-
11 πλανᾶν δυναμένων, ἐπὶ δὲ ταλαιπώρου ἡγεμονικοῦ
χάσκοντες καὶ καθεύδοντες, πᾶσαν φαντασίαν
παραπροσδεχόμεθα· ἡ γὰρ ζημία οὐ προσπίπτει.
12 Ὅταν οὖν θέλῃς γνῶναι, πῶς ἔχεις περὶ μὲν
τἀγαθὰ καὶ κακὰ ἀνειμένως, περὶ τἀδιάφορα δ᾽
ἐσπευσμένος, ἐπίστησον πῶς ἔχεις πρὸς τὸ
ἐκτυφλωθῆναι καὶ πῶς πρὸς τὸ ἐξαπατηθῆναι
καὶ γνώσῃ ὅτι μακρὰν εἶ τοῦ ὡς δεῖ πεπονθέναι
13 περὶ ἀγαθῶν καὶ κακῶν. "ἀλλὰ πολλῆς ἔχει
χρείαν παρασκευῆς καὶ πόνου πολλοῦ καὶ μαθη-
μάτων." τί οὖν; ἐλπίζεις ὅτι τὴν μεγίστην
14 τέχνην ἀπὸ ὀλίγων ἔστιν ἀναλαβεῖν; καίτοι
αὐτὸς μὲν ὁ προηγούμενος λόγος τῶν φιλοσόφων
λίαν ἐστὶν ὀλίγος. εἰ θέλεις γνῶναι, ἀνάγνωθι
15 τὰ Ζήνωνος καὶ ὄψει. τί γὰρ ἔχει μακρὸν

---

¹ Schegk : ῥήξας S.

---

¹ *i.e.*, in the sense of basing action upon only such impressions as have been tested and found to be trustworthy.

to contemplate both itself and its opposite? Therefore, the first and greatest task of the philosopher is
to test the impressions and discriminate between
them, and to apply [1] none that has not been tested.
You all see in the matter of coinage, in which it is
felt that we have some interest, how we have even invented an art, and how many means the tester employs
to test the coinage—sight, touch, smell, finally hearing; he throws the denarius down and then listens
to the sound, and is not satisfied with the sound it
makes on a single test, but, as a result of his constant
attention to the matter, he catches the tune, like a
musician. Thus, where we feel that it makes a good
deal of difference to us whether we go wrong or do
not go wrong, there we apply any amount of attention
to discriminating between things that are capable of
making us go wrong, but in the case of our governing
principle, poor thing, we yawn and sleep and errone-
ously accept any and every external impression; for
here the loss that we suffer does not attract our
attention.

When, therefore, you wish to realize how careless
you are about the good and the evil, and how zealous
you are about that which is indifferent, observe how
you feel about physical blindness on the one hand,
and mental delusion on the other, and you will find
out that you are far from feeling as you ought
about things good and things evil. "Yes, but this
requires much preparation, and much hard work, and
learning many things." Well, what then? Do you
expect it to be possible to acquire the greatest art
with a slight effort? And yet the chief doctrine of
the philosophers is extremely brief. If you would
know, read what Zeno has to say and you will see.

εἰπεῖν ὅτι "τέλος ἐστὶ τὸ ἕπεσθαι θεοῖς, οὐσία
16 δ' ἀγαθοῦ χρῆσις οἵα δεῖ φαντασιῶν"; λέγε "τί
οὖν ἐστι θεὸς καὶ τί φαντασία; καὶ τί ἐστι
φύσις ἡ ἐπὶ μέρους καὶ τί ἐστι φύσις ἡ τῶν
17 ὅλων;" ἤδη μακρόν. ἂν οὖν ἐλθὼν Ἐπίκουρος
εἴπῃ, ὅτι ἐν σαρκὶ δεῖ εἶναι τὸ ἀγαθόν, πάλιν
μακρὸν γίνεται καὶ ἀνάγκη ἀκοῦσαι τί τὸ προηγούμενόν ἐστιν ἐφ' ἡμῶν, τί τὸ ὑποστατικὸν καὶ
οὐσιῶδες. ὅτι τὸ κοχλίου ἀγαθὸν οὐκ εἰκὸς
εἶναι ἐν τῷ κελύφει, τὸ οὖν τοῦ ἀνθρώπου εἰκός;
18 σὺ δ' αὐτὸς τί κυριώτερον ἔχεις, Ἐπίκουρε; τί
ἐστιν ἐν σοὶ τὸ βουλευόμενον, τὸ ἐπισκεπτό-
μενον ἕκαστα, τὸ περὶ τῆς σαρκὸς αὐτῆς ὅτι
19 τὸ προηγούμενόν ἐστιν[1] ἐπικρῖνον; τί δὲ καὶ
λύχνον ἅπτεις καὶ πονεῖς ὑπὲρ ἡμῶν καὶ τηλικαῦτα βιβλία γράφεις; ἵνα μὴ ἀγνοήσωμεν
ἡμεῖς τὴν ἀλήθειαν; τίνες ἡμεῖς; τί πρὸς σὲ
ὄντες; οὕτω μακρὸς ὁ λόγος γίνεται.

κα'. Πρὸς τοὺς θαυμάζεσθαι θέλοντας.

1 Ὅταν τις ἣν δεῖ στάσιν ἔχῃ ἐν τῷ βίῳ, ἔξω
2 οὐ κέχηνεν. ἄνθρωπε, τί θέλεις σοι γενέσθαι;
ἐγὼ μὲν ἀρκοῦμαι, ἂν ὀρέγωμαι καὶ ἐκκλίνω
κατὰ φύσιν, ἂν ὁρμῇ καὶ ἀφορμῇ χρῶμαι ὡς
πέφυκα, ἂν προθέσει,[2] ἂν ἐπιβολῇ, ἂν συγ-

---

[1] τὸ after ἐστιν deleted by Usener.
[2] Meibom (Wolf): προσθέσει S.

For what is there lengthy in his statement: "To follow the gods ·is man's end, and the essence of good is the proper use of external impressions"? Ask, "What, then, is God, and what is an external impression? And what is nature in the individual and nature in the universe?" You already have a lengthy statement. If Epicurus should come and say that the good ought to be in the flesh, again the explanation becomes lengthy, and you must be told what is the principal faculty within us, and what our substantial, and what our essential, nature is. Since it is not probable that the good of a snail lies in its shell, is it, then, probable that the good of man lies in his flesh? But take your own case, Epicurus; what more masterful faculty do you yourself possess? What is that thing within you which takes counsel, which examines into all things severally, which, after examining the flesh itself, decides that it is the principal matter? And why do you light a lamp and toil in our behalf, and write such quantities of books? Is it that we may not fail to know the truth? Who are we? And what are we to you? And so the argument becomes lengthy.

CHAPTER XXI

To those who would be admired

WHEN a man has his proper station in life, he is not all agape for things beyond it. Man, what is it you want to have happen to you? As for myself, I am content if I exercise desire and aversion in accordance with nature, if I employ choice and refusal as my nature is, and similarly employ purpose and design

καταθέσει. τί οὖν ἡμῖν ὀβελίσκον καταπιὼν
3 περιπατεῖς; "ἤθελον, ἵνα με καὶ οἱ ἀπαντῶντες
θαυμάζωσιν καὶ ἐπακολουθοῦντες ἐπικραυ-
4 γάζωσιν· ὦ μεγάλου φιλοσόφου." τίνες εἰσὶν
οὗτοι, ὑφ' ὧν θαυμάζεσθαι θέλεις; οὐχ οὗτοί
εἰσι, περὶ ὧν εἴωθας λέγειν ὅτι μαίνονται; τί
οὖν; ὑπὸ τῶν μαινομένων θαυμάζεσθαι θέλεις;

κβ'. Περὶ τῶν προλήψεων.

1 Προλήψεις κοιναὶ πᾶσιν ἀνθρώποις εἰσίν· καὶ
πρόληψις προλήψει οὐ μάχεται. τίς γὰρ ἡμῶν
οὐ τίθησιν, ὅτι τὸ ἀγαθὸν συμφέρον ἐστὶ καὶ
αἱρετὸν καὶ ἐκ πάσης αὐτὸ περιστάσεως δεῖ
μετιέναι καὶ διώκειν; τίς δ' ἡμῶν οὐ τίθησιν,
ὅτι τὸ δίκαιον καλόν ἐστι καὶ πρέπον; πότ'
2 οὖν ἡ μάχη γίνεται; περὶ τὴν ἐφαρμογὴν τῶν
3 προλήψεων ταῖς ἐπὶ μέρους οὐσίαις, ὅταν ὁ μὲν
εἴπῃ "καλῶς ἐποίησεν, ἀνδρεῖός ἐστιν" "οὔ,
ἀλλ' ἀπονενοημένος." ἔνθεν ἡ μάχη γίνεται
4 τοῖς ἀνθρώποις πρὸς ἀλλήλους. αὕτη ἐστὶν ἡ
Ἰουδαίων καὶ Σύρων καὶ Αἰγυπτίων καὶ Ῥωμαίων
μάχη, οὐ περὶ τοῦ ὅτι τὸ ὅσιον πάντων προ-
τιμητέον καὶ ἐν παντὶ μεταδιωκτέον, ἀλλὰ πότερόν
ἐστιν ὅσιον τοῦτο τὸ χοιρείον φαγεῖν ἢ ἀνόσιον.
5 ταύτην τὴν μάχην εὑρήσετε καὶ Ἀγαμέμνονος
καὶ Ἀχιλλέως. κάλει γὰρ αὐτοὺς εἰς τὸ μέσον.
τί λέγεις σύ, ὦ Ἀγάμεμνον; οὐ δεῖ γενέσθαι

---

[1] Of one with a stiff and self-important bearing. Our
equivalent phrase is "to swallow a ramrod."

and assent. Why, then, do you walk around in our presence as though you had swallowed a spit?[1] "It has always been my wish that those who meet me should admire me and as they follow me should exclaim, 'O the great philosopher!'" Who are those people by whom you wish to be admired? Are they not these about whom you are in the habit of saying that they are mad? What then? Do you wish to be admired by the mad?

CHAPTER XXII

Of our preconceptions

PRECONCEPTIONS are common to all men, and one preconception does not contradict another. For who among us does not assume that the good is profitable and something to be chosen, and that in every circumstance we ought to seek and pursue it? And who among us does not assume that righteousness is beautiful and becoming? When, then, does contradiction arise? It arises in the application of our preconceptions to the particular cases, when one person says, "He did nobly, he is brave"; another, "No, but he is out of his mind." Thence arises the conflict of men with one another. This is the conflict between Jews and Syrians and Egyptians and Romans, not over the question whether holiness should be put before everything else and should be pursued in all circumstances, but whether the particular act of eating swine's flesh is holy or unholy. This, you will find, was also the cause of conflict between Agamemnon and Achilles. Come, summon them before us. What do you say, Agamemnon? Ought

143

τὰ δέοντα καὶ τὰ καλῶς ἔχοντα ; "δεῖ μὲν οὖν."

6 σὺ δὲ τί λέγεις, ὦ Ἀχιλλεῦ ; οὐκ ἀρέσκει σοι
γίνεσθαι τὰ καλῶς ἔχοντα ; "ἐμοὶ μὲν οὖν
πάντων μάλιστα ἀρέσκει." ἐφαρμόσατε οὖν

7 τὰς προλήψεις. ἐντεῦθεν ἡ ἀρχὴ μάχης. ὁ
μὲν λέγει "οὐ χρὴ ἀποδιδόναι με τὴν Χρυσηίδα
τῷ πατρί," ὁ δὲ λέγει "δεῖ μὲν οὖν." πάντως
ὁ ἕτερος αὐτῶν κακῶς ἐφαρμόζει τὴν πρόληψιν

8 τοῦ δέοντος. πάλιν ὁ μὲν λέγει "οὐκοῦν, εἴ με
δεῖ ἀποδοῦναι τὴν Χρυσηίδα, δεῖ με λαβεῖν ὑμῶν
τινος τὸ γέρας," ὁ δέ "τὴν ἐμὴν οὖν λάβῃς
ἐρωμένην ;" "τὴν σήν" φησίν. "ἐγὼ οὖν
μόνος—;" "ἀλλ' ἐγὼ μόνος μὴ ἔχω ;" οὕτως μάχη
γίνεται.

9 Τί οὖν ἐστι τὸ παιδεύεσθαι ; μανθάνειν τὰς
φυσικὰς προλήψεις ἐφαρμόζειν ταῖς ἐπὶ μέρους
οὐσίαις καταλλήλως τῇ φύσει καὶ λοιπὸν διελεῖν,

10 ὅτι τῶν ὄντων τὰ μέν ἐστιν ἐφ' ἡμῖν, τὰ δὲ οὐκ
ἐφ' ἡμῖν· ἐφ' ἡμῖν μὲν προαίρεσις καὶ πάντα
τὰ προαιρετικὰ ἔργα, οὐκ ἐφ' ἡμῖν δὲ τὸ σῶμα,
τὰ μέρη τοῦ σώματος, κτήσεις, γονεῖς, ἀδελφοί,

11 τέκνα, πατρίς, ἁπλῶς οἱ κοινωνοί. ποῦ οὖν
θῶμεν τὸ ἀγαθόν ; ποίᾳ οὐσίᾳ αὐτὸ ἐφαρμό-

12 σομεν ; τῇ ἐφ' ἡμῖν ;—Εἶτα οὐκ ἔστιν ἀγαθὸν
ὑγίεια καὶ ἀρτιότης καὶ ζωή, ἀλλ' οὐδὲ τέκνα

not that to be done which is proper, and that which is noble? "Indeed it ought." And what do you say, Achilles? Do you not agree that what is noble ought to be done? "As for me, I agree most emphatically with that principle." Very well, then, apply your preconceptions to the particular cases. It is just there the conflict starts. The one says, "I ought not to be compelled to give back Chryseis to her father," while the other says, "Indeed you ought." Most certainly one of the two is making a bad application of the preconception "what one ought to do." Again, the one of them says, "Very well, if I ought to give back Chryseis, then I ought to take from some one of you the prize *he* has won," and the other replies, "Would you, then, take the woman I love?" "Yes, the woman you love," the first answers. "Shall I, then, be the only one—?" "But shall I be the only one to have nothing?" So a conflict arises.

What, then, does it mean to be getting an education? It means to be learning how to apply the natural preconceptions to particular cases, each to the other in conformity with nature, and, further, to make the distinction, that some things are under our control while others are not under our control. Under our control are moral purpose and all the acts of moral purpose; but not under our control are the body, the parts of the body, possessions, parents, brothers, children, country—in a word, all that with which we associate. Where, then, shall we place "the good"? To what class of things are we going to apply it? To the class of things that are under our control?—What, is not health, then, a good thing, and a sound body, and life? Nay, and not even

οὐδὲ γονεῖς οὐδὲ πατρίς ;—Καὶ τίς σου ἀνέξεται ;
13 μεταθῶμεν οὖν αὐτὸ πάλιν ἐνθάδε. ἐνδέχεται
οὖν βλαπτόμενον καὶ ἀποτυγχάνοντα τῶν ἀγαθῶν
εὐδαιμονεῖν ;—Οὐκ ἐνδέχεται.—Καὶ τηρεῖν[1] τὴν
πρὸς τοὺς κοινωνοὺς οἵαν δεῖ ἀναστροφήν ; καὶ
πῶς ἐνδέχεται ; ἐγὼ γὰρ πέφυκα πρὸς τὸ ἐμὸν
14 συμφέρον. εἰ συμφέρει μοι ἀγρὸν ἔχειν, συμφέρει
μοι καὶ ἀφελέσθαι αὐτὸν τοῦ πλησίον· εἰ συμφέρει μοι ἱμάτιον ἔχειν, συμφέρει μοι καὶ κλέψαι
αὐτὸ ἐκ βαλανείου. ἔνθεν πόλεμοι, στάσεις,
15 τυραννίδες, ἐπιβουλαί. πῶς δ᾿ ἔτι δυνήσομαι
ἀποδιδόναι[2] τὸ πρὸς τὸν Δία καθῆκον ; εἰ γὰρ
βλάπτομαι καὶ ἀτυχῶ, οὐκ ἐπιστρέφεταί μου.
καὶ "τί μοι καὶ αὐτῷ, εἰ οὐ δύναταί μοι βοηθῆσαι ;" καὶ πάλιν "τί μοι καὶ αὐτῷ, εἰ θέλει
μ᾿ ἐν τοιούτοις εἶναι ἐν οἷς εἰμι ;" ἄρχομαι λοιπὸν
16 μισεῖν αὐτόν. τί οὖν ναοὺς ποιοῦμεν, τί οὖν
ἀγάλματα, ὡς κακοῖς δαίμοσιν, ὡς πυρετῷ τῷ
Διί ; καὶ πῶς ἔτι Σωτὴρ καὶ πῶς Ὑέτιος καὶ
πῶς Ἐπικάρπιος ; καὶ μήν, ἂν ἐνταῦθά που
θῶμεν τὴν οὐσίαν τοῦ ἀγαθοῦ, πάντα ταῦτα
ἐξακολουθεῖ.

17   Τί οὖν ποιήσωμεν ;—Αὕτη ἐστὶ ζήτησις τοῦ
φιλοσοφοῦντος τῷ ὄντι καὶ ὠδίνοντος· νῦν ἐγὼ
18 οὐχ ὁρῶ τί ἐστι τὸ ἀγαθὸν καὶ τὸ κακόν· οὐ
μαίνομαι ; ναί· ἀλλ᾿ ἂν[3] ἐνταῦθά που θῶ τὸ
ἀγαθόν, ἐν τοῖς προαιρετικοῖς, πάντες μου κατα-
γελάσονται. ἥξει τις γέρων πολιὸς χρυσοῦς

---

[1] Added by Kronenberg.   [2] Suggested by Schenkl.
[3] Added by Schenkl.

---

[1] Cf. I. 19, 6, an altar of Fever in Rome.

children, or parents, or country?—And who will tolerate you if you deny that? Therefore, let us transfer the designation "good" to these things. But is it possible, then, for a man to be happy if he sustains injury and fails to get that which is good?—It is not possible.—And to maintain the proper relations with his associates? And how can it be possible? For it is my nature to look out for my own interest. If it is my interest to have a farm, it is my interest to take it away from my neighbour; if it is my interest to have a cloak, it is my interest also to steal it from a bath. This is the source of wars, seditions, tyrannies, plots. And again, how shall I any longer be able to perform my duty towards Zeus? For if I sustain injury and am unfortunate, he pays no heed to me. And then we hear men saying, "What have I to do with him, if he is unable to help us?" And again, "What have I to do with him, if he wills that I be in such a state as I am now?" The next step is that I begin to hate him. Why, then, do we build temples to the gods, and make statues of them, as for evil spirits—for Zeus as for a god of Fever?[1] And how can he any longer be "Saviour," and "Rain-bringer," and "Fruit-giver?" And, in truth, if we set the nature of the good somewhere in this sphere, all these things follow.

What, then, shall we do?—This is a subject of enquiry for the man who truly philosophizes and is in travail of thought. Says such a man to himself, "I do not now see what is the good and what is the evil; am I not mad?" Yes, but suppose I set the good somewhere here, among the things that the will controls, all men will laugh at me. Some white-haired old man with many a gold ring on his fingers

δακτυλίους ἔχων πολλούς, εἶτα ἐπισείσας τὴν
κεφαλὴν ἐρεῖ " ἄκουσόν μου, τέκνον· δεῖ μὲν καὶ
φιλοσοφεῖν, δεῖ δὲ καὶ ἐγκέφαλον ἔχειν· ταῦτα
19 μωρά ἐστιν. σὺ παρὰ τῶν φιλοσόφων μανθάνεις
συλλογισμόν, τί δέ σοι ποιητέον ἐστίν, σὺ
20 κάλλιον οἶδας ἢ οἱ φιλόσοφοι." ἄνθρωπε, τί
οὖν μοι ἐπιτιμᾷς, εἰ οἶδα ; τούτῳ τῷ ἀνδραπόδῳ
21 τί εἴπω ; ἂν σιωπῶ, ῥήγνυται ἐκεῖνος. ὡς δεῖ
λέγειν ὅτι " σύγγνωθί μοι ὡς τοῖς ἐρῶσιν· οὐκ
εἰμὶ ἐμαυτοῦ, μαίνομαι."

κγ΄. Πρὸς Ἐπίκουρον.

1 Ἐπινοεῖ καὶ Ἐπίκουρος ὅτι φύσει ἐσμὲν κοινωνικοί, ἀλλ' ἅπαξ ἐν τῷ κελύφει θεὶς τὸ ἀγαθὸν
2 ἡμῶν οὐκέτι δύναται ἄλλο οὐδὲν εἰπεῖν. πάλιν
γὰρ ἐκείνου λίαν κρατεῖ, ὅτι οὐ δεῖ ἀπεσπασμένον
οὐδὲν τῆς τοῦ ἀγαθοῦ οὐσίας οὔτε θαυμάζειν
οὔτ' ἀποδέχεσθαι· καὶ καλῶς αὐτοῦ κρατεῖ.
3 πῶς οὖν ἔτι κοινωνικοί¹ ἐσμεν, οἷς μὴ φυσικὴ
ἔστι πρὸς τὰ ἔγγονα φιλοστοργία ; διὰ τί ἀπο-
συμβουλεύεις τῷ σοφῷ τεκνοτροφεῖν ; τί φοβῇ
4 μὴ διὰ ταῦτα εἰς λύπας ἐμπέσῃ ; διὰ γὰρ τὸν
Μῦν² τὸν ἔσω τρεφόμενον ἐμπίπτει ; τί οὖν
αὐτῷ μέλει, ἂν Μυΐδιον μικρὸν ἔσω κατακλαίῃ
5 αὐτοῦ ; ἀλλ' οἶδεν, ὅτι, ἂν ἅπαξ γένηται παιδίον,

---

¹ Wolf : ὑπονοητικοί S.
² Bentley : μῦν S and the editions.

---

¹ The reference here is clearly to Mys ("Mouse"), a
favourite slave of Epicurus, who was brought up in his
house, and took an active part in his philosophical studies,

will come along, and then he will shake his head and say, " Listen to me, my son ; one ought of course to philosophize, but one ought also to keep one's head ; this is all nonsense. You learn a syllogism from the philosophers, but you know better than the philosophers what you ought to do." Man, why, then, do you censure me, if I know? What shall I say to this slave ? If I hold my peace, the fellow bursts with indignation. So I must say, " Forgive me as you would lovers ; I am not my own master ; I am mad."

CHAPTER XXIII

In answer to Epicurus

EVEN Epicurus understands that we are by nature social beings, but having once set our good in the husk which we wear, he cannot go on and say anything inconsistent with this. For, he next insists emphatically upon the principle that we ought neither to admire nor to accept anything that is detached from the nature of the good ; and he is right in so doing. But how, then, can we still be social beings, if affection for our own children is not a natural sentiment? Why do you dissuade the wise man from bringing up children ? Why are you afraid that sorrow will come to him on their account ? What, does sorrow come to him on account of his house-slave Mouse ? [1] Well, what does it matter to him if his little Mouse in his home begins to cry ? Nay he knows, that if once a child is born,

as Bentley saw (cf. *Trans. Amer. Philol. Assoc.*, LII., 451). There is no evidence to support the common explanation that Epicurus had compared children to mice.

οὐκέτι ἐφ' ἡμῖν ἐστι μὴ στέργειν μηδὲ φροντίζειν
6 ἐπ' αὐτῷ. διὰ τοῦτο φησὶν οὐδὲ πολιτεύσεσθαι¹
τὸν νοῦν ἔχοντα· οἶδεν γὰρ τίνα δεῖ ποιεῖν τὸν
πολιτευόμενον· ἐπείτοι εἰ ὡς ἐν μυίαις μέλλεις
7 ἀναστρέφεσθαι, τί κωλύει; ἀλλ' ὅμως² εἰδὼς
ταῦτα τολμᾷ λέγειν ὅτι "μὴ ἀναιρώμεθα τέκνα."
ἀλλὰ πρόβατον μὲν οὐκ ἀπολείπει τὸ αὑτοῦ
ἔγγονον οὐδὲ λύκος, ἄνθρωπος δ' ἀπολείπει; τί
8 θέλεις; μωροὺς ἡμᾶς εἶναι ὡς τὰ πρόβατα; οὐδ'
ἐκεῖνα ἀπολείπει. θηριώδεις ὡς τοὺς λύκους;
9 οὐδ' ἐκεῖνοι ἀπολείπουσιν. ἄγε, τίς δέ σοι πεί-
θεται ἰδὼν παιδίον αὑτοῦ κλαῖον ἐπὶ τὴν γῆν
10 πεπτωκός; ἐγὼ μὲν οἶμαι ὅτι εἰ καὶ ἐμαντεύσατο
ἡ μήτηρ σου καὶ ὁ πατήρ, ὅτι μέλλεις ταῦτα
λέγειν, οὐκ ἄν σε ἔρριψαν.

κδ'. Πῶς πρὸς τὰς περιστάσεις ἀγωνιστέον;

1   Αἱ περιστάσεις εἰσὶν αἱ τοὺς ἄνδρας δεικνύου-
σαι. λοιπὸν ὅταν ἐμπέσῃ περίστασις, μέμνησο
ὅτι ὁ θεός σε ὡς ἀλείπτης τραχεῖ νεανίσκῳ συμβέ-
2 βληκεν.³—Ἵνα τί; φησίν.—Ἵνα Ὀλυμπιονίκης
γένῃ· δίχα δ' ἱδρῶτος οὐ γίγνεται. ἐμοὶ μὲν
οὐδεὶς δοκεῖ κρείσσονα ἐσχηκέναι περίστασιν ἧς σὺ
ἔσχηκας, ἂν θέλῃς ὡς ἀθλητὴς νεανίσκῳ χρῆσθαι.

---

¹ Upton (after Schegk): πολιτεύσασθαι S.
² Kronenberg: ὁ μὴ S.   ³ Wolf: βέβληκεν S.

---

¹ Since flies have no social organization or relationships,
and there is nothing to compel one to live like a man, and
not like an unsocial animal, except one's own sense of fitness
of things.

it is no longer in our power not to love it or to care for it. For the same reason Epicurus says that a man of sense does not engage in politics either; for he knows what the man who engages in politics has to do—since, of course, if you are going to live among men as though you were a fly among flies,[1] what is to hinder you? Yet, despite the fact that he knows this, he still has the audacity to say, "Let us not bring up children." But a sheep does not abandon its own offspring, nor a wolf; and yet does a man abandon his? What do you wish us to do? Would you have us be foolish as sheep? But even they do not desert their offspring. Would you have us be fierce as wolves? But even they do not desert their offspring. Come now, who follows your advice when he sees his child fallen on the ground and crying? Why, in my opinion, your mother and your father, even if they had divined that you were going to say such things, would not have exposed you!

CHAPTER XXIV

How should we struggle against difficulties?

It is difficulties that show what men are. Consequently, when a difficulty befalls, remember that God, like a physical trainer, has matched you with a rugged young man. What for? some one says, So that you may become an Olympic victor; but that cannot be done without sweat. To my way of thinking no one has got a finer difficulty than the one which you have got, if only you are willing to make use of it as an athlete makes use of a young

3 καὶ νῦν ἡμεῖς γε εἰς τὴν Ῥώμην κατάσκοπον
πέμπομεν. οὐδεὶς δὲ δειλὸν κατάσκοπον πέμπει,
ἵν᾽, ἂν μόνον ἀκούσῃ ψόφου καὶ σκιάν ποθεν ἴδῃ,
τρέχων ἔλθῃ τεταραγμένος καὶ λέγων ἤδη παρεῖναι
4 τοὺς πολεμίους. οὕτως νῦν καὶ σὺ ἂν ἐλθὼν ἡμῖν
εἴπῃς "φοβερὰ τὰ ἐν Ῥώμῃ πράγματα, δεινόν ἐστι
θάνατος, δεινόν ἐστι φυγή, δεινὸν λοιδορία, δεινὸν
5 πενία· φεύγετε ἄνδρες, πάρεισιν οἱ πολέμιοι,"
ἐροῦμέν σοι "ἄπελθε, σεαυτῷ μαντεύου· ἡμεῖς
τοῦτο μόνον ἡμάρτομεν, ὅτι τοιοῦτον κατάσκοπον
ἐπέμπομεν."

6 Πρὸ σοῦ κατάσκοπος ἀποσταλεὶς Διογένης
ἄλλα ἡμῖν ἀπήγγελκεν. λέγει ὅτι ὁ θάνατος οὐκ
ἔστι κακόν, οὐδὲ γὰρ αἰσχρόν· λέγει ὅτι ἀδοξία
7 ψόφος ἐστὶ μαινομένων ἀνθρώπων. οἷα δὲ περὶ
πόνου, οἷα δὲ περὶ ἡδονῆς, οἷα περὶ πενίας εἴρηκεν
οὗτος ὁ κατάσκοπος. τὸ δὲ γυμνητεύειν [1] λέγει
ὅτι κρεῖσσόν ἐστι πάσης περιπορφύρου· τὸ δ᾽ ἐπ᾽
ἀστρώτῳ πέδῳ καθεύδειν λέγει ὅτι μαλακωτάτη
8 κοίτη ἐστίν. καὶ ἀπόδειξιν φέρει περὶ ἑκάστου
τὸ θάρσος τὸ αὑτοῦ, τὴν ἀταραξίαν, τὴν ἐλευθερίαν, εἶτα καὶ τὸ σωμάτιον στίλβον καὶ συνε-
9 στραμμένον. "οὐδείς," φησίν, "πολέμιος ἐγγύς
ἐστιν· πάντα εἰρήνης γέμει." πῶς, ὦ Διόγενες ;
"ἰδού," φησίν, "μή τι βέβλημαι, μή τι τέτρωμαι,
10 μή τινα πέφευγα ;" τοῦτ᾽ ἔστιν οἷος δεῖ κατάσκοπος, σὺ δ᾽ ἡμῖν ἐλθὼν ἄλλα ἐξ ἄλλων λέγεις.

[1] Bentley : γυμνάσιον εἶναι S : γυμνὸν εἶναι s.

man to wrestle with. And now we are sending you
to Rome as a scout, to spy out the land.[1] But no
one sends a coward as a scout, that, if he merely
hears a noise and sees a shadow anywhere, he may
come running back in terror and report "The enemy
is already upon us." So now also, if you should
come and tell us, "The state of things at Rome is
fearful; terrible is death, terrible is exile, terrible
is reviling, terrible is poverty; flee, sirs, the enemy
is upon us!" we shall say to you, "Away, prophesy
to yourself! Our one mistake was that we sent a
man like you as a scout."

Diogenes, who before you was sent forth as a scout,
has brought us back a different report. He says,
"Death is not an evil, since it is not dishonourable"; he says, "Ill repute is a noise made by
madmen." And what a report this scout has made
us about toil and about pleasure and about poverty!
He says, "To be naked is better than any scarlet
robe; and to sleep on the bare ground," he says,
"is the softest couch." And he offers as a proof of
each statement his own courage, his tranquillity, his
freedom, and finally his body, radiant with health
and hardened. "There is no enemy near," says
he; "all is full of peace." How so, Diogenes?
"Why, look!" says he, "I have not been struck
with any missile, have I, or received any wound?
I have not fled from anyone, have I?" This is
what it means to be a proper scout, but you return
and tell us one thing after another. Will you not

---

[1] Domitian had banished the philosophers from Rome;
the young man is, therefore, being sent from Nicopolis to
learn what is going on there that might be of interest to the
cause of philosophy.

οὐκ ἀπελεύσῃ πάλιν καὶ ὄψει ἀκριβέστερον δίχα
τῆς δειλίας ;

11 Τί οὖν ποιήσω ;—Τί ποιεῖς, ἐκ πλοίου ὅταν
ἐξίῃς ; μή τι τὸ πηδάλιον αἴρεις, μή τι τὰς
κώπας ; τί οὖν αἴρεις ; τὰ σά, τὴν λήκυθον, τὴν
πήραν. καὶ νῦν ἂν ἦς μεμνημένος τῶν σῶν,
12 οὐδέποτε τῶν ἀλλοτρίων ἀντιποιήσῃ. λέγει σοι
" θὲς τὴν πλατύσημον." ἰδοὺ στενόσημος. " θὲς
καὶ ταύτην" ἰδοὺ ἱμάτιον μόνον. " θὲς τὸ ἱμάτιον"
13 ἰδοὺ γυμνός. " ἀλλὰ φθόνον μοι κινεῖς." λάβε
τοίνυν ὅλον τὸ σωμάτιον. ᾧ δύναμαι ῥῖψαι τὸ
14 σωμάτιον, ἔτι τοῦτον φοβοῦμαι ; ἀλλὰ κληρο-
νόμον μ' οὐκ ἀπολείψει. τί οὖν ; ἐπελαθόμην
ὅτι τούτων οὐδὲν ἐμὸν ἦν ; πῶς οὖν ἐμὰ αὐτὰ
λέγομεν ; ὡς τὸν κράβαττον ἐν τῷ πανδοκείῳ.
ἂν οὖν ὁ πανδοκεὺς ἀποθανὼν ἀπολίπῃ σοι τοὺς
κραβάττους· ἂν δ' ἄλλῳ, ἐκεῖνος ἕξει, σὺ δ' ἄλλον
15 ζητήσεις· ἂν οὖν μὴ εὕρῃς, χαμαὶ κοιμήσῃ μόνον
θαρρῶν καὶ ῥέγκων καὶ μεμνημένος ὅτι ἐν τοῖς
πλουσίοις καὶ βασιλεῦσι καὶ τυράννοις αἱ τραγῳδίαι τόπον ἔχουσιν, οὐδεὶς δὲ πένης τραγῳδίαν
16 συμπληροῖ εἰ μὴ ὡς χορευτής. οἱ δὲ βασιλεῖς
ἄρχονται μὲν ἀπ' ἀγαθῶν·

στέψατε δώματα·

εἶτα περὶ τρίτον ἢ τέταρτον μέρος·

ἰὼ Κιθαιρών, τί μ' ἐδέχου ;

---

[1] The reference must be to the Emperor Domitian, but
Epictetus discreetly uses no name.
[2] Worn by senators.   [3] Worn by knights.
[4] Worn by ordinary citizens.   [5] From an unknown play.

go away again and observe more accurately, without this cowardice?

What am I to do, then?—What do you do when you disembark from a ship? You do not pick up the rudder, do you, or the oars? What do you pick up, then? Your own luggage, your oil-flask, your wallet. So now, if you are mindful of what is your own property, you will never lay claim to that which is another's. He [1] says to you, "Lay aside your broad scarlet hem" [2] Behold, the narrow hem.[3] "Lay aside this also." Behold, the plain toga.[4] "Lay aside your toga." Behold, I am naked. "But you arouse my envy." Well, then, take the whole of my paltry body. Do I any longer fear the man to whom I can throw my body? But he will not leave me as his heir. What then? Did I forget that none of these things is my own? How, then, do we call them "my own"? Merely as we call the bed in the inn "my own." If, then, the inn-keeper dies and leaves you the beds, you will have them; but if he leaves them to someone else, *he* will have them, and *you* will look for another bed. If, then, you do not find one, you will have to sleep on the ground; only do so with good courage, snoring and remembering that tragedies find a place among the rich and among kings and tyrants, but no poor man fills a tragic rôle except as a member of the chorus. Now the kings commence in a state of prosperity:

"Hang the palace with garlands"; [5]

then, about the third or fourth act, comes—

"Alas, Cithaeron, why didst thou receive me?" [6]

[6] Sophocles, *Oedipus Rex*, 1390. Cithaeron was the mountain on which the infant Oedipus had been exposed to die.

17 ἀνδράποδον, ποῦ οἱ στέφανοι, ποῦ τὸ διάδημα;
18 οὐδέν σε ὠφελοῦσιν οἱ δορυφόροι; ὅταν οὖν ἐκείνων
τινὶ προσίῃς, τούτων μέμνησο, ὅτι τραγῳδῷ προσ-
έρχῃ, οὐ τῷ ὑποκριτῇ, ἀλλ᾽ αὐτῷ τῷ Οἰδίποδι.
19 "ἀλλὰ μακάριος ὁ δεῖνα· μετὰ πολλῶν γὰρ
περιπατεῖ." κἀγὼ συγκατατάττω ἐμαυτὸν σὺν
τοῖς πολλοῖς καὶ μετὰ πολλῶν περιπατῶ. τὸ δὲ
20 κεφάλαιον· μέμνησο ὅτι ἡ θύρα ἤνοικται. μὴ γίνου
τῶν παιδίων δειλότερος, ἀλλ᾽ ὡς ἐκεῖνα, ὅταν
αὐτοῖς μὴ ἀρέσκῃ τὸ πρᾶγμα, λέγει "οὐκέτι
παίξω," καὶ σύ, ὅταν σοι φαίνηταί τινα εἶναι
τοιαῦτα, εἰπὼν "οὐκέτι παίξω," ἀπαλλάσσου,
μένων δὲ μὴ θρήνει.

κε΄. Πρὸς τὸ αὐτό.

1   Εἰ ταῦτα ἀληθῆ ἐστι καὶ μὴ βλακεύομεν μηδ᾽
ὑποκρινόμεθα ὅτι τὸ ἀγαθὸν τοῦ ἀνθρώπου ἐν
προαιρέσει καὶ τὸ κακόν, τὰ δ᾽ ἄλλα πάντα οὐδὲν
πρὸς ἡμᾶς, τί ἔτι ταρασσόμεθα, τί ἔτι φοβούμεθα;
2 περὶ ἃ ἐσπουδάκαμεν, τούτων ἐξουσίαν οὐδεὶς ἔχει·
ὧν ἐξουσίαν οἱ ἄλλοι ἔχουσιν, τούτων οὐκ ἐπι-
3 στρεφόμεθα. ποῖον ἔτι πρᾶγμα ἔχομεν;—Ἀλλὰ
ἔντειλαί μοι.—Τί σοι ἐντείλωμαι; ὁ Ζεύς σοι οὐκ
ἐντέταλται; οὐ δέδωκέν σοι τὰ μὲν σὰ ἀκώλυτα
καὶ ἀπαραπόδιστα, τὰ δὲ μὴ σὰ κωλυτὰ καὶ
4 παραποδιστά; τίνα οὖν ἐντολὴν ἔχων ἐκεῖθεν

---

[1] That is, rules of conduct which will guide the inquirer
in dealing with these two classes of things.

Slave, where are your crowns, where your diadem?
Do your guards avail you not at all? When,
therefore, you approach one of those great men,
remember all this—that you are approaching a tragic
character, not the actor, but Oedipus himself.
"Nay, but so-and-so is blessed; for he has many
companions to walk with." So have I; I fall in line
with the multitude and have many companions to
walk with. But, to sum it all up: remember that
the door has been thrown open. Do not become a
greater coward than the children, but just as they
say, "I won't play any longer," when the thing
does not please them, so do you also, when things
seem to you to have reached that stage, merely say,
"I won't play any longer," and take your departure;
but if you stay, stop lamenting.

CHAPTER XXV

Upon the same theme

IF all this is true and we are not silly nor merely
playing a part when we say, "Man's good and
man's evil lies in moral choice, and all other things
are nothing to us," why are we still distressed and
afraid? Over the things that we seriously care for
no one has authority; and the things over which
other men have authority do not concern us. What
kind of thing have we left to discuss?—"Nay, give
me directions." [1]—What directions shall I give you?
Has not Zeus given you directions? Has he not
given you that which is your own, unhindered and
unrestrained, while that which is not your own is
subject to hindrance and restraint? What direc-

ἐλήλυθας, ποῖον διάταγμα ; τὰ σὰ τήρει ἐκ παντὸς
τρόπου, τῶν ἀλλοτρίων μὴ ἐφίεσο. τὸ πιστὸν
σόν, τὸ αἰδῆμον σόν·[1] τίς οὖν ἀφελέσθαι δύναταί
σου ταῦτα ; τίς κωλύσει χρῆσθαι αὐτοῖς ἄλλος
εἰ μὴ σύ ; σὺ δὲ πῶς ; ὅταν περὶ τὰ μὴ σαυτοῦ
5 σπουδάσῃς, τὰ σαυτοῦ ἀπώλεσας. τοιαύτας
ἔχων ὑποθήκας καὶ ἐντολὰς παρὰ τοῦ Διὸς ποίας
ἔτι παρ' ἐμοῦ θέλεις ; κρείσσων εἰμὶ ἐκείνου, ἀξιο-
6 πιστότερος ; ἀλλὰ ταύτας τηρῶν ἄλλων τινῶν
προσδέῃ ; ἀλλ' ἐκεῖνος οὐκ ἐντέταλται ταῦτα ;
φέρε τὰς προλήψεις, φέρε τὰς ἀποδείξεις τὰς
τῶν φιλοσόφων, φέρε ἃ πολλάκις ἤκουσας, φέρε
δ' ἃ εἶπας αὐτός, φέρε ἃ ἀνέγνως, φέρε ἃ
ἐμελέτησας.

7 Μέχρις οὖν τίνος ταῦτα τηρεῖν καλῶς ἔχει καὶ
8 τὴν παιδιὰν μὴ λύειν ; μέχρις ἂν κομψῶς διεξά-
γηται. ἐν Σατορναλίοις λέλογχεν βασιλεύς·
ἔδοξε γὰρ παῖξαι ταύτην τὴν παιδιάν. προστάσσει
"σὺ πίε, σὺ κέρασον, σὺ ᾆσον, σὺ ἄπελθε, σὺ
ἐλθέ." ὑπακούω, ἵνα μὴ παρ' ἐμὲ λύηται ἡ παιδιά.
9 "ἀλλὰ σὺ ὑπολάμβανε ὅτι ἐν κακοῖς εἶ." οὐχ
ὑπολαμβάνω· καὶ τίς μ' ἀναγκάσει ὑπολαμβά-
10 νειν ; πάλιν συνεθέμεθα παῖξαι τὰ περὶ Ἀγα-
μέμνονα καὶ Ἀχιλλέα. καταταγεὶς Ἀγαμέμνων
λέγει μοι "πορεύου πρὸς τὸν Ἀχιλλέα καὶ
11 ἀπόσπασον τὴν Βρισηίδα." πορεύομαι. "ἔρχου."
ἔρχομαι. ὡς γὰρ ἐπὶ τῶν ὑποθετικῶν λόγων

---

[1] τὸ αἰδῆμον σόν supplied by Upton from his 'codex.'

---

[1] The idea seems to be that all these preconceptions,
demonstrations, *etc.*, will be found to be based upon the
"promptings and directions" of Zeus.

tions, then, did you bring with you when you came from him into this world, what kind of an order? Guard by every means that which is your own, but do not grasp at that which is another's. Your faithfulness is your own, your self-respect is your own; who, then, can take these things from you? Who but yourself will prevent you from using them? But you, how do you act? When you seek earnestly that which is not your own, you lose that which is your own. Since you have such promptings and directions from Zeus, what kind do you still want from me? Am I greater than he, or more trustworthy? But if you keep these commands of his, do you need any others besides? But has he not given you these directions? Produce your preconceptions, produce the demonstrations of the philosophers, produce what you have often heard, and produce what you have said yourself, produce what you have read, produce what you have practised.[1]

How long, then, is it well to keep these precepts and not to break up the game? As long as it is played pleasantly. At the Saturnalia a king is chosen by lot; for it has been decided to play this game. The king gives his commands: "You drink, you mix wine, you sing, you go, you come." I obey, so as not to be the one to break up the game. "Come, suppose that you are in an evil plight." I do not so suppose; and who is there to compel me so to suppose? Again, we have agreed to play the story of Agamemnon and Achilles. The one who has been appointed to play the part of Agamemnon says to me, "Go to Achilles, and drag away Briseis." I go. He says, "Come," and I come. For as we

ἀναστρεφόμεθα, οὕτως δεῖ καὶ ἐπὶ τοῦ βίου.
"ἔστω νύξ." ἔστω. "τί οὖν; ἡμέρα ἐστίν;"
12 οὔ· ἔλαβον γὰρ ὑπόθεσιν τοῦ νύκτα εἶναι. "ἔστω
σε ὑπολαμβάνειν ὅτι νύξ ἐστιν." ἔστω. "ἀλλὰ
13 καὶ ὑπόλαβε ὅτι νύξ ἐστιν." οὐκ ἀκολουθεῖ τῇ
ὑποθέσει. οὕτως καὶ ἐνταῦθα. "ἔστω σε εἶναι
δυστυχῆ." ἔστω. "ἆρ' οὖν ἀτυχὴς εἶ;" ναί. "τί
οὖν; κακοδαιμονεῖς;" ναί. "ἀλλὰ καὶ ὑπόλαβε
ὅτι ἐν κακοῖς εἶ." οὐκ ἀκολουθεῖ τῇ ὑποθέσει·
καὶ ἄλλος με κωλύει.

14 Μέχρι πόσου οὖν ὑπακουστέον τοῖς τοιούτοις;
μέχρις ἂν οὐ λυσιτελῇ, τοῦτο δ' ἔστιν μέχρις ἂν
15 οὐ σῴζω τὸ πρέπον καὶ κατάλληλον. λοιπὸν οἱ
μέν εἰσι κακαύστηροι[1] καὶ κακοστόμαχοι καὶ
λέγουσιν "ἐγὼ οὐ δύναμαι παρὰ τούτῳ δειπνεῖν,
ἵν' αὐτοῦ ἀνέχομαι καθ' ἡμέραν διηγουμένου, πῶς
ἐν Μυσίᾳ ἐπολέμησεν. 'διηγησάμην σοι, ἀδελφέ,
πῶς ἐπὶ τὸν λόφον ἀνέβην· πάλιν ἄρχομαι
16 πολιορκεῖσθαι.'" ἄλλος λέγει "ἐγὼ δειπνῆσαι
θέλω μᾶλλον καὶ ἀκούειν αὐτοῦ ὅσα θέλει ἀδολε-
17 σχοῦντος." καὶ σὺ σύγκρινε ταύτας τὰς ἀξίας·
μόνον μηδὲν βαρούμενος ποίει, μὴ θλιβόμενος μηδ'
ὑπολαμβάνων ἐν κακοῖς εἶναι· τοῦτο γὰρ οὐδείς σε
18 ἀναγκάζει. καπνὸν πεποίηκεν ἐν τῷ οἰκήματι;

---

[1] Wendland : καταύστηροι S.

---

[1] That is, we accept our hypothesis as long as we can do
so in reason; so in life we must be guided by reason.

[2] A reverent form of reference to Zeus. See also I. 30, 1.

[3] The course of argument seems to be: I can assume that
it is night and reason in a manner consistent with that
assumption; but if it *really is* day, I cannot assume that it

behave in the matter of hypothetical proposals, so
we ought to behave in life also.[1] "Let it be
night." So be it. "What then? Is it day?"
No, for I have accepted the assumption that it is
night. "Let us suppose that you assume it to be
night." So be it. "But go on and assume that it *is*
night." That is not consistent with the hypothesis.
So also in the present case. "Let us suppose that
you are unhappy." So be it. "Are you, then,
unfortunate?" Yes. "What then? Are you
troubled with ill-fortune?" Yes. "But go on and
assume that you *are* in a wretched plight." That
is not consistent with the hypothesis; moreover,
there is Another[2] who forbids me so to think.[3]

How long, then, should we obey such commands?
As long as it is beneficial, and that means, as long
as I preserve what is becoming and consistent.
Further, some men are unduly crabbed and have too
sharp tongues and say, "I cannot dine at this
fellow's house, where I have to put up with his
telling every day how he fought in Moesia: 'I have
told you, brother, how I climbed up to the crest of
the hill; well now, I begin to be besieged again.'"
But another says, "I would rather dine and hear
him babble all he pleases." And it is for you to
compare these estimates; only do nothing as one
burdened, or afflicted, or thinking that he is in a
wretched plight; for no one forces you to this.
Has some one made a smoke in the house? If he

really is night, for that is no longer a mere hypothesis, but
the statement of a falsehood. I simply "play the game" as
long as we are dealing with hypotheses, but must "break
up the game" if required to make a false statement about
actual facts.

ἂν μέτριον, μενῶ· ἂν λίαν πολύν, ἐξέρχομαι. τούτου γὰρ μεμνῆσθαι καὶ κρατεῖν, ὅτι ἡ θύρα ἤνοι-
19 κται. ἀλλὰ " μὴ οἴκει ἐν Νικοπόλει." οὐκ οἰκῶ.
" μηδ' ἐν Ἀθήναις." οὐδ' ἐν Ἀθήναις. " μηδ' ἐν
20 Ῥώμῃ." οὐδ' ἐν Ῥώμῃ. " ἐν Γυάροις οἴκει." οἰκῶ.
ἀλλὰ πολύς μοι καπνὸς φαίνεται τὸ ἐν Γυάροις
οἰκεῖν. ἀποχωρῶ, ὅπου μ' οὐδεὶς κωλύσει οἰκεῖν·
21 ἐκείνη γὰρ ἡ οἴκησις παντὶ ἤνοικται. καὶ τὸ τελευταῖον χιτωνάριον, τοῦτ' ἔστι τὸ σωμάτιον, τούτου
22 ἀνωτέρω οὐδενὶ οὐδὲν εἰς ἐμὲ ἔξεστιν. διὰ τοῦτο
ὁ Δημήτριος εἶπεν τῷ Νέρωνι " ἀπειλεῖς μοι
23 θάνατον, σοὶ δ' ἡ φύσις." ἂν δὲ τὸ σωμάτιον
θαυμάσω, δοῦλον ἐμαυτὸν παραδέδωκα· ἂν τὸ
24 κτησείδιον, δοῦλον. εὐθὺς γὰρ αὐτὸς κατ' ἐμαυτοῦ
δηλῶ, τίνι ἁλωτός εἰμι. ὡς ὁ ὄφις ἐὰν συσπᾷ τὴν
κεφαλήν, λέγω " ἐκεῖνο αὐτοῦ τύπτε ὃ φυλάσσει."
καὶ σὺ γίγνωσκε, ὅτι ὃ ἂν φυλάσσειν ἐθέλῃς, κατ'
25 ἐκεῖνο ἐπιβήσεταί σοι ὁ κύριος. τούτων μεμνημένος τίνα ἔτι κολακεύσεις ἢ φοβήσῃ ;

26 Ἀλλὰ θέλω καθῆσθαι ὅπου οἱ συγκλητικοί.—
Ὁρᾷς ὅτι σὺ σαυτῷ στενοχωρίαν παρέχεις, σὺ
27 σαυτὸν θλίβεις ;—Πῶς οὖν ἄλλως θεωρήσω
καλῶς ἐν τῷ ἀμφιθεάτρῳ ;—Ἄνθρωπε, καὶ μὴ
θεώρει καὶ οὐ μὴ θλιβῇς. τί πράγματα ἔχεις ;
ἢ μικρὸν ἔκδεξαι καὶ ἀχθείσης τῆς θεωρίας
κάθισον εἰς τοὺς τῶν συγκλητικῶν τόπους καὶ

---

[1] A small island off Attica in the Aegean, used as a place
of exile during the Empire. The ordinary form is Γύαρος.
[2] He refers to the grave.

has made a moderate amount of smoke I shall stay; if too much, I go outside. For one ought to remember and hold fast to this, that the door stands open. But some one says, "Do not dwell in Nicopolis." I agree not to dwell there. "Nor in Athens." I agree not to dwell in Athens, either. "Nor in Rome." I agree not to dwell in Rome, either. "Dwell in Gyara."[1] I agree to dwell there. But to dwell in Gyara seems to me to be like a great quantity of smoke in the house. I leave for a place where no one will prevent me from dwelling; for that dwelling-place stands open to every man.[2] And as for the last inner tunic, that is, my paltry body, beyond *that* no one has any authority over *me*. That is why Demetrius said to Nero, "You threaten me with death, but nature threatens you." If I admire my paltry body, I have given myself away as a slave; if I admire my paltry property, I have given myself away as a slave; for at once I show thereby to my own hurt what I can be caught with. Just as when the snake draws in his head, I say, "Strike that part of him which he is protecting"; so do you be assured that your master will attack you at that point which you particularly wish to protect. If you remember all this, whom will you flatter or fear any more?

But I wish to sit where the senators do.—Do you realize that you are making close quarters for yourself, that you are crowding yourself?—How else, then, shall I have a good view in the amphitheatre?—Man, do not become spectator and you will not be crowded. Why do you make trouble for yourself? Or else wait a little while, and when the show is over sit down among the seats

28 ἡλιάζου. καθόλου γὰρ ἐκείνου μέμνησο, ὅτι
ἑαυτοὺς θλίβομεν, ἑαυτοὺς στενοχωροῦμεν, τοῦτ'
ἔστιν τὰ δόγματα ἡμᾶς θλίβει καὶ στενοχωρεῖ.

29 ἐπεὶ τί ἐστιν αὐτὸ τὸ λοιδορεῖσθαι; παραστὰς
λίθον λοιδόρει· καὶ τί ποιήσεις; ἂν οὖν τις ὡς
λίθος ἀκούῃ, τί ὄφελος τῷ λοιδοροῦντι; ἂν δ'
ἔχῃ τὴν ἀσθένειαν τοῦ λοιδορουμένου ὁ λοιδορῶν

30 ἐπιβάθραν, τότε ἀνύει. "περίσχισον αὐτόν."
τί λέγεις αὐτόν; τὸ ἱμάτιον λάβε, περίσχισον.

31 "ὕβριν σοι πεποίηκα." καλῶς σοι γένοιτο. ταῦτα ἐμελέτα Σωκράτης, διὰ τοῦτο ἓν ἔχων
πρόσωπον ἀεὶ διετέλει. ἡμεῖς δὲ θέλομεν πάντα
μᾶλλον ἀσκεῖν καὶ μελετᾶν ἢ ὅπως ἀπαραπό-

32 διστοι καὶ ἐλεύθεροι ἐσόμεθα. "παράδοξα λέγουσιν οἱ φιλόσοφοι." ἐν δὲ ταῖς ἄλλαις τέχναις
οὐκ ἔστι παράδοξα; καὶ τί παραδοξότερόν ἐστιν
ἢ κεντεῖν τινος τὸν ὀφθαλμόν, ἵνα ἴδῃ; εἴ τις
ἀπείρῳ τῶν ἰατρικῶν τοῦτο εἶπεν, οὐκ ἂν κατε-

33 γέλα τοῦ λέγοντος; τί οὖν θαυμαστὸν εἰ καὶ ἐν
φιλοσοφίᾳ πολλὰ τῶν ἀληθῶν παράδοξα φαίνεται
τοῖς ἀπείροις;

κϛ'. Τίς ὁ βιωτικὸς νόμος;[1]

1 Ἀναγιγνώσκοντος δὲ τοὺς ὑποθετικοὺς ἔφη·
Νόμος ὑποθετικός ἐστι καὶ οὗτος τὸ ἀκόλουθον
τῇ ὑποθέσει παραδέχεσθαι. πολὺ πρότερον δὲ

---

[1] One of the typical forms of argumentation upon which
the Stoics laid great stress. The subject is treated at
considerable length in I. 7.

of the senators and sun yourself. For in general remember this—that we crowd ourselves, we make close quarters for ourselves, that is to say, the decisions of our will crowd us and make us close quarters. Why, what is this matter of being reviled? Take your stand by a stone and revile it; and what effect will you produce? If, then, a man listens like a stone, what profit is there to the reviler? But if the reviler has the weakness of the reviled as a point of vantage, then he does accomplish something. "Strip him." Why do you say '*him*'? Take his cloak and strip that off. "I have outraged you." Much good may it do you! This is what Socrates practised, and that is why he always wore the same expression on his face. But we prefer to practise and rehearse anything rather than how to be untrammelled and free. "The philosophers talk paradoxes," you say. But are there not paradoxes in the other arts? And what is more paradoxical than to lance a man in the eye in order that he may see? If anyone said this to a man who was inexperienced in the art of surgery, would he not laugh at the speaker? What is there to be surprised at, then, if in philosophy also many things which are true appear paradoxical to the inexperienced?

CHAPTER XXVI

What is the rule of life?

As some one was reading the hypothetical arguments,[1] Epictetus said, This also is a law governing hypotheses—that we must accept what the hypothesis or premiss demands. But much more important is

νόμος βιωτικός ἐστιν οὗτος τὸ ἀκόλουθον τῇ
2 φύσει πράττειν. εἰ γὰρ ἐπὶ πάσης ὕλης καὶ περιστάσεως βουλόμεθα τηρῆσαι τὸ κατὰ φύσιν, δῆλον
ὅτι ἐν παντὶ στοχαστέον τοῦ μήτε τὸ ἀκόλουθον
ἡμᾶς ἐκφυγεῖν μήτε παραδέξασθαι τὸ μαχόμενον.
3 πρῶτον οὖν ἐπὶ τῆς θεωρίας γυμνάζουσιν ἡμᾶς
οἱ φιλόσοφοι ὅπου ῥᾷον, εἶτα οὕτως ἐπὶ τὰ
χαλεπώτερα ἄγουσιν· ἐνταῦθα γὰρ οὐδέν ἐστι τὸ
ἀνθέλκον ὡς πρὸς τὸ ἀκολουθῆσαι τοῖς διδασκο-
μένοις, ἐπὶ δὲ τῶν βιωτικῶν πολλὰ τὰ περισπῶντα.
4 γελοῖος οὖν ὁ λέγων πρῶτον βούλεσθαι ἐπ' ἐκεί-
νων· οὐ γὰρ ῥᾴδιον ἄρχεσθαι ἀπὸ τῶν χαλεπω-
5 τέρων. καὶ τοῦτον ἀπολογισμὸν ἔδει φέρειν πρὸς
τοὺς γονεῖς τοὺς ἀγανακτοῦντας ἐπὶ τῷ φιλοσοφεῖν
τὰ τέκνα. " οὐκοῦν ἁμαρτάνω, πάτερ, καὶ οὐκ οἶδα
τὸ ἐπιβάλλον ἐμαυτῷ καὶ προσῆκον· εἰ μὲν οὐδὲ
μαθητόν ἐστιν οὐδὲ διδακτόν, τί μοι ἐγκαλεῖς;
εἰ δὲ διδακτόν, δίδασκε· εἰ δὲ σὺ μὴ δύνασαι,
ἄφες με μαθεῖν παρὰ τῶν λεγόντων εἰδέναι.
6 ἐπεὶ τί δοκεῖς; ὅτι θέλων περιπίπτω κακῷ καὶ
ἀποτυγχάνω τοῦ ἀγαθοῦ; μὴ γένοιτο. τί οὖν
7 ἐστι τὸ αἴτιον τοῦ ἁμαρτάνειν με; ἡ ἄγνοια. οὐ
θέλεις οὖν ἀποθῶμαι τὴν ἄγνοιαν; τίνα πώποτε
ὀργὴ ἐδίδαξε τὰ κυβερνητικά, τὰ μουσικά; τὰ
βιωτικὰ οὖν διὰ τὴν ὀργήν σου δοκεῖς ὅτι
μαθήσομαι; "
8   Ταῦτα ἐκείνῳ μόνῳ λέγειν ἔξεστι τῷ τοιαύτην
9 ἐπιβολὴν ἐνηνοχότι. εἰ δέ τις μόνον ἐπιδείκνυσθαι θέλων ἐν συμποσίῳ ὅτι οἶδεν τοὺς ὑποθετικοὺς ἀναγιγνώσκει ταῦτα καὶ προσέρχεται

the following law of life—that we must do what nature demands. For if we wish in every matter and circumstance to observe what is in accordance with nature, it is manifest that in everything we should make it our aim neither to avoid that which nature demands, nor to accept that which is in conflict with nature. The philosophers, therefore, exercise us first in the theory where there is less difficulty, and then after that lead us to the more difficult matters; for in theory there is nothing which holds us back from following what we are taught, but in the affairs of life there are many things which draw us away. He is ridiculous, then, who says that he wishes to begin with the latter; for it is not easy to begin with the more difficult things. And this is the defence that we ought to present to such parents as are angry because their children study philosophy. "Very well then, father, I go astray, not knowing what is incumbent upon me or what my duty is. Now if this is a thing that can neither be taught nor learned, why do you reproach me? But if it can be taught, teach me; and if you cannot do this, allow me to learn from those who profess to know. Really, what is your idea? That I intentionally fall into evil and miss the good? Far from it! What, then, is the cause of my going astray? Ignorance. Very well, do you not want me to put away my ignorance? Whom did anger ever teach the art of steering, or music? Do you think, then, that your anger will make me learn the art of living?"

Only he can so speak who has applied himself to philosophy in such a spirit. But if a man reads upon the subject and resorts to the philosophers merely because he wants to make a display at a

τοῖς φιλοσόφοις, οὗτος ἄλλο τι πράσσει ἢ ἵνα
αὐτὸν συγκλητικὸς παρακατακείμενος θαυμάσῃ;
10 ἐκεῖ γὰρ τῷ ὄντι αἱ μεγάλαι ὗλαί εἰσι καὶ οἱ
ἐνθάδε πλοῦτοι ἐκεῖ παίγνια δοκοῦσιν. διὰ τοῦτο ἐκεῖ δύσκολον κρατῆσαι τῶν αὑτοῦ φαντασιῶν,
11 ὅπου τὰ ἐκσείοντα[1] μεγάλα. ἐγώ τινα οἶδα
κλαίοντα Ἐπαφροδίτου τῶν γονάτων ἁπτόμενον
καὶ λέγοντα ταλαιπωρεῖν· ἀπολελεῖφθαι γὰρ
αὐτῷ μηδέν, εἰ μὴ ἑκατὸν πεντήκοντα μυριάδας.
12 τί οὖν ὁ Ἐπαφρόδιτος; κατεγέλασεν ὡς ὑμεῖς;
οὔ· ἀλλ' ἐπιθαυμάσας λέγει "τάλας, πῶς οὖν
ἐσιώπας, πῶς ἐκαρτέρεις;"
13 Ταράξας[2] δὲ τὸν ἀναγιγνώσκοντα τοὺς ὑποθετικοὺς καὶ γελάσαντος τοῦ ὑποθεμένου αὐτῷ τὴν
ἀνάγνωσιν Σεαυτοῦ, ἔφη, καταγελᾷς· οὐ προεγύ-
μνασας τὸν νεανίσκον οὐδ' ἔγνως εἰ δύναται τούτοις παρακολουθεῖν, ἀλλ' ὡς ἀναγνώστῃ αὐτῷ
14 χρῇ.[3] τί οὖν, ἔφη, μὴ[4] δυναμένῃ διανοίᾳ συμπεπλεγμένου ἐπικρίσει παρακολουθεῖν ἔπαινον
πιστεύομεν, ψόγον πιστεύομεν, ἐπίκρισιν περὶ
τῶν καλῶς ἢ κακῶς γινομένων; κἄν τινα κακῶς
λέγῃ, οὗτος ἐπιστρέφεται, κἂν ἐπαινῇ τινα, ἐπαί-
ρεται· ἐν τοῖς οὕτως μικροῖς μὴ εὑρίσκων τὸ
15 ἑξῆς; αὕτη οὖν ἀρχὴ τοῦ φιλοσοφεῖν, αἴσθησις
τοῦ ἰδίου ἡγεμονικοῦ πῶς ἔχει· μετὰ γὰρ τὸ

---

[1] Schweighäuser: ἐκεῖ ὄντα S.   [2] Schenkl: . . ράξας S.
[3] Upton: χρᾷ S.   [4] Schweighäuser: τῆι S.

---

[1] *i.e.*, in the simple life of Nicopolis it is easy to use philosophic doctrines to live by; in Rome the temptation is strong
to use them for achieving social distinction.
[2] That is, the reason; compare note on I. 15, 4.

banquet of his knowledge of hypothetical arguments, what else is he doing but trying to win the admiration of some senator sitting by his side? For there in Rome are found in truth the great resources, while the riches of Nicopolis look to them like mere child's-play.[1] Hence it is difficult there for a man to control his own external impressions, since the distracting influences at Rome are great. I know a certain man who clung in tears to the knees of Epaphroditus and said that he was in misery; for he had nothing left but a million and a half sesterces. What, then, did Epaphroditus do? Did he laugh at him as you are laughing? No; he only said, in a tone of amazement, "Poor man, how, then, *did* you manage to keep silence? How *did* you endure it?"

Once when he had disconcerted the student who was reading the hypothetical arguments, and the one who had set the other the passage to read laughed at him, Epictetus said to the latter, "You are laughing at yourself. You did not give the young man a preliminary training, nor discover whether he was able to follow these arguments, but you treat him merely as a reader. Why is it, then," he added, "that to a mind unable to follow a judgement upon a complex argument we entrust the assigning of praise or blame, or the passing of a judgement upon what is done well or ill? If such a person speaks ill of another, does the man in question pay any attention to him, or if he praises another, is the latter elated? when the one who is dispensing praise or blame is unable, in matters as trivial as these, to find the logical consequence? This, then, is a starting point in philosophy—a perception of the state of one's own governing principle[2]; for when once a man realizes

γνῶναι ὅτι ἀσθενῶς οὐκ ἔτι θελήσει χρῆσθαι
16 αὐτῷ πρὸς τὰ μεγάλα. νῦν δὲ μὴ δυνάμενοί
τινες τὸν ψωμὸν καταπίνειν σύνταξιν ἀγορά-
σαντες ἐπιβάλλονται ἐσθίειν. διὰ τοῦτο ἐμοῦσιν
ἢ ἀπεπτοῦσιν· εἶτα στρόφοι καὶ κατάρροιαι καὶ
17 πυρετοί. ἔδει δ' ἐφιστάνειν, εἰ δύνανται. ἀλλ'
ἐν μὲν θεωρίᾳ ῥᾴδιον ἐξελέγξαι τὸν οὐκ εἰδότα,
ἐν δὲ τοῖς κατὰ τὸν βίον οὔτε παρέχει ἑαυτόν
18 τις ἐλέγχῳ τόν τ' ἐξελέγξαντα μισοῦμεν. ὁ δὲ
Σωκράτης ἔλεγεν ἀνεξέταστον βίον μὴ ζῆν.

κζ΄. Ποσαχῶς αἱ φαντασίαι γίνονται καὶ τίνα
πρόχειρα πρὸς αὐτὰς[1] βοηθήματα παρα-
σκευαστέον;

1 Τετραχῶς αἱ φαντασίαι γίνονται ἡμῖν· ἢ γὰρ
ἔστι τινὰ καὶ οὕτως φαίνεται ἢ οὐκ ὄντα οὐδὲ φαίνεται ὅτι ἔστιν ἢ ἔστι καὶ οὐ φαίνεται ἢ οὐκ ἔστι
2 καὶ φαίνεται. λοιπὸν ἐν πᾶσι τούτοις εὐστοχεῖν
ἔργον ἐστὶ τοῦ πεπαιδευμένου. ὅ τι δ' ἂν ᾖ τὸ
θλῖβον, ἐκείνῳ δεῖ προσάγειν τὴν βοήθειαν. εἰ
σοφίσματα ἡμᾶς Πυρρώνεια καὶ Ἀκαδημαικὰ
τὰ θλίβοντά ἐστιν, ἐκείνοις προσάγωμεν τὴν
3 βοήθειαν· εἰ αἱ τῶν πραγμάτων πιθανότητες,
καθ' ἃς φαίνεταί τινα ἀγαθὰ οὐκ ὄντα, ἐκεῖ τὴν
βοήθειαν ζητῶμεν· εἰ ἔθος ἐστὶ τὸ θλῖβον, πρὸς

---

[1] Meibom (after Wolf): αὐτὰ S.

[1] cf. Plato, Apology, 38 A: ὁ δὲ ἀνεξέταστος βίος οὐ βιωτὸς
ἀνθρώπῳ.

that it is weak, he will no longer wish to employ it upon great matters. But as it is, some who are unable to swallow the morsel buy a whole treatise and set to work to eat that. Consequently they throw up, or have indigestion; after that come colics and fluxes and fevers. But they ought first to have considered whether they have the requisite capacity. However, in a matter of theory it is easy enough to confute the man who does not know, but in the affairs of life a man does not submit himself to confutation, and we hate the person who has confuted us. But Socrates used to tell us not to live a life unsubjected to examination.[1]

CHAPTER XXVII.

In how many ways do the external impressions arise, and what aids should we have ready at hand to deal with them?

THE external impressions come to us in four ways; for either things are, and seem so to be; or they are not, and do not seem to be, either; or they are, and do not seem to be; or they are not, and yet seem to be. Consequently, in all these cases it is the business of the educated man to hit the mark. But whatever be the thing that distresses us, against that we ought to bring up our reinforcements. If the things that distress us are sophisms of Pyrrho and the Academy, let us bring up our reinforcements against them; if they are the plausibilities of things, whereby we are led to think that certain things are good when they are not, let us seek reinforcements at that point; if the thing that distresses us is a habit,

4 ἐκεῖνο τὴν βοήθειαν ἀνευρίσκειν πειρατέον. τί
οὖν πρὸς ἔθος ἔστιν εὑρίσκειν βοήθημα; τὸ
5 ἐναντίον ἔθος. ἀκούεις τῶν ἰδιωτῶν λεγόντων
"τάλας ἐκεῖνος, ἀπέθανεν· ἀπώλετο ὁ πατὴρ
αὐτοῦ, ἡ μήτηρ· ἐξεκόπη, ἀλλὰ καὶ ἄωρος καὶ
6 ἐπὶ ξένης." ἄκουσον τῶν ἐναντίων λόγων, ἀπόσπασον σεαυτὸν τούτων τῶν φωνῶν, ἀντίθες τῷ
ἔθει τὸ ἐναντίον ἔθος. πρὸς τοὺς σοφιστικοὺς
λόγους τὰ λογικὰ καὶ τὴν ἐν τούτοις γυμνασίαν
καὶ τριβήν, πρὸς τὰς τῶν πραγμάτων πιθανό-
τητας τὰς προλήψεις ἐναργεῖς ἐσμηγμένας καὶ
προχείρους ἔχειν δεῖ.

7 Ὅταν θάνατος φαίνηται κακόν,[1] πρόχειρον
ἔχειν ὅτι τὰ κακὰ ἐκκλίνειν καθήκει καὶ ἀν-
8 αγκαῖον ὁ θάνατος. τί γὰρ ποιήσω; ποῦ γὰρ
αὐτὸν φύγω; ἔστω ἐμὲ εἶναι Σαρπηδόνα τὸν
τοῦ Διός, ἵν' οὕτως γενναίως εἴπω "ἀπελθὼν
ἢ αὐτὸς ἀριστεῦσαι θέλω ἢ ἄλλῳ παρασχεῖν
ἀφορμὴν τοῦ ἀριστεῦσαι· εἰ μὴ δύναμαι κατορ-
θῶσαί τι αὐτός, οὐ φθονήσω ἄλλῳ τοῦ ποιῆσαί
τι γενναῖον." ἔστω ταῦτα ὑπὲρ ἡμᾶς, ἐκεῖνο οὐ
9 πίπτει εἰς ἡμᾶς; καὶ ποῦ φύγω τὸν θάνατον;
μηνύσατέ μοι τὴν χώραν, μηνύσατε ἀνθρώπους,
εἰς οὓς ἀπέλθω, εἰς οὓς οὐ παραβάλλει, μηνύσατε

---

¹ Meibom (after Wolf): καλὸν S.

---

[1] And therefore not an evil.
[2] A paraphrase of Homer, *Iliad*, XII. 328.

we should try to hunt up the reinforcements with
which to oppose that. What reinforcements, then,
is it possible to find with which to oppose habit?
Why, the contrary habit. You hear the common
folk saying, "That poor man! He is dead; his
father perished, and his mother; he was cut off, yes,
and before his time, and in a foreign land." Listen
to the arguments on the other side, tear yourself
away from these expressions, set over against one
habit the contrary habit. To meet sophistic arguments we must have the processes of logic and the
exercise and the familiarity with these; against the
plausibilities of things we must have our preconceptions clear, polished like weapons, and ready at
hand.

When death appears to be an evil, we must have
ready at hand the argument that it is our duty to
avoid evils, and that death is an inevitable thing.[1]
For what can I do? Where shall I go to escape
it? Suppose that I am Sarpedon the son of Zeus,
in order that I may nobly say, as he did: "Seeing
that I have left my home for the war, I wish either
to win the prize of valour myself, or else to give
someone else the chance to win it; if I am unable
to succeed in something myself, I shall not begrudge
another the achievement of some noble deed."[2]
Granted that such an act as Sarpedon's is beyond us,
does not the other alternative fall within the
compass of our powers?[3] And where can I go to
escape death? Show me the country, show me the
people to whom I may go, upon whom death does
not come; show me a magic charm against it. If

[3] *i.e.*, if we cannot act as nobly as Sarpedon, we can
at least think rationally about death, counting it no evil.

ἐπαοιδήν· εἰ μὴ ἔχω, τί με θέλετε ποιεῖν; οὐ
10 δύναμαι τὸν θάνατον ἀποφυγεῖν· τὸ φοβεῖσθαι
αὐτὸν μὴ ἀποφύγω, ἀλλ᾽ ἀποθάνω πενθῶν καὶ
τρέμων ; αὕτη γὰρ γένεσις πάθους θέλειν τι καὶ
11 μὴ γίνεσθαι. ἔνθεν ἂν μὲν δύνωμαι τὰ ἐκτὸς
μετατιθέναι πρὸς τὴν βούλησιν τὴν ἐμαυτοῦ,
μετατίθημι· εἰ δὲ μή, τὸν ἐμποδίζοντα ἐκτυ-
12 φλῶσαι θέλω. πέφυκε γὰρ ὁ ἄνθρωπος μὴ ὑπομένειν ἀφαιρεῖσθαι τοῦ ἀγαθοῦ, μὴ ὑπομένειν
13 περιπίπτειν τῷ κακῷ. εἶτα τὸ τελευταῖον, ὅταν
μήτε τὰ πράγματα μεταθεῖναι δυνηθῶ μήτε τὸν
ἐμποδίζοντα ἐκτυφλῶσαι, κάθημαι καὶ στένω καὶ
ὃν δύναμαι λοιδορῶ, τὸν Δία καὶ τοὺς θεοὺς τοὺς
ἄλλους· εἰ γὰρ μὴ ἐπιστρέφονταί μου, τί ἐμοὶ καὶ
14 αὐτοῖς ; "ναί· ἀλλ᾽ ἀσεβὴς ἔσῃ." τί οὖν μοι
χεῖρον ἔσται, ὧν ἔστι μοι νῦν ; τὸ σύνολον
ἐκείνου μεμνῆσθαι, ὅτι, ἐὰν μὴ ἐν τῷ αὐτῷ ᾖ τὸ
εὐσεβὲς καὶ συμφέρον, οὐ δύναται σωθῆναι τὸ
εὐσεβὲς ἔν τινι. ταῦτα οὐ δοκεῖ ἐπείγοντα ;
15 Ἐρχέσθω καὶ ἀπαντάτω Πυρρώνειος καὶ Ἀκα-
δημαικός. ἐγὼ μὲν γὰρ τὸ ἐμὸν μέρος οὐκ ἄγω
σχολὴν πρὸς ταῦτα οὐδὲ δύναμαι συνηγορῆσαι
16 τῇ συνηθείᾳ. εἰ καὶ περὶ ἀγριδίου πραγμάτιον
εἶχον, ἄλλον ἂν παρεκάλεσα τὸν συνηγορήσοντα.
17 τίνι οὖν ἀρκοῦμαι ; τῷ κατὰ τὸν τόπον. πῶς
μὲν αἴσθησις γίνεται, πότερον δι᾽ ὅλων ἢ ἀπὸ
μέρους, ἴσως οὐκ οἶδα ἀπολογίσασθαι, ταράσσει
δέ με ἀμφότερα. ὅτι δ᾽ ἐγὼ καὶ σὺ οὐκ ἐσμὲν οἱ
18 αὐτοί, λίαν ἀκριβῶς οἶδα. πόθεν τοῦτο ; οὐδέ-

174

I have none, what do you wish me to do? I cannot avoid death. Instead of avoiding the fear of it, shall I die in lamentation and trembling? For the origin of sorrow is this—to wish for something that does not come to pass. Therefore, if I can change externals according to my own wish, I change them; but if I cannot, I am ready to tear out the eyes of the man who stands in my way. For it is man's nature not to endure to be deprived of the good, not to endure to fall into the evil. Then, finally, when I can neither change the circumstances, nor tear out the eyes of the man who stands in my way, I sit down and groan, and revile whom I can—Zeus and the rest of the gods; for if they do not care for me, what are they to me? "Yes," you say, "but that will be impious of you." What, then, shall I get that is worse than what I have now? In short, we must remember this—that unless piety and self-interest be conjoined, piety cannot be maintained in any man. Do not these considerations seem urgent?

Let the follower of Pyrrho or of the Academy come and oppose us. Indeed I, for my part, have no leisure for such matters, nor can I act as advocate to the commonly received opinion. If I had a petty suit about a mere bit of land, I should have called in some one else to be my advocate. With what evidence, then, am I satisfied? With that which belongs to the matter in hand. To the question how perception arises, whether through the whole body, or from some particular part, perhaps I do not know how to give a reasonable answer, and both views perplex me. But that you and I are not the same persons, I know very certainly. Whence do I get this knowledge? When I want to swallow

ποτε καταπίνειν τι θέλων ἐκεῖ φέρω τὸν ψωμόν,
ἀλλ᾽ ὧδε· οὐδέποτ᾽ ἄρτον θέλων λαβεῖν τὸ σάρον
ἔλαβον, ἀλλ᾽ ἀεὶ ἐπὶ τὸν ἄρτον ἔρχομαι ὡς πρὸς
19 σκοπόν.[1] ὑμεῖς δ᾽ αὐτοὶ οἱ τὰς αἰσθήσεις ἀναιροῦντες ἄλλο τι ποιεῖτε ; τίς ὑμῶν εἰς βαλανεῖον
20 ἀπελθεῖν θέλων εἰς μυλῶνα ἀπῆλθεν ;—Τί οὖν ;
οὐ δεῖ κατὰ δύναμιν καὶ τούτων ἀντέχεσθαι, τοῦ
τηρῆσαι τὴν συνήθειαν, τοῦ πεφράχθαι πρὸς τὰ
21 κατ᾽ αὐτῆς ;—Καὶ τίς ἀντιλέγει ; ἀλλὰ τὸν
δυνάμενον, τὸν σχολάζοντα· τὸν δὲ τρέμοντα καὶ
ταρασσόμενον καὶ ῥηγνύμενον ἔσωθεν τὴν καρδίαν
ἄλλῳ τινὶ δεῖ προσευκαιρεῖν.

κη΄. Ὅτι οὐ δεῖ χαλεπαίνειν ἀνθρώποις, καὶ
τίνα τὰ μικρὰ καὶ μεγάλα ἐν ἀνθρώποις ;

1 Τί ἐστιν αἴτιον τοῦ συγκατατίθεσθαί τινι ; τὸ
2 φαίνεσθαι ὅτι ὑπάρχει. τῷ οὖν φαινομένῳ ὅτι
οὐχ ὑπάρχει συγκατατίθεσθαι οὐχ οἷόν τε. διὰ
τί ; ὅτι ἡ φύσις αὕτη[2] ἐστὶ τῆς διανοίας, τοῖς
μὲν ἀληθέσιν ἐπινεύειν, τοῖς δὲ ψευδέσι δυσαρε-
3 στεῖν, πρὸς δὲ τὰ ἄδηλα ἐπέχειν. τίς τούτου
πίστις ; "πάθε, εἰ δύνασαι, νῦν ὅτι νύξ ἐστιν."
οὐχ οἷόν τε. "ἀπόπαθε ὅτι ἡμέρα ἐστίν." οὐχ
οἷόν τε. "πάθε ἢ ἀπόπαθε ἀπὸ τοῦ ἀρτίους
4 εἶναι τοὺς ἀστέρας." οὐχ οἷόν τε. ὅταν οὖν τις

---

[1] Schweighäuser : προκόπτων S.   [2] Wolf : αὐτ* S.

---

[1] The accompanying gesture explained the allusion, which
was probably to the eye and the mouth, as in II. 20, 28.
A Cynic like Diogenes would very likely have illustrated
his point in a somewhat coarser fashion; and this is not
impossible in the present instance.
[2] The Pyrrhonists, or Sceptics.

something, I never take the morsel to that place
but to this¹; when I wish to take bread I never
take sweepings, but I always go after the bread as to
a mark. And do you yourselves,² who take away
the evidence of the senses, do anything else? Who
among you when he wishes to go to a bath goes to
a mill instead?—What then? Ought we not to the
best of our ability hold fast also to this—maintain,
that is, the commonly received opinion, and be
on our guard against the arguments that seek to
overthrow it?—And who disputes that? But only
the man who has the power and the leisure should
devote himself to these studies; while the man who
is trembling and perplexed and whose heart is
broken within him, ought to devote his leisure to
something else.

CHAPTER XXVIII

*That we ought not to be angry with men; and what are
the little things and the great among men?*

WHAT is the reason that we assent to anything?
The fact that it appears to us to be so. It is
impossible, therefore, to assent to the thing that
appears not to be so. Why? Because this is the
nature of the intellect—to agree to what is true, to
be dissatisfied with what is false, and to withhold
judgement regarding what is uncertain. What is
the proof of this? "Feel, if you can, that it is now
night." That is impossible. "Put away the feeling
that it is day." That is impossible. "Either feel
or put away the feeling that the stars are even
in number." That is impossible. When, therefore,

συγκατατίθεται τῷ ψεύδει, ἴσθι ὅτι οὐκ ἤθελεν
ψεύδει συγκαταθέσθαι· πᾶσα γὰρ ψυχὴ ἄκουσα
5 στέρεται τῆς ἀληθείας, ὡς λέγει Πλάτων· ἀλλὰ
ἔδοξεν αὐτῷ τὸ ψεῦδος ἀληθές. ἄγε ἐπὶ δὲ τῶν
πράξεων τί ἔχομεν τοιοῦτον οἷον ἐνθάδε τὸ
ἀληθὲς ἢ τὸ ψεῦδος ; τὸ καθῆκον καὶ παρὰ τὸ
καθῆκον, τὸ συμφέρον καὶ τὸ ἀσύμφορον, τὸ κατ'
6 ἐμὲ καὶ οὐ κατ' ἐμὲ καὶ ὅσα τούτοις ὅμοια. " οὐ
δύναται οὖν τις δοκεῖν μέν, ὅτι συμφέρει αὐτῷ,
7 μὴ αἱρεῖσθαι δ' αὐτό ; " οὐ δύναται. πῶς ἡ
λέγουσα

καὶ μανθάνω μὲν οἷα δρᾶν μέλλω κακά,
θυμὸς δὲ κρείσσων τῶν ἐμῶν βουλευμάτων ;

ὅτι αὐτὸ τοῦτο, τῷ θυμῷ χαρίσασθαι καὶ
τιμωρήσασθαι τὸν ἄνδρα, συμφορώτερον ἡγεῖται
8 τοῦ σῶσαι τὰ τέκνα. " ναί· ἀλλ' ἐξηπάτηται."
δεῖξον αὐτῇ ἐναργῶς ὅτι ἐξηπάτηται καὶ οὐ
ποιήσει· μέχρι δ' ἂν οὐ μὴ δεικνύῃς, τίνι ἔχει
9 ἀκολουθῆσαι ἢ τῷ φαινομένῳ ; οὐδενί. τί οὖν
χαλεπαίνεις αὐτῇ, ὅτι πεπλάνηται ἡ ταλαίπωρος
περὶ τῶν μεγίστων καὶ ἔχις ἀντὶ ἀνθρώπου γέγονεν ; οὐχὶ δ', εἴπερ ἄρα, μᾶλλον ἐλεεῖς, ὡς
τοὺς τυφλοὺς ἐλεοῦμεν, ὡς τοὺς χωλούς, οὕτως
τοὺς τὰ κυριώτατα τετυφλωμένους καὶ ἀποκεχω-
λωμένους ;
10 Ὅστις οὖν τούτου μέμνηται καθαρῶς ὅτι
ἀνθρώπῳ μέτρον πάσης πράξεως τὸ φαινόμενον
(λοιπὸν ἢ καλῶς φαίνεται ἢ κακῶς· εἰ καλῶς,

---

[1] A rather free paraphrase of Plato, *Sophistes*, 228 c.
[2] Euripides, *Medea*, 1078-1079 ; translated by Way.

a man assents to a falsehood, rest assured that it was not his wish to assent to it as false; "for every soul is unwillingly deprived of the truth," as Plato says[1]; it only seemed to him that the false was true. Well now, in the sphere of actions what have we corresponding to the true and the false here in the sphere of perceptions? Duty and what is contrary to duty, the profitable and the unprofitable, that which is appropriate to me and that which is not appropriate to me, and whatever is similar to these. "Cannot a man, then, think that something is profitable to him, and yet not choose it?" He cannot. How of her who says,

> Now, now, I learn what horrors I intend:
> But passion overmastereth sober thought?[2]

It is because the very gratification of her passion and the taking of vengeance on her husband she regards as more profitable than the saving of her children. "Yes, but she is deceived." Show her clearly that she is deceived, and she will not do it; but so long as you do not show it, what else has she to follow but that which appears to her to be true? Nothing. Why, then, are you angry with her, because the poor woman has gone astray in the greatest matters, and has been transformed from a human being into a viper? Why do you not, if anything, rather pity her? As we pity the blind and the halt, why do we not pity those who have been made blind and halt in their governing faculties?

Whoever, then, bears this clearly in mind, that the measure of man's every action is the impression of his senses (now this impression may be formed

ἀνέγκλητός ἐστιν· εἰ κακῶς, αὐτὸς ἐζημίωται·
οὐ δύναται γὰρ ἄλλος μὲν εἶναι ὁ πεπλανημένος,
ἄλλος δ' ὁ βλαπτόμενος), οὐδενὶ ὀργισθήσεται,
οὐδενὶ χαλεπανεῖ, οὐδένα λοιδορήσει, οὐδένα
μέμψεται, οὐ μισήσει, οὐ προσκόψει οὐδενί.
11 ὥστε καὶ τὰ οὕτω μεγάλα καὶ δεινὰ ἔργα ταύτην
ἔχει τὴν ἀρχήν, τὸ φαινόμενον; ταύτην οὐδ'
12 ἄλλην. ἡ Ἰλιὰς οὐδέν ἐστιν ἢ φαντασία καὶ
χρῆσις φαντασιῶν. ἐφάνη τῷ Ἀλεξάνδρῳ ἀπά-
γειν τοῦ Μενελάου τὴν γυναῖκα, ἐφάνη τῇ
13 Ἑλένῃ ἀκολουθῆσαι αὐτῷ. εἰ οὖν ἐφάνη τῷ
Μενελάῳ παθεῖν ὅτι κέρδος ἐστὶ τοιαύτης γυναικὸς στερηθῆναι, τ ἂν ἐγένετο; ἀπολώλει ἡ
14 Ἰλιὰς οὐ μόνον ἀλλὰ καὶ ἡ Ὀδύσσεια.—Ἐκ
τοιούτου οὖν μικροῦ πράγματος ἤρτηται τὰ
τηλικαῦτα;—Τίνα δὲ καὶ λέγεις τὰ τηλικαῦτα;
πολέμους καὶ στάσεις καὶ ἀπωλείας πολλῶν
ἀνθρώπων καὶ κατασκαφὰς πόλεων; καὶ τί μέγα
15 ἔχει ταῦτα;—Οὐδέν;—Τί δ' ἔχει μέγα πολλοὺς
βοῦς ἀποθανεῖν καὶ πολλὰ πρόβατα καὶ πολλὰς
καλιὰς χελιδόνων ἢ πελαργῶν ἐμπρησθῆναι καὶ
16 κατασκαφῆναι;—Ὅμοια οὖν ἐστι ταῦτα ἐκείνοις;—Ὁμοιότατα. σώματα ἀπώλετο ἀνθρώ-
πων· καὶ βοῶν καὶ προβάτων. οἰκημάτια
17 ἐνεπρήσθη ἀνθρώπων· καὶ πελαργῶν νεοσσιαί.
τί μέγα ἢ δεινόν; ἢ δεῖξόν μοι τί διαφέρει οἰκία

---

[1] *i.e.*, not merely does suffering always follow error, but
it is also morally unthinkable that one man's error can cause
another "suffering," in the Stoic sense; or, in other words,
no man can be injured (as Socrates believed; *cf.* I. 29, 18)
or made to "suffer" except by his own act (*cf.* § 23). It is
this fundamental moral postulate of the Stoics which led
them to classify so many of the ills of life which one person

rightly or wrongly; if rightly, the man is blameless; if wrongly, the man himself pays the penalty; for it is impossible that the man who has gone astray, is one person, while the man who suffers is another [1]),— whoever remembers this, I say, will not be enraged at anyone, will not be angry with anyone, will not revile anyone, will not blame, nor hate, nor take offence at anyone. So you conclude that such great and terrible things have their origin in this—the impression of one's senses? In this and nothing else. The *Iliad* is nothing but a sense-impression and a poet's use of sense-impressions. There came to Alexander an impression to carry off the wife of Menelaus, and an impression came to Helen to follow him. Now if an impression had led Menelaus to feel that it was a gain to be deprived of such a wife, what would have happened? We should have lost not merely the *Iliad*, but the *Odyssey* as well.— Then do matters of such great import depend upon one that is so small?—But what do you mean by "matters of such great import"? Wars and factions and deaths of many men and destructions of cities? And what is there great in all this?—What, nothing great in this?—Why, what is there great in the death of many oxen and many sheep and the burning and destruction of many nests of swallows or storks?—Is there any similarity between this and that?—A great similarity. Men's bodies perished in the one case, and bodies of oxen and sheep in the other. Petty dwellings of men were burned, and so were nests of storks. What is there great or dreadful about that? Or else show me in what

does actually cause to another as not real evils (*cf.* §§ 26–8), but ἀδιάφορα, "things indifferent." *cf.* I. 9, 13 ; I. 30, 2, etc.

ἀνθρώπου καὶ νεοσσιὰ πελαργοῦ ὡς οἴκησις.—

18 Ὅμοιον οὖν ἐστι πελαργὸς καὶ ἄνθρωπος ;—Τί
λέγεις ; κατὰ τὸ σῶμα ὁμοιότατον· πλὴν ὅτι μὲν
ἐκ δοκῶν καὶ κεραμίδων καὶ πλίνθων οἰκοδομεῖται
τὰ οἰκίδια, ἡ δ' ἐκ ῥάβδων καὶ πηλοῦ.

19 Οὐδενὶ οὖν διαφέρει ἄνθρωπος πελαργοῦ ;—
Μὴ γένοιτο· ἀλλὰ τούτοις οὐ διαφέρει.—Τίνι

20 οὖν διαφέρει ;—Ζήτει καὶ εὑρήσεις, ὅτι ἄλλῳ
διαφέρει. ὅρα μὴ τῷ παρακολουθεῖν οἷς ποιεῖ,
ὅρα μὴ τῷ κοινωνικῷ, μὴ τῷ πιστῷ, τῷ αἰδήμονι,

21 τῷ ἀσφαλεῖ, τῷ συνετῷ. ποῦ οὖν τὸ μέγα ἐν
ἀνθρώποις κακὸν καὶ ἀγαθόν ; ὅπου ἡ διαφορά.
ἂν σῴζηται τοῦτο καὶ περιτετειχισμένον μένῃ
καὶ μὴ διαφθείρηται τὸ αἰδῆμον μηδὲ τὸ πιστὸν
μηδὲ τὸ συνετόν, τότε σῴζεται καὶ αὐτός· ἂν δ'
ἀπολλύηταί τι τούτων καὶ ἐκπολιορκῆται, τότε

22 καὶ αὐτὸς ἀπόλλυται. καὶ τὰ μεγάλα πράγματα ἐν τούτῳ ἐστίν. ἔπταισεν μεγάλα ὁ Ἀλέξανδρος, ὅτ' ἐπῆλθον ναυσὶν[1] οἱ Ἕλληνες καὶ
ὅτε ἐπόρθουν τὴν Τροίαν καὶ ὅτε οἱ ἀδελφοὶ

23 αὐτοῦ ἀπώλλυντο ; οὐδαμῶς· δι' ἀλλότριον γὰρ
ἔργον πταίει οὐδείς· ἀλλὰ τότε πελαργῶν νεοσ-
σιαὶ ἐπορθοῦντο. πταῖσμα δ' ἦν, ὅτε ἀπώλεσε
τὸν αἰδήμονα, τὸν πιστόν, τὸν φιλόξενον, τὸν κό-

24 σμιον. πότ' ἔπταισεν ὁ Ἀχιλλεύς ; ὅτε ἀπέθανεν

---

[1] C. Schenkl: ἐπῆλθ* φασιν S.

respect a man's house and a stork's nest differ as a place of habitation.—Is there any similarity between a stork and a man?—What is that you say? As far as the body is concerned, a great similarity; except that the petty houses of men are made of beams and tiles and bricks, but the nest of a stork is made of sticks and clay.

Does a man, then, differ in no wise from a stork? —Far from it; but in these matters he does not differ.—In what wise, then, does he differ?—Seek and you will find that he differs in some other respect. See whether it be not in his understanding what he does, see whether it be not in his capacity for social action, in his faithfulness, his self-respect, his steadfastness, his security from error, his intelligence. Where, then, is the great evil and the great good among men? Just where the difference is; and if that element wherein the difference lies be preserved and stands firm and well fortified on every side, and neither his self-respect, nor his faithfulness, nor his intelligence be destroyed, then the man also is preserved; but if any of these qualities be destroyed or taken by storm, then the man also is destroyed. And it is in this sphere that the great things are. Did Alexander come to his great fall when the Hellenes assailed Troy with their ships, and when they were devastating the land, and when his brothers were dying? Not at all; for no one comes to his fall because of another's deed; but what went on then was merely the destruction of storks' nests. Nay, he came to his fall when he lost his self-respect, his faithfulness, his respect for the laws of hospitality, his decency of behaviour. When did Achilles come to his fall?

ὁ Πάτροκλος ; μὴ γένοιτο· ἀλλ' ὅτε ὠργίζετο, ὅτε
κορασίδιον ἔκλαεν, ὅτ' ἐπελάθετο ὅτι πάρεστιν
οὐκ ἐπὶ τὸ ἐρωμένας κτᾶσθαι, ἀλλ' ἐπὶ τὸ πολε-
25 μεῖν. ταῦτ' ἐστὶ τὰ ἀνθρωπικὰ πταίσματα, τοῦτό
ἐστιν ἡ πολιορκία, τοῦτό ἐστι κατασκαφή, ὅταν
τὰ δόγματα τὰ ὀρθὰ καθαιρῆται, ὅταν ἐκεῖνα
26 διαφθείρηται.—Ὅταν οὖν γυναῖκες ἄγωνται καὶ
παιδία αἰχμαλωτίζηται καὶ ὅταν αὐτοὶ κατασφά-
27 ζωνται, ταῦτα οὐκ ἔστι κακά ;—Πόθεν τοῦτο
προσδοξάζεις ; κἀμὲ δίδαξον.—Οὔ· ἀλλὰ πόθεν
28 σὺ λέγεις ὅτι οὐκ ἔστι κακά ;—Ἔλθωμεν ἐπὶ
τοὺς κανόνας, φέρε τὰς προλήψεις.

Διὰ τοῦτο γὰρ οὐκ ἔστιν ἱκανῶς θαυμάσαι τὸ
γινόμενον. ὅπου βάρη κρῖναι θέλομεν, οὐκ εἰκῇ
29 κρίνομεν· ὅπου τὰ εὐθέα καὶ στρεβλά, οὐκ εἰκῇ.
ἁπλῶς ὅπου διαφέρει ἡμῖν γνῶναι τὸ κατὰ τὸν
τόπον ἀληθές, οὐδέποθ' ἡμῶν οὐδεὶς οὐδὲν εἰκῇ
30 ποιήσει. ὅπου δὲ τὸ πρῶτον καὶ μόνον αἴτιόν
ἐστι τοῦ κατορθοῦν ἢ ἁμαρτάνειν, τοῦ εὐροεῖν ἢ
δυσροεῖν, τοῦ ἀτυχεῖν ἢ εὐτυχεῖν, ἐνθάδε μόνον
εἰκαῖοι καὶ προπετεῖς. οὐδαμοῦ ὅμοιόν τι ζυγῷ,
οὐδαμοῦ ὅμοιόν τι κανόνι, ἀλλά τι ἐφάνη καὶ
31 εὐθὺς ποιῶ τὸ φανέν. κρείσσων γάρ εἰμι τοῦ
Ἀγαμέμνονος ἢ τοῦ Ἀχιλλέως, ἵν' ἐκεῖνοι μὲν
διὰ τὸ ἀκολουθῆσαι τοῖς φαινομένοις τοιαῦτα
κακὰ ποιήσωσι καὶ πάθωσιν, ἐμοὶ δὲ ἀρκῇ[1] τὸ

[1] μὴ before ἀρκῇ deleted by Schweighäuser.

When Patroclus died? Far from it; but when Achilles himself was enraged, when he was crying about a paltry damsel, when he forgot that he was there, not to get sweethearts, but to make war. These are the falls that come to mankind, this is the siege of their city, this is the razing of it—when their correct judgements are torn down, when these are destroyed.—Then when women are driven off into captivity, and children are enslaved, and when the men themselves are slaughtered, are not all these things evils?—Where do you get the justification for adding this opinion? Let me know also.—No, on the contrary, do *you* let *me* know where you get the justification for saying that they are not evils?—Let us turn to our standards, produce your preconceptions.

For this is why I cannot be sufficiently astonished at what men do. In a case where we wish to judge of weights, we do not judge at haphazard; where we wish to judge what is straight and what is crooked, we do not judge at haphazard; in short, where it makes any difference to us to know the truth in the case, no one of us will do anything at haphazard. Yet where there is involved the first and only cause of acting aright or erring, of prosperity or adversity, of failure or success, there alone are we haphazard and headlong. There I have nothing like a balance, there nothing like a standard, but some sense-impression comes and immediately I go and act upon it. What, am I any better than Agamemnon or Achilles—are they because of following the impressions of their senses to do and suffer such evils, while I am to be satisfied with the impression of my senses? And

32 φαινόμενον; καὶ ποία τραγῳδία ἄλλην ἀρχὴν
ἔχει; Ἀτρεὺς Εὐριπίδου τί ἐστιν; τὸ φαινόμενον. Οἰδίπους Σοφοκλέους τί ἐστιν; τὸ φαινό-
33 μενον. Φοῖνιξ; τὸ φαινόμενον. Ἱππόλυτος;
τὸ φαινόμενον. τούτου οὖν μηδεμίαν ἐπιμέλειαν
ποιεῖσθαι τίνος ὑμῖν δοκεῖ; τίνες δὲ λέγονται οἱ
παντὶ τῷ φαινομένῳ ἀκολουθοῦντες;—Μαινό-
μενοι.—Ἡμεῖς οὖν ἄλλο τι ποιοῦμεν;

κθ′. Περὶ εὐσταθείας

1 Οὐσία τοῦ ἀγαθοῦ προαίρεσις ποιά, τοῦ κακοῦ
2 προαίρεσις ποιά. τί οὖν τὰ ἐκτός; ὗλαι τῇ
προαιρέσει, περὶ ἃς ἀναστρεφομένη τεύξεται τοῦ
3 ἰδίου ἀγαθοῦ ἢ κακοῦ. πῶς τοῦ ἀγαθοῦ τεύξεται;
ἂν τὰς ὕλας μὴ θαυμάσῃ. τὰ γὰρ περὶ τῶν
ὑλῶν δόγματα ὀρθὰ μὲν ὄντα ἀγαθὴν ποιεῖ τὴν
προαίρεσιν, στρεβλὰ δὲ καὶ διεστραμμένα κακήν.
4 τοῦτον τὸν νόμον ὁ θεὸς τέθεικεν καὶ φησίν "εἴ
τι ἀγαθὸν θέλεις, παρὰ σεαυτοῦ λάβε." σὺ
λέγεις "οὔ· ἀλλὰ παρ' ἄλλου." μή, ἀλλὰ παρὰ
5 σεαυτοῦ. λοιπὸν ὅταν ἀπειλῇ ὁ τύραννος καί
με[1] καλῇ, λέγω "τίνι ἀπειλεῖ;" ἂν λέγῃ "δήσω
σε," φημὶ ὅτι "ταῖς χερσὶν ἀπειλεῖ καὶ τοῖς
6 ποσίν." ἂν λέγῃ "τραχηλοκοπήσω σε," λέγω
"τῷ τραχήλῳ ἀπειλεῖ." ἂν λέγῃ "ἐς φυλακὴν

---

[1] Wolf: καὶ μὴ S.

---

[1] i.e., the proper control to exercise over one's haphazard
sense-impressions.

what tragedy has any other source than this? What is the *Atreus* of Euripides? His sense-impression. The *Oedipus* of Sophocles? His sense-impression. The *Phoenix*? His sense-impression. The *Hippolytus*? His sense-impression. What kind of a man, then, do you think he is who pays no attention to this matter[1]? What are those men called who follow every impression of their senses?—Madmen.—Are we, then, acting differently?

CHAPTER XXIX

Of steadfastness

THE essence of the good is a certain kind of moral purpose, and that of the evil is a certain kind of moral purpose. What, then, are the external things? They are materials for the moral purpose, in dealing with which it will find its own proper good or evil. How will it find the good? If it does not admire the materials. For the judgements about the materials, if they be correct, make the moral purpose good, but if they be crooked and awry, they make it evil. This is the law which God has ordained, and He says, " If you wish any good thing, get it from yourself." You say, " No, but from someone else." Do not so, but get it from yourself. For the rest, when the tyrant threatens and summons me, I answer " Whom are you threatening?" If he says, " I will put you in chains," I reply, " He is threatening my hands and my feet." If he says, " I will behead you," I answer, " He is threatening my neck." If he says,

σε βαλῶ," "ὅλῳ τῷ σαρκιδίῳ·" κἂν ἐξορισμὸν
7 ἀπειλῇ, τὸ αὐτό.—Σοὶ οὖν οὐδὲν ἀπειλεῖ ;—Εἰ
πέπονθα ὅτι ταῦτα οὐδέν ἐστι πρὸς ἐμέ, οὐδέν·
8 εἰ δὲ φοβοῦμαί τι τούτων, ἐμοὶ ἀπειλεῖ. τίνα
λοιπὸν δέδοικα ; τὸν τίνων ὄντα κύριον ; τῶν ἐπ'
ἐμοί ; οὐδὲ εἷς ἐστιν. τῶν οὐκ ἐπ' ἐμοί ; καὶ τί
μοι αὐτῶν μέλει ;
9 Ὑμεῖς οὖν οἱ φιλόσοφοι διδάσκετε καταφρονεῖν
τῶν βασιλέων ;—Μὴ γένοιτο. τίς ἡμῶν διδάσκει
ἀντιποιεῖσθαι πρὸς αὐτούς, ὧν ἐκεῖνοι[1] ἔχουσιν
10 ἐξουσίαν ; τὸ σωμάτιον λάβε, τὴν κτῆσιν λάβε,
τὴν φήμην λάβε, τοὺς περὶ ἐμὲ λάβε. ἄν τινας
τούτων ἀναπείθω ἀντιποιεῖσθαι, τῷ ὄντι ἐγκα-
11 λείτω μοι. "ναί· ἀλλὰ καὶ τῶν δογμάτων
ἄρχειν θέλω." καὶ τίς σοι ταύτην τὴν ἐξουσίαν
δέδωκεν ; ποῦ δύνασαι νικῆσαι δόγμα ἀλλότριον ;
12 "προσάγων," φησίν, "αὐτῷ φόβον νικήσω."
ἀγνοεῖς ὅτι αὐτὸ αὐτὸ ἐνίκησεν, οὐχ ὑπ' ἄλλου
ἐνικήθη· προαίρεσιν δὲ οὐδὲν ἄλλο νικῆσαι
13 δύναται, πλὴν αὐτὴ ἑαυτήν. διὰ τοῦτο καὶ ὁ
τοῦ θεοῦ νόμος κράτιστός ἐστι καὶ δικαιότατος·
τὸ κρεῖσσον ἀεὶ περιγινέσθω τοῦ χείρονος.
14 "κρείττονές εἰσιν οἱ δέκα τοῦ ἑνός." πρὸς τί ;
πρὸς τὸ δῆσαι, πρὸς τὸ ἀποκτεῖναι, πρὸς τὸ
ἀπαγαγεῖν ὅπου θέλουσιν, πρὸς τὸ ἀφελέσθαι
τὰ ὄντα. νικῶσιν τοίνυν οἱ δέκα τὸν ἕνα ἐν
15 τούτῳ, ἐν ᾧ κρείσσονές εἰσιν. ἐν τίνι οὖν χείρονές
εἰσιν ; ἂν ὁ μὲν ἔχῃ δόγματα ὀρθά, οἱ δὲ μή.

[1] Schweighäuser: τῶν ἐκείνων S.

"I will throw you into prison," I say, "He is threatening my whole paltry body"; and if he threatens me with exile, I give the same answer.— Does he, then, threaten *you* not at all?—If I feel that all this is nothing to me,—not at all; but if I am afraid of any of these threats, it is I whom he threatens. Who is there left, then, for me to fear? The man who is master of what? The things that are under my control? But there is no such man. The man who is master of the things that are not under my control? And what do I care for them?

Do you philosophers, then, teach us to despise our kings?—Far from it. Who among us teaches you to dispute their claim to the things over which they have authority? Take my paltry body, take my property, take my reputation, take those who are about me. If I persuade any to lay claim to these things, let some man truly accuse me. "Yes, but I wish to control your judgements also." And who has given you this authority? How can you have the power to overcome another's judgement? "By bringing fear to bear upon him," he says, "I shall overcome him." You fail to realize that the judgement overcame itself, it was not overcome by something else; and nothing else can overcome moral purpose, but it overcomes itself. For this reason too the law of God is most good and most just: "Let the better always prevail over the worse." "Ten are better than one," you say. For what? For putting in chains, for killing, for dragging away where they will, for taking away a man's property. Ten overcome one, therefore, in the point in which they are better. In what, then, are they worse? If the one has correct judge-

τί οὖν; ἐν τούτῳ δύνανται νικῆσαι; πόθεν; εἰ
δ' ἱστάμεθα ἐπὶ ζυγοῦ, οὐκ ἔδει τὸν βαρύτερον
καθελκύσαι;

16 Σωκράτης οὖν ἵνα πάθῃ ταῦτα ὑπ' Ἀθηναίων;
—Ἀνδράποδον, τί λέγεις τὸ Σωκράτης; ὡς ἔχει
τὸ πρᾶγμα λέγε· ἵν' οὖν τὸ Σωκράτους πραγ-
μάτιον¹ ἀπαχθῇ καὶ συρῇ ὑπὸ τῶν ἰσχυροτέρων
εἰς δεσμωτήριον καὶ κώνειόν τις δῷ τῷ σωματίῳ
17 τῷ Σωκράτους κἀκεῖνο ἀποψυγῇ²; ταῦτά σοι
φαίνεται θαυμαστά, ταῦτα ἄδικα, ἐπὶ τούτοις
ἐγκαλεῖς τῷ θεῷ; οὐδὲν οὖν εἶχε Σωκράτης ἀντὶ
18 τούτων; ποῦ ἦν ἡ οὐσία αὐτῷ τοῦ ἀγαθοῦ; τίνι
προσσχῶμεν³; σοὶ ἢ αὐτῷ; καὶ τί λέγει ἐκεῖνος;
"ἐμὲ δ' Ἄνυτος καὶ Μέλητος ἀποκτεῖναι μὲν
δύνανται, βλάψαι δ' οὔ." καὶ πάλιν "εἰ ταύτῃ
19 τῷ θεῷ φίλον, ταύτῃ γινέσθω." ἀλλὰ δεῖξον
ὅτι χείρονα ἔχων δόγματα κρατεῖ τοῦ κρείττονος
ἐν δόγμασιν. οὐ δείξεις· οὐδ' ἐγγύς. νόμος γὰρ
τῆς φύσεως καὶ τοῦ θεοῦ οὗτος· τὸ κρεῖσσον ἀεὶ
περιγινέσθω τοῦ χείρονος. ἐν τίνι; ἐν ᾧ κρεῖσσόν
20 ἐστιν. σῶμα σώματος ἰσχυρότερον, οἱ πλείονες
21 τοῦ ἑνός, ὁ κλέπτης τοῦ μὴ κλέπτου. διὰ τοῦτο
κἀγὼ τὸν λύχνον ἀπώλεσα, ὅτι ἐν τῷ ἀγρυπνεῖν
μου κρείσσων ἦν ὁ κλέπτης. ἀλλ' ἐκεῖνος

---

¹ σωμάτιον the edition of Salamanca: Bentley also seems
to have questioned the word, but compare III. i. 16.
² Koraes: ἀποφύγηι S.
³ Schweighäuser after Schegk: προσχῶμεν S.

---

[1] The interlocutor takes the case of Socrates as proving
that a question of right cannot be settled by weighing
judgements in the ordinary fashion, i.e., by counting votes.
[2] Plato, Apology, 30 c.

ments, and the ten have not. What then? Can they overcome in this point? How can they? But if we are weighed in the balance, must not the heavier draw down the scales?

So that a Socrates may suffer what he did at the hands of the Athenians?[1]—Slave, why do you say "Socrates"? Speak of the matter as it really is and say: That the paltry body of Socrates may be carried off and dragged to prison by those who were stronger than he, and that some one may give hemlock to the paltry body of Socrates, and that it may grow cold and die? Does this seem marvellous to you, does this seem unjust, for this do you blame God? Did Socrates, then, have no compensation for this? In what did the essence of the good consist for him? To whom shall we listen, to you or to Socrates himself? And what does *he* say? "Anytus and Meletus can kill me, but they cannot hurt me."[2] And again, "If so it is pleasing to God, so let it be."[3] But do you prove that one who holds inferior judgements prevails over the man who is superior in point of judgements. You will not be able to prove this; no, nor even come near proving it. For this is a law of nature and of God: "Let the better always prevail over the worse." Prevail in what? In that in which it is better. One body is stronger than another body; several persons are stronger than one; the thief is stronger than the man who is not a thief. That is why I lost my lamp,[4] because in the matter of keeping awake the thief was better than I was. However, he bought a lamp for a very

[3] Plato, *Crito*, 43 D.
[4] See I. 18, 15.

τοσούτου ὠνήσατο λύχνον· ἀντὶ λύχνου κλέπτης
ἐγένετο, ἀντὶ λύχνου ἄπιστος, ἀντὶ λύχνου
θηριώδης. τοῦτο ἔδοξεν αὐτῷ λυσιτελεῖν.

22 Ἔστω· ἀλλ' εἴληπταί μού τις τοῦ ἱματίου
καὶ ἕλκει μ' εἰς τὴν ἀγοράν, εἶτα ἐπικραυγάζουσιν
ἄλλοι "φιλόσοφε, τί σε ὠφέληκε τὰ δόγματα;
ἰδοὺ σύρῃ εἰς τὸ δεσμωτήριον, ἰδοὺ μέλλεις
23 τραχηλοκοπεῖσθαι." καὶ ποίαν ἔπραξα ἂν εἰσα-
γωγήν, ἵν', ἂν ἰσχυρότερος ἐπιλάβηταί μου τοῦ
ἱματίου, μὴ σύρωμαι; ἵνα, ἄν με δέκα περι-
σπάσαντες εἰς τὸ δεσμωτήριον ἐμβάλωσιν, μὴ
24 ἐμβληθῶ; ἄλλο οὖν οὐδὲν ἔμαθον; ἔμαθον, ἵνα
πᾶν τὸ γινόμενον ἴδω ὅτι, ἂν ἀπροαίρετον ᾖ,
25 οὐδέν ἐστι πρὸς ἐμέ.—πρὸς τοῦτο οὖν οὐκ
ὠφέλησαι; τί οὖν ἐν ἄλλῳ ζητεῖς τὴν ὠφέλειαν
26 ἢ ἐν ᾧ ἔμαθες;—καθήμενος λοιπὸν ἐν τῇ φυλακῇ
λέγω "οὗτος ὁ ταῦτα κραυγάζων οὔτε τοῦ
σημαινομένου ἀκούει οὔτε τῷ λεγομένῳ παρακολουθεῖ οὔτε ὅλως μεμέληκεν αὐτῷ εἰδέναι
περὶ τῶν φιλοσόφων τί λέγουσιν ἢ τί ποιοῦσιν.
27 ἄφες αὐτόν." "ἀλλ' ἔξελθε πάλιν ἀπὸ τῆς
φυλακῆς." εἰ μηκέτι χρείαν ἔχητέ μου ἐν τῇ
φυλακῇ, ἐξέρχομαι· ἂν πάλιν σχῆτε, εἰσε-
28 λεύσομαι. μέχρι τίνος; μέχρις ἂν οὗ λόγος
αἱρῇ συνεῖναί με τῷ σωματίῳ· ὅταν δὲ μὴ αἱρῇ,
29 λάβετε αὐτὸ καὶ ὑγιαίνετε. μόνον μὴ ἀλογίστως,
μόνον μὴ μαλακῶς, μὴ ἐκ τῆς τυχούσης προ-

---

[1] Epictetus seems to stop and address himself somewhat
abruptly, but the connection of this and the next sentence is
not entirely clear. Schweighäuser thought that they were
addressed to some one of his pupils.

high price; for a lamp he became a thief, for a lamp he became faithless, for a lamp he became beast-like. This seemed to him to be profitable!

Very well; but now someone has taken hold of me by my cloak and pulls me into the market-place, and then others shout at me, "Philosopher, what good have your judgements done you? See, you are being dragged off to prison; see, you are going to have your head cut off." And what kind of *Introduction to Philosophy* could I have studied, which would prevent me from being dragged off, if a man who is stronger than I am should take hold of my cloak? Or would prevent me from being thrown into the prison, if ten men should hustle me and throw me unto it? Have I, then, learned nothing else? I have learned to see that everything which happens, if it be outside the realm of my moral purpose, is nothing to me.—Have you, then, derived no benefit from this principle for the present case?[1] Why, then, do you seek your benefit in something other than that in which you have learned that it is?— Well, as I sit in the prison I say, "The fellow who shouts this at me neither understands what is meant, nor follows what is said, nor has he taken any pains at all to know what philosophers say, or what they do. Don't mind him." "But come out of the prison again." If you have no further need of me in the prison, I shall come out; if you ever need me there again, I shall go back in. For how long? For so long as reason chooses that I remain with my paltry body; but when reason does not so choose, take it and good health to you! Only let me not give up my life irrationally, only let me not give up my life faintheartedly, or from some casual pretext. For

φάσεως. πάλιν γὰρ ὁ θεὸς οὐ βούλεται· χρείαν
γὰρ ἔχει κόσμου τοιούτου, τῶν ἐπὶ γῆς ἀνα-
στρεφομένων τοιούτων. ἐὰν δὲ σημήνῃ τὸ ἀνα-
κλητικὸν ὡς τῷ Σωκράτει, πείθεσθαι δεῖ τῷ
σημαίνοντι ὡς στρατηγῷ.

30 Τί οὖν; λέγειν δεῖ ταῦτα πρὸς τοὺς πολλούς;
31 —Ἵνα τί; οὐ γὰρ ἀρκεῖ τὸ αὐτὸν πείθεσθαι;
τοῖς γὰρ παιδίοις, ὅταν προσελθόντα κροτῇ καὶ
λέγῃ "σήμερον Σατορνάλια ἀγαθά," λέγομεν
"οὐκ ἔστιν ἀγαθὰ ταῦτα"; οὐδαμῶς· ἀλλὰ καὶ
32 αὐτοὶ ἐπικροτοῦμεν. καὶ σὺ τοίνυν, ὅταν μετα-
πεῖσαί τινα μὴ δύνῃ, γίγνωσκε ὅτι παιδίον ἐστὶ
καὶ ἐπικρότει αὐτῷ· ἂν δὲ μὴ τοῦτο θέλῃς,[1]
σιώπα λοιπόν.

33 Τούτων δεῖ μεμνῆσθαι καὶ κληθέντα εἴς τινα
τοιαύτην περίστασιν εἰδέναι, ὅτι ἐλήλυθεν ὁ
34 καιρὸς τοῦ ἀποδεῖξαι, εἰ πεπαιδεύμεθα. νέος
γὰρ ἀπὸ σχολῆς ἀπιὼν εἰς περίστασιν ὅμοιός
ἐστι τῷ μεμελετηκότι συλλογισμοὺς ἀναλύειν, κἄν
τις εὔλυτον[2] αὐτῷ προτείνῃ, λέγει "μᾶλλόν μοι
πεπλεγμένον κομψῶς προτείνατε, ἵνα γυμνασθῶ."
καὶ οἱ ἀθληταὶ τοῖς κούφοις νεανίσκοις δυσ-
35 αρεστοῦσιν· "οὐ βαστάζει με," φησίν. "οὗτός
ἐστιν εὐφυὴς νέος." οὔ· ἀλλὰ καλέσαντος τοῦ
καιροῦ κλάειν δεῖ καὶ λέγειν "ἤθελον ἔτι
μανθάνειν." τίνα; εἰ ταῦτα οὐκ ἔμαθες ὥστ'[3]

<hr>

[1] Wolf after Schegk: θέλῃι S.   [2] Reiske: εὔλογον S.
[3] Meibom: οὐχ ὥστ' S.

<hr>

[1] Equivalent to our greeting, "Merry Christmas!" In
what follows it would appear that the clapping of hands
upon this occasion was a kind of salutation, somewhat like
the kiss at Easter among Greek Orthodox Christians.

again, God does not so desire; for He has need of
such a universe, and of such men who go to and
fro upon earth. But if He gives the signal to
retreat, as He did to Socrates, I must obey Him
who gives the signal, as I would a general.

What then? Must I say these things to the
multitude? For what purpose? Is it not sufficient
for a man himself to believe them? For example,
when the children come up to us and clap their
hands and say, "To-day is the good Saturnalia," [1]
do we say to them, "All this is not good"? Not
at all; but we too clap our hands to them. And
do you too, therefore, when you are unable to make
a man change his opinion, realize that he is a child
and clap your hands to him; but if you do not want
to do this, you have merely to hold your peace.

All this a man ought to remember, and when he
is summoned to meet some such difficulty, he ought
to know that the time has come to show whether
we are educated. For a young man leaving school
and facing a difficulty is like one who has practised
the analysis of syllogisms, and if someone propounds
him one that is easy to solve, he says, "Nay, rather
propound me one that is cunningly involved, so that
I may get exercise from it." Also the athletes are
displeased with the youths of light weight: "He
cannot lift me," says one. "Yonder is a sturdy young
man." Oh no; but when the crisis calls,[2] he has to
weep and say, "I wanted to keep on learning."
Learning what? If you do not learn these things
so as to be able to manifest them in action, what did

[2] That is, when, instead of an exercise for practice, he
has to meet an actual contestant, or a practical difficulty
in life.

195

36 ἔργῳ δεῖξαι, πρὸς τί αὐτὰ ἔμαθες; ἐγώ τινα
οἶμαι τῶν καθημένων ἐνταῦθα ὠδίνειν αὐτὸν
ἐφ᾽ ἑαυτοῦ καὶ λέγειν "ἐμοὶ νῦν περίστασιν μὴ
ἔρχεσθαι τοιαύτην, ὁποία τούτῳ ἐλήλυθεν; ἐμὲ
νῦν κατατριβῆναι καθήμενον ἐν γωνίᾳ δυνάμενον
στεφανωθῆναι Ὀλύμπια; πότε τις ἐμοὶ καταγ-
γελεῖ τοιοῦτον ἀγῶνα;" οὕτως ἔχειν ἔδει πάντας
37 ὑμᾶς. ἀλλ᾽ ἐν μὲν τοῖς Καίσαρος μονομάχοις
εἰσί τινες οἱ ἀγανακτοῦντες ὅτι οὐδεὶς αὐτοὺς
προάγει οὐδὲ ζευγνύει καὶ εὔχονται τῷ θεῷ καὶ
προσέρχονται τοῖς ἐπιτρόποις δεόμενοι μονο-
μαχῆσαι, ἐξ ὑμῶν δ᾽ οὐδεὶς φανήσεται τοιοῦτος;
38 ἤθελον πλεῦσαι ἐπ᾽ αὐτὸ τοῦτο καὶ ἰδεῖν, τί μου
39 ποιεῖ ὁ ἀθλητής, πῶς μελετᾷ τὴν ὑπόθεσιν. "οὐ
θέλω," φησίν, "τοιαύτην." ἐπὶ σοὶ γάρ ἐστι
λαβεῖν ἣν θέλεις ὑπόθεσιν; δέδοταί σοι σῶμα
τοιοῦτο, γονεῖς τοιοῦτοι, ἀδελφοὶ τοιοῦτοι, πατρὶς
τοιαύτη, τάξις ἐν αὐτῇ τοιαύτη· εἶτά μοι λέγεις
ἐλθὼν "ἄλλαξόν μοι τὴν ὑπόθεσιν." εἶτα οὐκ
ἔχεις ἀφορμὰς πρὸς τὸ χρήσασθαι τοῖς [1] δοθεῖσιν;
40 σόν ἐστι προτεῖναι, ἐμὸν μελετῆσαι καλῶς. οὔ·
ἀλλὰ "μὴ τοιοῦτό μοι προβάλῃς τροπικόν, ἀλλὰ
τοιοῦτον· μὴ τοιαύτην ἐπενέγκῃς τὴν ἐπιφοράν,
41 ἀλλὰ τοιαύτην." ἔσται χρόνος τάχα, ἐν ᾧ οἱ
τραγῳδοὶ οἰήσονται ἑαυτοὺς εἶναι προσωπεῖα καὶ
ἐμβάδας καὶ τὸ σύρμα. ἄνθρωπε, ταῦτα ὕλην
42 ἔχεις καὶ ὑπόθεσιν. φθέγξαι τι, ἵνα εἰδῶμεν
πότερον τραγῳδὸς εἶ ἢ γελωτοποιός· κοινὰ γὰρ

---

[1] Supplied by Schenkl.

---

[1] Objecting, that is, to a hypothetical syllogism of a particular kind and proposing another, more to his own liking.

you learn them for? I fancy that someone among these who are sitting here is in travail within his own soul and is saying, "Alas, that such a difficulty does not come to me *now* as that which has come to this fellow! Alas, that now I must be worn out sitting in a corner, when I might be crowned at Olympia! When will someone bring me word of such a contest?" You ought all to be thus minded. But among the gladiators of Caesar there are some who complain because no one brings them out, or matches them with an antagonist, and they pray God and go to their managers, begging to fight in single combat; and yet will no one of you display a like spirit? I wanted to sail to Rome for this very purpose and to see what my athlete is doing, what practice he is following in his task. "I do not want," says he, "this kind of a task." What, is it in your power to take any task you want? You have been given such a body, such parents, such brothers, such a country, such a position in it; and then do you come to me and say, "Change the task for me"? What, do you not possess resources to enable you to utilize that which has been given? You ought to say, "It is yours to set the task, mine to practise it well." No, but you *do* say, "Do not propose to me such-and-such a hypothetical syllogism, but rather such-and-such a one;[1] do not urge upon me such-and-such a conclusion, but rather such-and-such a one." A time will soon come when the tragic actors will think that their masks and buskins and the long robe are themselves. Man, all these things you have as a subject-matter and a task. Say something, so that we may know whether you are a tragic actor or a buffoon; for both of these have

43 ἔχουσι τὰ ἄλλα ἀμφότεροι. διὰ τοῦτο ἂν ἀφέλῃ
τις αὐτοῦ καὶ τὰς ἐμβάδας καὶ τὸ προσωπεῖον
καὶ ἐν εἰδώλῳ αὐτὸν προαγάγῃ, ἀπώλετο ὁ
τραγῳδὸς ἢ μένει; ἂν φωνὴν ἔχῃ, μένει.

44 Καὶ ἐνθάδε. "λάβε ἡγεμονίαν." λαμβάνω
καὶ λαβὼν δεικνύω, πῶς ἄνθρωπος ἀναστρέφεται
45 πεπαιδευμένος. "θὲς τὴν πλατύσημον καὶ ἀνα-
λαβὼν ῥάκη πρόσελθε ἐν προσώπῳ τοιούτῳ."
τί οὖν; οὐ δέδοταί μοι καλὴν φωνὴν εἰσενεγκεῖν;
46 "πῶς οὖν ἀναβαίνεις νῦν;" ὡς μάρτυς ὑπὸ τοῦ
47 θεοῦ κεκλημένος. "ἔρχου σὺ καὶ μαρτύρησόν
μοι· σὺ γὰρ ἄξιος εἶ προαχθῆναι μάρτυς ὑπ'
ἐμοῦ. μή τι τῶν ἐκτὸς τῆς προαιρέσεως ἀγαθόν
ἐστιν ἢ κακόν; μή τινα βλάπτω; μή τι ἐπ'
ἄλλῳ τὴν ὠφέλειαν ἐποίησα τὴν ἑκάστου ἢ ἐπ'
48 αὐτῷ;" τίνα μαρτυρίαν δίδως τῷ θεῷ; "ἐν
δεινοῖς εἰμι, κύριε, καὶ δυστυχῶ, οὐδείς μου ἐπιστρέφεται, οὐδείς μοι δίδωσιν οὐδέν, πάντες
49 ψέγουσιν, κακολογοῦσιν." ταῦτα μέλλεις μαρτυρεῖν καὶ καταισχύνειν τὴν κλῆσιν ἣν κέκληκεν,
ὅτι σε ἐτίμησεν ταύτην τὴν τιμὴν καὶ ἄξιον
ἡγήσατο προσαγαγεῖν εἰς μαρτυρίαν τηλικαύτην;
50 Ἀλλ' ἀπεφήνατο ὁ ἔχων τὴν ἐξουσίαν "κρίνω
σε ἀσεβῆ καὶ ἀνόσιον εἶναι." τί σοι γέγονεν;
51 "ἐκρίθην ἀσεβὴς καὶ ἀνόσιος εἶναι." ἄλλο οὐδέν; "οὐδέν." εἰ δὲ περὶ συνημμένου τινὸς ἐπι-
κεκρίκει καὶ ἐδεδώκει ἀπόφασιν "τὸ εἰ ἡμέρα

---

¹ The toga with a broad stripe of red which was worn
by men of senatorial rank.

everything but their lines in common. Therefore, if one should take away from him both his buskins and his mask, and bring him on the stage as a mere shade of an actor, is the tragic actor lost, or does he abide? If he has a voice, he abides.

And so it is in actual life. "Take a governorship." I take it and having done so I show how an educated man comports himself. "Lay aside the laticlave,[1] and having put on rags come forward in a character to correspond." What then? Has it not been given me to display a fine voice. "In what rôle, then, do you mount the stage now?" As a witness summoned by God. God says, "Go you and bear witness for Me; for you are worthy to be produced by me as a witness. Is any of those things which lie outside the range of the moral purpose either good or evil? Do I injure any man? Have I put each man's advantage under the control of any but himself?" What kind of witness do you bear for God? "I am in sore straits, O Lord, and in misfortune; no one regards me, no one gives me anything, all blame me and speak ill of me." Is this the witness that you are going to bear, and is this the way in which you are going to disgrace the summons which He gave you, in that He bestowed this honour upon you and deemed you worthy to be brought forward in order to bear testimony so important?

But the one who has authority over you declares, "I pronounce you impious and profane." What has happened to you? "I have been pronounced impious and profane." Nothing else? "Nothing." But if he had passed judgement upon some hypothetical syllogism and had made a declaration, "I judge

ἐστίν, φῶς ἐστιν κρίνω ψεῦδος εἶναι," τί ἐγεγόνει
τῷ συνημμένῳ; τίς ἐνθάδε κρίνεται, τίς κατα-
κέκριται; τὸ συνημμένον ἢ ὁ ἐξαπατηθεὶς περὶ
52 αὐτοῦ; οὗτος οὖν τίς ποτε ὁ ἔχων ἐξουσίαν τοῦ
ἀποφήνασθαί τι περὶ σοῦ; οἶδεν τί ἐστι τὸ
εὐσεβὲς ἢ τὸ ἀσεβές; μεμελέτηκεν αὐτό; μεμά-
53 θηκεν; ποῦ; παρὰ τίνι; εἶτα μουσικὸς μὲν οὐκ
ἐπιστρέφεται αὐτοῦ ἀποφαινομένου περὶ τῆς
νήτης ὅτι ἐστὶν ὑπάτη οὐδὲ γεωμετρικός, ἂν
ἐπικρίνῃ τὰς ἀπὸ κέντρου πρὸς τὸν κύκλον
54 προσπιπτούσας μὴ εἶναι ἴσας· ὁ δὲ ταῖς ἀληθείαις πεπαιδευμένος ἀνθρώπου ἀπαιδεύτου ἐπι-
στραφήσεται ἐπικρίνοντός τι περὶ ὁσίου καὶ
ἀνοσίου καὶ ἀδίκου καὶ δικαίου;

Ὦ πολλῆς ἀδικίας τῶν πεπαιδευμένων. ταῦτα
55 οὖν ἔμαθες ἐνταῦθα; οὐ θέλεις τὰ μὲν λογάρια
τὰ περὶ τούτων ἄλλοις ἀφεῖναι, ἀταλαιπώροις
ἀνθρωπαρίοις, ἵν' ἐν γωνίᾳ καθεζόμενοι μισθάρια
λαμβάνωσιν ἢ γογγύζωσιν, ὅτι οὐδεὶς αὐτοῖς παρέχει οὐδέν, σὺ δὲ χρῆσθαι παρελθὼν οἷς ἔμαθες;
56 οὐ γὰρ λογάριά ἐστι τὰ λείποντα νῦν, ἀλλὰ γέμει
τὰ βιβλία τῶν Στωικῶν λογαρίων. τί οὖν τὸ
λεῖπόν ἐστιν; ὁ χρησόμενος, ὁ ἔργῳ μαρτυρήσων
57 τοῖς λόγοις. τοῦτό μοι τὸ πρόσωπον ἀνάλαβε,
ἵνα μηκέτι παλαιοῖς ἐν τῇ σχολῇ παραδείγμασι
χρώμεθα, ἀλλὰ ἔχωμέν τι καὶ καθ' ἡμᾶς παρά-

---

[1] The lowest string had, however, the highest note in
pitch, and *vice versa*.

the statement, 'If it is day, there is light,' to be false," what has happened to the hypothetical syllogism? Who is being judged in this case, who has been condemned? The hypothetical syllogism, or the man who has been deceived in his judgement about it? Who in the world, then, is this man who has authority to make any declaration about you? Does he know what piety or impiety is? Has he pondered the matter? Has he learned it? Where? Under whose instruction? And yet a musician pays no attention to him, if he declares that the lowest string is the highest,[1] nor does a geometrician, if the man decides that the lines extending from the centre to the circumference of a circle are not equal; but shall the truly educated man pay attention to an uninstructed person when he passes judgement on what is holy and unholy, and on what is just and unjust?

How great is the injustice committed by the educated in so doing! Is this, then, what you have learned here? Will you not leave to others, mannikins incapable of taking pains, the petty quibbles about these things, so that they may sit in a corner and gather in their petty fees, or grumble because nobody gives them anything, and will you not yourself come forward and make use of what you have learned? For what is lacking now is not quibbles; nay, the books of the Stoics are full of quibbles. What, then, is the thing lacking now? The man to make use of them, the man to bear witness to the arguments by his acts. This is the character I would have you assume, that we may no longer use old examples in the school, but may have some example from our own time

58 δεῖγμα. ταῦτα οὖν τίνος ἐστὶ θεωρεῖν; τοῦ
σχολάζοντος. ἔστι γὰρ φιλοθεώρόν τι ζῷον ὁ
59 ἄνθρωπος. ἀλλ' αἰσχρόν ἐστι θεωρεῖν ταῦτα
οὕτως ὡς οἱ δραπέται· ἀλλ' ἀπερισπάστως
καθῆσθαι καὶ ἀκούειν νῦν μὲν τραγῳδοῦ νῦν δὲ
κιθαρῳδοῦ, οὐχ ὡς ἐκεῖνοι ποιοῦσιν. ἅμα μὲν
ἐπέστη καὶ ἐπῄνεσεν τὸν τραγῳδόν, ἅμα δὲ περι-
εβλέψατο· εἶτα ἄν τις φθέγξηται κύριον, εὐθὺς
60 σεσόβηνται, ταράσσονται. αἰσχρόν ἐστιν οὕτως
καὶ τοὺς φιλοσόφους θεωρεῖν τὰ ἔργα τῆς φύσεως.
τί γάρ ἐστι κύριος; ἄνθρωπος ἀνθρώπου κύριος
οὐκ ἔστιν, ἀλλὰ θάνατος καὶ ζωὴ καὶ ἡδονὴ καὶ
61 πόνος. ἐπεὶ χωρὶς τούτων ἄγαγέ μοι τὸν Καίσαρα καὶ ὄψει πῶς εὐσταθῶ. ὅταν δὲ μετὰ
τούτων ἔλθῃ βροντῶν καὶ ἀστράπτων, ἐγὼ δὲ
ταῦτα φοβῶμαι, τί ἄλλο ἢ ἐπέγνωκα τὸν κύριον
62 ὡς ὁ δραπέτης; μέχρι δ' ἂν οὐ τινα ἀνοχὴν ἀπὸ
τούτων ἔχω, ὡς δραπέτης ἐφίσταται θεάτρῳ
οὕτως κἀγώ· λούομαι, πίνω, ᾄδω, πάντα δὲ μετὰ
63 φόβου καὶ ταλαιπωρίας. ἐὰν δ' ἐμαυτὸν ἀπο-
λύσω τῶν δεσποτῶν, τοῦτ' ἔστιν ἐκείνων, δι' ἃ
οἱ δεσπόται εἰσὶ φοβεροί, ποῖον ἔτι πρᾶγμα ἔχω,
ποῖον ἔτι κύριον;
64   Τί οὖν; κηρύσσειν δεῖ ταῦτα πρὸς πάντας;—
Οὔ, ἀλλὰ τοῖς ἰδιώταις συμπεριφέρεσθαι καὶ
λέγειν "οὗτος ὃ αὑτῷ ἀγαθὸν οἴεται τοῦτο κἀμοὶ
65 συμβουλεύει· συγγιγνώσκω αὐτῷ." καὶ γὰρ

---

[1] The runaway slave, always apprehensive that his master
may suddenly appear, is nervous and distraught, giving only
half his mind to the spectacle before him.

[2] One who sang to his own accompaniment upon the
cithara or harp.

also. Whose part is it, then, to contemplate these matters? The part of him who devotes himself to learning; for man is a kind of animal that loves contemplation. But it is disgraceful to contemplate these things like runaway slaves;[1] nay, sit rather free from distractions and listen, now to tragic actor and now to the citharoede,[2] and not as those runaways do. For at the very moment when one of them is paying attention and praising the tragic actor, he takes a glance around, and then if someone mentions the word "master," they are instantly all in a flutter and upset. It is disgraceful for men who are philosophers to contemplate the works of nature in this spirit. For what is a "master"? One man is not master of another man, but death and life and pleasure and hardship are his masters. So bring Caesar to me, if he be *without* these things, and you shall see how steadfast I am. But when he comes *with* them, thundering and lightening, and I am afraid of them, what else have I done but recognized my master, like the runaway slave? But so long as I have, as it were, only a respite from these threats, I too am acting like a runaway slave who is a spectator in a theatre; I bathe, I drink, I sing, but I do it all in fear and misery. But if I emancipate myself from my masters, that is, from those things which render masters terrifying, what further trouble do I have, what master any more?

What then? Must I proclaim this to all men? No, but I must treat with consideration those who are not philosophers by profession, and say, "This man advises for me that which he thinks good in his own case; therefore I excuse him." For Socrates

Σωκράτης συνεγίγνωσκεν τῷ ἐπὶ τῆς φυλακῆς
κλάοντι, ὅτε ἔμελλεν πίνειν τὸ φάρμακον, καὶ
66 λέγει " ὡς γενναίως ἡμᾶς ἀποδεδάκρυκεν." μή
τι οὖν ἐκείνῳ λέγει ὅτι " διὰ τοῦτο τὰς γυναῖκας
ἀπελύσαμεν "; ἀλλὰ τοῖς γνωρίμοις, τοῖς δυνα-
μένοις αὐτὰ ἀκοῦσαι· ἐκείνῳ δὲ συμπεριφέρεται
ὡς παιδίῳ.

λ'. Τί δεῖ πρόχειρον ἔχειν ἐν ταῖς
περιστάσεσιν ;

1 Ὅταν εἰσίῃς πρός τινα τῶν ὑπερεχόντων,
μέμνησο ὅτι καὶ ἄλλος ἄνωθεν βλέπει τὰ γιγνό-
μενα καὶ ὅτι ἐκείνῳ σε δεῖ μᾶλλον ἀρέσκειν ἢ
2 τούτῳ. ἐκεῖνος οὖν σου πυνθάνεται " φυγὴν καὶ
φυλακὴν καὶ δεσμὰ καὶ θάνατον καὶ ἀδοξίαν τί
3 ἔλεγες ἐν τῇ σχολῇ ;" " ἐγὼ ἀδιάφορα." " νῦν
οὖν τίνα αὐτὰ λέγεις ; μή τι ἐκεῖνα ἠλλάγη ;"
" οὔ." " σὺ οὖν ἠλλάγης ;" " οὔ." " λέγε οὖν
τίνα ἐστὶν ἀδιάφορα." " τὰ ἀπροαίρετα." [1] " λέγε
καὶ τὰ ἑξῆς." " ἀπροαίρετα οὐδὲν πρὸς ἐμέ."
4 " λέγε καὶ τὰ ἀγαθὰ τίνα ὑμῖν ἐδόκει ;" " προαίρεσις οἵα δεῖ καὶ χρῆσις φαντασιῶν." " τέλος
5 δὲ τί ;" " τὸ σοὶ ἀκολουθεῖν." " ταῦτα καὶ νῦν
λέγεις ;" " ταῦτα καὶ νῦν λέγω." ἄπιθι λοιπὸν
ἔσω θαρρῶν καὶ μεμνημένος τούτων καὶ ὄψει

---

[1] τὰ ἀπροαίρετα supplied by Upton from his "codex."

---

[1] Slightly modified from Plato, *Phaedo*, 116D.
[2] Slightly modified from Plato, *Phaedo*, 117D.

excused the jailor who wept for him when he was about to drink the poison, and said, " How generously he has wept for us!"[1] Does he, then, say to the jailor, " This is why we sent the women away"?[2] No, but he makes this latter remark to his intimate friends, to those who were fit to hear it; but the jailor he treats with consideration like a child.

CHAPTER XXX

What aid ought we to have ready at hand in difficulties?

WHEN you come into the presence of some prominent man, remember that Another[3] looks from above on what is taking place, and that you must please Him rather than this man. He, then, who is above asks of you, " In your school what did you call exile and imprisonment and bonds and death and disrepute?" " I called them ' things indifferent.' " " What, then, do you call them now? Have they changed at all?" " No." " Have you, then, changed?" " No." " Tell me, then, what things are 'indifferent.'" " Those that are independent of the moral purpose." " Tell me also what follows." " Things independent of the moral purpose are nothing to me." " Tell me also what you thought were 'the good things.'" " A proper moral purpose and a proper use of external impressions." " And what was the 'end'?" " To follow Thee." " Do you say all that even now?" " I say the same things even now." Then enter in, full of confidence and mindful of all this, and you shall see

---

[3] That is, God. Compare note on I. 25, 13.

τί ἐστι νέος μεμελετηκὼς ἃ δεῖ ἐν ἀνθρώποις
6 ἀμελετήτοις. ἐγὼ μὲν νὴ τοὺς θεοὺς φαντάζομαι
ὅτι πείσῃ τὸ τοιοῦτον "τί οὕτως μεγάλα καὶ
7 πολλὰ παρασκευαζόμεθα πρὸς τὸ μηδέν; τοῦτο
ἦν ἡ ἐξουσία; τοῦτο τὰ πρόθυρα, οἱ κοιτωνῖται,
οἱ ἐπὶ τῆς μαχαίρας; τούτων ἔνεκα τοὺς πολλοὺς
λόγους ἤκουον; ταῦτα οὐδὲν ἦν, ἐγὼ δ' ὡς μεγάλα
παρεσκευαζόμην."

what it means to be a young man who has studied what he ought, when he is in the presence of men who have not studied. As for me, by the gods, I fancy that you will feel somewhat like this: "Why do we make such great and elaborate preparations to meet what amounts to nothing? Was this what authority amounted to? Was this what the vestibule, the chamberlains, the armed guards amounted to? Was it for all this that I listened to those long discourses? Why, all this never amounted to anything, but I was preparing for it as though it were something great."

BOOK II

B̄

ΚΕΦΑΛΑΙΑ ΤΟΥ B̄ ΒΙΒΛΙΟΥ

---

[1] Upton: λ'γων S.
[2] Supplied by Schweighäuser.

BOOK II

Chapters of the Second Book

α΄. Ὅτι οὐ μάχεται τὸ θαρρεῖν τῷ εὐλαβεῖσθαι.

1 Παράδοξον μὲν τυχὸν φαίνεταί τισιν τὸ ἀξιού-
μενον ὑπὸ τῶν φιλοσόφων, ὅμως δὲ σκεψώμεθα
κατὰ δύναμιν, εἰ ἀληθές ἐστι τὸ δεῖν[1] ἅμα μὲν εὐλα-
2 βῶς ἅμα δὲ θαρροῦντως πάντα ποιεῖν. ἐναντίον γάρ
πως δοκεῖ τῷ θαρραλέῳ τὸ εὐλαβές, τὰ δ' ἐναντία
3 οὐδαμῶς συνυπάρχει. τὸ δὲ φαινόμενον πολλοῖς
ἐν τῷ τόπῳ παράδοξον δοκεῖ μοι τοιούτου τινὸς
ἔχεσθαι· εἰ μὲν γὰρ πρὸς ταὐτὰ ἠξιοῦμεν χρῆσθαι
τῇ τ' εὐλαβείᾳ καὶ τῷ θάρσει, δικαίως ἂν ἡμᾶς
4 ἠτιῶντο ὡς τὰ ἀσύνακτα συνάγοντας. νῦν δὲ
τί δεινὸν ἔχει τὸ λεγόμενον; εἰ γὰρ ὑγιῆ ταῦτ'
ἐστι τὰ πολλάκις μὲν εἰρημένα, πολλάκις δ'
ἀποδεδειγμένα, ὅτι ἡ οὐσία τοῦ ἀγαθοῦ ἔστιν ἐν
χρήσει φαντασιῶν καὶ τοῦ κακοῦ ὡσαύτως, τὰ
δ' ἀπροαίρετα οὔτε τὴν τοῦ κακοῦ δέχεται φύσιν
5 οὔτε τὴν τοῦ ἀγαθοῦ, τί παράδοξον ἀξιοῦσιν οἱ
φιλόσοφοι, εἰ λέγουσιν "ὅπου μὲν τὰ ἀπροαίρετα,
ἐκεῖ τὸ θάρσος ἔστω σοι, ὅπου δὲ τὰ προαιρετικά,
6 ἐκεῖ ἡ εὐλάβεια"; εἰ γὰρ ἐν κακῇ προαιρέσει τὸ

---

[1] τὸ δεῖν Elter: τόδε. ἵν' S.

CHAPTER I

That confidence does not conflict with caution

Perhaps the following contention of the philosophers appears paradoxical to some, but nevertheless let us to the best of our ability consider whether it is true that "we ought to do everything both cautiously and confidently at the same time." For caution seems to be in a way contrary to confidence, and contraries are by no means consistent. But that which appears to many to be paradoxical in the matter under discussion seems to me to involve something of this sort: If we demanded that a man should employ both caution and confidence in regard to the same things, then we would be justly charged with uniting qualities that are not to be united. But, as a matter of fact, what is there strange about the saying? For if the statements which have often been made and often proved are sound, namely that "the nature of the good as well as of the evil lies in a use of the impressions of the senses, but the things which lie outside the province of the moral purpose admit neither the nature of the evil, nor the nature of the good"; what is there paradoxical about the contention of the philosophers, if they say, "Where the things that lie outside the province of the moral purpose are involved, there show confidence, but where the things that lie within the province of the moral purpose are involved, there show caution"? For if the evil lies in an evil exercise of the moral

κακόν, πρὸς μόνα ταῦτα χρῆσθαι ἄξιον εὐλαβείᾳ·
εἰ δὲ τὰ ἀπροαίρετα καὶ μὴ ἐφ' ἡμῖν οὐδὲν πρὸς

7 ἡμᾶς, πρὸς ταῦτα τῷ θάρσει χρηστέον. καὶ
οὕτως ἅμα μὲν εὐλαβεῖς ἅμα δὲ θαρραλέοι ἐσόμεθα
καὶ νὴ Δία διὰ τὴν εὐλάβειαν θαρραλέοι. διὰ γὰρ
τὸ εὐλαβεῖσθαι τὰ ὄντως κακὰ συμβήσεται
θαρρεῖν ἡμῖν πρὸς τὰ μὴ οὕτως ἔχοντα.

8 Λοιπὸν ἡμεῖς τὸ τῶν ἐλάφων πάσχομεν· ὅτε
φοβοῦνται καὶ φεύγουσιν αἱ ἔλαφοι τὰ πτερά, ποῦ
τρέπονται καὶ πρὸς τίνα ἀναχωροῦσιν ὡς ἀσφαλῆ ;
πρὸς τὰ δίκτυα· καὶ οὕτως ἀπόλλυνται ἐναλ-

9 λάξασαι τὰ φοβερὰ καὶ τὰ θαρραλέα. οὕτως
καὶ ἡμεῖς ποῦ χρώμεθα τῷ φόβῳ; πρὸς τὰ ἀπροαίρετα. ἐν τίσιν πάλιν θαρροῦντες ἀναστρεφόμεθα
ὡς οὐδενὸς ὄντος δεινοῦ ; ἐν τοῖς προαιρετικοῖς.

10 ἐξαπατηθῆναι ἢ προπεσεῖν ἢ ἀναίσχυντόν τι
ποιῆσαι ἢ μετ' ἐπιθυμίας αἰσχρᾶς ὀρεχθῆναί
τινος οὐδὲν διαφέρει ἡμῖν, ἂν μόνον ἐν τοῖς ἀπροαι-
ρέτοις¹ εὐστοχῶμεν. ὅπου δὲ θάνατος ἢ φυγὴ ἢ
πόνος ἢ ἀδοξία, ἐκεῖ τὸ ἀναχωρητικόν, ἐκεῖ τὸ

11 σεσοβημένον. τοιγαροῦν ὥσπερ εἰκὸς τοὺς
περὶ τὰ μέγιστα διαμαρτάνοντας τὸ μὲν φύσει θαρραλέον θρασὺ κατασκευάζομεν, ἀπονενοημένον,
ἰταμόν, ἀναίσχυντον, τὸ δ' εὐλαβὲς φύσει καὶ

---

¹ Upton from his " codex ": ἀπροαιρετικοῖς S.

---

¹ The beaters used to frighten deer into the nets by
stretching a cord, with brightly coloured feathers on it, across
the safe openings in the wood. Compare Vergil, *Georgics*, III.
372 ; *cf. Aen.*, XII. 750., " (In Scythia) men drive them (stags)
not (into nets, as they do here) with the terrors of the
crimson feather."

purpose, it is only in regard to matters of this kind that it is right to employ caution; but if the things which lie outside the province of the moral purpose and are not under our control are nothing to us, we ought to employ confidence in regard to them. And so we shall be at one and the same time both cautious and confident, yes, and, by Zeus, confident because of our caution. For because we are cautious about the things which are really evil, the result will be that we shall have confidence in regard to the things which are not of that nature.

However, we act like deer: when the hinds are frightened by the feathers [1] and run away from them, where do they turn, and to what do they fly for refuge as a safe retreat? Why, to the nets; and so they perish because they have confused the objects of fear with the objects of confidence. So it is with us also; where do we show fear? About the things which lie outside the province of the moral purpose. Again, in what do we behave with confidence as if there were no danger? In the things which lie within the province of the moral purpose. To be deceived, or to act impetuously, or to do something shameless, or with base passion to desire something, makes no difference to us, if only in the matters which lie outside the province of the will we succeed in our aim. But where death, or exile, or hardship, or ignominy faces us, there we show the spirit of running away, there we show violent agitation. Therefore, as might be expected of those men who err in matters of the greatest concern, we transform our natural confidence into boldness, desperateness, recklessness, shamelessness, while our natural caution and self-respect we transform into

αἰδῆμον δειλὸν καὶ ταπεινόν, φόβων καὶ ταραχῶν
12 μεστόν. ἂν γάρ τις ἐκεῖ μεταθῇ τὸ εὐλαβές, ὅπου
προαίρεσις καὶ ἔργα προαιρέσεως, εὐθὺς ἅμα τῷ
θέλειν εὐλαβεῖσθαι καὶ ἐπ' αὐτῷ κειμένην ἕξει
τὴν ἔκκλισιν· ἂν δ' ὅπου τὰ μὴ ἐφ' ἡμῖν ἐστι καὶ
ἀπροαίρετα, πρὸς τὰ ἐπ' ἄλλοις ὄντα τὴν ἔκκλισιν
ἔχων ἀναγκαίως φοβήσεται, ἀκαταστατήσει,
13 ταραχθήσεται. οὐ γὰρ θάνατος ἢ πόνος φοβερόν,
ἀλλὰ τὸ φοβεῖσθαι πόνον ἢ θάνατον. διὰ
τοῦτο ἐπαινοῦμεν τὸν εἰπόντα ὅτι

οὐ κατθανεῖν γὰρ δεινόν, ἀλλ' αἰσχρῶς θανεῖν.

14 Ἔδει οὖν πρὸς μὲν τὸν θάνατον τὸ θάρσος
ἐστράφθαι, πρὸς δὲ τὸν φόβον τοῦ θανάτου τὴν
εὐλάβειαν· νῦν δὲ τὸ ἐναντίον πρὸς μὲν τὸν θάνατον τὴν φυγήν, πρὸς δὲ τὸ περὶ αὐτοῦ δόγμα τὴν
ἀνεπιστρεψίαν καὶ τὸ ἀμελὲς [1] καὶ τὸ ἀδιαφορη-
15 τικόν. ταῦτα δ' ὁ Σωκράτης καλῶς ποιῶν
μορμολύκεια ἐκάλει. ὡς γὰρ τοῖς παιδίοις τὰ
προσωπεῖα φαίνεται δεινὰ καὶ φοβερὰ δι' ἀπειρίαν,
τοιοῦτόν τι καὶ ἡμεῖς πάσχομεν πρὸς τὰ πράγματα
δι' οὐδὲν ἄλλο ἢ ὥσπερ καὶ τὰ παιδία πρὸς τὰς
16 μορμολυκείας. τί γάρ ἐστι παιδίον; ἄγνοια. τί
ἐστι παιδίον; ἀμαθία. ἐπεὶ ὅπου οἶδεν, κἀκεῖνα
17 οὐδὲν ἡμῶν ἔλαττον ἔχει· θάνατος τί ἐστιν·
μορμολύκειον. στρέψας αὐτὸ κατάμαθε· ἰδού,

---

[1] Kronenberg: ἀφειδὲς S.

---

[1] From an unknown tragic poet (Nauck, *Fragm. Trag
Adesp.*, 88); included also among the *Monostichs* of
Menander, 504.

[2] Plato, *Phaedo* 77E; compare *Crito* 46C. Epictetus seems

216

cowardice and abjectness, full of fears and perturbations. For if a man should transfer his caution to the sphere of the moral purpose and the deeds of the moral purpose, then along with the desire to be cautious he will also at once have under his control the will to avoid; whereas, if he should transfer his caution to those matters which are not under our control and lie outside the province of the moral purpose, inasmuch as he is applying his will to avoid towards those things which are under the control of others, he will necessarily be subject to fear, instability, and perturbation. For it is not death or hardship that is a fearful thing, but the fear of hardship or death. That is why we praise the man who said

Not death is dreadful, but a shameful death.[1]

Our confidence ought, therefore, to be turned toward death, and our caution toward the fear of death; whereas we do just the opposite—in the face of death we turn to flight, but about the formation of a judgement on death we show carelessness, disregard, and unconcern. But Socrates did well to call all such things "bugbears."[2] For just as masks appear fearful and terrible to children because of inexperience, in some such manner we also are affected by events, and this for the same reason that children are affected by bugbears. For what is a child? Ignorance. What is a child? Want of instruction. For where a child has knowledge, he is no worse than we are. What is death? A bugbear. Turn it about and learn what it is; see,

to use μορμολύκειον and μορμολυκεία in the unusual sense of a terrifying form of mask.

πῶς οὐ δάκνει· τὸ σωμάτιον δεῖ χωρισθῆναι τοῦ
πνευματίου, ὡς πρότερον ἐκεχώριστο, ἢ νῦν ἢ
ὕστερον. τί οὖν ἀγανακτεῖς, εἰ νῦν; εἰ γὰρ μὴ
18 νῦν, ὕστερον. διὰ τί; ἵνα ἡ περίοδος ἀνύηται τοῦ
κόσμου· χρείαν γὰρ ἔχει τῶν μὲν ἐνισταμένων,
19 τῶν δὲ μελλόντων, τῶν δ᾽ ἠνυσμένων. πόνος τί
ἐστιν; μορμολύκειον. στρέψον αὐτὸ καὶ κατά-
μαθε. τραχέως κινεῖται τὸ σαρκίδιον, εἶτα πάλιν
λείως. ἄν σοι μὴ λυσιτελῇ, ἡ θύρα ἤνοικται·
20 ἄν λυσιτελῇ, φέρε. πρὸς πάντα γὰρ ἠνοῖχθαι
δεῖ τὴν θύραν, καὶ πρᾶγμα οὐκ ἔχομεν.

21 Τίς οὖν τούτων τῶν δογμάτων καρπός; ὅνπερ
δεῖ κάλλιστόν τ᾽ εἶναι καὶ πρεπωδέστατον τοῖς
τῷ ὄντι παιδευομένοις, ἀταραξία ἀφοβία ἐλευ-
22 θερία. οὐ γὰρ τοῖς πολλοῖς περὶ τούτων πιστευ-
τέον, οἳ λέγουσιν μόνοις ἐξεῖναι παιδεύεσθαι τοῖς
ἐλευθέροις, ἀλλὰ τοῖς φιλοσόφοις μᾶλλον, οἳ
23 λέγουσι μόνους τοὺς παιδευθέντας ἐλευθέρους εἶναι.
—Πῶς τοῦτο;—Οὕτως· νῦν ἄλλο τί ἐστιν
ἐλευθερία ἢ τὸ ἐξεῖναι ὡς βουλόμεθα διεξάγειν;
"οὐδέν." λέγετε δή μοι, ὦ ἄνθρωποι, βούλεσθε
ζῆν ἁμαρτάνοντες; "οὐ βουλόμεθα." οὐδεὶς
24 τοίνυν ἁμαρτάνων ἐλεύθερός ἐστιν. βούλεσθε
ζῆν φοβούμενοι, βούλεσθε λυπούμενοι, βούλεσθε
ταρασσόμενοι; "οὐδαμῶς." οὐδεὶς ἄρα οὔτε

---

[1] A favourite idea of the Stoics (Zeno in Diog. Laert. VII.
137; Marcus Aurelius V. 13 and 32; X. 7, 2; XI. 2).
Briefly expressed, it is a theory of "cyclical regeneration"
(Marc. Aur. XI. 2), *i.e.*, that all things repeat themselves
in periodic cycles. *Cf.* Norden, *Geburt des Kindes* (1924), 31.
[2] "Freedom" in the days of the older Greek philosophers
connoted primarily the exercise of political rights, but in

it does not bite. The paltry body must be separated from the bit of spirit, either now or later, just as it existed apart from it before. Why are you grieved, then, if it be separated now? For if it be not separated now, it will be later. Why? So that the revolution of the universe may be accomplished;[1] for it has need of the things that are now coming into being, and the things that shall be, and the things that have been accomplished. What is hardship? A bugbear. Turn it about and learn what it is. The poor flesh is subjected to rough treatment, and then again to smooth. If you do not find this profitable, the door stands open; if you do find it profitable, bear it. For the door must be standing open for every emergency, and then we have no trouble.

What, then, is the fruit of these doctrines? Precisely that which must needs be both the fairest and the most becoming for those who are being truly educated—tranquillity, fearlessness, freedom. For on these matters we should not trust the multitude, who say, "Only the free can be educated," but rather the philosophers, who say, "Only the educated are free."—How is that?— Thus: At this time[2] is freedom anything but the right to live as we wish? "Nothing else." Tell me, then, O men, do you wish to live in error? "We do not." Well, no one who lives in error is free. Do you wish to live in fear, in sorrow, in turmoil? "By no means." Well then, no man who

the time of Epictetus, under the Roman rule, it meant nothing more than the privilege to live the kind of life that one pleased under the authority of the Imperial government. There is a play also on the double meaning of free, *i.e.*, in a social and in a moral sense.

φοβούμενος οὔτε λυπούμενος οὔτε ταρασσόμενος
ἐλεύθερός ἐστιν, ὅστις δ' ἀπήλλακται λυπῶν
καὶ φόβων καὶ ταραχῶν, οὗτος τῇ αὐτῇ ὁδῷ
25 καὶ τοῦ δουλεύειν ἀπήλλακται. πῶς οὖν ἔτι
ὑμῖν πιστεύσομεν, ὦ φίλτατοι νομοθέται; οὐκ
ἐπιτρέπομεν παιδεύεσθαι, εἰ μὴ τοῖς ἐλευθέροις;
οἱ φιλόσοφοι γὰρ λέγουσιν ὅτι οὐκ ἐπιτρέπομεν
ἐλευθέροις εἶναι εἰ μὴ τοῖς πεπαιδευμένοις, τοῦτό
26 ἐστιν ὁ θεὸς οὐκ ἐπιτρέπει.—Ὅταν οὖν στρέψῃ τις
ἐπὶ στρατηγοῦ τὸν αὑτοῦ δοῦλον, οὐδὲν ἐποίησεν;
—Ἐποίησεν.—Τί;—Ἔστρεψεν τὸν αὑτοῦ δοῦλον
ἐπὶ στρατηγοῦ.—Ἄλλο οὐδέν;—Ναί· καὶ εἰκο-
27 στὴν αὑτοῦ δοῦναι ὀφείλει.—Τί οὖν; ὁ ταῦτα
παθὼν οὐ γέγονεν ἐλεύθερος;—Οὐ μᾶλλον ἢ
28 ἀτάραχος. ἐπεὶ σὺ ὁ ἄλλους στρέφειν δυνάμενος
οὐδένα ἔχεις κύριον; οὐκ ἀργύριον, οὐ κοράσιον,
οὐ παιδάριον, οὐ τὸν τύραννον, οὐ φίλον τινὰ τοῦ
τυράννου; τί οὖν τρέμεις ἐπί τινα τοιαύτην ἀπιὼν
περίστασιν;

29 Διὰ τοῦτο λέγω πολλάκις "ταῦτα μελετᾶτε καὶ
ταῦτα πρόχειρα ἔχετε, πρὸς τίνα δεῖ τεθαρρηκέναι
καὶ πρὸς τίνα εὐλαβῶς διακεῖσθαι, ὅτι πρὸς τὰ
ἀπροαίρετα θαρρεῖν, εὐλαβεῖσθαι τὰ προαιρετικά."
30 —Ἀλλ' οὐκ ἀνέγνων σοι οὐδ' ἔγνως τί ποιῶ;—
31 Ἐν τίνι; ἐν λεξειδίοις. ἔχε σου τὰ λεξείδια·
δεῖξον, πῶς ἔχεις πρὸς ὄρεξιν καὶ ἔκκλισιν, εἰ μὴ

---

[1] Part of the ceremony of manumission in Roman law.
The tax of "five per cent." mentioned just below is the fee
that had to be paid to the State.

[2] The words of a pupil who has read and correctly
interpreted some passage set him, or has read aloud to
Epictetus some essay of his own composition.

is in fear, or sorrow, or turmoil, is free, but whoever
is rid of sorrows and fears and turmoils, this man is
by the self-same course rid also of slavery. How,
then, shall we any longer trust you, O dearest
lawgivers? Do we allow none but the free to get
an education? For the philosophers say, "We do
not allow any but the educated to be free"; that is,
God does not allow it.—When, therefore, in the
presence of the praetor a man turns his own slave
about, has he done nothing?[1]—He has done
something.—What?—He has turned his slave about
in the presence of the praetor.—Nothing more?—
Yes, he is bound to pay a tax of five per cent. of the
slave's value.—What then? Has not the man to
whom this has been done become free?—He has no
more become free than he has acquired peace of
mind. You, for example, who are able to turn
others about, have *you* no master? Have you not
as your master money, or a mistress, or a boy
favourite, or the tyrant, or some friend of the tyrant?
If not, why do you tremble when you go to face some
circumstance involving those things?

That is why I say over and over again, "Practise
these things and have them ready at hand, that is,
the knowledge of what you ought to face with
confidence, and what you ought to face with
caution—that you ought to face with confidence
that which is outside the province of the moral
purpose, with caution that which is within the
province of the moral purpose."—But have I not
read to you, and do you not know what I am
doing?[2]—What have you been engaged upon?
Trifling phrases! Keep your trifling phrases!
Show me rather how you stand in regard to desire

ἀποτυγχάνεις ὧν θέλεις, εἰ μὴ περιπίπτεις οἷς οὐ
θέλεις. ἐκεῖνα δὲ τὰ περιόδια, ἂν νοῦν ἔχῃς, ἄρας
32 πού ποτε ἀπαλείψεις.—Τί οὖν; Σωκράτης οὐκ
ἔγραφεν;—Καὶ τίς τοσαῦτα; ἀλλὰ πῶς; ἐπεὶ
μὴ ἐδύνατο ἔχειν ἀεὶ τὸν ἐλέγχοντα αὐτοῦ τὰ
δόγματα ἢ ἐλεγχθησόμενον ἐν τῷ μέρει, αὐτὸς
ἑαυτὸν ἤλεγχεν καὶ ἐξήταζεν καὶ ἀεὶ μίαν γέ τινα
33 πρόληψιν ἐγύμναζεν χρηστικῶς. ταῦτα γράφει
φιλόσοφος· λεξείδια δὲ καὶ "ἦ δ' ὅς," "ἦν δ' ἐγώ,"[1]
ἄλλοις ἀφίησι, τοῖς ἀναισθήτοις ἢ τοῖς μακαρίοις,
τοῖς σχολὴν ἄγουσιν ὑπὸ ἀταραξίας ἢ τοῖς μηδὲν
τῶν ἑξῆς ὑπολογιζομένοις διὰ μωρίαν.

34   Καὶ νῦν καιροῦ καλοῦντος ἐκεῖνα δείξεις ἀπελθὼν καὶ ἀναγνώσῃ καὶ ἐμπερπερεύσῃ; "ἰδού,
35 πῶς διαλόγους συντίθημι." μή, ἄνθρωπε, ἀλλ'
ἐκεῖνα μᾶλλον "ἰδού, πῶς ὀρεγόμενος οὐκ ἀποτυγχάνω. ἰδού, πῶς ἐκκλίνων οὐ περιπίπτω.
φέρε θάνατον καὶ γνώσῃ· φέρε πόνους, φέρε
δεσμωτήριον, φέρε ἀδοξίαν, φέρε καταδίκην."
36 αὕτη ἐπίδειξις νέου ἐκ σχολῆς ἐληλυθότος. τἄλλα δ' ἄλλοις ἄφες, μηδὲ φωνήν τις ἀκούσῃ σου
περὶ αὐτῶν ποτε μηδ', ἂν ἐπαινέσῃ τις ἐπ' αὐτοῖς,
ἀνέχου, δόξον δὲ μηδεὶς εἶναι καὶ εἰδέναι μηδέν.

---

[1] Kronenberg: ἡ ὁδὸς ἦν λέγ** S (λέγω Sc).

---

[1] A very strange passage, for it was generally believed
that Socrates did not write. Still there seems to have been
some doubt on the question (Diog. Laert. I. 16 makes the
statement that he did not write as resting "on the
authority of some"), and the style of writing which
Epictetus here describes seems not to have been intended for
publication, so that it may be possible that Socrates wrote
copiously, but only as a philosophical exercise, and not for
others to read.

and aversion, whether you do not fail to get what you wish, or do not fall into what you do not wish. As for those trifling periods of yours, if you are wise, you will take them away somewhere and blot them out.—What then? Did not Socrates write?—Yes, who wrote as much as he?[1] But how? Since he could not have always at hand someone to test his judgements, or to be tested by him in turn, he was in the habit of testing and examining himself, and was always in a practical way trying out some particular primary conception. That is what a philosopher writes; but trifling phrases, and "said he," "said I"[2] he leaves to others, to the stupid or the blessed, those who by virtue of their tranquillity live at leisure, or those who by virtue of their folly take no account of logical conclusions.

And now, when the crisis calls, will you go off and make an exhibition of your compositions, and give a reading from them, and boast, "See, how I write dialogues"? Do not so, man, but rather boast as follows: "See how in my desire I do not fail to get what I wish. See how in my aversions I do not fall into things that I would avoid. Bring on death and you shall know; bring on hardships, bring on imprisonment, bring on disrepute, bring on condemnation." This is the proper exhibition of a young man come from school. Leave other things to other people; neither let anyone ever hear a word from you about them, nor, if anyone praises you for them, do you tolerate it, but let yourself be accounted a no-body and a know-nothing. Show

---

[2] Characteristic expressions in dialogue, an especially popular type of composition for philosophy which aspired to a refined literary form; compare the critical note.

37 μόνον τοῦτο εἰδὼς φαίνου, πῶς μήτ᾽ ἀποτύχῃς
38 ποτὲ μήτε περιπέσῃς. ἄλλοι μελετάτωσαν
δίκας, ἄλλοι προβλήματα, ἄλλοι συλλογισμούς·
σὺ ἀποθνήσκειν, σὺ δεδέσθαι, σὺ στρεβλοῦσθαι,
39 σὺ ἐξορίζεσθαι. πάντα ταῦτα θαρροῦντως, πε-
ποιθότως τῷ κεκληκότι σε ἐπ᾽ αὐτά, τῷ ἄξιον
τῆς χώρας ταύτης κεκρικότι, ἐν ᾗ καταταχθεὶς
ἐπιδείξεις, τίνα δύναται λογικὸν ἡγεμονικὸν πρὸς
40 τὰς ἀπροαιρέτους δυνάμεις ἀντιταξάμενον. καὶ
οὕτως τὸ παράδοξον ἐκεῖνο οὐκέτι οὔτ᾽ ἀδύνατον
φανεῖται οὔτε παράδοξον, ὅτι ἅμα μὲν εὐλαβεῖσθαι δεῖ ἅμα δὲ θαρρεῖν, πρὸς μὲν τὰ ἀπροαίρετα
θαρρεῖν, ἐν δὲ τοῖς προαιρετικοῖς εὐλαβεῖσθαι.

β΄. Περὶ ἀταραξίας.

1 Ὅρα σὺ ὁ ἀπιὼν ἐπὶ τὴν δίκην, τί θέλεις
2 τηρῆσαι καὶ ποῦ θέλεις ἀνύσαι. εἰ γὰρ προαίρεσιν θέλεις τηρῆσαι κατὰ φύσιν ἔχουσαν, πᾶσά
σοι ἀσφάλεια, πᾶσά σοι εὐμάρεια, πρᾶγμα οὐκ
3 ἔχεις. τὰ γὰρ ἐπὶ σοὶ αὐτεξούσια καὶ φύσει
ἐλεύθερα θέλων τηρῆσαι καὶ τούτοις ἀρκούμενος
τίνος ἔτι ἐπιστρέφῃ; τίς γὰρ αὐτῶν κύριος, τίς
4 αὐτὰ δύναται ἀφελέσθαι; εἰ θέλεις αἰδήμων
εἶναι καὶ πιστός, τίς οὐκ ἐάσει σε; εἰ θέλεις μὴ

that you know this only—how you may never either fail to get what you desire or fall into what you avoid. Let others practise lawsuits, others problems, others syllogisms; do you practise how to die, how to be enchained, how to be racked, how to be exiled. Do all these things with confidence, with trust in Him who has called you to face them and deemed you worthy of this position, in which having once been placed you shall exhibit what can be achieved by a rational governing principle when arrayed against the forces that lie outside the province of the moral purpose. And thus the paradox of which we were speaking will no longer appear either impossible or paradoxical, namely, that at the same time we ought to be both cautious and confident, confident in regard to those things that lie outside the province of the moral purpose, and cautious in regard to those things that lie within the province of the moral purpose.

CHAPTER II

On tranquillity

CONSIDER, you who are going to court, what you wish to maintain and wherein you wish to succeed; for if you wish to maintain freedom of moral purpose in its natural condition, all security is yours, every facility yours, you have no trouble. For if you are willing to keep guard over those things which are under your direct authority and by nature free, and if you are satisfied with them, what else do you care about? For who is master of them, who can take them away from you? If you wish to be self-respecting and honourable, who is it that will not allow you?

κωλύεσθαι μηδ' ἀναγκάζεσθαι, τίς σε ἀναγκάσει
ὀρέγεσθαι ὧν οὐ δοκεῖ σοι, τίς ἐκκλίνειν ἃ μὴ
5 φαίνεταί σοι; ἀλλὰ τί; πράξει μέν σοί τινα ἃ
δοκεῖ φοβερὰ εἶναι· ἵνα δὲ καὶ ἐκκλίνων αὐτὰ
6 πάθῃς, πῶς δύναται ποιῆσαι; ὅταν οὖν ἐπὶ σοὶ
ᾖ τὸ ὀρέγεσθαι καὶ ἐκκλίνειν, τίνος ἔτι ἐπι-
7 στρέφῃ; τοῦτό σοι προοίμιον, τοῦτο διήγησις,
τοῦτο πίστις, τοῦτο νίκη, τοῦτο ἐπίλογος, τοῦτο
εὐδοκίμησις.

8 Διὰ τοῦτο ὁ Σωκράτης πρὸς τὸν ὑπομιμνή-
σκοντα, ἵνα παρασκευάζηται πρὸς τὴν δίκην,
ἔφη "οὐ δοκῶ οὖν σοι ἅπαντι τῷ βίῳ πρὸς τοῦτο
9 παρασκευάζεσθαι;"—"Ποίαν παρασκευήν;"—
"Τετήρηκα," φησίν, "τὸ ἐπ' ἐμοί."—"Πῶς
οὖν;" "Οὐδὲν οὐδέποτ' ἄδικον οὔτ' ἰδίᾳ οὔτε
10 δημοσίᾳ ἔπραξα." εἰ δὲ θέλεις καὶ τὰ ἐκτὸς
τηρῆσαι, τὸ σωμάτιον καὶ τὸ οὐσίδιον καὶ τὸ ἀξιω-
μάτιον, λέγω σοι· ἤδη αὐτόθεν παρασκευάζου τὴν
δυνατὴν παρασκευὴν πᾶσαν καὶ λοιπὸν σκέπτου
11 καὶ τὴν φύσιν τοῦ δικαστοῦ καὶ τὸν ἀντίδικον. εἰ
γονάτων ἅψασθαι δεῖ, γονάτων ἅψαι· εἰ κλαῦ-
12 σαι, κλαῦσον· εἰ οἰμῶξαι, οἴμωξον. ὅταν γὰρ
ὑποθῇς τὰ σὰ τοῖς ἐκτός, δούλευε τὸ λοιπὸν καὶ
μὴ ἀντισπῶ καὶ ποτὲ μὲν θέλε δουλεύειν, ποτὲ
13 δὲ μὴ θέλε, ἀλλ' ἁπλῶς καὶ ἐξ ὅλης τῆς διανοίας
ἢ ταῦτα ἢ ἐκεῖνα· ἢ ἐλεύθερος ἢ δοῦλος, ἢ πεπαιδευμένος ἢ ἀπαίδευτος, ἢ γενναῖος ἀλεκτρυὼν ἢ
ἀγεννής, ἢ ὑπόμενε τυπτόμενος, μέχρις ἂν ἀπο-

---

[1] A somewhat free version of what Xenophon records in
his *Apology*, 2 f.

If you wish not to be hindered nor compelled, what man will compel you to desire what does not seem to you to be desirable, to avoid what you do not feel should be avoided? Well, what then? The judge will do some things to you which are thought to be terrifying; but how can he make you try to avoid what you suffer? When, therefore, desire and aversion are under your own control, what more do you care for? This is your introduction, this the setting forth of your case, this your proof, this your victory, this your peroration, this your approbation.

That is why Socrates, in reply to the man who was reminding him to make preparation for his trial, said, "Do you not feel, then, that with my whole life I am making preparation for this?"—"What kind of preparation?"—"I have maintained," says he, "that which is under my control."—"How then?"—"I have never done anything that was wrong either in my private or in my public life."[1] But if you wish to maintain also what is external, your paltry body and your petty estate and your small reputation, I have this to say to you: Begin this very moment to make all possible preparation, and furthermore study the character of your judge and your antagonist. If you must clasp men's knees, clasp them; if you must wail, then wail; if you must groan, then groan. For when you subject what is your own to externals, then from henceforth be a slave, and stop letting yourself be drawn this way and that, at one moment wishing to be a slave, at another not, but be either this or that simply and with all your mind, either a free man or a slave, either educated or uneducated, either a spirited fighting cock or a spiritless one,

227

θάνῃς, ἢ ἀπαγόρευσον εὐθύς. μή σοι γένοιτο
πληγὰς πολλὰς λαβεῖν καὶ ὕστερον ἀπαγορεῦ-
14 σαι. εἰ δ' αἰσχρὰ ταῦτα, αὐτόθεν ἤδη δίελε " ποῦ
φύσις κακῶν καὶ ἀγαθῶν ; οὗ καὶ ἀλήθεια. ὅπου
ἀλήθεια καὶ οὗ [1] φύσις, ἐκεῖ τὸ εὐλαβές· ὅπου ἡ
ἀλήθεια, ἐκεῖ τὸ θαρραλέον, ὅπου ἡ φύσις."
15 Ἐπεί τοι δοκεῖς, ὅτι τὰ ἐκτὸς τηρῆσαι θέλων
Σωκράτης παρελθὼν ἂν ἔλεγε " ἐμὲ δ' Ἄνυτος
καὶ Μέλητος ἀποκτεῖναι μὲν δύνανται, βλάψαι
16 δ' οὔ"; οὕτω μωρὸς ἦν, ἵνα μὴ ἴδῃ ὅτι αὕτη ἡ
ὁδὸς ἐνταῦθα οὐ φέρει, ἀλλ' ἄλλη ; τί οὖν ἐστιν,
17 ὅτι οὐκ ἔχει λόγον καὶ προσερεθίζειν [2] ; ὡς ὁ
ἐμὸς Ἡράκλειτος περὶ ἀγριδίου πραγματίου
ἔχων ἐν Ῥόδῳ καὶ ἀποδείξας τοῖς δικασταῖς ὅτι
δίκαια λέγει ἐλθὼν ἐπὶ τὸν ἐπίλογον ἔφη ὅτι
" ἀλλ' οὔτε δεήσομαι ὑμῶν οὔτ' ἐπιστρέφομαι, τί
μέλλετε κρίνειν· ὑμεῖς τε μᾶλλον οἱ κρινόμενοί
ἐστε ἢ ἐγώ." καὶ οὕτως κατέστρεψε τὸ πραγμά-
18 τιον. τίς χρεία ; μόνον μὴ δέου, μὴ προστίθει
δ' ὅτι " καὶ οὐ δέομαι," εἰ μή τι καιρός ἐστιν
ἐπίτηδες ἐρεθίσαι τοὺς δικαστὰς ὡς Σωκράτει.
19 καὶ σὺ εἰ τοιοῦτον ἐπίλογον παρασκευάζῃ, τί
20 ἀναβαίνεις, τί ὑπακούεις ; εἰ γὰρ σταυρωθῆναι

---

[1] Schegk : οὐ S.
[2] Bentley : προσερεθίζει S.

---

[1] These last three sentences make no satisfactory sense in
themselves, and none of the numerous emendations which
have been offered seem convincing, while at the same time
they interrupt the course of the argument where they stand.
It would appear, as Schenkl suggests, that they constitute
a seriously mutilated section of the preceding chapter
(possibly from the very end), which by some accident has
become imbedded in an alien context.

either endure to be beaten until you die, or give in at once. Far be it from you to receive many blows and yet at the last give in! But if that is disgraceful, begin this very moment to decide the question, "Where is the nature of good and evil to be found? Where truth also is. Where truth and where nature are, there is caution; where truth is, there is confidence, where nature is." [1]

Why, do you think that if Socrates had wished to maintain his external possessions he would have come forward and said, "Anytus and Meletus are able indeed to kill me, but they cannot harm me"? Was he so foolish as not to see that this course does not lead to that goal, but elsewhere? Why is it unreasonable, then, to add also a word of provocation? Just as my friend Heracleitus, who had an unimportant lawsuit about a small piece of land in Rhodes; after he had pointed out the justice of his claim he went on to the peroration in which he said, "But neither will I entreat you, nor do I care what your decision is going to be, and it is you who are on trial rather than I." And so he ruined his case. What is the use of acting like that? Merely make no entreaties, but do not add the words "Yes, and I make no entreaties," unless the right time has come for you, as it did for Socrates, deliberately to provoke your judges. If you, for your part, are preparing a peroration of that sort, why do you mount the platform at all, why answer the summons? [2] For if you wish to be crucified, wait and the cross

---

[2] That is, it is a sheer waste of effort to speak in so provocative a manner as to invite condemnation. If that is what you wish, simply do nothing at all and you will gain your end.

θέλεις, ἔκδεξαι καὶ ἥξει ὁ σταυρός· εἰ δ᾽ ὑπακοῦσαι λόγος αἱρεῖ καὶ πεῖσαι τό γε παρ᾽ αὑτόν,
τὰ ἐξῆς τούτῳ ποιητέον τηροῦντι μέντοι τὰ ἴδια.

21 Ταύτῃ καὶ γελοῖόν ἐστι τὸ λέγειν "ὑπόθου μοι."
τί σοι ὑποθῶμαι; ἀλλὰ "ποίησόν μου τὴν διά-
νοιαν ὅ τι ἂν ἀποβαίνῃ πρὸς τοῦτο ἁρμόσασθαι."

22 ἐπεὶ ἐκεῖνό γε ὅμοιόν ἐστιν οἷον εἰ ἀγράμματος
λέγοι "εἰπέ μοι τί γράψω, ὅταν μοι προβληθῇ

23 τι ὄνομα." ἂν γὰρ εἴπω ὅτι Δίων, εἶτα παρελθὼν
ἐκεῖνος αὐτῷ προβάλῃ μὴ τὸ Δίωνος ὄνομα,

24 ἀλλὰ τὸ Θέωνος, τί γένηται; τί γράψῃ; ἀλλ᾽ εἰ
μὲν μεμελέτηκας γράφειν, ἔχεις καὶ παρασκευάσασθαι[1] πρὸς πάντα τὰ ὑπαγορευόμενα· εἰ δὲ
μή, τί σοι ἐγὼ νῦν ὑποθῶμαι; ἂν γὰρ ἄλλο τι
ὑπαγορεύῃ τὰ πράγματα, τί ἐρεῖς ἢ τί πράξεις;

25 τούτου οὖν τοῦ καθολικοῦ μέμνησο καὶ ὑποθήκης
οὐκ ἀπορήσεις. ἐὰν δὲ πρὸς τὰ ἔξω χάσκῃς,
ἀνάγκη σε ἄνω καὶ κάτω κυλίεσθαι πρὸς τὸ

26 βούλημα τοῦ κυρίου. τίς δ᾽ ἐστὶ κύριος; ὁ τῶν
ὑπὸ σοῦ τινος σπουδαζομένων ἢ ἐκκλινομένων
ἔχων ἐξουσίαν.

γ΄. Πρὸς τοὺς συνιστάντας τινὰς τοῖς
φιλοσόφοις

1 Καλῶς ὁ Διογένης πρὸς τὸν ἀξιοῦντα γράμματα παρ᾽ αὐτοῦ λαβεῖν συστατικὰ "ὅτι μὲν
ἄνθρωπος," φησίν, "εἶ, καὶ ἰδὼν γνώσεται· εἰ δ᾽

---

[1] Upton from his "codex"   παρασκευάσαι S.

will come; but if reason decides that you should answer the summons and do your best to have what you say carry conviction, you must act in accordance therewith, but always maintaining what is your own proper character.

Looked at in this way it is also absurd to say, "Advise me." What advice am I to give you? Nay, say rather, "Enable my mind to adapt itself to whatever comes." Since the other expression is just as if an illiterate should say, "Tell me what to write when some name is set me to write." For if I say, "Write Dio," and then his teacher comes along and sets him not the name "Dio," but "Theo," what will happen? What will he write? But if you have practised writing, you are able also to prepare yourself for everything that is dictated to you; if you have not practised, what advice can I now offer you? For if circumstances dictate something different, what will you say or what will you do? Bear in mind, therefore, this general principle and you will not be at a loss for a suggestion. But if you gape open-mouthed at externals, you must needs be tossed up and down according to the will of your master. And who is your master? He who has authority over any of the things upon which you set your heart or which you wish to avoid.

CHAPTER III

To those who recommend persons to the philosophers

THAT is an excellent answer of Diogenes to the man who asked for a letter of recommendation from him: "That you are a man," he says, "he will

ἀγαθὸς ἢ κακός, εἰ μὲν ἔμπειρός ἐστι διαγνῶναι
τοὺς ἀγαθοὺς καὶ κακούς, γνώσεται, εἰ δ' ἄπειρος,
2 οὐδ' ἂν μυριάκις γράψω αὐτῷ." ὅμοιον γὰρ
ὥσπερ εἰ δραχμὴ συσταθῆναί τινι ἠξίου, ἵνα
δοκιμασθῇ. εἰ ἀργυρογνωμονικός ἐστιν, σὺ σαυ-
3 τὴν συστήσεις. ἔδει οὖν τοιοῦτόν τι ἔχειν ἡμᾶς
καὶ ἐν τῷ βίῳ οἷον ἐπ' ἀργυρίου, ἵν' εἰπεῖν δύνωμαι καθάπερ ὁ ἀργυρογνώμων λέγει "φέρε ἣν
4 θέλεις δραχμὴν καὶ διαγνώσομαι." ἀλλ' ἐπὶ
συλλογισμῶν "φέρε ὃν θέλεις καὶ διακρινῶ σοι
τὸν ἀναλυτικόν¹ τε καὶ μή." διὰ τί; οἶδα γὰρ
ἀναλύειν συλλογισμούς· ἔχω τὴν δύναμιν, ἣν
ἔχειν δεῖ τὸν ἐπιγνωστικὸν τῶν περὶ συλλο-
5 γισμοὺς κατορθούντων. ἐπὶ δὲ τοῦ βίου τί ποιῶ;
νῦν μὲν λέγω ἀγαθόν, νῦν δὲ κακόν. τί τὸ αἴτιον;
τὸ ἐναντίον ἢ ἐπὶ τῶν συλλογισμῶν, ἀμαθία καὶ
ἀπειρία.

δ'. Πρὸς τὸν ἐπὶ μοιχείᾳ ποτὲ κατειλημμένον

1 Λέγοντος αὐτοῦ ὅτι Ὁ ἄνθρωπος πρὸς πίστιν
γέγονεν καὶ τοῦτο ὁ ἀνατρέπων ἀνατρέπει τὸ
ἴδιον τοῦ ἀνθρώπου, ἐπεισῆλθέν τις τῶν δοκούν-
των φιλολόγων, ὃς κατείληπτό ποτε μοιχὸς ἐν

---

¹ This is Wolf's interpretation of the rare word ἀναλυτικός,
i.e., as referring to a syllogism. But Upton, Schweighäuser,
and others take it in the sense of "a person who is capable of
analyzing syllogisms." The former interpretation fits the
preceding sentence better, the latter the following sentence.
As in § 3 the assayer of silver and the assayer of character
are blended, so here apparently the transition from the
syllogism to those who handle it is made somewhat abruptly.

know at a glance; but whether you are a good or a bad man he will discover if he has the skill to distinguish between good and bad, and if he is without that skill he will not discover the facts, even though I write him thousands of times." For it is just as though a drachma asked to be recommended to someone, in order to be tested. If the man in question is an assayer of silver, you will recommend yourself. We ought, therefore, to have also in everyday life the sort of thing that we have in the case of silver, so that I may be able to say, as the assayer of silver says, "Bring me any drachma you please, and I will appraise it." Now in the case of syllogisms I say, "Bring me any you please and I will distinguish for you between the one that is capable of analysis and the one that is not."[1] How so? Because, I know how to analyze syllogisms myself; I have the faculty which the man must have who is going to appraise those who handle syllogisms properly. But in everyday life what do I do? Sometimes I call a thing good, and sometimes bad. What is the reason? The opposite of what was true in the case of syllogisms, namely, ignorance and inexperience.

CHAPTER IV

To the man who had once been caught in adultery

As Epictetus was remarking that man is born to fidelity, and that the man who overthrows this is overthrowing the characteristic quality of man, there entered one who had the reputation of being a scholar, and who had once been caught in the city

233

2 τῇ πόλει. ὁ δ' 'Αλλ' ἄν, φησίν, ἀφέντες τοῦτο
τὸ πιστόν, πρὸς ὃ πεφύκαμεν, ἐπιβουλεύωμεν τῇ
γυναικὶ τοῦ γείτονος, τί ποιοῦμεν; τί γὰρ ἄλλο
ἢ ἀπόλλυμεν καὶ ἀναιροῦμεν; τίνα; τὸν πιστόν,
3 τὸν αἰδήμονα, τὸν ὅσιον. ταῦτα μόνα; γειτνί-
ασιν δ' οὐκ ἀναιροῦμεν, φιλίαν δ' οὔ, πόλιν δ'
οὔ; εἰς τίνα δὲ χώραν αὐτοὺς κατατάσσομεν;
ὡς τίνι σοι χρῶμαι, ἄνθρωπε; ὡς γείτονι, ὡς
φίλῳ; ποίῳ τινί; ὡς πολίτῃ; τί σοι πιστεύσω;
4 εἶτα σκευάριον μὲν εἰ ἦς οὕτως σαπρόν, ὥστε
σοι πρὸς μηδὲν δύνασθαι χρῆσθαι, ἔξω ἂν ἐπὶ
τὰς κοπρίας ἐρρίπτου καὶ οὐδ' ἐκεῖθεν ἄν τίς σε
5 ἀνῃρεῖτο· εἰ δ' ἄνθρωπος ὢν οὐδεμίαν χώραν
δύνασαι ἀποπληρῶσαι ἀνθρωπικήν, τί σε ποιή-
σομεν; ἔστω γάρ, φίλου οὐ δύνασαι τόπον ἔχειν.
δούλου δύνασαι; καὶ τίς σοι πιστεύσει; οὐ
θέλεις οὖν ῥιφῆναί που καὶ αὐτὸς ἐπὶ κοπρίαν
6 ὡς σκεῦος ἄχρηστον, ὡς κόπριον; εἶτα ἐρεῖς
"οὐδείς μου ἐπιστρέφεται, ἀνθρώπου φιλολό-
γου"; κακὸς γὰρ εἶ καὶ ἄχρηστος. οἷον εἰ οἱ
σφῆκες[1] ἠγανάκτουν, ὅτι οὐδεὶς αὐτῶν ἐπιστρέφεται, ἀλλὰ φεύγουσι πάντες κἄν τις δύνηται,
7 πλήξας κατέβαλεν. σὺ κέντρον ἔχεις τοιοῦτον,
ὥστε ὃν ἂν πλήξῃς εἰς πράγματα καὶ ὀδύνας
ἐμβάλλειν. τί σε θέλεις ποιήσωμεν; οὐκ ἔχεις
ποῦ τεθῇς.
8 Τί οὖν; οὐκ εἰσὶν αἱ γυναῖκες κοιναὶ φύσει;
κἀγὼ λέγω. καὶ γὰρ τὸ χοιρίδιον κοινὸν τῶν

---

[1] Upton: σκώληκες S.

---

[1] A not uncommon social theory in antiquity, to which the
Stoics also subscribed (Diog. Laert. VII. 33 and 131); but

in the act of adultery. But, goes on Epictetus, if we abandon this fidelity to which we are by nature born, and make designs against our neighbour's wife, what are we doing? Why, what but ruining and destroying? Whom? The man of fidelity, of self-respect, of piety. Is that all? Are we not overthrowing also neighbourly feeling, friendship, the state? In what position are we placing ourselves? As what am I to treat you, fellow? As a neighbour, as a friend? Of what kind? As a citizen? What confidence am I to place in you? If you were a vessel so cracked that it was impossible to use you for anything, you would be cast forth upon the dunghills and even from there no one would pick you up; but if, although a man, you cannot fill a man's place, what are we going to do with you? For, assuming that you cannot hold the place of a friend, can you hold that of a slave? And who is going to trust you? Are you not willing, therefore, that you too should be cast forth upon some dunghill as a useless vessel, as a piece of dung? For all that will you say, "Nobody cares for me, a scholar!"? No, for you are an evil man, and useless. It is just as if the wasps complained that nobody cares for them, but all run away from them, and, if anyone can, he strikes them and knocks them down. You have such a sting that you involve in trouble and pain whomever you strike. What do you want us to do with you? There is no place where you can be put.

What then, you say; are not women by nature common property?[1] I agree. And the little pig is

Epictetus accepts the doctrine only with such limitations as make it compatible with ordinary matrimonal institutions. Compare also frag. 15, where he recurs to the topic.

κεκλημένων· ἀλλ' ὅταν μέρη γένηται, ἂν σοι
φανῇ, ἀνάρπασον ἀνελθὼν¹ τὸ τοῦ παρακατα-
κειμένου μέρος, λάθρα κλέψον ἢ παρακαθεὶς τὴν
χεῖρα λίχνευε, κἂν μὴ δύνῃ τοῦ κρέως ἀποσπά-
σαι, λίπαινε τοὺς δακτύλους καὶ περίλειχε.
καλὸς συμπότης καὶ σύνδειπνος Σωκρατικός.
9 ἄγε, τὸ δὲ θέατρον οὐκ ἔστι κοινὸν τῶν πολιτῶν ;
ὅταν οὖν καθίσωσιν, ἐλθών, ἄν σοι φανῇ, ἔκβαλέ
10 τινα αὐτῶν. οὕτως καὶ αἱ γυναῖκες φύσει κοιναί.
ὅταν δ' ὁ νομοθέτης ὡς ἑστιάτωρ διέλῃ αὐτάς, οὐ
θέλεις καὶ αὐτὸς ἴδιον μέρος ζητεῖν, ἀλλὰ τὸ
ἀλλότριον ὑφαρπάζεις καὶ λιχνεύεις ; " ἀλλὰ
11 φιλόλογός εἰμι καὶ Ἀρχέδημον νοῶ." Ἀρχέδημον τοίνυν νοῶν μοιχὸς ἴσθι καὶ ἄπιστος καὶ
ἀντὶ ἀνθρώπου λύκος ἢ πίθηκος. τί γὰρ
κωλύει;

ε΄. Πῶς συνυπάρχει μεγαλοφροσύνη καὶ ἐπιμέλεια ;

1 Αἱ ὗλαι ἀδιάφοροι, ἡ δὲ χρῆσις αὐτῶν οὐκ
2 ἀδιάφορος. πῶς οὖν τηρήσῃ τις ἅμα μὲν τὸ
εὐσταθὲς καὶ ἀτάραχον, ἅμα δὲ τὸ ἐπιμελὲς καὶ
μὴ εἰκαῖον μηδ' ἐπισεσυρμένον ; ἂν μιμῆται

---

¹ ἐλθὼν Upton : ἀπελθὼν Schenkl.

¹ The reference is probably to the *Symposia* by Plato and
Xenophon.
² Possibly the Stoic philosopher of Tarsus (Plut. *de Exil.* 14),
but more likely the rhetorician who commented upon a portion

the common property of the invited guests; but
when portions have been assigned, if it so pleases
you, approach and snatch up the portion of the guest
who reclines at your side, steal it secretly, or slip in
your hand and glut your greed, and if you cannot
tear off a piece of the meat, get your fingers greasy
and lick them. A fine companion you would make
at a feast, and a dinner-guest worthy of Socrates![1]
Come now, is not the theatre the common property
of the citizens? When, therefore, they are seated
there, go, if it so pleases you, and throw someone of
them out of his seat. In the same way women also
are by nature common property. But when the law-
giver, like a host at a banquet, has apportioned them,
are you not willing like the rest to look for your own
portion instead of filching away and glutting your
greed upon that which is another's? "But I am a
scholar and understand Archedemus."[2] Very well
then, understand Archedemus and be an adulterer
and faithless and a wolf or an ape instead of a man;
for what is there to prevent you?

CHAPTER V

How are magnanimity and carefulness compatible?

MATERIALS are indifferent, but the use which we
make of them is not a matter of indifference. How,
therefore, shall a man maintain steadfastness and
peace of mind, and at the same time the careful
spirit and that which is neither reckless nor
negligent? If he imitates those who play at dice.

of Aristotle's *Rhetoric* (Quintilian, III. 6. 31 and 33), if these
be really different persons, which is not entirely certain.

3 τοὺς κυβεύοντας. αἱ ψῆφοι ἀδιάφοροι, οἱ κύβοι
ἀδιάφοροι· πόθεν οἶδα, τί μέλλει πίπτειν; τῷ
πεσόντι δ' ἐπιμελῶς καὶ τεχνικῶς χρῆσθαι, τοῦτο

4 ἤδη ἐμὸν ἔργον ἐστίν. οὕτως τοίνυν τὸ μὲν
προηγούμενον καὶ ἐπὶ τοῦ βίου ἔργον ἐκεῖνο·
δίελε τὰ πράγματα καὶ διάστησον καὶ εἰπὲ "τὰ

5 ἔξω οὐκ ἐπ' ἐμοί· προαίρεσις ἐπ' ἐμοί. ποῦ
ζητήσω τὸ ἀγαθὸν καὶ τὸ κακόν; ἔσω ἐν τοῖς
ἐμοῖς." ἐν δὲ τοῖς ἀλλοτρίοις μηδέποτε μήτ'
ἀγαθὸν ὀνομάσῃς μήτε κακὸν μήτ' ὠφέλειαν μήτε
βλάβην μήτ' ἄλλο τι τῶν τοιούτων.

6 Τί οὖν; ἀμελῶς τούτοις χρηστέον; οὐδαμῶς.
τοῦτο γὰρ πάλιν τῇ προαιρέσει κακόν ἐστι καὶ

7 ταύτῃ¹ παρὰ φύσιν. ἀλλ' ἅμα μὲν ἐπιμελῶς,
ὅτι ἡ χρῆσις οὐκ ἀδιάφορον, ἅμα δ' εὐσταθῶς καὶ

8 ἀταράχως, ὅτι ἡ ὕλη οὐ διαφέρουσα. ὅπου γὰρ
τὸ διαφέρον, ἐκεῖ οὔτε κωλῦσαί μέ τις δύναται
οὔτ' ἀναγκάσαι. ὅπου κωλυτὸς καὶ ἀναγκαστός
εἰμι, ἐκείνων ἡ μὲν τεῦξις οὐκ ἐπ' ἐμοὶ οὐδ'
ἀγαθὸν ἢ κακόν, ἡ χρῆσις δ' ἢ κακὸν ἢ ἀγαθόν,

9 ἀλλ' ἐπ' ἐμοί. δύσκολον δὲ μῖξαι καὶ συναγαγεῖν
ταῦτα, ἐπιμέλειαν τοῦ προσπεπονθότος ταῖς ὕλαις
καὶ εὐστάθειαν τοῦ ἀνεπιστρεπτοῦντος, πλὴν οὐκ
ἀδύνατον. εἰ δὲ μή, ἀδύνατον τὸ εὐδαιμονῆσαι.

10 ἀλλ' οἷόν τι ἐπὶ τοῦ πλοῦ ποιοῦμεν. τί μοι
δύναται; τὸ ἐκλέξασθαι τὸν κυβερνήτην, τοὺς

11 ναύτας, τὴν ἡμέραν, τὸν καιρόν. εἶτα χειμὼν

---

¹ ταύτην τὴν S: ταύτῃ s: τὴν deleted by Schenkl.

238

The counters are indifferent, the dice are indifferent;
how am I to know what is going to fall? But to
make a careful and skilful use of what has fallen,
that is now my task.[1] In like manner, therefore,
the principal task in life is this: distinguish matters
and weigh them one against another, and say to
yourself, "Externals are not under my control;
moral choice is under my control. Where am I to
look for the good and the evil? Within me, in that
which is my own." But in that which is another's
never employ the words "good" or "evil," or
"benefit" or "injury," or anything of the sort.

What then? Are these externals to be used
carelessly? Not at all. For this again is to the
moral purpose an evil and thus unnatural to it.
They must be used carefully, because their use is
not a matter of indifference, and at the same time
with steadfastness and peace of mind, because the
material is indifferent. For in whatever really concerns us, there no man can either hinder or compel
me. The attainment of those things in which I can
be hindered or compelled is not under my control and
is neither good nor bad, but the use which I make
of them is either good or bad, and that is under my
control. It is, indeed, difficult to unite and combine
these two things—the carefulness of the man who is
devoted to material things and the steadfastness
of the man who disregards them, but it is not impossible. Otherwise happiness were impossible.
But we act very much as though we were on a
voyage. What is possible for me? To select the
helmsman, the sailors, the day, the moment. Then

---

[1] *Cf.* Menander in the *Adelphoe* of Terence, 740 f.:

> Si illud quod maxume opus est iactu non cadit,
> Illud quod cecidit forte, id arte ut corrigas.

ἐμπέπτωκεν. τί οὖν ἔτι μοι μέλει ; τὰ γὰρ ἐμὰ
ἐκπεπλήρωται. ἄλλου ἐστὶν ἡ ὑπόθεσις, τοῦ
12 κυβερνήτου. ἀλλὰ καὶ ἡ ναῦς καταδύεται. τί
οὖν ἔχω ποιῆσαι ; ὃ δύναμαι, τοῦτο μόνον ποιῶ·
μὴ φοβούμενος ἀποπνίγομαι οὐδὲ κεκραγὼς οὐδ'
ἐγκαλῶν τῷ θεῷ, ἀλλ' εἰδώς, ὅτι τὸ γενόμενον
13 καὶ φθαρῆναι δεῖ. οὐ γάρ εἰμι αἰών, ἀλλ'
ἄνθρωπος, μέρος τῶν πάντων ὡς ὥρα ἡμέρας.
ἐνστῆναί με δεῖ ὡς τὴν ὥραν καὶ παρελθεῖν ὡς
14 ὥραν. τί οὖν μοι διαφέρει πῶς παρέλθω, πότερον
πνιγεὶς ἢ πυρέξας ; διὰ γὰρ τοιούτου τινὸς δεῖ
παρελθεῖν με.

15   Τοῦτο ὄψει ποιοῦντας καὶ τοὺς σφαιρίζοντας
ἐμπείρως. οὐδεὶς αὐτῶν διαφέρεται περὶ τοῦ
ἁρπαστοῦ ὡς περὶ ἀγαθοῦ ἢ κακοῦ, περὶ δὲ τοῦ
16 βάλλειν καὶ δέχεσθαι. λοιπὸν ἐν τούτῳ ἡ εὐ-
ρυθμία, ἐν τούτῳ ἡ τέχνη, τὸ τάχος, ἡ εὐγνω-
μοσύνη, ἵν' ἐγώ, μηδ' ἂν τὸν κόλπον ἐκτείνω,
δύναμαι¹ λαβεῖν αὐτό, ὁ δέ, ἂν βάλω, λαμβά-
17 νει. ἂν δὲ μετὰ ταραχῆς καὶ φόβου δεχώμεθα
ἢ βάλλωμεν αὐτό, ποία ἔτι παιδιά, ποῦ δέ τις
εὐσταθήσει, ποῦ δέ τις τὸ ἐξῆς ὄψεται ἐν αὐτῇ ;
ἀλλ' ὁ μὲν ἐρεῖ "βάλε," ὁ δὲ² "μὴ βάλῃς," ὁ
δὲ "μὴ ἀναβάλῃς."³   τοῦτο δὴ μάχη ἐστὶ καὶ οὐ
παιδιά.

¹ Koraes : δύνωμαι S.
² ὁ δὲ added by Upton after Wolf.
³ Oldfather–Capps : ἀνέβαλες S : μίαν ἔβαλες Sc : ἀνάλαβῃς
Richards.

¹ A variety of ball-playing among the Greeks consisted in
tossing the ball back and forth between partners or team-
mates (often in response to a call, Plutarch, *Alex.* 39, 3),
while their opponents tried to get the ball away (Galen,
de Parvae Pilae Exercitio, 2), somewhat as in the American

a storm comes down upon us. Very well, what further concern have I? For my part has been fulfilled. The business belongs to someone else, that is, the helmsman. But, more than that, the ship goes down. What, then, have I to do? What I can; that is the only thing I do; I drown without fear, neither shrieking nor crying out against God, but recognizing that what is born must also perish. For I am not eternal, but a man; a part of the whole, as an hour is part of a day. I must come on as the hour and like an hour pass away. What difference, then, is it to me how I pass away, whether by drowning or by a fever? For by something of the sort I must needs pass away.

This is what you will see skilful ball players doing also. None of them is concerned about the ball as being something good or bad, but about throwing and catching it. Accordingly, form has to do with that, skill with that, and speed, and grace; where I cannot catch the ball even if I spread out my cloak, the expert catches it if I throw. Yet if we catch or throw the ball in a flurry or in fear, what fun is there left, and how can a man be steady, or see what comes next in the game? But one player will say " Throw ! " another, " Don't throw ! " and yet another, " Don't throw it up ! " [1] That, indeed, would be a strife and not a game.

games Keep-away and Basket-ball. An interesting series of calls used in the game is given by Antiphanes in *Athenaeus*, I. 15a, one of which, ἄνω, "Up!", may be the short form of the positive of the call given in the text here. On the ball-teams at Sparta see M. N. Tod, *Annual of the British School at Athens*, 1903-4, 63 ff. Possibly one might read ἀναβάλῃ, "Don't wait!" or "Don't stall!" which would fit the context admirably, although the use of βάλλω in different senses within the same sentence would appear rather strange.

18 Τοιγαροῦν Σωκράτης ἤδει σφαιρίζειν. πῶς;
παίζειν ἐν τῷ δικαστηρίῳ. "λέγε μοι," φησίν,
" Ἄνυτε, πῶς με φῂς θεὸν οὐ νομίζειν; οἱ δαί-
μονές σοι τίνες εἶναι δοκοῦσιν; οὐχὶ ἤτοι θεῶν
παῖδές εἰσιν ἢ ἐξ ἀνθρώπων καὶ θεῶν μεμιγμένοι
19 τινές;" ὁμολογήσαντος δὲ "τίς οὖν σοι δοκεῖ
δύνασθαι ἡμιόνους μὲν ἡγεῖσθαι εἶναι, ὄνους δὲ
μή;" ὡς ἁρπαστίῳ παίζων. καὶ τί ἐκεῖ ἐν μέσῳ
ἁρπάστιον τότ᾽ ἦν¹; τὸ δεδέσθαι, τὸ φυγαδευθῆναι, τὸ πιεῖν φάρμακον, τὸ γυναικὸς ἀφαιρε-
20 θῆναι, τὸ τέκνα ὀρφανὰ καταλιπεῖν. ταῦτα ἦν
ἐν μέσῳ οἷς ἔπαιζεν, ἀλλ᾽ οὐδὲν ἧττον ἔπαιζεν
καὶ ἐσφαίριζεν εὐρύθμως. οὕτως καὶ ἡμεῖς τὴν
μὲν ἐπιμέλειαν σφαιριστικωτάτην, τὴν δ᾽ ἀδια-
21 φορίαν ὡς ὑπὲρ ἁρπαστίου. δεῖ γὰρ πάντως
περί τινα τῶν ἐκτὸς ὑλῶν φιλοτεχνεῖν, ἀλλ᾽ οὐκ
ἐκείνην ἀποδεχόμενον, ἀλλ᾽ οἵα ἂν ᾖ ἐκείνη, τὴν
περὶ αὐτὴν φιλοτεχνίαν ἐπιδεικνύοντα. οὕτως καὶ
ὁ ὑφάντης οὐκ ἔρια ποιεῖ, ἀλλ᾽ οἷα ἂν παραλάβῃ
22 περὶ αὐτὰ φιλοτεχνεῖ. ἄλλος σοι δίδωσι τροφὰς
καὶ κτῆσιν καὶ αὐτὰ ταῦτα δύναται ἀφελέσθαι
καὶ τὸ σωμάτιον αὐτό. σὺ λοιπὸν παραλαβὼν
23 τὴν ὕλην ἐργάζου. εἶτα ἂν ἐξέλθῃς μηδὲν παθών,

¹ Elter: ἁρπάστιον τὸ ζῆν S.

---

¹ A term originally used of any spiritual power, and in
early Greek often of the greatest gods, but in classical and
Hellenistic times coming generally to be restricted to spiritual
essences of a lower rank. There is no adequate English word
which can be used in translation.
² A free paraphrase of the argument in Plato's *Apology*,
26ε ff., obviously from memory, for the questions were put
by Socrates, not to Anytus, but to Meletus.—Socrates had

In that sense, then, Socrates knew how to play
ball. How so? He knew how to play in the law-
court. "Tell me," says he, "Anytus, what do you
mean when you say that I do not believe in God.
In your opinion who are the *daemones*? [1]
Are they
not either the offspring of the gods or a hybrid race,
the offspring of men and gods?" And when Anytus
had agreed to that statement Socrates went on,
"Who, then, do you think, can believe that mules
exist, but not asses?" [2] In so speaking he was like
a man playing ball. And at that place and time
what was the ball that he was playing with? Imprisonment, exile, drinking poison, being deprived
of wife, leaving children orphans. These were the
things with which he was playing, but none the
less he played and handled the ball in good form.
So ought we also to act, exhibiting the ball-player's
carefulness about the game, but the same indifference about the object played with, as being a mere
ball. For a man ought by all means to strive to
show his skill in regard to some of the external
materials, yet without making the material a part
of himself, but merely lavishing his skill in regard
to it, whatever it may be. So also the weaver does
not make wool, but he lavishes his skill on whatever
wool he receives. Another [3] gives you sustenance
and property and can likewise take them away, yes,
and your paltry body itself. Do you accordingly
accept the material and work it up. Then if you
come forth without having suffered any harm, the

been charged with denying the existence of the gods, but at
the same time introducing new *daemones*. If, however,
daemones are merely offspring of gods, then it is impossible
that both charges could be true of any sane man.

[3] That is, God.

οἱ μὲν ἄλλοι ἀπαντῶντές σοι συγχαρήσονται ὅτι
ἐσώθης, ὁ δ' εἰδὼς βλέπειν τὰ τοιαῦτα, ἂν μὲν
ἴδῃ ὅτι εὐσχημόνως ἀνεστράφης ἐν τούτῳ, ἐπαι-
νέσει καὶ συνησθήσεται· ἂν δὲ δι' ἀσχημοσύνην
τινὰ διασεσωσμένον, τὰ ἐναντία. ὅπου γὰρ τὸ
χαίρειν εὐλόγως, ἐκεῖ καὶ τὸ συγχαίρειν.

24 Πῶς οὖν λέγεται τῶν ἐκτός τινα κατὰ φύσιν
καὶ παρὰ φύσιν ; ὥσπερ ἂν εἰ ἀπόλυτοι ἦμεν.
τῷ γὰρ ποδὶ κατὰ φύσιν εἶναι ἐρῶ τὸ καθαρῷ
εἶναι, ἀλλ', ἂν αὐτὸν ὡς πόδα λάβῃς καὶ ὡς μὴ
ἀπόλυτον, καθήξει αὐτὸν καὶ εἰς πηλὸν ἐμβαίνειν
καὶ ἀκάνθας πατῆσαι καὶ ἔστιν ὅτε ἀποκοπῆναι
ὑπὲρ τοῦ ὅλου· εἰ δὲ μή, οὐκέτι ἔσται πούς.
25 τοιοῦτόν τι καὶ ἐφ' ἡμῶν ὑπολαβεῖν δεῖ. τί εἶ ;
ἄνθρωπος. εἰ μὲν ὡς ἀπόλυτον σκοπεῖς, κατὰ
φύσιν ἐστὶ ζῆσαι μέχρι γήρως, πλουτεῖν, ὑγιαί-
νειν. εἰ δ' ὡς ἄνθρωπον σκοπεῖς καὶ μέρος ὅλου
τινός, δι' ἐκεῖνο τὸ ὅλον νῦν μέν σοι νοσῆσαι
καθήκει, νῦν δὲ πλεῦσαι καὶ κινδυνεῦσαι, νῦν δ'
ἀπορηθῆναι, πρὸ ὥρας δ' ἔστιν ὅτ' ἀποθανεῖν.
26 τί οὖν ἀγανακτεῖς ; οὐκ οἶδας ὅτι ὡς ἐκεῖνος
οὐκέτι ἔσται πούς, οὕτως οὐδὲ σὺ ἄνθρωπος ; τί
γάρ ἐστιν ἄνθρωπος ; μέρος πόλεως, πρώτης μὲν
τῆς ἐκ θεῶν καὶ ἀνθρώπων, μετὰ ταῦτα δὲ τῆς
ὡς ἔγγιστα λεγομένης, ἥ τί ἐστι μικρὸν τῆς ὅλης
27 μίμημα. " νῦν οὖν ἐμὲ κρίνεσθαι ;" νῦν οὖν
ἄλλον πυρέσσειν, ἄλλον πλεῖν, ἄλλον ἀποθνή-

---

[1] That is, things which are natural for the part of a whole
to endure, appear unnatural, if that same part regards itself
as a separate and independent entity.

[2] That is, existing separate and *per se*.

others who meet you will congratulate you on your escape, but the man who knows how to observe such matters, if he sees that you have exhibited good form in this affair, will praise you and rejoice with you; but if he sees that you owe your escape to some dishonourable action, he will do the opposite. For where a man may rejoice with good reason, there others may rejoice with him.

How, then, can it be said that some externals are natural, and others unnatural? It is just as if we were detached from them.[1] For I will assert of the foot as such that it is natural for it to be clean, but if you take it as a foot, and not as a thing detached,[2] it will be appropriate for it to step into mud and trample on thorns and sometimes to be cut off for the sake of the whole body; otherwise it will no longer be a foot. We ought to hold some such view also about ourselves. What are you? A man. Now if you regard yourself as a thing detached, it is natural for you to live to old age, to be rich, to enjoy health. But if you regard yourself as a man and as a part of some whole, on account of that whole it is fitting for you now to be sick, and now to make a voyage and run risks, and now to be in want, and on occasion to die before your time. Why, then, are you vexed? Do you not know that as the foot, if detached, will no longer be a foot, so you too, if detached, will no longer be a man? For what is a man? A part of a state; first of that state which is made up of gods and men, and then of that which is said to be very close to the other, the state that is a small copy of the universal state. "Must I, then, be put on trial now?" Well, would you have someone else be sick of a fever now, some-

σκειν, ἄλλον κατακεκρίσθαι ; ἀδύνατον γὰρ ἐν
τοιούτῳ σώματι, ἐν τούτῳ τῷ περιέχοντι, τούτοις
τοῖς συζῶσιν μὴ συμπίπτειν ἄλλοις ἄλλα τοιαῦ-
28 τα. σὸν οὖν ἔργον ἐλθόντα εἰπεῖν ἃ δεῖ, δια-
θέσθαι ταῦτα ὡς ἐπιβάλλει. εἶτα ἐκεῖνος λέγει
29 "κρίνω¹ σε ἀδικεῖν." "εὖ σοι γένοιτο. ἐποίησα
ἐγὼ τὸ ἐμόν, εἰ δὲ καὶ σὺ τὸ σὸν ἐποίησας, ὄψει
αὐτός." ἔστι γάρ τις κἀκείνου κίνδυνος, μή σε
λανθανέτω.

ϛʹ. Περὶ ἀδιαφορίας.

1   Τὸ συνημμένον ἀδιάφορον· ἡ κρίσις ἡ περὶ
αὐτοῦ οὐκ ἀδιάφορος, ἀλλ' ἢ ἐπιστήμη ἢ δόξα ἢ
ἀπάτη. οὕτως τὸ ζῆν ἀδιάφορον, ἡ χρῆσις οὐκ
2 ἀδιάφορος. μή ποτ' οὖν, ὅταν εἴπῃ τις ὑμῖν
ἀδιαφορεῖν καὶ ταῦτα, ἀμελεῖς γίνεσθε, μήθ'
ὅταν εἰς ἐπιμέλειάν τις ὑμᾶς παρακαλῇ, ταπεινοὶ
3 καὶ τὰς ὕλας τεθαυμακότες. καλὸν δὲ καὶ τὸ
εἰδέναι τὴν αὐτοῦ παρασκευὴν καὶ δύναμιν, ἵν' ἐν
οἷς μὴ παρεσκεύασαι, ἡσυχίαν ἄγῃς μηδ' ἀγα-
νακτῇς, εἴ τινες ἄλλοι πλεῖόν σου ἔχουσιν ἐν
4 ἐκείνοις. καὶ γὰρ σὺ ἐν συλλογισμοῖς πλεῖον
ἀξιώσεις σεαυτὸν ἔχειν κἂν ἀγανακτῶσιν ἐπὶ
τούτῳ, παραμυθήσῃ αὐτούς· "ἐγὼ ἔμαθον, ὑμεῖς

¹ Blass: κρινῶ S.

one else go on a voyage, someone else die, someone else be condemned? For it is impossible in such a body as ours, in this universe that envelops us, among these fellow-creatures of ours, that such things should not happen, some to one man and some to another. It is your task, therefore, to step forward and say what you should, to arrange these matters as is fitting. Then the judge says, "I adjudge you guilty." I reply, "May it be well with you. I have done my part; and it is for you to see whether you have done yours." For the judge too runs a risk, do not forget that.

CHAPTER VI

Of indifference in things

THE hypothetical syllogism in itself is a matter of indifference; yet the judgement about it is not indifferent, but is either knowledge, or opinion, or delusion. In like manner, although life is a matter of indifference, the use which you make of it is not a matter of indifference. Therefore, when someone tells you, "These things also are indifferent," do not become careless, and when someone exhorts you to be careful, do not become abject and overawed by material things. It is good also to know one's own training and capacity, so that where you have had no training you may keep quiet and not be annoyed if some other persons outshine you in those matters. For you in your turn will expect to outshine them in syllogisms, and if they are annoyed at that, you will console them by saying, "I have learned this,

5 δ' οὔ." οὕτως καί, ὅπου τινὸς χρεία τριβῆς, μὴ
ζήτει τὸ ἀπ' αὐτῆς¹ περιγινόμενον, ἀλλ' ἐκείνου
μὲν παραχώρει τοῖς περιτετριμμένοις, σοὶ δ'
ἀρκείτω τὸ εὐσταθεῖν.

6 "Ἄπελθε καὶ ἄσπασαι τὸν δεῖνα." "ἀσπά-
ζομαι."² "πῶς;" "οὐ ταπεινῶς." "ἀλλ' ἐξε-
κλείσθης."³ "διὰ θυρίδος γὰρ οὐκ ἔμαθον
εἰσέρχεσθαι· ὅταν δὲ κεκλειμένην εὕρω τὴν
θύραν, ἀνάγκη μ' ἢ ἀποχωρῆσαι ἢ διὰ τῆς
7 θυρίδος εἰσελθεῖν." "ἀλλὰ καὶ λάλησον αὐτῷ."
8 "λαλῶ." "τίνα τρόπον"; "οὐ ταπεινῶς." "ἀλλ'
οὐκ ἐπέτυχες." μὴ γὰρ σὸν τοῦτο τὸ ἔργον ἦν;
ἀλλ' ἐκείνου. τί οὖν ἀντιποιῇ τοῦ ἀλλοτρίου;
ἀεὶ μεμνημένος ὅ τι σὸν καὶ τί ἀλλότριον οὐ
9 ταραχθήσῃ. διὰ τοῦτο καλῶς ὁ Χρύσιππος
λέγει ὅτι "μέχρις ἂν ἄδηλά μοι ᾖ τὰ ἑξῆς, ἀεὶ
τῶν εὐφυεστέρων ἔχομαι πρὸς τὸ τυγχάνειν
τῶν κατὰ φύσιν· αὐτὸς γάρ μ' ὁ θεὸς ἐποίησεν
10 τούτων ἐκλεκτικόν. εἰ δέ γε ᾔδειν ὅτι νοσεῖν μοι
καθείμαρται νῦν, καὶ ὥρμων ἂν ἐπ' αὐτό· καὶ
γὰρ ὁ πούς, εἰ φρένας εἶχεν, ὥρμα ἂν ἐπὶ τὸ
πηλοῦσθαι."

11   Ἐπεί τοι τίνος ἕνεκα γίνονται στάχυες; οὐχ
ἵνα καὶ ξηρανθῶσιν; ἀλλὰ ξηραίνονται μέν, οὐχ
ἵνα δὲ καὶ θερισθῶσιν; οὐ γὰρ ἀπόλυτοι γίνον-
12 ται. εἰ οὖν αἴσθησιν εἶχον, εὔχεσθαι αὐτοὺς

---

¹ Elter : ἀπὸ τῆς χρείας S.   ² Added by Schenkl.
³ Schenkl : ἐξεκλείσθην S.

---

¹ Compare *Stoic. Vet. Fragm.* III. 46, frag. 191. Von Arnim
thinks that only the last few words are a literal quotation
from Chrysippus.

and you have not.' So also in a case where some
acquired skill is needed, do not seek that which
only practice can give, but leave that to those who
have acquired the knack, and be content yourself to
remain steadfast.

"Go and salute so-and-so." "I salute him."
"How?" "In no abject spirit." "But the door
was shut in your face." "Yes, for I have not
learned how to crawl in at the window; but when
I find the door closed, I must either go away or
crawl in at the window." "But go and *do* speak
to him." "I do so speak." "In what manner?"
"In no abject spirit." "But you did not get what
you wanted." Surely that was not your business,
was it? Nay, it was his. Why, then, lay claim to
that which is another's? If you always bear in
mind what is your own and what is another's, you
will never be disturbed. Therefore Chrysippus[1]
well says, "As long as the consequences are not
clear to me, I cleave ever to what is better adapted
to secure those things that are in accordance with
nature; for God himself has created me with the
faculty of choosing things. But if I really knew
that it was ordained for me to be ill at this present
moment, I would even seek illness; for the foot
also, if it had a mind, would seek to be covered with
mud."[2]

For example, why do heads of grain grow? Is it
not that they may also become dry? But when
they become dry, is it not that they may also be
harvested? Since they do not grow for themselves
alone. If, therefore, they had feeling, ought they

---

[2] That is, if the owner of it found it necessary to step into
the mud ; *cf.* II. 5, 24.

ἔδει, ἵνα μὴ θερισθῶσιν μηδέποτε; τοῦτο δὲ
κατάρα ἐστὶν ἐπὶ σταχύων τὸ μηδέποτε θερι-
13 σθῆναι. οὕτως ἴστε ὅτι καὶ ἐπ' ἀνθρώπων
κατάρα ἐστὶ τὸ μὴ ἀποθανεῖν· ὅμοιον τῷ μὴ
14 πεπανθῆναι, μὴ θερισθῆναι. ἡμεῖς δ' ἐπειδὴ οἱ
αὐτοί ἐσμεν, ἅμα μὲν οὓς δεῖ θερισθῆναι, ἅμα δὲ
καὶ αὐτῷ τούτῳ παρακολουθοῦντες ὅτι θεριζό-
μεθα, διὰ τοῦτο ἀγανακτοῦμεν. οὔτε γὰρ ἴσμεν
τίνες ἐσμὲν οὔτε μεμελετήκαμεν τὰ ἀνθρωπικὰ
15 ὡς ἱππικοὶ τὰ ἱππικά. ἀλλὰ Χρυσάντας μὲν
παίειν μέλλων τὸν πολέμιον, ἐπειδὴ τῆς σάλ-
πιγγος ἤκουσεν ἀνακαλούσης, ἀνέσχεν· οὕτως
προυργιαίτερον ἔδοξεν αὐτῷ τὸ τοῦ στρατηγοῦ
16 πρόσταγμα ἢ τὸ ἴδιον ποιεῖν· ἡμῶν δ' οὐδεὶς
θέλει οὐδὲ τῆς ἀνάγκης καλούσης εὐλύτως
ὑπακοῦσαι αὐτῇ, ἀλλὰ κλάοντες καὶ στένοντες
πάσχομεν ἃ πάσχομεν καὶ περιστάσεις αὐτὰ
17 καλοῦντες. ποίας περιστάσεις, ἄνθρωπε; εἰ
περιστάσεις λέγεις τὰ περιεστηκότα, πάντα
περιστάσεις εἰσίν· εἰ δ' ὡς δύσκολα καλεῖς,
ποίαν δυσκολίαν ἔχει τὸ γενόμενον φθαρῆναι;
18 τὸ δὲ φθεῖρον ἢ μάχαιρά ἐστιν ἢ τροχὸς ἢ
θάλασσα ἢ κεραμὶς ἢ τύραννος. τί σοι μέλει,
ποίᾳ ὁδῷ καταβῇς εἰς Ἅιδου; ἴσαι πᾶσαί εἰσιν.
19 εἰ δὲ θέλεις ἀκοῦσαι τἀληθῆ, συντομωτέρα ἣν
πέμπει ὁ τύραννος. οὐδέποτ' οὐδεὶς τύραννος ἐξ
μησίν τινα ἔσφαξεν, πυρετὸς δὲ καὶ ἐνιαυτῷ
πολλάκις. ψόφος ἐστὶ πάντα ταῦτα καὶ κόμπος
κενῶν ὀνομάτων.

---

[1] Xenophon, *Cyropaedia*, IV. 1, 3.
[2] *i.e.*, the rack.

to pray that they should never at all be harvested?
But never to be harvested at all is a curse for heads
of grain. In like manner I would have you know
that in the case of men as well it is a curse never
to die; it is like never growing ripe, never being
harvested. But, since we are ourselves those who
must both be harvested and also be aware of the
very fact that we are being harvested, we are angry
on that account. For we neither know who we are,
nor have we studied what belongs to man, as horse-
men study what belongs to horses. But Chrysantas,
when he was on the point of striking the foe,
refrained because he heard the bugle sounding the
recall;[1] it seemed so much more profitable to him
to do the bidding of his general than to follow his
own inclination. Yet no one of us is willing, even
when necessity calls, to obey her readily, but what
we suffer we suffer with fears and groans, and call it
"circumstances." What do you mean by "circumstances," man? If you call "circumstances" your
surroundings, all things are "circumstances"; but if
you use the word of hardships, what hardship is involved when that which has come into being is
destroyed? The instrument of destruction is a
sword, or a wheel,[2] or the sea, or a tile, or a tyrant.
What concern is it to you by what road you descend
to the House of Hades? They are all equal.[3] But
if you care to hear the truth, the road by which the
tyrant sends you is the shorter. No tyrant ever
took six months to cut a man's throat, but a fever
often takes more than a year. All these things are
a mere noise and a vaunting of empty names.

[3] A popular saying variously ascribed to Anaxagoras,
Aristippus, Diogenes, and others.

20 " Τῇ κεφαλῇ κινδυνεύω ἐπὶ Καίσαρος." ἐγὼ δ'
οὐ κινδυνεύω, ὃς οἰκῶ ἐν Νικοπόλει, ὅπου σεισμοὶ
τοσοῦτοι ; σὺ δ' αὐτὸς ὅταν διαπλέῃς τὸν Ἀδρίαν,

21 τί κινδυνεύεις ; οὐ τῇ κεφαλῇ ; " ἀλλὰ καὶ τῇ
ὑπολήψει κινδυνεύω." τῇ σῇ ; πῶς ; τίς γάρ σε
ἀναγκάσαι δύναται ὑπολαβεῖν τι ὧν οὐ θέλεις ;
ἀλλὰ τῇ ἀλλοτρίᾳ ; καὶ ποῖός ἐστι κίνδυνος σὸς

22 ἄλλους τὰ ψεύδη ὑπολαβεῖν ; " ἀλλ' ἐξορισθῆναι κινδυνεύω." τί ἐστιν ἐξορισθῆναι ; ἀλλαχοῦ εἶναι ἢ ἐν Ῥώμῃ ; " ναί." τί οὖν ; " ἂν εἰς
Γύαρα πεμφθῶ ; " ἄν σοι ποιῇ, ἀπελεύσῃ· εἰ
δὲ μή, ἔχεις ποῦ ἀντὶ Γυάρων ἀπέλθῃς, ὅπου
κἀκεῖνος ἐλεύσεται, ἄν τε θέλῃ ἄν τε μή, ὁ

23 πέμπων σε εἰς Γύαρα. τί λοιπὸν ὡς ἐπὶ μεγάλα
ἀνέρχῃ ; μικρότερά ἐστι τῆς παρασκευῆς, ἵν'
εἴπῃ νέος εὐφυὴς ὅτι " οὐκ ἦν τοσούτου τοσούτων
μὲν ἀκηκοέναι, τοσαῦτα δὲ γεγραφέναι, τοσούτῳ
δὲ χρόνῳ παρακεκαθικέναι γεροντίῳ οὐ πολλοῦ

24 ἀξίῳ." μόνον ἐκείνης τῆς διαιρέσεως μέμνησο,
καθ' ἣν διορίζεται τὰ σὰ καὶ οὐ τὰ σά. μή ποτ'

25 ἀντιποιήσῃ τινὸς τῶν ἀλλοτρίων. βῆμα καὶ φυλακὴ τόπος ἐστὶν ἑκάτερον, ὁ μὲν ὑψηλός, ὁ δὲ
ταπεινός· ἡ προαίρεσις δ' ἴση, ἂν ἴσην αὐτὴν ἐν [1]
ἑκατέρῳ φυλάξαι θέλῃς, δύναται φυλαχθῆναι.

26 καὶ τότ' ἐσόμεθα ζηλωταὶ Σωκράτους, ὅταν ἐν

27 φυλακῇ δυνώμεθα παιᾶνας γράφειν. μέχρι δὲ
νῦν ὡς ἔχομεν, ὅρα εἰ ἠνεσχόμεθ' ἂν ἐν τῇ φυλακῇ ἄλλου τινὸς ἡμῖν λέγοντος " θέλεις ἀναγνῶ

---

[1] Supplied by Schweighäuser.

[1] Gyara or Gyaros was a little island east of Attica, used
as a place of banishment in the early empire. Compare
I. 25, 19 f., etc.

252

" I run the risk of my life in Caesar's presence."
But do I not run a risk by living in Nicopolis, where
there are so many earthquakes? And what risk do
you yourself take when you cross the Adriatic?
Do you not risk your life? " But I also risk my
opinion at court." Your own opinion? How so?
Why, who can compel you to opine anything against
your will? But do you mean some other man's
opinion? And what kind of risk is it of yours that
others should entertain false opinions? " But I run
the risk of banishment." What is banishment? To
be somewhere else than in Rome? " Yes." What
then? " Suppose I am sent to Gyara." [1] If it is to
your good, you will go; if not, you have a place to
which you may go instead of Gyara—where he too
will go, whether he will or no, who is sending you
to Gyara. Then why do you go up to Rome as
though it were some great thing? It amounts to
less than your preparation for it; so that a young
man of parts may say, " It was not worth so much
to have listened to so many lectures, and to have
written so many exercises, and to have sat so long
at the side of a little old man, who was not worth
very much himself." Only remember that distinction which is drawn between what is yours and
what is not yours. Never lay claim to anything that
is not your own. A platform and a prison is each a
place, the one high, and the other low; but your
moral purpose can be kept the same, if you wish to
keep it the same, in either place. And then we
shall be emulating Socrates, when we are able to
write paeans in prison. But considering what has
been our state hitherto, I wonder if we should have
endured it, had some one else said to us in prison,

σοι παιᾶνας"· "τί μοι πράγματα παρέχεις; οὐκ
οἶδας τὰ ἔχοντά με κακά; ἐν τούτοις γάρ μοι
ἔστιν—" ἐν τίσιν οὖν; "ἀποθνήσκειν μέλλω."
ἄνθρωποι δ' ἄλλοι ἀθάνατοι ἔσονται;

ζ. Πῶς μαντευτέον;

1 Διὰ τὸ ἀκαίρως μαντεύεσθαι πολλοὶ καθήκοντα
2 πολλὰ παραλείπομεν. τί γὰρ ὁ μάντις δύναται
πλέον ἰδεῖν θανάτου ἢ κινδύνου ἢ νόσου ἢ ὅλως
3 τῶν τοιούτων; ἂν οὖν δέῃ κινδυνεῦσαι ὑπὲρ τοῦ
φίλου, ἂν δὲ καὶ ἀποθανεῖν ὑπὲρ αὐτοῦ καθήκῃ,
ποῦ μοι καιρὸς ἔτι μαντεύεσθαι; οὐκ ἔχω τὸν
μάντιν ἔσω τὸν εἰρηκότα μοι τὴν οὐσίαν τοῦ
ἀγαθοῦ καὶ τοῦ κακοῦ, τὸν ἐξηγημένον τὰ σημεῖα
4 ἀμφοτέρων; τί οὖν ἔτι χρείαν ἔχω τῶν σπλάγχνων ἢ τῶν οἰωνῶν; ἀλλ' ἀνέχομαι λέγοντος
ἐκείνου "συμφέρει σοι"; τί γάρ ἐστι συμφέρον
5 οἶδεν; τί ἐστιν ἀγαθὸν οἶδεν; μεμάθηκεν ὥσπερ
τὰ σημεῖα τῶν σπλάγχνων οὕτως σημεῖα τίνα
ἀγαθῶν καὶ κακῶν; εἰ γὰρ τούτων οἶδεν σημεῖα,
καὶ καλῶν καὶ αἰσχρῶν οἶδεν καὶ δικαίων καὶ
6 ἀδίκων. ἄνθρωπε, σύ μοι λέγε τί σημαίνεται,
ζωὴ ἢ θάνατος, πενία ἢ πλοῦτος· πότερον δὲ

---

¹ The idea seems to be: We go to a diviner in order to
find out what acts to avoid if we would escape evils to
ourselves. But the things in life that are accounted our chief
ills are death, danger, illness, and the like. These evils one
must sometimes, in self-respect, accept, and they are in fact,

"Would you like to have me read you paeans?"
"Why bother me? Do you not know the trouble
that I am in? What, is it possible for me in this
condition——?" In what condition, then? "I am
about to die." But will other men be immortal?

CHAPTER VII

How should one employ Divination?

BECAUSE we employ divination when there is no
occasion for it, many of us neglect many of the
duties of life. For what can the diviner see that is
of greater import than death,[1] or danger, or illness,
or in general such things as these? If, then, it
becomes necessary for me to risk my life for my
friend, and if it becomes my duty even to die for
him, where do I find beyond that any occasion to
employ divination? Have I not within me the
diviner that has told me the true nature of good and
of evil, that has set forth the signs characteristic of
both of them? What further use have I, then, of
entrails, or of birds? But when he says, "It is
expedient for you," do I accept it? Why, does
he know what is expedient? Does he know what
is good? Has he learned the signs characteristic of
things good and things evil, as he has the signs
characteristic of entrails? For if he knows the
signs characteristic of these, he knows also those of
things honourable and base, and right and wrong.
Man, it is for you to tell me what is indicated by
signs—life or death, poverty or wealth ; but whether

not evils at all. Hence the petty things about which men
consult the diviner fall into insignificance.

συμφέρει ταῦτα ἢ ἀσύμφορά ἐστιν, σοῦ μέλλω

7 πυνθάνεσθαι; διὰ τί ἐν γραμματικοῖς οὐ λέγεις;
ἐνθάδ' οὖν, ὅπου πάντες ἄνθρωποι πλανώμεθα

8 καὶ πρὸς ἀλλήλους μαχόμεθα; διὰ τοῦτο ἡ
γυνὴ καλῶς εἶπεν ἡ πέμψαι θέλουσα τῇ
Γρατίλλῃ ἐξωρισμένῃ τὸ πλοῖον τῶν ἐπιμηνίων
κατὰ τὸν εἰπόντα ὅτι "Ἀφαιρήσεται αὐτὰ
Δομιτιανός," "Μᾶλλον θέλω," φησίν, "ἵν'
ἐκεῖνος αὐτὰ ἀφέληται ἢ ἵν' ἐγὼ μὴ πέμψω."

9 Τί οὖν ἡμᾶς ἐπὶ τὸ οὕτω[1] συνεχῶς μαντεύεσθαι
ἄγει; ἡ δειλία, τὸ φοβεῖσθαι τὰς ἐκβάσεις. διὰ
τοῦτο κολακεύομεν τοὺς μάντεις· "κληρονομήσω,
κύριε, τὸν πατέρα;" "ἴδωμεν· ἐπεκθυσώμεθα."
"ναί, κύριε, ὡς ἡ τύχη θέλει." εἶτ' ἂν[2] εἴπῃ
"κληρονομήσεις," ὡς παρ' αὐτοῦ τὴν κληρονομίαν
εἰληφότες εὐχαριστοῦμεν αὐτῷ. διὰ τοῦτο κἀ-

10 κεῖνοι λοιπὸν ἐμπαίζουσιν ἡμῖν. τί οὖν; δεῖ δίχα
ὀρέξεως ἔρχεσθαι καὶ ἐκκλίσεως, ὡς ὁ ὁδοιπόρος
πυνθάνεται παρὰ τοῦ ἀπαντήσαντος, ποτέρα τῶν
ὁδῶν φέρει, οὐκ ἔχων ὄρεξιν πρὸς τὸ[3] τὴν δεξιὰν
μᾶλλον φέρειν ἢ τὴν ἀριστεράν· οὐ γὰρ τούτων

11 τινὰ ἀπελθεῖν θέλει ἀλλὰ τὴν φέρουσαν. οὕτως
ἔδει καὶ ἐπὶ τὸν θεὸν ἔρχεσθαι ὡς ὁδηγόν, ὡς τοῖς
ὀφθαλμοῖς χρώμεθα, οὐ παρακαλοῦντες αὐτοὺς
ἵνα τὰ τοιαῦτα μᾶλλον ἡμῖν δεικνύωσιν, ἀλλ' οἷα
ἐνδείκνυνται τούτων τὰς φαντασίας δεχόμενοι.

12 νῦν δὲ τρέμοντες τὸν ὀρνιθάριον κρατοῦμεν καὶ

---

[1] Schenkl: τούτ * * S.   [2] Kronenberg: ἐπὰν S.
[3] Supplied by Upton.

---

[1] That is, on a subject about which you do not profess to
know anything.

these things are expedient or inexpedient, am I going to ask of you? Why don't you speak on points of grammar?[1] Well then, on *this* matter, in which we mortals are all astray and in conflict with one another, you *do* speak? Wherefore, that was an admirable answer which the woman gave who wished to send a boatload of supplies to Gratilla after she had been exiled. To a man who said, "Domitian will confiscate them," she replies, "I should rather have him confiscate them than myself fail to send them."

What, then, induces us to employ divination so constantly? Cowardice, fear of the consequences. This is why we flatter the diviners, saying: "Master, shall I inherit my father's property?" "Let us see; let us offer a sacrifice about that matter." "Yes, master, as fortune wills." Then if the diviner says, "You will inherit the property," we thank him as though we had received the inheritance from *him*. That is why they in their turn go on making mock of us. Well, what then? We ought to go to them without either desire or aversion, just as the wayfarer asks the man who meets him which of two roads leads to his destination, without any desire to have the right-hand road lead there any more than the left-hand road; for he does not care to travel one particular road of the two, but merely the one that leads to his destination. So also we ought to go to God as a guide, making use of Him as we make use of our eyes; we do not call upon them to show us such-and-such things by preference, but we accept the impressions of precisely such things as they reveal to us. But as it is, we tremble before the bird-augur, lay hold upon him, and appealing to him

ὡς[1] θεὸν ἐπικαλούμενοι δεόμεθα αὐτοῦ· "κύριε,
13 ἐλέησον· ἐπίτρεψόν μοι ἐξελθεῖν." ἀνδράποδον,
ἄλλο γάρ τι θέλεις ἢ τὸ ἄμεινον ; ἄλλο οὖν τι
14 ἄμεινον ἢ τὸ τῷ θεῷ δοκοῦν ; τί τὸ ὅσον ἐπὶ σοὶ
διαφθείρεις τὸν κριτήν, παράγεις τὸν σύμβουλον ;

η΄. Τίς οὐσία τοῦ ἀγαθοῦ ;

1   Ὁ θεὸς ὠφέλιμος· ἀλλὰ καὶ τἀγαθὸν ὠφέλιμον.
εἰκὸς οὖν, ὅπου ἡ οὐσία τοῦ θεοῦ, ἐκεῖ εἶναι καὶ
2 τὴν τοῦ ἀγαθοῦ. τίς οὖν οὐσία θεοῦ ; σάρξ ; μὴ
γένοιτο. ἀγρός ; μὴ γένοιτο. φήμη ; μὴ γένοιτο.
3 νοῦς, ἐπιστήμη, λόγος ὀρθός. ἐνταῦθα τοίνυν
ἁπλῶς ζήτει τὴν οὐσίαν τοῦ ἀγαθοῦ. ἐπεί τοι
μή τι αὐτὴν ἐν φυτῷ ζητεῖς ; οὔ. μή τι ἐν
ἀλόγῳ ; οὔ. ἐν λογικῷ οὖν ζητῶν τί ἔτι ἀλλαχοῦ
ζητεῖς ἢ ἐν τῇ παραλλαγῇ τῇ πρὸς τὰ ἄλογα ;
4 τὰ φυτὰ οὐδὲ φαντασίαις χρηστικά ἐστιν. διὰ
τοῦτο οὐ λέγεις ἐπ' αὐτῶν τὸ ἀγαθόν. δεῖται
5 οὖν τὸ ἀγαθὸν χρήσεως φαντασιῶν. ἆρά γε
μόνης ; εἰ γὰρ μόνης, λέγε καὶ ἐν τοῖς ἄλλοις
ζῴοις τὰ ἀγαθὰ εἶναι καὶ εὐδαιμονίαν καὶ κακο-
6 δαιμονίαν. νῦν δ' οὐ λέγεις καὶ καλῶς ποιεῖς· εἰ

as if he were a god, we beg of him, saying: "Master, have mercy; grant that I come off safe." You slave! What, do you want anything but what is best for you? Is anything else best for you than what pleases God? Why do you do all that in you lies to corrupt your judge, to mislead your counsellor?

CHAPTER VIII

What is the true nature of the good?

GOD is helpful; but the good also is helpful. It would seem, therefore, that the true nature of the good will be found to be where we find that of God to be. What, then, is the true nature of God? Flesh? Far from it! Land? Far from it! Fame? Far from it! It is intelligence, knowledge, right reason. Here, therefore, and only here, shall you seek the true nature of the good. Surely you do not seek it at all in a plant, do you? No. Nor in an irrational creature? No. If, then, you seek it in that which is rational, why do you keep on seeking it somewhere else than in that which differentiates the rational from the irrational? Plants are incapable of dealing even with external impressions; for that reason you do not speak of the "good" in referring to them. The good requires, therefore, the faculty of using external impressions. Can that be all that it requires? For, if that be all, then you must assert that things good, and happiness and unhappiness, are to be found in the other animals as well as in man. But, as a matter of fact, you do not so assert, and you are right; for even if they have in

γὰρ καὶ τὰ μάλιστα χρῆσιν φαντασιῶν ἔχει,
ἀλλὰ παρακολούθησίν γε τῇ χρήσει τῶν φαντασιῶν οὐκ ἔχει. καὶ εἰκότως· ὑπηρετικὰ γὰρ
7 γέγονεν ἄλλοις, οὐκ αὐτὰ προηγούμενα. ὁ ὄνος
ἐπεὶ γέγονεν μή τι προηγουμένως; οὔ· ἀλλ' ὅτι
νώτου χρείαν εἴχομεν βαστάζειν τι δυναμένου.
ἀλλὰ νὴ Δία καὶ περιπατοῦντος αὐτοῦ χρείαν
εἴχομεν· διὰ τοῦτο προσείληφε καὶ τὸ χρῆσθαι
φαντασίαις· ἄλλως γὰρ περιπατεῖν οὐκ ἐδύνατο.
8 καὶ λοιπὸν αὐτοῦ που πέπαυται. εἰ δὲ καὶ αὐτός
που προσειλήφει παρακολούθησιν[1] τῇ χρήσει
τῶν φαντασιῶν, καὶ δῆλον ὅτι κατὰ λόγον οὐκέτ'
ἂν ἡμῖν ὑπετέτακτο οὐδὲ τὰς χρείας ταύτας
παρεῖχεν, ἀλλ' ἦν ἂν ἴσος ἡμῖν καὶ ὅμοιος.
9   Οὐ θέλεις οὖν ἐκεῖ ζητεῖν τὴν οὐσίαν τοῦ
ἀγαθοῦ, οὗ μὴ παρόντος ἐπ' οὐδενὸς τῶν ἄλλων
10 θέλεις λέγειν τὸ ἀγαθόν; "τί[2] οὖν; οὐκ ἔστι
θεῶν ἔργα κἀκεῖνα;" ἔστιν, ἀλλ' οὐ προηγού-
11 μενα οὐδὲ μέρη θεῶν. σὺ δὲ προηγούμενον εἶ,
σὺ ἀπόσπασμα εἶ τοῦ θεοῦ· ἔχεις τι ἐν σεαυτῷ
μέρος ἐκείνου. τί οὖν ἀγνοεῖς σου τὴν συγγέ-
12 νειαν; τί οὐκ οἶδας, πόθεν ἐλήλυθας; οὐ θέλεις
μεμνῆσθαι, ὅταν ἐσθίῃς, τίς ὢν ἐσθίεις καὶ τίνα
τρέφεις; ὅταν συνουσίᾳ χρῇ, τίς ὢν χρῇ; ὅταν
ὁμιλίᾳ; ὅταν γυμνάζῃ, ὅταν διαλέγῃ, οὐκ οἶδας

---

[1] Schenkl: παρακολουθῇ S.
[2] Upton: εἰ S.

---

[1] That is, things that are an end in themselves, like man,
in the characteristic Stoic anthropocentric view. *Cf.* also II.
10, 3.
[2] That is, the ass went no further in the development of
its faculties.

the highest degree the faculty of using external impressions, still they do not have the faculty of understanding, at all events, their use of the external impressions. And with good reason; for they are born to serve others, and are not themselves of primary importance.[1] The ass, for example, is not born to be of primary importance, is it? No; but because we had need of a back that was able to carry something. But, by Zeus, we had need that it should be able also to walk around; therefore it has further received the faculty of using external impressions; for otherwise it would not be able to walk around. And at about that stage there was an end.[2] But if it, like man, had somehow received the faculty of understanding the use of its external impressions, it is also clear that consequently it would no longer be subject to us, nor would it be performing these services, but would be our equal and our peer.

Will you not, therefore, seek the true nature of the good in that quality the lack of which in all creatures other than man prevents you from using the term "good" of any of these? "But what then? Are not those creatures also works of God?" They are, but they are not of primary importance, nor portions of Divinity. But you are a being of primary importance; you are a fragment of God; you have within you a part of Him. Why, then, are you ignorant of your own kinship? Why do you not know the source from which you have sprung? Will you not bear in mind, whenever you eat, who you are that eat, and whom you are nourishing? Whenever you indulge in intercourse with women, who you are that do this? Whenever you mix in society, whenever you take physical exercise, whenever you

ὅτι θεὸν τρέφεις, θεὸν γυμνάζεις ; θεὸν περιφέρεις,
13 τάλας, καὶ ἀγνοεῖς. δοκεῖς με λέγειν ἀργυροῦν
τινα ἢ χρυσοῦν ἔξωθεν ; ἐν σαυτῷ φέρεις αὐτὸν
καὶ μολύνων οὐκ αἰσθάνῃ ἀκαθάρτοις μὲν δια-
14 νοήμασι, ῥυπαραῖς δὲ πράξεσι. καὶ ἀγάλματος
μὲν τοῦ θεοῦ παρόντος οὐκ ἂν τολμήσαις τι τούτων ποιεῖν ὧν ποιεῖς. αὐτοῦ δὲ τοῦ θεοῦ παρόντος ἔσωθεν καὶ ἐφορῶντος πάντα καὶ ἐπακούοντος οὐκ αἰσχύνῃ ταῦτα ἐνθυμούμενος καὶ ποιῶν,
ἀναίσθητε τῆς αὐτοῦ φύσεως καὶ θεοχόλωτε ;

15 Λοιπὸν ἡμεῖς τί φοβούμεθα ἐκπέμποντες νέον
ἐπί τινας πράξεις ἐκ τῆς σχολῆς, μὴ ἄλλως
ποιήσῃ τι, μὴ ἄλλως φάγῃ, μὴ ἄλλως συνου-
σιάσῃ, μὴ ταπεινώσῃ αὐτὸν ῥάκη περιτεθέντα,¹
16 μὴ ἐπάρῃ ² κομψὰ ἱμάτια ; οὗτος οὐκ οἶδεν
αὑτοῦ θεόν, οὗτος οὐκ οἶδεν, μετὰ τίνος ἀπέρ-
χεται. ἀλλ' ἀνεχόμεθα λέγοντος "αὑτοῦ σε
17 ἤθελον ἔχειν" ; ἐκεῖ τὸν θεὸν οὐκ ἔχεις ; εἶτ'
18 ἄλλον τινὰ ζητεῖς ἐκεῖνον ἔχων ; ἢ ἄλλα σοι
ἐρεῖ ἐκεῖνος ἢ ταῦτα ; ἀλλ' εἰ μὲν τὸ ἄγαλμα ἦς
τὸ Φειδίου, ἢ Ἀθηνᾶ ἢ ὁ Ζεύς, ἐμέμνησο ἂν καὶ
σαυτοῦ καὶ τοῦ τεχνίτου καὶ εἴ τινα αἴσθησιν
εἶχες, ἐπειρῶ ἂν μηδὲν ἀνάξιον ποιεῖν τοῦ κατα-
σκευάσαντος μηδὲ σεαυτοῦ, μηδ' ἐν ἀπρεπεῖ
19 σχήματι φαίνεσθαι τοῖς ὁρῶσι· νῦν δέ σε ὅτι ὁ
Ζεὺς πεποίηκεν, διὰ τοῦτο ἀμελεῖς οἷόν τινα

---

¹ Wolf: περιτιθέντα S.   ² Reiske: ἐπάγηι S.

---

¹ Referring to the chryselephantine statues at Athens and
at Olympia, upon which the fame of Pheidias principally
rested. The statue of Athena held a Nike in the out-
stretched right hand; *cf.* § 20 below.

converse, do you not know that you are nourishing
God, exercising God? You are bearing God about
with you, you poor wretch, and know it not! Do
you suppose I am speaking of some external God,
made of silver or gold? It is within yourself that
you bear Him, and do not perceive that you are
defiling Him with impure thoughts and filthy actions.
Yet in the presence of even an image of God you
would not dare to do anything of the things you are
now doing. But when God Himself is present within
you, seeing and hearing everything, are you not
ashamed to be thinking and doing such things as
these, O insensible of your own nature, and object
of God's wrath!

Again, when we send a young man forth from the
school to sundry activities, why are we afraid that
he will do something amiss—eat amiss, have intercourse with women amiss, be abased if dressed in rags
or conceited if he has on fine clothes? This fellow
does not know the God within him, this fellow does
not know the companion with whom he is setting
forth. Nay, can we allow him to say, "O God,
would that I had Thee here"? Have you not God
there, where you are? And when you have Him, do
you seek for someone else? Or will He have other
commands for you than these? Nay, if you were a
statue of Pheidias, his Athena or his Zeus,[1] you
would have remembered both yourself and your
artificer, and if you had any power of perception
you would have tried to do nothing unworthy of
him that had fashioned you, nor of yourself, and you
would have tried not to appear in an unbecoming
attitude before the eyes of men; but as it is, because
Zeus has made you, do you on that account not care

δείξεις σεαυτόν; καὶ τί ὁ τεχνίτης τῷ τεχνίτῃ
ὅμοιος ἢ τὸ κατασκεύασμα τῷ κατασκευάσματι;
20 καὶ ποῖον ἔργον τεχνίτου εὐθὺς ἔχει τὰς δυνάμεις
ἐν ἑαυτῷ, ἃς ἐμφαίνει διὰ τῆς κατασκευῆς; οὐχὶ
λίθος ἐστὶν ἢ χαλκὸς ἢ χρυσὸς ἢ ἐλέφας; καὶ ἡ
Ἀθηνᾶ ἡ Φειδίου ἅπαξ ἐκτείνασα τὴν χεῖρα καὶ
τὴν Νίκην ἐπ᾽ αὐτῆς δεξαμένη ἕστηκεν οὕτως
ὅλῳ τῷ αἰῶνι, τὰ δὲ τοῦ θεοῦ κινούμενα, ἔμ-
21 πνοα, χρηστικὰ φαντασιῶν, δοκιμαστικά. τούτου
τοῦ δημιουργοῦ κατασκεύασμα ὢν καταισχύνεις
αὐτό; τί δ᾽; ὅτι οὐ μόνον σε κατεσκεύασεν,
ἀλλὰ καὶ σοὶ μόνῳ ἐπίστευσεν καὶ παρακατέθετο,
22 οὐδὲ τούτου μεμνήσῃ, ἀλλὰ καὶ καταισχυνεῖς
τὴν ἐπιτροπήν; εἰ δέ σοι ὀρφανόν τινα ὁ θεὸς
23 παρέθετο, οὕτως ἂν αὐτοῦ ἠμέλεις; παραδέδωκέ
σοι σεαυτὸν καὶ λέγει "οὐκ εἶχον ἄλλον πιστό-
τερόν σου· τοῦτόν μοι φύλασσε τοιοῦτον οἷος
πέφυκεν, αἰδήμονα, πιστόν, ὑψηλόν, ἀκατά-
πληκτον, ἀπαθῆ, ἀτάραχον." εἶτα σὺ οὐ
φυλάσσεις;
24 "Ἀλλ᾽ ἐροῦσιν· 'πόθεν ἡμῖν οὗτος ὀφρῦν
ἐνήνοχεν καὶ σεμνοπροσωπεῖ;'" οὔπω κατ᾽
ἀξίαν. ἔτι γὰρ οὐ θαρρῶ οἷς ἔμαθον καὶ
συγκατεθέμην· ἔτι τὴν ἀσθένειαν τὴν ἐμαυτοῦ
25 φοβοῦμαι. ἐπεί τοι ἄφετέ με θαρρῆσαι καὶ τότε
ὄψεσθε βλέμμα οἷον δεῖ καὶ σχῆμα οἷον δεῖ, τότε

---

[1] See the note on p. 262.

what manner of person you show yourself to be?
And yet what comparison is there between the one
artificer and the other, or between the one work of
art and the other? And what work of an artificer
has forthwith within itself the faculties which its
workmanship discloses? Is it not mere stone, or
bronze, or gold, or ivory? And the Athena of
Pheidias, when once it had stretched out its hand
and received the Nike[1] upon it, stands in this attitude
for all time to come; but the works of God are
capable of movement, have the breath of life, can
make use of external impressions, and pass judgement upon them. Do you dishonour the workmanship of this Craftsman, when you are yourself that
workmanship? Nay more, do you go so far as to
forget, not only that He fashioned you, but also
that He entrusted and committed you to yourself
alone, and moreover, by forgetting, do you dishonour your trust? Yet if God had committed
some orphan to your care, would you so neglect
Him? He has delivered your own self into your
keeping, saying, "I had no one more faithful than
you; keep this man for me unchanged from the character with which nature endowed him—reverent,
faithful, high-minded, undismayed, unimpassioned,
unperturbed." After that do you fail so to keep
him?

"But men will say, 'Where do you suppose our
friend here got his proud look and his solemn
countenance?'" Ah, but my bearing is not yet what
it should be! For I still lack confidence in what I
have learned and agreed to; I am still afraid of my
own weakness. Just let me gain confidence and
then you will see the right look in my eye and the

ὑμῖν δείξω τὸ ἄγαλμα, ὅταν τελειωθῇ, ὅταν
26 στιλπνωθῇ. τί δοκεῖτε; ὀφρῦν; μὴ γένοιτο.
μὴ γὰρ ὁ Ζεὺς ὁ ἐν Ὀλυμπίᾳ ὀφρῦν ἀνέσπακεν;
ἀλλὰ πέπηγεν αὐτοῦ τὸ βλέμμα, οἷον δεῖ εἶναι
τοῦ ἐροῦντος

  οὐ γὰρ ἐμὸν παλινάγρετον οὐδ᾽ ἀπατηλόν.

27 τοιοῦτον ὑμῖν δείξω ἐμαυτόν, πιστόν, αἰδήμονα,
28 γενναῖον, ἀτάραχον. μή τι οὖν ἀθάνατον, ἀγή-
ρων, μή τι ἄνοσον; ἀλλ᾽ ἀποθνήσκοντα θείως,
νοσοῦντα θείως. ταῦτα ἔχω, ταῦτα δύναμαι·
29 τὰ δ᾽ ἄλλα οὔτ᾽ ἔχω οὔτε δύναμαι. δείξω ὑμῖν
νεῦρα φιλοσόφου· ποῖα νεῦρα; ὄρεξιν ἀναπότευκτον, ἔκκλισιν ἀπερίπτωτον, ὁρμὴν καθήκουσαν, πρόθεσιν ἐπιμελῆ, συγκατάθεσιν ἀπρόπτω-
τον. ταῦτα ὄψεσθε.

θ΄. Ὅτι οὐ δυνάμενοι τὴν ἀνθρώπου ἐπαγγελίαν
πληρῶσαι τὴν φιλοσόφου προσλαμβάνομεν

1 Οὐκ ἔστι τὸ τυχὸν αὐτὸ μόνον ἀνθρώπου ἐπ-
2 αγγελίαν πληρῶσαι. τί γάρ ἐστιν ἄνθρωπος;
Ζῷον, φησί, λογικόν, θνητόν. Εὐθὺς ἐν τῷ
λογικῷ τίνων χωριζόμεθα; Τῶν θηρίων. Καὶ
τίνων ἄλλων; Τῶν προβάτων καὶ τῶν ὁμοίων.
3 Ὅρα οὖν μή τί πως ὡς θηρίον ποιήσῃς· εἰ δὲ μή,
ἀπώλεσας τὸν ἄνθρωπον, οὐκ ἐπλήρωσας τὴν

---

[1] Homer, *Iliad*, I. 526, Bryant's translation.
[2] That is, what a person or a thing promises or is expected
to perform. In rendering ἐπαγγελία the same word has been
retained throughout the chapter, even in unusual colloca-
tions, so as to preserve clearly the point of the analogy.

right bearing; then, when the statue is finished and polished, I will show it to you. What do you think of it? A lofty air, say you? Heaven forbid! For the Zeus at Olympia does not show a proud look, does he? No, but his gaze is steady, as befits one who is about to say,

No word of mine can be revoked or prove untrue.[1]

Of such character will I show myself to you—faithful, reverent, noble, unperturbed. You do not mean, therefore, immortal, or ageless, or exempt from disease? No, but one who dies like a god, who bears disease like a god. This is what I have; this is what I can do; but all else I neither have nor can do. I will show you the sinews of a philosopher What do you mean by sinews? A desire that fails not of achievement, an aversion proof against encountering what it would avoid, an appropriate choice, a thoughtful purpose, a well-considered assent. This is what you shall see.

CHAPTER IX

That although we are unable to fulfil the profession of a man, we adopt that of a philosopher

It is no simple task, this of fulfilling merely the profession [2] of a man. For what is a man? A rational, mortal animal, someone says. To begin with, from what are we distinguished by the rational element? From the wild beasts. And from what else? From sheep and the like. See to it, then, that you never act like a wild beast; if you do, you will have destroyed the man in you, you have not fulfilled

ἐπαγγελίαν. ὅρα μή τι ὡς πρόβατον· εἰ δὲ μή,
4 καὶ οὕτως ἀπώλετο ὁ ἄνθρωπος. τίνα οὖν
ποιοῦμεν ὡς πρόβατα ; ὅταν τῆς γαστρὸς ἕνεκα,
ὅταν τῶν αἰδοίων, ὅταν εἰκῇ, ὅταν ῥυπαρῶς, ὅταν
ἀνεπιστρέπτως, ποῦ ἀπεκλίναμεν ; ἐπὶ τὰ πρό-
5 βατα. τί ἀπωλέσαμεν ; τὸ λογικόν. ὅταν μαχί-
μως καὶ βλαβερῶς καὶ θυμικῶς καὶ ὠστικῶς,
6 ποῦ ἀπεκλίναμεν ; ἐπὶ τὰ θηρία. λοιπὸν οἱ μὲν
ἡμῶν μεγάλα θηρία εἰσίν, οἱ δὲ θηρίδια κακοήθη
καὶ μικρά, ἐφ᾽[1] ὧν ἔστιν εἰπεῖν "λέων με καὶ
7 φαγέτω." διὰ πάντων δὲ τούτων ἀπόλλυται ἡ
8 τοῦ ἀνθρώπου ἐπαγγελία. πότε γὰρ σῴζεται
συμπεπλεγμένον ; ὅταν τὴν ἐπαγγελίαν πληρώσῃ, ὥστε σωτηρία συμπεπλεγμένου ἐστὶ τὸ ἐξ
ἀληθῶν συμπεπλέχθαι. πότε διεζευγμένον ;
ὅταν τὴν ἐπαγγελίαν πληρώσῃ. πότε αὐλοί,
9 πότε λύρα, πότε ἵππος, πότε κύων ; τί οὖν
θαυμαστόν, εἰ καὶ ἄνθρωπος ὡσαύτως μὲν
10 σῴζεται, ὡσαύτως δ᾽ ἀπόλλυται ; αὔξει δ᾽
ἕκαστον καὶ σῴζει τὰ κατάλληλα ἔργα· τὸν
τέκτονα τὰ τεκτονικά, τὸν γραμματικὸν τὰ
γραμματικά. ἂν δ᾽ ἐθίσῃ γράφειν ἀγραμμάτως,
ἀνάγκη καταφθείρεσθαι καὶ ἀπόλλυσθαι τὴν
11 τέχνην. οὕτως τὸν μὲν αἰδήμονα σῴζει τὰ αἰδήμονα ἔργα, ἀπολλύει δὲ τὰ[2] ἀναιδῆ· τὸν δὲ

---

[1] Wolf: ἀφ᾽ S.   [2] Wolf: τὸν S.

---

[1] Referring to the proverb, "Let a lion devour me, and
not a fox," ascribed to Aesop, *Prov.* 15 (*Paroemiographi
Graeci*, II. 230). As it is considered to be a greater misfortune to be killed by a mean and small animal than by
a great one, so malignant and petty people are more hateful
than the strong and fierce.

your profession. See to it that you never act like a
sheep; if you do, the man in you is destroyed in this
way also. Well, when do we act like sheep? When
we act for the sake of the belly, or of our sex-organs,
or at random, or in a filthy fashion, or without due
consideration, to what level have we degenerated?
To the level of sheep. What have we destroyed?
The reason. When we act pugnaciously, and injuri-
ously, and angrily, and rudely, to what level have
we degenerated? To the level of the wild beasts.
Well, the fact is that some of us *are* wild beasts of a
larger size, while others are little animals, malignant
and petty, which give us occasion to say, "Let it be
a lion that devours me!" [1] By means of all these
actions the profession of a man is destroyed. For
when is a complex thing preserved? When it
fulfils its profession; consequently, the salvation
of a complex thing is to be composed of parts that
are true. When is a discrete [2] thing preserved?
When it fulfils its profession. When are flutes, a
lyre, a horse, a dog preserved? What is there to
be surprised at, then, if a man also is preserved in
the same way and in the same way destroyed?
Now deeds that correspond to his true nature
strengthen and preserve each particular man;
carpentry does that for the carpenter, grammatical
studies for the grammarian. But if a man acquires
the habit of writing ungrammatically, his art must
necessarily be destroyed and perish. So modest
acts preserve the modest man, whereas immodest
acts destroy him; and faithful acts preserve the

[2] A thing viewed as a separate entity existing *per se*, not
as a mere component part of something else.

12 πιστὸν τὰ πιστὰ καὶ τὰ ἐναντία ἀπολλύει. καὶ
τοὺς ἐναντίους πάλιν ἐπαύξει τὰ ἐναντία· τὸν
ἀναίσχυντον ἀναισχυντία,[1] τὸν ἄπιστον ἀπιστία,[1]
τὸν λοίδορον λοιδορία, τὸν ὀργίλον ὀργή, τὸν
φιλάργυρον αἱ ἀκατάλληλοι λήψεις καὶ δόσεις.

13 Διὰ τοῦτο παραγγέλλουσιν οἱ φιλόσοφοι μὴ ἀρκεῖσθαι μόνῳ τῷ μαθεῖν, ἀλλὰ καὶ μελέτην
14 προσλαμβάνειν, εἶτα ἄσκησιν. πολλῷ γὰρ χρόνῳ
τὰ ἐναντία ποιεῖν εἰθίσμεθα καὶ τὰς ὑπολήψεις
τὰς ἐναντίας ταῖς ὀρθαῖς χρηστικὰς ἔχομεν. ἂν
οὖν μὴ καὶ τὰς ὀρθὰς χρηστικὰς ποιήσωμεν,
οὐδὲν ἄλλο ἢ ἐξηγηταὶ ἐσόμεθα ἀλλοτρίων
15 δογμάτων. ἄρτι γὰρ τίς ἡμῶν οὐ δύναται
τεχνολογῆσαι περὶ ἀγαθῶν καὶ κακῶν; ὅτι τῶν
ὄντων τὰ μὲν ἀγαθά, τὰ δὲ κακά, τὰ δ' ἀδιάφορα·
ἀγαθὰ μὲν οὖν ἀρεταὶ καὶ τὰ μετέχοντα τῶν
ἀρετῶν· κακὰ τὰ δ' ἐναντία· ἀδιάφορα δὲ
16 πλοῦτος, ὑγεία, δόξα. εἶτ' ἂν μεταξὺ λεγόντων
ἡμῶν ψόφος μείζων γένηται ἢ τῶν παρόντων τις
17 καταγελάσῃ ἡμῶν, ἐξεπλάγημεν. ποῦ ἐστιν,
φιλόσοφε, ἐκεῖνα ἃ ἔλεγες; πόθεν αὐτὰ προφερό-
μενος ἔλεγες; ἀπὸ τῶν χειλῶν αὐτόθεν. τί οὖν
ἀλλότρια βοηθήματα μολύνεις; τί κυβεύεις περὶ
18 τὰ μέγιστα; ἄλλο γάρ ἐστιν ὡς εἰς ταμιεῖον
ἀποθέσθαι ἄρτους καὶ οἶνον, ἄλλο ἐστὶ φαγεῖν.
τὸ βρωθὲν ἐπέφθη, ἀνεδόθη, νεῦρα ἐγένετο, σάρκες,

---

[1] Supplied by Upton from his " codex."

faithful man while acts of the opposite character destroy him. And again, acts of the opposite character strengthen men of the opposite character; shamelessness strengthens the shameless man, faithlessness the faithless, abuse the abusive, wrath the wrathful, a disproportion between what he receives and what he pays out the miserly.

That is why the philosophers admonish us not to be satisfied with merely learning, but to add thereto practice also, and then training. For in the course of years we have acquired the habit of doing the opposite of what we learn and have in use opinions which are the opposite of the correct ones. If, therefore, we do not also put in use the correct opinions, we shall be nothing but the interpreters of other men's judgements. For who is there among us here and now that cannot give a philosophical discourse about good and evil? It will run like this: Of things that be, some are good, others evil, and others indifferent; now good things are virtues and everything that partakes in the virtues; evil are the opposite; while indifferent are wealth, health, reputation. Then, if we are interrupted in the midst of our speech by some unusually loud noise, or if someone in the audience laughs at us, we are upset. Where, you philosopher, are the things you are talking about? Where did you get what you were just saying? From your lips, and that is all. Why, then, do you pollute the helpful principles that are not your own? Why do you gamble about matters of the very utmost concern? For to store away bread and wine in a pantry is one thing, and to eat them is another. What is eaten is digested, distributed, becomes sinews, flesh, bones,

ὀστέα, αἷμα, εὔχροια, εὔπνοια. τὰ ἀποκείμενα
ὅταν μὲν θελήσῃς ἐκ προχείρου λαβὼν δεῖξαι
δύνασαι, ἀπ᾽ αὐτῶν δέ σοι ὄφελος οὐδὲν εἰ μὴ
19 μέχρι τοῦ δοκεῖν ὅτι ἔχεις. τί γὰρ διαφέρει
ταῦτα ἐξηγεῖσθαι ἢ τὰ τῶν ἑτεροδόξων;
τεχνολόγει νῦν καθίσας τὰ Ἐπικούρου καὶ τάχα
ἐκείνου χρηστικώτερον τεχνολογήσεις. τί οὖν
Στωικὸν λέγεις σεαυτόν, τί ἐξαπατᾷς τοὺς
πολλούς, τί ὑποκρίνῃ Ἰουδαῖον ὢν Ἕλλην [1];
20 οὐχ ὁρᾷς, πῶς ἕκαστος λέγεται Ἰουδαῖος, πῶς
Σύρος, πῶς Αἰγύπτιος; καὶ ὅταν τινὰ ἐπαμ-
φοτερίζοντα ἴδωμεν, εἰώθαμεν λέγειν " οὐκ ἔστιν
Ἰουδαῖος, ἀλλ᾽ ὑποκρίνεται." ὅταν δ᾽ ἀναλάβῃ
τὸ πάθος τὸ τοῦ βεβαμμένου καὶ ᾑρημένου, τότε
21 καὶ ἔστι τῷ ὄντι καὶ καλεῖται Ἰουδαῖος. οὕτως
καὶ ἡμεῖς παραβαπτισταί,[2] λόγῳ μὲν Ἰουδαῖοι,
ἔργῳ δ᾽ ἄλλο τι, ἀσυμπαθεῖς πρὸς τὸν λόγον,
μακρὰν ἀπὸ τοῦ χρῆσθαι τούτοις ἃ λέγομεν, ἐφ᾽
22 οἷς ὡς εἰδότες αὐτὰ ἐπαιρόμεθα. οὕτως οὐδὲ τὴν
τοῦ ἀνθρώπου ἐπαγγελίαν πληρῶσαι δυνάμενοι
προσλαμβάνομεν τὴν τοῦ φιλοσόφου, τηλικοῦτο

---

[1] Schenkl: ιουδαῖος ὢν ἕλληνας S.
[2] παραβαπτισταί Salmasius, perhaps correctly.

---

[1] It would appear (especially from the expression "counterfeit 'baptists'" below) that Epictetus is here speaking really
of the Christians, who were in his time not infrequently
confused with the Jews. (But it should be observed that
the text translated here is an emendation, for the MS. says
"the part of Greeks when you are a Jew," which may
possibly be defended on the understanding that, in the
parlance of Epictetus, a Jew is one who does not follow
reason as his sole guide.)

The sense of this much vexed passage I take to be: True

blood, a good complexion, easy breathing. What is stored away you can readily take and show whenever you please, but you get no good from it except in so far as you are reputed to possess it. For how much better is it to set forth these principles than those of other schools of thought? Sit down now and give a philosophical discourse upon the principles of Epicurus, and perhaps you will discourse more effectively than Epicurus himself. Why, then, do you call yourself a Stoic, why do you deceive the multitude, why do you act the part of a Jew,[1] when you are a Greek? Do you not see in what sense men are severally called Jew, Syrian, or Egyptian? For example, whenever we see a man halting between two faiths, we are in the habit of saying, "He is not a Jew, he is only acting the part." But when he adopts the attitude of mind of the man who has been baptized and has made his choice, then he both is a Jew in fact and is also called one. So we also are counterfeit "baptists," ostensibly Jews, but in reality something else, not in sympathy with our own reason, far from applying the principles which we profess, yet priding ourselves upon them as being men who know them. So, although we are unable even to fulfil the profession of man, we take on the additional profession of the philosopher

Jews (*i.e.* Christians) are a very marked class of men because of the rigorous consistency between their faith and their practice. But there are some who for one reason or another (possibly in order to avail themselves of the charity which the Christians dispensed to the poor, as Schweighäuser suggests,—like the so-called "rice Christians") profess a faith which they do not practise. It is this class, then, which Epictetus has in mind when he bitterly calls himself and his pupils "counterfeit 'baptists.'"

φορτίον, οἷον εἴ τις δέκα λίτρας ἆραι μὴ δυνάμενος
τὸν τοῦ Αἴαντος λίθον βαστάζειν ἤθελεν.

ιʹ. Πῶς ἀπὸ τῶν ὀνομάτων τὰ καθήκοντα
ἔστιν εὑρίσκειν;

1 Σκέψαι τίς εἶ. τὸ πρῶτον ἄνθρωπος, τοῦτο δ'
ἔστιν οὐδὲν ἔχων κυριώτερον προαιρέσεως, ἀλλὰ
ταύτῃ τὰ ἄλλα ὑποτεταγμένα, αὐτὴν δ' ἀδού-
2 λευτον καὶ ἀνυπότακτον. σκόπει οὖν, τίνων
κεχώρισαι κατὰ λόγον. κεχώρισαι θηρίων,
3 κεχώρισαι προβάτων. ἐπὶ τούτοις πολίτης εἶ
τοῦ κόσμου καὶ μέρος αὐτοῦ, οὐχ ἓν τῶν ὑπηρε-
τικῶν, ἀλλὰ τῶν προηγουμένων· παρακολου-
θητικὸς γὰρ εἶ τῇ θείᾳ διοικήσει καὶ τοῦ ἑξῆς
4 ἐπιλογιστικός. τίς οὖν ἐπαγγελία πολίτου;
μηδὲν ἔχειν ἰδίᾳ συμφέρον, περὶ μηδενὸς βουλεύε-
σθαι ὡς ἀπόλυτον, ἀλλ' ὥσπερ ἄν, εἰ ἡ χεὶρ
ἢ ὁ ποὺς λογισμὸν εἶχον καὶ παρηκολούθουν
τῇ φυσικῇ κατασκευῇ, οὐδέποτ' ἂν ἄλλως
ὥρμησαν ἢ ὠρέχθησαν ἢ ἐπανενεγκόντες ἐπὶ τὸ
5 ὅλον. διὰ τοῦτο καλῶς λέγουσιν οἱ φιλόσοφοι
ὅτι εἰ προῄδει ὁ καλὸς καὶ ἀγαθὸς τὰ ἐσόμενα,
συνήργει ἂν καὶ τῷ νοσεῖν καὶ τῷ ἀποθνήσκειν
καὶ τῷ πηροῦσθαι, αἰσθανόμενός γε, ὅτι ἀπὸ τῆς

---

[1] The huge one with which he beat down Aeneas. Homer,
Iliad, VII. 264.
[2] *Cf.* II. 8, 6 f. and note.

—so huge a burden! It is as though a man who was unable to raise ten pounds wanted to lift the stone of Aias.[1]

CHAPTER X

How is it possible to discover a man's duties from the designations which he bears?

CONSIDER who you are. To begin with, a Man; that is, one who has no quality more sovereign than moral choice, but keeps everything else subordinate to it, and this moral choice itself free from slavery and subjection. Consider, therefore, what those things are from which you are separated by virtue of the faculty of reason. You are separated from wild beasts, you are separated from sheep. In addition to this you are a citizen of the world, and a part of it, not one of the parts destined for service, but one of primary importance;[2] for you possess the faculty of understanding the divine administration of the world, and of reasoning upon the consequences thereof. What, then, is the profession of a citizen? To treat nothing as a matter of private profit, not to plan about anything as though he were a detached unit, but to act like the foot or the hand, which, if they had the faculty of reason and understood the constitution of nature, would never exercise choice or desire in any other way but by reference to the whole. Hence the philosophers well say that if the good and excellent man knew what was going to happen, he would help on the processes of disease and death and maiming, because he would realize that this allotment comes from the orderly

275

τῶν ὅλων διατάξεως τοῦτο ἀπονέμεται, κυριώτερον
δὲ τὸ ὅλον τοῦ μέρους καὶ ἡ πόλις τοῦ πολίτου.
6 νῦν δ' ὅτι οὐ προγιγνώσκομεν, καθήκει τῶν πρὸς
ἐκλογὴν εὐφυεστέρων ἔχεσθαι, ὅτι καὶ πρὸς τοῦτο
γεγόναμεν.

7 Μετὰ τοῦτο μέμνησο, ὅτι υἱὸς εἶ. τίς τούτου
τοῦ προσώπου ἐπαγγελία; πάντα τὰ¹ αὑτοῦ
ἡγεῖσθαι τοῦ πατρός, πάντα ὑπακούειν, μηδέποτε
ψέξαι πρός τινα μηδὲ βλαβερόν τι αὐτῷ εἰπεῖν ἢ
πρᾶξαι, ἐξίστασθαι ἐν πᾶσιν καὶ παραχωρεῖν
συνεργοῦντα κατὰ δύναμιν.

8 Μετὰ τοῦτο ἴσθι ὅτι καὶ ἀδελφὸς εἶ. καὶ πρὸς
τοῦτο δὲ τὸ πρόσωπον ὀφείλεται παραχώρησις,
εὐπείθεια, εὐφημία, μηδέποτ' ἀντιποιήσασθαί
τινος πρὸς αὐτὸν² τῶν ἀπροαιρέτων, ἀλλ' ἡδέως
ἐκεῖνα προίεσθαι, ἵν' ἐν τοῖς προαιρετικοῖς πλέον
9 ἔχῃς. ὅρα γὰρ οἷόν ἐστιν ἀντὶ θίδρακος, ἂν
οὕτως τύχῃ, καὶ καθέδρας αὐτὸν εὐγνωμοσύνην
κτήσασθαι, ὅση ἡ πλεονεξία.

10 Μετὰ ταῦτα εἰ βουλευτὴς πόλεώς τινος, ὅτι
βουλευτής· εἰ νέος, ὅτι νέος· εἰ πρεσβύτης, ὅτι
11 πρεσβύτης· εἰ πατήρ, ὅτι πατήρ. ἀεὶ γὰρ
ἕκαστον τῶν τοιούτων ὀνομάτων εἰς ἐπιλογισμὸν
12 ἐρχόμενον ὑπογράφει τὰ οἰκεῖα ἔργα. ἐὰν δ'
ἀπελθὼν ψέγῃς σου τὸν ἀδελφόν, λέγω σοι "ἐπε-
13 λάθου, τίς εἶ καὶ τί σοι ὄνομα." εἶτα εἰ μὲν

---

¹ Reiske.
² Wolf: ἑαυτὸν S.

---

¹ πλέον ἔχειν (πλεονεξία), "getting the best of it," usually
had a bad sense, but there *is* a πλεονεξία which should attract
the good man.

arrangement of the whole, and the whole is more sovereign than the part, and the state more sovereign than the citizen. But as it is, seeing that we do not know beforehand what is going to happen, it is our duty to cleave to that which is naturally more fit to be chosen, since we are born for this purpose.

Next bear in mind that you are a Son. What is the profession of this character? To treat everything that is his own as belonging to his father, to be obedient to him in all things, never to speak ill of him to anyone else, nor to say or do anything that will harm him, to give way to him in everything and yield him precedence, helping him as far as is within his power.

Next know that you are also a Brother. Upon this character also there is incumbent deference, obedience, kindly speech, never to claim as against your brother any of the things that lie outside the realm of your free moral choice, but cheerfully to give them up, so that in the things that *do* lie within the realm of your free moral choice you may have the best of it.[1] For see what it is, at the price of a head of lettuce, if it so chance, or of a seat, for you to acquire his goodwill—how greatly you get the best of it there!

Next, if you sit in the town council of some city, remember that you are a councillor; if you are young, remember that you are young; if old, that you are an elder; if a father, that you are a father. For each of these designations, when duly considered, always suggests the acts that are appropriate to it. But if you go off and speak ill of your brother, I say to you, " You have forgotten who you are and what your designation is." Why, if you

χαλκεὺς ὢν ἐχρῶ τῇ σφύρᾳ ἄλλως, ἐπιλελη-
σμένος ἂν ἦς τοῦ χαλκέως· εἰ δὲ τοῦ ἀδελφοῦ
ἐπελάθου καὶ ἀντὶ ἀδελφοῦ ἐχθρὸς ἐγένου, οὐδὲν
14 ἀντ' οὐδενὸς ἠλλάχθαι φανεῖ σεαυτῷ[1] ; εἰ δ' ἀντὶ
ἀνθρώπου, ἡμέρου ζῴου καὶ κοινωνικοῦ, θηρίον
γέγονας βλαβερόν, ἐπίβουλον, δηκτικόν, οὐδὲν
ἀπολώλεκας ; ἀλλὰ δεῖ σε κέρμα ἀπολέσαι, ἵνα
ζημιωθῇς, ἄλλου δ' οὐδενὸς ἀπώλεια ζημιοῖ τὸν
15 ἄνθρωπον ; εἶτα[2] γραμματικὴν μὲν ἀποβαλὼν ἢ
μουσικὴν ζημίαν ἂν[3] ἡγοῦ τὴν ἀπώλειαν αὐτῆς·
εἰ δ' αἰδῶ καὶ καταστολὴν καὶ ἡμερότητα ἀπο-
16 βαλεῖς, οὐδὲν ἡγῇ τὸ πρᾶγμα ; καίτοι ἐκεῖνα
μὲν παρ' ἔξωθέν τινα καὶ ἀπροαίρετον αἰτίαν
ἀπόλλυται, ταῦτα δὲ παρ' ἡμᾶς· καὶ ἐκεῖνα μὲν
οὔτ' ἔχειν καλόν ἐστιν[4] οὔτ' ἀπολλύειν αἰσχρόν
ἐστιν, ταῦτα δὲ καὶ μὴ ἔχειν καὶ ἀπολλύειν καὶ
17 αἰσχρόν ἐστι καὶ ἐπονείδιστον καὶ ἀτύχημα. τί
ἀπολλύει ὁ τὰ τοῦ κιναίδου πάσχων ; τὸν ἄνδρα.
ὁ δὲ διατιθείς ; πολλὰ μὲν καὶ ἄλλα καὶ αὐτὸς δ'
18 οὐδὲν ἧττον τὸν ἄνδρα. τί ἀπολλύει ὁ μοιχεύων ;
τὸν αἰδήμονα, τὸν ἐγκρατῆ, τὸν κόσμιον, τὸν πολίτην, τὸν γείτονα. τί ἀπολλύει ὁ ὀργιζόμενος ; ἄλλο
19 τι. ὁ φοβούμενος ; ἄλλο τι. οὐδεὶς δίχα ἀπωλείας καὶ ζημίας κακός ἐστιν. λοιπὸν εἰ τὴν ζημίαν
ζητεῖς ἐν κέρματι, πάντες οὗτοι ἀβλαβεῖς, ἀζή-
μιοι, ἂν οὕτως τύχῃ, καὶ ὠφελούμενοι καὶ

---

[1] Schenkl : φανεῖς ἑαυτῶι S.   [2] Schenkl : εἰ S.
[3] Supplied by Koraes.
[4] καλόν ἐστιν supplied by Schenkl.

were a smith and used your hammer amiss, you
would have forgotten the smith you were; but if
you forget the brother you are, and become an
enemy instead of a brother, will you seem to
yourself to have exchanged nothing for nothing?
And if, instead of being a man, a gentle and
social being, you have become a wild beast, a mis-
chievous, treacherous, biting animal, have you lost
nothing? What, must you lose a bit of pelf so as to
suffer damage, and does the loss of nothing else
damage a man? Yet, if you lost your skill in the
use of language or in music, you would regard the
loss of it as damage; but if you are going to lose
self-respect and dignity and gentleness, do you
think that does not matter? And yet those former
qualities are lost from some external cause that is
beyond the power of our will, but these latter are
lost through our own fault; and it is neither noble
to have nor disgraceful to lose these former qualities, but not to have these latter, or having had
them to lose them, is a disgrace and a reproach and
a calamity. What is lost by the victim of unnatural
lust? His manhood. And by the agent? Beside
a good many other things he also loses his manhood
no less than the other. What does the adulterer
lose? He loses the man of self-respect that was,
the man of self-control, the gentleman, the citizen,
the neighbour. What does the man lose who is
given to anger? Something else. Who is given
to fear? Something else. No one is evil without
loss and damage. Furthermore, if you look for
your loss in pelf, all those whom I have just mentioned suffer neither injury nor loss; nay, if it so
chance, they even get gain and profit, when, through

κερδαίνοντες, ὅταν διά τινος τούτων τῶν ἔργων
20 κέρμα αὐτοῖς προσγένηται. ὅρα δ᾽ εἰ ἐπὶ
κερμάτιον πάντα ἀνάγεις, ὅτι οὐδ᾽ ὁ τὴν ῥινά
σοι ἀπολλύων ἔσται βεβλαμμένος.—Ναί, φησίν,
21 κεκολόβωται γὰρ τὸ σῶμα.—Ἄγε, ὁ δὲ τὴν
ὄσφρασίαν αὐτὴν ἀπολωλεκὼς οὐδὲν ἀπολλύει;
ψυχῆς οὖν δύναμις οὐκ ἔστιν οὐδεμία, ἣν ὁ μὲν
κτησάμενος ὠφελεῖται, ὁ δ᾽ ἀποβαλὼν ζημιοῦται;
22 —Ποίαν καὶ λέγεις;—Οὐδὲν ἔχομεν αἰδῆμον
φύσει;—Ἔχομεν.—Ὁ τοῦτο ἀπολλύων οὐ ζημιοῦται, οὐδενὸς στερίσκεται, οὐδὲν ἀποβάλλει
23 τῶν πρὸς αὐτόν; οὐκ ἔχομεν φύσει τι πιστόν,
φύσει στερκτικόν, φύσει ὠφελητικόν, ἀλλήλων
φύσει ἀνεκτικόν; ὅστις οὖν εἰς ταῦτα περιορᾷ
ζημιούμενον ἑαυτόν, οὗτος ᾖ ἀβλαβὴς καὶ
ἀζήμιος;
24 Τί οὖν; μὴ βλάψω τὸν βλάψαντα;—Πρῶτον
μὲν ἰδού, τί ἐστι βλάβη καὶ μνήσθητι ὧν
25 ἤκουσας παρὰ τῶν φιλοσόφων. εἰ γὰρ τὸ
ἀγαθὸν ἐν προαιρέσει καὶ τὸ κακὸν ὡσαύτως ἐν
προαιρέσει, βλέπε μὴ τοιοῦτ᾽ ἐστιν ὃ λέγεις· "τί
26 οὖν; ἐπειδὴ ἐκεῖνος ἑαυτὸν ἔβλαψεν πρὸς ἐμέ τι
ἄδικον ποιήσας, ἐγὼ ἐμαυτὸν μὴ βλάψω πρὸς
27 ἐκεῖνον ἄδικόν τι ποιήσας;" τί οὖν οὐ τοιοῦτόν τι
φανταζόμεθα, ἀλλ᾽ ὅπου τι σωματικὸν ἐλάττωμα
ἢ¹ εἰς κτῆσιν, ἐκεῖ ἡ βλάβη, ὅπου εἰς τὴν
28 προαίρεσιν, οὐδεμία βλάβη; οὔτε γὰρ τὴν

¹ Supplied by Wolf.

some of their deeds just mentioned, they also acquire pelf. But observe that if you make paltry pelf your standard for everything, not even the man who loses his nose will in your eyes have suffered an injury.—"Oh yes, he has," someone says, " for his body is mutilated."—Come now, and does the man who has lost his entire sense of smell lose nothing? Is there, then, no such thing as a faculty of the mind, the possession of which means gain to a man, and the loss, injury?—What faculty do you mean? Have we not a natural sense of self-respect?—We have.—Does not the man who destroys this suffer a loss, is he not deprived of something, does he not lose something that belonged to him? Do we not have a natural sense of fidelity, a natural sense of affection, a natural sense of helpfulness, a natural sense of keeping our hands off one another? Shall, therefore, the man who allows himself to suffer loss in such matters, be regarded as having suffered neither injury nor loss?

Well, what then? Am I not to injure the man who has injured me?—First consider what injury is, and call to mind what you have heard the philosophers say. For if the good lies in moral purpose, and the evil likewise in moral purpose, see if what you are saying does not come to something like this, " Well, what then? Since so-and-so has injured himself by doing me some wrong, shall I not injure myself by doing him some wrong?" Why, then, do we not represent the case to ourselves in some such light as that? Instead of that, where there is some loss affecting our body or our property, there we count it injury; but is there no injury where the loss affects our moral purpose?

κεφαλὴν ἀλγεῖ ὁ ἐξαπατηθεὶς ἢ ἀδικήσας οὔτε
τὸν ὀφθαλμὸν οὔτε τὸ ἰσχίον, οὔτε τὸν ἀγρὸν
29 ἀπολλύει. ἡμεῖς δ' ἄλλο οὐδὲν ἐθέλομεν ἢ
ταῦτα· τὴν προαίρεσιν δὲ πότερον αἰδήμονα καὶ
πιστὴν ἕξομεν ἢ ἀναίσχυντον καὶ ἄπιστον, οὐδ'
ἐγγὺς διαφερόμεθα πλὴν μόνον ἐν τῇ σχολῇ μέχρι
30 τῶν λογαρίων. τοιγαροῦν μέχρι τῶν λογαρίων
προκόπτομεν, ἔξω δ' αὐτῶν οὐδὲ τὸ ἐλάχιστον.

ια'. Τίς ἀρχὴ φιλοσοφίας ;

1   Ἀρχὴ φιλοσοφίας παρά γε τοῖς ὡς δεῖ καὶ κατὰ
θύραν ἁπτομένοις αὐτῆς συναίσθησις τῆς αὐτοῦ
ἀσθενείας καὶ ἀδυναμίας περὶ τὰ ἀναγκαῖα.
2 ὀρθογωνίου μὲν γὰρ τριγώνου ἢ διέσεως ἡμιτονίου[1]
οὐδεμίαν φύσει ἔννοιαν ἥκομεν ἔχοντες, ἀλλ' ἔκ
τινος τεχνικῆς παραλήψεως διδασκόμεθα ἕκαστον
αὐτῶν καὶ διὰ τοῦτο οἱ μὴ εἰδότες αὐτὰ οὐδ' οἴονται
3 εἰδέναι. ἀγαθοῦ δὲ καὶ κακοῦ καὶ καλοῦ καὶ
αἰσχροῦ καὶ πρέποντος καὶ ἀπρεποῦς καὶ εὐδαιμονίας καὶ προσήκοντος καὶ ἐπιβάλλοντος καὶ
ὅ τι δεῖ ποιῆσαι καὶ ὅ τι οὐ δεῖ ποιῆσαι τίς οὐκ
4 ἔχων ἔμφυτον ἔννοιαν ἐλήλυθεν ; διὰ τοῦτο
πάντες χρώμεθα τοῖς ὀνόμασιν καὶ ἐφαρμόζειν

---

[1] ἢ ἡμιτονίου s, perhaps rightly.

For the man who has been deceived or who has done some wrong has no pain in his head, or his eye, or his hip, neither does he lose his land. But these are the things we care for and nothing else; yet the question whether we are going to have a moral purpose characterized by self-respect and good faith, or by shamelessness and bad faith, does not so much as begin to disturb us, except only in so far as we make it a topic of trivial discussion in the classroom. Therefore, so far as our trivial discussions go, we do make some progress, but, apart from them, not even the very least.

CHAPTER XI

What is the beginning of philosophy?

THE beginning of philosophy with those who take it up as they should, and enter in, as it were, by the gate, is a consciousness of a man's own weakness and impotence with reference to the things of real consequence in life. For we come into being without any innate concept of a right-angled triangle, or of a half-tone musical interval, but by a certain systematic method of instruction we are taught the meaning of each of these things, and for that reason those who do not know them also do not fancy that they do. But, on the other hand, who has come into being without an innate concept of what is good and evil, honourable and base, appropriate and inappropriate, and happiness, and of what is proper and falls to our lot, and what we ought to do and what we ought not to do? Wherefore, we all use these terms and endeavour to adapt our preconceptions

283

πειρώμεθα τὰς προλήψεις ταῖς ἐπὶ μέρους οὐσίαις.
5 καλῶς ἐποίησεν, δεόντως, οὐ δεόντως· ἠτύχησεν,
εὐτύχησεν· ἄδικός ἐστιν, δίκαιός ἐστιν. τίς
ἡμῶν φείδεται τούτων τῶν ὀνομάτων; τίς ἡμῶν
ἀναβάλλεται τὴν χρῆσιν αὐτῶν μέχρι μάθῃ καθάπερ τῶν περὶ τὰς γραμμὰς ἢ τοὺς φθόγγους οἱ οὐκ
6 εἰδότες; τούτου δ' αἴτιον τὸ ἥκειν ἤδη τινὰ ὑπὸ
τῆς φύσεως κατὰ τὸν τόπον ὥσπερ δεδιδαγ-
μένους, ἀφ' ὧν ὁρμώμενοι καὶ τὴν οἴησιν προσ-
7 ειλήφαμεν. Νὴ Δία γὰρ φύσει ¹ οὐκ οἶδα ἐγὼ τὸ
καλὸν καὶ τὸ αἰσχρόν; οὐκ ἔχω ἔννοιαν αὐτοῦ;—
Ἔχεις.—Οὐκ ἐφαρμόζω τοῖς ἐπὶ μέρους;—Ἐφαρ-
8 μόζεις.—Οὐ καλῶς οὖν ἐφαρμόζω;—Ἐνταῦθά
ἐστι τὸ ζήτημα πᾶν καὶ οἴησις ἐνταῦθα προσγίνε-
ται. ἀφ' ὁμολογουμένων γὰρ ὁρμώμενοι τούτων ἐπὶ
τὸ ἀμφισβητούμενον προάγουσιν ὑπὸ τῆς ἀκαταλ-
9 λήλου ἐφαρμογῆς. ὡς εἴ γε καὶ τοῦτο ἔτι πρὸς ἐκεί-
10 νοις ἐκέκτηντο, τί ἐκώλυε αὐτοὺς εἶναι τελείους; νῦν
δ' ἐπεὶ δοκεῖς ὅτι καὶ καταλλήλως ἐφαρμόζεις τὰς
προλήψεις τοῖς ἐπὶ μέρους, εἰπέ μοι, πόθεν τοῦτο
λαμβάνεις;—Ὅτι δοκεῖ μοι.—Τουτὶ ² οὖν τινι οὐ
δοκεῖ, καὶ οἴεται καὶ αὐτὸς ἐφαρμόζειν καλῶς· ἢ
11 οὐκ οἴεται;—Οἴεται.—Δύνασθε οὖν περὶ ὧν τὰ
μαχόμενα δοξάζετε ἀμφότεροι καταλλήλως ἐφαρ-
12 μόζειν τὰς προλήψεις;—Οὐ δυνάμεθα.—Ἔχεις

¹ Schenkl (note): Διὰ γὰρ φησίν S.
² Schenkl: τούτωι S.

284

about them to the individual instances. "He has done well, as he ought, or as he ought not; he has been unfortunate, or fortunate; he is a wicked man, or he is a just man"—who of us refrains from expressions of this kind? Who of us waits before he uses them until he has learned what they mean, as those who have no knowledge of lines or sounds wait before they use the terms relating to them? The reason is that we come into the world with a certain amount of instruction upon this matter already given us, as it were, by nature, and that starting with this we have added thereto our opinion.—Yes, by Zeus, for do I in my own case not have by gift of nature knowledge of what is noble and base; do I not have a concept of the matter?—You do.—Do I not apply it to individual instances?—You do.—Do I not, then, apply it properly?—There lies the whole question, and there opinion comes in. For men start with these principles upon which they are agreed, but then, because they make an unsuitable application of them, get into disputes. Since if, in addition to having the principles themselves, they really possessed also the faculty of making suitable application of the same, what could keep them from being perfect? But now, since you think that you can also apply your preconceptions suitably to the individual cases, tell me, whence do you get this gift?—It is because I think so.—But on this precise point someone else does not think so, and yet he too fancies that he is applying the principles properly, does he not?—He does so fancy.—Can both of you, then, be making suitable applications of your preconceptions in the matters upon which your opinions are at variance?—We cannot.—Can you,

285

οὖν δεῖξαί τι ἡμῖν πρὸς τὸ αὐτὰς ἐφαρμόζειν
ἄμεινον ἀνωτέρω τοῦ δοκεῖν σοι ; ὁ δὲ μαινόμενος
ἄλλα τινὰ ποιεῖ ἢ τὰ δοκοῦντά οἱ καλά ; κἀκείνῳ
οὖν ἀρκεῖ τοῦτο τὸ κριτήριον ;—Οὐκ ἀρκεῖ.—
Ἐλθὲ[1] οὖν ἐπί τι ἀνωτέρω τοῦ δοκεῖν.—Τί τοῦτό
ἐστιν ;

13 Ἰδ᾽ ἀρχὴ φιλοσοφίας· αἴσθησις μάχης τῆς πρὸς
ἀλλήλους τῶν ἀνθρώπων καὶ ζήτησις τοῦ παρ᾽ ὃ
γίνεται ἡ μάχη καὶ κατάγνωσις καὶ ἀπιστία πρὸς
τὸ ψιλῶς δοκοῦν, ἔρευνα δέ τις περὶ τὸ δοκοῦν εἰ
ὀρθῶς δοκεῖ καὶ εὕρεσις κανόνος τινός, οἷον ἐπὶ
βαρῶν τὸν ζυγὸν εὕρομεν, οἷον ἐπὶ εὐθέων καὶ
14 στρεβλῶν τὴν στάθμην.—Τοῦτ᾽ ἔστιν ἀρχὴ φιλοσοφίας ; πάντα καλῶς ἔχει τὰ δοκοῦντα ἅπασι ;
Καὶ πῶς δυνατὸν τὰ μαχόμενα καλῶς ἔχειν ;
15 οὐκοῦν οὐ πάντα.—Ἀλλὰ τὰ ἡμῖν δοκοῦντα ;[2] τί
μᾶλλον ἢ τὰ Σύροις, τί μᾶλλον ἢ τὰ Αἰγυπτίοις,
τί μᾶλλον ἢ τὰ ἐμοὶ φαινόμενα ἢ τὰ τῷ δεῖνι ;—
Οὐδὲν μᾶλλον.—Οὐκ ἄρα ἀρκεῖ τὸ δοκοῦν ἑκάστῳ
πρὸς τὸ εἶναι· οὐδὲ γὰρ ἐπὶ βαρῶν ἢ μέτρων
ψιλῇ τῇ ἐμφάσει ἀρκούμεθα, ἀλλὰ κανόνα τινὰ
16 ἐφ᾽ ἑκάστου εὕρομεν· ἐνταῦθ᾽ οὖν οὐδεὶς κανὼν
ἀνωτέρω τοῦ δοκεῖν ; καὶ πῶς οἷόν τε ἀτέκμαρτα
εἶναι καὶ ἀνεύρετα τὰ ἀναγκαιότατα ἐν ἀνθρώποις ;

---

[1] *Sc.*: ἐλθὼν S.
[2] Kronenberg : οὐκοῦν οὐ πάντα, ἀλλὰ τὰ ἡμῖν δοκοῦντα. S
(and Schenkl).

---

[1] " Each man " (ἕκαστος, as below, § 15) would have been
a more logical form for this question, for it is clear from the
context that Epictetus is not speaking here of the actual
correctness of any opinion universally held, but only of *any*
opinion held by *any* man.

then, show us anything higher than your own opinion which will make it possible for us to apply our preconceptions better? And does the madman do anything else but that which seems to him to be good? Is this criterion, then, sufficient in his case also?—It is not.—Go, therefore, to something higher than your own opinion, and tell us what that is.

Behold the beginning of philosophy!—a recognition of the conflict between the opinions of men, and a search for the origin of that conflict, and a condemnation of mere opinion, coupled with scepticism regarding it, and a kind of investigation to determine whether the opinion is rightly held, together with the invention of a kind of standard of judgement, as we have invented the balance for the determination of weights, or the carpenter's rule for the determination of things straight and crooked.— Is this the beginning of philosophy? Is everything right that every man thinks?[1] Nay, how is it possible for conflicting opinions to be right? Consequently, not all opinions are right.—But are *our* opinions right? Why ours, rather than those of the Syrians; why ours, rather than those of the Egyptians; why ours, rather than my own, or those of so-and-so?—There is no reason why.—Therefore, the opinion which each man holds is not a sufficient criterion for determining the truth; for also in the case of weights and measures we are not satisfied with the mere appearance, but we have invented a certain standard to test each. In the present case, then, is there no standard higher than opinion? And yet how can it possibly be that matters of the utmost consequence among men should be unde-

17 —Ἔστιν οὖν.—Καὶ διὰ τί οὐ ζητοῦμεν αὐτὸν καὶ
ἀνευρίσκομεν καὶ ἀνευρόντες λοιπὸν ἀπαραβάτως
χρώμεθα δίχα αὐτοῦ μηδὲ τὸν δάκτυλον ἐκτεί-
18 νοντες; τοῦτο γάρ, οἶμαι, ἐστὶν ὃ εὑρεθὲν ἀπαλ-
λάσσει μανίας τοὺς μόνῳ τῷ δοκεῖν μέτρῳ πάντων
χρωμένους, ἵνα λοιπὸν ἀπό τινων γνωρίμων καὶ
διευκρινημένων ὁρμώμενοι χρώμεθα ἐπὶ τῶν ἐπὶ
μέρους διηρθρωμέναις ταῖς προλήψει.

19   Τίς ὑποπέπτωκεν οὐσία περὶ ἧς ζητοῦμεν;—
20 Ἡδονή.—Ὕπαγε αὐτὴν τῷ κανόνι, βάλε εἰς τὸν
ζυγόν. τὸ ἀγαθὸν δεῖ εἶναι τοιοῦτον, ἐφ' ᾧ θαρρεῖν
ἄξιον καὶ ᾧ πεποιθέναι;—Δεῖ.—Ἀβεβαίῳ οὖν
21 τινι θαρρεῖν ἄξιον;—Οὔ.—Μή τι οὖν βέβαιον ἡ
ἡδονή;—Οὔ.—Ἆρον οὖν καὶ βάλε ἔξω ἐκ τοῦ
ζυγοῦ καὶ ἀπέλασον τῆς χώρας τῶν ἀγαθῶν μακράν.
22 εἰ δ' οὐκ ὀξυβλεπτεῖς καὶ ἕν σοι ζυγὸν οὐκ ἀρκεῖ,
φέρε ἄλλο. ἐπὶ τῷ ἀγαθῷ ἄξιον ἐπαίρεσθαι;—
Ναί.—Ἐφ' ἡδονῇ οὖν παρούσῃ ἄξιον ἐπαίρεσθαι;
βλέπε μὴ εἴπῃς ὅτι ἄξιον· εἰ δὲ μή, οὐκέτι σε
οὐδὲ τοῦ ζυγοῦ ἄξιον ἡγήσομαι.

23   Οὕτως κρίνεται τὰ πράγματα καὶ ἵσταται τῶν
24 κανόνων ἡτοιμασμένων· καὶ τὸ φιλοσοφεῖν τοῦτό
ἐστιν, ἐπισκέπτεσθαι καὶ βεβαιοῦν τοὺς κανόνας,
25 τὸ δ' ἤδη χρῆσθαι τοῖς ἐγνωσμένοις τοῦτο τοῦ
καλοῦ καὶ ἀγαθοῦ ἔργον ἐστίν.

288

terminable and undiscoverable.—Therefore, there *is* some standard.—Then why do we not look for it and find it, and when we have found it thenceforth use it unswervingly, not so much as stretching out our finger without it? For this is something, I think, the discovery of which frees from madness those who use only opinion as the measure of all things, so that thenceforward, starting with certain principles that are known and clearly discriminated, we may use in the judgement of specific cases an organically articulated system of preconceived ideas.

What subject has arisen that we wish to investigate?—Pleasure.—Subject it to the standard, put it into the balance. Should the good be the sort of thing that we can properly have confidence and trust in?—It should.—Can we properly have confidence, then, in something that is insecure?—No.—Pleasure contains no element of security, does it?—No.—Away with it, then, and throw it out of the balance, and drive it far away from the region of things good. But if you are not endowed with keen eyesight and if one balance is not enough for you, bring another. Can one properly feel elated over the good?—Yes.—Can one properly feel elated, then, over the moment's pleasure? See that you do not say that it is proper; if you do, I shall no longer regard you as a proper person even to have a balance!

And so are matters judged and weighed, if we have the standards ready with which to test them; and the task of philosophy is this—to examine and to establish the standards; but to go ahead and use them after they have become known is the task of the good and excellent man.

ιβ'. Περὶ τοῦ διαλέγεσθαι.

1   Ἃ μὲν δεῖ μαθόντα εἰδέναι χρῆσθαι λόγῳ, ἠκρί-
βωται ὑπὸ τῶν ἡμετέρων· περὶ δὲ τὴν χρῆσιν
αὐτῶν τὴν προσήκουσαν τελέως ἀγύμναστοί ἐσμεν.
2 δὸς γοῦν ᾧ θέλεις ἡμῶν ἰδιώτην τινὰ τὸν προσδια-
λεγόμενον· καὶ οὐχ εὑρίσκει χρήσασθαι αὐτῷ,
ἀλλὰ μικρὰ κινήσας τὸν ἄνθρωπον, ἂν παρὰ
σκέλος¹ ἀπαντᾷ ἐκεῖνος, οὐκέτι δύναται μεταχει-
ρίσασθαι, ἀλλ' ἢ λοιδορεῖ λοιπὸν ἢ καταγελᾷ καὶ
λέγει " ἰδιώτης ἐστίν· οὐκ ἔστιν αὐτῷ χρήσασθαι."
3 ὁ δ' ὁδηγός, ὅταν λάβῃ τινὰ πλανώμενον, ἤγαγεν
ἐπὶ τὴν ὁδὸν τὴν δέουσαν, οὐχὶ καταγελάσας ἢ
4 λοιδορησάμενος ἀπῆλθεν. καὶ σὺ δεῖξον αὐτῷ
τὴν ἀλήθειαν καὶ ὄψει ὅτι ἀκολουθεῖ. μέχρι δ'
ἂν οὐ μὴ δεικνύῃς, μὴ ἐκείνου καταγέλα, ἀλλὰ
μᾶλλον αἰσθάνου τῆς ἀδυναμίας τῆς αὐτοῦ.
5   Πῶς οὖν ἐποίει Σωκράτης; αὐτὸν ἠνάγκαζεν
τὸν προσδιαλεγόμενον αὐτῷ μαρτυρεῖν, ἄλλου δ'
οὐδενὸς ἐδεῖτο μάρτυρος. τοιγαροῦν ἐξῆν αὐτῷ
λέγειν ὅτι " τοὺς μὲν ἄλλους ἐῶ χαίρειν, ἀεὶ δὲ τῷ
ἀντιλέγοντι ἀρκοῦμαι μάρτυρι· καὶ τοὺς μὲν ἄλλους οὐκ ἐπιψηφίζω, τὸν δὲ προσδιαλεγόμενον
6 μόνον." οὕτω γὰρ ἐναργῆ ἐτίθει τὰ ἀπὸ τῶν
ἐννοιῶν, ὥστε πάνθ' ὁντιναοῦν συναισθανόμενον
7 τῆς μάχης ἀναχωρεῖν ἀπ' αὐτῆς. " Ἆρά γε ὁ

---

¹ παρὰ μέλος (" off the tune, out of harmony ") s, perhaps
correctly.

---

¹ A free paraphrase of Plato, *Gorgias*, 474A; compare
also 472c. A still freer paraphrase of the same general
idea appears in II. 26, 6.

CHAPTER XII

Upon the art of argumentation

WHAT a man ought to learn before he will know how to conduct an argument has been precisely defined by the philosophers of our school; but as to the proper use of what we have learned we are still utterly inexperienced. At all events, give to anyone of us you please some layman with whom to carry on an argument; he will find no way of dealing with him, but after moving the man a little, in case the latter thwarts him, our man gives up trying to handle him, and thereafter either reviles him, or laughs him to scorn, and remarks, "He is a mere layman; it is impossible to do anything with him." But the real guide, whenever he finds a person going astray, leads him back to the right road, instead of leaving him with a scornful laugh or an insult. So also do you show him the truth and you will see that he follows. But so long as you do not show him the truth, do not laugh him to scorn, but rather recognize your own incapacity.

How did Socrates act? He used to force the man who was arguing with him to be his witness, and never needed any other witness. That is why he could say, "I can dispense with all the others, and am always satisfied to have my fellow-disputant for a witness; and the votes of the rest I do not take, but only that of my fellow-disputant." [1] For he used to make so clear the consequences which followed from the concepts, that absolutely everyone realized the contradiction involved and gave up the battle. "And so does the man who feels envy

φθονῶν χαίρει ;"—" Οὐδαμῶς, ἀλλὰ μᾶλλον
λυπεῖται." ἀπὸ τοῦ ἐναντίου ἐκίνησε τὸν πλησίον.
" Τί δ'; ἐπὶ κακοῖς δοκεῖ σοι εἶναι λύπη ὁ φθόνος;
8 καὶ τί ὁ φθόνος ἐστὶ κακῶν ;" οὐκοῦν ἐκεῖνον
ἐποίησεν εἰπεῖν ὅτι λύπη ἐστὶν ἐπ' ἀγαθοῖς ὁ
φθόνος. " Τί δέ; φθονοίη ἄν τις τοῖς οὐδὲν πρὸς
9 αὑτόν;"—" Οὐδαμῶς." καὶ οὕτως ἐκπεπλη-
ρωκὼς τὴν ἔννοιαν καὶ διηρθρωκὼς ἀπηλλάσ-
σετο, οὐ λέγων ὅτι " ὅρισαί μοι τὸν φθόνον," εἶτα
ὁρισαμένου " κακῶς ὡρίσω· οὐ γὰρ ἀντακολουθεῖ
10 τῷ κεφαλαιώδει τὸ ὁρικόν·" ῥήματα τεχνικὰ καὶ
διὰ τοῦτο τοῖς ἰδιώταις φορτικὰ καὶ δυσπαρα-
κολούθητα, ὧν ἡμεῖς ἀποστῆναι οὐ δυνάμεθα.
11 ἐξ ὧν δ' αὐτὸς ὁ ἰδιώτης ἐπακολουθῶν ταῖς
αὑτοῦ φαντασίαις παραχωρῆσαι δύναιτ' ἄν τι
ἢ ἀθετῆσαι, οὐδαμῶς διὰ τούτων αὐτὸν κινῆσαι
12 δυνάμεθα. καὶ λοιπὸν εἰκότως συναισθανόμενοι
ταύτης ἡμῶν τῆς ἀδυναμίας ἀπεχόμεθα τοῦ
13 πράγματος, ὅσοις γ' ἐστί τι εὐλαβείας. οἱ δὲ
πολλοὶ καὶ εἰκαῖοι συγκαθέντες εἴς τι τοιοῦτον
φύρονται καὶ φύρουσι καὶ τὰ τελευταῖα
λοιδορήσαντες καὶ λοιδορηθέντες ἀπέρχονται.

14   Τὸ πρῶτον δὲ τοῦτο καὶ μάλιστα ἴδιον Σωκράτους μηδέποτε παροξυνθῆναι ἐν λόγῳ, μηδέποτε
λοίδορον προενέγκασθαι μηδέν, μηδέποθ' ὑβρι-

---

[1] Based on Xenophon, *Memorabilia*, III. 9, 8, and Plato, *Philebus*, 48B, and following.

rejoice in it?"[1]—"Not at all; but he experiences pain rather than joy." (By the contradiction in terms he has moved the other party to the argument.) "Very well, does envy seem to you to be feeling of pain at evils? And yet what envy is there of evils?" (Consequently, he has made his opponent say that envy is a feeling of pain at good things.) "Very well, would a man feel envy about matters that did not concern him in the least?"—"Not at all." And so he filled out and articulated the concept, and after that went his way; he did not start in by saying, "Define envy for me," and then, when the other had defined it, remark, "That is a bad definition you have made, for the definition term does not fit the subject defined." Those are technical terms, and for that reason wearisome to the layman and hard for him to follow, and yet we are unable to dispense with them. But as to terms which the layman could himself follow, and so, by the assistance of his own external impressions, be able to accept or reject some proposition—we are absolutely unable to move him by their use. The result is that, recognizing this incapacity of ours, we naturally refrain from attempting the matter, those of us, I mean, who are at all cautious. But the rash multitude of men, when once they have let themselves in for something of this sort, get confused themselves and confuse others, and finally, after reviling their opponents and being themselves reviled, they walk away.

Now this was the first and most characteristic thing about Socrates, that he never got wrought up during an argument, never used any term of abuse

στικόν, ἀλλὰ τῶν λοιδορούντων ἀνέχεσθαι καὶ
15 παύειν μάχην. εἰ θέλετε γνῶναι, πόσην ἐν
τούτῳ δύναμιν εἶχεν, ἀνάγνωτε τὸ Ξενοφῶντος
Συμπόσιον καὶ ὄψεσθε πόσας μάχας διαλέλυκεν.
16 διὰ τοῦτο εἰκότως καὶ παρὰ τοῖς ποιηταῖς ἐν
μεγίστῳ ἐπαίνῳ λέλεκται τὸ

> αἶψά τε καὶ μέγα νεῖκος ἐπισταμένως κατέ-
> παυσεν.

17   Τί οὖν; οὐ λίαν ἐστὶ νῦν ἀσφαλὲς τὸ πρᾶγμα
καὶ μάλιστα ἐν Ῥώμῃ. τὸν γὰρ ποιοῦντα αὐτὸ
οὐκ ἐν γωνίᾳ δηλονότι δεήσει ποιεῖν, ἀλλὰ προσελθόντα ὑπατικῷ τινι, ἂν οὕτως τύχῃ, πλουσίῳ
πυθέσθαι αὐτοῦ "ἔχεις μοι εἰπεῖν, ὦ οὗτος, ᾧ
18 τινι τοὺς ἵππους τοὺς σεαυτοῦ παρέδωκας;"
"ἔγωγε." "ἆρα τῷ τυχόντι καὶ ἀπείρῳ ἱππι-
κῆς;" "οὐδαμῶς." "τί δ'; ᾧ τινι τὸ χρυσίον
ἢ τὸ ἀργύριον ἢ τὴν ἐσθῆτα;" "οὐδὲ ταῦτα τῷ
19 τυχόντι." "τὸ σῶμα δὲ τὸ σαυτοῦ ἤδη τινὶ
ἔσκεψαι ἐπιτρέψαι εἰς ἐπιμέλειαν αὐτοῦ;" "πῶς
γὰρ οὔ;" "ἐμπείρῳ δηλονότι καὶ τούτῳ ἀλειπτι-
20 κῆς ἢ ἰατρικῆς;" "πάνυ μὲν οὖν." "πότερον
ταῦτά σοι τὰ κράτιστά ἐστιν ἢ καὶ ἄλλο τι
ἐκτήσω πάντων ἄμεινον;" "ποῖον καὶ λέγεις;"
"τὸ αὐτοῖς νὴ Δία τούτοις χρώμενον καὶ δοκιμάζον ἕκαστον καὶ βουλευόμενον." "ἆρά γε τὴν
21 ψυχὴν λέγεις;" "ὀρθῶς ὑπέλαβες. ταύτην γάρ

---

¹ Hesiod, *Theogony*, 87.

or insolence, but endured the abuse of others, and put an end to strife. If you wish to know how great was the faculty he had in this field, read the *Symposium* of Xenophon, and you will see how many cases of strife he settled. Therefore, and with good reason, among the poets also very high praise has been accorded to the following sentiment:

"Soon doth he shrewdly make an end of a quarrel though weighty."[1]

Well, what then? Nowadays this activity is not a very safe one, and especially so in Rome. For the man who engages in it will clearly be under obligation not to do it in a corner, but he must go up to some rich person of consular rank, if it so chance, and ask him, "You there, can you tell to whose care you have entrusted your horses?" "I can, indeed," answers the man. "Is it, then, some chance comer, a man who knows nothing about the care of horses?" "Not at all." "And what then? Can you tell me to whom you have entrusted your gold, or your silver, or your clothing?" "I have not entrusted these, either, to a chance comer." "And have you ever thought about entrusting your body to someone to look after it?" "Why, certainly." "And, of course, he too is a man of special skill in the art of physical training, or medicine, is he not?" "Yes, indeed." "Are these your most valuable possessions, or have you something else that is better than all of them?" "Just what do you mean?" "That, by Zeus, which utilizes these other things, and puts each of them to the test, and exercises deliberation?" "Ah so, you are talking about my soul, are you?" "You have

τοι καὶ λέγω." "πολὺ νὴ Δία τῶν ἄλλων τοῦτο
22 ἄμεινον δοκῶ μοι κεκτῆσθαι." "ἔχεις οὖν εἰπεῖν,[1]
ὅτῳ τρόπῳ τῆς ψυχῆς ἐπιμεμέλησαι ; οὐ γὰρ
εἰκῇ χῶς[2] ἔτυχεν εἰκός σε οὕτως σοφὸν ὄντα
καὶ ἐν τῇ πόλει δόκιμον τὸ κράτιστον τῶν σεαυτοῦ περιορᾶν ἀμελούμενον καὶ ἀπολλύμενον."
23 "οὐδαμῶς." "ἀλλ' αὐτὸς ἐπιμέλησαι αὐτοῦ ;
24 πότερον μαθὼν παρά του ἢ εὑρὼν αὐτός ;" ὧδε
λοιπὸν ὁ κίνδυνος, μὴ πρῶτον μὲν εἴπῃ "τί δέ σοι
μέλει, βέλτιστε ; κύριός[3] μου εἶ ;" εἶτ' ἂν ἐπι-
μείνῃς πράγματα παρέχων, διαράμενος κονδύλους
25 σοι δῷ. τούτου τοῦ πράγματος ἤμην ποτὲ
ζηλωτὴς καὶ αὐτός, πρὶν εἰς ταῦτα ἐμπεσεῖν.

ιγ΄. Περὶ τοῦ ἀγωνιᾶν.

1 Οταν ἀγωνιῶντα ἴδω ἄνθρωπον, λέγω· οὗτος
τί ποτε θέλει ; εἰ μὴ τῶν οὐκ ἐφ' αὑτῷ τι ἤθελεν,
2 πῶς ἂν ἔτι ἠγωνία ; διὰ τοῦτο καὶ ὁ κιθαρῳδὸς
μόνος μὲν ᾄδων οὐκ ἀγωνιᾷ, εἰς θέατρον δ' εἰσερχόμενος, κἂν λίαν εὔφωνος ᾖ καὶ καλῶς κιθα-
ρίζῃ· οὐ γὰρ ᾆσαι μόνον θέλει καλῶς, ἀλλὰ καὶ
εὐδοκιμῆσαι, τοῦτο δ' οὐκέτι ἐστὶν ἐπ' αὐτῷ.
3 λοιπὸν οὗ μὲν ἡ ἐπιστήμη αὐτῷ πρόσεστιν, ἐκεῖ

---

[1] Schenkl: ἡμῖν S (εἰπεῖν ἡμῖν s).
[2] Schenkl: γ' ὡς S.   [3] C. Schenkl: τίς S.

understood me aright, for it is precisely this that I am talking about." "By Zeus, I regard this as far and away the most valuable of all my possessions." "Can you, then, tell in what way you have taken care of your soul? For it is not to be supposed that as wise a man as yourself and one so honoured in the city is recklessly and at random allowing the very best of his possessions to go to ruin through neglect." "Certainly not." "But have you yourself taken care of that possession? Did you learn how to take care of it from somebody else, or did you discover how yourself?" Then comes the danger that first he will say, "What is that to you, good sir? Are you my master?" and after that, if you persist in annoying him, that he will lift his fist and give you a blow. This was a pursuit that I too was very fond of once upon a time, before I fell to my present estate.

CHAPTER XIII

Of anxiety

WHEN I see a man in anxiety, I say to myself, What can it be that this fellow wants? For if he did not want something that was outside of his control, how could he still remain in anxiety? That is why the citharoede when singing all alone shows no anxiety, but does so when he enters the theatre, even though he has a very beautiful voice and plays the cithara admirably; for he does not wish merely to sing well, but also to win applause, and that is no longer under his control. Accordingly, where he has skill, there he shows confidence. Set before him

τὸ θάρσος· φέρε ὃν θέλεις ἰδιώτην καὶ οὐκ ἐπι-
στρέφεται· ὅπου δ' οὐκ οἶδεν οὐδὲ μεμελέτηκεν,
4 ἐκεῖ ἀγωνιᾷ. τί δ' ἔστι τοῦτο; οὐκ οἶδεν, τί
ἔστιν ὄχλος οὐδὲ τί ὄχλου ἔπαινος· ἀλλὰ τὴν
νήτην μὲν τύπτειν ἔμαθεν καὶ τὴν ὑπάτην, ἔπαινος δ' ὁ παρὰ τῶν πολλῶν τί ἐστι καὶ τίνα
δύναμιν ἔχει ἐν βίῳ οὔτε οἶδεν οὔτε μεμελέτηκεν
5 αὐτό. ἀνάγκη λοιπὸν τρέμειν καὶ ὠχριᾶν.

Κιθαρῳδὸν μὲν οὖν οὐ δύναμαι εἰπεῖν μὴ εἶναι,
ὅταν ἴδω τινὰ φοβούμενον, ἄλλο δέ τι δύναμαι
6 εἰπεῖν καὶ οὐδὲ ἕν, ἀλλὰ πολλά. καὶ πρῶτον
πάντων ξένον αὐτὸν καλῶ καὶ λέγω· οὗτος ὁ
ἄνθρωπος οὐκ οἶδεν ποῦ τῆς γῆς ἐστιν, ἀλλ' ἐκ
τοσούτου χρόνου ἐπιδημῶν ἀγνοεῖ τοὺς νόμους
τῆς πόλεως καὶ τὰ ἔθη καὶ τί ἔξεστι καὶ τί οὐκ
ἔξεστιν· ἀλλ' οὐδὲ νομικόν τινα παρέλαβεν
πώποτε τὸν ἐροῦντα αὐτῷ καὶ ἐξηγησόμενον τὰ
7 νόμιμα· ἀλλὰ διαθήκην μὲν οὐ γράφει μὴ εἰδὼς
πῶς δεῖ γράφειν ἢ παραλαβὼν τὸν εἰδότα οὐδ'
ἐγγύην ἄλλως σφραγίζεται ἢ ἀσφάλειαν γράφει,
ὀρέξει δὲ χρῆται δίχα νομικοῦ καὶ ἐκκλίσει καὶ
8 ὁρμῇ καὶ ἐπιβολῇ καὶ προθέσει. πῶς δίχα
νομικοῦ; οὐκ οἶδεν ὅτι θέλει τὰ μὴ διδόμενα καὶ
οὐ θέλει τὰ ἀναγκαῖα καὶ οὐκ οἶδεν οὔτε τὰ ἴδια
οὔτε τὰ ἀλλότρια. εἰ δέ γ' ᾔδει, οὐδέποτ' ἂν
ἐνεποδίζετο, οὐδέποτ' ἐκωλύετο, οὐκ ἂν ἠγωνία.

any layman that you please, and the musician pays no attention to him ; but in a matter of which he has no knowledge, and which he has never studied, there he is in anxiety. What is the meaning of this? Why, he simply does not know what a crowd is, or the applause of a crowd ; to be sure, he has learned how to strike the lowest and the highest strings on the cithara, but what the praise of the multitude is, and what function it has in life, that he neither knows nor has studied. Hence he must needs tremble and turn pale.

Now then, I cannot say that the man is not a citharoede, when I see anyone in a state of fear, but I can say something else of him, and, indeed, not one thing only, but a number of things. And first of all, I call him a stranger and say : This man does not know where in the world he is, but though he has been living here so long a time, he is ignorant of the laws of the city and its customs, what he is allowed to do and what he is not allowed to do. Nay more, he has never even called in a lawyer to tell him and explain to him what are the usages conformable with law ; yet he does not write a will without knowing how he ought to write it or else calling in an expert, nor does he just casually affix his seal to a bond or give a written guarantee ; but without the services of a lawyer he exercises desire and aversion and choice and design and purpose. How do I mean " without the services of a lawyer "? Why, he does not know that he is wishing for things that are not vouchsafed him, and wishing to avoid the inevitable, and he does not know either what is his own or what is another's. Did he but know, he would never feel hindered, never constrained, would

9 πῶς γὰρ οὔ ; φοβεῖταί τις οὖν ὑπὲρ τῶν μὴ κακῶν ;—Οὔ.—Τί δ'; ὑπὲρ τῶν κακῶν μέν, ἐπ'
10 αὐτῷ δ' ὄντων ὥστε μὴ συμβῆναι ;—Οὐδαμῶς.—
Εἰ οὖν τὰ μὲν ἀπροαίρετα οὔτ' ἀγαθὰ οὔτε κακά,
τὰ προαιρετικὰ δὲ πάντα ἐφ' ἡμῖν καὶ οὔτ' ἀφελέσθαι τις ἡμῶν αὐτὰ δύναται οὔτε περιποιῆσαι
ἃ οὐ θέλομεν αὐτῶν, ποῦ ἔτι τόπος ἀγωνίας ;
11 ἀλλὰ περὶ τοῦ σωματίου ἀγωνιῶμεν, ὑπὲρ τοῦ
κτησιδίου, περὶ τοῦ τί δόξει τῷ Καίσαρι, περὶ
τῶν ἔσω δ' οὐδενός. μή τι περὶ τοῦ μὴ ψεῦδος
ὑπολαβεῖν ;—Οὔ· ἐπ' ἐμοὶ γάρ ἐστιν.—Μή τι
τοῦ ὁρμῆσαι παρὰ φύσιν ;—Οὐδὲ περὶ τούτου.—
12 Ὅταν οὖν ἴδῃς τινὰ ὠχριῶντα, ὡς ὁ ἰατρὸς ἀπὸ
τοῦ χρώματος λέγει "τούτου ὁ σπλὴν πέπονθε,
τούτου δὲ τὸ ἧπαρ," οὕτως καὶ σὺ λέγε "τούτου
ὄρεξις καὶ ἔκκλισις πέπονθεν, οὐκ εὐοδεῖ, φλεγ-
13 μαίνει." χρῶμα γὰρ οὐ μεταβάλλει οὐδὲν ἄλλο
οὐδὲ τρόμον ποιεῖ οὐδὲ ψόφον τῶν ὀδόντων οὐδὲ
μετοκλάζει καὶ ἐπ' ἀμφοτέρους πόδας ἵζει.¹

14 διὰ τοῦτο Ζήνων μὲν Ἀντιγόνῳ μέλλων ἐντυγχάνειν οὐκ ἠγωνία· ἃ γὰρ οὗτος ἐθαύμαζεν, τούτων
οὐδενὸς εἶχεν ἐκεῖνος ἐξουσίαν, ὧν δ' εἶχεν ἐκεῖνος
15 οὐκ ἐπεστρέφετο οὗτος· Ἀντίγονος δὲ Ζήνωνι
μέλλων ἐντυγχάνειν ἠγωνία, καὶ εἰκότως· ἤθελε
γὰρ ἀρέσκειν αὐτῷ, τοῦτο δ' ἔξω ἔκειτο· οὗτος δ'

---

¹ Homer, *Iliad*, XIII. 281 ; that is, the coward in ambush
is restless and cannot keep in one position.

not be anxious. How could he? Is any man in fear about things that are not evil?—No.—What then? Is he in fear about things that are evil, indeed, but that are in his own power to prevent?—Not at all.— If, then, things indifferent are neither good nor bad, but all matters of moral purpose are under our control, and no man can either take them away from us, or bring upon us such of them as we do not wish, what room is there left for anxiety? Yet we are anxious about our wretched body, about our trifling estate, about what Caesar will think, but are anxious about none of the things that are within us. We are not anxious about not conceiving a false opinion, are we?—No, for that is under my control.—Or about making a choice contrary to nature?—No, not about this, either.—Then, whenever you see a man looking pale, just as the physician judging from the complexion says, "This man's spleen is affected, and this man's liver," so do you also say, "This man's desire and aversion are affected, he is not getting along well, he is feverish." For there is nothing else that changes a man's complexion, or makes him tremble, or his teeth to chatter, or to

> "Shift from knee to knee and rest on either foot." [1]

That is why Zeno was not anxious when he was about to meet Antigonus; for over none of the things that Zeno regarded highly did Antigonus have power, and what Antigonus did have power over Zeno cared nothing about. But Antigonus was anxious when he was about to meet Zeno, and very naturally so; for he wanted to please him, and that lay outside of his control; yet Zeno did not care about pleasing *him*, any more than any other

ἐκείνῳ οὐκ ἤθελεν, οὐδὲ γὰρ ἄλλος τις τεχνίτης τῷ ἀτέχνῳ.

16 Ἐγώ σοι ἀρέσαι θέλω ; ἀντὶ τίνος ; οἶδας γὰρ τὰ μέτρα, καθ' ἃ κρίνεται ἄνθρωπος ὑπ' ἀνθρώπου ; μεμέληκέ¹ σοι γνῶναι, τί ἐστιν ἀγαθὸς ἄνθρωπος καὶ τί κακὸς καὶ πῶς ἑκάτερον γίγνε-

17 ται ; διὰ τί οὖν σὺ αὐτὸς ἀγαθὸς οὐκ εἶ ;—Πῶς, φησίν, οὐκ εἰμί ;—Ὅτι οὐδεὶς ἀγαθὸς πενθεῖ οὐδὲ στενάζει, οὐδεὶς οἰμώζει, οὐδεὶς ὠχριᾷ καὶ τρέμει οὐδὲ λέγει " πῶς μ' ἀποδέξεται, πῶς μου

18 ἀκούσει ; " ἀνδράποδον, ὡς ἂν αὐτῷ δοκῇ. τί οὖν σοὶ μέλει περὶ τῶν ἀλλοτρίων ; νῦν οὐκ ἐκείνου ἁμάρτημά ἐστι τὸ κακῶς ἀποδέξασθαι τὰ παρὰ σοῦ ;—Πῶς γὰρ οὔ ;—Δύναται δ' ἄλλου μὲν εἶναι ἁμάρτημα, ἄλλου δὲ κακόν ;—Οὔ.—Τί

19 οὖν ἀγωνιᾷς ὑπὲρ τῶν ἀλλοτρίων ;—Ναί· ἀλλ' ἀγωνιῶ, πῶς ἐγὼ αὐτῷ λαλήσω.—Εἶτ' οὐκ ἔξεστι γὰρ ὡς θέλεις αὐτῷ λαλῆσαι ;—Ἀλλὰ

20 δέδοικα μὴ ἐκκρουσθῶ.—Μή τι γράφειν μέλλων τὸ Δίωνος ὄνομα δέδοικας μὴ ἐκκρουσθῆς ;— Οὐδαμῶς.—Τί τὸ αἴτιον ; οὐχ ὅτι μεμελέτηκας γράφειν ;—Πῶς γὰρ οὔ ;—Τί δ' ; ἀναγιγνώσκειν μέλλων οὐχ ὡσαύτως ἂν εἶχες ;—Ὡσαύτως.—Τί τὸ αἴτιον ; ὅτι πᾶσα τέχνη ἰσχυρόν τι ἔχει καὶ

21 θαρραλέον ἐν τοῖς ἑαυτῆς. λαλεῖν οὖν οὐ μεμελέτηκας ; καὶ τί ἄλλο ἐμελέτας ἐν τῇ σχολῇ ;— Συλλογισμοὺς καὶ μεταπίπτοντας.—Ἐπὶ τί ;

---

¹ Schenkl : μεμελέτηκε S.

artist cares about pleasing one who has no knowledge of his art.

Do I care to please you? What do I gain thereby?
For do you know the standards according to which
man is judged by man? Have you been concerned
to know what a good man is, and what an evil man,
and how each becomes what he is? Why, then, are
you not a good man yourself?—How do you make
out, he answers, that I am not a good man?—Why,
because no good man grieves or groans, no good
man laments, no good man turns pale and trembles,
or asks, "How will he receive me? How will he
listen to me?" You slave! He will receive you
and listen to you as seems best to *him.* Why, then, are
you concerned about things that are not your own?
Now is it not his own fault if he gives a bad reception
to what you have to say?—Of course.—Is it possible
for one man to make the mistake and yet another
suffer the harm?—No.—Why, then, are you anxious
over what is not your own?—That is all very well,
but I am anxious over how I shall speak to him.—
What, are you not privileged to speak to him as you
please?—Yes, but I am afraid that I shall be disconcerted.—You are not afraid of being disconcerted
when you are about to write the name Dio, are you?
—No, not at all.— What is the reason? Is it not that
you have practised writing?—Yes, of course.—What
then? If you were about to read something, would
you not feel the same way about it?—Quite the
same.—What is the reason? Why, because every art
has an element of strength and confidence inside its
own field. Have you, then, not practised speaking?
And what else did you practise in your school?
—Syllogisms and arguments involving equivocal

303

οὐχ ὥστε ἐμπείρως διαλέγεσθαι ; τὸ δ' ἐμπείρως
ἐστὶν οὐχὶ εὐκαίρως καὶ ἀσφαλῶς καὶ συνετῶς,
ἔτι δ' ἀπταίστως καὶ ἀπαραποδίστως, ἐπὶ πᾶσι
22 δὲ τούτοις τεθαρρηκότος ;—Ναί.—Ἱππεὺς οὖν
ὢν εἰς πεδίον ἐληλυθὼς πρὸς πεζὸν ἀγωνιᾷς,
ὅπου σὺ μεμελέτηκας, ἐκεῖνος δ' ἀμελέτητός
ἐστιν ;—Ναί· ἀλλὰ ἐξουσίαν ἔχει ἀποκτεῖναί
23 με.—Λέγε οὖν τὰ ἀληθῆ, δύστηνε, καὶ μὴ ἀλαζο-
νεύου μηδὲ φιλόσοφος εἶναι ἀξίου μηδὲ ἀγνόει
σου τοὺς κυρίους, ἀλλὰ μέχρις ἂν ἔχῃς ταύτην
τὴν λαβὴν τὴν ἀπὸ τοῦ σώματος, ἀκολούθει
24 παντὶ τῷ ἰσχυροτέρῳ. λέγειν δὲ Σωκράτης ἐμελέτα ὁ πρὸς τοὺς τυράννους οὕτως διαλεγόμενος,
ὁ πρὸς τοὺς δικαστάς, ὁ ἐν τῷ δεσμωτηρίῳ.
λέγειν Διογένης μεμελετήκει ὁ πρὸς Ἀλέξανδρον
οὕτως λαλῶν, ὁ πρὸς Φίλιππον, ὁ πρὸς τοὺς
πειρατάς, ὁ πρὸς τὸν ὠνησάμενον αὐτόν[1] . . .
25
26 ἐκείνοις, οἷς μεμέληκεν,[2] τοῖς θαρροῦσι· σὺ δ' ἐπὶ
τὰ σαυτοῦ βάδιζε καὶ ἐκείνων ἀποστῆς μηδέποτε·
εἰς τὴν γωνίαν ἀπελθὼν κάθησο καὶ πλέκε
συλλογισμοὺς καὶ ἄλλῳ πρότεινε·
27   οὐκ ἔστι δ' ἐν σοὶ πόλεος[3] ἡγεμὼν ἀνήρ.

---

[1] The editors have noted a lacuna here.
[2] Schweighäuser : μεμελέτηκεν S.
[3] C. Schenkl : πόλεως S.

premisses.—To what end? Was it not to enable you to conduct an argument skilfully? And does not "skilfully" mean seasonably and securely and intelligently, and, more than that, without making mistakes and without embarrassment, and, in addition to all this, with confidence?—Surely.—Well then, if you are on horseback and have ridden out upon the plain against a man who is on foot, are you in anxiety, assuming that you are in practice and the other is not?—Yes, that is all very well, but Caesar has authority to put me to death.—Then tell the truth, wretch, and do not brag, nor claim to be a philosopher, nor fail to recognize your masters; but as long as you let them have this hold on you through your body, follow everyone that is stronger than you are. But Socrates used to practise speaking to some purpose—Socrates, who discoursed as he did to the Tyrants,[1] to his judges, and in the prison. Diogenes had practised speaking—Diogenes, who talked to Alexander as he did, to Philip, to the pirates, to the man who had bought him . . . [Leave such matters] to those who are seriously interested in them, to the brave; but do you walk away to your own concerns and never depart from them again; go into your corner and sit down, and spin syllogisms and propound them to others:

"In thee the State hath found no leader true."[2]

---

[1] The "Thirty Tyrants," who ruled in Athens a short while before the death of Socrates.

[2] A verse of unknown authorship.

ιδ'. Πρὸς Νάσωνα.

1 Εἰσελθόντος τινὸς τῶν Ῥωμαικῶν μετὰ υἱοῦ
καὶ ἐπακούοντος ἑνὸς ἀναγνώσματος Οὗτος, ἔφη,
ὁ τρόπος ἐστὶ τῆς διδασκαλίας καὶ ἀπεσιώπησεν.

2 ἀξιοῦντος δ' ἐκείνου εὑρεῖν τὰ ἑξῆς, Κόπον ἔχει,
ἔφη, πᾶσα τέχνη τῷ ἰδιώτῃ καὶ ἀπείρῳ αὐτῆς,

3 ὅταν παραδιδῶται. καὶ τὰ μὲν ἀπὸ τῶν τεχνῶν
γινόμενα τήν τε χρείαν εὐθὺς ἐνδείκνυται πρὸς ὃ
γέγονεν καὶ τὰ πλεῖστα αὐτῶν ἔχει τι καὶ ἀγωγὸν

4 καὶ ἐπίχαρι. καὶ γὰρ σκυτεὺς πῶς μὲν μανθάνει τις
παρεῖναι καὶ παρακολουθεῖν ἀτερπές,[1] τὸ δ' ὑπό-

5 δημα χρήσιμον καὶ ἰδεῖν ἄλλως οὐκ ἀηδές. καὶ
τέκτονος ἡ μὲν μάθησις ἀνιαρὰ μάλιστα τῷ ἰδιώτῃ
παρατυγχάνοντι, τὸ δ' ἔργον ἐπιδείκνυσι τὴν

6 χρείαν τῆς τέχνης. πολὺ δὲ μᾶλλον ἐπὶ μουσικῆς
ὄψει αὐτό· ἂν γὰρ παρῇς τῷ διδασκομένῳ, φανεῖταί
σοι πάντων ἀτερπέστατον τὸ μάθημα, τὰ μέντοι
ἀπὸ τῆς μουσικῆς ἡδέα καὶ ἐπιτερπῆ τοῖς ἰδιώταις
ἀκούειν.

7 Καὶ ἐνταῦθα τὸ μὲν ἔργον τοῦ φιλοσοφοῦντος
τοιοῦτόν τι φανταζόμεθα, ὅτι δεῖ τὴν αὐτοῦ
βούλησιν συναρμόσαι τοῖς γινομένοις, ὡς μήτε τι
τῶν γινομένων ἀκόντων ἡμῶν γίνεσθαι μήτε τῶν

8 μὴ γινομένων θελόντων ἡμῶν μὴ γίνεσθαι. ἐξ οὗ
περίεστι τοῖς συστησαμένοις αὐτὸ ἐν ὀρέξει μὴ

---

[1] Upton: ἀπρεπές S.

---

[1] Apparently named Naso, to judge from the title to this
chapter. A Julius Naso, the son of a man of letters, is
mentioned not infrequently in the correspondence of the
younger Pliny. See *Prosop. Imp. Romani*, II. p. 202, no. 293.

CHAPTER XIV

To Naso

ONCE when a certain Roman citizen [1] accompanied by his son had come in and was listening to one of his readings, Epictetus said : This is the style of my teaching, and then lapsed into silence. But when the other requested to know what came next, he replied : Instruction in the technique of any art is boring to the layman who has had no experience in it. Now the products of the arts show immediately their use towards the purpose for which they are made, and most of them possess also a certain attractiveness and charm. For example, to stand by and watch the process by which a shoemaker learns his trade is, indeed, not pleasant, yet the shoe is useful and not an unpleasant thing to look at either. And the process of education in the case of a carpenter is especially tiresome to the layman who happens to be watching, but the work which the carpenter does shows the use of his art. You will find the same much more true in the case of music ; for if you are standing by when someone is taking a lesson, the process of instruction will strike you as the most unpleasant of all, yet the results of music are sweet and pleasing to the ear of the layman. So also in our own case, we picture the work of the philosopher to be something like this : He should bring his own will into harmony with what happens, so that neither anything that happens happens against our will, nor anything that fails to happen fails to happen when we wish it to happen. The result of this for those who have so ordered the work

ἀποτυγχάνειν, ἐν ἐκκλίσει δὲ μὴ περιπίπτειν,
ἀλύπως, ἀφόβως, ἀταράχως διεξάγειν καθ' αὑτὸν
μετὰ τῶν κοινωνῶν τηροῦντα τὰς σχέσεις τάς τε
φυσικὰς καὶ ἐπιθέτους, τὸν υἱόν, τὸν πατέρα, τὸν
ἀδελφόν, τὸν πολίτην, τὸν ἄνδρα, τὴν γυναῖκα,
τὸν γείτονα, τὸν σύνοδον, τὸν ἄρχοντα, τὸν
ἀρχόμενον.

9   Τὸ ἔργον τοῦ φιλοσοφοῦντος τοιοῦτόν τι φανταζόμεθα. λοιπὸν ἐφεξῆς τούτῳ ζητοῦμεν, πῶς
10 ἔσται τοῦτο. ὁρῶμεν οὖν ὅτι ὁ τέκτων μαθών τινα
γίνεται τέκτων, ὁ κυβερνήτης μαθών τινα γίνεται
κυβερνήτης. μή ποτ' οὖν καὶ ἐνθάδε οὐκ ἀπαρκεῖ
τὸ βούλεσθαι καλὸν καὶ ἀγαθὸν γενέσθαι, χρεία
δὲ καὶ μαθεῖν τινα ; ζητοῦμεν οὖν τίνα ταῦτα.
11 λέγουσιν οἱ φιλόσοφοι, ὅτι μαθεῖν δεῖ πρῶτον
τοῦτο, ὅτι ἔστι θεὸς καὶ προνοεῖ τῶν ὅλων καὶ
οὐκ ἔστι λαθεῖν αὐτὸν οὐ μόνον ποιοῦντα, ἀλλ'
οὐδὲ διανοούμενον ἢ ἐνθυμούμενον· εἶτα ποῖοί
12 τινες εἰσίν. οἷοι γὰρ ἂν ἐκεῖνοι εὑρεθῶσιν, τὸν
ἐκείνοις ἀρέσοντα καὶ πεισθησόμενον ἀνάγκη
13 πειρᾶσθαι κατὰ δύναμιν ἐξομοιοῦσθαι ἐκείνοις· εἰ
πιστόν ἐστι τὸ θεῖον, καὶ τοῦτον εἶναι πιστόν· εἰ
ἐλεύθερον, καὶ τοῦτον ἐλεύθερον· εἰ εὐεργετικόν,
καὶ τοῦτον εὐεργετικόν· εἰ μεγαλόφρον, καὶ τοῦτον
μεγαλόφρονα· ὡς θεοῦ τοίνυν ζηλωτὴν τὰ ἐξῆς
πάντα καὶ ποιεῖν καὶ λέγειν.

14   Πόθεν οὖν ἄρξασθαι δεῖ ;—Ἂν συγκαθῇς, ἐρῶ

308

of philosophy is that in desire they are not disappointed, and in aversion they do not fall into what they would avoid; that each person passes his life to himself, free from pain, fear, and perturbation, at the same time maintaining with his associates both the natural and the acquired relationships, those namely of son, father, brother, citizen, wife, neighbour, fellow-traveller, ruler, and subject.

Something like this is our picture of the work of the philosopher. The next thing after this is that we seek the means of achieving it. We see, then, that the carpenter becomes a carpenter by first learning something, the helmsman becomes a helmsman by first learning something. May it not be, then, that in our case also it is not sufficient to wish to become noble and good, but that we are under the necessity of learning something first? We seek, then, what this is. Now the philosophers say that the first thing we must learn is this: That there is a God, and that He provides for the universe, and that it is impossible for a man to conceal from Him, not merely his actions, but even his purposes and his thoughts. Next we must learn what the gods are like; for whatever their character is discovered to be, the man who is going to please and obey them must endeavour as best he can to resemble them. If the deity is faithful, he also must be faithful; if free, he also must be free; if beneficent, he also must be beneficent; if high-minded, he also must be high-minded, and so forth; therefore, in everything he says and does, he must act as an imitator of God.

Where, then, ought I to start?—If you enter upon this task, I will say that in the first place you

σοι ὅτι πρῶτον δεῖ σε τοῖς ὀνόμασι παρακολουθεῖν.
—Ὥστ᾽ ἐγὼ νῦν οὐ παρακολουθῶ τοῖς ὀνόμασιν;
15 —Οὐ παρακολουθεῖς.—Πῶς οὖν χρῶμαι αὐτοῖς;—
Οὕτως ὡς οἱ ἀγράμματοι ταῖς ἐγγραμμάτοις
φωναῖς, ὡς τὰ κτήνη ταῖς φαντασίαις· ἄλλο γάρ
16 ἐστι χρῆσις, ἄλλο παρακολούθησις. εἰ δ᾽ οἴει
παρακολουθεῖν, φέρε ὃ θέλεις ὄνομα καὶ βασανί-
17 σωμεν αὐτούς, εἰ παρακολουθοῦμεν.—Ἀλλ᾽ ἀνια-
ρὸν τὸ ἐξελέγχεσθαι πρεσβύτερον ἄνθρωπον ἤδη
κἂν οὕτως τύχῃ τὰς τρεῖς στρατείας ἐστρατευμένον.
18 —Οἶδα κἀγώ. νῦν γὰρ σὺ ἐλήλυθας πρὸς ἐμὲ ὡς
μηδενὸς δεόμενος. τίνος δ᾽ ἂν καὶ φαντασθείης
ὡς ἐνδέοντος; πλουτεῖς, τέκνα ἔχεις, τυχὸν καὶ
γυναῖκα, καὶ οἰκέτας πολλούς, ὁ Καῖσάρ σε οἶδεν,
ἐν Ῥώμῃ πολλοὺς φίλους κέκτησαι, τὰ καθήκοντα
ἀποδίδως, οἶδας τὸν εὖ ποιοῦντα ἀντευποιῆσαι καὶ
19 τὸν κακῶς ποιοῦντα κακῶς ποιῆσαι. τί σοι λείπει;
ἂν οὖν σοι δείξω, ὅτι τὰ ἀναγκαιότατα καὶ
μέγιστα πρὸς εὐδαιμονίαν, καὶ ὅτι μέχρι δεῦρο
πάντων μᾶλλον ἢ τῶν προσηκόντων ἐπιμεμέλησαι,
καὶ τὸν κολοφῶνα ἐπιθῶ·[1] οὔτε τί θεός ἐστιν οἶδας

---

[1] Upton's "codex": πείθω S.

---

[1] By the municipal law of Caesar (*C. I. L.* I², 593 = Dessau,
Inscr. Lat., 6085, § 89), a man to be eligible to the Senate of
a municipality must have served three campaigns in the
cavalry, or six in the infantry, and it is probable that this
provision is referred to here. *Cf.* IV. 1, 37-40, and on
the *tres militiae equestres* see Mommsen : *Römisches Staatsrecht*,
III. (1887), 543, n. 2-4 ; 549, n. 1. On the other hand the
scholiast (probably Arethas, see Schenkl, pp. lxxii. ff.)
on § 17 apparently took this to mean that Naso had once
been a commanding officer (for the corrupt διὰ τὸν ἄσκνα
λέγει κ.τ.λ., one ought probably to read something like

ought to understand the meaning of terms.—So you imply that I do not now understand the meaning of terms?—You do not.—How comes it, then, that I use them?—Why, you use them as the illiterate use written speech, as the cattle use external impressions; for use is one thing, and understanding another. But if you think you understand terms, propose any term you please, and let us put ourselves to the test, to see whether we understand it.—But it is unpleasant to be subjected to an examination when one is already somewhat advanced in years, and, if it so chance, has served his three campaigns.[1]—I realize that myself. For now you have come to me like a man who stood in need of nothing. But what could anyone even imagine you to be in need of? You are rich, you have children, possibly also a wife, and many slaves; Caesar knows you, you have many friends in Rome, you perform the duties incumbent upon you, and when a man has done you either good or harm you know how to pay him back in kind. What do you still lack? If, therefore, I show you that what you lack are things most necessary and important for happiness, and that hitherto you have devoted your attention to everything but what was appropriate for you to do, and if I add the colophon,[2]

στρατηγὸν Νάσωνα λέγει, ἦν γὰρ τῶν μεγάλων τῆς Ῥώμης), although this can hardly have been more than a guess on his part.

[2] *i.e.* the finishing touch; a word (sometimes derived from the ancient city Colophon because of a tradition that its efficient cavalry gave the finishing stroke in every war in which it was engaged [Strabo, XIV. i, 28], but more probably a common noun in the sense of "tip," "summit," "finishing point,") used to indicate the title and other explanatory data when entered at the end of a work.

οὔτε τί ἄνθρωπος οὔτε τί ἀγαθὸν οὔτε τί κακόν,
20 καὶ τὸ μὲν τῶν ἄλλων ἴσως ἀνεκτόν, ὅτι δ' αὐτὸς
αὐτὸν ἀγνοεῖς, πῶς δύνασαι ἀνασχέσθαι μου καὶ
21 ὑποσχεῖν τὸν ἔλεγχον καὶ παραμεῖναι; οὐδαμῶς,
ἀλλ' εὐθὺς ἀπαλλάσσῃ χαλεπῶς ἔχων. καίτοι τί
σοι ἐγὼ κακὸν πεποίηκα; εἰ μὴ καὶ τὸ ἔσοπτρον
τῷ αἰσχρῷ, ὅτι δεικνύει αὐτὸν αὐτῷ οἷός ἐστιν· εἰ
μὴ καὶ ὁ ἰατρὸς τὸν νοσοῦντα ὑβρίζει,[1] ὅταν εἴπῃ
αὐτῷ " ἄνθρωπε, δοκεῖς μηδὲν ἔχειν, πυρέσσεις δέ·
ἀσίτησον σήμερον, ὕδωρ πίε·" καὶ οὐδεὶς λέγει " ὦ
22 δεινῆς ὕβρεως." ἐὰν δέ τινι εἴπῃς " αἱ ὀρέξεις σου
φλεγμαίνουσιν, αἱ ἐκκλίσεις ταπειναί εἰσιν, αἱ
ἐπιβολαὶ ἀνομολογούμεναι, αἱ ὁρμαὶ ἀσύμφωναι
τῇ φύσει, αἱ ὑπολήψεις εἰκαῖαι καὶ ἐψευσμέναι,"
εὐθὺς ἐξελθὼν λέγει " ὕβρισέν με."
23 Τοιαῦτά ἐστι τὰ ἡμέτερα ὡς ἐν πανηγύρει. τὰ
μὲν κτήνη πραθησόμενα ἄγεται καὶ οἱ βόες, οἱ δὲ
πολλοὶ τῶν ἀνθρώπων οἱ μὲν ὠνησόμενοι οἱ δὲ
πωλήσοντες· ὀλίγοι δέ τινές εἰσιν οἱ κατὰ θέαν
ἐρχόμενοι τῆς πανηγύρεως, πῶς τοῦτο γίνεται καὶ
διὰ τί καὶ τίνες οἱ τιθέντες τὴν πανήγυριν καὶ ἐπὶ
24 τίνι. οὕτως καὶ ἐνθάδ' ἐν τῇ πανηγύρει ταύτῃ· οἱ
μέν τινες ὡς κτήνη οὐδὲν πλέον πολυπραγμονοῦσι
τοῦ χόρτου· ὅσοι γὰρ περὶ κτῆσιν καὶ ἀγροὺς καὶ
οἰκέτας καὶ ἀρχάς τινας ἀναστρέφεσθε, ταῦτα
25 οὐδὲν ἄλλο ἢ χόρτος ἐστίν· ὀλίγοι δ' εἰσὶν οἱ πανη-
γυρίζοντες ἄνθρωποι φιλοθεάμονες. "τί ποτ'

---

[1] C. Schenkl: ὅταν αὐτὸν ὑβρίζῃ S (the first two words
deleted in the Cambridge ed. of 1655).

---

[1] A famous comparison, ascribed to Pythagoras. See Cicero,
Tuscul. Disp. v. 9; Diog. Laert. VIII. 8; Iamblichus, *Vita
Pythagori*, 58. *Cf.* Menander, frg. 481κ (Allinson, p. 442).

saying: You know neither what God is, nor what man is, nor what good, nor what evil is—if I say that you are ignorant of these other matters you may possibly endure that; but if I say that you do not understand your own self, how can you possibly bear with me, and endure and abide my questioning? You cannot do so at all, but immediately you go away offended. And yet what harm have I done you? None at all, unless the mirror also does harm to the ugly man by showing him what he looks like; unless the physician insults the patient, when he says to him, "Man, you think there is nothing the matter with you; but you have a fever; fast to-day and drink only water"; and no one says, "What dreadful insolence!" Yet if you tell a man, "Your desires are feverish, your attempts to avoid things are humiliating, your purposes are inconsistent, your choices are out of harmony with your nature, your conceptions are hit-or-miss and false," why, immediately he walks out and says, "He insulted me."

Our position is like that of those who attend a fair.[1] Cattle and oxen are brought there to be sold, and most men engage in buying and selling, while there are only a few who go merely to see the fair, how it is conducted, and why, and who are promoting it, and for what purpose. So it is also in this "fair" of the world in which we live; some persons, like cattle, are interested in nothing but their fodder; for to all of you that concern yourselves with property and lands and slaves and one office or another, all this is nothing but fodder! And few in number are the men who attend the fair because they are fond of the spectacle. "What,

οὖν ἐστιν ὁ κόσμος, τίς αὐτὸν διοικεῖ. οὐδείς·
26 καὶ πῶς οἷόν τε πόλιν μὲν ἢ οἶκον μὴ δύνασθαι
διαμένειν μηδ᾽ ὀλιγοστὸν χρόνον δίχα τοῦ διοι-
κοῦντος καὶ ἐπιμελομένου, τὸ δ᾽ οὕτως μέγα καὶ
καλὸν κατασκεύασμα εἰκῇ καὶ ὡς ἔτυχεν οὕτως
27 εὐτάκτως ¹ οἰκονομεῖσθαι ; ἔστιν οὖν ὁ διοικῶν.
ποῖός τις καὶ πῶς ὁ διοικῶν ; ἡμεῖς δὲ τίνες ὄντες
ὑπ᾽ αὐτοῦ γεγόναμεν καὶ πρὸς τί ἔργον ; ἀρά γ᾽
ἔχομέν τινα ἐπιπλοκὴν πρὸς αὐτὸν καὶ σχέσιν ἢ
28 οὐδεμίαν ; " ταῦτ᾽ ἔστιν ἃ πάσχουσιν οὗτοι οἱ
ὀλίγοι· καὶ λοιπὸν τούτῳ μόνῳ σχολάζουσι τῷ
29 τὴν πανήγυριν ἱστορήσαντας ² ἀπελθεῖν. τὶ οὖν ;
καταγελῶνται ὑπὸ τῶν πολλῶν· καὶ γὰρ ἐκεῖ οἱ
θεαταὶ ὑπὸ τῶν ἐμπόρων· καὶ εἰ τὰ κτήνη συναί-
σθησίν τινα εἶχεν, κατεγέλα ἂν ³ τῶν ἄλλο τι
τεθαυμακότων ἢ τὸν χόρτον.

ιε΄. Πρὸς τοὺς σκληρῶς τισιν ὧν ἔκριναν
ἐμμένοντας.

1   Ὅταν ἀκούσωσί τινες τούτων τῶν λόγων, ὅτι
βέβαιον εἶναι δεῖ καὶ ἡ μὲν προαίρεσις ἐλεύθερον
φύσει καὶ ἀνανάγκαστον, τὰ δ᾽ ἄλλα κωλυτά,

---

¹ Bentley : ἀτάκτως S.   ² Salmasius : ἱστορήσαντ᾽ S.
³ Added by Upton from his "codex."

then, is the universe," they ask, "and who governs
it? No one? Yet how can it be that, while it is
impossible for a city or a household to remain even
a very short time without someone to govern and
care for it, nevertheless this great and beautiful
structure should be kept in such orderly arrangement by sheer accident and chance? There must
be, therefore, One who governs it. What kind of
a being is He, and how does He govern it? And
what are we, who have been created by Him, and
for what purpose were we created? Do we, then,
really have some contact and relation with Him
or none at all?" That is the way these few are
affected; and thenceforward they have leisure for
this one thing only—to study well the "fair"
of life before they leave it. With what result,
then? They are laughed to scorn by the crowd,
quite as in the real fair the mere spectators
are laughed at by the traffickers; yes, and if the
cattle themselves had any comprehension like
ours of what was going on, they too would laugh at
those who had wonder and admiration for anything
but their fodder!

CHAPTER XV

*To those who cling obstinately to the judgements
which they have once formed*

SOME men, when they hear the following precepts:
That one ought to be steadfast, and that the moral
purpose is naturally free and not subject to compulsion, while everything else is liable to inter-

315

ἀναγκαστά, δοῦλα, ἀλλότρια, φαντάζονται ὅτι
δεῖ παντὶ τῷ κριθέντι ὑπ' αὐτῶν ἀπαραβάτως
2 ἐμμένειν. ἀλλὰ πρῶτον ὑγιὲς εἶναι δεῖ τὸ κεκρι-
μένον. θέλω γὰρ εἶναι τόνους ἐν σώματι, ἀλλ'
3 ὡς ὑγιαίνοντι, ὡς ἀθλοῦντι· ἂν δέ μοι φρενιτικοῦ
τόνους ἔχων ἐνδεικνύῃ καὶ ἀλαζονεύῃ ἐπ' αὐτοῖς,
ἐρῶ σοι ὅτι "ἄνθρωπε, ζήτει τὸν θεραπεύσοντα.
τοῦτο οὐκ εἰσὶ τόνοι, ἀλλ' ἀτονία."

4 Ἕτερον τρόπον τοιοῦτόν τι καὶ ἐπὶ τῆς ψυχῆς
πάσχουσιν οἱ παρακούοντες τῶν λόγων τούτων.
οἷον καὶ ἐμός τις ἑταῖρος ἐξ οὐδεμιᾶς αἰτίας ἔκρι-
5 νεν ἀποκαρτερεῖν. ἔγνων ἐγὼ ἤδη τρίτην ἡμέραν
ἔχοντος αὐτοῦ τῆς ἀποχῆς καὶ ἐλθὼν ἐπυνθανό-
6 μην τί ἐγένετο.—Κέκρικα, φησίν.—'Ἀλλ' ὅμως
τί σε ἦν τὸ ἀναπεῖσαν; εἰ γὰρ ὀρθῶς ἔκρινας,
ἰδοὺ παρακαθήμεθά σοι καὶ συνεργοῦμεν, ἵν'
7 ἐξέλθῃς· εἰ δ' ἀλόγως ἔκρινας, μετάθου.—Τοῖς
κριθεῖσιν ἐμμένειν δεῖ.—Τί ποιεῖς, ἄνθρωπε; οὐ
πᾶσιν, ἀλλὰ τοῖς ὀρθῶς. ἐπεὶ παθὼν ἄρτι ὅτι
νύξ ἐστιν, ἄν σοι δοκῇ, μὴ μετατίθεσο, ἀλλ'
ἔμμενε καὶ λέγε ὅτι τοῖς κριθεῖσιν ἐμμένειν δεῖ.
8 οὐ θέλεις τὴν ἀρχὴν στῆσαι καὶ τὸν θεμέλιον,
τὸ κρίμα σκέψασθαι πότερον ὑγιὲς ἢ οὐχ ὑγιές,
καὶ οὕτως λοιπὸν ἐποικοδομεῖν αὐτῷ τὴν εὐ-
9 τονίαν, τὴν ἀσφάλειαν; ἂν δὲ σαπρὸν ὑποστήσῃ

316

ference and compulsion, subject to others and not our own—some men, I say, fancy that whenever they have formed a judgement they ought to stand by it immovably. And yet the first requirement is that the judgement formed be a sound one. For I want vigour in the body, but it must be the vigour of the body in a state of health and physical exercise; whereas, if you show me that you possess the vigour of a madman, and boast about it, I will say to you, " Man, look for someone to cure you. This is not vigour, but feebleness."

The following is another way in which the minds of those are affected who hear these precepts amiss. For example, a friend of mine for no reason at all made up his mind to starve himself to death. I learned about it when he was already in the third day of his fasting, and went and asked what had happened.—I have decided, he answered.—Very well, but still what was it that induced you to make up your mind? For if your judgement was good, see, we are at your side and ready to help you to make your exit from this life; but if your judgement was irrational, change it.—I must abide by my decisions. —Why, man, what are you about? You mean not *all* your decisions, but only the right ones. For example, if you are convinced at this moment that it is night, do not change your opinion, if that seems best to you, but abide by it and say that you ought to abide by your decisions! Do you not wish to make your beginning and your foundation firm, that is, to consider whether your decision is sound or unsound, and only after you have done that proceed to rear thereon the structure of your determination and your firm resolve? But if you lay a rotten and

317

καὶ καταπῖπτον, οὐκ οἰκοδομημάτιον,[1] ὅσῳ δ'
ἂν πλείονα καὶ ἰσχυρότερα ἐπιθῇς, τοσούτῳ
10 θᾶττον κατενεχθήσεται. ἄνευ πάσης αἰτίας
ἐξάγεις ἡμῖν ἄνθρωπον ἐκ τοῦ ζῆν φίλον καὶ
συνήθη, τῆς αὐτῆς πόλεως πολίτην καὶ τῆς
11 μεγάλης καὶ τῆς μικρᾶς· εἶτα φόνον ἐργαζόμενος
καὶ ἀπολλύων ἄνθρωπον μηδὲν ἠδικηκότα λέγεις
12 ὅτι τοῖς κριθεῖσιν ἐμμένειν δεῖ. εἰ δ' ἐπῆλθέν
σοί πώς ποτ' ἐμὲ ἀποκτεῖναι, ἔδει σε ἐμμένειν
τοῖς κριθεῖσιν;

13 Ἐκεῖνος μὲν οὖν μόγις μετεπείσθη. τῶν δὲ
νῦν τινας οὐκ ἔστι μεταθεῖναι. ὥστε μοι δοκῶ
ὃ πρότερον ἠγνόουν νῦν εἰδέναι, τί ἐστι τὸ ἐν τῇ
συνηθείᾳ λεγόμενον· μωρὸν οὔτε πεῖσαι οὔτε
14 ῥῆξαι ἔστιν. μή μοι γένοιτο φίλον ἔχειν σοφὸν
μωρόν. δυσμεταχειριστότερον[2] οὐδέν ἐστιν.
"κέκρικα." καὶ γὰρ οἱ μαινόμενοι· ἀλλ' ὅσῳ
βεβαιότερον κρίνουσι τὰ οὐκ ὄντα, τοσούτῳ
15 πλείονος ἐλλεβόρου δέονται. οὐ θέλεις τὰ τοῦ
νοσοῦντος ποιεῖν καὶ τὸν ἰατρὸν παρακαλεῖν;
"νοσῶ, κύριε· βοήθησόν μοι. τί με δεῖ ποιεῖν
16 σκέψαι· ἐμόν ἐστι πείθεσθαί σοι." οὕτως καὶ
ἐνταῦθ'· "ἃ δεῖ με ποιεῖν οὐκ οἶδα, ἐλήλυθα
δὲ μαθησόμενος." οὔ, ἀλλὰ "περὶ τῶν ἄλλων

---

[1] C. Schenkl and Elter: οἰκοδόμημά τι ὄν S. Perhaps οὐκ
(or οὐ καὶ) οἰκοδομητέον (or οἰκοδομητέον τί) after Schegk.
[2] Wolf: δυσμεταχείριστον S.

---

[1] That is, the Universe, in Stoic parlance.
[2] Is amenable neither to reason nor force; will neither
bend nor break.

crumbling foundation, you cannot rear thereon even
a small building, but the bigger and the stronger
your superstructure is the more quickly it will fall
down. Without any reason you are taking out of
this life, to our detriment, a human being who is
a familiar friend, a citizen of the same state, both
the large state [1] and the small; and then, though
in the act of murder, and while engaged in the
destruction of a human being that has done
no wrong, you say that you " must abide by
your decisions "! But if the idea ever entered
your head to kill *me*, would you have to abide by
your decisions?

Well, it was hard work to persuade that man;
but there are some men of to-day whom it is impossible to move. So that I feel that I now know
what I formerly did not understand—the meaning
of the proverb, "A fool you can neither persuade
nor break." [2] God forbid that I should ever have
for a friend a wise fool ! [3] There is nothing harder
to handle. "I have decided," he says! Why yes,
and so have madmen; but the more firm their
decision is about what is false, the more hellebore [4]
they need. Will you not act like a sick man, and
summon a physician? " I am sick, sir; help me.
Consider what I ought to do; it is my part to obey
you." So also in the present instance. "I know
not what I ought to be doing, but I have come to
find out." Thus one should speak. No, but this
is what one hears, "Talk to me about anything else,

---

[3] A loquacious and argumentatively stubborn person. In
the original this sentence makes a trimeter scazon, and hence
is probably a quotation from some satirical poem.

[4] Commonly used in antiquity as a remedy for insanity.

17 μοι λέγε· τοῦτο δὲ κέκρικα." περὶ ποίων ἄλλων;
τί γάρ ἐστι μεῖζον ἢ προὐργιαίτερον τοῦ πει-
σθῆναί σε, ὅτι οὐκ ἀρκεῖ τὸ κεκρικέναι καὶ τὸ
μὴ μεταθέσθαι; οὗτοι οἱ μανικοὶ τόνοι, οὐχ
18 ὑγιεινοί. "ἀποθανεῖν θέλω, ἄν με τοῦτο ἀναγ-
κάσῃς." διὰ τί, ἄνθρωπε; τί ἐγένετο; "κέκρικα." ἐσώθην, ὅτι οὐ κέκρικας ἐμὲ ἀποκτεῖναι.
19 "ἀργύριον οὐ λαμβάνω." διὰ τί; "κέκρικα."
ἴσθι ὅτι ᾧ τόνῳ νῦν χρῇ πρὸς τὸ μὴ λαμβάνειν,
οὐδὲν κωλύει σε ἀλόγως ποτὲ ῥέψαι πρὸς τὸ
λαμβάνειν καὶ πάλιν λέγειν ὅτι "κέκρικα,"
20 ὥσπερ ἐν νοσοῦντι καὶ ῥευματιζομένῳ σώματι
ποτὲ μὲν ἐπὶ ταῦτα ποτὲ δ' ἐπ' ἐκεῖνα ῥέπει
τὸ ῥεῦμα. οὕτως καὶ ἀσθενὴς ψυχή, ὅπου μὲν
κλίνει, ἄδηλον ἔχει· ὅταν δὲ καὶ τόνος προσῇ
τῷ κλίματι τούτῳ καὶ τῇ φορᾷ, τότε γίνεται
τὸ κακὸν ἀβοήθητον καὶ ἀθεράπευτον.

ιϛ'. Ὅτι οὐ μελετῶμεν χρῆσθαι τοῖς περὶ
ἀγαθῶν καὶ κακῶν δόγμασιν.

1 Ποῦ τὸ ἀγαθόν;—Ἐν προαιρέσει.—Ποῦ τὸ
κακόν;—Ἐν προαιρέσει.—Ποῦ τὸ οὐδέτερον;—
2 Ἐν τοῖς ἀπροαιρέτοις.—Τί οὖν; μέμνηταί τις
ἡμῶν ἔξω τούτων τῶν λόγων; μελετᾷ τις αὐτὸς

---

[1] Cf. § 12 above.
[2] Probably the criticism of some Cynic philosopher
addressed to Epictetus.

but on this point I have made my decision." "Anything else" indeed! Why, what is more important
or more to your advantage than to be convinced
that it is not sufficient for a man merely to have
reached decisions, and to refuse to change? These
are the sinews of madness, not health. "If you
force me to this, I would gladly die." What for,
man? What has happened? "I have decided!"
It was fortunate for me that you did not decide
to kill me!¹ Or again, another says, "I take
no money for my services."² Why so? "Because I have decided." Rest assured that there
is nothing to prevent you from some day turning
irrationally to taking money for your services, and
that with the same vehemence with which you now
refuse to take it, and then saying again, "I have
decided"; precisely as in a diseased body, suffering
from a flux, the flux inclines now in this direction
and now in that. Such is also the sick mind; it
is uncertain which way it is inclined, but when
vehemence also is added to this inclination and
drift, then the evil gets past help and past cure."

CHAPTER XVI

*That we do not practise the application of our
judgements about things good and evil*

WHEREIN lies the good?—In moral purpose.—
Wherein lies evil?—In moral purpose.—Wherein
lies that which is neither good nor evil?—In the
things that lie outside the domain of moral purpose.
—Well, what of it? Does any one of us remember
these statements outside the classroom? Does any

321

ἐφ' αὑτοῦ τοῦτον τὸν τρόπον ἀποκρίνεσθαι τοῖς
πράγμασιν ὡς ἐπὶ τῶν ἐρωτημάτων; "ἆρά γε
ἡμέρα ἐστίν;" "ναί." "τί δέ; νὺξ ἐστιν;"
"οὔ." "τί δ'; ἄρτιοί εἰσιν οἱ ἀστέρες;" "οὐκ
3 ἔχω λέγειν." ὅταν σοι προφαίνηται ἀργύριον,
μεμελέτηκας ἀποκρίνεσθαι τὴν δέουσαν ἀπόκρισιν, ὅτι "οὐκ ἀγαθόν"; ἤσκηκας ἐν ταύταις ταῖς
4 ἀποκρίσεσιν ἢ πρὸς μόνα τὰ σοφίσματα; τί οὖν
θαυμάζεις, εἰ, ὅπου μὲν μεμελέτηκας, ἐκεῖ κρείττων γένῃ σεαυτοῦ, ὅπου δ' ἀμελετήτως ἔχεις,
5 ἐκεῖ δ' ὁ αὐτὸς διαμένεις; ἐπεὶ διὰ τί ὁ ῥήτωρ
εἰδὼς ὅτι γέγραφε καλῶς, ὅτι ἀνείληφε τὰ
γεγραμμένα, φωνὴν εἰσφέρων ἡδεῖαν ὅμως ἔτι
6 ἀγωνιᾷ; ὅτι οὐκ ἀρκεῖται τῷ μελετῆσαι. τί οὖν
θέλει; ἐπαινεθῆναι ὑπὸ τῶν παρόντων. πρὸς μὲν
οὖν τὸ δύνασθαι μελετᾶν ἤσκηται, πρὸς ἔπαινον
7 δὲ καὶ ψόγον οὐκ ἤσκηται. πότε γὰρ ἤκουσεν
παρά τινος, τί ἐστιν ἔπαινος,[1] τί ἐστι ψόγος,
τίς ἑκατέρου φύσις; τοὺς ποίους τῶν ἐπαίνων
διωκτέον ἢ τοὺς ποίους τῶν ψόγων φευκτέον; πότε
δ' ἐμελέτησεν ταύτην τὴν μελέτην ἀκόλουθον
8 τούτοις τοῖς λόγοις; τί οὖν ἔτι θαυμάζεις, εἰ,
ὅπου μὲν ἔμαθεν, ἐκεῖ διαφέρει τῶν ἄλλων, ὅπου
δ' οὐ μεμελέτηκεν, ἐκεῖ τοῖς πολλοῖς ὁ αὐτός
9 ἐστιν; ὡς ὁ κιθαρῳδὸς οἶδεν κιθαρίζειν, ᾄδει
καλῶς, στατὸν ἔχει καλὸν καὶ ὅμως εἰσερχόμενος
τρέμει· ταῦτα γὰρ οἶδεν, ὄχλος δὲ τί ἐστιν οὐκ

[1] τί ἐστιν ἔπαινος added by Wolf.

---

[1] The answers to these questions are obvious and are
given without hesitation. Questions about the facts of life,
about good and evil, like the following, should be answered
with equal promptness and conviction.

one of us when by himself practise answering facts in the way he answers these questions? "So it is day, is it?" "Yes." "What then? Is it night?" "No." "What then? Is the number of the stars even?" "I cannot say." [1] When you are shown money, have you practised giving the proper answer, namely, that it is not a good thing? Have you trained yourself in answers of this kind, or merely to answer sophisms? Why, then, are you surprised to find that in the fields in which you have practised you surpass yourself, but in that in which you have not practised you remain the same? For why is it that the orator, although he knows that he has composed a good speech, has memorized what he has written and is bringing a pleasing voice to his task, is still anxious despite all that? Because he is not satisfied with the mere practice of oratory. What, then, does he want? He wants to be praised by his audience. Now he has trained himself with a view to being able to practise oratory, but he has not trained himself with reference to praise and blame. For when did he ever hear any one say what praise is, what blame is, and what is the nature of each? What kinds of praise are to be sought, and what kinds of blame are to be avoided? And when did he ever go through this course of training in accordance with these principles? Why, then, are you any longer surprised because he surpasses all others in the field in which he has studied, but in that in which he has not practised he is no better than the multitude? He is like a citharoede who knows how to play to the harp, sings well, has a beautiful flowing gown, and still trembles when he comes upon the stage; for all that has gone before he knows, but

10 οἶδεν οὐδ' ὄχλου βοὴ οὐδὲ κατάγελως. ἀλλ' οὐδ'
αὐτὸ τὸ ἀγωνιᾶν τί ἐστιν οἶδεν, πότερον ἡμέτερον
ἔργον ἐστὶν ἢ ἀλλότριον, ἔστιν αὐτὸ παῦσαι ἢ
οὐκ ἔστιν. διὰ τοῦτο ἐὰν μὲν ἐπαινεθῇ, φυση-
θεὶς ἐξῆλθεν· ἐὰν δὲ καταγελασθῇ, τὸ φυση-
μάτιον ἐκεῖνο ἐκεντήθη καὶ προσεκάθισεν.

11   Τοιοῦτόν τι καὶ ἡμεῖς πάσχομεν. τίνα θαυμάζομεν; τὰ ἐκτός. περὶ τίνα σπουδάζομεν;
περὶ τὰ ἐκτός. εἶτ' ἀπορούμεν, πῶς φοβούμεθα
12 ἢ πῶς ἀγωνιῶμεν; τί οὖν ἐνδέχεται, ὅταν τὰ
ἐπιφερόμενα κακὰ ἡγώμεθα; οὐ δυνάμεθα μὴ
13 φοβεῖσθαι, οὐ δυνάμεθα μὴ ἀγωνιᾶν. εἶτα λέγομεν "κύριε ὁ θεός, πῶς μὴ ἀγωνιῶ;" μωρέ,
χεῖρας οὐκ ἔχεις; οὐκ ἐποίησέν σοι αὐτὰς ὁ θεός;
εὔχου νῦν καθήμενος, ὅπως αἱ μύξαι σου μὴ
ῥέωσιν· ἀπόμυξαι μᾶλλον καὶ μὴ ἐγκάλει. τί οὖν;
14 ἐνταῦθά σοι οὐδὲν δέδωκεν; οὐ δέδωκέ σοι καρτερίαν, οὐ δέδωκέ σοι μεγαλοψυχίαν, οὐ δέδωκεν
ἀνδρείαν; τηλικαύτας ἔχων χεῖρας ἔτι ζητεῖς
15 τὸν ἀπομύξοντα; ἀλλ' οὐδὲ μελετῶμεν ταῦτα
οὐδ' ἐπιστρεφόμεθα. ἐπεὶ δότε μοι ἕνα, ᾧ μέλει
πῶς τι ποιήσῃ, ὃς ἐπιστρέφεται οὐ τοῦ τυχεῖν
τινος, ἀλλὰ τῆς ἐνεργείας τῆς αὑτοῦ. τίς περι-
πατῶν τῆς ἐνεργείας τῆς αὑτοῦ ἐπιστρέφεται;
τίς βουλευόμενος αὐτῆς τῆς βουλῆς, οὐχὶ δὲ τοῦ

what a crowd is he does not know, nor what the shouting and the scornful laughter of a crowd are. Nay, he does not even know what this anxiety itself is, whether it is something that we can control, or beyond our powers, whether he can stop it or not. That is why, if he is praised, he goes off the stage all puffed up; but if he is laughed to scorn, that poor windbag of his conceit is pricked and flattens out.

We too experience something of the same kind. What do we admire? Externals. What are we in earnest about? About externals. Are we, then, at a loss to know how it comes about that we are subject to fear and anxiety? Why, what else can possibly happen, when we regard impending events as things evil? We cannot help but be in fear, we cannot help but be in anxiety. And then we say, "O Lord God, how may I escape anxiety?" Fool, have you not hands? Did not God make them for you? Sit down now and pray forsooth that the mucus in your nose may not run! Nay, rather wipe your nose and do not blame God! What then? Has he given you nothing that helps in the present case? Has he not given you endurance, has he not given you magnanimity, has he not given you courage? When you have such serviceable hands as these do you still look for someone to wipe your nose? But these virtues we neither practise nor concern ourselves withal. Why, show me one single man who cares *how* he does something, who is concerned, not with getting something, but with his own action. Who is there that is concerned with his own action while he is walking around? Who, when he is planning, is concerned with the plan

16 τυχεῖν ἐκείνου περὶ οὗ βουλεύεται; κἂν μὲν
τύχῃ, ἐπῆρται καὶ λέγει "πῶς γὰρ ἡμεῖς καλῶς
ἐβουλευσάμεθα; οὐκ ἔλεγόν σοι, ἀδελφέ, ὅτι
ἀδύνατόν ἐστιν ἡμῶν τι σκεψαμένων μὴ οὕτως
ἐκβῆναι;" ἂν δ' ἑτέρως χωρήσῃ, τεταπείνωται
τάλας, οὐχ εὑρίσκει οὐδὲ τί εἴπῃ περὶ τῶν γεγονότων. τίς ἡμῶν τούτου ἕνεκα μάντιν παρέ-
17 λαβεν; τίς ἡμῶν¹ ἐνεκοιμήθη ὑπὲρ ἐνεργείας;
τίς; ἕνα μοι δότε, ἵνα ἴδω τοῦτον, ὃν ἐκ πολλοῦ
χρόνου ζητῶ, τὸν ταῖς ἀληθείαις εὐγενῆ καὶ εὐφυᾶ·
εἴτε νέον εἴτε πρεσβύτερον, δότε.

18   Τί οὖν ἔτι θαυμάζομεν εἰ περὶ μὲν τὰς ὕλας
τετρίμμεθα, ἐν δὲ ταῖς ἐνεργείαις ταπεινοί, ἀσχή-
μονες, οὐδενὸς ἄξιοι, δειλοί, ἀταλαίπωροι, ὅλοι
ἀτυχήματα; οὐ γὰρ μεμέληκεν ἡμῖν οὐδὲ μελε-
19 τῶμεν. εἰ δὲ μὴ τὸν θάνατον ἢ τὴν φυγὴν
ἐφοβούμεθα, ἀλλὰ τὸν φόβον, ἐμελετῶμεν ἂν
ἐκείνοις μὴ περιπίπτειν ἃ φαίνεται ἡμῖν κακά.
20 νῦν δ' ἐν μὲν τῇ σχολῇ γοργοὶ καὶ κατάγλωσσοι,
κἂν ζητημάτιον ἐμπέσῃ περί τινος τούτων, ἱκανοὶ
τὰ ἑξῆς ἐπελθεῖν· ἕλκυσον δ' εἰς χρῆσιν καὶ
εὑρήσεις τάλανας ναυαγούς. προσπεσέτω φαντασία ταρακτικὴ καὶ γνώσῃ, τί ἐμελετῶμεν καὶ
21 πρὸς τί ἐγυμναζόμεθα. λοιπὸν ὑπὸ² τῆς ἀμε-
λετησίας προσεπισωρεύομεν ἀεί τινα καὶ προσ-

----

¹ οὐκ after ἡμῶν in S was deleted by Wolf.
² Wolf : ἐπὶ S.

----

¹ Referring to a dream oracle like that of Asclepius, but
the text is somewhat uncertain.

itself, and not with getting what he is planning about? And then if he gets it, he is all set up and says, "Yes, indeed, what a fine plan we made! Did I not tell you, brother, that, if there was anything at all in my views, it was impossible for the plan to fall out otherwise?" But if the plan goes the other way, he is humble and wretched, and cannot even find any explanation of what has happened. Who of us ever called in a seer for a case of this kind? Who of us ever slept in a temple [1] for enlightenment about our action? Who? Show me but one, that I may see him, the man that I have long been looking for, the truly noble and gifted man; be he young or old, only show him!

Why, then, do we wonder any longer that, although in material things we are thoroughly experienced, nevertheless in our actions we are dejected, unseemly, worthless, cowardly, unwilling to stand the strain, utter failures one and all? For we have not troubled ourselves about these matters in time past, nor do we even now practise them. Yet if we were afraid, not of death or exile, but of fear itself, then we should practise how not to encounter those things that appear evil to us. But as it is, we are fiery and fluent in the schoolroom, and if some trivial question about one of these points comes up, we are able to pursue the logical consequences; yet drag us into practical application, and you will find us miserable shipwrecked mariners. Let a disturbing thought come to us and you will find out what we have been practising and for what we have been training! As a result, because of our lack of practice, we are ever going out of our way to heap up terrors and to make them out greater

22 πλάσσομεν μείζονα τῶν καθεστώτων. εὐθὺς ἐγώ,
ὅταν πλέω, κατακύψας εἰς τὸν βυθὸν ἢ τὸ
πέλαγος περιβλεψάμενος καὶ μὴ ἰδὼν γῆν ἐξ-
ίσταμαι καὶ φανταζόμενος, ὅτι ὅλον με δεῖ τὸ
πέλαγος τοῦτο ἐκπιεῖν, ἂν ναυαγήσω, οὐκ ἐπέρ-
χεταί μοι, ὅτι μοι τρεῖς ξέσται ἀρκοῦσιν. τί
οὖν με ταράσσει; τὸ πέλαγος; οὔ, ἀλλὰ τὸ
23 δόγμα. πάλιν ὅταν σεισμὸς γένηται, φαντάζομαι
ὅτι ἡ πόλις ἐπιπίπτειν μοι μέλλει· οὐ γὰρ ἀρκεῖ
μικρὸν λιθάριον, ἵν' ἔξω μου τὸν ἐγκέφαλον βάλῃ;

24   Τίνα οὖν ἐστι τὰ βαροῦντα καὶ ἐξιστάντα ἡμᾶς;
τίνα γὰρ ἄλλα ἢ τὰ δόγματα; τὸν γὰρ ἐξιόντα
καὶ ἀπαλλαττόμενον τῶν συνήθων καὶ ἑταίρων
καὶ τόπων καὶ συναναστροφῆς τί ἐστι τὸ βαροῦν
25 ἄλλο ἢ δόγμα; τὰ γοῦν παιδία εὐθὺς ὅταν κλαύσῃ
μικρὰ τῆς τιτθῆς ἀπελθούσης, πλακούντιον λα-
26 βόντα ἐπιλέλησται. θέλεις οὖν καὶ ἡμεῖς τοῖς
παιδίοις ὁμοιωθῶμεν[1]; οὔ, νὴ τὸν Δία. οὐ γὰρ
ὑπὸ πλακουντίου τοῦτο πάσχειν ἀξιῶ, ἀλλ' ὑπὸ
27 δογμάτων ὀρθῶν. τίνα δ' ἐστὶ ταῦτα; ἃ δεῖ τὸν
ἄνθρωπον ὅλην τὴν ἡμέραν μελετῶντα μηδενὶ προσ-
πάσχειν τῶν ἀλλοτρίων, μηθ' ἑταίρῳ μήτε τόπῳ
μήτε γυμνασίοις, ἀλλὰ μηδὲ τῷ σώματι τῷ αὐτοῦ,
μεμνῆσθαι δὲ τοῦ νόμου καὶ τοῦτον πρὸ ὀφθαλμῶν
28 ἔχειν. τίς δ' ὁ νόμος ὁ θεῖος; τὰ ἴδια τηρεῖν, τῶν
ἀλλοτρίων μὴ ἀντιποιεῖσθαι, ἀλλὰ διδομένοις μὲν
χρῆσθαι, μὴ διδόμενα δὲ μὴ ποθεῖν, ἀφαιρουμένου
δέ τινος ἀποδιδόναι εὐλύτως καὶ αὐτόθεν, χάριν

───────────
[1] Koraes: ὁμοῶμεν S.

328

than they actually are. For example, whenever I go to sea, on gazing down into the deep or looking around upon the expanse of waters and seeing no land, I am beside myself, fancying that if I am wrecked I shall have to swallow this whole expanse of waters; but it does not occur to me that three pints are enough. What is it, then, that disturbs me? The expanse of sea? No, but my judgement. Again, when there is an earthquake, I fancy that the whole city is going to fall upon me; what, is not a little stone enough to knock my brains out?

What, then, are the things that weigh upon us and drive us out of our senses? Why, what else but our judgements? For when a man goes hence abandoning the comrades, the places, and the social relations to which he is accustomed, what else is the burden that is weighing him down but a judgement? Children, indeed, when they cry a little because their nurse has left, forget their troubles as soon as they get a cookie. Would you, therefore, have *us* resemble children? No, by Zeus! For I claim that we should be influenced in this way, not by a cookie, but by true judgements. And what are these? The things which a man ought to practise all day long, without being devoted to what is not his own, either comrade, or place, or gymnasia, nay, not even to his own body; but he should remember the law and keep that before his eyes. And what is the law of God? To guard what is his own, not to lay claim to what is not his own, but to make use of what is given him, and not to yearn for what has not been given; when something is taken away, to give it up readily and with-

εἰδότα οὗ ἐχρήσατο χρόνου, εἰ θέλεις μὴ κλάειν [1]
29 τὴν τιτθὴν καὶ μάμμην. τί γὰρ διαφέρει, τίνος
ἥττων ἐστὶ καὶ ἐκ τίνος κρέμαται; τί κρείττων εἶ
τοῦ διὰ κοράσιον κλάοντος, εἰ διὰ γυμνασίδιον καὶ
στωίδια καὶ νεανισκάρια καὶ τοιαύτην διατριβὴν
30 πενθεῖς; ἄλλος ἐλθὼν ὅτι οὐκέτι τὸ τῆς Δίρκης
ὕδωρ πίνειν μέλλει. τὸ γὰρ Μάρκιον χεῖρόν ἐστι
τοῦ τῆς Δίρκης; "ἀλλ' ἐκεῖνό μοι σύνηθες ἦν."
31 καὶ τοῦτο πάλιν ἔσται σοι σύνηθες. εἶτ' ἂν μὲν
τοιούτῳ προσπάθῃς, καὶ τοῦτο πάλιν κλαῖε καὶ
ζήτει στίχον ὅμοιον τῷ Εὐριπίδου ποιῆσαι

θερμάς τε τὰς Νέρωνος Μάρκιόν θ' ὕδωρ.

ἴδε πῶς τραγῳδία γίνεται, ὅταν εἰς μωροὺς
ἀνθρώπους πράγματα τὰ [2] τυγχάνοντ' ἐμπέσῃ.
32 "Πότε οὖν Ἀθήνας πάλιν ὄψομαι καὶ τὴν
ἀκρόπολιν;" τάλας, οὐκ ἀρκεῖ σοι ἃ βλέπεις καθ'
ἡμέραν; κρεῖττόν τι ἔχεις ἢ μεῖζον ἰδεῖν τοῦ ἡλίου,
τῆς σελήνης, τῶν ἄστρων, τῆς γῆς ὅλης, τῆς
33 θαλάσσης; εἰ δὲ δὴ παρακολουθεῖς τῷ διοικοῦντι
τὰ ὅλα κἀκεῖνον ἐν σαυτῷ περιφέρεις, ἔτι ποθεῖς
λιθάρια καὶ πέτραν κομψήν; ὅταν οὖν μέλλῃς
ἀπολιπεῖν αὐτὸν τὸν ἥλιον καὶ τὴν σελήνην, τί
34 ποιήσεις; κλαύσεις καθήμενος ὡς τὰ παιδία; τί

---

[1] Shaftesbury : καλεῖν S.
[2] Added by Schweighäuser.

---

[1] The fountain of Dirce was at Thebes; the Marcian
aqueduct brought good water to Rome at this time.
[2] A parody upon the *Phoenissae*, 368: "The gymnasia in
which I was reared and the water of Dirce." Polyneices
is speaking.

out delay, being grateful for the time in which he had the use of it — all this if you do not wish to be crying for your nurse and your mammy! For what difference does it make what object a man has a weakness for and depends upon? In what respect are you superior to the man who weeps for a maid, if you grieve for a trivial gymnasium, a paltry colonnade, a group of youngsters, and that way of spending your time? Someone else comes and grieves because he is no longer going to drink the water of Dirce.[1] What, is the water of the Marcian aqueduct inferior to that of Dirce? "Nay, but I was accustomed to that water." And you will get accustomed to this in turn. And then, if you become addicted to something of this kind, weep for this too in turn, and try to write a line after the pattern of that of Euripides:

To Nero's baths and Marcian founts once more.[2]

Behold how tragedy arises, when everyday events befall fools!

"When, then, shall I see Athens once more and the Acropolis?" Poor man, are you not satisfied with what you are seeing every day? Have you anything finer or greater to look at than the sun, the moon, the stars, the whole earth, the sea? And if you really understand Him that governs the universe, and bear Him about within you, do you yet yearn for bits of stone and a pretty rock?[3] When, therefore, you are about to leave the sun and the moon, what will you do? Will you sit and cry as little children cry? What was it you did at

[3] The rock of the Acropolis and the marble buildings upon it.

οὖν ἐν τῇ σχολῇ ἐποίεις, τί ἤκουες, τί ἐμάνθανες ;
τί σαυτὸν φιλόσοφον ἐπέγραφες ἐξὸν τὰ ὄντα
ἐπιγράφειν ; ὅτι " εἰσαγωγὰς ἔπραξά τινας καὶ
Χρυσίππεια ἀνέγνων, φιλοσόφου δ᾽ οὐδὲ θύραν
35 παρῆλθον. ποῦ γάρ μοι μέτεστι τούτου τοῦ
πράγματος, οὗ Σωκράτει μετῆν τῷ οὕτως
ἀποθανόντι, οὕτως ζήσαντι ; οὐ Διογένει μετῆν ; "
36 ἐπινοεῖς τούτων τινὰ κλάοντα ἢ ἀγανακτοῦντα,
ὅτι τὸν δεῖνα οὐ μέλλει βλέπειν οὐδὲ τὴν δεῖνα
οὐδ᾽ ἐν Ἀθήναις ἔσεσθαι ἢ ἐν Κορίνθῳ, ἀλλ᾽, ἂν
37 οὕτως τύχῃ, ἐν Σούσοις ἢ ἐν Ἐκβατάνοις ; ᾧ γὰρ
ἔξεστιν ἐξελθεῖν, ὅταν θέλῃ, τοῦ συμποσίου καὶ
μηκέτι παίζειν, ἔτι οὗτος ἀνιᾶται μένων ; οὐχὶ δ᾽
ὡς παιδία¹ παραμένει, μέχρις ἂν ψυχαγωγῆται ;
38 ταχύ γ᾽ ἂν ὁ τοιοῦτος ὑπομείναι φυγήν τινα
φυγεῖν εἰς ἄπαντα ἢ τὴν ἐπὶ θανάτῳ κατακριθείς.
39   Οὐ θέλεις ἤδη ὡς τὰ παιδία ἀπογαλακτισθῆναι
καὶ ἅπτεσθαι τροφῆς στερεωτέρας μηδὲ κλάειν
40 μάμμας καὶ τιτθάς, γραῶν ἀποκλαύματα ; " ἀλλ᾽
ἐκείνας ἀπαλλασσόμενος ἀνιάσω."   σὺ αὐτὰς
ἀνιάσεις ; οὐδαμῶς, ἀλλ᾽ ὅπερ καὶ σέ, τὸ δόγμα.
τί οὖν ἔχεις ποιῆσαι ; ἔξελε, τὸ δ᾽ ἐκείνων, ἂν εὖ
ποιῶσιν, αὐταὶ ἐξελοῦσιν· εἰ δὲ μή, οἰμώξουσι δι᾽
41 αὐτάς.   ἄνθρωπε, τὸ λεγόμενον τοῦτο ἀπονοήθητι²
ἤδη ὑπὲρ εὐροίας, ὑπὲρ ἐλευθερίας, ὑπὲρ μεγα-

---

¹ Gataker (supported by Bentley and Upton), παιδιᾷ S.
Compare the very close parallel in I. 24, 20, and for the
frequent use by Epictetus of illustrations from the character
and behaviour of children see E. Kenner: *Das Kind. Ein
Gleichnissmittel bei Epiktet*, München, 1905, 54 ff.

---

¹ Did no serious work in philosophy. For the figure of
speech compare IV. 1, 177.

school? What was it you heard and learned? Why did you record yourself as a philosopher when you might have recorded the truth in these words: "I studied a few introductions, and did some reading in Chrysippus, but I did not even get past the door of a philosopher?"[1] Since what part have I in that business in which Socrates, who died so nobly, and so nobly lived, had a part? Or in that in which Diogenes had a part?" Can you imagine one of these men crying or fretting because he is not going to see such-and-such a man, or such-and-such a woman, or to live in Athens or in Corinth, but, if it so happen, in Susa or in Ecbatana? What, does he who is at liberty to leave the banquet when he will, and to play the game no longer, keep on annoying himself by staying? Does he not stay, like children, only as long as he is entertained? Such a man would be likely, forsooth, to endure going into exile for life or the exile of death, if this were his sentence.

Are you not willing, at this late date, like children, to be weaned and to partake of more solid food, and not to cry for mammies and nurses—old wives' lamentations? "But if I leave, I shall cause those women sorrow?" *You* cause them sorrow? Not at all, but it will be the same thing that causes sorrow to you yourself—bad judgement.[2] What, then, can you do? Get rid of that judgement, and, if they do well, they will themselves get rid of their judgement; otherwise, they will come to grief and have only themselves to thank for it. Man, do something desperate, as the expression goes, now if never before, to achieve peace, freedom, and high-

[2] This point is especially well brought out in *Encheiridion*, 5.

λοψυχίας. ἀνάτεινόν ποτε τὸν τράχηλον ὡς
12 ἀπηλλαγμένος δουλείας, τόλμησον ἀναβλέψας
πρὸς τὸν θεὸν εἰπεῖν ὅτι " χρῶ μοι λοιπὸν εἰς ὃ ἂν
θέλης· ὁμογνωμονῶ σοι, σός[1] εἰμι· οὐδὲν παραι-
τοῦμαι τῶν σοὶ δοκούντων· ὅπου θέλεις, ἄγε· ἣν
θέλεις ἐσθῆτα περίθες. ἄρχειν με θέλεις, ἰδιω-
τεύειν, μένειν, φεύγειν, πένεσθαι, πλουτεῖν ; ἐγώ
σοι ὑπὲρ ἁπάντων τούτων πρὸς τοὺς ἀνθρώπους
13 ἀπολογήσομαι· δείξω τὴν ἑκάστου φύσιν οἵα
14 ἐστίν." οὔ· ἀλλ' ἔνδον ὡς κοράσια[2] καθήμενος
ἐκδέχου σου τὴν μάμμην, μέχρις σε χορτάσῃ. ὁ
Ἡρακλῆς εἰ τοῖς ἐν οἴκῳ παρεκάθητο, τίς ἂν ἦν ;
Εὐρυσθεὺς καὶ οὐχὶ Ἡρακλῆς. ἄγε, πόσους δὲ
περιερχόμενος τὴν οἰκουμένην συνήθεις ἔσχεν,
φίλους ; ἀλλ' οὐδὲν φίλτερον τοῦ θεοῦ· διὰ τοῦτο
ἐπιστεύθη Διὸς υἱὸς εἶναι καὶ ἦν. ἐκείνῳ τοίνυν
πειθόμενος περιῄει καθαίρων ἀδικίαν καὶ ἀνομίαν.
15 ἀλλ' οὐκ εἶ Ἡρακλῆς καὶ οὐ δύνασαι καθαίρειν τὰ
ἀλλότρια κακά, ἀλλ' οὐδὲ Θησεύς, ἵνα τὰ τῆς
Ἀττικῆς καθάρῃς· τὰ σαυτοῦ κάθαρον. ἐντεῦθεν
ἐκ τῆς διανοίας ἔκβαλε ἀντὶ Προκρούστου καὶ
Σκίρωνος λύπην, φόβον, ἐπιθυμίαν, φθόνον,
ἐπιχαιρεκακίαν, φιλαργυρίαν, μαλακίαν, ἀκρα-

---

[1] Salmasius : ἴσος S.

[2] Capps: ἐν βοὸς κοιλίᾳ S (retained by Schenkl), "in a
cow's belly," which might conceivably be a contemptuous
expression for a cradle, or baby-basket, but I know of no
evidence to support this view.

---

[1] Compare the critical note.

mindedness. Lift up your neck at last like a man escaped from bondage, be bold to look towards God and say, " Use me henceforward for whatever Thou wilt; I am of one mind with Thee; I am Thine; I crave exemption from nothing that seems good in Thy sight; where Thou wilt, lead me; in what raiment Thou wilt, clothe me. Wouldst Thou have me to hold office, or remain in private life; to remain here or go into exile; to be, poor or be rich ? I will defend all these Thy acts before men; I will show what the true nature of each thing is." Nay, you will not; sit rather in the house as girls do [1] and wait for your mammy until she feeds you! If Heracles had sat about at home, what would he have amounted to? He would have been Eurystheus [2] and no Heracles. Come, how many acquaintances and friends did he have with him as he went up and down through the whole world ? Nay, he had no dearer friend than God. That is why he was believed to be a son of God, and was. It was therefore in obedience to His will that he went about clearing away wickedness and lawlessness. But you are no Heracles, you say, and you cannot clear away the wickedness of other men, nay, nor are you even a Theseus, to clear away the ills of Attica merely. Very well, clear away your own then. From just here, from out your own mind, cast not Procrustes and Sciron, [3] but grief, fear, desire, envy, joy at others' ills; cast out greed, effeminacy, incontinency. These

[2] The craven, stay-at-home king, under whose orders Heracles performed his "labours."
[3] Two famous robbers who infested the road between Athens and Megara and were given their just deserts by Theseus.

16 σίαν. ταῦτα δ' οὐκ ἔστιν ἄλλως ἐκβαλεῖν, εἰ μὴ
πρὸς μόνον τὸν θεὸν ἀποβλέποντα, ἐκείνῳ μόνῳ
προσπεπονθότα, τοῖς ἐκείνου προστάγμασι καθω-
17 σιωμένον. ἂν δ' ἄλλο τι θέλῃς, οἰμώζων καὶ
στένων ἀκολουθήσεις τῷ ἰσχυροτέρῳ ἔξω ζητῶν
ἀεὶ τὴν εὔροιαν καὶ μηδέποτ' εὑρεῖν δυνάμενος.
ἐκεῖ γὰρ αὐτὴν ζητεῖς, οὗ μή ἐστιν, ἀφεὶς ἐκεῖ
ζητεῖν, ὅπου ἐστίν.

ιζ'. Πῶς ἐφαρμοστέον τὰς προλήψεις τοῖς ἐπὶ
μέρους ;

1 Τί πρῶτόν ἐστιν ἔργον τοῦ φιλοσοφοῦντος ;
ἀποβαλεῖν οἴησιν· ἀμήχανον γάρ, ἅ τις εἰδέναι
2 οἴεται, ταῦτα ἄρξασθαι μανθάνειν. τὰ μὲν οὖν
ποιητέα καὶ οὐ ποιητέα καὶ ἀγαθὰ καὶ κακὰ καὶ
καλὰ καὶ αἰσχρὰ πάντες ἄνω καὶ κάτω λαλοῦντες
ἐρχόμεθα πρὸς τοὺς φιλοσόφους, ἐπὶ τούτοις ἐπαι-
νοῦντες ψέγοντες, ἐγκαλοῦντες μεμφόμενοι, περὶ
ἐπιτηδευμάτων καλῶν καὶ αἰσχρῶν ἐπικρίνοντες
3 καὶ διαλαμβάνοντες. τίνος δ' ἕνεκα προσερχόμεθα
τοῖς φιλοσόφοις ; μαθησόμενοι[1] ἃ οὐκ οἰόμεθα
εἰδέναι. τίνα δ' ἐστὶ ταῦτα ; τὰ θεωρήματα. ἃ
γὰρ λαλοῦσιν οἱ φιλόσοφοι μαθεῖν θέλομεν οἱ μὲν[2]
ὡς κομψὰ καὶ δριμέα, οἱ δ', ἵν' ἀπ' αὐτῶν περιποιή-
4 σωνται. γελοῖον οὖν τὸ οἴεσθαι, ὅτι ἄλλα μέν
τις μαθεῖν βούλεται, ἄλλα δὲ μαθήσεται, ἢ λοιπὸν
5 ὅτι προκόψει τις ἐν οἷς οὐ μανθάνει. τὸ δ' ἐξα-

---

[1] Added by Schenkl.
[2] οἱ μὲν added by Schweighäuser.

---

[1] *i.e.*, of conceit in one's own opinion.

things you cannot cast out in any other way than
by looking to God alone, being specially devoted
to Him only, and consecrated to His commands.
But if you wish anything else, with lamentation and
groaning you will follow that which is stronger than
you are, ever seeking outside yourself for peace, and
never able to be at peace. For you seek peace
where it is not, and neglect to seek it where it is.

CHAPTER XVII

*How ought we adjust our preconceptions to individual
instances?*

WHAT is the first business of one who practises
philosophy? To get rid of thinking that one
knows [1]; for it is impossible to get a man to begin
to learn that which he thinks he knows. However, as we go to the philosophers we all babble
hurly-burly about what ought to be done and what
ought not, good and evil, fair and foul, and on these
grounds assign praise and blame, censure and repre-
hension, passing judgement on fair and foul practices,
and discriminating between them. But what do we
go to the philosophers for? To learn what we do
not think we know. And what is that? General
principles. For some of us want to learn what the
philosophers are saying, thinking it will be witty
and shrewd, others, because they wish to profit
thereby. But it is absurd to think that when a man
wishes to learn one thing he will actually learn
something else, or, in short, that a man will make
progress in anything without learning it. But the

πατῶν τοὺς πολλοὺς τοῦτ' ἔστιν, ὅπερ καὶ
Θεόπομπον τὸν ῥήτορα, ὅς που[1] καὶ Πλάτωνι
6 ἐγκαλεῖ ἐπὶ τῷ βούλεσθαι ἕκαστα ὁρίζεσθαι. τί
γὰρ λέγει ; "οὐδεὶς ἡμῶν πρὸ σοῦ ἔλεγεν ἀγαθὸν
ἢ δίκαιον ; ἢ μὴ παρακολουθοῦντες τί ἐστι τούτων
ἕκαστον ἀσήμως καὶ κενῶς ἐφθεγγόμεθα[2] τὰς
7 φωνάς ;" τίς γάρ σοι λέγει, Θεόπομπε, ὅτι
ἐννοίας οὐκ εἴχομεν ἑκάστου τούτων φυσικὰς καὶ
προλήψεις ; ἀλλ' οὐχ οἷόν τ' ἐφαρμόζειν τὰς
προλήψεις ταῖς καταλλήλοις οὐσίαις μὴ διαρθρώ-
σαντα αὐτὰς καὶ αὐτὸ τοῦτο σκεψάμενον, ποίαν
8 τινὰ ἑκάστη αὐτῶν οὐσίαν ὑποτακτέον. ἐπεὶ
τοιαῦτα λέγε καὶ πρὸς τοὺς ἰατρούς· "τίς γὰρ
ἡμῶν οὐκ ἔλεγεν ὑγιεινόν τι καὶ νοσερόν, πρὶν
Ἱπποκράτη γενέσθαι ; ἢ κενῶς τὰς φωνὰς ταύτας
9 ἀπηχοῦμεν ;" ἔχομεν γάρ τινα καὶ ὑγιεινοῦ πρόληψιν. ἀλλ' ἐφαρμόσαι οὐ δυνάμεθα. διὰ τοῦτο
ὁ μὲν λέγει "ἀνάτεινον," ὁ δὲ λέγει "δὸς τροφήν·"
καὶ ὁ μὲν λέγει "φλεβοτόμησον," ὁ δὲ λέγει
"σικύασον." τί τὸ αἴτιον ; ἄλλο γε ἢ ὅτι
τὴν τοῦ ὑγιεινοῦ πρόληψιν οὐ δύναται καλῶς
ἐφαρμόσαι τοῖς ἐπὶ μέρους ;
10 Οὕτως ἔχει καὶ ἐνθάδ' ἐπὶ τῶν κατὰ τὸν βίον.
ἀγαθὸν καὶ κακὸν καὶ συμφέρον καὶ ἀσύμφορον
τίς ἡμῶν οὐ λαλεῖ ; τίς γὰρ ἡμῶν οὐκ ἔχει τού-

---

[1] Wolf and Koraes : ὅπου S.
[2] Schegk and Salmasius : φθεγγόμεθα S.

---

[1] Almost certainly the same as Theopompus of Chios, the
pupil of Isocrates, more generally known to us as an historian,
but also famous in his own time in his declamations (ἐπι-

338

multitude are under the same misapprehension as was Theopompus, the orator,[1] who actually censures Plato for wishing to define every term. Well, what does he say? "Did none of us before your time ever use the words 'good' or 'just'? Or, without understanding what each of these terms severally mean, did we merely utter them as vague and empty sounds?" Why, who tells you, Theopompus, that we did not have a natural conception of each term, that is, a preconceived idea of it? But it is impossible to adjust our preconceived ideas to the appropriate facts without having first systematized them and having raised precisely this question— what particular fact is to be classified under each preconception. Suppose, for example, that you make the same sort of remark to the physicians: "Why, who among us did not use terms 'healthy' and 'diseased' before Hippocrates was born? Or were we merely making an empty noise with these sounds?" For, of course, we have a certain pre-conception of the idea "healthy." But we are unable to apply it. That is why one person says, "Keep abstaining from food," and another, "Give nourishment"; again, one says, "Cut a vein," and another says, "Use the cupping-glass." What is the reason? Is it really anything but the fact that a person is unable properly to apply the preconceived idea of "healthy" to the specific instances?

So it stands here also, in the affairs of life. Who among us has not upon his lips the words "good" and "evil," "advantageous" and "disadvantageous"? For who among us does not have a preconceived

δεικτικοὶ λόγοι). The following quotation is probably from the *Diatribe against Plato* (Athen. XI. 508c).

τῶν ἑκάστου πρόληψιν ; ἆρ᾽ οὖν διηρθρωμένην καὶ
11 τελείαν ; τοῦτο δεῖξον. "πῶς δείξω ;" ἐφάρ-
μοσον αὐτὴν καλῶς ταῖς ἐπὶ μέρους οὐσίαις.
εὐθὺς τοὺς ὅρους Πλάτων μὲν ὑποτάσσει τῇ τοῦ
χρησίμου προλήψει, σὺ δὲ τῇ τοῦ ἀχρήστου.
12 δυνατὸν οὖν ἐστιν ἀμφοτέρους ὑμᾶς ἐπιτυγχά-
νειν ; πῶς οἷόν τε ; τῇ δὲ τοῦ πλούτου οὐσίᾳ
οὐχ ὁ μέν τις ἐφαρμόζει τὴν τοῦ ἀγαθοῦ πρόληψιν, ὁ δ᾽ οὔ ; τῇ δὲ τῆς ἡδονῆς, τῇ δὲ τῆς
13 ὑγείας ; καθόλου γὰρ εἰ πάντες οἱ τὰ ὀνόματα
λαλοῦντες μὴ κενῶς ἴσμεν ἕκαστα τούτων καὶ
μηδεμιᾶς ἐπιμελείας περὶ τὴν διάρθρωσιν τῶν
προλήψεων δεόμεθα, τί διαφερόμεθα, τί πολε-
μοῦμεν, τί ψέγομεν ἀλλήλους ;
14   Καὶ τί μοι νῦν τὴν πρὸς ἀλλήλους μάχην
παραφέρειν καὶ ταύτης μεμνῆσθαι ; σὺ αὐτὸς εἰ
ἐφαρμόζεις καλῶς τὰς προλήψεις, διὰ τί δυσροεῖς,
15 διὰ τί ἐμποδίζῃ ; ἀφῶμεν ἄρτι τὸν δεύτερον τόπον
τὸν περὶ τὰς ὁρμὰς καὶ τὴν κατὰ ταύτας περὶ
τὸ καθῆκον φιλοτεχνίαν. ἀφῶμεν καὶ τὸν τρίτον
16 τὸν περὶ τὰς συγκαταθέσεις. χαρίζομαί σοι
ταῦτα πάντα. στῶμεν ἐπὶ τοῦ πρώτου καὶ σχεδὸν αἰσθητὴν παρέχοντος τὴν ἀπόδειξιν τοῦ μὴ
17 ἐφαρμόζειν καλῶς τὰς προλήψεις. νῦν σὺ θέλεις
τὰ δυνατὰ καὶ τὰ σοὶ δυνατά ; τί οὖν ἐμποδίζῃ ;
διὰ τί δυσροεῖς ; νῦν οὐ φεύγεις τὰ ἀναγκαῖα ;

---

[1] The word, δυσροεῖν, is the opposite of the technical term
εὐροεῖν (τὸ εὐροῦν, εὐροία), which is a metaphor which is derived from
the even flow of quiet waters.

[2] The three fields, according to Epictetus, are, 1. ὄρεξις,
desire ; 2. ὁρμή, choice ; 3. συγκατάθεσις, assent. Compare
III. 2.

idea of each of these terms? Very well, is it fitted
into a system and complete? Prove that it is.
"How shall I prove it?" Apply it properly to
specific facts. To start with, Plato classifies defini-
tions under the preconception "the useful," but you
classify them under that of "the useless." Is it,
then, possible for both of you to be right? How
can that be? Does not one man apply his preconceived idea of "the good" to the fact of wealth,
while another does not? And another to that of
pleasure, and yet another to that of health? Indeed,
to sum up the whole matter, if all of us who have
these terms upon our lips possess no mere empty
knowledge of each one severally, and do not need
to devote any pains to the systematic arrangement
of our preconceived ideas, why do we disagree, why
fight, why blame one another?

And yet what need is there for me to bring
forward now our strife with one another and make
mention of that? Take your own case; if you apply
properly your preconceived ideas, why are you
troubled,[1] why are you hampered? Let us pass by
for the moment the second field of study[2]—that
which has to do with our choices and the discussion
of what is our duty in regard to them. Let us pass
by also the third—that which has to do with our
assents. I make you a present of all this. Let us
confine our attention to the first field, one which
allows an almost palpable proof that you do not
properly apply your preconceived ideas. Do you
at this moment desire what is possible in general
and what is possible for you in particular? If so,
why are you hampered? Why are you troubled?
Are you not at this moment trying to escape what

341

διὰ τί οὖν περιπίπτεις τινί, διὰ τί δυστυχεῖς ; διὰ
τί θέλοντός σού τι οὐ γίνεται καὶ μὴ θέλοντος
18 γίνεται ; ἀπόδειξις γὰρ αὕτη μεγίστη δυσροίας
καὶ κακοδαιμονίας. θέλω τι καὶ οὐ γίνεται· καὶ
τί ἐστιν ἀθλιώτερον ἐμοῦ ; οὐ θέλω τι καὶ
γίνεται· καὶ τί ἐστιν ἀθλιώτερον ἐμοῦ ;
19 Τοῦτο καὶ ἡ Μήδεια οὐχ ὑπομείνασα ἦλθεν
ἐπὶ τὸ ἀποκτεῖναι τὰ τέκνα. μεγαλοφυῶς κατά
γε τοῦτο. εἶχε γὰρ ἣν δεῖ φαντασίαν, οἷόν ἐστι
20 τὸ ἃ θέλει τινι μὴ προχωρεῖν. " εἶτα οὕτως
τιμωρήσομαι τὸν ἀδικήσαντά με καὶ ὑβρίσαντα.
καὶ τί ὄφελος τοῦ κακῶς οὕτως διακειμένου ;
πῶς οὖν γένηται ; ἀποκτείνω μὲν τὰ τέκνα.
21 ἀλλὰ καὶ ἐμαυτὴν τιμωρήσομαι. καὶ τί μοι
μέλει ; " τοῦτ' ἐστιν ἔκπτωσις ψυχῆς μεγάλα
νεῦρα ἐχούσης. οὐ γὰρ ᾔδει, ποῦ κεῖται τὸ
ποιεῖν ἃ θέλομεν, ὅτι τοῦτο οὐκ ἔξωθεν δεῖ
λαμβάνειν οὐδὲ τὰ πράγματα μετατιθέντα καὶ
22 μεθαρμοζόμενον. μὴ θέλε τὸν ἄνδρα, καὶ οὐδὲν
ὧν θέλεις οὐ γίνεται. μὴ θέλε αὐτὸν ἐξ ἅπαντός
σοι συνοικεῖν, μὴ θέλε μένειν ἐν Κορίνθῳ καὶ
ἁπλῶς μηδὲν ἄλλο θέλε ἢ ἃ ὁ θεὸς θέλει. καὶ
τίς σε κωλύσει, τίς ἀναγκάσει ; οὐ μᾶλλον ἢ
τὸν Δία.
23 Ὅταν τοιοῦτον ἔχῃς ἡγεμόνα καὶ τοιούτῳ
συνθέλῃς καὶ συνορέγῃ, τί φοβῇ ἔτι μὴ ἀπο-
24 τύχῃς ; χάρισαί σου τὴν ὄρεξιν καὶ τὴν ἔκκλισιν

---

[1] What follows is a free paraphrase of Euripides, *Medea*,
790 ff.

is inevitable? If so, why do you fall into any trouble, why are you unfortunate? Why is it that when you want something it does not happen, and when you do not want it, it does happen? For this is the strongest proof of trouble and misfortune. I want something, and it does not happen; and what creature is more wretched than I? I do not want something, and it does happen; and what creature is more wretched than I?

Medea, for example, because she could not endure this, came to the point of killing her children. In this respect at least hers was the act of a great spirit. For she had the proper conception of what it means for anyone's wishes not to come true. "Very well, then," says she,[1] "in these circumstances I shall take vengeance upon the man who has wronged and insulted me. Yet what good do I get out of his being in such an evil plight? How can that be accomplished? I kill my children. But I shall be punishing myself also. Yet what do I care?" This is the outbursting of a soul of great force. For she did not know where the power lies to do what we wish—that we cannot get this from outside ourselves, nor by disturbing and deranging things. Give up wanting to keep your husband, and nothing of what you want fails to happen. Give up wanting him to live with you at any cost. Give up wanting to remain in Corinth, and, in a word, give up wanting anything but what God wants. And who will prevent you, who will compel you? No one, any more than anyone prevents or compels Zeus.

When you have such a leader as Zeus and identify your wishes and your desires with His, why are you still afraid that you will fail? Give to poverty and

343

πενία καὶ πλούτῳ· ἀποτεύξῃ, περιπεσῇ.¹ ἀλλ'
ὑγιείᾳ· δυστυχήσεις· ἀρχαῖς, τιμαῖς, πατρίδι,
φίλοις, τέκνοις, ἁπλῶς ἄν τινι τῶν ἀπροαιρέτων.
25 ἀλλὰ τῷ Διὶ χάρισαι αὐτάς,² τοῖς ἄλλοις θεοῖς·
ἐκείνοις παράδος, ἐκεῖνοι κυβερνάτωσαν, μετ'
26 ἐκείνων τετάχθωσαν· καὶ ποῦ ἔτι δυσροήσεις;
εἰ δὲ φθονεῖς, ἀταλαίπωρε, καὶ ἐλεεῖς καὶ ζηλοτυ-
πεῖς καὶ τρέμεις καὶ μίαν ἡμέραν οὐ διαλείπεις,
ἐν ᾗ οὐ κατακλάεις καὶ σαυτοῦ καὶ τῶν θεῶν,
27 καὶ τί ἔτι λέγεις ³ πεπαιδεῦσθαι; ποίαν παι-
δείαν, ἄνθρωπε; ὅτι συλλογισμοὺς ἔπραξας,
μεταπίπτοντας; οὐ θέλεις ἀπομαθεῖν, εἰ δυνατόν,
πάντα ταῦτα καὶ ἄνωθεν ἄρξασθαι συναισθανό-
28 μενος ὅτι μέχρι νῦν οὐδ' ἥψω τοῦ πράγματος, καὶ
λοιπὸν ἔνθεν ἀρξάμενος προσοικοδομεῖν τὰ ἑξῆς,
πῶς μηδὲν ἔσται σοῦ μὴ θέλοντος, θέλοντος ⁴
μηδὲν οὐκ ἔσται;

29 Δότε μοι ἕνα νέον κατὰ ταύτην τὴν ἐπιβολὴν
ἐληλυθότα εἰς σχολήν, τούτου τοῦ πράγματος
ἀθλητὴν γενόμενον καὶ λέγοντα ὅτι "ἐμοὶ τὰ
μὲν ἄλλα πάντα χαιρέτω, ἀρκεῖ δ' εἰ ἐξέσται
ποτὲ ἀπαραποδίστῳ καὶ ἀλύπῳ διαγαγεῖν καὶ
ἀνατεῖναι τὸν τράχηλον πρὸς τὰ πράγματα ὡς
ἐλεύθερον καὶ εἰς τὸν οὐρανὸν ἀναβλέπειν ὡς
φίλον τοῦ θεοῦ μηδὲν φοβούμενον τῶν συμβῆναι
30 δυναμένων." δειξάτω τις ὑμῶν αὐτὸν τοιοῦτον,
ἵνα εἴπω· ἔρχου, νεανίσκε, εἰς τὰ σά· σοὶ γὰρ

---

¹ Wolf: περί*** S.   ² Schweighäuser : αὐτά S.
³ Wolf: ἐπιλέγεις S.   ⁴ Supplied by Schweighäuser.

to wealth your aversion and your desire: you will fail to get what you wish, and you will fall into what you would avoid. Give them to health; you will come to grief; so also if you give them to offices, honours, country, friends, children, in short to anything that lies outside the domain of moral purpose. But give them to Zeus and the other gods; entrust them to their keeping, let them exercise the control; let your desire and your aversion be ranged on their side—and how can you be troubled any longer? But if you show envy, wretched man, and pity, and jealousy, and timidity, and never let a day pass without bewailing yourself and the gods, how can you continue to say that you have been educated? What kind of education, man, do you mean? Because you have worked on syllogisms, and arguments with equivocal premisses? Will you not unlearn all this, if that be possible, and begin at the beginning, realizing that hitherto you have not even touched the matter; and for the future, beginning at this point, add to your foundations that which comes next in order—provision that nothing shall be that you do not wish, and that nothing shall fail to be that you *do* wish?

Give me but one young man who has come to school with this purpose in view, who has become an athlete in this activity, saying, " As for me, let everything else go; I am satisfied if I shall be free to live untrammelled and untroubled, to hold up my neck in the face of facts like a free man, and to look up to heaven as a friend of God, without fear of what may possibly happen." Let one of you show me such a person, so that I can say to him: Enter, young man, into your own, for it is your

εἵμαρται κοσμῆσαι φιλοσοφίαν, σά ἐστι ταῦτα
31 τὰ κτήματα, σὰ τὰ βιβλία, σοὶ οἱ λόγοι. εἶθ᾽,
ὅταν τοῦτον ¹ ἐκπονήσῃ καὶ καταθλήσῃ τὸν
τόπον, πάλιν ἐλθών μοι εἰπάτω "ἐγὼ θέλω μὲν
καὶ ἀπαθὴς εἶναι καὶ ἀτάραχος, θέλω δ᾽ ὡς
εὐσεβὴς καὶ φιλόσοφος καὶ ἐπιμελὴς εἰδέναι τί
μοι πρὸς θεούς ἐστι καθῆκον, τί πρὸς γονεῖς, τί
πρὸς ἀδελφούς, τί πρὸς τὴν πατρίδα, τί πρὸς
32 ξένους." ἔρχου καὶ ἐπὶ τὸν δεύτερον τόπον· σός
33 ἐστι καὶ οὗτος. "ἀλλ᾽ ἤδη καὶ τὸν δεύτερον
τόπον ἐκμεμελέτηκα. ἤθελον δ᾽ ἀσφαλῶς
ἔχειν ² καὶ ἀσείστως ³ καὶ οὐ μόνον ἐγρηγορώς,
ἀλλὰ καὶ καθεύδων καὶ οἰνωμένος καὶ ἐν μελαγ-
χολίᾳ." σὺ θεὸς εἶ, ὦ ἄνθρωπε, σὺ μεγάλας
ἔχεις ἐπιβολάς.

34 Οὔ· ἀλλ᾽ "ἐγὼ θέλω γνῶναι, τί λέγει Χρύσιππος ἐν τοῖς περὶ τοῦ Ψευδομένου." οὐκ
ἀπάγξῃ μετὰ τῆς ἐπιβολῆς ταύτης, τάλας ; καὶ
τί σοι ὄφελος ἔσται ; πενθῶν ἅπαν ἀναγνώσῃ
35 καὶ τρέμων πρὸς ἄλλους ἐρεῖς. οὕτως καὶ ὑμεῖς
ποιεῖτε. "θέλεις ἀναγνῶ σοι, ἀδελφέ, καὶ σὺ
ἐμοί ;" "θαυμαστῶς, ἄνθρωπε, γράφεις·" καὶ
" σὺ μεγάλως εἰς τὸν Ξενοφῶντος χαρακτῆρα,"
36 " σὺ εἰς τὸν Πλάτωνος," "σὺ εἰς τὸν Ἀντισθέ-
νους." εἶτ᾽ ἀλλήλοις ὀνείρους διηγησάμενοι
πάλιν ἐπὶ ταὐτὰ ἐπανέρχεσθε· ὡσαύτως ὀρέ-

---

¹ Schegk and Upton : τοιοῦτον S.
² Added by Sc.   ³ Wolf : ἀσίτως S.

---

¹ Compare I. 18, 23.
² A stock sophism in the form: If a person says, " I am
lying," does he lie or tell the truth ? If he is lying, he
is telling the truth ; if he is telling the truth, he is lying. Cf.

destiny to adorn philosophy, yours are these possessions, yours these books, yours these discourses.
Then, when he has worked his way through this
first field of study and mastered it like an athlete,
let him come to me again and say, " I want, it is
true, to be tranquil and free from turmoil, but I
want also, as a god-fearing man, a philosopher and
a diligent student, to know what is my duty towards
the gods, towards parents, towards brothers, towards
my country, towards strangers." Advance now to
the second field of study ; this also is yours. " Yes,
but I have already studied this second field. What
I wanted was to be secure and unshaken, and that
not merely in my waking hours, but also when
asleep, and drunk, and melancholy-mad."[1] Man,
you are a god, great are the designs you cherish !

No, that is not the way it goes, but someone says,
" I wish to know what Chrysippus means in his
treatise on *The Liar*." [2] If that is your design, go
hang, you wretch ! And what good will knowing
that do you ? With sorrow you will read the whole
treatise, and with trembling you will talk about
it to others. This is the way you also, my hearers,
behave. You say : " Shall I read aloud to you,
brother, and you to me ? " [3] " Man, you write
wonderfully." And again, " You have a great gift
for writing in the style of Xenophon," " You for
that of Plato," " You for that of Antisthenes." And
then, when you have told dreams to one another,
you go back to the same things again ; you have

Von Arnim, *Stoicorum Veterum Fragmenta*, II. 92, frag. 280 ff.
Chrysippus is said to have written six books on the subject,
Diog. Laer. VII. 196. *Cf.* Pease on Cic. *De Div.* II. 11.

[3] That is, each his own compositions, in expectation of
mutual compliments. *Cf.* Hor. *Ep.* II. 2, 87 ff.

γεσθε, ὡσαύτως ἐκκλίνετε, ὁμοίως ὁρμᾶτε, ἐπι-
βάλλεσθε, προτίθεσθε,[1] ταὐτὰ[2] εὔχεσθε, περὶ
37 ταὐτὰ σπουδάζετε. εἶτα οὐδὲ ζητεῖτε τὸν ὑπο-
μνήσοντα ὑμᾶς, ἀλλ' ἄχθεσθε, ἐὰν ἀκούητε
τούτων. εἶτα λέγετε "ἀφιλόστοργος γέρων·
ἐξερχομένου μου οὐκ ἔκλαυσεν οὐδ' εἶπεν 'εἰς
οἵαν περίστασιν ἀπέρχῃ μοι,[3] τέκνον· ἂν σωθῇς,
38 ἅψω λύχνους.'" ταῦτ' ἔστι τὰ τοῦ φιλοστόργου;
μέγα σοι ἀγαθὸν ἔσται σωθέντι τοιούτῳ καὶ
λύχνων ἄξιον. ἀθάνατον γὰρ εἶναί σε δεῖ καὶ
ἄνοσον.

39   Ταύτην οὖν, ὅπερ λέγω, τὴν οἴησιν τὴν τοῦ
δοκεῖν εἰδέναι τι τῶν χρησίμων ἀποβαλόντας[4]
ἔρχεσθαι δεῖ πρὸς τὸν λόγον, ὡς πρὸς τὰ γεω-
40 μετρικὰ προσάγομεν, ὡς πρὸς τὰ μουσικά. εἰ
δὲ μή, οὐδ' ἐγγὺς ἐσόμεθα τῷ προκόψαι, κἂν
πάσας τὰς εἰσαγωγὰς[5] καὶ τὰς συντάξεις τὰς
Χρυσίππου μετὰ τῶν Ἀντιπάτρου καὶ Ἀρχεδήμου
διέλθωμεν.

ιη'. Πῶς ἀγωνιστέον πρὸς τὰς φαντασίας;

1   Πᾶσα ἕξις καὶ δύναμις ὑπὸ τῶν καταλλήλων
ἔργων συνέχεται καὶ αὔξεται, ἡ περιπατητικὴ
ὑπὸ τοῦ περιπατεῖν, ἡ τροχαστικὴ ὑπὸ τοῦ
2 τρέχειν. ἂν θέλῃς ἀναγνωστικὸς εἶναι, ἀναγί-
γνωσκε· ἂν γραφικός, γράφε. ὅταν δὲ τριάκοντα

---

[1] Wolf : προστίθεσθε S.   [2] Schegk and Wolf : ταῦτα S.
[3] Koraes : ἀπέρχομαι S.   [4] Koraes : ἀποβάλλοντας S.
[5] Reiske : συναγωγάς S.

[1] Compare I. 19, 24.

exactly the same desires as before, the same
aversions, in the same way you make your choices,
your designs, and your purposes, you pray for the
same things and are interested in the same things.
In the second place, you do not even look for
anybody to give you advice, but you are annoyed
if you are told what I am telling you. Again, you
say: "He is an old man without the milk of human
kindness in him; he did not weep when I left, nor
say, 'I fear you are going into a very difficult
situation, my son; if you come through safely, I
will light lamps.'" [1] Is this what a man with the
milk of human kindness in him would say? It will
be a great piece of good luck for a person like you
to come through safely, a thing worth lighting
lamps to celebrate! Surely you ought to be
free from death and free from disease!

It is this conceit of fancying that we know something useful, that, as I have said, we ought to
cast aside before we come to philosophy, as we do
in the case of geometry and music. Otherwise we
shall never even come near to making progress, even
if we go through all the Introductions and the
Treatises of Chrysippus, with those of Antipater and
Archedemus thrown in!

CHAPTER XVIII

How must we struggle against our external impressions?

EVERY habit and faculty is confirmed and
strengthened by the corresponding actions, that
of walking by walking, that of running by running.
If you wish to be a good reader, read; if you wish
to be a good writer, write. If you should give up

ἐφεξῆς ἡμέρας μὴ ἀναγνῷς, ἀλλ' ἄλλο τι πράξῃς,
3 γνώσῃ τὸ γινόμενον. οὕτως κἂν ἀναπέσῃς δέκα
ἡμέρας, ἀναστὰς ἐπιχείρησον μακροτέραν ὁδὸν
περιπατῆσαι καὶ ὄψει, πῶς σου τὰ σκέλη παρα-
4 λύεται. καθόλου οὖν εἴ τι ποιεῖν ἐθέλῃς, ἑκτικὸν
ποίει αὐτό· εἴ τι μὴ ποιεῖν ἐθέλῃς, μὴ ποίει αὐτό,
ἀλλ' ἔθισον ἄλλο τι πράττειν μᾶλλον ἀντ' αὐτοῦ.
5 οὕτως ἔχει καὶ ἐπὶ τῶν ψυχικῶν· ὅταν ὀργισθῇς,
γίγνωσκε ὅτι οὐ μόνον σοι τοῦτο γέγονεν κακόν,
ἀλλ' ὅτι καὶ τὴν ἕξιν ηὔξησας καὶ ὡς πυρὶ
6 φρύγανα παρέβαλες. ὅταν ἡττηθῇς τινος ἐν
συνουσίᾳ, μὴ τὴν μίαν ἧτταν ταύτην λογίζου,
ἀλλ' ὅτι καὶ τὴν ἀκρασίαν σου τέτροφας, ἐπηύ-
7 ξησας. ἀδύνατον γὰρ ἀπὸ τῶν καταλλήλων
ἔργων μὴ καὶ τὰς ἕξεις καὶ τὰς δυνάμεις τὰς μὲν
ἐμφύεσθαι μὴ πρότερον οὔσας, τὰς δ' ἐπιτείνεσθαι
καὶ ἰσχυροποιεῖσθαι.

8 Οὕτως ἀμέλει καὶ τὰ ἀρρωστήματα ὑποφύε-
σθαι λέγουσιν οἱ φιλόσοφοι. ὅταν γὰρ ἅπαξ
ἐπιθυμήσῃς ἀργυρίου, ἂν μὲν προσαχθῇ λόγος
εἰς αἴσθησιν ἄξων[1] τοῦ κακοῦ, πέπαυταί τε ἡ
ἐπιθυμία καὶ τὸ ἡγεμονικὸν ἡμῶν εἰς τὸ ἐξαρχῆς
9 ἀποκατέστη· ἐὰν δὲ μηδὲν προσαγάγῃς εἰς θερα-
πείαν, οὐκέτι εἰς ταὐτὰ ἐπάνεισιν, ἀλλὰ πάλιν
ἐρεθισθὲν ὑπὸ τῆς καταλλήλου φαντασίας θᾶττον
ἢ πρότερον ἐξήφθη πρὸς τὴν ἐπιθυμίαν. καὶ
τούτου συνεχῶς γινομένου τυλοῦται λοιπὸν καὶ

---

[1] Wolf: ἀξιῶν S.

reading for thirty days one after the other, and
be engaged in something else, you will know what
happens. So also if you lie in bed for ten days, get
up and try to take a rather long walk, and you will
see how wobbly your legs are. In general, therefore, if you want to do something, make a habit
of it ; if you want not to do something, refrain from
doing it, and accustom yourself to something else
instead. The same principle holds true in the
affairs of the mind also ; when you are angry, you
may be sure, not merely that this evil has befallen
you, but also that you have strengthened the habit,
and have, as it were, added fuel to the flame.
When you have yielded to someone in carnal intercourse, do not count merely this one defeat, but
count also the fact that you have fed your incon-
tinence, you have given it additional strength. For
it is inevitable that some habits and faculties should,
in consequence of the corresponding actions, spring
up, though they did not exist before, and that others
which were already there should be intensified and
made strong.

In this way, without doubt, the infirmities of our
mind and character spring up, as the philosophers
say. For when once you conceive a desire for
money, if reason be applied to bring you to a
realization of the evil, both the passion is stilled and
our governing principle is restored to its original
authority ; but if you do not apply a remedy, your
governing principle does not revert to its previous
condition, but, on being aroused again by the corresponding external impression, it bursts into the flame
of desire more quickly than it did before. And
if this happens over and over again, the next stage

10 τὸ ἀρρώστημα βεβαιοῖ τὴν φιλαργυρίαν. ὁ γὰρ
πυρέξας, εἶτα παυσάμενος οὐχ ὁμοίως ἔχει τῷ
πρὸ τοῦ πυρέξαι, ἂν μή τι θεραπευθῇ εἰς ἅπαν.
11 τοιοῦτόν τι καὶ ἐπὶ τῶν τῆς ψυχῆς παθῶν
γίνεται. ἴχνη τινὰ καὶ μώλωπες ἀπολείπονται
ἐν αὐτῇ, οὓς εἰ μή τις ἐξαλείψῃ καλῶς, πάλιν
κατὰ τῶν αὐτῶν μαστιγωθεὶς οὐκέτι μώλωπας,
12 ἀλλ' ἕλκη ποιεῖ. εἰ οὖν θέλεις μὴ εἶναι ὀργίλος,
μὴ τρέφε σου τὴν ἕξιν, μηδὲν αὐτῇ παράβαλλε
αὐξητικόν. τὴν πρώτην ἡσύχασον καὶ τὰς
13 ἡμέρας ἀρίθμει ἃς οὐκ ὠργίσθης. "καθ' ἡμέραν
εἰώθειν ὀργίζεσθαι, νῦν παρ' ἡμέραν, εἶτα παρὰ
δύο, εἶτα παρὰ τρεῖς." ἂν δὲ καὶ τριάκοντα παρα-
λίπῃς, ἐπίθυσον τῷ θεῷ. ἡ γὰρ ἕξις ἐκλύεται
τὴν πρώτην, εἶτα καὶ παντελῶς ἀναιρεῖται.
14 "σήμερον οὐκ ἐλυπήθην οὐδ' αὔριον οὐδ' ἐφεξῆς
διμήνῳ καὶ τριμήνῳ· ἀλλὰ προσέσχον γενομένων
τινῶν ἐρεθιστικῶν." γίγνωσκε ὅτι κομψῶς σοί
ἐστιν.

15 Σήμερον καλὸν ἰδὼν ἢ καλὴν οὐκ εἶπον αὐτὸς
ἐμαυτῷ ὅτι "ὤφελόν τις μετὰ ταύτης ἐκοιμήθη"
καὶ "μακάριος ὁ ἀνὴρ αὐτῆς·" ὁ γὰρ τοῦτ' εἰπὼν
16 "μακάριος" καὶ "ὁ μοιχός"· οὐδὲ τὰ ἑξῆς ἀναζω-
γραφῶ, παροῦσαν αὐτὴν καὶ ἀποδυομένην καὶ
17 παρακατακλινομένην. καταψῶ τὴν κορυφήν μου
καὶ λέγω· εὖ, Ἐπίκτητε, κομψὸν σοφισμάτιον
ἔλυσας, πολλῷ κομψότερον τοῦ Κυριεύοντος.
18 ἂν δὲ καὶ βουλομένου τοῦ γυναικαρίου καὶ νεύον-

---

¹ See II. 19, especially 1–9.

is that a callousness results and the infirmity strengthens the avarice. For the man who has had a fever, and then recovered, is not the same as he was before the fever, unless he has experienced a complete cure. Something like this happens also with the affections of the mind. Certain imprints and weals are left behind on the mind, and unless a man erases them perfectly, the next time he is scourged upon the old scars, he has weals no longer but wounds. If, therefore, you wish not to be hot-tempered, do not feed your habit, set before it nothing on which it can grow. As the first step, keep quiet and count the days on which you have not been angry. "I used to be angry every day, after that every other day, then every third, and then every fourth day." If you go as much as thirty days without a fit of anger, sacrifice to God. For the habit is first weakened and then utterly destroyed. "To-day I was not grieved" (and so the next day, and thereafter for two or three months); "but I was on my guard when certain things happened that were capable of provoking grief." Know that things are going splendidly with you.

To-day when I saw a handsome lad or a handsome woman I did not say to myself, "Would that a man might sleep with her," and "Her husband is a happy man," for the man who uses the expression "happy" of the husband means "Happy is the adulterer" also; I do not even picture to myself the next scene—the woman herself in my presence, disrobing and lying down by my side. I pat myself on the head and say, Well done, Epictetus, you have solved a clever problem, one much more clever than the so-called "Master"[1]: But when the wench is

τος καὶ προσπέμποντος, ἂν δὲ καὶ ἁπτομένου καὶ
συνεγγίζοντος ἀπόσχωμαι καὶ νικήσω, τοῦτο μὲν
ἤδη τὸ σόφισμα ὑπὲρ τὸν Ψευδόμενον, ὑπὲρ τὸν
Ἡσυχάζοντα. ἐπὶ τούτῳ καὶ μέγα φρονεῖν ἄξιον.
οὐκ ἐπὶ τῷ τὸν Κυριεύοντα ἐρωτῆσαι.

19 Πῶς οὖν γένηται τοῦτο; θέλησον ἀρέσαι αὐτός
ποτε σεαυτῷ, θέλησον καλὸς φανῆναι τῷ θεῷ·
ἐπιθύμησον καθαρὸς μετὰ καθαροῦ σαυτοῦ γενέ-
20 σθαι καὶ μετὰ τοῦ θεοῦ. εἶθ' ὅταν προσπίπτῃ
σοί τις φαντασία τοιαύτη, Πλάτων μὲν ὅτι ἴθι
ἐπὶ τὰς ἀποδιοπομπήσεις, ἴθι ἐπὶ θεῶν ἀποτρο-
21 παίων ἱερὰ ἱκέτης· ἀρκεῖ κἂν ἐπὶ τὰς τῶν καλῶν
καὶ ἀγαθῶν ἀνδρῶν συνουσίας ἀποχωρήσας πρὸς
τούτῳ γίνῃ ἀντεξετάζων, ἄν τε τῶν ζώντων τινὰ
22 ἔχῃς ἄν τε τῶν ἀποθανόντων. ἄπελθε πρὸς
Σωκράτη καὶ ἴδε αὐτὸν συγκατακείμενον Ἀλκι-
βιάδῃ καὶ διαπαίζοντα αὐτοῦ τὴν ὥραν. ἐνθυμή-
θητι οἵαν νίκην ποτὲ ἔγνω ἐκεῖνος νενικηκότα
ἑαυτόν, οἷα Ὀλύμπια, πόστος ἀφ' Ἡρακλέους
ἐγένετο· ἵνα τις, νὴ τοὺς θεούς, δικαίως
ἀσπάζηται αὐτὸν "χαῖρε, παράδοξε," οὐχὶ τοὺς
σαπροὺς τούτους πύκτας καὶ παγκρατιαστὰς
οὐδὲ τοὺς ὁμοίους αὐτοῖς, τοὺς μονομάχους·
23 ταῦτα ἀντιθεὶς νικήσεις τὴν φαντασίαν, οὐχ

---

[1] For *The Liar* see on II. 17, 34. "The Quiescent" was
the somewhat desperate solution of Chrysippus for the
sorites fallacy. On being asked whether two grains made a
heap, then three, and so forth, he would finally stop
answering the questions at all ! Cicero, *Acad. Post.* II. 93.

[2] *Laws*, IX. 854B (slightly modified).

[3] Plato, *Symposium*, 218D ff.

[4] As traditional founder and first victor at the Olympic
games ; all others might be enumerated in order beginning

not only willing, but nods to me and sends for me, yes, and when she even lays hold upon me and snuggles up to me, if I still hold aloof and conquer, this has become a solved problem greater than *The Liar*, and *The Quiescent*.[1] On this score a man has a right to be proud indeed, but not about his proposing " The Master " problem.

How, then, may this be done? Make it your wish finally to satisfy your own self, make it your wish to appear beautiful in the sight of God. Set your desire upon becoming pure in the presence of your pure self and of God. " Then when an external impression of that sort comes suddenly upon you," says Plato,[2] " go and offer an expiatory sacrifice, go and make offering as a suppliant to the sanctuaries of the gods who avert evil "; it is enough if you only withdraw " to the society of the good and excellent men," and set yourself to comparing your conduct with theirs, whether you take as your model one of the living, or one of the dead. Go to Socrates and mark him as he lies down beside Alcibiades[3] and makes light of his youthful beauty. Bethink yourself how great a victory he once won and knew it himself, like an Olympic victory, and what his rank was, counting in order from Heracles[4]; so that, by the gods, one might justly greet him with the salutation, " Hail, wondrous man ! " for he was victor over something more than these rotten boxers and pancratiasts, and the gladiators who resemble them. If you confront your external impression with such thoughts, you will overcome it, and not

with him, although the ordinary count was from Coroebus of Elis, supposed to have been winner of the footrace in 776 B.C.

24 ἑλκυσθήσῃ ὑπ' αὐτῆς. τὸ πρῶτον δ' ὑπὸ τῆς
ὀξύτητος μὴ συναρπασθῇς, ἀλλ' εἰπὲ " ἔκδεξαί
με μικρόν, φαντασία· ἄφες ἴδω τίς εἶ καὶ περὶ
25 τίνος, ἄφες σε δοκιμάσω." καὶ τὸ λοιπὸν μὴ
ἐφῇς αὐτῇ προάγειν ἀναζωγραφούσῃ τὰ ἑξῆς.
εἰ δὲ μή, οἴχεταί σε ἔχουσα ὅπου ἂν θέλῃ. ἀλλὰ
μᾶλλον ἄλλην τινὰ ἀντεισάγαγε καλὴν καὶ
γενναίαν φαντασίαν καὶ ταύτην τὴν ῥυπαρὰν
26 ἔκβαλε. κἂν ἐθισθῇς οὕτως γυμνάζεσθαι, ὄψει,
οἷοι ὦμοι γίνονται, οἷα νεῦρα, οἷοι τόνοι· νῦν δὲ
μόνον τὰ λογάρια καὶ πλέον οὐδὲ ἕν.

27 Οὗτός ἐστιν ὁ ταῖς ἀληθείαις ἀσκητὴς ὁ
πρὸς τὰς τοιαύτας φαντασίας γυμνάζων ἑαυτόν.
28 μεῖνον, τάλας, μὴ συναρπασθῇς. μέγας ὁ ἀγών
ἐστιν, θεῖον τὸ ἔργον, ὑπὲρ βασιλείας, ὑπὲρ
29 ἐλευθερίας, ὑπὲρ εὐροίας, ὑπὲρ ἀταραξίας. τοῦ
θεοῦ μέμνησο, ἐκεῖνον ἐπικαλοῦ βοηθὸν καὶ
παραστάτην ὡς τοὺς Διοσκόρους ἐν χειμῶνι οἱ
πλέοντες. ποῖος γὰρ μείζων χειμὼν ἢ ὁ ἐκ
φαντασιῶν ἰσχυρῶν καὶ ἐκκρουστικῶν τοῦ λόγου·
αὐτὸς γὰρ ὁ χειμὼν τί ἄλλο ἐστὶν ἢ φαντασία ;
30 ἐπεί τοι ἆρον τὸν φόβον τοῦ θανάτου καὶ φέρε
ὅσας θέλεις βροντὰς καὶ ἀστραπὰς καὶ γνώσῃ,
ὅση γαλήνη ἐστὶν ἐν τῷ ἡγεμονικῷ καὶ εὐδία.
31 ἂν δ' ἅπαξ ἡττηθεὶς εἴπῃς ὅτι ὕστερον νικήσεις,
εἶτα πάλιν τὸ αὐτό, ἴσθι ὅτι οὕτως ποθ' ἕξεις
κακῶς καὶ ἀσθενῶς, ὥστε μηδ' ἐφιστάνειν ὕστερον

---

[1] That is, reason.

be carried away by it. But, to begin with, be not swept off your feet, I beseech you, by the vividness of the impression, but say, "Wait for me a little, O impression; allow me to see who you are, and what you are an impression of; allow me to put you to the test." And after that, do not suffer it to lead you on by picturing to you what will follow. Otherwise, it will take possession of you and go off with you wherever it will. But do you rather introduce and set over against it some fair and noble impression, and throw out this filthy one. And if you form the habit of taking such exercises, you will see what mighty shoulders you develop, what sinews, what vigour; but as it is, you have merely your philosophic quibbles, and nothing more.

The man who exercises himself against such external impressions is the true athlete in training. Hold, unhappy man; be not swept along with your impressions! Great is the struggle, divine the task; the prize is a kingdom, freedom, serenity, peace. Remember God; call upon Him to help you and stand by your side, just as voyagers, in a storm, call upon the Dioscuri. For what storm is greater than that stirred up by powerful impressions which unseat the reason? As for the storm itself, what else is it but an external impression? To prove this, just take away the fear of death, and then bring on as much thunder and lightning as you please, and you will realize how great is the calm, how fair the weather, in your governing principle.[1] But if you be once defeated and say that by and by you will overcome, and then a second time do the same thing, know that at last you will be in so wretched a state and so weak that by and by you will not so

357

ὅτι ἁμαρτάνεις, ἀλλὰ καὶ ἀπολογίας ἄρξῃ πορί-
32 ζειν ὑπ ρ τοῦ πράγματος· καὶ τότε βεβαιώσεις
τὸ τοῦ Ἡσιόδου, ὅτι ἀληθές ἐστιν

αἰεὶ δ' ἀμβολιεργὸς ἀνὴρ ἄτῃσι παλαίει.

ιθ'. Πρὸς τοὺς μέχρι λόγου μόνον ἀναλαμ-
βάνοντας τὰ τῶν φιλοσόφων.

1 Ὁ κυριεύων λόγος ἀπὸ τοιούτων τινῶν ἀφορμῶν
ἠρωτῆσθαι φαίνεται· κοινῆς γὰρ οὔσης μάχης
τοῖς τρισὶ τούτοις πρὸς ἄλληλα, τῷ πᾶν παρεληλυθὸς ἀληθὲς ἀναγκαῖον εἶναι καὶ τῷ δυνατῷ
ἀδύνατον μὴ ἀκολουθεῖν καὶ τῷ δυνατὸν[1] εἶναι
ὃ οὔτ' ἔστι ἀληθὲς οὔτ' ἔσται, συνιδὼν τὴν
μάχην ταύτην ὁ Διόδορος τῇ τῶν πρώτων δυεῖν
πιθανότητι συνεχρήσατο πρὸς παράστασιν τοῦ
μηδὲν εἶναι δυνατόν, ὃ οὔτ' ἔστιν ἀληθὲς οὔτ'
2 ἔσται. λοιπὸν ὁ μέν τις ταῦτα τηρήσει τῶν
δυεῖν, ὅτι ἔστι τέ τι δυνατόν, ὃ οὔτ' ἔστιν ἀληθὲς
οὔτ' ἔσται, καὶ δυνατῷ ἀδύνατον οὐκ ἀκολουθεῖ·
οὐ πᾶν δὲ παρεληλυθὸς ἀληθὲς ἀναγκαῖόν ἐστιν,

[1] Before this word there is an erasure of two letters
in S.

---

[1] *Works and Days*, 413.
[2] So called because thought to be unanswerable ; it involved the questions of " the possible " and " the necessary,"
in other words, chance and fate, freewill and determination.
The matter was first set forth in a note contributed to
Upton's edition of Epictetus by James Harris, and re-
published, with additions, by Schweighäuser. Definitive
is the discussion by Eduard Zeller, *Sitzungsber. der Berliner*

much as notice that you are doing wrong, but you will even begin to offer arguments in justification of your conduct; and then you will confirm the truth of the saying of Hesiod:

Forever with misfortunes dire must he who loiters cope.[1]

CHAPTER XIX

To those who take up the teachings of the philosophers only to talk about them

THE "Master argument"[2] appears to have been propounded on the strength of some such principles as the following. Since there is a general contradiction with one another[3] between these three propositions, to wit: (1) Everything true as an event in the past is necessary, and (2) An impossible does not follow a possible, and (3) What is not true now and never will be, is nevertheless possible, Diodorus, realizing this contradiction, used the plausibility of the first two propositions to establish the principle, Nothing is possible which is neither true now nor ever will be. But one man will maintain, among the possible combinations of two at a time, the following, namely, (3) Something is possible, which is not true now and never will be, and (2) An impossible does not follow a possible; yet he will not grant the third proposition (1), Everything true as an event in the past is necessary, which is what

Akad. 1882, 151–9. See also his *Philosophie der Griechen*[4], II, 1, 269–70. For the context in which these problems appear, see also Von Arnim, *Stoicorum Veterum Fragmenta*, I. 109; II. 92 f.

[3] That is, any two are supposed to contradict the third.

καθάπερ οἱ περὶ Κλεάνθην φέρεσθαι δοκοῦσιν,
3 οἷς ἐπὶ πολὺ συνηγόρησεν Ἀντίπατρος. οἱ δὲ
τἄλλα δύο, ὅτι δυνατόν τ' ἐστίν, ὃ οὔτ' ἔστιν
ἀληθὲς οὔτ' ἔσται, καὶ πᾶν παρεληλυθὸς ἀληθὲς
ἀναγκαῖόν ἐστιν, δυνατῷ δ' ἀδύνατον ἀκολουθεῖ.
4 τὰ τρία δ' ἐκεῖνα τηρῆσαι ἀμήχανον διὰ τὸ
κοινὴν εἶναι αὐτῶν μάχην.

5 Ἂν οὖν τίς μου πύθηται "σὺ δὲ ποῖα αὐτῶν
τηρεῖς;" ἀποκρινοῦμαι πρὸς αὐτὸν ὅτι οὐκ οἶδα·
παρείληφα δ' ἱστορίαν τοιαύτην, ὅτι Διόδωρος
μὲν ἐκεῖνα ἐτήρει, οἱ δὲ περὶ Πανθοίδην οἶμαι
καὶ Κλεάνθην τὰ ἄλλα, οἱ δὲ περὶ Χρύσιππον
6 τὰ ἄλλα. "σὺ οὖν τί;" οὐδὲ γέγονα πρὸς
τούτῳ, τῷ βασανίσαι τὴν ἐμαυτοῦ φαντασίαν
καὶ συγκρῖναι τὰ λεγόμενα καὶ δόγμα τι ἐμαυτοῦ
ποιήσασθαι κατὰ τὸν τόπον. διὰ τοῦτο οὐδὲν
7 διαφέρω τοῦ γραμματικοῦ. "τίς ἦν ὁ τοῦ
Ἕκτορος πατήρ;" "Πρίαμος." "τίνες ἀδελφοί;"
"Ἀλέξανδρος καὶ Δηίφοβος." "μήτηρ δ' αὐτῶν
τίς;" "Ἑκάβη. παρείληφα ταύτην τὴν ἱστορίαν." "παρὰ τίνος;" "παρ' Ὁμήρου. γράφει
δὲ περὶ τῶν αὐτῶν δοκῶ καὶ Ἑλλάνικος καὶ εἴ
8 τις ἄλλος τοιοῦτος." κἀγὼ περὶ τοῦ Κυριεύοντος
τί ἄλλο ἔχω ἀνωτέρω; ἀλλ' ἂν ὦ κενός, μάλιστα
ἐπὶ συμποσίῳ καταπλήσσομαι τοὺς παρόντας,
9 ἐξαριθμούμενος τοὺς γεγραφότας. "γέγραφεν
δὲ καὶ Χρύσιππος θαυμαστῶς ἐν τῷ πρώτῳ περὶ

---

[1] That is, deny (2) that "An impossible does *not* follow a
possible."

[2] That is, each pair is in conflict with the third.

Cleanthes and his group, whom Antipater has stoutly supported, seem to think. But others will maintain the other two propositions, (3) A thing is possible which is not true now and never will be, and (1) Everything true as an event in the past is necessary, and then will assert that, An impossible *does* follow a possible.[1] But there is no way by which one can maintain all three of these propositions, because of their mutual contradiction.[2]

If, then, someone asks me, "But which pair of these do you yourself maintain?" I shall answer him that I do not know; but I have received the following account: Diodorus used to maintain one pair, Panthoides and his group, I believe, and Cleanthes another, and Chrysippus and his group the third. "What, then, is *your* opinion?" I do not know, and I was not made for this purpose—to test my own external impression upon the subject, to compare the statements of others, and to form a judgement of my own. For this reason I am no better than the grammarian. When asked, "Who was the father of Hector?" he replied, "Priam." "Who were his brothers?" "Alexander and Deïphobus." "And who was their mother?" "Hecuba. This is the account that I have received." "From whom?" "From Homer," he said. "And Hellanicus also, I believe, writes about these same matters, and possibly others like him." And so it is with me about the "Master Argument"; what further have I to say about it? But if I am a vain person, I can astonish the company, especially at a banquet, by enumerating those who have written on the subject. "Chrysippus also has written admirably on this topic in the first book of his treatise

Δυνατῶν. καὶ Κλεάνθης δ' ἰδίᾳ γέγραφεν περὶ
τούτου καὶ Ἀρχέδημος. γέγραφεν δὲ καὶ Ἀντίπατρος, οὐ μόνον δ' ἐν τοῖς περὶ Δυνατῶν, ἀλλὰ
10 καὶ κατ' ἰδίαν ἐν τοῖς περὶ τοῦ Κυριεύοντος. οὐκ
ἀνέγνωκας τὴν σύνταξιν;" "οὐκ ἀνέγνωκα."
"ἀνάγνωθι." καὶ τί ὠφεληθήσεται; φλυαρό-
τερος ἔσται καὶ ἀκαιρότερος ἢ νῦν ἐστιν. σοὶ
γὰρ τί ἄλλο προσγέγονεν ἀναγνόντι; ποῖον
δόγμα πεποίησαι κατὰ τὸν τόπον; ἀλλ' ἐρεῖς
ἡμῖν Ἑλένην καὶ Πρίαμον καὶ τὴν τῆς Καλυψοῦς
νῆσον τὴν οὔτε γενομένην οὔτ' ἐσομένην.

11 Καὶ ἐνταῦθα μὲν οὐδὲν μέγα τῆς ἱστορίας
κρατεῖν, ἴδιον δὲ δόγμα μηδὲν πεποιῆσθαι. ἐπὶ
τῶν ἠθικῶν δὲ πάσχομεν αὐτὸ πολὺ μᾶλλον ἢ
12 ἐπὶ τούτων. "εἰπέ μοι περὶ ἀγαθῶν καὶ κακῶν."
"ἄκουε·

Ἰλιόθεν με φέρων ἄνεμος Κικόνεσσι πέλασσεν.

13 τῶν ὄντων τὰ μέν ἐστιν ἀγαθά, τὰ δὲ κακά, τὰ
δ' ἀδιάφορα. ἀγαθὰ μὲν οὖν αἱ ἀρεταὶ καὶ τὰ
μετέχοντα αὐτῶν, κακὰ δὲ κακίαι καὶ τὰ μετέχοντα κακίας, ἀδιάφορα δὲ τὰ μεταξὺ τούτων,
πλοῦτος, ὑγίεια, ζωή, θάνατος, ἡδονή, πόνος."
14 "πόθεν οἶδας;" "Ἑλλάνικος λέγει ἐν τοῖς
Αἰγυπτιακοῖς." τί γὰρ διαφέρει τοῦτο εἰπεῖν ἢ
ὅτι Διογένης ἐν τῇ Ἠθικῇ ἢ Χρύσιππος ἢ
Κλεάνθης; βεβασάνικας οὖν τι αὐτῶν καὶ δόγμα

---

[1] That is, instead of speaking from your own knowledge
or belief, you will merely recite the opinions of others.

[2] Homer, *Od.*, IX. 39. The inappropriate quotation (as
with Hellanicus below) shows the absurdity of such a
treatment of ethical questions.

On Things Possible. And Cleanthes has written a special work on the subject, and Archedemus. Antipater also has written, not only in his book *On Things Possible*, but also a separate monograph in his discussion of *The Master Argument*. Have you not read the treatise?" "I have not read it." "Then read it." And what good will it do him? He will be more trifling and tiresome than he is already. You, for example, what have you gained by the reading of it? What judgement have you formed on the subject? Nay, you will tell us of Helen, and Priam, and the island of Calypso[1] which never was and never will be!

And in the field of literary history, indeed, it is of no great consequence that you master the received account without having formed any judgement of your own. But in questions of conduct we suffer from this fault much more than we do in literary matters. "Tell me about things good and evil." "Listen:

The wind that blew me from the Trojan shore
Brought me to the Ciconians.[2]

Of things some are good, others bad, and yet others indifferent. Now the virtues and everything that shares in them are good, while vices and everything that shares in vice are evil, and what falls in between these, namely, wealth, health, life, death, pleasures, pain, are indifferent." "Where do you get that knowledge?" "Hellanicus says so in his *History of Egypt*." For what difference does it make whether you say this, or that Diogenes says so in his *Treatise on Ethics*, or Chrysippus, or Cleanthes? Have you, then, tested any of these statements and

15 σεαυτοῦ πεποίησαι; δείκνυε πῶς εἴωθας ἐν πλοίῳ
χειμάζεσθαι.¹ μέμνησαι ταύτης τῆς διαιρέσεως,
ὅταν ψοφήσῃ τὸ ἱστίον καὶ ἀνακραυγάσαντί σοι
κακόσχολός πως² παραστὰς εἴπῃ "λέγε μοι
τοὺς θεούς σοι οἷα³ πρῴην ἔλεγες· μή τι κακία⁴

16 ἐστὶ τὸ ναυαγῆσαι, μή τι κακίας μετέχον;" οὐκ
ἄρας ξύλον ἐνσείσεις αὐτῷ; "τί ἡμῖν καὶ σοί,
ἄνθρωπε; ἀπολλύμεθα καὶ σὺ ἐλθὼν παίζεις."

17 ἂν δέ σε ὁ⁵ Καῖσαρ μεταπέμψηται κατηγο-
ρούμενον, μέμνησαι τῆς διαιρέσεως· ἂν τίς σοι
εἰσιόντι καὶ ὠχριῶντι ἅμα καὶ τρέμοντι προσ-
ελθὼν εἴπῃ "τί τρέμεις, ἄνθρωπε; περὶ τίνων
σοί ἐστιν ὁ λόγος; μή τι ἔσω ὁ Καῖσαρ ἀρετὴν

18 καὶ κακίαν τοῖς εἰσερχομένοις δίδωσι;" "τί μοι
ἐμπαίζεις καὶ σὺ πρὸς τοῖς ἐμοῖς κακοῖς;"
"ὅμως, φιλόσοφε, εἰπέ μοι, τί τρέμεις; οὐχὶ
θάνατός ἐστι τὸ κινδυνευόμενον ἢ δεσμωτήριον
ἢ πόνος τοῦ σώματος ἢ φυγὴ ἢ ἀδοξία; τί γὰρ
ἄλλο; μή τι κακία, μή τι μέτοχον κακίας; σὺ

19 οὖν τίνα ταῦτα ἔλεγες;" "τί ἐμοὶ καὶ σοί,
ἄνθρωπε; ἀρκεῖ ἐμοὶ τὰ ἐμὰ κακά." καὶ καλῶς
λέγεις. ἀρκεῖ γάρ σοι τὰ σὰ κακά, ἡ ἀγένεια,
ἡ δειλία, ἡ ἀλαζονεία, ἣν ἠλαζονεύου ἐν τῇ σχολῇ
καθήμενος. τί τοῖς ἀλλοτρίοις ἐκαλλωπίζου; τί
Στωικὸν ἔλεγες σεαυτόν;

¹ Restored by Bentley from Gellius, *Noctes Atticae*, I. 2, 8:
γυμνάζεσθαι *S*.   ² Preserved by Gellius: om. *S*.
³ Bentley: σοι, & Gellius, οἷα *S*.
⁴ Bentley: κακεία Gellius, κακίας *S*.
⁵ Preserved by Gellius: om. *S*.

have you formed your own judgement upon them?
Show me how you are in the habit of conducting
yourself in a storm on board ship. Do you bear
in mind this logical distinction between good and
evil when the sail crackles, and you have screamed
and some fellow-passenger, untimely humorous,
comes up and says, "Tell me, I beseech you by
the gods, just what you were saying a little while
ago. Is it a vice to suffer shipwreck? Is there
any vice in that?" Will you not pick up a piece of
wood and cudgel him? "What have we to do with
you, fellow? We are perishing and you come and
crack jokes!" And if Caesar sends for you to
answer an accusation, do you bear in mind this
distinction? Suppose someone approaches you when
you are going in pale and trembling, and says,
"Why are you trembling, fellow? What is the
affair that concerns you? Does Caesar inside the
palace bestow virtue and vice upon those who
appear before him?" "Why do you also make
mock of me and add to my other ills?" "But yet,
philosopher, tell me, why are you trembling? Is
not the danger death, or prison, or bodily pain, or
exile, or disrepute? Why, what else can it be?
Is it a vice at all, or anything that shares in
vice? What was it, then, that *you* used to call
these things?" "What have I to do with you,
fellow? My own evils are enough for me." And
in that you are right. For your own evils *are*
enough for you—your baseness, your cowardice, the
bragging that you indulged in when you were sitting in the lecture room. Why did you pride yourself upon things that were not your own? Why
did you call yourself a Stoic?

20 Τηρεῖτε οὕτως ἑαυτοὺς ἐν οἷς ἐπράσσετε καὶ
εὑρήσετε τίνος ἔσθ' αἱρέσεως. τοὺς πλείστους
ὑμῶν Ἐπικουρείους εὑρήσετε, ὀλίγους τινὰς
21 Περιπατητικοὺς καὶ τούτους ἐκλελυμένους. ποῦ
γὰρ ἵν' ὑμεῖς τὴν ἀρετὴν πᾶσιν τοῖς ἄλλοις ἴσην
ἢ καὶ κρείττονα ἔργῳ ὑπολάβητε; Στωικὸν δὲ
22 δείξατέ μοι, εἴ τινα ἔχητε. ποῦ ἢ πῶς; ἀλλὰ
τὰ λογάρια τὰ Στωικὰ λέγοντας μυρίους. τὰ
γὰρ Ἐπικούρεια αὐτοὶ οὗτοι χεῖρον λέγουσι;
τὰ γὰρ Περιπατητικὰ οὐ καὶ αὐτὰ ὁμοίως ἀκρι-
23 βοῦσιν; τίς οὖν ἐστι Στωικός; ὡς λέγομεν
ἀνδριάντα Φειδιακὸν τὸν τετυπωμένον κατὰ τὴν
τέχνην τὴν Φειδίου, οὕτως τινά μοι δείξατε κατὰ
24 τὰ δόγματα ἃ λαλεῖ τετυπωμένον. δείξατέ μοί
τινα νοσοῦντα καὶ εὐτυχοῦντα, κινδυνεύοντα
καὶ εὐτυχοῦντα, ἀποθνήσκοντα καὶ εὐτυχοῦντα,
πεφυγαδευμένον καὶ εὐτυχοῦντα, ἀδοξοῦντα καὶ
εὐτυχοῦντα. δείξατ'· ἐπιθυμῶ τινα νὴ τοὺς
25 θεοὺς ἰδεῖν Στωικόν. ἀλλ' οὐκ ἔχετε τὸν τετυπωμένον δεῖξαι· τόν γε τυπούμενον δείξατε, τὸν
ἐπὶ ταῦτα κεκλικότα. εὐεργετήσατέ με· μὴ
φθονήσητε ἀνθρώπῳ γέροντι ἰδεῖν θέαμα, ὃ μέχρι
26 νῦν οὐκ εἶδον. οἴεσθε ὅτι τὸν Δία τὸν Φειδίου
δείξετε ἢ τὴν Ἀθηνᾶν, ἐλεφάντινον καὶ χρυσοῦν
κατασκεύασμα; ψυχὴν δειξάτω τις ὑμῶν
ἀνθρώπου θέλοντος ὁμογνωμονῆσαι τῷ θεῷ καὶ
μηκέτι μήτε θεὸν μήτ' ἄνθρωπον μέμφεσθαι, μὴ
ἀποτυχεῖν τινος, μὴ περιπεσεῖν τινι, μὴ ὀργι-

---

¹ An early Christian scholiast remarks at this point
"And I would fain see a monk."

Observe yourselves thus in your actions and you will find out to what sect of the philosophers you belong. You will find that most of you are Epicureans, some few Peripatetics, but these without any backbone; for wherein do you in fact show that you consider virtue equal to all things else, or even superior? But as for a Stoic, show me one if you can! Where, or how? Nay, but you can show me thousands who recite the petty arguments of the Stoics. Yes, but do these same men recite the petty arguments of the Epicureans any less well? Do they not handle with the same precision the petty arguments of the Peripatetics also? Who, then, is a Stoic? As we call a statue "Pheidian" that has been fashioned according to the art of Pheidias, in that sense show me a man fashioned according to the judgements which he utters. Show me a man who though sick is happy, though in danger is happy, though dying is happy, though condemned to exile is happy, though in disrepute is happy. Show him! By the gods, I would fain see a Stoic![1] But you cannot show me a man completely so fashioned; then show me at least one who is becoming so fashioned, one who has begun to tend in that direction; do me this favour; do not begrudge an old man the sight of that spectacle which to this very day I have never seen. Do you fancy that you are going to show me the Zeus or the Athena of Pheidias, a creation of ivory and gold? Let one of you show me the soul of a man who wishes to be of one mind with God, and never again to blame either God or man, to fail in nothing that he would achieve, to fall into nothing that he would avoid, to be free from anger, envy

σθῆναι, μὴ φθονῆσαι, μὴ ζηλοτυπῆσαι (τί γὰρ
27 δεῖ περιπλέκειν ;), θεὸν ἐξ ἀνθρώπου ἐπιθυμοῦντα
γενέσθαι καὶ ἐν τῷ σωματίῳ τούτῳ τῷ νεκρῷ
περὶ τῆς πρὸς τὸν Δία κοινωνίας βουλευόμενον.
28 δείξατε. ἀλλὰ οὐκ ἔχετε. τί οὖν αὐτοῖς ἐμπαί-
ζετε καὶ τοὺς ἄλλους κυβεύετε ; καὶ περιθέμενοι
σχῆμα ἀλλότριον περιπατεῖτε κλέπται καὶ
λωποδύται τούτων τῶν οὐδὲν προσηκόντων
ὀνομάτων καὶ πραγμάτων ;

29   Καὶ νῦν ἐγὼ μὲν παιδευτής εἰμι ὑμέτερος, ὑμεῖς
δὲ παρ' ἐμοὶ παιδεύεσθε. κἀγὼ μὲν ἔχω ταύτην
τὴν ἐπιβολήν, ἀποτελέσαι ὑμᾶς ἀκωλύτους,
ἀναναγκάστους, ἀπαραποδίστους, ἐλευθέρους,
εὐροοῦντας, εὐδαιμονοῦντας, εἰς τὸν θεὸν ἀφο-
ρῶντας ἐν παντὶ καὶ μικρῷ καὶ μεγάλῳ· ὑμεῖς
δὲ ταῦτα μαθησόμενοι καὶ μελετήσοντες πάρεστε.
30 διὰ τί οὖν οὐκ ἀνύετε τὸ ἔργον, εἰ καὶ ὑμεῖς
ἔχετ' ἐπιβολὴν οἵαν δεῖ κἀγὼ πρὸς τῇ ἐπιβολῇ
καὶ παρασκευὴν οἵαν δεῖ ; τί τὸ λεῖπόν ἐστιν ;
31 ὅταν ἴδω τέκτονα, ᾧτῳ [1] ὕλη πάρεστιν παρα-
κειμένη, ἐκδέχομαι τὸ ἔργον. καὶ ἐνθάδε τοίνυν
ὁ τέκτων ἐστίν, ἡ ὕλη ἐστίν· τί ἡμῖν λείπει ;
32 οὐκ ἔστι διδακτὸν τὸ πρᾶγμα ; διδακτόν. οὐκ
ἔστιν οὖν ἐφ' ἡμῖν ; μόνον μὲν οὖν τῶν ἄλλων
πάντων. οὔτε πλοῦτός ἐστιν ἐφ' ἡμῖν οὔθ'
ὑγίεια οὔτε δόξα οὔτε ἄλλο τι ἁπλῶς πλὴν ὀρθὴ
χρῆσις φαντασιῶν. τοῦτο ἀκώλυτον φύσει μό-
33 νον, τοῦτο ἀνεμπόδιστον. διὰ τί οὖν οὐκ ἀνύετε ;
εἴπατέ μοι τὴν αἰτίαν. ἢ γὰρ παρ' ἐμὲ γίνεται ἢ

----

[1] Schenkl: ὅτ' ἂν S (ὅταν corr.).

and jealousy—but why use circumlocutions?—a man who has set his heart upon changing from a man into a god, and although he is still in this paltry body of death, does none the less have his purpose set upon fellowship with Zeus. Show him to me! But you cannot. Why, then, do you mock your own selves and cheat everybody else? And why do you put on a guise that is not your own and walk about as veritable thieves and robbers who have stolen these designations and properties that in no sense belong to you?

And so now I am your teacher, and you are being taught in my school. And my purpose is this—to make of you a perfect work, secure against restraint, compulsion, and hindrance, free, prosperous, happy, looking to God in everything both small and great; and you are here with the purpose of learning and practising all this. Why, then, do you not complete the work, if it is true that you on your part have the right kind of purpose and I on my part, in addition to the purpose, have the right kind of preparation? What is it that is lacking? When I see a craftsman who has material lying ready at hand, I look for the finished product. Here also, then, is the craftsman, and here is the material; what do we yet lack? Cannot the matter be taught? It can. Is it, then, not under our control? Nay, it is the only thing in the whole world that *is* under our control. Wealth is not under our control, nor health, nor fame, nor, in a word, anything else except the right use of external impressions. This alone is by nature secure against restraint and hindrance. Why, then, do you not finish the work? Tell me the reason. For it lies either in me, or in

παρ' ὑμᾶς ἢ παρὰ τὴν φύσιν τοῦ πράγματος.
αὐτὸ τὸ πρᾶγμα ἐνδεχόμενον καὶ μόνον ἐφ' ἡμῖν.
λοιπὸν οὖν ἢ παρ' ἐμέ ἐστιν ἢ παρ' ὑμᾶς ἤ, ὅπερ
34 ἀληθέστερον, παρ' ἀμφοτέρους. τί οὖν; θέλετε
ἀρξώμεθά ποτε τοιαύτην ἐπιβολὴν κομίζειν ἐνταῦθα; τὰ μέχρι νῦν ἀφῶμεν. ἀρξώμεθα μόνον,
πιστεύσατέ μοι, καὶ ὄψεσθε.

κ'. Πρὸς Ἐπικουρείους καὶ Ἀκαδημαϊκούς.

1   Τοῖς ὑγιέσι καὶ ἐναργέσιν ἐξ ἀνάγκης καὶ οἱ
ἀντιλέγοντες προσχρῶνται· καὶ σχεδὸν τοῦτο
μέγιστον ἄν τις ποιήσαιτο τεκμήριον τοῦ ἐναργές
τι εἶναι, τὸ ἐπάναγκες εὑρίσκεσθαι καὶ τῷ
2 ἀντιλέγοντι συγχρήσασθαι αὐτῷ· οἷον εἴ τις
ἀντιλέγοι τῷ εἶναί τι καθολικὸν ἀληθές, δῆλον
ὅτι τὴν ἐναντίαν ἀπόφασιν οὗτος ὀφείλει ποι-
ήσασθαι· οὐδέν ἐστι καθολικὸν ἀληθές. ἀνδρά-
3 ποδον, οὐδὲ τοῦτο. τί γὰρ ἄλλο ἐστὶ τοῦτο ἢ οἷον
4 εἴ τι ἔστι καθολικόν, ψεῦδός ἐστιν; πάλιν ἄν τις
παρελθὼν λέγῃ "γίγνωσκε, ὅτι οὐδέν ἐστι
γνωστόν, ἀλλὰ πάντα ἀτέκμαρτα," ἢ ἄλλος
ὅτι "πίστευσόν μοι καὶ ὠφεληθήσῃ· οὐδὲν δεῖ
ἀνθρώπῳ πιστεύειν," ἢ πάλιν ἄλλος "μάθε παρ'
5 ἐμοῦ, ἄνθρωπε, ὅτι οὐδὲν ἐνδέχεται μαθεῖν· ἐγώ

---

¹ In § 29.

² The essential position of the philosophers of the New or
Middle Academy as exemplified by Arcesilaus and Carneades,
which Epictetus attacks here, was the denial of the possibility of knowledge, or of the existence of any positive
proof, and the maintenance of an attitude of suspended
judgement.

you, or in the nature of the thing. The thing itself is possible and is the only thing that is under our control. Consequently, then, the fault lies either in me, or in you, or, what is nearer the truth, in us both. What then? Would you like to have us at last begin to introduce here a purpose such as I have described?[1] Let us let bygones be bygones. Only let us begin, and, take my word for it, you shall see.

CHAPTER XX

Against Epicureans and Academics [2]

THE propositions which are true and evident must of necessity be employed even by those who contradict them; and one might consider as perhaps the strongest proof of a proposition being evident the fact that even the man who contradicts it finds himself obliged at the same time to employ it. For example, if a man should contradict the proposition that there is a universal statement which is true, it is clear that he must assert the contrary, and say: No universal statement is true. Slave, this is not true, either. For what else does this assertion amount to than: If a statement is universal, it is false? Again, if a man comes forward and says, " I would have you know that nothing is knowable, but that everything is uncertain "; or if someone else says, " Believe me, and it will be to your advantage, when I say: One ought not to believe a man at all "; or again, someone else, " Learn from me, man, that it is impossible to learn anything; it

σοι λέγω τοῦτο καὶ διδάξω σε, ἐὰν θέλῃς·" τίνι
οὖν τούτων διαφέρουσιν οὗτοι—τίνες ποτέ;—οἱ
Ἀκαδημαϊκοὺς αὐτοὺς λέγοντες; "ὦ ἄνθρωποι, συγκατάθεσθε ὅτι οὐδεὶς συγκατατίθεται·
πιστεύσατε ἡμῖν ὅτι οὐδεὶς πιστεύει οὐδενί."

6   Οὕτως καὶ Ἐπίκουρος, ὅταν ἀναιρεῖν θέλῃ τὴν
φυσικὴν κοινωνίαν ἀνθρώποις πρὸς ἀλλήλους,
7 αὐτῷ τῷ ἀναιρουμένῳ συγχρῆται. τί γὰρ λέγει;
"μὴ ἐξαπατᾶσθε, ἄνθρωποι, μηδὲ παράγεσθε
μηδὲ διαπίπτετε· οὐκ ἔστι φυσικὴ κοινωνία τοῖς
λογικοῖς πρὸς ἀλλήλους· πιστεύσατέ μοι. οἱ
δὲ τὰ ἕτερα λέγοντες ἐξαπατῶσιν ὑμᾶς καὶ
8 παραλογίζονται." τί οὖν σοι μέλει; ἄφες ἡμᾶς
ἐξαπατηθῆναι. μή τι χεῖρον ἀπαλλάξεις, ἂν
πάντες οἱ ἄλλοι πεισθῶμεν, ὅτι φυσική ἐστιν
ἡμῖν κοινωνία πρὸς ἀλλήλους καὶ ταύτην δεῖ
παντὶ τρόπῳ φυλάσσειν; καὶ πολὺ κρεῖσσον
9 καὶ ἀσφαλέστερον. ἄνθρωπε, τί ὑπὲρ ἡμῶν
φροντίζεις, τί δι' ἡμᾶς ἀγρυπνεῖς, τί λύχνον
ἅπτεις, τί ἐπανίστασαι, τί τηλικαῦτα βιβλία
συγγράφεις; μή τις ἡμῶν ἐξαπατηθῇ περὶ θεῶν
ὡς ἐπιμελουμένων ἀνθρώπων ἢ μή τις ἄλλην
10 οὐσίαν ὑπολάβῃ τοῦ ἀγαθοῦ ἢ ἡδονήν; εἰ γὰρ
οὕτως ταῦτα ἔχει, βαλὼν κάθευδε καὶ τὰ τοῦ
σκώληκος ποίει, ὧν ἄξιον ἔκρινας σεαυτόν· ἔσθιε
καὶ πῖνε καὶ συνουσίαζε καὶ ἀφόδευε καὶ ῥέγκε.
11 τί δὲ σοὶ μέλει, πῶς οἱ ἄλλοι ὑπολήψονται περὶ
τούτων, πότερον ὑγιῶς ἢ οὐχ ὑγιῶς; τί γὰρ σοὶ

is I who tell you this and I will prove it to you, if you
wish," what difference is there between these persons
and—whom shall I say?—those who call themselves
Academics? "O men," say the Academics, "give
your assent to the statement that no man assents to
any statement; believe *us* when we say that no man
can believe anybody."

So also Epicurus, when he wishes to do away
with the natural fellowship of men with one another,
at the same time makes use of the very principle
that he is doing away with. For what does he
say? "Be not deceived, men, nor led astray, nor
mistaken; there is no natural fellowship with
one another among rational beings; believe me.
Those who say the contrary are deceiving you and
leading you astray with false reasons." Why do
you care, then? Allow us to be deceived. Will
you fare any the worse, if all the rest of us are
persuaded that we do have a natural fellowship with
one another, and that we ought by all means to
guard it? Nay, your position will be much better
and safer. Man, why do you worry about us, why
keep vigil on our account, why light your lamp, why
rise betimes, why write such big books? Is it to
keep one or another of us from being deceived into
the belief that the gods care for men, or is it
to keep one or another of us from supposing that
the nature of the good is other than pleasure? For
if this is so, off to your couch and sleep, and lead
the life of a worm, of which you have judged yourself worthy; eat and drink and copulate and defe-
cate and snore. What do you care how the rest of
mankind will think about these matters, or whether
their ideas be sound or not? For what have you to

καὶ ἡμῖν; τῶν γὰρ προβάτων σοι μέλει, ὅτι
παρέχει ἡμῖν αὐτὰ καρησόμενα καὶ ἀμελχθη-
12 σόμενα καὶ τὸ τελευταῖον κατακοπησόμενα; οὐχὶ
δ' εὐκταῖον ἦν, εἰ ἐδύναντο οἱ ἄνθρωποι κατα-
κηληθέντες καὶ ἐπασθέντες ὑπὸ τῶν Στωικῶν
ἀπονυστάζειν καὶ παρέχειν σοι καὶ τοῖς ὁμοίοις
καρησομένους καὶ ἀμελχθησομένους ἑαυτούς;
13 πρὸς γὰρ τοὺς Συνεπικουρείους ἔδει σε ταῦτα
λέγειν, οὐχὶ δὲ πρὸς ἐκείνους ἀποκρύπτεσθαι,
καὶ¹ πολὺ μάλιστ' ἐκείνους πρὸ πάντων ἀνα-
πείθειν, ὅτι φύσει κοινωνικοὶ γεγόναμεν, ὅτι
14 ἀγαθὸν ἡ ἐγκράτεια, ἵνα σοι πάντα τηρῆται; ἢ
πρός τινας μὲν δεῖ φυλάττειν ταύτην τὴν κοινωνίαν, πρός τινας δ' οὔ; πρὸς τίνας οὖν δεῖ
τηρεῖν; πρὸς τοὺς ἀντιτηροῦντας ἢ πρὸς τοὺς
παραβατικῶς αὐτῆς ἔχοντας; καὶ τίνες παρα-
βατικώτερον αὐτῆς ἔχουσιν ὑμῶν τῶν ταῦτα
διειληφότων;
15 Τί οὖν ἦν τὸ ἐγεῖρον αὐτὸν ἐκ τῶν ὕπνων καὶ
ἀναγκάζον γράφειν ἃ ἔγραφεν; τί γὰρ ἄλλο ἢ
τὸ πάντων τῶν ἐν ἀνθρώποις ἰσχυρότατον, ἡ
φύσις ἕλκουσα ἐπὶ τὸ αὐτῆς βούλημα ἄκοντα
16 καὶ στένοντα; "ὅτι γὰρ δοκεῖ σοι ταῦτα τὰ
ἀκοινώνητα, γράψον αὐτὰ καὶ ἄλλοις ἀπόλιπε
καὶ ἀγρύπνησον δι' αὐτὰ καὶ αὐτὸς ἔργῳ κατήγο-
17 ρος γενοῦ τῶν σαυτοῦ δογμάτων." εἶτα Ὀρέστην
μὲν ὑπὸ Ἐρινύων ἐλαυνόμενον φῶμεν ἐκ τῶν
ὕπνων ἐξεγείρεσθαι· τούτῳ δ' οὐ χαλεπώτεραι
αἱ Ἐρινύες καὶ Ποιναί; ἐξήγειρον καθεύδοντα
καὶ οὐκ εἴων ἠρεμεῖν, ἀλλ' ἠνάγκαζον ἐξαγγέλ-
λειν τὰ αὐτοῦ κακὰ ὥσπερ τοὺς Γάλλους ἡ μανία

¹ Added by Wolf.

do with us? Come, do you interest yourself in
sheep because they allow themselves to be shorn by
us, and milked, and finally to be butchered and cut
up? Would it not be desirable if men could be
charmed and bewitched into slumber by the Stoics
and allow themselves to be shorn and milked by
you and your kind? Is not this something that you
ought to have said to your fellow Epicureans
only and to have concealed your views from out-
siders, taking special pains to persuade them, of
all people, that we are by nature born with a sense
of fellowship, and that self-control is a good thing,
so that everything may be kept for you? Or ought
we to maintain this fellowship with some, but not
with others? With whom, then, ought we to maintain it? With those who reciprocate by maintaining
it with us, or with those who are transgressors of it?
And who are greater transgressors of it than you
Epicureans who have set up such doctrines?

What, then, was it that roused Epicurus from his
slumbers and compelled him to write what he did?
What else but that which is the strongest thing in
men—nature, which draws a man to do her will
though he groans and is reluctant? "For," says
she, "since you hold these anti-social opinions,
write them down and bequeathe them to others and
give up your sleep because of them and become
in fact yourself the advocate to denounce your own
doctrines." Shall we speak of Orestes as being
pursued by the Furies and roused from his slumbers?
But are not the Furies and the Avengers that
beset Epicurus more savage? They roused him
from sleep and would not let him rest, but compelled
him to herald his own miseries, just as madness and

375

18 καὶ ὁ οἶνος. οὕτως ἰσχυρόν τι καὶ ἀνίκητόν
ἐστιν ἡ φύσις ἡ ἀνθρωπίνη. πῶς γὰρ δύναται
ἄμπελος μὴ ἀμπελικῶς κινεῖσθαι, ἀλλ' ἐλαικῶς,
ἢ ἐλαία πάλιν μὴ ἐλαικῶς, ἀλλ' ἀμπελικῶς ;

19 ἀμήχανον, ἀδιανόητον. οὐ τοίνυν οὐδ' ἄνθρωπον
οἷόν τε παντελῶς ἀπολέσαι τὰς κινήσεις τὰς
ἀνθρωπικὰς καὶ οἱ ἀποκοπτόμενοι τάς γε προθυμίας τὰς τῶν ἀνδρῶν ἀποκόψασθαι οὐ δύναν-

20 ται. οὕτως καὶ Ἐπίκουρος τὰ μὲν ἀνδρὸς πάντ'
ἀπεκόψατο καὶ τὰ οἰκοδεσπότου καὶ πολίτου
καὶ φίλου, τὰς δὲ προθυμίας τὰς ἀνθρωπικὰς
οὐκ ἀπεκόψατο· οὐ γὰρ ἠδύνατο, οὐ μᾶλλον ἢ
οἱ ἀταλαίπωροι Ἀκαδημαϊκοὶ τὰς αἰσθήσεις τὰς
αὑτῶν ἀποβαλεῖν ἢ ἀποτυφλῶσαι δύνανται καίτοι τοῦτο μάλιστα πάντων ἐσπουδακότες.

21 Ὢ τῆς[1] ἀτυχίας· λαβών τις παρὰ τῆς
φύσεως μέτρα καὶ κανόνας εἰς ἐπίγνωσιν τῆς
ἀληθείας οὐ προσφιλοτεχνεῖ τούτοις προσθεῖναι
καὶ προσεξεργάσασθαι τὰ λείποντα, ἀλλὰ πᾶν
τοὐναντίον, εἴ τι καὶ ἔχει[2] γνωριστικὸν τῆς

22 ἀληθείας, ἐξαιρεῖν πειρᾶται καὶ ἀπολλύειν. τί
λέγεις, φιλόσοφε ; τὸ εὐσεβὲς καὶ τὸ ὅσιον ποῖόν
τί σοι φαίνεται ; "ἂν θέλῃς, κατασκευάσω ὅτι
ἀγαθόν." ναὶ κατασκεύασον, ἵν' οἱ πολῖται ἡμῶν
ἐπιστραφέντες τιμῶσι τὸ θεῖον καὶ παύσωνταί
ποτε ῥαθυμοῦντες περὶ τὰ μέγιστα. "ἔχεις οὖν

23 τὰς κατασκευάς ;" ἔχω καὶ χάριν οἶδα. "ἐπεὶ

---

[1] Schenkl : τί (σ added later) ἢ S.
[2] Schenkl : ἐκεῖ S.

---

[1] Priests of Cybele who mutilated themselves in frenzy.

wine compel the Galli.[1] Such a powerful and invincible thing is the nature of man. For how can a vine be moved to act, not like a vine, but like an olive, or again an olive to act, not like an olive, but like a vine? It is impossible, inconceivable. Neither, then, is it possible for a man absolutely to lose the affections of a man, and those who cut off their bodily organs are unable to cut off the really important thing—their sexual desires. So with Epicurus: he cut off everything that characterizes a man, the head of a household, a citizen, and a friend, but he did not succeed in cutting off the desires of human beings; for that he could not do, any more than the easy-going [2] Academics are able to cast away or blind their own sense-perceptions, although they have made every effort to do so.

Ah, what a misfortune! A man has received from nature measures and standards for discovering the truth, and then does not go on and take the pains to add to these and to work out additional principles to supply the deficiencies, but does exactly the opposite, endeavouring to take away and destroy whatever faculty he does possess for discovering the truth. What do you say, philosopher? What is your opinion of piety and sanctity? "If you wish, I shall prove that it is good." By all means, prove it, that our citizens may be converted and may honour the Divine and at last cease to be indifferent about the things that are of supreme importance. "Do you, then, possess the proofs?" I do, thank heaven. "Since, then, you are quite satisfied with

[2] That is, unwilling to think matters through to a logical end. The meaning of the expression comes out clearly in the following section.

οὖν ταῦτά σοι λίαν ἀρέσκει, λάβε τὰ ἐναντία·
ὅτι θεοὶ οὔτ' εἰσίν, εἴ τε καὶ εἰσίν, οὐκ ἐπιμε-
λοῦνται ἀνθρώπων οὐδὲ κοινόν τι ἡμῖν ἐστι πρὸς
αὐτοὺς τό τ' εὐσεβὲς τοῦτο καὶ ὅσιον παρὰ τοῖς
πολλοῖς ἀνθρώποις λαλούμενον κατάψευσμά
ἐστιν ἀλαζόνων ἀνθρώπων καὶ σοφιστῶν ἢ νὴ
Δία νομοθετῶν εἰς φόβον καὶ ἐπίσχεσιν τῶν
24 ἀδικούντων." εὖ, φιλόσοφε· ὠφέλησας ἡμῶν
τοὺς πολίτας, ἀνεκτήσω τοὺς νέους ῥέποντας ἤδη
25 πρὸς καταφρόνησιν τῶν θείων. "τί οὖν; οὐκ
ἀρέσκει σοι ταῦτα; λάβε νῦν, πῶς ἡ δικαιοσύνη
οὐδέν ἐστι, πῶς ἡ αἰδὼς μωρία ἐστίν, πῶς πατὴρ
26 οὐδέν ἐστιν, πῶς ὁ υἱὸς οὐδέν ἐστιν." εὖ, φιλό-
σοφε· ἐπίμενε, πεῖθε τοὺς νέους, ἵνα πλείονας
ἔχωμεν ταῦτά σοι πεπονθότας καὶ λέγοντας. ἐκ
τούτων τῶν λόγων ηὐξήθησαν ἡμῖν αἱ εὐνομού-
μεναι πόλεις, Λακεδαίμων διὰ τούτους τοὺς
λόγους ἐγένετο, Λυκοῦργος ταῦτα τὰ πείσματα
ἐνεποίησεν αὐτοῖς διὰ τῶν νόμων αὐτοῦ καὶ τῆς
παιδείας, ὅτι οὔτε τὸ δουλεύειν αἰσχρόν ἐστι
μᾶλλον ἢ καλὸν οὔτε τὸ ἐλευθέρους εἶναι καλὸν
μᾶλλον ἢ αἰσχρόν, οἱ ἐν Θερμοπύλαις ἀποθα-
νόντες διὰ ταῦτα τὰ δόγματα ἀπέθανον, Ἀθηναῖοι
δὲ τὴν πόλιν διὰ ποίους ἄλλους λόγους ἀπέλιπον ;
27 εἶτα οἱ λέγοντες ταῦτα γαμοῦσι καὶ παιδοποιοῦνται καὶ πολιτεύονται καὶ ἱερεῖς καθιστᾶσιν
αὐτοὺς καὶ προφήτας. τίνων ; τῶν οὐκ ὄντων·
καὶ τὴν Πυθίαν ἀνακρίνουσιν αὐτοί, ἵνα τὰ ψευδῆ
πύθωνται, καὶ ἄλλοις τοὺς χρησμοὺς ἐξηγοῦνται.
ὦ μεγάλης ἀναισχυντίας καὶ γοητείας.

---

[1] The Athenians twice abandoned their city, once in 480 B.C.,
and again in 479 B.C., rather than submit to the Persians.

all this, hear the contrary : The gods do not exist,
and even if they do, they pay no attention to men,
nor have we any fellowship with them, and hence
this piety and sanctity which the multitude talk about
is a lie told by impostors and sophists, or, I swear,
by legislators to frighten and restrain evildoers."
Well done, philosopher! You have conferred a
service upon our citizens, you have recovered our
young men who were already inclining to despise
things divine. "What then? Does not all this
satisfy you? Learn now how righteousness is
nothing, how reverence is folly, how a father is
nothing, how a son is nothing." Well done,
philosopher! Keep at it; persuade the young men,
that we may have more who feel and speak as you
do. It is from principles like these that our well-
governed states have grown great! Principles like
these have made Sparta what it was! These are
the convictions which Lycurgus wrought into the
Spartans by his laws and his system of education,
namely that neither is slavery base rather than
noble, nor freedom noble rather than base! Those
who died at Thermopylae died because of these
judgements regarding slavery and freedom! And
for what principles but these did the men of Athens
give up their city? [1] And then those who talk thus
marry and beget children and fulfil the duties of
citizens and get themselves appointed priests and
prophets! Priests and prophets of whom? Of
gods that do not exist! And they themselves consult the Pythian priestess—in order to hear lies
and to interpret the oracles to others! Oh what
monstrous shamelessness and imposture!

28 Ἄνθρωπε, τί ποιεῖς; αὐτὸς σεαυτὸν ἐξελέγχεις
καθ' ἡμέραν καὶ οὐ θέλεις ἀφεῖναι τὰ ψυχρὰ
ταῦτα ἐπιχειρήματα; ἐσθίων ποῦ φέρεις τὴν χεῖρα;
εἰς τὸ στόμα ἢ εἰς τὸν ὀφθαλμόν; λουόμενος ποῦ
ἐμβαίνεις; πότε τὴν χύτραν εἶπες λοπάδα ἢ τὴν

29 τορύνην ὀβελίσκον; εἴ τινος αὐτῶν δοῦλος ἤμην,
εἰ καὶ ἔδει με καθ' ἡμέραν ὑπ' αὐτοῦ ἐκδέρεσθαι,
ἐγὼ ἂν αὐτὸν ἐστρέβλουν. "βάλε ἐλάδιον,
παιδάριον, εἰς τὸ βαλανεῖον." ἔβαλον ἂν γάριον
καὶ ἀπελθὼν κατὰ τῆς κεφαλῆς αὐτοῦ κατέχεον.
"τί τοῦτο;" "φαντασία μοι ἐγένετο ἐλαίου
ἀδιάκριτος, ὁμοιοτάτη, νὴ τὴν σὴν τύχην."

30 "δὸς ὧδε τὴν πτισάνην." ἤνεγκα ἂν αὐτῷ
γεμίσας παροψίδα ὀξογάρου. "οὐκ ᾔτησα τὴν
πτισάνην;" "ναί, κύριε· τοῦτο πτισάνη ἐστίν."
"τοῦτο οὐκ ἔστιν ὀξόγαρον;" "τί μᾶλλον ἢ
πτισάνη;" "λάβε καὶ ὀσφράνθητι, λάβε καὶ
γεῦσαι." "πόθεν οὖν οἶδας, εἰ αἱ αἰσθήσεις

31 ἡμᾶς ψεύδονται;" τρεῖς, τέσσαρας, τῶν συν-
δούλων εἰ ἔσχον ὁμονοοῦντας, ἀπάγξασθαι ἂν
αὐτὸν ἐποίησα ῥηγνύμενον ἢ μεταθέσθαι. νῦν δ'
ἐντρυφῶσιν ἡμῖν τοῖς μὲν παρὰ τῆς φύσεως διδομένοις πᾶσι χρώμενοι, λόγῳ δ' αὐτὰ ἀναιροῦντες.

32 Εὐχάριστοί γ' ἄνθρωποι καὶ αἰδήμονες. εἰ
μηδὲν ἄλλο καθ' ἡμέραν ἄρτους ἐσθίοντες τολμῶσι
λέγειν ὅτι "οὐκ οἴδαμεν, εἰ ἔστι τις Δημήτηρ ἢ

33 Κόρη ἢ Πλούτων." ἵνα μὴ λέγω, ὅτι νυκτὸς καὶ

---

¹ There is an abrupt transition here from the Epicureans
to the Academics.

² Demeter and Kore represent agriculture and the "corn-
spirit." Pluto is added as the personification of the darkness
of earth out of which the plants spring, and as the spouse of

Man, what are you doing?[1] You are confuting your own self every day, and are you unwilling to give up these frigid attempts of yours? When you eat, where do you bring your hand? To your mouth, or to your eye? When you take a bath, into what do you step? When did you ever call the pot a plate, or the ladle a spit? If I were slave to one of these men, even if I had to be soundly flogged by him every day, I would torment him. "Boy, throw a little oil into the bath." I would have thrown a little fish sauce in, and as I left would pour it down on his head. "What does this mean?" "I had an external impression that could not be distinguished from olive oil; indeed, it was altogether like it. I swear by your fortune." "Here, give me the gruel." I would have filled a side dish with vinegar and fish sauce and brought it to him. "Did I not ask for the gruel?" "Yes, master; this is gruel." "Is not this vinegar and fish sauce?" "How so, any more than gruel." "Take and smell it, take and taste it." "Well, how do you know, if the senses deceive us?" If I had had three or four fellow-slaves who felt as I did, I would have made him burst with rage and hang himself, or else change his opinion. But as it is, such men are toying with us; they use all the gifts of nature, while in theory doing away with them.

Grateful men indeed and reverential! Why, if nothing else, at least they eat bread every day, and yet have the audacity to say, "We do not know if there is a Demeter, or a Kore, or a Pluto"[2]; not to

Kore, or else, possibly, because he suggests the death of the grain of corn before the new shoot appears. *Cf. I. Corinth.* xv. 36: "That which thou sowest is not quickened, except it die."

ἡμέρας ἀπολαύοντες καὶ μεταβολῶν τοῦ ἔτους
καὶ ἄστρων καὶ θαλάσσης καὶ γῆς καὶ τῆς παρ'
ἀνθρώπων συνεργείας ὑπ' οὐδενὸς τούτων οὐδὲ
κατὰ ποσὸν ἐπιστρέφονται, ἀλλὰ μόνον ἐξεμέσαι
τὸ προβλημάτιον ζητοῦσι καὶ τὸν στόμαχον γυ-
34 μνάσαντες ἀπελθεῖν ἐν βαλανείῳ.¹ τί δ' ἐροῦσι
καὶ περὶ τίνων ἢ πρὸς τίνας καὶ τί ἔσται αὐτοῖς
ἐκ τῶν λόγων τούτων, οὐδὲ κατὰ βραχὺ πεφρον-
τίκασι· μή τι νέος εὐγενὴς ἀκούσας τῶν λόγων
τούτων πάθῃ τι ὑπ' αὐτῶν ἢ καὶ παθὼν πάντ'
35 ἀπολέσῃ τὰ τῆς εὐγενείας σπέρματα· μή τινι
μοιχεύοντι ἀφορμὰς παράσχωμεν τοῦ ἀπαναι-
σχυντῆσαι πρὸς τὰ γινόμενα· μή τις τῶν νοσφι-
ζομένων τὰ δημόσια εὑρεσιλογίας τινὸς ἐπιλάβηται
ἀπὸ τῶν λόγων τούτων· μή τις τῶν αὑτοῦ γονέων
ἀμελῶν θράσος τι καὶ ἀπὸ τούτων προσλάβῃ.

Τί οὖν κατὰ σὲ ἀγαθὸν ἢ κακόν, αἰσχρὸν² ἢ
36 καλόν; ταῦτα ἢ ταῦτα; τί οὖν; ἔτι τούτων
τις ἀντιλέγει τινὶ ἢ λόγον δίδωσιν ἢ λαμβάνει
37 ἢ μεταπείθειν πειρᾶται; πολὺ νὴ Δία μᾶλλον
τοὺς κιναίδους ἐλπίσαι τις ἂν μεταπείσειν ἢ
τοὺς ἐπὶ τοσοῦτον ἀποκεκωφωμένους καὶ ἀποτε-
τυφλωμένους.

κα΄. Περὶ ἀνομολογίας.

1 Τῶν περὶ αὑτοὺς κακῶν³ τὰ μὲν ῥᾳδίως ὁμο-
λογοῦσιν ἄνθρωποι, τὰ δ' οὐ ῥᾳδίως. οὐδεὶς οὖν

---

¹ εἰς βαλανεῖον Schenkl, but cf. I. 11, 32.
² Added by Wolf.
³ τῶν . . . κακῶν transferred by Wendland from the end of
the preceding chapter.

mention that, although they enjoy night and day, the changes of the year and the stars and the sea and the earth and the co-operation of men, they are not moved in the least by any one of these things, but look merely for a chance to belch out their trivial "problem," and after thus exercising their stomach to go off to the bath. But what they are going to say, or what they are going to talk about, or to whom, and what their hearers are going to get out of these things that they are saying, all this has never given them a moment's concern. I greatly fear that a noble-spirited young man may hear these statements and be influenced by them, or, having been influenced already, may lose all the germs of the nobility which he possessed; that we may be giving an adulterer grounds for brazening out his acts; that some embezzler of public funds may lay hold of a specious plea based upon these theories; that someone who neglects his own parents may gain additional affrontery from them.

What, then, in your opinion is good or bad, base or noble? This or that? What then? Is there any use in arguing further against any of these persons, or giving them a reason, or listening to one of theirs, or trying to convert them? By Zeus, one might much rather hope to convert a filthy degenerate than men who have become so deaf and blind!

CHAPTER XXI

Of inconsistency

SOME of their faults men readily admit, but others not so readily. Now no one will admit that he is

ὁμολογήσει ὅτι ἄφρων ἐστὶν ἢ ἀνόητος, ἀλλὰ πᾶν
τοὐναντίον πάντων ἀκούσεις λεγόντων "ὤφελον
2 ὡς φρένας ἔχω οὕτως καὶ τύχην εἶχον." δειλοὺς
δὲ ῥᾳδίως ἑαυτοὺς ὁμολογοῦσι καὶ λέγουσιν "ἐγὼ
δειλότερός εἰμι, ὁμολογῶ· τὰ δ' ἄλλ' οὐχ
3 εὑρήσεις με μωρὸν ἄνθρωπον." ἀκρατῆ οὐ ῥᾳδίως
ὁμολογήσει τις, ἄδικον οὐδ' ὅλως, φθονερὸν οὐ
4 πάνυ ἢ περίεργον, ἐλεήμονα οἱ πλεῖστοι. τί οὖν
τὸ αἴτιον ; τὸ μὲν κυριώτατον ἀνομολογία καὶ
ταραχὴ ἐν τοῖς περὶ ἀγαθῶν καὶ κακῶν, ἄλλοις δ'
ἄλλα αἴτια καὶ σχεδὸν ὅσα ἂν αἰσχρὰ φαντά-
5 ζωνται, ταῦτα οὐ πάνυ ὁμολογοῦσι· τὸ δὲ δειλὸν
εἶναι εὐγνώμονος ἤθους φαντάζονται καὶ τὸ ἐλεήμονα, τὸ δ' ἠλίθιον εἶναι παντελῶς ἀνδραπόδου·
καὶ τὰ περὶ κοινωνίαν δὲ πλημμελήματα οὐ πάνυ
6 προσίενται. ἐπὶ δὲ τῶν πλείστων ἁμαρτημάτων
κατὰ τοῦτο μάλιστα φέρονται ἐπὶ τὸ ὁμολογεῖν
αὐτά, ὅτι φαντάζονταί τι ἐν αὐτοῖς εἶναι ἀκούσιον
7 καθάπερ ἐν τῷ δειλῷ καὶ ἐλεήμονι. κἂν ἀκρατῆ
που [1] παρομολογῇ τις αὐτόν, ἔρωτα προσέθηκεν,
ὥστε συγγνωσθῆναι ὡς ἐπ' ἀκουσίῳ. τὸ δ'
ἄδικον οὐδαμῶς φαντάζονται ἀκούσιον. ἔνι τι
καὶ τῷ ζηλοτύπῳ, ὡς οἴονται, τοῦ ἀκουσίου. διὰ
τοῦτο καὶ περὶ τούτου παρομολογοῦσιν.

8 Ἐν οὖν τοιούτοις ἀνθρώποις ἀναστρεφόμενον,
οὕτως τεταραγμένοις, οὕτως οὐκ εἰδόσιν οὔθ' ὅ τι
λέγουσιν οὔθ' ὅ τι ἔχουσιν κακὸν ἢ εἰ [2] ἔχουσιν ἢ

---

[1] Shaftesbury: τι· οὐ S.   [2] Supplied by Schenkl.

foolish or unintelligent, but, quite the contrary, you hear everyone say, " I wish I had as much luck as I have sense." But they readily admit that they are timid, and say, " I am a bit timid, I admit; but in general you will not find me to be a fool." A man will not readily admit that he is incontinent, not at all that he is unjust, and will never admit that he is envious or meddlesome; but most men will admit that they are moved by pity. What is the reason for this? The principal reason is confusion of thought and an unwillingness to admit a fault in matters which involve good and evil; but, apart from that, different people are affected by different motives, and, as a rule, they will never admit anything that they conceive to be disgraceful; timidity, for example, they conceive to be an indication of a prudent disposition, and the same is true of pity, but stupidity they conceive to be a slave's quality altogether; also they will never plead guilty to offences against society. Now in the case of most errors, the principal reason why men are inclined to admit them is because they conceive that there is an involuntary element in them, as, for instance, in timidity and pity. And if a man ever does, grudgingly, admit that he is incontinent, he adds that he is in love, expecting to be excused as for an involuntary act. But injustice they do not at all conceive of as involuntary. In jealousy there is also, as they fancy, an element of the involuntary, and therefore this too is a fault which men grudgingly admit.

When such are the men we live among—so confused, so ignorant both of what they mean by " evil " and what evil quality they have, or whether they have one, or, if so, how they come to have it, or

παρὰ τί ἔχουσιν ἢ πῶς παύσονται αὐτῶν, καὶ
αὐτὸν οἶμαι ἐφιστάνειν ἄξιον συνεχὲς " μὴ που καὶ
9 αὐτὸς εἷς εἰμι ἐκείνων; τίνα φαντασίαν ἔχω περὶ
ἐμαυτοῦ ; πῶς ἐμαυτῷ χρῶμαι ; μή τι καὶ αὐτὸς
ὡς φρονίμῳ, μή τι καὶ αὐτὸς ὡς ἐγκρατεῖ ; μὴ
καὶ αὐτὸς λέγω ποτὲ ταῦτα, ὅτι εἰς τὸ ἐπιὸν
10 πεπαίδευμαι ; ἔχω ἣν δεῖ συναίσθησιν τὸν μηδὲν
εἰδότα, ὅτι οὐδὲν οἶδα ; ἔρχομαι πρὸς τὸν διδάσκαλον ὡς ἐπὶ τὰ χρηστήρια πείθεσθαι παρε-
σκευασμένος ; ἢ καὶ αὐτὸς κορύζης μεστὸς εἰς τὴν
σχολὴν εἰσέρχομαι μόνην τὴν ἱστορίαν μαθησόμενος καὶ τὰ βιβλία νοήσων, ἃ πρότερον οὐκ ἐνό-
ουν, ἂν δ' οὕτως τύχῃ, καὶ ἄλλοις ἐξηγησόμενος ;"
11 ἄνθρωπ', ἐν οἴκῳ διαπεπύκτευκας τῷ δουλαρίῳ,
τὴν οἰκίαν ἀνάστατον πεποίηκας, τοὺς γείτονας
συντετάραχας· καὶ ἔρχῃ μοι καταστολὰς ποιήσας
ὡς σοφὸς καὶ καθήμενος κρίνεις, πῶς ἐξηγησάμην
τὴν λέξιν, πρὸς[1] τί ποτ' ἐφλυάρησα τὰ ἐπελθόντα
12 μοι ; φθονῶν ἐλήλυθας, τεταπεινωμένος, ὅτι σοι
ἐξ οἴκου φέρεται οὐδέν, καὶ κάθῃ μεταξὺ λεγο-
μένων τῶν λόγων αὐτὸς οὐδὲν ἄλλο ἐνθυμούμενος ἢ
13 πῶς ὁ πατὴρ τὰ πρὸς σε ἢ πῶς ὁ ἀδελφός. "τί[2]
λέγουσιν οἱ ἐκεῖ ἄνθρωποι περὶ ἐμοῦ ; νῦν οἴονταί
με προκόπτειν καὶ λέγουσιν ὅτι 'ἥξει ἐκεῖνος

---

[1] Reiske and Koraes : πῶς S.
[2] Salmasius : τὰ S.

---

[1] Evidently the student depended upon his home for his
supplies.

how they will get rid of it—among such men I
wonder whether it is not worth while for us also to
watch ourselves, each one asking himself the
questions : " Is it possible that I too am one of these
people? What conceit am I cherishing regarding
myself? How do I conduct myself? Do I for my
part act like a wise man? Do I for my part act like
a man of self-control? Do I for my part ever say
that I have been educated to meet whatever comes?
Have I the consciousness, proper to a man who
knows nothing, that I do know nothing? Do I go
to my teacher, like one who goes to consult an
oracle, prepared to obey? Or do I, too, like a
sniffling child, go to school to learn only the history
of philosophy and to understand the books which I
did not understand before, and, if chance offers, to
explain them to others?" Man, at home you have
fought a regular prize-fight with your slave, you
have driven your household into the street, you have
disturbed your neighbours' peace ; and now do you
come to me with a solemn air, like a philosopher,
and sitting down pass judgement on the explanation
I gave of the reading of the text and on the
application, forsooth, of the comments I made as I
babbled out whatever came into my head? You
have come in a spirit of envy, in a spirit of
humiliation because nothing is being sent you from
home,[1] and you sit there while the lecture is going
on, thinking, on your part, of nothing in the world
but how you stand with your father or your brother!
You reflect : " What are my people at home
saying about me? At this moment they are
thinking that I am making progress in my studies,
and they are saying ' He will know everything

14 πάντα εἰδώς.' ἤθελόν πώς ποτε πάντα μαθὼν
ἐπανελθεῖν, ἀλλὰ πολλοῦ πόνου χρεία καὶ οὐδεὶς
οὐδὲν πέμπει καὶ ἐν Νικοπόλει σαπρῶς λούει τὰ
βαλανεῖα καὶ ἐν οἴκῳ κακῶς καὶ ὧδε κακῶς."

15 Εἶτα λέγουσιν "οὐδεὶς ὠφελεῖται ἐκ τῆς
σχολῆς." τίς γὰρ ἔρχεται εἰς σχολήν, τίς γάρ,
ὡς θεραπευθησόμενος ; τίς ὡς παρέξων αὑτοῦ τὰ
δόγματα ἐκκαθαρθησόμενα, τίς συναισθησόμενος

16 τίνων δεῖται ; τί οὖν θαυμάζετ᾽, εἰ ἃ φέρετ᾽ εἰς
τὴν σχολήν, αὐτὰ ταῦτα ἀποφέρετε πάλιν ; οὐ
γὰρ ὡς ἀποθησόμενοι ἢ ἐπανορθώσοντες ἢ

17 ἀλλ᾽ ἀντ᾽ αὐτῶν ληψόμενοι ἔρχεσθε. πόθεν ;
οὐδ᾽ ἐγγύς. ἐκεῖνο γοῦν βλέπετε μᾶλλον, εἰ
ἐφ᾽ ὃ ἔρχεσθε τοῦτο ὑμῖν γίνεται. θέλετε λαλεῖν
περὶ τῶν θεωρημάτων. τί οὖν ; οὐ φλυαρότεροι
γίνεσθε ; οὐχὶ δὲ παρέχει τινὰ ὕλην ὑμῖν πρὸς
τὸ ἐπιδείκνυσθαι τὰ θεωρημάτια ; οὐ [1] συλλογισμοὺς ἀναλύετε, μεταπίπτοντας ; οὐκ ἐφοδεύετε
Ψευδομένου λήμματα, ὑποθετικούς ; τί οὖν ἔτι
ἀγανακτεῖτε εἰ ἐφ᾽ ἃ πάρεστε, ταῦτα λαμβάνετε ;

18 " ναί· ἀλλ᾽ ἂν ἀποθάνῃ μου τὸ παιδίον ἢ ὁ
ἀδελφὸς ἢ ἐμὲ ἀποθνήσκειν δέῃ ἢ στρεβλοῦσθαι,

19 τί με τὰ τοιαῦτα [2] ὠφελήσει ; " μὴ γὰρ ἐπὶ τοῦτο
ἦλθες, μὴ γὰρ τούτου ἕνεκά μοι παρακάθησαι, μὴ
γὰρ διὰ τοῦτό ποτε λύχνον ἧψας ἢ ἠγρύπνησας ;

---

[1] Supplied by Wolf.   [2] Meibom: μετὰ ταῦτα S.

[1] See II. 17, 34, and note.

when he comes back home!' I did want, at one time, I suppose, to learn everything before going back home, but that requires a great deal of hard work, and nobody sends me anything, and at Nicopolis they have rotten accommodations at the baths, and my lodgings are bad, and the school here is bad."

And then people say: "Nobody gets any good from going to school." Well, who goes to school— who, I repeat—with the expectation of being cured? Who with the expectation of submitting his own judgements for purification? Who with the expectation of coming to a realization of what judgements he needs? Why, then, are you surprised, if you carry back home from your school precisely the judgements you bring to it? For you do not come with the expectation of laying them aside, or of correcting them, or of getting others in exchange for them. Not at all, nor anything like it. Look rather to this at least—whether you are getting what you came for. You want to be able to speak fluently about philosophic principles. Well, are you not becoming more of an idle babbler? Do not these petty philosophic principles supply you with material for making exhibitions? Do you not resolve syllogisms, and arguments with equivocal premisses? Do you not examine the assumptions in *The Liar*[1] syllogism, and in hypothetical syllogisms? Why, then, are you still vexed, if you are getting what you came for? "Yes, but if my child or my brother dies, or if I must die, or be tortured, what good will such things do me?" But was it really for this that you came? Is it really for this that you sit by my side? Did you ever really light your lamp, or work late at

ἢ εἰς τὸν περίπατον ἐξελθὼν προέβαλές ποτε
σαυτῷ φαντασίαν τινὰ ἀντὶ συλλογισμοῦ καὶ
20 ταύτην κοινῇ ἐφωδεύσατε; ποῦ ποτε; εἶτα
λέγετε "ἄχρηστα τὰ θεωρήματα." τίσιν; τοῖς
οὐχ ὡς δεῖ χρωμένοις. τὰ γὰρ κολλύρια οὐκ
ἄχρηστα τοῖς ὅτε δεῖ καὶ ὡς δεῖ ἐγχριομένοις, τὰ
μαλάγματα δ᾽ οὐκ ἄχρηστα, οἱ ἁλτῆρες οὐκ
ἄχρηστοι, ἀλλὰ τισὶν ἄχρηστοι, τισὶν πάλιν
21 χρήσιμοι. ἄν μου πυνθάνῃ νῦν "χρήσιμοί εἰσιν
οἱ συλλογισμοί;" ἐρῶ σοι ὅτι χρήσιμοι, κἂν
θέλῃς, ἀποδείξω πῶς. "ἐμὲ οὖν τι ὠφελήκασιν;"
ἄνθρωπε, μὴ γὰρ ἐπύθου, εἰ σοὶ χρήσιμοι, ἀλλὰ
22 καθόλου; πυθέσθω μου καὶ ὁ δυσεντερικός, εἰ
χρήσιμον ὄξος, ἐρῶ ὅτι χρήσιμον. "ἐμοὶ οὖν
χρήσιμον;" ἐρῶ "οὔ. ζήτησον πρῶτον σταλῆναί
σου τὸ ῥεῦμα, τὰ ἑλκύδρια ἀπουλωθῆναι." καὶ
ὑμεῖς, ἄνδρες, τὰ ἕλκη πρῶτον θεραπεύετε, τὰ
ῥεύματα ἐπιστήσατε, ἠρεμήσατε τῇ διανοίᾳ,
ἀπερίσπαστον αὐτὴν ἐνέγκατε εἰς τὴν σχολήν·
καὶ γνώσεσθε οἵαν ἰσχὺν ὁ λόγος ἔχει.

κβ΄. Περὶ φιλίας.

1   Περὶ ἅ τις ἐσπούδακεν, φιλεῖ ταῦτα εἰκότως.
μή τι οὖν περὶ τὰ κακὰ ἐσπουδάκασιν οἱ ἄνθρωποι; οὐδαμῶς. ἀλλὰ μή τι περὶ τὰ μηδὲν πρὸς

390

night, for this? Or when you went out into the
covered walk did you ever set before yourself,
instead of a syllogism, some external impression and
examine this with your fellow-students? When did
you ever do that? And then you say, "The
principles are useless." To whom? To those who
do not use them properly. For instance, eye-salves
are not useless to those who rub them on when and
as they ought, and poultices are not useless,
jumping-weights are not useless; but they are
useless to some people, and, on the other hand,
useful to others. If you ask me now, "Are our
syllogisms useful?" I will tell you that they are,
and, if you wish, I will show how they are useful.
"Have they, then, helped *me* at all?" Man, you
did not ask, did you? whether they are useful to
you, but whether they are useful in general? Let
the man who is suffering from dysentery ask me
whether vinegar is useful; I will tell him that it is
useful. "Is it useful, then, to me?" I will say,
"No. Seek first to have your discharge stopped,
the little ulcers healed." So do you also, men, first
cure your ulcers, stop your discharges, be tranquil in
mind, bring it free from distraction into the school;
and then you will know what power reason has.

CHAPTER XXII

Of friendship

WHATEVER a man is interested in he naturally
loves. Now do men take an interest in things evil?
Not at all. Well, and do they take an interest in
things which in no respect concern them? No, not

2 αὐτούς; οὐδὲ περὶ ταῦτα. ὑπολείπεται τοίνυν
3 περὶ μόνα τὰ ἀγαθὰ ἐσπουδακέναι αὐτούς· εἰ
δ᾽ ἐσπουδακέναι, καὶ φιλεῖν ταῦτα. ὅστις οὖν
ἀγαθῶν ἐπιστήμων ἐστίν, οὗτος ἂν καὶ φιλεῖν
εἰδείη· ὁ δὲ μὴ δυνάμενος διακρῖναι τὰ ἀγαθὰ
ἀπὸ τῶν κακῶν καὶ τὰ οὐδέτερα ἀπ᾽ ἀμφοτέρων
πῶς ἂν ἔτι οὗτος φιλεῖν δύναιτο; τοῦ φρονίμου
τοίνυν ἐστὶ μόνου τὸ φιλεῖν.

4 Καὶ πῶς; φησίν· ἐγὼ γὰρ ἄφρων ὢν ὅμως
5 φιλῶ μου τὸ παιδίον.—Θαυμάζω μὲν νὴ τοὺς
θεούς, πῶς καὶ τὸ πρῶτον ὡμολόγηκας ἄφρονα
εἶναι σεαυτόν. τί γάρ σοι λείπει; οὐ χρῇ
αἰσθήσει, οὐ φαντασίας διακρίνεις, οὐ τροφὰς
προσφέρῃ τὰς ἐπιτηδείους τῷ σώματι, οὐ σκέπην,
6 οὐκ οἴκησιν; πόθεν οὖν ὁμολογεῖς ἄφρων εἶναι;
ὅτι νὴ Δία πολλάκις ἐξίστασαι ὑπὸ τῶν φαντασιῶν καὶ ταράττῃ καὶ ἡττῶσίν σε αἱ πιθανότητες
αὐτῶν· καὶ ποτὲ μὲν ταῦτα ἀγαθὰ ὑπολαμβάνεις,
εἶτα ἐκεῖνα αὐτὰ κακά, ὕστερον δ᾽ οὐδέτερα· καὶ
ὅλως λυπῇ, φοβῇ, φθονεῖς, ταράσσῃ, μεταβάλλῃ·
7 διὰ ταῦτα ὁμολογεῖς ἄφρων εἶναι. ἐν δὲ τῷ
φιλεῖν οὐ μεταβάλλῃ; ἀλλὰ πλοῦτον μὲν καὶ
ἡδονὴν καὶ ἁπλῶς αὐτὰ τὰ πράγματα ποτὲ μὲν
ἀγαθὰ ὑπολαμβάνεις εἶναι, ποτὲ δὲ κακά· ἀνθρώπους δὲ τοὺς αὐτοὺς οὐχὶ ποτὲ μὲν ἀγαθούς, ποτὲ
δὲ κακοὺς καὶ ποτὲ μὲν οἰκείως ἔχεις, ποτὲ δ᾽

in these, either. It remains, therefore, that men take an interest in good things only; and if they take an interest in them, they love them. Whoever, then, has knowledge of good things, would know how to love them too; but when a man is unable to distinguish things good from things evil, and what is neither good nor evil from both the others, how could he take the next step and have the power to love? Accordingly, the power to love belongs to the wise man and to him alone.

How so? says someone; for I am foolish myself, but yet I love my child.—By the gods, I am surprised at you; at the very outset you have admitted that you are foolish. For something is lacking in you; what is it? Do you not use sense perception, do you not distinguish between external impressions, do you not supply the nourishment for your body that is suitable to it, and shelter, and a dwelling? How comes it, then, that you admit you are foolish? Because, by Zeus, you are frequently bewildered and disturbed by your external impressions, and overcome by their persuasive character; and at one moment you consider these things good, and then again you consider them, though the very same, evil, and later on as neither good nor evil; and, in a word, you are subject to pain, fear, envy, turmoil, and change; that is why you are foolish, as you admit you are. And in loving are you not changeable? But as for wealth, and pleasure, and, in a word, material things, do you not consider them at one moment good, at another bad? And do you not consider the same persons at one moment good, and at another bad, and do you not at one moment feel friendly towards them, and at another unfriendly,

ἐχθρῶς αὐτοῖς, καὶ ποτὲ μὲν ἐπαινεῖς, ποτὲ δὲ
8 ψέγεις ;—Ναὶ καὶ ταῦτα πάσχω.—Τί οὖν ; ὁ
ἐξηπατημένος περί τινος δοκεῖ σοι φίλος εἶναι
αὐτοῦ ;—Οὐ πάνυ.—Ὁ δὲ μεταπτώτως ἑλόμενος
αὐτὸν εἶναι εὔνους ¹ αὐτῷ ;—Οὐδ' οὗτος.—Ὁ δὲ
νῦν λοιδορῶν μέν τινα, ὕστερον δὲ θαυμάζων ;—
9 Οὐδ' οὗτος.—Τί οὖν ; κυνάρια οὐδέποτ' εἶδες σαί-
νοντα καὶ προσπαίζοντα ἀλλήλοις, ἵν' εἴπῃς
"οὐδὲν φιλικώτερον" ; ἀλλ' ὅπως ἴδῃς, τί ἐστι
10 φιλία, βάλε κρέας εἰς μέσον καὶ γνώσῃ. βάλε
καὶ σοῦ καὶ τοῦ παιδίου μέσον ἀγρίδιον καὶ
γνώσῃ, πῶς σὲ τὸ παιδίον ταχέως κατορύξαι
θέλει καὶ σὺ τὸ παιδίον εὔχῃ ἀποθανεῖν. εἶτα
σὺ πάλιν "οἶον ἐξέθρεψα τεκνίον· πάλαι ἐκφέ-
11 ρει." βάλε κορασίδιον κομψὸν καὶ αὐτὸ ὁ
γέρων φιλεῖ κἀκεῖνος ὁ νέος· ἂν δέ, δοξάριον. ἂν
δὲ κινδυνεῦσαι δέῃ, ἐρεῖς τὰς φωνὰς τὰς τοῦ
Ἀδμήτου πατρός·

> θέλεις βλέπειν φῶς, πατέρα δ' οὐ θέλειν
> δοκεῖς ; ²

12 οἴει ὅτι ἐκεῖνος οὐκ ἐφίλει τὸ ἴδιον παιδίον, ὅτε
μικρὸν ἦν, οὐδὲ πυρέσσοντος αὐτοῦ ἠγωνία οὐδ'
ἔλεγεν πολλάκις ὅτι "ὤφελον ἐγὼ μᾶλλον
ἐπύρεσσον" ; εἶτα ἐλθόντος τοῦ πράγματος καὶ

---

¹ Wolf: εὔνουν S.
² Quoted from memory. That of Euripides give χαίρεις
δρῶν . . . χαίρειν δοκεῖς. That of Epictetus gives both
versions, but the correct version, preceding the incorrect,
was bracketed by Elter.

---

¹ Euripides, *Alcestis*, 691, Browning's translation. *Cf.* the
critical note. Admetus had been reproaching his father for
not being willing to die in his stead.

and at one moment praise them, while at another
you blame them?—Yes, I am subject to exactly
these emotions.—What then? Do you think that
the man who has been deceived about someone can
be his friend?—No, indeed.—And can the man
whose choice of a friend is subject to change show
good will to that friend?—No, neither can he.—
And the man who now reviles someone, and later
on admires him?—No, neither can he.—What
then? Did you never see dogs fawning on one
another and playing with one another, so that you
say, "Nothing could be more friendly"? But to
see what their friendship amounts to, throw a piece
of meat between them and you will find out. Throw
likewise between yourself and your son a small piece
of land, and you will find out how much your son
wants to bury you, the sooner the better, and how
earnestly you pray for your son's death. Then you
will change your mind again and say, "What a child
I have brought up! All this time he has been ready
to carry me to my grave." Throw between you a
pretty wench, and the old man as well as the young
one falls in love with her; or, again, a bit of glory.
And if you have to risk your life you will say what
the father of Admetus did:

> "Thou joyest seeing daylight: dost suppose
>   Thy father joys not too?"[1]

Do you imagine that he did not love his own child
when it was small, and that he was not in agony
when it had the fever, and that he did not say over
and over again, "If only I had the fever instead"?
And then, when the test comes and is upon him,

13 ἐγγίσαντος ὅρα οἵας φωνὰς ἀφιᾶσιν. ὁ Ἐτεοκλῆς
καὶ ὁ Πολυνείκης οὐκ ἦσαν ἐκ τῆς αὐτῆς μητρὸς
καὶ τοῦ αὐτοῦ πατρός ; οὐκ ἦσαν συντεθραμμένοι,
συμβεβιωκότες, συμπεπαικότες,[1] συγκεκοιμη-
μένοι, πολλάκις ἀλλήλους καταπεφιληκότες ;
ὥστ᾽ εἴ τις οἶμαι εἶδεν αὐτούς, κατεγέλασεν ἂν
τῶν φιλοσόφων ἐφ᾽ οἷς περὶ φιλίας παραδοξο-
14 λογοῦσιν. ἀλλ᾽ ἐμπεσούσης εἰς τὸ μέσον ὥσπερ
κρέως τῆς τυραννίδος ὅρα οἷα λέγουσι·

> ποῦ ποτε στήσῃ πρὸ πύργων ;—ὡς τί μ᾽ εἰρώ-
> τας τόδε ;[2]—
> ἀντιτάξομαι κτενῶν σε.—κἀμὲ τοῦδ᾽ ἔρως ἔχει.

καὶ εὔχονται εὐχὰς τοιάσδε.

15 Καθόλου γάρ—μὴ ἐξαπατᾶσθε—πᾶν ζῷον
οὐδενὶ οὕτως ᾠκείωται ὡς τῷ ἰδίῳ συμφέροντι.
ὅ τι ἂν οὖν πρὸς τοῦτο φαίνηται αὐτῷ ἐμποδίζειν,
ἄν τ᾽ ἀδελφὸς ᾖ τοῦτο ἄν τε πατὴρ ἄν τε τέκνον
ἄν τ᾽ ἐρώμενος ἄν τ᾽ ἐραστής, μισεῖ, προβάλ-
16 λεται, καταρᾶται. οὐδὲν γὰρ οὕτως φιλεῖν
πέφυκεν ὡς τὸ αὐτοῦ συμφέρον· τοῦτο πατὴρ
καὶ ἀδελφὸς καὶ συγγενεῖς καὶ πατρὶς καὶ θεός.
17 ὅταν γοῦν εἰς τοῦτο ἐμποδίζειν ἡμῖν οἱ θεοὶ
δοκῶσιν, κἀκείνους λοιδοροῦμεν καὶ τὰ ἰδρύματα
αὐτῶν καταστρέφομεν καὶ τοὺς ναοὺς ἐμπιπρῶ-
μεν, ὥσπερ Ἀλέξανδρος ἐκέλευσεν ἐμπρησθῆναι
18 τὰ Ἀσκλήπεια ἀποθανόντος τοῦ ἐρωμένου. διὰ
τοῦτο ἂν μὲν ἐν ταὐτῷ τις θῇ τὸ συμφέρον καὶ

---

[1] Reiske (simul luserunt Schegk): συμπεπαιχότες Bentley,
Koraes : συμπεπωκότες S, Schenkl.
[2] (εἰρώτας) Bentley : ἐρωτᾶις. τῶιδ᾽ S. Cf. the marginal

just see what words he utters! Were not Eteocles
and Polyneices born of the same mother and the same
father? Had they not been brought up together,
lived together, played together, slept together, many
a time kissed one another? So that I fancy if anyone
had seen them, he would have laughed at the
philosophers for their paradoxical views on friendship.
But when the throne was cast between them, like a
piece of meat between the dogs, see what they say:

> *Eteo.* Where before the wall dost mean to stand?
> *Poly.* Why asked thou this of me?
> *Eteo.* I shall range myself against thee.
> *Poly.* Mine is also that desire![1]

Such also are the prayers they utter.[2]

It is a general rule—be not deceived—that every
living thing is to nothing so devoted as to its own
interest. Whatever, then, appears to it to stand in
the way of this interest, be it a brother, or father,
or child, or loved one, or lover, the being hates,
accuses, and curses it. For its nature is to love
nothing so much as its own interest; this to it
is father and brother and kinsmen and country and
God. When, for instance, we think that the gods
stand in the way of our attainment of this, we revile
even them, cast their statues to the ground, and
burn their temples, as Alexander ordered the temples
of Asclepius to be burned when his loved one died.[3]
For this reason, if a man puts together in one scale

---

[1] Euripides, *Phoenissae*, 621 f.
[2] In vv. 1365 ff. and 1373 ff., where each prays that he
may kill his brother.
[3] Hephaestion; *cf.* Arrian, *Anabasis*, VII. 14, 5.

---

gloss ἐρωτᾷς in Marc. 471 on *Phoenissae*, 621, where the MSS.
give ἱστορεῖς, and *Trans. Am. Philol. Assoc.*, LII. 49.

τὸ ὅσιον καὶ τὸ καλὸν καὶ πατρίδα καὶ γονεῖς
καὶ φίλους, σῴζεται ταῦτα πάντα· ἂν δ' ἀλλαχοῦ μὲν τὸ συμφέρον, ἀλλαχοῦ δὲ τοὺς φίλους
καὶ τὴν πατρίδα καὶ τοὺς συγγενεῖς καὶ αὐτὸ τὸ
δίκαιον, οἴχεται πάντα ταῦτα καταβαρούμενα
19 ὑπὸ τοῦ συμφέροντος. ὅπου γὰρ ἂν τὸ "ἐγὼ"
καὶ τὸ "ἐμόν," ἐκεῖ ἀνάγκη ῥέπειν τὸ ζῷον· εἰ
ἐν σαρκί, ἐκεῖ τὸ κυριεῦον εἶναι· εἰ ἐν προαιρέσει,
20 ἐκεῖ¹ εἶναι· εἰ ἐν τοῖς ἐκτός, ἐκεῖ. εἰ τοίνυν ἐκεῖ
εἰμι ἐγώ, ὅπου ἡ προαίρεσις, οὕτως μόνως καὶ
φίλος ἔσομαι οἷος δεῖ καὶ υἱὸς καὶ πατήρ. τοῦτο
γάρ μοι συνοίσει τηρεῖν τὸν πιστόν, τὸν αἰδήμονα, τὸν ἀνεκτικόν, τὸν ἀφεκτικὸν καὶ συνεργη-
21 τικόν, φυλάσσειν τὰς σχέσεις· ἂν δ' ἀλλαχοῦ μὲν
ἐμαυτὸν θῶ, ἀλλαχοῦ δὲ τὸ καλόν, οὕτως ἰσχυρὸς
γίνεται ὁ Ἐπικούρου λόγος, ἀποφαίνων ἢ μηδὲν
εἶναι τὸ καλὸν ἢ εἰ ἄρα τὸ ἔνδοξον.

22 Διὰ ταύτην τὴν ἄγνοιαν καὶ Ἀθηναῖοι καὶ
Λακεδαιμόνιοι διεφέροντο καὶ Θηβαῖοι πρὸς ἀμφοτέρους καὶ μέγας βασιλεὺς πρὸς τὴν Ἑλλάδα
καὶ Μακεδόνες πρὸς ἀμφοτέρους καὶ νῦν Ῥωμαῖοι
πρὸς Γέτας καὶ ἔτι πρότερον τὰ ἐν Ἰλίῳ διὰ
23 ταῦτα ἐγένετο. ὁ Ἀλέξανδρος τοῦ Μενελάου
ξένος ἦν, καὶ εἴ τις αὐτοὺς εἶδεν φιλοφρονου-
μένους ἀλλήλους, ἠπίστησεν ἂν τῷ λέγοντι οὐκ
εἶναι φίλους αὐτούς. ἀλλ' ἐβλήθη εἰς τὸ μέσον
μερίδιον, κομψὸν γυναικάριον, καὶ περὶ αὐτοῦ
24 πόλεμος. καὶ νῦν ὅταν ἴδῃς φίλους, ἀδελφοὺς

---

¹ Upton (after Schegk) : ἐκεῖνο S.

---

¹ That is, the things with which a man identifies himself
and his personal interest.

his interest and righteousness and what is honourable and country and parents and friends, they are all safe; but if he puts his interest in one scale, and in the other friends and country and kinsmen and justice itself, all these latter are lost because they are outweighed by his interest. For where one can say "I" and "mine," to that side must the creature perforce incline; if they[1] are in the flesh, there must the ruling power be; if they are in the moral purpose, there must it be; if they are in externals, there must it be. If, therefore, I am where my moral purpose is, then, and then only, will I be the friend and son and the father that I should be. For then this will be my interest—to keep my good faith, my self-respect, my forbearance, my abstinence, and my co-operation, and to maintain my relations with other men. But if I put what is mine in one scale, and what is honourable in the other, then the statement of Epicurus assumes strength, in which he declares that "the honourable is either nothing at all, or at best only what people hold in esteem."

It was through ignorance of this that the Athenians and Lacedaemonians quarrelled, and the Thebans with both of them, and the Great King with Greece, and the Macedonians with both of them, and in our days the Romans with the Getae, and yet earlier than any of these, what happened at Ilium was due to this. Alexander was a guest of Menelaus, and if anyone had seen their friendly treatment of one another, he would have disbelieved any man who said they were not friends. But there was thrown in between them a morsel, a pretty woman, and to win her war arose. So now, when you see friends,

ὁμονοεῖν δοκοῦντας, μὴ αὐτόθεν ἀποφήνῃ περὶ
τῆς φιλίας τι αὐτῶν μηδ᾽ ἂν ὀμνύωσιν μηδ᾽ ἂν
ἀδυνάτως ἔχειν λέγωσιν ἀπηλλάχθαι ἀλλήλων.
25 οὐκ ἔστι πιστὸν τὸ τοῦ φαύλου ἡγεμονικόν· ἀβέ-
βαιόν ἐστιν, ἄκριτον, ἄλλοθ᾽ ὑπ᾽ ἄλλης φαντα-
26 σίας νικώμενον. ἀλλ᾽ ἐξέτασον μὴ ταῦθ᾽ ἃ οἱ
ἄλλοι, εἰ ἐκ τῶν αὐτῶν γονέων καὶ ὁμοῦ ἀνατε-
θραμμένοι καὶ ὑπὸ τῷ αὐτῷ παιδαγωγῷ, ἀλλ᾽
ἐκεῖνο μόνον, ποῦ τὸ συμφέρον αὐτοῖς τίθενται,
27 πότερον ἐκτὸς ἢ ἐν προαιρέσει. ἂν ἐκτός, μὴ
εἴπῃς φίλους οὐ μᾶλλον ἢ πιστοὺς ἢ βεβαίους
ἢ θαρραλέους ἢ ἐλευθέρους, ἀλλὰ μηδ᾽ ἀνθρώ-
28 πους, εἰ νοῦν ἔχεις. οὐ γὰρ ἀνθρωπικὸν δόγμα
ἐστὶ τὸ ποιοῦν δάκνειν ἀλλήλους ἢ[1] λοιδορεῖσθαι καὶ τὰς ἐρημίας καταλαμβάνειν ἢ τὰς
ἀγορὰς ὡς θηρία[2] τὰ ὄρη, καὶ ἐν τοῖς δικαστη-
ρίοις ἀποδείκνυσθαι τὰ λῃστῶν· οὐδὲ τὸ ἀκρα-
τεῖς καὶ μοιχοὺς καὶ φθορεῖς ἀπεργαζόμενον·
οὐδ᾽ ὅσ᾽ ἄλλα πλημμελοῦσιν ἄνθρωποι κατ᾽
ἀλλήλων·[3] δι᾽ ἓν καὶ μόνον τοῦτο δόγμα, τὸ ἐν
τοῖς ἀπροαιρέτοις τίθεσθαι αὑτοὺς καὶ τὰ ἑαυτῶν.
29 ἂν δ᾽ ἀκούσῃς, ὅτι ταῖς ἀληθείαις οὗτοι οἱ ἄνθρωποι ἐκεῖ μόνον οἴονται τὸ ἀγαθὸν ὅπου προαίρεσις, ὅπου χρῆσις ὀρθὴ φαντασιῶν, μηκέτι
πολυπραγμονήσῃς μήτ᾽ εἰ υἱὸς καὶ πατήρ ἐστι

---

[1] Capps: καὶ S.
[2] θηρία supplied by Capps.
[3] The correct punctuation of this passage (colons after
ἀπεργαζόμενον and ἀλλήλων) is due to Capps.

or brothers, who seem to be of one mind, do not instantly make pronouncement about their friendship, not even if they swear to it, nor even if they say that they cannot be separated from one another. The ruling principle of the bad man is not to be trusted; it is insecure, incapable of judgement, a prey now to one external impression and now to another. Nay, do not make the same enquiry that most men do, asking whether two men are of the same parents, or were brought up together, or had the same school attendant, but this, and this only: Where do they put their interest—outside themselves, or in their moral purpose? If outside, call them not friends, any more than you would call them faithful, steadfast, courageous, or free; nay, call them not even human beings, if you are wise. For it is no judgement of human sort which makes them bite (that is revile) one another, and take to the desert (that is, to the market-place) as wild beasts take to the mountains, and in courts of law act the part of brigands; nor is it a judgement of human sort which makes them profligates and adulterers and corrupters; nor is it any such thing which makes men guilty of any of the many other crimes which they commit against one another; it is because of one single judgement, and this alone—because they put themselves and what belongs to themselves in the category of things which lie outside the sphere of moral purpose. But if you hear these men assert that in all sincerity they believe the good to be where moral purpose lies, and where there is the right use of external impressions, then you need no longer trouble yourself as to whether they are son and father, or brothers, or have been schoolmates

μήτ᾽ εἰ ἀδελφοὶ μήτ᾽ εἰ πολὺν χρόνον συμπεφοι-
τηκότες καὶ ἑταῖροι, ἀλλὰ μόνον αὐτὸ τοῦτο
γνοὺς θαρρῶν ἀποφαίνου, ὅτι φίλοι, ὥσπερ ὅτι
30 πιστοί, ὅτι δίκαιοι. ποῦ γὰρ ἀλλαχοῦ φιλία
ἢ ὅπου πίστις, ὅπου αἰδώς, ὅπου δόσις¹ τοῦ
καλοῦ, τῶν δ᾽ ἄλλων οὐδενός;
31   "᾽Αλλὰ τεθεράπευκέ με τοσούτῳ χρόνῳ· καὶ
οὐκ ἐφίλει με;" πόθεν οἶδας, ἀνδράποδον, εἰ
οὕτως τεθεράπευκεν ὡς τὰ ὑποδήματα σπογγίζει
τὰ ἑαυτοῦ, ὡς τὸ κτῆνος κτενίζει;² πόθεν οἶδας,
εἰ τὴν χρείαν σ᾽ ἀποβαλόντα τὴν τοῦ σκευαρίου
32 ῥίψει ὡς κατεαγὸς πινάκιον; "ἀλλὰ γυνή μου
ἐστὶ καὶ τοσούτῳ χρόνῳ συμβεβιώκαμεν." πόσῳ
δ᾽ ἡ ᾽Εριφύλη μετὰ τοῦ ᾽Αμφιαράου καὶ τέκνων
μήτηρ καὶ πολλῶν; ἀλλ᾽ ὅρμος ἦλθεν εἰς τὸ
33 μέσον. τί δ᾽ ἐστὶν ὅρμος; τὸ δόγμα τὸ περὶ τῶν
τοιούτων. ἐκεῖνο ἦν τὸ θηριῶδες, ἐκεῖνο τὸ δια-
κόπτον τὴν φιλίαν, τὸ οὐκ ἐῶν εἶναι γυναῖκα
34 γαμετήν, μητέρα³ μητέρα. καὶ ὑμῶν ὅστις
ἐσπούδακεν ἢ αὐτός τινι⁴ εἶναι φίλος ἢ ἄλλον
κτήσασθαι φίλον, ταῦτα τὰ δόγματα ἐκκοπτέτω,
ταῦτα μισησάτω, ταῦτα ἐξελασάτω ἐκ τῆς
35 ψυχῆς τῆς ἑαυτοῦ. καὶ οὕτως ἔσται πρῶτον
μὲν αὐτὸς ἑαυτῷ μὴ λοιδορούμενος, μὴ μαχό-
36 μενος, μὴ μετανοῶν, μὴ βασανίζων ἑαυτόν· ἔπειτα
καὶ ἑτέρῳ, τῷ μὲν ὁμοίῳ πάντη ἁπλοῦς,⁵ τοῦ
δ᾽ ἀνομοίου ἀνεκτικός, πρᾷος πρὸς αὐτόν, ἥμερος,

---

¹ διάδοσις Schweighäuser: δόσις καὶ λῆψις Shaftesbury:
θέσις Elter (after Schegk).   ² κτενίζει supplied by Capps.
³ τὴν before μητέρα deleted by Schenkl.
⁴ Schenkl (after Schegk): τις S.
⁵ Capps, combining πάντη (πάντῃ) of Schweighäuser and
ἁπλοῦς of the Salamanc edition: παντὶ ἁπλῶς S.

a long time and are comrades ; but though this is the
only knowledge you have concerning them, you may
confidently declare them "friends," just as you may
declare them "faithful" and "upright." For where
else is friendship to be found than where there is
fidelity, respect, a devotion[1] to things honourable
and to naught beside?

"But he has paid attention to me all these years ;
and did he not love me?" How do you know,
slave, whether he has paid attention to you just as he
sponges his shoes, or curries his horse? How do
you know but that, when you have lost your utility,
as that of some utensil, he will throw you away like
a broken plate? "But she is my wife and we have
lived together all these years." But how long did
Eriphyle live with Amphiaraus, yes, and bore him
children, and many of them? But a necklace came
in between them. And what does a necklace signify?
One's judgement about things like a necklace. That
was the brutish element, that was what sundered
the bond of love, what would not allow a woman to
be a wife, a mother to remain a mother. So let
every one of you who is eager to be a friend to
somebody himself, or to get somebody else for a
friend, eradicate these judgements, hate them, banish
them from his own soul. When this is done, first
of all, he will not be reviling himself, fighting with
himself, repenting, tormenting himself ; and, in the
second place, in relation to his comrade, he will be
always straightforward to one who is like him himself, while to one who is unlike he will be tolerant,
gentle, kindly, forgiving, as to one who is ignorant

---

[1] For δόσις in this sense (not in *L. and S.*), see *Thes. L.G.*
s.v. and especially R. Hirzel: *Untersuch. zu Cic. Philos.*
Schr. II. (1882). 563. n. 1 ; Bonhöffer 1890: 286, n. 1.

συγγνωμονικὸς ὡς πρὸς ἀγνοοῦντα, ὡς πρὸς δια-
πίπτοντα περὶ τῶν μεγίστων· οὐδενὶ χαλεπός,
ἅτ᾽ εἰδὼς ἀκριβῶς τὸ τοῦ Πλάτωνος, ὅτι πᾶσα
37 ψυχὴ ἄκουσα στέρεται τῆς ἀληθείας. εἰ δὲ μή,
τὰ μὲν ἄλλα πράξετε πάντα ὅσα οἱ φίλοι καὶ
συμπιεῖσθε καὶ συσκηνήσετε καὶ συμπλεύσετε
καὶ ἐκ τῶν αὐτῶν γεγενημένοι ἔσεσθε· καὶ γὰρ
οἱ ὄφεις. φίλοι δ᾽ οὔτ᾽ ἐκεῖνοι οὔθ᾽ ὑμεῖς, μέχρις
ἂν ἔχητε τὰ θηριώδη ταῦτα καὶ μιαρὰ δόγματα.

κγ΄. Περὶ τῆς τοῦ λέγειν δυνάμεως.

1 Βιβλίον πᾶς ἂν ἥδιον ἀναγνῷη[1] καὶ ῥᾷον τὸ
εὐσημοτέροις γράμμασι γεγραμμένον. οὐκοῦν
καὶ λόγους πᾶς ἄν τις ῥᾷον ἀκούσειε[2] τοὺς
εὐσχήμοσιν ἅμα καὶ εὐπρεπέσιν ὀνόμασι σεση-
2 μασμένους. οὐκ ἄρα τοῦτο ῥητέον, ὡς οὐδεμία
δύναμίς ἐστιν ἀπαγγελτική· τοῦτο γὰρ ἅμα
μὲν ἀσεβοῦς ἐστιν ἀνθρώπου, ἅμα δὲ δειλοῦ.
ἀσεβοῦς μέν, ὅτι τὰς παρὰ τοῦ θεοῦ χάριτας
ἀτιμάζει, ὥσπερ εἰ ἀνῄρει τὴν εὐχρηστίαν τῆς
ὁρατικῆς ἢ τῆς ἀκουστικῆς δυνάμεως ἢ αὐτῆς
3 τῆς φωνητικῆς. εἰκῇ οὖν σοι ὁ θεὸς ὀφθαλμοὺς
ἔδωκεν, εἰκῇ πνεῦμα ἐνεκέρασεν αὐτοῖς οὕτως
ἰσχυρὸν καὶ φιλότεχνον, ὥστε μακρὰν ἐξικνού-
μενον ἀναμάσσεσθαι τοὺς τύπους τῶν ὁρωμένων;

---

[1] Koraes : ἀναγνῶ ἢ S.   [2] Schenkl : ἀκούσει S.

[1] *Cf.* I. 28, 4.
[2] In Stoic physiology the spirit of vision connected the
central mind with the pupil of the eye, and sight was
produced by the action of this spirit upon external objects,

or is making a mistake in things of the greatest
importance; he will not be harsh with anybody,
because he knows well the saying of Plato, that
"every soul is unwillingly deprived of the truth." [1]
But if you fail to do this, you may do everything
else that friends do—drink together, and share the
same tent, and sail on the same ship—and you may
be sons of the same parents; yes, and so may snakes!
But they will never be friends and no more will you,
as long as you retain these brutish and abominable
judgements.

CHAPTER XXIII

Of the faculty of expression

EVERYONE would read with greater pleasure and
ease the book that is written in the clearer characters.
Therefore everyone would also listen with greater
ease to those discourses that are expressed in
appropriate and attractive language   We must not,
therefore, say that there is no faculty of expression,
for this is to speak both as an impious man and
as a coward.   As an impious man, because one is
thereby disparaging the gifts received from God, as
though one were denying the usefulness of the
faculty of vision, or that of hearing, or that of speech
itself.   Did God give you eyes to no purpose, did
He to no purpose put in them a spirit [2] so strong
and so cunningly devised that it reaches out to a
great distance and fashions the forms of whatever

not by the passive reception of rays. See L. Stein,
Psychologie der Stoa (1886), 127–9; *Erkenntnistheorie der Stoa*
(1888), 135 f.; A. Bonhöffer, *Epiktet und die Stoa* (1890), 123;
and for the origins of this general theory, J. I. Beare, *Greek
Theories of elementary Cognition* (1906), 11 ff.

4 καὶ ποῖος ἄγγελος οὕτως ὠκὺς καὶ ἐπιμελής; εἰκῇ
δὲ καὶ τὸν μεταξὺ ἀέρα οὕτως ἐνεργὸν ἐποίησεν καὶ
ἔντονον, ὥστε δι' αὐτοῦ τεινομένου[1] πως διικνεῖ-
σθαι τὴν ὅρασιν; εἰκῇ δὲ φῶς ἐποίησεν, οὗ μὴ
παρόντος οὐδενὸς τῶν ἄλλων ὄφελος ἦν;

5 Ἄνθρωπε, μήτ' ἀχάριστος ἴσθι μήτε πάλιν
ἀμνήμων τῶν κρεισσόνων, ἀλλ' ὑπὲρ μὲν τοῦ
ὁρᾶν καὶ ἀκούειν καὶ νὴ Δία ὑπὲρ αὐτοῦ
τοῦ ζῆν καὶ τῶν συνεργῶν πρὸς αὐτό, ὑπὲρ
καρπῶν ξηρῶν, ὑπὲρ οἴνου, ὑπὲρ ἐλαίου

6 εὐχαρίστει τῷ θεῷ· μέμνησο δ' ὅτι ἄλλο τί σοι
δέδωκεν κρεῖττον ἁπάντων τούτων, τὸ χρησό-
μενον αὐτοῖς, τὸ δοκιμάσον, τὸ τὴν ἀξίαν ἑκάστου

7 λογιούμενον. τί γάρ ἐστι τὸ ἀποφαινόμενον
ὑπὲρ ἑκάστης τούτων τῶν δυνάμεων, πόσου
τις ἀξία ἐστὶν αὐτῶν; μή τι αὐτὴ ἑκάστη ἡ
δύναμις; μή τι τῆς ὁρατικῆς ποτ' ἤκουσας λε-
γούσης τι περὶ ἑαυτῆς, μή τι τῆς ἀκουστικῆς;[2]
ἀλλ' ὡς διάκονοι καὶ δοῦλαι τεταγμέναι εἰσὶν

8 ὑπηρετεῖν τῇ χρηστικῇ τῶν φαντασιῶν. κἂν
πύθῃ, πόσου ἕκαστον ἄξιόν ἐστιν, τίνος πυνθάνῃ; τίς σοι ἀποκρίνεται; πῶς οὖν δύναταί τις
ἄλλη δύναμις κρείσσων εἶναι ταύτης, ἢ καὶ ταῖς
λοιπαῖς διακόνοις χρῆται καὶ δοκιμάζει αὐτὴ

9 ἕκαστα καὶ ἀποφαίνεται; τίς γὰρ ἐκείνων οἶδεν,
τίς ἐστιν αὐτὴ καὶ πόσου ἀξία; τίς ἐκείνων
οἶδεν, ὁπότε δεῖ χρῆσθαι αὐτῇ καὶ πότε μή;

---

[1] Wolf: γινομένου S.

[2] The words μή τι πυρῶν; μή τι κριθῶν; μή τι ἵππου; μή τι
κινός; "Or wheat, or barley, or a horse, or a dog?" which
follow at this point in S, were deleted by Schenkl (after
Schweighäuser) as being out of keeping with the context.

is seen? And what messenger is so swift and so
attentive as the eye? And did He to no purpose
make also the intervening air so active and so intent [1]
that the vision passes through it as through some
tense medium? And did He to no purpose create
light, without the presence of which all else were
useless?

Man, be neither ungrateful for these gifts, nor
yet forgetful of the better things, but for sight and
hearing, yes and, by Zeus, for life itself and for
what is conducive to it, for dry fruits, for wine, for
olive oil, give thanks unto God; and at the same
time remember that He has given you something
better than all these things—the faculty which can
make use of them, pass judgement upon them,
estimate the value of each. For what is that which,
in the case of each of these faculties, shows what it
is worth? [2] Is it each faculty itself? Did you ever
hear the faculty of sight say anything about itself?
Or the faculty of vision? No, but they have been
appointed as servants and slaves to minister to the
faculty which makes use of external impressions.
And if you ask, what each thing is worth, of whom
do you ask? Who is to answer you? How, then,
can any other faculty be superior to this which both
uses the rest as its servants, and itself passes judgement upon each several thing and pronounces upon
it? For which one of them knows what it is and
what it is worth? Which one of them knows when
one ought to use it, and when not? What is the

---

[1] That is, firm, taut, elastic, so as to be sensitive to the
action of the spirit of vision, and not dull and yielding like
mud or putty.

[2] For the general theme, see I. 1.

τίς ἐστιν ἡ ἀνοίγουσα καὶ κλείουσα τοὺς ὀφθαλμοὺς καὶ ἀφ' ὧν δεῖ ἀποστρέφουσα, τοῖς δὲ
προσάγουσα; ἡ ὁρατική; οὔ, ἀλλ' ἡ προαιρετική. τίς ἡ τὰ ὦτα ἐπικλείουσα καὶ ἀνοίγουσα;
10 τίς, καθ' ἣν περίεργοι καὶ πευθῆνες ἢ πάλιν
ἀκίνητοι ὑπὸ λόγου; ἡ ἀκουστική;[1] οὐκ ἄλλη
11 ἢ ἡ προαιρετικὴ δύναμις. εἶτ' αὐτὴ ἰδοῦσα, ὅτι
ἐν τυφλαῖς καὶ κωφαῖς ταῖς ἄλλαις ἁπάσαις
δυνάμεσίν ἐστι μηδέ τι ἄλλο συνορᾶν δυναμέναις
πλὴν αὐτὰ ἐκεῖνα τὰ ἔργα, ἐφ' οἷς τεταγμέναι
εἰσὶ διακονεῖν ταύτῃ καὶ ὑπηρετεῖν, αὐτὴ δὲ μόνη
ὀξὺ βλέπει καὶ τάς τ' ἄλλας καθορᾷ, πόσου
ἑκάστη ἀξία, καὶ αὑτήν, μέλλει ἡμῖν ἄλλο τι
ἀποφαίνεσθαι τὸ κράτιστον εἶναι ἢ αὑτήν; καὶ
12 τί ποιεῖ ἄλλο ὀφθαλμὸς ἀνοιχθεὶς ἢ ὁρᾷ; εἰ δὲ
δεῖ τὴν τοῦ τινος ἰδεῖν γυναῖκα καὶ πῶς, τίς
13 λέγει; ἡ προαιρετική. εἰ δὲ δεῖ πιστεῦσαι τοῖς
λεχθεῖσιν ἢ ἀπιστῆσαι καὶ πιστεύσαντα ἐρεθι-
14 σθῆναι ἢ μή, τίς λέγει; οὐχ ἡ προαιρετική; ἡ δὲ
φραστικὴ αὕτη καὶ καλλωπιστικὴ τῶν ὀνομάτων,
εἴ τις ἄρα ἰδία δύναμις, τί ἄλλο ποιεῖ ἤ, ὅταν
ἐμπέσῃ λόγος περί τινος, καλλωπίζει τὰ ὀνόματα
καὶ συντίθησιν ὥσπερ οἱ κομμωταὶ τὴν κόμην;
15 πότερον δ' εἰπεῖν ἄμεινον ἢ σιωπῆσαι καὶ οὕτως
ἄμεινον ἢ ἐκείνως καὶ τοῦτο πρέπον ἢ οὐ πρέπον,
καὶ τὸν καιρὸν ἑκάστου καὶ τὴν χρείαν τίς ἄλλη
λέγει ἢ ἡ προαιρετική; θέλεις οὖν αὐτὴν παρελ-
θοῦσαν αὑτῆς καταψηφίσασθαι;

---

[1] Upton from his "codex" (after Wolf): ἢ ἀκουστικοί S.

faculty that opens and closes the eyes, and turns them away from the things from which it should turn them, but directs them toward other things? The faculty of sight? No, but the faculty of moral purpose. What is the faculty that closes and opens the ears? What is that faculty by virtue of which men are curious and inquisitive, or again, unmoved by what is said? The faculty of hearing? No, it is none other than the faculty of moral purpose. When, then, this faculty sees that all the other faculties which surround it are blind and deaf, and unable to see anything but the very acts for which they have been appointed to serve and minister unto it, while it alone sees clearly and surveys, not only all the rest, determining what each is worth, but itself also, is it likely to pronounce that anything else is supreme but itself? And what else can the open eye do but see? But whether it ought to see someone's wife and how, what faculty tells it? That of moral purpose. And what faculty tells a man whether he ought to believe what he has been told, or disbelieve, and, if he believes, whether he ought to be provoked by it or not? Is it not that of moral purpose? And this faculty of speech and of the adornment of language, if it really is a separate faculty, what else does it do, when discourse arises about some topic, but ornament and compose the words, as hairdressers do the hair? But whether it is better to speak than to keep silence, and to do so in this way, or in that, and whether this is appropriate or not appropriate, and the proper occasion and utility of each action—what else tells us all this but the faculty of moral purpose? Would you, then, have it come forward and condemn itself?

16 "Τί οὖν," φησίν, "εἰ οὕτως τὸ πρᾶγμα ἔχει,
καὶ δύναται τὸ διακονοῦν κρεῖσσον εἶναι ἐκείνου
ᾧ διακονεῖ, ὁ ἵππος τοῦ ἱππέως ἢ ὁ κύων τοῦ
κυνηγοῦ ἢ τὸ ὄργανον τοῦ κιθαριστοῦ ἢ οἱ
ὑπηρέται τοῦ βασιλέως ;"—Τί ἐστι τὸ χρώμενον;
17 προαίρεσις. τί ἐπιμελεῖται πάντων ; προαίρεσις.
τί ὅλον ἀναιρεῖ τὸν ἄνθρωπον ποτὲ μὲν λιμῷ,
ποτὲ δ' ἀγχόνῃ, ποτὲ δὲ κατὰ κρημνοῦ ; προαί-
18 ρεσις. εἶτα τούτου τί ἰσχυρότερον ἐν ἀνθρώποις
ἐστίν ; καὶ πῶς οἷόν τε τοῦ ἀκωλύτου τὰ
19 κωλυόμενα ; τὴν ὁρατικὴν δύναμιν τίνα πέφυκεν
ἐμποδίζειν ; καὶ προαίρεσις καὶ ἀπροαίρετα.[1]
τὴν ἀκουστικὴν ταῦτά, τὴν φραστικὴν ὡσαύτως.
προαίρεσιν δὲ τί ἐμποδίζειν πέφυκεν ; ἀπροαίρετον οὐδέν, αὐτὴ δ' ἑαυτὴν διαστραφεῖσα. διὰ
τοῦτο κακία μόνη αὕτη γίνεται ἢ ἀρετὴ μόνη.
20 Εἶτα τηλικαύτη δύναμις οὖσα καὶ πᾶσι τοῖς
ἄλλοις ἐπιτεταγμένη παρελθοῦσα ἡμῖν λεγέτω
κράτιστον εἶναι τῶν ὄντων τὴν σάρκα. οὐδὲ εἰ
αὐτὴ ἡ σὰρξ ἑαυτὴν ἔλεγεν εἶναι κράτιστον,
21 ἠνέσχετο ἄν τις αὐτῆς. νῦν δὲ τί ἐστιν, 'Επί-
κουρε, τὸ ταῦτα ἀποφαινόμενον ; τὸ περὶ Τέλους
συγγεγραφός, τὸ τὰ Φυσικά, τὸ περὶ Κανόνος ;

---

[1] Salmasius : προαιρετά S.

---

[1] This passage is very obscure in the original and it may
well be that something is missing before § 16 which would
make the objector's question more plausible, or else after the
first part of the question, so that the remainder would belong
to the answer by Epictetus.   It is not impossible that the
whole paragraph, §§ 16–19, is derived from a separate context
and fitted in here rather badly by Arrian himself or by some

"What then," says an objector, "if the matter stands like *this*, and it *is* possible for that which serves to be superior to what it serves—the horse to the rider, or the dog to the hunter, or his instrument to the harper, or his servants to the king?"[1] Well, what faculty is it that uses the services of the rest in this way? Moral purpose. What is it that attends to everything? Moral purpose. What is it that destroys the whole man, sometimes by hunger, sometimes by a noose, sometimes by hurling him over a cliff? Moral purpose. Is there, then, anything stronger than this among men? Yet how can the things that are subject to hindrance be stronger than that which is unhindered? What are by their very nature capable of hindering the faculty of vision? Both moral purpose and things that lie outside its sphere. The same hinder vision; and so it is also with speech. But what is by its very nature capable of hindering moral purpose? Nothing that lies outside its sphere, but only itself when perverted. For this reason moral purpose becomes the only vice, or the only virtue.

Therefore, since it is so great a faculty and has been set over everything else, let *it* come before us and say that the flesh is of all things the most excellent. Nay, even if the flesh itself called itself most excellent, one would not have tolerated such a statement. But now what is it, Epicurus, that makes such a declaration? that composed the treatise *On the End*, or *The Physics*, or *On the Standard?*[2]

ancient reader or editor, because essentially it does no more than repeat the preceding paragraph.

[2] Famous works by Epicurus, of which the first treated ethics and the third epistomology, the "standard" being a standard of judgement or criterion.

τὸ τὸν πώγωνα καθεικός; τὸ γράφον, ὅτε
ἀπέθνησκεν, ὅτι "τὴν τελευταίαν ἄγοντες ἅμα
22 καὶ μακαρίαν ἡμέραν;" ἡ σὰρξ ἢ ἡ προαίρεσις;
εἶτα τούτου τι κρεῖσσον ἔχειν ὁμολογεῖς καὶ οὐ
μαίνῃ; οὕτως τυφλὸς ταῖς ἀληθείαις καὶ κωφὸς
εἶ;

23 Τί οὖν; ἀτιμάζει τις τὰς ἄλλας δυνάμεις; μὴ
γένοιτο. λέγει τις μηδεμίαν εἶναι χρείαν ἢ
προαγωγὴν ἔξω¹ τῆς προαιρετικῆς δυνάμεως;
μὴ γένοιτο. ἀνόητον, ἀσεβές, ἀχάριστον πρὸς
τὸν θεόν. ἀλλὰ τὴν ἀξίαν ἑκάστῳ ἀποδίδωσιν.

24 ἔστι γάρ τις καὶ ὄνου χρεία, ἀλλ' οὐχ ἡλίκη βοός·
ἔστι καὶ κυνός, ἀλλ' οὐχ ἡλίκη οἰκέτου· ἔστι
καὶ οἰκέτου, ἀλλ' οὐχ ἡλίκη τῶν πολιτῶν· ἔστι

25 καὶ τούτων, ἀλλ' οὐχ ἡλίκη τῶν ἀρχόντων. οὐ
μέντοι διὰ τὸ ἄλλα εἶναι κρείττονα καὶ ἣν
παρέχει τὰ ἕτερα χρείαν ἀτιμαστέον. ἔστι τις
ἀξία καὶ τῆς φραστικῆς δυνάμεως, ἀλλ' οὐχ

26 ἡλίκη τῆς προαιρετικῆς. ὅταν οὖν ταῦτα λέγω,
μή τις οἰέσθω ὅτι ἀμελεῖν ὑμᾶς ἀξιῶ φράσεως·
οὐδὲ γὰρ ὀφθαλμῶν οὐδ' ὤτων οὐδὲ χειρῶν οὐδὲ

27 ποδῶν οὐδ' ἐσθῆτος οὐδ' ὑποδημάτων. ἀλλ' ἄν
μου πυνθάνῃ "τί οὖν ἐστι κράτιστον τῶν ὄντων;"

---

¹ Supplied by Schenkl.

---

¹ That is, assume the rôle of a philosopher, compare I. 2,
29, and note.
² A slight variation from the standard form of the famous
saying of Epicurus on his death-bed. See Usener, *Epicurea*,
p. 143, 16 ff., and especially Diog. Laert. X. 10, 22: "And
when he was at the point of death, he wrote the following
letter to Idomeneus: 'We have written this letter to you on
a happy day to us, which is also the last day of our life. For

that caused you to let your beard grow long?[1]
that wrote as it was dying: "We are spending
what is our last and at the same time a happy
day?"[2] Was it the flesh or the moral purpose?
Come, do you confess that you have something
superior to the flesh, and you are not insane, either?
Are you, in all truth, so blind and deaf?

Well, what then? Does a man despise his
other faculties? Far from it! Does a man say
there is no use or advancement save in the faculty
of moral purpose? Far from it! That is unintelligent, impious, ungrateful towards God. Nay, he is
but assigning its true value to each thing. For there is
some use in an ass, but not as much as there is in
an ox; there is use also in a dog, but not as much
as there is in a slave; there is use also in a slave,
but not as much as there is in your fellow-citizens;
there is use also in these, but not as much as there
is in the magistrates. Yet because some things are
superior we ought not to despise the use which the
others give. There is a certain value also in the
faculty of eloquence, but it is not as great as that
of the faculty of moral purpose. When, therefore,
I say this, let no one suppose that I am bidding you
neglect speech, any more than I bid you neglect
eyes, or ears, or hands, or feet, or dress, or shoes.
But if you ask me, "What, then, is the highest of

strangury has attacked me, and also a dysentery, so violent
that nothing can be added to the violence of my sufferings.
But the cheerfulness of my mind, which arises from the
recollection of all my philosophical contemplations, counter-
balances all these afflictions. And I beg you to take care of
the children of Metrodorus, in a manner worthy of the
devotion shown by the youth to me, and to philosophy.'"
(Yonge's translation.)

413

τί εἴπω; τὴν φραστικήν; οὐ δύναμαι· ἀλλὰ τὴν
28 προαιρετικήν, ὅταν ὀρθὴ γένηται. τοῦτο γάρ
ἐστι τὸ κἀκείνῃ χρώμενον καὶ ταῖς ἄλλαις
πάσαις καὶ μικραῖς καὶ μεγάλαις δυνάμεσιν·
τούτου κατορθωθέντος ἀγαθὸς ἄνθρωπος γίνεται,[1]
29 ἀποτευχθέντος κακὸς ἄνθρωπος γίνεται· παρ' ὃ
ἀτυχοῦμεν, εὐτυχοῦμεν, μεμφόμεθ' ἀλλήλους,
εὐαρεστοῦμεν, ἁπλῶς ὃ λεληθὸς[2] μὲν κακοδαιμο-
νίαν ποιεῖται, τυχὸν δ' ἐπιμελείας εὐδαιμονίαν.

30   Τὸ δ' αἴρειν τὴν δύναμιν τῆς φραστικῆς καὶ
λέγειν μὴ εἶναι μηδεμίαν ταῖς ἀληθείαις οὐ μόνον
ἀχαρίστου ἐστὶ πρὸς τοὺς δεδωκότας, ἀλλὰ καὶ
31 δειλοῦ. ὁ γὰρ τοιοῦτος φοβεῖσθαί μοι δοκεῖ, μή,
εἴπερ ἐστί τις δύναμις κατὰ τὸν τόπον, οὐ
32 δυνηθῶμεν αὐτῆς καταφρονῆσαι. τοιοῦτοί εἰσι
καὶ οἱ λέγοντες μηδεμίαν εἶναι παραλλαγὴν
κάλλους πρὸς αἶσχος. εἶτα ὁμοίως ἦν κινηθῆναι
τὸν Θερσίτην ἰδόντα καὶ τὸν Ἀχιλλέα; ὁμοίως
33 τὴν Ἑλένην καὶ ἣν ἔτυχε[3] γυναῖκα; καὶ ταῦτα
μωρὰ καὶ ἄγροικα καὶ οὐκ εἰδότων τὴν ἑκάστου
φύσιν, ἀλλὰ φοβουμένων μὴ ἄν τις αἴσθηται τῆς
διαφορᾶς, εὐθὺς συναρπασθεὶς καὶ ἡττηθεὶς
34 ἀπέλθῃ. ἀλλὰ τὸ μέγα τοῦτο, ἀπολιπεῖν ἑκάστῳ
τὴν αὑτοῦ δύναμιν ἣν ἔχει καὶ ἀπολιπόντα ἰδεῖν
τὴν ἀξίαν τῆς δυνάμεως καὶ τὸ κράτιστον τῶν
ὄντων καταμαθεῖν καὶ τοῦτο ἐν παντὶ μεταδιώκειν,
περὶ τοῦτο ἐσπουδακέναι, πάρεργα τἆλλα πρὸς

---

[1] The word ἀγαθὸς before γίνεται was deleted by
Salmasius.

[2] Sb : λεληθὲν S : Schenkl suggests ἀμεληθέν : neglecta
Wolf.

[3] Upton : εἶχε S.

all things?" what shall I say? The faculty of eloquence? I cannot; but rather that of moral purpose,
when it becomes a *right* moral purpose. For it is this
which uses not only that faculty of eloquence but
also all the other faculties both small and great;
when this has been set right a man becomes good,
when it has failed a man becomes bad ; it is through
this that we are unfortunate, and are fortunate,
blame one another, and are pleased with one
another; in a word, it is this which, when ignored,
produces wretchedness, but when attended to produces happiness.

But to do away with the faculty of eloquence and
to say that in all truth it is nothing is the act not
merely of a man ungrateful to those who have given
it, but also cowardly. For such a person seems to
me to be afraid that, if there really is a faculty of
this kind, we may not be able to despise it. Such
also are those who assert that there is no difference
between beauty and ugliness. What! could a man
be affected in the same way by the sight of Thersites
and that of Achilles ? Or by the sight of Helen
and that of some ordinary woman ? But these are
the notions of foolish and boorish persons who do
not know the nature of each several thing, but are
afraid that if a man notices the superiority of the
faculty in question he will immediately be carried
away by it and come off worsted. Nay, the great
thing is this : to leave each in the possession of his
own proper faculty, and, so leaving him, to observe
the value of the faculty, and to learn what is the
highest of all things, and in everything to pursue
after this, to be zealous about this, treating all other
things as of secondary value in comparison with it,

τοῦτο πεποιημένον, οὐ μέντοι ἀμελοῦντα οὐδ'
35 ἐκείνων κατὰ δύναμιν. καὶ γὰρ ὀφθαλμῶν ἐπιμε-
λητέον, ἀλλ' οὐχ ὡς τοῦ κρατίστου, ἀλλὰ καὶ
τούτων διὰ τὸ κράτιστον· ὅτι ἐκεῖνο οὐκ ἄλλως
ἕξει κατὰ φύσιν εἰ μὴ ἐν τούτοις εὐλογιστοῦν καὶ
τὰ ἕτερα παρὰ τὰ ἕτερα αἱρούμενον.

36 Τί οὖν ἐστι τὸ γινόμενον; οἷον εἴ τις ἀπιὼν εἰς
τὴν πατρίδα τὴν ἑαυτοῦ καὶ διοδεύων πανδοκεῖον
καλὸν ἀρέσαντος αὐτῷ τοῦ πανδοκείου καταμένοι
37 ἐν τῷ πανδοκείῳ. ἄνθρωπε, ἐπελάθου σου τῆς
προθέσεως· οὐκ εἰς τοῦτο ὥδευες, ἀλλὰ διὰ τούτου.
" ἀλλὰ κομψὸν τοῦτο." πόσα δ' ἄλλα πανδοκεῖα
38 κομψά, πόσοι δὲ λειμῶνες· ἁπλῶς ὡς δίοδος. τὸ
δὲ προκείμενον ἐκεῖνο· εἰς τὴν πατρίδα ἐπανελθεῖν,
τοὺς οἰκείους ἀπαλλάξαι δέους, αὐτὸν τὰ τοῦ
πολίτου ποιεῖν, γῆμαι, παιδοποιεῖσθαι, ἄρξαι τὰς
39 νομιζομένας ἀρχάς. οὐ γὰρ τοὺς κομψοτέρους
ἡμῖν τόπους ἐκλεξόμενος ἐλήλυθας, ἀλλ' ἐν οἷς
ἐγένου καὶ ὧν κατατέταξαι πολίτης, ἐν τούτοις
ἀναστραφησόμενος. τοιοῦτόν τι καὶ ἐνταῦθά ἐστι
40 τὸ γινόμενον. ἐπεὶ διὰ λόγου καὶ τοιαύτης παρα-
δόσεως ἐλθεῖν ἐπὶ τὸ τέλειον δεῖ καὶ τὴν αὑτοῦ
προαίρεσιν ἐκκαθᾶραι καὶ τὴν δύναμιν τὴν χρηστικὴν τῶν φαντασιῶν ὀρθὴν κατασκευάσαι,
ἀνάγκη δὲ τὴν παράδοσιν γίνεσθαι διά τινων[1]
θεωρημάτων καὶ διὰ λέξεως ποιᾶς καὶ μετά τινος
41 ποικιλίας καὶ δριμύτητος τῶν θεωρημάτων, ὑπ'

---

[1] διά τινων Kronenberg: τῶν S.

---

[1] Compare the saying ascribed to Jesus by the Great
Mogul Akbar as inscribed on a gateway of the ruined city
Futtey-pore-Sikri in India. "Jesus had said : 'The world

though without neglecting these, as far as this is possible. For we must take care of our eyes too, yet not as the highest thing, but we must take care of them for the sake of the highest; because this latter will not have its natural perfection unless it uses the eyes with reason and chooses one thing instead of another.

What, then, generally takes place? Men act like a traveller on the way to his own country who stops at an excellent inn, and, since the inn pleases him, stays there. Man, you have forgotten your purpose; you were not travelling *to* this but *through* it.[1] "But this is a fine inn." And how many other inns are fine, and how many meadows—yet simply for passing through. But your purpose is the other thing, to return to your country, to relieve the fear of your kinsmen, to do the duties of a citizen yourself, to marry, bring up children, hold the customary offices. For you did not come into the world to select unusually fine places, I ween, but to live and go about your business in the place where you were born and were enrolled as a citizen. Something like this takes place also in the matter which we are considering. Since a man must advance to perfection through the spoken word and such instruction as you receive here, and must purify his own moral purpose and correct the faculty which makes use of external impressions, and since the instruction must necessarily be given by means of certain principles, and in a particular style, and with a certain variety and impressiveness in the

is but a bridge, over which you must pass, but must not linger to build your dwelling.'" See Resch, *Agrapha* (1906), no. 95, p. 292.

αὐτῶν τινες τούτων ἁλισκόμενοι καταμένουσιν
αὐτοῦ, ὁ μὲν ὑπὸ τῆς λέξεως, ὁ δ' ὑπὸ συλλογισμῶν, ὁ δ' ὑπὸ μεταπιπτόντων, ὁ δ' ὑπ' ἄλλου
τινὸς τοιούτου πανδοκείου, καὶ προσμείναντες
κατασήπονται ὡς παρὰ ταῖς Σειρῆσιν.

42   Ἄνθρωπε, τὸ προκείμενον ἦν σοι κατασκευάσαι
σαυτὸν χρηστικὸν ταῖς προσπιπτούσαις φαντασίαις κατὰ φύσιν, ἐν ὀρέξει ἀναπότευκτον, ἐν δ'
ἐκκλίσει ἀπερίπτωτον, μηδέποτ' ἀτυχοῦντα, μηδέποτε δυστυχοῦντα, ἐλεύθερον, ἀκώλυτον, ἀνανάγκαστον, συναρμόζοντα τῇ τοῦ Διὸς διοικήσει,
ταύτῃ πειθόμενον, ταύτῃ εὐαρεστοῦντα, μηδένα
μεμφόμενον, μηδέν' αἰτιώμενον, δυνάμενον εἰπεῖν
τούτους τοὺς στίχους ἐξ ὅλης ψυχῆς

   ἄγου δέ μ', ὦ Ζεῦ, καὶ σύ γ' ἡ Πεπρωμένη.¹

43 εἶτα τοῦτο τὸ προκείμενον ἔχων ἀρέσαντός σοι
λεξειδίου, ἀρεσάντων θεωρημάτων τινῶν αὐτοῦ
καταμένεις καὶ κατοικεῖν προαιρῇ ἐπιλαθόμενος
τῶν ἐν οἴκῳ καὶ λέγεις " ταῦτα κομψά ἐστιν";
τίς γὰρ λέγει μὴ εἶναι αὐτὰ κομψά; ἀλλ' ὡς
44 δίοδον, ὡς πανδοκεῖα. τί γὰρ κωλύει φράζοντα

---

¹ In *Encheiridion* 53 the other three verses are quoted :

   "To that goal long ago to me assigned.
   I'll follow and not falter ; if my will
   Prove weak and craven, still I'll follow on."

They are derived from a poem of Cleanthes (Von Arnim,
Stoicorum Veterum Fragmenta, I. frag. 527). For a somewhat
indifferent translation of them into Latin, see Seneca, *Epist.*,
107. 11, who adds as a fifth verse in the pointed style
characteristic of him : *Ducunt volentem fata, nolentem trahunt.*
"The willing are led by fate, the reluctant dragged." It is
not impossible that the sentiment here expressed may be

form of these principles, some persons are captivated by all these things and stay where they are ; one is captivated by style, another by syllogisms, another by arguments with equivocal premisses, another by some other " inn " of that sort, and staying there they moulder away as though they were among the Sirens.

Man, your purpose was to make yourself competent to use conformably with nature the external impressions that came to you, in desire not to fail in what you would attain, and in avoidance not to fall into what you would avoid, never suffering misfortune, never ill fortune, free, unhindered, unconstrained, conforming to the governance of Zeus, obeying this, well satisfied with this, blaming no one, charging no one, able to say with your whole heart the verses, beginning :

"Lead thou me on, O Zeus, and Destiny." [1]

And then, although you have this purpose, because some petty trick of style, or certain principles, catch your fancy, are you going to stay just where you are and choose to dwell there, forgetful of the things at home and saying " This is fine " ? Well, who says that it is not fine? But only like a passageway, like an "inn." For what is to prevent

one of the remote and probably unconscious inspirations of Cardinal Newman's celebrated hymn,

"Lead, Kindly Light, amid the encircling gloom
Lead Thou me on !"

For his mind being haunted by "some texts of this kind," *i.e.*, that "God meets those who go in His way," *etc.*, see Ward's *Life of John Henry Cardinal Newman*, I. 55.

ὡς Δημοσθένης ἀτυχεῖν ; τί δὲ κωλύει συλλογισμοὺς ἀναλύοντα ὡς Χρύσιππος ἄθλιον εἶναι,
πενθεῖν, φθονεῖν, ἁπλῶς ταράσσεσθαι, κακοδαι-
45 μονεῖν ; οὐδὲ ἕν. ὁρᾶς οὖν ὅτι πανδοκεῖα ἦν
ταῦτα οὐδενὸς ἄξια, τὸ δὲ προκείμενον ἄλλο ἦν.
46 ταῦτα ὅταν λέγω πρός τινας, οἴονταί με κατα-
βάλλειν τὴν περὶ τὸ λέγειν ἐπιμέλειαν ἢ τὴν περὶ
τὰ θεωρήματα. ἐγὼ δ' οὐ ταύτην καταβάλλω,
ἀλλὰ τὸ περὶ ταῦτ' ἀκαταληκτικῶς[1] ἔχειν καὶ
47 ἐνταῦθα τίθεσθαι τὰς αὑτῶν ἐλπίδας. εἴ τις
τοῦτο παριστὰς βλάπτει τοὺς ἀκούοντας, κἀμὲ
τίθεσθε ἕνα τῶν βλαπτόντων. οὐ δύναμαι δ'
ἄλλο βλέπων τὸ κράτιστον καὶ τὸ κυριώτατον
ἄλλο λέγειν εἶναι, ἵν' ὑμῖν χαρίσωμαι.

κδ΄. Πρός τινα τῶν οὐκ ἠξιωμένων ὑπ' αὐτοῦ.

1   Εἰπόντος αὐτῷ τινος ὅτι Πολλάκις ἐπιθυμῶν
σου ἀκοῦσαι ἦλθον πρὸς σὲ καὶ οὐδέποτέ μοι
2 ἀπεκρίνω· καὶ νῦν, εἰ δυνατόν, παρακαλῶ σε
εἰπεῖν τί μοι, Δοκεῖ σοι, ἔφη, καθάπερ ἄλλου
τινὸς εἶναι τέχνη οὕτως δὲ καὶ τοῦ λέγειν, ἣν ὁ
μὲν ἔχων ἐμπείρως ἐρεῖ, ὁ δὲ μὴ ἔχων ἀπείρως ;—
3 Δοκεῖ.—Οὐκοῦν ὁ μὲν διὰ τοῦ λέγειν αὐτός τε
ὠφελούμενος καὶ ἄλλους οἷός τε ὢν ὠφελεῖν οὗτος
ἐμπείρως ἂν λέγοι, ὁ δὲ βλαπτόμενος μᾶλλον καὶ
βλάπτων οὗτος ἄπειρος ἂν εἴη τῆς τέχνης ταύτης
τῆς τοῦ λέγειν ; εὕροις ἂν τοὺς μὲν βλαπτομένους

---

[1] Upton's "codex" : ταῦτα καταληκτικῶς S.

a man having the eloquence of Demosthenes and yet being unhappy, and what is to prevent him from analyzing syllogisms like Chrysippus, and yet being wretched, from sorrowing, envying, in a word, from being disturbed and miserable? Absolutely nothing. You see, then, that these were "inns" of no value, while your purpose was something else. When I speak thus to some people they think that I am disparaging the study of rhetoric or that of general principles. Yet I am not disparaging this, but only the habit of dwelling unceasingly on these matters and setting one's hopes in them. If a man does his hearers harm by presenting this view, set me down too as one of those who work harm. But when I see that one thing is highest and supreme, I cannot say the same of something else, in order to gratify you, my hearers.

CHAPTER XXIV

To one of those whom he did not deem worthy

Someone said to him: I have often come to you, wishing to hear you and you have never given me an answer; and now, if it be possible, I beg you to say something to me. He answered: Do you think that, just as in anything else there is an art, so there is also an art in speaking, and that he who has this art will speak with skill, while he who does not have it will speak without skill?—I do.—Then he who by speaking benefits himself and is able to benefit others would be speaking with skill, while he who confers injury rather than benefit would be without skill in this art of speaking? You would

4 τοὺς δ' ὠφελουμένους. οἱ δ' ἀκούοντες πάντες
ὠφελοῦνται ἀφ' ὧν ἀκούουσιν ἢ καὶ τούτων εὕροις
ἂν τοὺς μὲν ὠφελουμένους τοὺς δὲ βλαπτομένους ;
—Καὶ τούτων, ἔφη.—Οὐκοῦν καὶ ἐνταῦθα ὅσοι
μὲν ἐμπείρως ἀκούουσιν ὠφελοῦνται, ὅσοι δ' ἀπεί-
5 ρως βλάπτονται ;—Ὡμολόγει.—Ἔστιν ἄρα τις
ἐμπειρία καθάπερ τοῦ λέγειν οὕτως καὶ τοῦ
6 ἀκούειν ;—Ἔοικεν.—Εἰ δὲ βούλει, καὶ οὕτως
σκέψαι αὐτό. τὸ μουσικῶς ἅψασθαι τίνος σοι
7 δοκεῖ ;—Μουσικοῦ.—Τί δέ ; τὸν ἀνδριάντα ὡς
δεῖ κατασκευάσαι τίνος σοι φαίνεται ;—Ἀνδριαντοποιοῦ.—Τὸ ἰδεῖν ἐμπείρως οὐδεμιᾶς σοι προσ-
δεῖσθαι φαίνεται τέχνης ;—Προσδεῖται καὶ τοῦτο.
8 —Οὐκοῦν εἰ καὶ τὸ λέγειν ὡς δεῖ τοῦ ἐμπείρου
ἐστίν, ὁρᾶς ὅτι καὶ τὸ ἀκούειν ὠφελίμως τοῦ
9 ἐμπείρου ἐστίν ; καὶ τὸ μὲν τελείως καὶ ὠφελίμως.
εἰ βούλει, πρὸς τὸ παρὸν ἀφῶμεν, ἐπεὶ καὶ μακράν
10 ἐσμεν ἀμφότεροι παντὸς τοῦ τοιούτου· ἐκεῖνο δὲ
πᾶς ἄν τις ὁμολογήσαί μοι δοκεῖ, ὅτι ποσῆς γέ
τινος τριβῆς περὶ τὸ ἀκούειν προσδεῖται ὁ τῶν
φιλοσόφων ἀκουσόμενος. ἢ γὰρ οὔ ;
11 Περὶ τίνος οὖν λέγω πρὸς σέ ; δεῖξόν μοι. περὶ
τίνος ἀκοῦσαι δύνασαι ; περὶ ἀγαθῶν καὶ κακῶν ;
τίνος ; ἆρά γε ἵππου ;—Οὔ.—Ἀλλὰ βοός ;—Οὔ.
12 —Τί οὖν ; ἀνθρώπου ;—Ναί.—Οἴδαμεν οὖν, τί
ἐστιν ἄνθρωπος, τίς ἡ φύσις αὐτοῦ, τίς ἡ ἔννοια ;
ἔχομεν καὶ κατὰ ποσὸν περὶ τοῦτο[1] τὰ ὦτα

---

[1] Schweighäuser: τοῦ S.

find that some are injured and others benefited. And are all those who hear benefited by what they hear, or would you find that of them too some are benefited but others injured?—Yes, that is true of them also, he said.—Then in this case too are all those that show skill in listening benefited, but all those that do not show such skill are injured?—He agreed.—Is there, therefore, also a certain skill in listening, just as there is in speaking?—So it seems.—But, if you please, look at the matter from this angle also: whose part do you think it is to handle an instrument musically?—The musician's. —Very well, and whose part does it appear to you to be to make a statue properly?—The sculptor's.— Does it appear to you to require no art to look at a statue with skill?—This also requires art.—If, then, to speak as one ought is the part of a skilled person, do you see that to hear with benefit to himself is also the part of the skilled person? Now as for perfection and benefit, if you please, let us drop the consideration of them for the present, since both of us are far removed from anything of that sort; but this I think everyone would admit, that the man who is going to listen to the philosophers needs at least a certain amount of practice in listening. Is it not so?

What, then, shall I talk to you about? Tell me. What are you capable of hearing about? About things good and evil? Good and evil for what? Do you mean for a horse?—No.—Well then, for an ox?—No.—What then? For a man?—Yes.—Do we know, then, what a man is, what his nature is, what the concept of man is? And have we ears that are to any degree open with regard to this?

τετρημένα; ἀλλὰ φύσις τί ἐστιν ἐννοεῖς ἢ δύνασαι καὶ κατὰ ποσὸν ἀκολουθῆσαί μοι λέγοντι;
13 ἀλλ' ἀποδείξει χρήσομαι πρὸς σέ; πῶς; παρακολουθεῖς γὰρ αὐτῷ τούτῳ, τί ἐστιν ἀπόδειξις ἢ
πῶς τι ἀποδείκνυται ἢ διὰ τίνων; ἢ τίνα ὅμοια
14 μὲν ἀποδείξει ἐστίν, ἀπόδειξις δ' οὐκ ἔστιν; τί
γάρ ἐστιν ἀληθὲς οἶδας ἢ τί ἐστι ψεῦδος; τί τίνι
ἀκολουθεῖ, τί τίνι μάχεται ἢ ἀνομολογούμενόν
ἐστιν ἢ ἀσύμφωνον; ἀλλὰ κινῶ σε πρὸς φιλοσο-
15 φίαν; πῶς παραδεικνύω σοι τὴν μάχην τῶν
πολλῶν ἀνθρώπων, καθ' ἣν διαφέρονται περὶ
ἀγαθῶν καὶ κακῶν καὶ συμφερόντων καὶ ἀσυμφό-
ρων, αὐτὸ τοῦτο τί ἐστι μάχη οὐκ εἰδότι; ¹ δεῖξον
οὖν μοι, τί περανῶ διαλεγόμενός σοι. κίνησόν
16 μοι προθυμίαν. ὡς ἡ κατάλληλος πόα τῷ προ-
βάτῳ φανεῖσα προθυμίαν αὐτῷ κινεῖ πρὸς τὸ
φαγεῖν, ἂν δὲ λίθον ἢ ἄρτον παραθῇς, οὐ κινηθή-
σεται, οὕτως εἰσί τινες ἡμῖν φυσικαὶ προθυμίαι καὶ
πρὸς τὸ λέγειν, ὅταν ὁ ἀκουσόμενος φανῇ τις, ὅταν
αὐτὸς ἐρεθίσῃ. ἂν δ' ὡς λίθος ἢ χόρτος ᾖ παρακεί-
17 μενος, πῶς δύναται ἀνθρώπῳ ὄρεξιν κινῆσαι; ἡ
ἄμπελος μή τι λέγει τῷ γεωργῷ "ἐπιμελοῦ μου";
ἀλλ' αὐτὴ δι' αὑτῆς ἐμφαίνουσα, ὅτι ἐπιμεληθέντι
λυσιτελήσει αὐτῷ, ἐκκαλεῖται πρὸς τὴν ἐπιμέ-
18 λειαν. τὰ παιδία τὰ πιθανὰ καὶ δριμέα τίνα οὐκ
ἐκκαλεῖται πρὸς τὸ συμπαίζειν αὐτοῖς καὶ συν-
έρπειν καὶ πρὸς τὸ συμψελλίζειν; ὄνῳ δὲ τίς

¹ Reiske: εἰδότα S.

Nay, have you a conception of what nature is, or can you in any measure follow me when I speak? But shall I use a demonstration for you? How can I? For do you really understand what a proof is, or how anything is demonstrated, or by what means? Or what things resemble demonstration, but are not demonstration? Do you know, for instance, what is true, or what is false; what follows what, what contradicts, or is out of agreement, or out of harmony with what? But am I to interest you in philosophy? How shall I set before you the contradiction in the ideas of the multitude, which leads them to disagree about things good and evil, advantageous and disadvantageous, when you do not know what contradiction itself is? Show me, then, what I shall accomplish by a discussion with you. Arouse in me an eagerness for it. Just as suitable grass when shown to the sheep arouses in it an eagerness to eat, whereas if you set before it a stone or a loaf of bread,[1] it will not be moved to eat, so we have certain moments of natural eagerness for speech also, when the suitable hearer appears, and when he himself stimulates us. But when the would-be hearer by our side is like a stone, or grass, how can he arouse desire in the breast of a man? Does the vine say to the husbandman, "Pay attention to me"? Nay, but the vine by its very appearance shows that it will profit him to pay attention to it, and so invites him to devote his attention. Who is not tempted by attractive and wide-awake children to join their sports, and crawl on all fours with them, and talk baby talk with them? But who is

[1] The observation of nature is faulty; sheep will upon occasion eat bread, vegetables, and even meat.

425

προθυμεῖται συμπαίζειν ἢ συνογκᾶσθαι; καὶ γὰρ εἰ μικρόν, ὅμως ὀνάριόν ἐστιν.

19 Τί οὖν μοι οὐδὲν λέγεις;—Ἐκεῖνο μόνον ἔχω σοι εἰπεῖν, ὅτι ὁ ἀγνοῶν, τίς ἐστι καὶ ἐπὶ τί γέγονεν καὶ ἐν τίνι τούτῳ τῷ κόσμῳ καὶ μετὰ τίνων κοινωνῶν καὶ τίνα τὰ ἀγαθά ἐστι καὶ τὰ κακὰ καὶ τὰ καλὰ καὶ τὰ αἰσχρά, καὶ μήτε λόγῳ παρακολουθῶν μήτ' ἀποδείξει, μήτε τί ἐστιν ἀληθὲς ἢ τί ψεῦδος, μήτε διακρῖναι ταῦτα δυνά-μενος οὔτ' ὀρέξεται κατὰ φύσιν οὔτ' ἐκκλινεῖ οὔθ' ὁρμήσει οὔτ' ἐπιβαλεῖται, οὐ συγκαταθήσεται, οὐκ ἀνανεύσει, οὐκ ἐφέξει, τὸ σύνολον κωφὸς καὶ τυφλὸς περιελεύσεται δοκῶν μέν τις εἶναι, ὢν δ'

20 οὐδείς. νῦν γὰρ πρῶτον τοῦθ' οὕτως ἔχει; οὐχὶ ἐξ οὗ γένος ἀνθρώπων ἐστίν, ἐξ ἐκείνου πάντα τὰ ἁμαρτήματα καὶ τὰ ἀτυχήματα παρὰ ταύτην

21 τὴν ἄγνοιαν γεγένηται; Ἀγαμέμνων καὶ Ἀχιλ-λεὺς διὰ τί ἀλλήλοις διεφέροντο; οὐχὶ διὰ τὸ μὴ εἰδέναι, τίνα ἐστὶ συμφέροντα καὶ ἀσύμφορα; οὐχὶ ὁ μὲν λέγει, ὅτι συμφέρει ἀποδοῦναι τῷ πατρὶ τὴν Χρυσηΐδα, ὁ δὲ λέγει, ὅτι οὐ συμφέρει; οὐχὶ ὁ μὲν λέγει, ὅτι δεῖ αὐτὸν λαβεῖν τὸ ἄλλου γέρας, ὁ δέ, ὅτι οὐ δεῖ; οὐχὶ διὰ ταῦτα ἐπελά-

22 θοντο καὶ τίνες ἦσαν καὶ ἐπὶ τί ἐληλύθεσαν; ἔα, ἄνθρωπε, ἐπὶ τί ἐλήλυθας; ἐρωμένας κτησό-μενος ἢ πολεμήσων; "πολεμήσων." τίσι; τοῖς Τρωσὶν ἢ τοῖς Ἕλλησιν; "τοῖς Τρωσίν." ἀφεὶς

eager to play with an ass, or to join its braying? For however small it may be, it is still nothing but a little ass.

Why, then, have you nothing to say to me?—There is only one thing I can say to you—that the man who does not know who he is, and what he is born for, and what sort of a world this is that he exists in, and whom he shares it with ; and does not know what the good things are and what are the evil, what the noble and what the base ; and is unable to follow either reason or demonstration, or what is true and what is false, and cannot distinguish one from the other ; and will manifest neither desire, nor aversion, nor choice, nor purpose in accordance with nature ; will not assent, will not dissent, will not withhold judgement—such a man, to sum it all up, will go about deaf and blind, thinking that he is somebody, when he really is nobody. What! do you think that this is something new? Has it not been true from the time when the human race began to be, that every mistake and every misfortune has been due to this kind of ignorance? Why did Agamemnon and Achilles quarrel? Was it not because they did not know what things are expedient and what are inexpedient? Does not one of them say that it is expedient to give Chryseïs back to her father, while the other says that it is not expedient? Does not one of them say that he ought to get some other man's meed of honour, while the other says that he ought not? Is it not true that this made them forget who they were and what they had come for? Ho, there, man, what have you come for? To get sweethearts or to fight? "To fight." With whom? The Trojans or the Greeks? "The Trojans." Well, then, are you turning your back on

οὖν τὸν Ἕκτορα ἐπὶ τὸν βασιλέα τὸν σαυτοῦ
23 σπᾷς τὸ ξίφος; σὺ δ', ὦ βέλτιστε, ἀφεὶς τὰ τοῦ
βασιλέως ἔργα,

ᾧ λαοί τ' ἐπιτετράφαται καὶ τόσσα μέμηλεν,

περὶ κορασιδίου διαπυκτεύεις τῷ πολεμικωτάτῳ
τῶν συμμάχων, ὃν δεῖ παντὶ τρόπῳ περιέπειν
καὶ φυλάττειν; καὶ χείρων γίνῃ κομψοῦ ἀρχιε-
ρέως, ὃς τοὺς καλοὺς μονομάχους διὰ πάσης
ἐπιμελείας ἔχει; ὁρᾷς, οἷα ποιεῖ ἄγνοια περὶ τῶν
συμφερόντων;

24 "'Ἀλλὰ κἀγὼ πλούσιός εἰμι." μή τι οὖν τοῦ
Ἀγαμέμνονος πλουσιώτερος; "ἀλλὰ καὶ καλός
εἰμι." μή τι οὖν τοῦ Ἀχιλλέως καλλίων;
"ἀλλὰ καὶ κόμιον κομψὸν ἔχω." ὁ δ' Ἀχιλλεὺς
οὐ κάλλιον καὶ ξανθόν; καὶ οὐκ ἐκτένιζεν αὐτὸ
25 κομψῶς οὐδ' ἔπλασσεν. "ἀλλὰ καὶ ἰσχυρός
εἰμι." μή τι οὖν δύνασαι λίθον ἆραι ἡλίκον ὁ
Ἕκτωρ ἢ ὁ Αἴας; "ἀλλὰ καὶ εὐγενής." μή τι
ἐκ θεᾶς μητρός, μή τι πατρὸς ἐγγόνου Διός; τί
οὖν ἐκεῖνον ὠφελεῖ ταῦτα, ὅταν καθήμενος κλαίῃ
26 διὰ τὸ κορασίδιον; "ἀλλὰ ῥήτωρ εἰμί." ἐκεῖνος
δ' οὐκ ἦν; οὐ βλέπεις πῶς κέχρηται τοῖς δεινο-
τάτοις τῶν Ἑλλήνων περὶ λόγους Ὀδυσσεῖ καὶ
Φοίνικι, πῶς αὐτοὺς ἀστόμους πεποίηκε;

---

[1] Homer, *Iliad*, II. 25, translated by Bryant.
[2] The reference is obscure; possibly Chryses is meant
(Wolf and others), but this seems most unlikely, or there may
be a sneering allusion to some contemporary of the philosopher, who was excessively interested in gladiators (Schenkl).
I am inclined to think rather of Calchas, the high priest
of the Achaeans, who treats both Agamemnon and Achilles
with more civility than they would seem to deserve, at least

Hector and drawing your sword against your own king? As for you, O best of men, are you turning your back on your duties as king,

> Who has the charge of nations and sustains
> Such mighty cares,[1]

and for the sake of a paltry damsel engage in a fist-fight with the greatest warrior among your allies, a man whom you ought to honour and protect in every way? And do you sink below the level of an elegant high priest who treats the noble gladiators with all respect?[2] Do you see the sort of thing that ignorance of what is expedient leads to?

"But I too am rich." You are not, then, richer than Agamemnon, are you? "But I am also handsome." You are not, then, handsomer than Achilles, are you? "But I have also a fine head of hair." And did not Achilles have a finer, and golden hair, too? And did he not comb it elegantly and dress it up? "But I am also strong." You are not, then, able to lift as large a stone as Hector or Aias lifted, are you? "But I am also noble born." Your mother is not a goddess, is she, or your father of the seed of Zeus? What good, then, does all this do him when he sits in tears about the damsel? "But I am an orator." And was not he? Do you not observe how he has dealt with Odysseus and Phoenix, the most skilful of the Greeks in eloquence, how he stopped their mouths?[3]

in the opinion of Epictetus, who had no undue reverence for the great figures of the Epic.

[3] The reference is to the spirited and convincing speeches of Achilles (*Iliad*, IX.) in answer to the appeals of Odysseus and Phoenix.

27 Ταῦτά σοι μόνα ἔχω εἰπεῖν καὶ οὐδὲ ταῦτα
28 προθύμως.—Διὰ τί ;—Ὅτι με οὐκ ἠρέθισας. εἰς
τί γὰρ ἀπιδὼν ἐρεθισθῶ[1] ὡς οἱ ἱππικοὶ περὶ τοὺς
ἵππους τοὺς εὐφυεῖς ; εἰς τὸ σωμάτιον ; αἰσχρῶς
αὐτὸ πλάσσεις. εἰς τὴν ἐσθῆτα ; καὶ ταύτην
τρυφερὰν ἔχεις. εἰς σχῆμα, εἰς βλέμμα ; εἰς
29 οὐδέν. ὅταν ἀκοῦσαι θέλῃς φιλοσόφου, μὴ λέγε
αὐτῷ ὅτι "οὐδέν μοι λέγεις ;" ἀλλὰ μόνον
δείκνυε σαυτὸν οἷον τ᾽ [2] ἀκούειν καὶ ὄψει, πῶς
κινήσεις τὸν λέγοντα.

κε΄. Πῶς ἀναγκαῖα τὰ λογικά ;

1 Τῶν παρόντων δέ τινος εἰπόντος Πεῖσόν με,
ὅτι τὰ λογικὰ χρήσιμά ἐστιν, Θέλεις, ἔφη,
2 ἀποδείξω σοι τοῦτο ;—Ναί.—Οὐκοῦν λόγον μ᾽
ἀποδεικτικὸν διαλεχθῆναι δεῖ ;—Ὁμολογήσαντος
3 δὲ Πόθεν οὖν εἴσῃ, ἄν σε σοφίσωμαι ;—Σιωπή-
σαντος δὲ τοῦ ἀνθρώπου Ὁρᾷς, ἔφη, πῶς αὐτὸς
ὁμολογεῖς ὅτι ταῦτα ἀναγκαῖά ἐστιν, εἰ χωρὶς
αὐτῶν οὐδ᾽ αὐτὸ τοῦτο δύνασαι μαθεῖν, πότερον
ἀναγκαῖα ἢ οὐκ ἀναγκαῖά ἐστιν.

κϛ΄. Τί τὸ ἴδιον τοῦ ἁμαρτήματος ;

1 Πᾶν ἁμάρτημα μάχην περιέχει. ἐπεὶ γὰρ ὁ
ἁμαρτάνων οὐ θέλει ἁμαρτάνειν, ἀλλὰ κατορ-

[1] Wolf : ἐρεθίσω S.
[2] Schenkl : τοῦ S.

This is all I have to say to you, and even for this I have no heart.—Why so?—Because you have not stimulated me. For what is there in you that I may look at and be stimulated, as experts in horseflesh are stimulated when they see thoroughbred horses? At your paltry body? But you make it ugly by the shape which you give to it.[1] At your clothes? There is something too luxurious about them, also. At your air, at your countenance? I have nothing to look at. When you wish to hear a philosopher, do not ask him, "Have you nothing to say to me?" but only show yourself capable of hearing him, and you will see how you will stimulate the speaker.

CHAPTER XXV

How is logic necessary?

WHEN someone in his audience said, Convince me that logic is necessary, he answered: Do you wish me to demonstrate this to you?—Yes.—Well, then, must I use a demonstrative argument?—And when the questioner had agreed to that, Epictetus asked him, How, then, will you know if I impose upon you?—As the man had no answer to give, Epictetus said: Do you see how you yourself admit that all this instruction is necessary, if, without it, you cannot so much as know whether it is necessary or not?

CHAPTER XXVI

What is the distinctive characteristic of error?

EVERY error involves a contradiction. For since he who is in error does not wish to err, but to be right,

---

[1] That is, by pasture, overeating, or lack of exercise.

2 θῶσαι, δῆλον ὅτι ὃ μὲν θέλει οὐ ποιεῖ. τί γὰρ
ὁ κλέπτης θέλει πρᾶξαι; τὸ αὑτῷ συμφέρον.
οὐκ οὖν, εἰ ἀσύμφορόν ἐστιν αὑτῷ τὸ κλέπτειν,
3 ὃ μὲν θέλει ποιεῖ. πᾶσα δὲ ψυχὴ λογικὴ φύσει
διαβέβληται πρὸς μάχην· καὶ μέχρι μὲν ἂν μὴ
παρακολουθῇ τούτῳ, ὅτι ἐν μάχῃ ἐστίν, οὐδὲν
κωλύεται τὰ μαχόμενα ποιεῖν· παρακολουθή-
σαντα δὲ πολλὴ ἀνάγκη ἀποστῆναι τῆς μάχης
καὶ φυγεῖν οὕτως ὡς καὶ ἀπὸ τοῦ ψεύδους ἀνανεῦσαι πικρὰ ἀνάγκη τῷ αἰσθανομένῳ, ὅτι ψεῦδός
ἐστιν· μέχρι δὲ τοῦτο μὴ φαντάζηται, ὡς ἀληθεῖ
ἐπινεύει αὐτῷ.

4 Δεινὸς οὖν ἐν λόγῳ, ὁ δ' αὐτὸς καὶ προτρε-
πτικὸς καὶ ἐλεγκτικὸς οὗτος ὁ δυνάμενος ἑκάστῳ
παραδεῖξαι τὴν μάχην,[1] καθ' ἣν ἁμαρτάνει, καὶ
σαφῶς παραστῆσαι, πῶς ὃ θέλει οὐ ποιεῖ καὶ ὃ μὴ
5 θέλει ποιεῖ. ἂν γὰρ τοῦτο δείξῃ τις, αὐτὸς ἀφ'
αὑτοῦ ἀναποχωρήσει. μέχρι δὲ μὴ δεικνύῃς, μὴ
θαύμαζε, εἰ ἐπιμένει· κατορθώματος γὰρ φαντασίαν
6 λαμβάνων ποιεῖ αὐτό. διὰ τοῦτο καὶ Σωκράτης
ταύτῃ τῇ δυνάμει πεποιθὼς ἔλεγεν ὅτι "ἐγὼ
ἄλλον μὲν οὐδένα εἴωθα παρέχειν μάρτυρα ὧν
λέγω, ἀρκοῦμαι δ' ἀεὶ τῷ προσδιαλεγομένῳ καὶ
ἐκεῖνον ἐπιψηφίζω καὶ καλῶ μάρτυρα καὶ εἷς ὢν
7 οὗτος ἀρκεῖ μοι ἀντὶ πάντων." ᾔδει γάρ, ὑπὸ

it is clear that he is not doing what he wishes. For what does the thief wish to achieve? His own interest. Therefore, if thievery is against his interest, he is not doing what he wishes. Now every rational soul is by nature offended by contradiction; and so, as long as a man does not understand that he is involved in contradiction, there is nothing to prevent him from doing contradictory things, but when he has come to understand the contradiction, he must of necessity abandon and avoid it, just as a bitter necessity compels a man to renounce the false when he perceives that it is false; but as long as the falsehood does not appear, he assents to it as the truth.

He, then, who can show to each man the contradiction which causes him to err, and can clearly bring home to him how he is not doing what he wishes, and is doing what he does not wish, is strong in argument, and at the same time effective both in encouragement and refutation. For as soon as anyone shows a man this, he will of his own accord abandon what he is doing. But so long as you do not point this out, be not surprised if he persists in his error; for he does it because he has an impression that he is right. That is why Socrates, because he trusted in this faculty, used to say: " I am not in the habit of calling any other witness to what I say, but I am always satisfied with my fellow-disputant, and I call for his vote and summon him as a witness, and he, though but a single person, is sufficient for me in place of all men."[1] For Socrates knew what moves

---

[1] Compare II. 12, 5, and the note on that passage.

---

[1] Supplied by Wolf.

ARRIAN'S DISCOURSES OF EPICTETUS

τινος λογικὴ ψυχὴ κινεῖται, ὁμοίως [1] ζυγῷ ἐπιρ-
ρέψει,[2] ἄν τε θέλῃς ἄν τε μή. λογικῷ ἡγεμονικῷ δεῖξον μάχην καὶ ἀποστήσεται· ἂν δὲ μὴ
δεικνύῃς, αὐτὸς σαυτῷ μᾶλλον ἐγκάλει ἢ τῷ μὴ
πειθομένῳ.

[1] Added by Schweighäuser.
[2] Schenkl: ἐπιτρέψει or ἐπειθρέψει S. Many conjectural
restorations have been proposed.

434

a rational soul, and that like the beam of a balance it will incline,[1] whether you wish or no. Point out to the rational governing faculty a contradiction and it will desist; but if you do not point it out, blame yourself rather than the man who will not be persuaded.

[1] The text is very uncertain (see critical note). The general idea, however, is pretty clearly that expressed by Cicero, *Acad. Pri.* II. 38 ; *Ut enim necesse est lancem in libra ponderibus impositis deprimi, sic animum perspicuis cedere.*

INDEX

INDEX

438

INDEX

439

INDEX

440

INDEX

441

INDEX

Rhetoric, 421
Rhodes, 229
Robe, the long, of tragic actors, 197, 199
Romans, 81, 143, 399
Rome, 13, 65, 71, 73, 75, 85, 87, 131, 153, 163, 169, 197, 253, 295
Rufus (Musonius Rufus), 13, 59, 73
Rule of life, 165
Runner, 33

Salutation, 249
Sanctity, 377, 379
Sarpedon, 173
Saturnalia, 159, 195
Scholar, caught in adultery, 233 ff.
School attendant, 83, 85
School exercises, 75, 77, 169, 207, 221, 223, 253, 283, 303, 307, 321, 327, 331, 333, 345, 347, 387, 389
School, frequenter of, 89
School-respect, 27, 279, 281, 379, 403
Sciron, 335
Scourging, 15, 17
Scout, of philosophy, 153
Second field of study, 341, 345
Self-examination, 337
Self-interest, 131, 133, 147, 175, 397, 399, 401, 403
Self-love, 133
Self-respect, 27, 279, 281, 379, 403
Senate, 15, 19, 21
Senators, 163, 165
Sense impressions, 179, 181, 185, 187
Senses, evidence of, 177
Serenity, 27
Sheep, 151, 269, 425
Shoemaker, 307
Sick mind, 321
Sirens, 419
Slave and slavery, 67, 99, 131, 203, 221, 227, 381, 385, 413
Smith, 279
Smoke in the house, 161, 163
Snake, 163
Social relations, 309
Socrates, 23, 25, 35, 63 f., 71, 91, 95, 117, 131, 165, 171, 191, 195, 203, 205, 217, 223, 227, 229, 237, 243, 253, 291, 293, 305, 333, 355, 433
Soldiers, 105, 109
Son, duty of, 95, 277
Sophisms, 171
Sophocles, 187
Sorrow, 333
Soul, 103, 295, 297

Sparta, 379
Speech, 409; art of speaking, 421
Sponges, 85
Standard, The, by Epicurus, 411
Standard of judgement, 115, 185, 287, 289, 303, 377. See also *Criterion*.
Starving, 317, 411
State, of men and of gods, 245; small copy of universal state, 245
Steadfastness, 187 ff., 237, 239, 315 ff.
Stoics, 201, 273, 291, 365, 367, 375
Storks' nests, 181, 183
Strength of character, 39
Stupidity, 285
Style, 417, 419
Suicide, 15, 17, 67 f., 157, 163, 219, 317, 381, 411
Sun, 103, 133
Surgery, 165
Susa, 333
Swallows' nests, 181
Swine's flesh, 143
Syllogisms, 51 ff., 61, 149, 195, 197, 199, 201, 225, 233, 247, 303, 345, 389, 391, 413, 421
Sympathy in Nature, 101, 103
Symposium, The, of Xenophon, 295
Syrians, 81, 143, 273, 287

Tax for manumission of slave, 221
Teaching, skill in, 291, 293, 295
Technique, instruction in, 307
Theo, the name, 231
Theopompus, 339
Thermopylae, 379
Thersites, 415
Theseus, 335
Thief, 125, 127, 191, 433
Things Possible, works by Chrysippus and by Antipater, 363
Third field of study, 341, (347)
Thrasea, 13
Three campaigns, the, 310, 311
Timidity, 385
Tragedy, 35, 155, 187, 331
Tragic actor, 197, 199, 203
Tragic rôle, 155, 199
Tranquillity, 219, 223, 225
Transitoriness of life, 241
Traveller, 417, 419
Tribuneship, 135
Triptolemus, 35
Trojans, 427
Trojan shore, 363
Troy, 183

442

INDEX

PRINTED IN GREAT BRITAIN BY
RICHARD CLAY AND COMPANY, LTD.,
BUNGAY, SUFFOLK.

THE LOEB CLASSICAL LIBRARY

VOLUMES ALREADY PUBLISHED

Latin Authors

AMMIANUS MARCELLINUS. Translated by J. C. Rolfe. 3 Vols.

APULEIUS: THE GOLDEN ASS (METAMORPHOSES). W. Adlington (1566). Revised by S. Gaselee.

ST. AUGUSTINE: CITY OF GOD. 7 Vols. Vol. I. G. H. McCracken. Vol. VI. W. C. Greene.

ST. AUGUSTINE, CONFESSIONS OF. W. Watts (1631). 2 Vols.

ST. AUGUSTINE, SELECT LETTERS. J. H. Baxter.

AUSONIUS. H. G. Evelyn White. 2 Vols.

BEDE. J. E. King. 2 Vols.

BOETHIUS: TRACTS and DE CONSOLATIONE PHILOSOPHIAE. Rev. H. F. Stewart and E. K. Rand.

CAESAR: ALEXANDRIAN, AFRICAN and SPANISH WARS. A. G. Way.

CAESAR: CIVIL WARS. A. G. Peskett.

CAESAR: GALLIC WAR. H. J. Edwards.

CATO: DE RE RUSTICA; VARRO: DE RE RUSTICA. H. B. Ash and W. D. Hooper.

CATULLUS. F. W. Cornish; TIBULLUS. J. B. Postgate; PERVIGILIUM VENERIS. J. W. Mackail.

CELSUS: DE MEDICINA. W. G. Spencer. 3 Vols.

CICERO: BRUTUS, and ORATOR. G. L. Hendrickson and H. M. Hubbell.

[CICERO]: AD HERENNIUM. H. Caplan.

CICERO: DE ORATORE, etc. 2 Vols. Vol. I. DE ORATORE, Books I. and II. E. W. Sutton and H. Rackham. Vol. II. DE ORATORE, Book III. De Fato; Paradoxa Stoicorum; De Partitione Oratoria. H. Rackham.

CICERO: DE FINIBUS. H. Rackham.

CICERO: DE INVENTIONE, etc. H. M. Hubbell.

CICERO: DE NATURA DEORUM and ACADEMICA. H. Rackham.

CICERO: DE OFFICIIS. Walter Miller.

CICERO: DE REPUBLICA and DE LEGIBUS; SOMNIUM SCIPIONIS, Clinton W. Keyes.

CICERO: DE SENECTUTE, DE AMICITIA, DE DIVINATIONE. W. A. Falconer.

CICERO: IN CATILINAM, PRO FLACCO, PRO MURENA, PRO SULLA. Louis E. Lord.

CICERO: LETTERS to ATTICUS. E. O. Winstedt. 3 Vols.

CICERO: LETTERS TO HIS FRIENDS. W. Glynn Williams. 3 Vols.

CICERO: PHILIPPICS. W. C. A. Ker.

CICERO: PRO ARCHIA POST REDITUM, DE DOMO, DE HARUSPICUM RESPONSIS, PRO PLANCIO. N. H. Watts.

CICERO: PRO CAECINA, PRO LEGE MANILIA, PRO CLUENTIO, PRO RABIRIO. H. Grose Hodge.

CICERO: PRO CAELIO, DE PROVINCIIS CONSULARIBUS, PRO BALBO. R. Gardner.

CICERO: PRO MILONE, IN PISONEM, PRO SCAURO, PRO FONTEIO, PRO RABIRIO POSTUMO, PRO MARCELLO, PRO LIGARIO, PRO REGE DEIOTARO. N. H. Watts.

CICERO: PRO QUINCTIO, PRO ROSCIO AMERINO, PRO ROSCIO COMOEDO, CONTRA RULLUM. J. H. Freese.

CICERO: PRO SESTIO, IN VATINIUM. R. Gardner.

CICERO: TUSCULAN DISPUTATIONS. J. E. King.

CICERO: VERRINE ORATIONS. L. H. G. Greenwood. 2 Vols.

CLAUDIAN. M. Platnauer. 2 Vols.

COLUMELLA: DE RE RUSTICA. DE ARBORIBUS. H. B. Ash, E. S. Forster and E. Heffner. 3 Vols.

CURTIUS, Q.: HISTORY OF ALEXANDER. J. C. Rolfe. 2 Vols.

FLORUS. E. S. Forster; and CORNELIUS NEPOS. J. C. Rolfe.

FRONTINUS: STRATAGEMS and AQUEDUCTS. C. E. Bennett and M. B. McElwain.

FRONTO: CORRESPONDENCE. C. R. Haines. 2 Vols

GELLIUS, J. C. Rolfe. 3 Vols.

HORACE: ODES AND EPODES. C. E. Bennett.

HORACE: SATIRES, EPISTLES, ARS POETICA. H. R. Fairclough.

JEROME: SELECTED LETTERS. F. A. Wright.

JUVENAL and PERSIUS. G. G. Ramsay.

LIVY. B. O. Foster, F. G. Moore, Evan T. Sage, and A. C. Schlesinger and R. M. Geer (General Index). 14 Vols.

LUCAN. J. D. Duff.

LUCRETIUS. W. H. D. Rouse.

MARTIAL. W. C. A. Ker. 2 Vols.

MINOR LATIN POETS: from PUBLILIUS SYRUS to RUTILIUS NAMATIANUS, including GRATTIUS, CALPURNIUS SICULUS, NEMESIANUS, AVIANUS, and others with "Aetna" and the "Phoenix." J. Wight Duff and Arnold M. Duff.

OVID: THE ART OF LOVE and OTHER POEMS. J. H. Mozley.

2

OVID: FASTI. Sir James G. Frazer.

OVID: HEROIDES and AMORES. Grant Showerman.

OVID: METAMORPHOSES. F. J. Miller. 2 Vols.

OVID: TRISTIA and EX PONTO. A. L. Wheeler.

PERSIUS. Cf. JUVENAL.

PETRONIUS. M. Heseltine; SENECA; APOCOLOCYNTOSIS. W. H. D. Rouse.

PLAUTUS. Paul Nixon. 5 Vols.

PLINY: LETTERS. Melmoth's Translation revised by W. M. L. Hutchinson. 2 Vols.

PLINY: NATURAL HISTORY. H. Rackham and W. H. S. Jones. 10 Vols. Vols. I.–V. and IX. H. Rackham. Vols. VI. and VII. W. H. S. Jones.

PROPERTIUS. H. E. Butler.

PRUDENTIUS. H. J. Thomson. 2 Vols.

QUINTILIAN. H. E. Butler. 4 Vols.

REMAINS OF OLD LATIN. E. H. Warmington. 4 Vols. Vol. I. (ENNIUS AND CAECILIUS.) Vol. II. (LIVIUS, NAEVIUS, PACUVIUS, ACCIUS.) Vol. III. (LUCILIUS and LAWS OF XII TABLES.) (ARCHAIC INSCRIPTIONS.)

SALLUST. J. C. Rolfe.

SCRIPTORES HISTORIAE AUGUSTAE. D. Magie. 3 Vols.

SENECA: APOCOLOCYNTOSIS. Cf. PETRONIUS.

SENECA: EPISTULAE MORALES. R. M. Gummere. 3 Vols.

SENECA: MORAL ESSAYS. J. W. Basore. 3 Vols.

SENECA: TRAGEDIES. F. J. Miller. 2 Vols.

SIDONIUS: POEMS and LETTERS. W. B. ANDERSON. 2 Vols.

SILIUS ITALICUS. J. D. Duff. 2 Vols.

STATIUS. J. H. Mozley. 2 Vols.

SUETONIUS. J. C. Rolfe. 2 Vols.

TACITUS: DIALOGUES. Sir Wm. Peterson. AGRICOLA and GERMANIA. Maurice Hutton.

TACITUS: HISTORIES AND ANNALS. C. H. Moore and J. Jackson. 4 Vols.

TERENCE. John Sargeaunt. 2 Vols.

TERTULLIAN: APOLOGIA and DE SPECTACULIS. T. R. Glover. MINUCIUS FELIX. G. H. Rendall.

VALERIUS FLACCUS. J. H. Mozley.

VARRO: DE LINGUA LATINA. R. G. Kent. 2 Vols.

VELLEIUS PATERCULUS and RES GESTAE DIVI AUGUSTI. F. W. Shipley.

VIRGIL. H. R. Fairclough. 2 Vols.

VITRUVIUS: DE ARCHITECTURA. F. Granger. 2 Vols.

Greek Authors

ACHILLES TATIUS. S. Gaselee.

AELIAN: ON THE NATURE OF ANIMALS. A. F. Scholfield. 3 Vols.

AENEAS TACTICUS, ASCLEPIODOTUS and ONASANDER. The Illinois Greek Club.

AESCHINES. C. D. Adams.

AESCHYLUS. H. Weir Smyth. 2 Vols.

ALCIPHRON, AELIAN, PHILOSTRATUS: LETTERS. A. R. Benner and F. H. Fobes.

ANDOCIDES, ANTIPHON, Cf. MINOR ATTIC ORATORS.

APOLLODORUS. Sir James G. Frazer. 2 Vols.

APOLLONIUS RHODIUS. R. C. Seaton.

THE APOSTOLIC FATHERS. Kirsopp Lake. 2 Vols.

APPIAN: ROMAN HISTORY. Horace White. 4 Vols.

ARATUS. Cf. CALLIMACHUS.

ARISTOPHANES. Benjamin Bickley Rogers. 3 Vols. Verse trans.

ARISTOTLE: ART OF RHETORIC. J. H. Freese.

ARISTOTLE: ATHENIAN CONSTITUTION, EUDEMIAN ETHICS, VICES AND VIRTUES. H. Rackham.

ARISTOTLE: GENERATION OF ANIMALS. A. L. Peck.

ARISTOTLE: METAPHYSICS. H. Tredennick. 2 Vols.

ARISTOTLE: METEROLOGICA. H. D. P. Lee.

ARISTOTLE: MINOR WORKS. W. S. Hett. On Colours, On Things Heard, On Physiognomies, On Plants, On Marvellous Things Heard, Mechanical Problems, On Indivisible Lines, On Situations and Names of Winds, On Melissus, Xenophanes, and Gorgias.

ARISTOTLE: NICOMACHEAN ETHICS. H. Rackham.

ARISTOTLE: OECONOMICA and MAGNA MORALIA. G. C. Armstrong; (with Metaphysics, Vol. II.).

ARISTOTLE: ON THE HEAVENS. W. K. C. Guthrie.

ARISTOTLE: ON THE SOUL. PARVA NATURALIA. ON BREATH. W. S. Hett.

ARISTOTLE: CATEGORIES, ON INTERPRETATION, PRIOR ANALYTICS. H. P. Cooke and H. Tredennick.

ARISTOTLE: POSTERIOR ANALYTICS, TOPICS. H. Tredennick and E. S. Forster.

ARISTOTLE: ON SOPHISTICAL REFUTATIONS.
On Coming to be and Passing Away, On the Cosmos. E. S. Forster and D. J. Furley.

ARISTOTLE: PARTS OF ANIMALS. A. L. Peck; MOTION AND PROGRESSION OF ANIMALS. E. S. Forster.

4

ARISTOTLE: PHYSICS. Rev. P. Wicksteed and F. M. Cornford. 2 Vols.

ARISTOTLE: POETICS and LONGINUS. W. Hamilton Fyfe; DEMETRIUS ON STYLE. W. Rhys Roberts.

ARISTOTLE: POLITICS. H. Rackham.

ARISTOTLE: PROBLEMS. W. S. Hett. 2 Vols.

ARISTOTLE: RHETORICA AD ALEXANDRUM (with PROBLEMS. Vol. II.) H. Rackham.

ARRIAN: HISTORY OF ALEXANDER and INDICA. Rev. E. Iliffe Robson. 2 Vols.

ATHENAEUS: DEIPNOSOPHISTAE. C. B. GULICK. 7 Vols.

ST. BASIL: LETTERS. R. J. Deferrari. 4 Vols.

CALLIMACHUS: FRAGMENTS. C. A. Trypanis.

CALLIMACHUS, Hymns and Epigrams, and LYCOPHRON. A. W. Mair; ARATUS. G. R. MAIR.

CLEMENT of ALEXANDRIA. Rev. G. W. Butterworth.

COLLUTHUS. Cf. OPPIAN.

DAPHNIS AND CHLOE. Thornley's Translation revised by J. M. Edmonds; and PARTHENIUS. S. Gaselee.

DEMOSTHENES I.: OLYNTHIACS, PHILIPPICS and MINOR ORATIONS. I.–XVII. AND XX. J. H. Vince.

DEMOSTHENES II.: DE CORONA and DE FALSA LEGATIONE. C. A. Vince and J. H. Vince.

DEMOSTHENES III.: MEIDIAS, ANDROTION, ARISTOCRATES, TIMOCRATES and ARISTOGEITON, I. AND II. J. H. Vince.

DEMOSTHENES IV.–VI.: PRIVATE ORATIONS and IN NEAERAM. A. T. Murray.

DEMOSTHENES VII.: FUNERAL SPEECH, EROTIC ESSAY, EXORDIA and LETTERS. N. W. and N. J. DeWitt.

DIO CASSIUS: ROMAN HISTORY. E. Cary. 9 Vols.

DIO CHRYSOSTOM. J. W. Cohoon and H. Lamar Crosby. 5 Vols.

DIODORUS SICULUS. 12 Vols. Vols. I.–VI. C. H. Oldfather. Vol. VII. C. L. Sherman. Vols. IX. and X. R. M. Geer. Vol. XI. F. Walton.

DIOGENES LAERTIUS. R. D. Hicks. 2 Vols.

DIONYSIUS OF HALICARNASSUS: ROMAN ANTIQUITIES. Spelman's translation revised by E. Cary. 7 Vols.

EPICTETUS. W. A. Oldfather. 2 Vols.

EURIPIDES. A. S. Way. 4 Vols. Verse trans.

EUSEBIUS: ECCLESIASTICAL HISTORY. Kirsopp Lake and J. E. L. Oulton. 2 Vols.

GALEN: ON THE NATURAL FACULTIES. A. J. Brock.

THE GREEK ANTHOLOGY. W. R. Paton. 5 Vols.

GREEK ELEGY AND IAMBUS with the ANACREONTEA. J. M. Edmonds. 2 Vols.

THE GREEK BUCOLIC POETS (THEOCRITUS, BION, MOSCHUS). J. M. Edmonds.

GREEK MATHEMATICAL WORKS. Ivor Thomas. 2 Vols.

HERODES. Cf. THEOPHRASTUS: CHARACTERS.

HERODOTUS. A. D. Godley. 4 Vols.

HESIOD AND THE HOMERIC HYMNS. H. G. Evelyn White.

HIPPOCRATES and the FRAGMENTS OF HERACLEITUS. W. H. S. Jones and E. T. Withington. 4 Vols.

HOMER: ILIAD. A. T. Murray. 2 Vols.

HOMER: ODYSSEY. A. T. Murray. 2 Vols.

ISAEUS. E. W. Forster.

ISOCRATES. George Norlin and LaRue Van Hook. 3 Vols.

ST. JOHN DAMASCENE: BARLAAM AND IOASAPH. Rev. G. R. Woodward and Harold Mattingly.

JOSEPHUS. H. St. J. Thackeray and Ralph Marcus. 9 Vols. Vols. I.–VII.

JULIAN. Wilmer Cave Wright. 3 Vols.

LUCIAN. 8 Vols. Vols. I.–V. A. M. Harmon. Vol. VI. K. Kilburn.

LYCOPHRON. Cf. CALLIMACHUS.

LYRA GRAECA. J. M. Edmonds. 3 Vols.

LYSIAS. W. R. M. Lamb.

MANETHO. W. G. Waddell: PTOLEMY: TETRABIBLOS. F. E. Robbins.

MARCUS AURELIUS. C. R. Haines.

MENANDER. F. G. Allinson.

MINOR ATTIC ORATORS (ANTIPHON, ANDOCIDES, LYCURGUS, DEMADES, DINARCHUS, HYPEREIDES). K. J. Maidment and J. O. Burtt. 2 Vols.

NONNOS: DIONYSIACA. W. H. D. Rouse. 3 Vols.

OPPIAN, COLLUTHUS, TRYPHIODORUS. A. W. Mair.

PAPYRI. NON-LITERARY SELECTIONS. A. S. Hunt and C. C. Edgar. 2 Vols. LITERARY SELECTIONS (Poetry). D. L. Page.

PARTHENIUS. Cf. DAPHNIS and CHLOE.

PAUSANIAS: DESCRIPTION OF GREECE. W. H. S. Jones. 4 Vols. and Companion Vol. arranged by R. E. Wycherley.

PHILO. 10 Vols. Vols. I.–V.; F. H. Colson and Rev. G. H. Whitaker. Vols. VI.–IX.; F. H. Colson.

PHILO: two supplementary Vols. (*Translation only*.) Ralph Marcus.

PHILOSTRATUS: THE LIFE OF APOLLONIUS OF TYANA. F. C. Conybeare. 2 Vols.

PHILOSTRATUS: IMAGINES; CALLISTRATUS: DESCRIPTIONS. A. Fairbanks.

6

PHILOSTRATUS and EUNAPIUS: LIVES OF THE SOPHISTS. Wilmer Cave Wright.

PINDAR. Sir J. E. Sandys.

PLATO: CHARMIDES, ALCIBIADES, HIPPARCHUS, THE LOVERS, THEAGES, MINOS and EPINOMIS. W. R. M. Lamb.

PLATO: CRATYLUS, PARMENIDES, GREATER HIPPIAS, LESSER HIPPIAS. H. N. Fowler.

PLATO: EUTHYPHRO, APOLOGY, CRITO, PHAEDO, PHAEDRUS. H. N. Fowler.

PLATO: LACHES, PROTAGORAS, MENO, EUTHYDEMUS. W. R. M. Lamb.

PLATO: LAWS. Rev. R. G. Bury. 2 Vols.

PLATO: LYSIS, SYMPOSIUM, GORGIAS. W. R. M. Lamb.

PLATO: REPUBLIC. Paul Shorey. 2 Vols.

PLATO: STATESMAN, PHILEBUS. H. N. Fowler; ION. W. R. M. Lamb.

PLATO: THEAETETUS and SOPHIST. H. N. Fowler.

PLATO: TIMAEUS, CRITIAS, CLITOPHO, MENEXENUS, EPISTULAE. Rev. R. G. Bury.

PLUTARCH: MORALIA. 15 Vols. Vols. I.–V. F. C. Babbitt. Vol. VI. W. C. Helmbold. Vol. VII. P. H. De Lacy and B. Einarson. Vol. IX. E. L. Minar, Jr., F. H. Sandbach, W. C. Helmbold. Vol. X. H. N. Fowler. Vol. XII. H. Cherniss and W. C. Helmbold.

PLUTARCH: THE PARALLEL LIVES. B. Perrin. 11 Vols.

POLYBIUS. W. R. Paton. 6 Vols.

PROCOPIUS: HISTORY OF THE WARS. H. B. Dewing. 7 Vols.

PTOLEMY: TETRABIBLOS. Cf. MANETHO.

QUINTUS SMYRNAEUS. A. S. Way. Verse trans.

SEXTUS EMPIRICUS. Rev. R. G. Bury. 4 Vols.

SOPHOCLES. F. Storr. 2 Vols. Verse trans.

STRABO: GEOGRAPHY. Horace L. Jones. 8 Vols.

THEOPHRASTUS: CHARACTERS. J. M. Edmonds. HERODES, etc. A. D. Knox.

THEOPHRASTUS: ENQUIRY INTO PLANTS. Sir Arthur Hort, Bart. 2 Vols.

THUCYDIDES. C. F. Smith. 4 Vols.

TRYPHIODORUS. Cf. OPPIAN.

XENOPHON: CYROPAEDIA. Walter Miller. 2 Vols.

XENOPHON: HELLENICA, ANABASIS, APOLOGY, and SYMPOSIUM. C. L. Brownson and O. J. Todd. 3 Vols.

XENOPHON: MEMORABILIA and OECONOMICUS. E. C. Marchant.

XENOPHON: SCRIPTA MINORA. E. C. Marchant.

IN PREPARATION

Greek Authors

ARISTOTLE: HISTORY OF ANIMALS. A. L. Peck.
PLOTINUS: A. H. Armstrong.

Latin Authors

BABRIUS AND PHAEDRUS. Ben E. Perry.

DESCRIPTIVE PROSPECTUS ON APPLICATION

London   WILLIAM HEINEMANN LTD
Cambridge, Mass.   HARVARD UNIVERSITY PRESS

8